Hebrews

Reformed Expository Commentary

A Series

Series Editors

Richard D. Phillips
Philip Graham Ryken

Testament Editors

Iain M. Duguid, Old Testament
Daniel M. Doriani, New Testament

Hebrews

RICHARD D. PHILLIPS

P&R PUBLISHING

P.O. BOX 817 • PHILLIPSBURG • NEW JERSEY 08865-0817

Page design by Lakeside Design Plus

Printed in the United States of America

Library of Congress Cataloging-in-Publication Data

Phillips, Richard D. (Richard Davis), 1960–
    Hebrews / Richard D. Phillips.
        p. cm. — (Reformed expository commentary)
    Includes bibliographical references and index.
    ISBN-13:   978-0-87552-784-0
    ISBN-10:   0-87552-784-1
    1. Bible. N.T. Hebrews—Commentaries. I. Title. II. Series.

BS2775.53.P46 2006
227'.87077—dc22
                                                                    2005057513

To the memory of

James Montgomery Boice,
with thanks to God for his love of Christ
and his example as a faithful expositor
of God's mighty Word,

and to

the apostle and high priest
of our confession, Jesus Christ

Hebrews 3:1–3

Contents

SERIES INTRODUCTION

In every generation there is a fresh need for the faithful exposition of God's Word in the church. At the same time, the church must constantly do the work of theology: reflecting on the teaching of Scripture, confessing its doctrines of the Christian faith, and applying them to contemporary culture. We believe that these two tasks—the expositional and the theological—are interdependent. Our doctrine must derive from the biblical text, and our understanding of any particular passage of Scripture must arise from the doctrine taught in Scripture as a whole.

We further believe that these interdependent tasks of biblical exposition and theological reflection are best undertaken in the church, and most specifically in the pulpits of the church. This is all the more true since the study of Scripture properly results in doxology and praxis—that is, in praise to God and practical application in the lives of believers. In pursuit of these ends, we are pleased to present the Reformed Expository Commentary as a fresh exposition of Scripture for our generation in the church. We hope and pray that pastors, teachers, Bible study leaders, and many others will find this series to be a faithful, inspiring, and useful resource for the study of God's infallible, inerrant Word.

The Reformed Expository Commentary has four fundamental commitments. First, these commentaries aim to be *biblical*, presenting a comprehensive exposition characterized by careful attention to the details of the text. They are not exegetical commentaries—commenting word by word or even verse by verse—but integrated expositions of whole passages of Scripture. Each commentary will thus present a sequential, systematic treatment of an entire book of the Bible, passage by passage. Second, these commentaries are unashamedly *doctrinal*. We are committed to the Westminster Confession of Faith and Catechisms as containing the system of doctrine taught in the Scriptures of the Old and New Testaments. Each volume will teach, promote, and defend the doctrines of the Reformed faith as they are found in the Bible. Third, these commentaries are *redemptive-historical* in their orientation. We believe in the unity of the Bible and its central message of salvation in Christ. We are thus committed to a Christ-centered view of the Old Testament, in which its characters, events, regulations, and institutions are properly understood as pointing us to Christ and his gospel, as well as giving us examples to follow in living by faith. Fourth, these commentaries are *practical*, applying the text of Scripture to contemporary challenges of life—both public and private—with appropriate illustrations.

The contributors to the Reformed Expository Commentary are all pastor-scholars. As pastor, each author will first present his expositions in the pulpit ministry of his church. This means that these commentaries are rooted in the teaching of Scripture to real people in the church. While aiming to be scholarly, these expositions are not academic. Our intent is to be faithful, clear, and helpful to Christians who possess various levels of biblical and theological training—as should be true in any effective pulpit ministry. Inevitably this means that some issues of academic interest will not be covered. Nevertheless, we aim to achieve a responsible level of scholarship, seeking to promote and model this for pastors and other teachers in the church. Significant exegetical and theological difficulties, along with such historical and cultural background as is relevant to the text, will be treated with care.

We strive for a high standard of enduring excellence. This begins with the selection of the authors, all of whom have proven to be outstanding communicators of God's Word. But this pursuit of excellence is also reflected in a disciplined editorial process. Each volume is edited by both a series editor and a testament editor. The testament editors, Iain Duguid for the Old Testament and Daniel Doriani for the New Testament, are accomplished pastors and respected scholars who have taught at the seminary level. Their job is to ensure that each volume is sufficiently conversant with up-to-date scholarship and is faithful and accurate in its exposition of the text. As series editors, we oversee each volume to ensure its overall quality—including excellence of writing, soundness of teaching, and usefulness in application. Working together as an editorial team, along with the publisher, we are devoted to ensuring that these are the best commentaries our gifted authors can provide, so that the church will be served with trustworthy and exemplary expositions of God's Word.

It is our goal and prayer that the Reformed Expository Commentary will serve the church by renewing confidence in the clarity and power of Scripture and by upholding the great doctrinal heritage of the Reformed faith. We hope that pastors who read these commentaries will be encouraged in their own expository preaching ministry, which we believe to be the best and most biblical pattern for teaching God's Word in the church. We hope that lay teachers will find these commentaries among the most useful resources they rely upon for understanding and presenting the text of the Bible. And we hope that the devotional quality of these studies of Scripture will instruct and inspire each Christian who reads them in joyful, obedient discipleship to Jesus Christ.

May the Lord bless all who read the Reformed Expository Commentary. We commit these volumes to the Lord Jesus Christ, praying that the Holy Spirit will use them for the instruction and edification of the church, with thanksgiving to God the Father for his unceasing faithfulness in building his church through the ministry of his Word.

Richard D. Phillips
Philip Graham Ryken
Series Editors

PREFACE

One of the glories of the Bible is the way God takes a particular situation involving a particular group of people and uses it to speak with the greatest of relevance to people of all kinds, in all times, and in all places. The Book of Hebrews provides a great example of this principle. Written by an unknown apostolic leader to a group of Jewish Christians facing persecution in the mid-first century A.D., the words of this book speak to Christians everywhere about standing firm in Jesus Christ. Is there a message more relevant and necessary to the times in which we live?

Few studies can be more profitable to Christians today than that of the Epistle to the Hebrews. In this letter, God exhorts us to persevere in the faith, even in the face of trials. Hebrews tells us *why* we must press on—because of the surpassing supremacy of Jesus Christ—and *how* we must press on—through faith in Christ, like the faith of those who went before us. Hebrews warns us of the pitfalls common to every age and through which many make a shipwreck of their souls, reminding us as well of the many resources available to us in our pilgrimage through this life.

Most valuable of all, the Book of Hebrews offers a singular and matchless presentation of our Lord Jesus Christ. Showing forth Jesus' supremacy to the angels, to Moses, to Joshua, and to Aaron, the author of Hebrews brings out features of Jesus' portrait that are found nowhere else in the New Testament. Especially in his detailed description of Jesus as our perfect high priest—the most pointed presentation of this office found in all of sacred Scripture—we learn how and why Jesus "is able to save to the uttermost those who draw near to God through him" (Heb. 7:25).

The student of Hebrews will gain detailed knowledge of Old Testament Israel and biblical insight regarding God's intention in the old covenant. Here we see covenant theology laid bare as it is biblically centered on Christ and his work. In Hebrews we gain superior insight into God's own view of sacred Scripture; Hebrews consists largely of expositions of Old Testament passages, and in these expositions we survey the contours of how inspiration and inerrancy work out in practice. Furthermore, since Hebrews is not so much a treatise as a sermon—the writer describes it as "my word of exhortation" (Heb. 13:22)—pastors and other leaders in Christ's flock receive a helpful model of biblical exhortation and encouragement.

My goal in writing these studies is the same expressed so well by the writer of Hebrews himself: "Let us hold fast the confession of our hope without wavering, for he who promised is faithful. And let us consider how to stir up one another to love and good works" (Heb. 10:23–24). May God bless these studies to all who read them—that you may trust firmly in Jesus Christ until the end, giving glory to his blessed name.

These messages were first preached in the early morning services of Tenth Presbyterian Church in Philadelphia from September 1999 to July 2001. Most of them were preached during our weekly communion service, and I will always be grateful to God that my first pulpit ministry involved the regular communing with God's people in the presence of Christ. Perhaps my fondest memory from that time was administering the sacrament weekly to James Montgomery Boice, then my senior pastor. His humble godliness and love for our Savior made an indelible impact on my heart. These studies are lovingly dedicated to his memory, with praise to God and with thanks for the example Dr. Boice set as a Christian, a pastor, and an expositor of Scripture.

Such is my esteem for the Book of Hebrews that I preached these messages again in the evening services of First Presbyterian Church of Coral Springs/Margate, Florida. To all the faithful and beloved brothers and sisters in this great church, I offer my heartfelt thanks for their constant love and support. I am thankful, as well, for the careful editing of my colleagues Phil Ryken and Dan Doriani, and for the many fine labors of my friends at P&R Publishing. I thank with special gratitude my wife Sharon, whose devotion to Christ and ministry to me make my service to God possible, and our five children, Hannah, Matthew, Jonathan, Ellie, and Lydia. Finally, I give thanks to God for the wonderful gift of his only Son to be the Lamb and the Priest who offered the sacrifice for the forgiveness of my sins, and on whose present intercession I wholly rely. To him be glory forever.

Hebrews

STANDING FIRM IN CHRIST

PART 1

The Supremacy of Christ

1

GOD'S FINAL WORD

Hebrews 1:1–2

Long ago, at many times and in many ways, God spoke to our
fathers by the prophets, but in these last days he has spoken to us
by his Son. (Heb. 1:1–2)

A scene from Jesus' life and ministry wonderfully depicts what the Book of Hebrews is all about. Matthew 17 tells us that Jesus took his three closest disciples up onto the mount, where they saw him transfigured in glory, speaking with Moses and Elijah. Peter proposed building a tabernacle for the veneration of these three spiritual giants. But just then the Shekinah glory cloud enveloped them in brightness and the voice of God said, "This is my beloved Son, with whom I am well pleased; listen to him" (Matt. 17:5). When the disciples rose from their terror, they did not see either Moses or Elijah, but they saw Jesus alone. A. W. Pink comments: "The glory associated with Moses and Elijah was so eclipsed by the infinitely greater glory connected with Christ, that they faded from view."[1]

1. A. W. Pink, *An Exposition of Hebrews* (Grand Rapids: Baker, 1954), 29.

This is what the Book of Hebrews is about—the supremacy of Christ, along with the sufficiency of his work and the necessity of faith in him for salvation.

BACKGROUND TO THE BOOK OF HEBREWS

We should begin studying a book with a consideration of its background. Who wrote the Book of Hebrews? To whom was it written and when? What prompted the writing of the letter, what is its literary genre, and on what basis is it included in the biblical canon?

When we consider the authorship of Hebrews, we must first observe that the answer is not stated in the letter itself. There is no opening greeting, nor do the closing remarks identify the writer. There is, however, no shortage of candidates for the honor of authorship.

Throughout church history there has been a strong impulse to name the apostle Paul as the author of Hebrews. There seem to be two main reasons for this, the first of which is that much of the letter's content sounds Pauline. Hebrews 13:23 refers to Timothy, one of Paul's protégés, and chapter 10's theme of joy amidst suffering strongly reminds us of Paul. Therefore, it is argued, the author of Hebrews must at least have been a member of the Pauline circle. The second reason to support Paul has to do with the canonicity of the book. The inclusion of Hebrews in the Bible was not without controversy, and arguments for Paul's authorship naturally strengthened its case dramatically.

Nonetheless, there are many indications that Paul almost certainly did not write Hebrews. First, in all of Paul's other letters he identifies himself, blatantly asserting his apostolic authority. The writer of Hebrews does not identify himself, although some speculate that because of Jewish hostility Paul may have wanted to remain anonymous. More telling is the nature of the Greek in Hebrews, which is of a high literary style in striking contrast to Paul's more common Greek. The structure of Hebrews, with its interspersed exhortations, contrasts with Paul's tendency to save practical applications for the letter's end. Most conclusive is the statement of Hebrews 2:3, which says the author's message "was attested to us by those who heard." In other words, the writer received his message from those who heard it firsthand from Jesus. This is the very thing

Paul always denies in his letters, insisting that he received his revelation directly from the Lord and not from the other apostles (see Gal. 1:12).

With Paul ruled out, other candidates are drawn from his circle and include Luke, Silas, and Priscilla. Most persuasive are the arguments in favor of Barnabas and Apollos. Hebrews 13:22 describes the letter as a "word of exhortation," and Barnabas's name means "son of exhortation." Not only was Barnabas a close associate of Paul, but as a Levite he would likely have had the kind of interest in the Jewish priesthood that shows up in Hebrews. An even more intriguing suggestion was made by Martin Luther in favor of Paul's sometime associate Apollos. Acts 18:24 identifies him as "an eloquent man, competent in the Scriptures," which qualifies him to write such an extraordinary epistle. Furthermore, Apollos hailed from Alexandria, and Hebrews shows an interest in theological themes known to have been popular there.

So who wrote Hebrews? In the end, we must agree with the ancient scholar Origen, who concluded, "Who wrote the epistle is known to God alone."[2] All we can say with confidence is that it came from an apostolic figure who was likely a colleague of the apostle Paul. It did not please the Holy Spirit to have us know the human author's identity, so we must content ourselves with knowing that the letter is the Word of God.

Also important is the identity of the recipients. The title "To the Hebrews" is not in the text, although it is found in all the earliest manuscripts. This, along with the letter's content, argues persuasively that these were Jewish Christians who were under pressure to renounce the faith and return to Judaism.

As to their location, the two main options are Palestine and Rome. Those who argue for a Palestinian audience point out that Christians are known to have suffered at the hands of their fellow Jews, and also point to the detailed references to the Jewish temple ritual. Since the discovery of the Dead Sea Scrolls, some have tried to show similarities to the writings of the Essene community in the Judean desert. Opposing this theory is the fact that all of the Old Testament citations in Hebrews are from the Septuagint, the Greek version common in that time, which was not used in Palestine as much as elsewhere. Also opposing a Palestinian background is the statement that the recipients of the letter had only heard of Jesus secondhand (see Heb. 2:3).

2. Eusebius, *The History of the Church*, trans. G. A. Williamson (New York: Penguin, 1965), 6.25.

Furthermore, Hebrews 12:4 states that earlier persecutions did not involve the shedding of blood, whereas those in Palestine certainly did from the very beginning.

Scholarly consensus has recently shifted in the direction of Rome. Clement of Rome, writing around A.D. 95, shows close familiarity with Hebrews, and the books of Acts and Romans speak of a large Jewish church in Rome from early on. The Jewish Christians there were persecuted in A.D. 49 under the emperor Claudius, and then again in the 60s under Nero. What we know of the former of these persecutions seems to fit the description of 10:32–34 and 12:4 (in that Claudius's persecution involved loss of property and imprisonment, but not bloodshed), and the anticipation of violence fits the latter, with Nero's notorious violence against Christians. Finally, there is the statement of Hebrews 13:24, "Those who come from Italy send you greetings." It could be that a pastor now in Rome was writing to Jewish believers in Palestine. But the more natural reason for Italian Christians to send their greetings is that the readers were themselves from Italy.

If Rome was the location of the audience, then the letter would have been written shortly before A.D. 64, when Nero's persecution broke out. Under almost all theories, Hebrews was written prior to A.D. 70, when Jerusalem and its temple were destroyed by the Romans. Not only does Hebrews speak of the temple rituals as a present reality, but it is hard to imagine its writer passing up such an opportunity as the fall of Jerusalem to prove the passing away of the old covenant religion.

The purpose of Hebrews is made clear by its content. The writer warns Christians not to fall back from faith in Christ in the midst of trials and exhorts them instead to press on to full maturity. The letter should not be thought of as a theological treatise, but as a sermon written by a pastor to a congregation from which he is separated. The writer describes it as "my word of exhortation" (13:22). His method is to point out the supremacy of Christ over everything to which the readers might be tempted to turn; he is superior to angels, to Moses and the prophets, to Aaron and the Levitical priests, to the blood sacrifices of the old covenant, and to the tabernacle and temple themselves. Since Jesus is the true messenger, the true prophet, the true priest, and the true sacrifice, to renounce him is to lose salvation altogether. Therefore, the readers must hold fast to Jesus Christ.

The author's plea is summed up in Hebrews 10:23: "Let us hold fast the confession of our hope without wavering, for he who promised is faithful."

The final matter of background to consider is the place of Hebrews in the New Testament canon. The early church's basic test of canonicity was proof of apostolicity. This did not mean that a book had to be written by an apostle, as is shown by the ready inclusion of Mark, Luke, Acts, and other books. It was sufficient for the author to be an associate of an apostle, so long as the teaching was apostolic in character. We should not think, however, that it was the church that created the canon, since really it was exactly the opposite. The canon—that is, the apostolic teaching of the New Testament writings—created the church. Hywel Jones aptly summarizes, "The canon was drawn up . . . by way of response to the effect which sacred literature had on those who heard it. The church's formal acknowledgement of a piece of literature was an 'Amen' to the Holy Spirit's testimony in it, and not a bestowing of its own *imprimatur*."[3]

Any introduction to Hebrews ought to conclude with an appreciation of its outstanding excellence. Here the last word is best given to John Calvin, who wrote in the dedication of his commentary: "Since the Epistle addressed to the Hebrews contains a full discussion of the eternal divinity of Christ, His supreme government, and only priesthood (which are the main points of heavenly wisdom), and as these things are so explained in it, that the whole power and work of Christ are set forth in the most graphic way, it rightly deserves to have the place and honor of an invaluable treasure in the Church."[4]

GOD HAS SPOKEN

As soon as we begin the Book of Hebrews, we encounter what is perhaps the single most important statement that could be made in our time: "God spoke" (Heb. 1:1). This is one of the most vital things people today need to know. Ours is a relativistic age; as many as 70 percent of Americans insist that there are no absolutes, whether in matters of truth or morality. Secular society having removed God, there no longer is a heavenly voice to speak

---

3. Hywel R. Jones, *Let's Study Hebrews* (Edinburgh: Banner of Truth, 2002), xiii.
4. John Calvin, *New Testament Commentaries*, 12 vols. (Grand Rapids: Eerdmans, 1994), 12:ix.

with clarity and authority. The price we have paid is the loss of truth, and with truth, hope. Even when it comes to those things we think we know, we now consider them mere constructs of thought amidst the constant flux of uncertain knowledge and belief. Really, we are told, we don't know anything for sure, nor can we.

All this is especially the case when it comes to our knowledge of God himself. Can we know our Creator, if there is one? Is there a Savior to help us? Unless God has spoken, we cannot even be sure he is there; unless God is there, there is no ultimate hope for us as individuals, and no answer for the ultimate problem of death. Job asks, "Can you find out the deep things of God?" (11:7) and answers No. By definition, God is beyond the realm of our senses, from which all our self-gained knowledge has to come. Therefore, if God is there and wants us to know him—if he has an answer, a plan, or a salvation—he is going to have to speak to us. And he must speak in a way we can understand. Therefore, there is nothing more important, nothing more essential, than what Hebrews says in its very first verse: "God has spoken."

This is the uniform testimony of the Bible about itself, that it is God's very Word. The Bible's books were written by human authors, who spoke and wrote in human language. But the Bible insists that through them God himself spoke and speaks to us still. Peter explained, "Men spoke from God as they were carried along by the Holy Spirit" (2 Peter 1:21). This is what we refer to as the Bible's *inspiration*. God has communicated to us through the Holy Spirit's leading of its human authors. The point is not that these books contain the inspired insights of men; the point is exactly the opposite. Indeed, we might better speak of the Bible not as being *in*spired but as being *ex*pired. It is God's Word as from his very mouth, given through the Holy Spirit's work in the lives of human servants. This is what Paul emphasizes in 2 Timothy 3:16, where he says, "All Scripture is breathed out by God."

The divine authorship of Holy Scripture needs to be emphasized today, especially since contemporary scholarship tends to focus on the human authors. It is right, of course, to realize the human contours God used to give different shape to different Bible books. Moses had his own experience and calling and personality and gifts, and God used them to craft a particular message in the books that Moses wrote. The same is true of Paul and

John and all the other biblical writers. But while the Bible itself affirms this, its own emphasis is on divine authorship. Hebrews 1:1 says that God spoke "at many times and in many ways," and that God employed "the prophets" to do this. But in all of this it was still God who spoke. It is not Moses who spoke in Genesis, nor David who spoke in the Psalms, nor Paul who spoke in Romans. God spoke in the Bible, and we must regard all Scripture as his holy Word.

The Book of Hebrews gives the Bible's own slant on the process of revelation. Whenever the writer cites Scripture, it is never the human author whom he credits but the divine Author. In Hebrews 2:12 he cites Psalm 22:22 and ascribes it to Jesus Christ speaking in the Old Testament. Hebrews 3:7–11 cites Psalm 95, but prefaces it not by saying "as David said," but "as the Holy Spirit says." So it goes all through Hebrews. The point is not to deny the significance of the Bible's human authors, but to show that our emphasis, following the Bible's own emphasis, must always be on God speaking in his Word.

This has several important implications. First, if God speaks in the Bible, then the Bible carries divine *authority*. Today, many want to set aside the Bible's teachings when they collide with current cultural standards. But just as God commands our obedience, so he also demands that we humbly obey his Word. There is nothing so important for Christians to recover today as the awe and respect that Scripture deserves as God's own revelation to us.

Second, if God wrote the Bible, then it is enduringly *relevant*. After all, if God does not change—and by nature he cannot—then his Word does not change either. It is true that some things said in the Bible were intended only for its original recipients. God told Moses, not us, to "Go down to Egypt." But the teaching given all through the Bible—on God's character, on sin and on his moral standards, on the good news of salvation and how it comes to us—abides forever for the simple reason that God abides forever. The writer of Hebrews says in chapter 13 that Christian standards of conduct remain the same because "Jesus Christ is the same yesterday and today and forever" (13:8).

God not only spoke in the Bible to those who first received it, but he speaks as well to those who read it today. This is emphasized in Hebrews. In Hebrews 3:7, for instance, the writer cites Psalm 95, written a thousand years before, and writes, "as the Holy Spirit *says.*" He uses the present tense. It is not merely what the Holy Spirit *said* back when David wrote it, but what the Holy Spirit says now as God speaks to those who read it. This is why the Bible is fully relevant to all our needs today.

Third, since God has spoken in the Bible, even though he did so with great diversity—"at many times and in many ways"—we also hold to the *unity* of the Bible. The Bible consists of sixty-six books written over at least thirteen hundred years by over forty different people. And yet it is one book with one unified message. James Boice explains:

> These people were not alike. Some were kings. Others were statesmen, priests, prophets, a tax collector, a physician, a tentmaker, fishermen. . . . Yet together they produced a volume that is a marvelous unity in its doctrine, historical viewpoints, ethics and expectations. It is, in short, a single story of divine redemption begun in Israel, centered in Jesus Christ and culminating at the end of history. . . . Behind the efforts of the more than forty human authors is the one perfect, sovereign and guiding mind of God.[5]

This provides us with an important interpretive principle, namely, that Scripture is best interpreted by Scripture itself. Since the Bible is one message spoken by God, we should understand the teaching in one passage in light of the way that teaching is given elsewhere in Scripture. To be sure, the Bible's message is progressively revealed, so that the gospel appears in bud in the Old Testament and in bloom only in the New Testament. Many doctrines are therefore progressively revealed. Nonetheless, the clear teaching God gives in one place constrains our interpretation of the same subject elsewhere in the Bible. This is most relevant to our study of Hebrews, where the author not only finds numerous Old Testament passages to be relevant to his readers, but under the Holy Spirit's control also gives us an authoritative guide as to how we should understand them (as well as the whole Old Testament).

5. James Montgomery Boice, *Foundations of the Christian Faith* (Downers Grove, Ill.: InterVarsity, 1986), 58–59.

THE FINAL REVELATION IN GOD'S SON

These opening verses tell us not merely that God has spoken, but that his final and definitive revelation is in and through his Son, Jesus Christ. The writer makes this point through three contrasts in Hebrews 1:1–2. First, there is the *when* of revelation: "long ago," in contrast to "in these last days." Second, there is the *to whom* of revelation, "to our fathers," versus "to us." Third, there is the *how* of revelation, namely, "at many times and in many ways . . . by the prophets," versus "by his Son."

The author's point, which is the burden of the entire Book of Hebrews, is to show the superiority of Christianity to the old covenant religion. He wastes no time getting to this point, arguing the supremacy of Christ over the prophets. This supremacy does not in any way malign the Old Testament faith. Unlike pagan religions, it was a legitimate revelation and a true faith. In the Old Testament "God spoke," and it was God-given religion. Nonetheless, Christ is superior and with his coming there is now no excuse for reverting back to Judaism.

The author describes former revelation as coming "at many times and in many ways." His point is not merely the diversity of revelation in the Old Testament, but its fragmentary, incomplete, and gradual character. Take any one book of the Old Testament—perhaps Genesis, with its rich scenes of creation, fall, and redemption; or Esther, with her courageous faith in an unseen God; or Psalms, with its heart-lifting poetry—and you will read true divine revelation, even necessary revelation. But each book is fragmentary and incomplete. The Old Testament is unfulfilled. It expectantly longs for the answer that comes in Jesus Christ. By contrast, God's revelation in Christ is not partial or incomplete. This is why the Christian era is described as "these last days." The point is not that Jesus is about to come back any minute, as many take this to mean (though other New Testament passages tell us to have this perspective), but that this is the age of fulfillment when God's revelation has been made complete. This is what makes the *when* of Christian revelation so much better. Calvin comments, "It was not a part of the Word that Christ brought, but the last closing Word."[6]

6. Calvin, *New Testament Commentaries,* 12:6.

Another reason for the superiority of the Christian faith is the contrast in the channel of its revelation, that is, the *how*. In the Old Testament, God spoke by the prophets, but in the New he speaks by his own Son. One could hardly find a greater group of spiritual giants than the prophets of the Old Testament. Moses, Elijah, Isaiah, Jeremiah—these were outstanding bearers of divine truth. Yet how they pale compared to the very Son of God come to earth. As Jesus put it, "He who comes from above is above all. He who is of the earth belongs to the earth and speaks in an earthly way. He who comes from heaven is above all" (John 3:31).

The revelation in Christ, then, given not merely to our forefathers but preserved for us in Scripture, is superior to that given formerly through the prophets. Martin Luther concludes: "If the word of the prophets is accepted, how much more ought we to seize the gospel of Christ, since it is not a prophet speaking to us but the Lord of the prophets, not a servant but a son, not an angel but God."[7]

JESUS THE TRUTH

Whenever we think of Jesus as the ultimate, final truth, we may remember the confrontation at his trial before Pontius Pilate. The Roman governor had demanded to know if Jesus really thought himself a king. Jesus replied that his kingdom was not of this world. When Pilate responded doubtfully, Jesus related his kingship to the revelation of God's truth in the world. He said, "For this purpose I was born and for this purpose I have come into the world—to bear witness to the truth" (John 18:37). Christ reigns through God's Word, because in Christ God has fully and ultimately revealed himself.

What a confrontation that was! Pilate represented the philosophy and wisdom of the world, with its relativism and cruel utilitarianism. Pilate was not able to accept that there could be truth at all. Looking into the very face of God's Son, through whom God has revealed the ultimate truth, Pilate replied, "What is truth?" (John 18:38). This not only shows that what we call postmodernity, with its denial of truth, is really nothing new, but it also

---

7. Martin Luther, cited in Philip E. Hughes, *A Commentary on the Epistle to the Hebrews* (Grand Rapids: Eerdmans, 1977), 37.

dramatizes the tragedy of our unbelieving world. Jesus put it this way: "This is the judgment: the light has come into the world, and people loved the darkness rather than the light because their deeds were evil" (John 3:19). There before Pilate stood the very Truth of God, and there was Pilate denying even the possibility of truth.

Pilate thought he was judging Jesus, but with the Truth before him it was the governor who really was on trial. The same is true today. When you read or hear God's message through his Son Jesus Christ, you stand before the Truth. If you reject him, God's final Word, you consign yourself to darkness—the darkness of spiritual blindness now and the eternal darkness that comes in God's final judgment.

But if you look to Jesus Christ, and if in him you see and believe the very Truth of God, then God's redemptive work of the ages will be fulfilled in you. "At many times and in many ways," God began preparing the world through the prophets for the coming of his Son. Why? So that in these last days—these days of God's redemptive fulfillment in Jesus Christ—we might enter into the fullness of salvation. This is what Jesus said to the disciples as they struggled to know the truth on the night of his arrest. "I am the way, and the truth, and the life," he told them (John 14:6). And so he is for us. When we receive Jesus as the Truth, then he becomes the Way for us to enter into Life everlasting. This is why Jesus is God's final Word, and why even if all else in this world is lost we must hold fast to him in faith.

2

PROPHET, PRIEST, AND KING

Hebrews 1:2–4

He is the radiance of the glory of God and the exact imprint of his
nature, and he upholds the universe by the word of his power.
(Heb. 1:3)

*I*t is hard for us to understand how remarkable it was for the first generation of Christians to put their faith in Jesus Christ. This is especially true of the Jews who had not personally known Jesus but converted to Christianity. We can imagine the kind of arguments that unbelieving Jews would have employed to dissuade their new faith. They would have pointed out that Jesus was just a man, the son of a poor carpenter from a backwater village in Galilee. They might have echoed Nathaniel's comment, "Can anything good come out of Nazareth?" (John 1:46). It was a time of unrest and of heady passions, they may have pointed out, and this man Jesus was just one of many zealous leaders of his day. Worst of all, his failure as a Messiah was proved by his humiliating execution as the worst sort of criminal. The fact that he was crucified—the most despicable of all deaths—proved that he was rejected by God. Jesus may have been a decent enough man, though he obviously got carried away by his short-lived fame. The real problem was his fanatical disciples, who made outlandish claims about his resurrection and started a heretical religion that actually worshiped the poor man.

If this is the kind of argument the Jewish Christians were subjected to, it likely was a potent one. Especially since believing on Christ came at such a high cost—exclusion from Jewish society and perhaps even violent persecution in the days to come—many might have reconsidered their religious options.

The Epistle to the Hebrews was written because of this kind of pressure. Then, as now, faith in Jesus came at a price. You could not be a Christian without carrying a cross and suffering at the hands of the world. Therefore, it had to be worth it to believe on Jesus Christ. This is what the writer of Hebrews wanted to impress upon his readers. In the book's opening lines, he directs us to the supremacy of our Lord. He knows that if we perceive Jesus in the marvel of his person and his work—as God's Son and as our Savior—then instead of doubting or trembling in fear we will respond with words like those from the great hymn: "I know whom I have believed, and am persuaded that he is able to keep that which I've committed unto him against that day."

Verses 2–3 contain seven statements of Christ's supremacy. This number seems deliberate, because verses 5–14 go on to list seven Old Testament citations that are ascribed to Christ. Seven was the number for perfection or completion, and that is the writer's point here: the perfect supremacy of Christ. Furthermore, the seven statements of verses 2 and 3 may be organized along the lines of the three great Old Testament offices that are perfected and completed in Christ: prophet, priest, and king. This is a helpful and biblical way of thinking about our Lord. He is prophet in that he perfectly reveals God to us. He is priest in offering himself for our sins, cleansing us, and interceding for us with God. He is our king, reigning now in heaven and ruling over us as our Sovereign Lord.

CHRIST AS THE TRUE KING

It is with the last of these, Christ as king, that the writer of Hebrews begins his sevenfold exclamation of the supremacy of Christ. Verse 2 says, "In these last days he has spoken to us by his Son, whom he appointed the heir of all things, through whom also he created the world." In these first two of the seven statements, we see Jesus as Lord both in his person and in his work.

First, he is "appointed the heir of all things." This is something that follows from Christ's being God's only Son. In Israel, it was the firstborn son who had the right of inheritance. This means that "as the heir, all things already belong to the Son in principle, just as they will actually and finally be his at the end."[1] This was God the Father's appointment, his purpose in creation: that his Son should be blessed and glorified in receiving all things. This is also the ultimate purpose of our redemption: "His inheritance is the innumerable company of the redeemed and the universe renewed by virtue of his triumphant work of reconciliation."[2]

The writer of Hebrews goes on to say, "through whom also he created the world." Jesus Christ, God's Son, is Lord and King because of his divine role in creation. Not only was the world made for him, but it was made by him. There can hardly be a stronger claim for lordship than this. If you are the one who made something, and for whom it was made, then you are its rightful lord. So it is in the case of Jesus Christ. Paul says the same thing in Colossians 1:16: "For by him all things were created, in heaven and on earth, visible and invisible, whether thrones or dominions or rulers or authorities—all things were created through him and for him." Hebrews 1:3 adds that even now "he upholds the universe by the word of his power."

Those Jewish Christians who first received this letter were being tempted to renounce Christianity. But Jesus fulfills and gathers to himself all that the office of king ever meant in Israel. He is the true king, the Lord of all, and the faithful of Israel are those who worship and serve him.

We need to embrace the same truth. Jesus is king over the church and over the Christian people, no less than when the Israelites of David's day looked to his authority and obeyed his commands. But how seldom people think of Jesus this way. When he walked upon this earth in his humanity, Jesus did not look like a king. He did not ride a great stallion; his coming was not heralded by trumpets; he did not hold court in a palace of gold. This is why people scoffed at his kingship. Pontius Pilate said, "Are you the King of the Jews?" It was not so much a question as a taunt. Jesus replied, "My

---

1. Donald A. Hagner, *Encountering the Book of Hebrews* (Grand Rapids: Baker, 2002), 41.
2. Philip E. Hughes, *A Commentary on the Epistle to the Hebrews* (Grand Rapids: Eerdmans, 1977), 37.

kingdom is not of this world" (John 18:33, 36). Does this mean that while you have to respect earthly rulers, you can afford to ignore Jesus' kingdom since it is merely spiritual? James M. Boice answers,

> Nothing is farther from the truth, for when we say that Christ's kingdom is not of this world, what we are really saying is that Christ's kingdom is of heaven and therefore has an even greater claim over us than do the earthly kingdoms we know so well. . . . Over these is Christ, and we flout His kingship not merely at the peril of our fortune and lives but at the peril of our eternal souls.[3]

Jesus was appointed heir of all things, which were made through him and are even now sustained by him. But this is seen only by God's Word, and only with the eyes of faith. Jesus is enthroned, not upon an earthly throne, but "at the right hand of the Majesty on high" (Heb. 1:3). We can see this only by faith. Believing on Christ as our king, we must obey him by faith, and we must be comforted amidst our trials in the knowledge that one day soon he will come to manifest his kingdom over all creation, destroying his enemies with the rod of his might (Ps. 2:9), and inviting his faithful servants to enter into the joy of his kingdom (Matt. 25:21). As the writer of Hebrews points out in 2:8–9, quoting from Psalm 8, "At present, we do not yet see everything in subjection to him." This is the cause of our unbelief and fear. But by faith we know that he is even now "crowned with glory and honor," and someday soon every eye will see him, every knee will bow, and every tongue confess that Jesus Christ is Lord (Phil. 2:10–11).

CHRIST AS THE FINAL PROPHET

This passage exalts Christ not only as Lord of all, but also as the One who perfectly reveals God in all his glory. He is the true king, but also the final prophet: "He is the radiance of the glory of God and the exact imprint of his nature" (Heb. 1:3).

Hot and brilliant as the sun is in the heavens, we would never see it or feel its warmth without the radiating beams that come to the earth. So it is with

---

3. James Montgomery Boice, *The Gospel of John* (Grand Rapids: Zondervan, 1985), 1278.

God and his Son, who is the radiance of his glory. Without the Son we remain in the dark regarding the glory of God. But with the Son we have an ideal, indeed, a perfect revelation of God. Paul said in 2 Corinthians 4:6 that we see "the light of the knowledge of the glory of God in the face of Jesus Christ." We do not see God in Christ through drawings that purport to represent his features, much less through an actor who tries to represent the way Jesus must have been. We see God in Christ through the Bible's teaching of his person and work, of his holy zeal and compassionate love, of his heavenly words and mighty, saving works.

As the Son, Jesus is a better revelation than that which came through the prophets. It is one thing to know a chosen servant. You can learn a lot about a master by what you see in those who work for him. But as Martyn Lloyd-Jones explains, "A servant may be able to say everything that is right about his lord and master, he may know him well and intimately, but he can never represent him in the way that the son can. The son is a manifestation of the father by being what he is. Thus our Lord himself, while here on earth, represented and manifested the name of God in a way that is incomparable and greater than all others, because he is the Son of God."[4] John 1:18 tells us, in a striking assertion of Jesus' deity: "No one has ever seen God; the only God, who is at the Father's side, he has made him known."

Jesus is the perfect prophet—the one who fully reveals God's glory—because he is not only similar to God the Father, but also is "the exact imprint of his nature." The Greek word here is *charaktēr*, which gives us the word "character." It refers to the stamp or imprint made by a die or seal. The best example is a coin with the imprint of a ruler's face; in the same way, Jesus bears God's image or imprint. Paul says, "He is the image of the invisible God" (Col. 1:15). The point is the trustworthiness with which Jesus reveals God to us. There is an exact correspondence between what we see in him and what is true of God. "Whoever has seen me has seen the Father," Jesus explained (John 14:9).

Furthermore, Jesus "upholds the universe by the word of his power" (Heb. 1:3). Jesus wields divine power because as God's Son he is fully

---

4. D. Martyn Lloyd-Jones, *Safe in the World* (Wheaton, Ill.: Crossway, 1988), 60–61.

God. As the true and great and final prophet, he is able not merely to reveal God's will but also to establish God's will upon the earth.

This description of Jesus as the great and final prophet helps us to gain a proper understanding of the relationship of the Old Testament to the New. The reason the Hebrew Christians should not revert from Christ back to Judaism is not that the Old Testament was wrong. Through the long line of prophets, God left his people with his revelation for their salvation. But the chief message of that revelation was of a Savior yet to come, the true prophet who would not only point to salvation but would also accomplish it. Isaiah spoke of a child who would be born, a son who would be given, and said that he would be called "Wonderful Counselor" (Isa. 9:6). He added, "The Spirit of the LORD shall rest upon him, the Spirit of wisdom and understanding, the Spirit of counsel and might, the Spirit of knowledge and the fear of the LORD. And his delight shall be in the fear of the LORD" (Isa. 11:2–3). The way to be a true follower of Isaiah and the other prophets was and is to believe their message, to receive in faith the One for whom they prayed, who is the head of their order and the fulfillment of their age-old longing.

CHRIST AS THE PERFECT PRIEST

We need to give homage to Jesus, God's Son, as the King who is Lord of all. And we need to listen to him as the true and final prophet who perfectly reveals God's glory. But there is a third office Jesus perfects and completes, that of the priest. Apart from his ministry in this office we may bow to God, and we may listen to God, but we can never be accepted by God and draw near to his presence. Therefore, the writer of Hebrews tells us that Jesus is the true and perfect priest, who makes atonement for our sins. He writes, "After making purification for sins, he sat down at the right hand of the Majesty on high" (Heb. 1:3).

The theme of Christ's priestly office will occupy much of the Book of Hebrews, and it is a message we must understand if we want to be saved. Jesus fulfills the priestly office because he offers the one true sacrifice to take away our sin. This is what the angel said about him to Joseph even before his birth: "You shall call his name Jesus, for he will save his people from their sins" (Matt. 1:21). Yes, Jesus rules within us by his spirit, and he speaks to us as prophet through the gospel. But these are possible only because as Lamb of God he laid down his life for our sins, making purification for us upon the cross. Then, as the true and final priest, he went into heaven to present his own blood to God to secure our full, perfect, and final forgiveness.

This sevenfold exclamation of praise to God's Son is completed with the statement that "he sat down at the right hand of the Majesty on high" (Heb. 1:3). There were no seats in the temple at Jerusalem. The priests offered sacrifices for the purification of the people day and night without ceasing because the problem of sin had not yet been solved. They never sat down. But when God's Son, the true priest whom the old covenant priests merely represented, shed his blood for us, his atoning sacrifice was the one to which all the others had merely pointed. He sat down, because there was no more sacrifice to be made, God's Son having offered his infinitely holy and precious blood once for all. That being the case, if the readers of Hebrews wanted the benefits of the Old Testament sacrifices, then they must not turn away from Christ but hold fast to his death for their salvation.

God's Son "sat down at the right hand of the Majesty on high" (Heb. 1:3). Since this is a throne, naturally we think of his kingly office. But it is also as our priest that Jesus takes up his heavenly royal seat. The King who rules on the throne of heaven is the very priest who sacrificed himself for our salvation and whose presence there bears everlasting testimony to our forgiveness. As Charles Wesley says in his great hymn "Arise, My Soul, Arise":

> Five bleeding wounds he bears,
>   received on Calvary;
> they pour effectual prayers,
>   they strongly plead for me.
> "Forgive him, O forgive," they cry,
>   "forgive him, O forgive," they cry,
> "nor let that ransomed sinner die!"[5]

5. Charles Wesley, "Arise, My Soul, Arise," 1742.

CROWN HIM WITH MANY CROWNS

Verse 4 completes what in the Greek text is a single sentence that runs from the beginning of verse 1. It says, "Having become as much superior to angels as the name he has inherited is more excellent than theirs." This seems like an odd ending, but there are two explanations. The first is that Jewish spirituality in that day had an excessively high view of angels. The Jews connected angels with the great events of the Old Testament, believing that God gave Moses the law through angelic mediation and that it was an angel voice that spoke to Moses from the burning bush (Ex. 3:2).

The writer of Hebrews does not quarrel with these facts but rather with their interpretation. He acknowledges that angels are ministering spirits God sends for our help (Heb. 1:14). But that God employed angels does not mean that we should exalt them, as many Jews seem to have been doing. The angels, like the prophets, were servants of the old covenant. But Jesus Christ is the Son who fulfills the old covenant. He is the Christ, the Messiah, which means "Anointed One." He fulfills the three anointed offices of the Old Testament: prophet, priest, and king. Therefore, the only way to fulfill all that the Old Testament taught, the only way to realize all that the Israelite fathers had looked to with hope, was to trust in the Son of God, Jesus Christ. Upon the throne of heaven, he is exalted above even the angels, and his name—that is, his title or position—is more excellent than theirs.

There is another possible reason why the writer brings in angels, one that resonates with our own spiritual environment. People are fascinated by angels. Book about angels are bestsellers, and many people adorn themselves with angelic jewelry. The reason is that people know they need a mediator with God. They need someone to open a doorway to heaven and to the blessing and power of God. They need supernatural help for their otherwise insurmountable problems. People in the first-century church, just as in our own time, found in angels an appealing and non-demanding form of spiritual hope and comfort (see Col. 2:18). The fact that we don't know much about angels makes them attractive for our veneration; we can fill in the details as we want them to be.

What this passage reveals about Jesus Christ is a cause for much greater comfort and hope than we could ever gain through the mystical worship of angels. When the Bible presents God's Son as the true prophet and priest and king, God is showing us that Jesus Christ is and does all that our souls could ever need. Jesus Christ is the Messiah, the long-expected Anointed One, who enters into the God-given offices of the Old Testament so that he might save us to the uttermost. Charles Hodge expresses this well, explaining how Jesus Christ perfectly fulfills all our needs so that we might enter with him into the blessings of eternal life:

> We as fallen men, ignorant, guilty, polluted, and helpless, need a Saviour who is a prophet to instruct us; a priest to atone and to make intercession for us; and a king to rule over and protect us. And the salvation which we receive at his hands includes all that a prophet, priest, and king in the highest sense of those terms can do. We are enlightened in the knowledge of the truth; we are reconciled unto God by the sacrificial death of his Son; and we are delivered from the power of Satan and introduced into the kingdom of God; all of which supposes that our Redeemer is to us at once prophet, priest, and king.[6]

Jesus is the perfect and all-sufficient answer from God for our everlasting blessing. The significance of this for the original readers is obvious: If you have a Savior like this, you never let him go. If you have to lose your job, your family, your possessions—even your life—then so be it. Jesus said, "Whoever would save his life will lose it, but whoever loses his life for my sake will save it. For what does it profit a man if he gains the whole world and loses or forfeits himself?" (Luke 9:24–25). What great profit it is, then, to gain Christ, and eternal life with him, even if all the world needs to be lost.

What this passage tells us about Christ reminds us not merely *that* we must hold to him in faith, but also *how* to draw near to him in faith. This comes through our understanding of his three offices as prophet and priest and king.

Jesus is our King. We need to be ruled and governed, protected and led. Let us therefore bow before him and crown him Lord of all, flying his banner at the gates of our hearts and forsaking all other kingdoms and rulers. Jesus is our Prophet. We need truth; he is the Truth and he speaks the

6. Charles Hodge, *Systematic Theology*, 3 vols. (Grand Rapids: Eerdmans, 1993), 2:461.

truth. Let us therefore come to his Word seeking light and forsaking all the false prophets who would lead us astray. Jesus is our Priest. So we should readily come to him for cleansing, for forgiveness, for interceding prayers, and for a full and loving reconciliation with God the Father. Let us therefore confess our great need for his blood and for his ongoing priestly intercession in heaven. Let us lay hold of the cross, forsaking all claim to any merit of our own. In all these ways, through his three offices, let us commit ourselves to Jesus Christ alone, who is able to save us to the uttermost, to the glory of God the Father.

3

SUPERIOR TO ANGELS

Hebrews 1:4—9

For to which of the angels did God ever say, "You are my Son,
today I have begotten you"? Or again, "I will be to him a father,
and he shall be to me a son"? (Heb. 1:5)

ngels are "in." If you go to your local bookstore you will find
legions of books, jewelry, and trinkets celebrating these
winged spirits. When it comes to the media, it is certainly
true that angels are "in." Probably most well known is the popular 1990s
television show *Touched by an Angel*, in which viewers encountered all too
human angels serving as heavenly psychologists, proclaiming a soothing
message of love from an all-embracing, nonjudgmental God. This is a far
cry from the biblical presentation of angels, who are anything but advo-
cates of a morally loose, tolerant deity. Angels appeal to our age because
they seem to offer us access to heavenly blessings without having to deal
directly with heaven's God himself.

Ours is not the only time when false or inappropriate attitudes toward
angels were held. Among many Jews in the first century there was an
unhealthy emphasis on angels, in part because of the excellent things

said of them in Scripture. While angels are not to be thought of frivolously, neither are they to hold an improper place in our devotion.

Probably the main reason why the author of Hebrews needed to emphasize Christ's superiority to the angels has to do with angels' association with the old covenant given at Mount Sinai. In Hebrews 2:2 we see an example of this teaching, where it is said that the Old Testament law was "declared by angels." Acts 7:53 tells us that the law was "delivered by angels," so that their mediation of the law at Sinai does have biblical support.

In saying that Christ is superior to the angels, the author is again emphasizing the superiority of the new covenant over the old, and therefore the folly of turning back from the gospel. He makes this point here by means of seven Old Testament quotations. This is the pattern we will see all through Hebrews, and the writer sets an example for us in the authority he grants to Scripture. In this chapter we will look at the first five of these citations, from Hebrews 1:4 to 1:9, which together prove the superiority of God's Son to the angels.

Superior Because of a Better Name

The argument of these verses is straightforward: by means of these Old Testament prophecies and teachings, the writer of Hebrews demonstrates the claim of verse 4, that Jesus became "as much superior to angels as the name he has inherited is more excellent than theirs." Christ's supremacy rests upon his inheritance of the name "Son of God." The author's greater burden is to show the superiority of the new covenant to the old, the gospel to the law, that covenant which is mediated by Christ to the covenant mediated by angels. His purpose is to persuade his readers not to fall back from Christianity to the old and now obsolete religion.

The basic reason for Christ's exaltation over the angels is stated in verse 4, that he inherited the superior name, that is, the name of God's Son. This is reinforced in the next two citations, from Psalm 2 and 2 Samuel 7. Psalm 2 is an explicitly "messianic" psalm, referring in verse 2 to "the Anointed One." The early Christians made a strong connection between its statement that "the kings of the earth set themselves, and the rulers take counsel together, against the Lord and against his anointed" (v. 2), and the trial and condemnation of Jesus Christ.[1] Most important is the verse quoted in our passage, "The LORD said to me, 'You are my Son; today I have begotten you'" (v. 7).

This raises the question as to when Jesus inherited the name "Son of God," as Hebrews 1:4 says, or when he was begotten as God's Son (Heb. 1:5, citing Ps. 2:7). After all, was he not the only begotten Son of God from before all worlds? Isn't that the point of John 3:16, that "God so loved the world, that he gave his [one and] only Son"? In what way, then, did Christ *inherit* the name "Son of God"?

There are several times in Jesus' life and ministry when a heavenly voice was heard proclaiming him to be God's Son. For instance, when the angel Gabriel announced the birth of a son to the virgin Mary, he said, "He will be great and will be called the Son of the Most High" (Luke 1:32). Some commentators therefore conclude that it was in his incarnation that Jesus was appointed or declared Son of God. Similarly, when Jesus was baptized by John the Baptist, we are told that the voice of God himself was audibly heard, saying, "This is my beloved Son, with whom I am well pleased" (Matt. 3:17). Therefore some mark this, the inauguration of Christ's public ministry, as his proclamation as Son. Again, when Jesus was transfigured in glory before the three disciples, God's voice was heard, "This is my beloved Son, with whom I am well pleased" (Matt. 17:5).

About one thing we must be clear: Jesus is eternally Son of God. He did not become Son of God at or subsequent to his incarnation. J. I. Packer explains that the relationship of the "God-man to the Father while He was on earth was not a new relationship occasioned by the incarnation, but the continuation in time of the eternal relationship between the Son and the Father in heaven. As in heaven, so on earth."[2] Thus Paul says in Romans 1:3–4 that according to Jesus' human nature he is called son of David, but according to his divine nature he is the Son of God. Likewise, John 1:14 tells us that in the incarnation "the Word became flesh and dwelt among us," and as a result we saw the "glory as of the only Son from the Father."

---

1. For an outline of the significance of Psalm 2 to the early church, see Donald A. Hagner, *Encountering the Book of Hebrews* (Grand Rapids: Baker, 2002), 47.

2. J. I. Packer, *Knowing God* (Downers Grove, Ill.: InterVarsity, 1979), 54–55.

So, if Jesus is eternally Son of God, what do we make of the statement in Psalm 2:7 that "today I have begotten you"? Fortunately, the New Testament helps us elsewhere, as is often the case. One of the principles of interpretation that the writer of Hebrews strictly follows is that Scripture interprets Scripture. We call this principle *the analogy of faith.* In the case of Psalm 2:7 we are helped by the apostle Paul, who cited it in his sermon at Pisidian Antioch: "We bring you the good news that what God promised to the fathers, this he has fulfilled to us their children by raising Jesus, as also it is written in the second Psalm, 'You are my Son, today I have begotten you' " (Acts 13:32–33).

This refers to Christ's resurrection, and the idea of begetting here is that of declaring or manifesting to the full. Paul amplifies this in Romans 1:4, writing that Jesus "was declared to be the Son of God in power according to the Spirit of holiness by his resurrection from the dead, Jesus Christ our Lord." Here, then, is why those first-century Christians must hold fast to their faith in Christ, as must we: when God raised our Lord Jesus from the dead, having been crucified for our sins, God the Father brought him into his inheritance, manifesting before all the world his status as divine Son.

This idea of inheritance is key to the point of these verses. When we think of someone inheriting riches or a name, it has nothing to do with the merit or achievement of that person. Quite often, heirs are unworthy people who lack the very qualities that allowed their forebearer to amass his fortune. To be an heir simply means that you were born in an advantageous position and will not have to work for a living like the rest of us.

But that was not the way it was seen in Scripture, nor in the ancient world in which the original readers of this letter lived. In Roman society, when a son came of age, and if he was approved as a man by his father, he would be ceremonially received and bestowed with his name. So it was in Christ's resurrection: by raising him from the dead, God gave final approval to him who had perfectly fulfilled the law and obediently endured the cross, bestowing on him the name "Son of God" with the Father's divine and supernatural signature. Furthermore, in the ancient world sons inevitably entered into their father's occupation and business. Today, very few of us follow in our father's footsteps. But back then this is what it meant to be a son. To be accepted and approved as son meant all these things—approval, inheritance, and fitness to take up the business of the father. James Montgomery Boice writes,

> The resurrection of Jesus Christ establishes the doctrine of our Lord's deity. When he lived upon earth Jesus claimed to be equal with God and that God would raise him from the dead three days after his execution by the Jewish and Roman authorities. . . . The resurrection is God's seal on Christ's claim to divinity. Jesus was "designated Son of God in power according to the Spirit of holiness by his resurrection from the dead" (Rom. 1:4).[3]

By means of the resurrection, God the Father declared that Jesus Christ, and he alone, is the worthy heir and the true Son of God.

The second citation, from 2 Samuel 7:14, serves to augment the point made by the first: "I will be to him a father, and he shall be to me a son." This was originally spoken by the prophet Nathan, as God's response to King David's godly desire to build a temple for the Lord. In this famous passage God promised David that he would always have an heir, and that his son would build God's house. As with many Old Testament prophecies, this had a near and an ultimate fulfillment. On the one hand it applied to Solomon, who built the temple and whom God treated with fatherly affection. But there were things said of this son that could not be true of any merely human descendant of David, especially the statement that "I will establish the throne of his kingdom forever" (2 Sam. 7:13). This connects the prophecy forward to David's greater Son, Jesus Christ, of whom God says, "I will be to him a father, and he shall be to me a son." John Owen explains that this expresses "the paternal care of God over Christ in his kingdom, and the dearness of Christ himself unto him."[4]

The point, then, is, "To which of the angels did God ever say things like this?" The answer is that God said such things to none of the angels, and since he specially dignified Jesus Christ with the name of his own Son, Christ must be recognized as superior. That being the case, to whom should we

---

3. James Montgomery Boice, *Foundations of the Christian Faith* (Downers Grove, Ill.: InterVarsity, 1986), 342–43.

4. John Owen, *An Exposition of the Epistle to the Hebrews*, 7 vols. (Edinburgh: Banner of Truth, 1991), 3:145.

turn for salvation? Whom shall we worship as our Lord and whom shall we follow, except the one proclaimed worthy to be heir and Son of God? Jesus taught, "No one comes to the Father except through me" (John 14:6), for his salvation is that of the only begotten Son.

Superior Because He Is Worshiped

Hebrews 1:6 gives the second argument for Christ's superiority, namely, that the angels are commanded to worship him. To prove this, the writer cites either Psalm 97:7 or Deuteronomy 32:43, both of which include the statement he has in mind: "And again, when he brings the firstborn into the world, he says, 'Let all God's angels worship him.'" In the Hebrew text, the angels are referred to as *elohim*, or gods, a not uncommon Old Testament way of speaking of the angels as heavenly beings. The Greek translation, the Septuagint, translates it as "angels," and it is from there that our author cites; since he writes under the inspiration of the Holy Spirit, our text tells us the correct interpretation of Psalm 97:7 and Deuteronomy 32:43.

First, we have the writer's own introductory statement: "When he brings the firstborn into the world," to which he adds God's command that the angels should worship him. This probably refers to the coming of Jesus in his first advent, beginning with the virgin birth. Perhaps the most spectacular part of that first Christmas was the choir of angels singing praise. Angels also rejoiced at the open tomb, and again at Jesus' ascension into heaven. The Book of Revelation reveals that the angels forever worship the Son who is lion and lamb as he sits upon his throne (see Rev. 5:5–6).

Furthermore, the writer of Hebrews speaks of Christ as God's "firstborn," and it is for this that he is worshiped. The point here seems to be Jesus' special status over all the created realm. It does not mean that Jesus is first among creatures, but rather that he is exalted above the creatures. The idea is again that of inheritance and unique dignity. F. F. Bruce explains, "He is called firstborn because he exists before all creation and because all creation is his heritage."[5]

5. F. F. Bruce, *The Epistle to the Hebrews*, rev. ed., New International Commentary on the New Testament (Grand Rapids: Eerdmans, 1990), 56.

Great as the angels are, they are still creatures. So when the firstborn enters the world, it is no surprise to see them as chief among his worshipers. This was God's command and their delight. It shows that Jesus is the One we ought to worship, the One we want to trust and follow. Far from worshiping the angels, we should follow their example and worship God's Son.

SUPERIOR BECAUSE OF HIS DIVINE SOVEREIGNTY

Third, the writer of Hebrews points out that Christ is superior because of his divine sovereignty. This is the point of the brief citation in verse 7, as well as of the longer one in verses 8 and 9.

Verse 7 cites Psalm 104:4, saying, "Of the angels he says, 'He makes his angels winds, and his ministers a flame of fire.'" This is a description of the angels as servants, even glorious ones. We should not despise angels; it is to God's glory that these are the kinds of servants and ministers he creates and deploys. Bruce writes, "Angels are portrayed as executing the divine commands with the swiftness of wind and the strength of fire."[6] We would not want to toy with angels. Though their glory is lesser than the Son's, it is a very significant glory. Everywhere they appear in the Bible they strike fear into men's hearts. In the Book of Revelation, even the apostle John was tempted to worship the angel who appeared to him. "You must not do that!" the angel rebuked him. "Worship God" (Rev. 19:10).

Nevertheless, as great and mighty and glorious as angels are, they minister while Christ sits enthroned. They have servanthood, and he has sovereignty. Therefore, the statement of their glory as servants is set against another Old Testament citation in verses 8 and 9, from Psalm 45:6–7, which exults in Christ's sovereign glory: "But of the Son he says, 'Your throne, O God, is forever and ever, the scepter of uprightness is the scepter of your kingdom. You have loved righteousness and hated wickedness; therefore God, your God, has anointed you with the oil of gladness beyond your companions.'"

Christ's enthronement was central to the Old Testament expectation. This theme starts in passages like Psalm 2 and 2 Samuel 7, which our author

6. Ibid., 58.

has already brought into play. But it continues all through the Old Testament. Isaiah rested the hope of his generation on God's promise of a Savior: "For to us a child is born, to us a son is given; and the government shall be upon his shoulder, and his name shall be called Wonderful Counselor, Mighty God, Everlasting Father, Prince of Peace. Of the increase of his government and of peace there will be no end, on the throne of David and over his kingdom, to establish it and to uphold it with justice and with righteousness from this time forth and forevermore" (Isa. 9:6–8). This is what the angel told Mary would be accomplished through her virgin-born Son: "He will be great and will be called the Son of the Most High. And the Lord God will give to him the throne of his father David, and he will reign over the house of Jacob forever, and of his kingdom there will be no end" (Luke 1:32–33).

All this was anticipated in the remarkable lines of Psalm 45. This is a wedding psalm, depicting a royal bride as she prepares to enter into marriage with the king: "All glorious is the princess in her chamber, with robes interwoven with gold. In many-colored robes she is led to the king" (Ps. 45:13–14). The psalm begins with words that express the throbbing in her heart: the bride celebrates his handsome looks, his royal splendor and majesty, his mighty strength, and the dignity of his cause (Ps. 45:1–5). But then verse 6 explodes the bounds of propriety. The psalm suddenly exclaims of the king, "Your throne, O God, is forever and ever." This verse is an intense example of what is true of the Old Testament as a whole, that it demands fulfillment in the coming of Jesus Christ. However a Jewish scribe might explain away this statement, no king of Judah could live up to this acclamation. Only Jesus Christ, the son of David and the Son of God, can fulfill this boast of an eternal reign that is perfect in righteousness. The writer of Hebrews is teaching us how to read the Old Testament (and particularly the Psalms), namely, to read it through a Christ-colored lens—promising and anticipating, portraying and celebrating the coming of Jesus Christ. The handling of the Psalms by the author of Hebrews shows us what Jesus himself taught the forlorn disciples on the Emmaus road: "That everything written about me in the Law of Moses and the Prophets and the Psalms must be fulfilled" (Luke 24:44).

Just as the opening verses of Hebrews (Heb. 1:1–3) introduced the anointed offices of Jesus—prophet, priest, and king—Psalm 45 goes on to speak of this royal groom's anointing: "You have loved righteousness and hated wickedness. Therefore God, your God, has anointed you with the oil of gladness beyond your companions" (v. 7). There could hardly be a clearer reference to the Messiah—the Anointed One. He is identified as God: "Your throne, O God, is forever and ever" (Ps. 45:6). But it is "God, your God," who anoints him. Not only does this provide an important Old Testament foreshadowing of the doctrine of the Trinity, but it stunningly asserts that the true king of glory, the true Messiah in whom righteousness will come to reign, is one with God himself.

Note, too, the basis for this exaltation—the Messiah's perfect righteousness. The psalm says, "The scepter of uprightness is the scepter of your kingdom. You have loved righteousness and hated wickedness" (Heb. 1:8–9; Ps. 45:6–7). This is why Jesus is exalted; this is why he is anointed as Messiah and Savior, because in his righteousness he is worthy to reign as God's Son and is able to save sinners.

All this being true, to whom else will we turn for the righteousness we so desperately lack, but need if we are to stand in God's judgment? Who else will reign over this earth to establish righteousness? To what power, to what authority, will we run seeking safety and refuge, except the One whom God has enthroned forever, who bears the title, "You, O God," whose scepter is that of righteousness, and who, at the end of days, will establish righteousness upon the earth?

"I Have Become Your Father"

The five Old Testament citations in Hebrews 1:5–9 amply prove the writer's point that Jesus is superior to the angels, and therefore worthy of our adoration. He is superior because his name is greater, Son of God; he is superior because he is worshiped by the angels themselves; and he is superior because of his royal sovereignty and divine anointing.

It is one thing, however, to acknowledge Christ's greatness and worthiness to be praised, and another to come to him personally seeking your own salvation. The writer has proved the former, but the latter is his goal, that is, that we should hold fast to Jesus Christ as Savior and Lord.

In all of these Old Testament citations, God the Father acts and ordains with regard to Jesus Christ. He appoints and declares Jesus as Son and heir;

he commands angels to worship him; he enthrones him on the eternal throne of righteousness. Why? Because the Father loves the Son and wants to exalt and bless him, just as the Son loves the Father and wants him to be praised.

But there was another reason for all these things, a reason that is amazing and thrilling. God appointed and exalted and enthroned his Son so that we might be reconciled to him and enter into salvation through the Son as a mediator. This is why the eternal Son became man, and as man was declared Son of God in power—it was for our sakes, because of his love for us. God's Son became like us, so that we might become like him through his resurrection.

If you have believed on Jesus Christ as God's Son and come to him to be your Savior, then these verses speak not merely to him but also to you. You, in the quiet of your heart, hear God's tender voice say these precious, dear words of verse 5 to you: "You are my son, today I have become your Father." Forevermore, you may call God Father, with all the security and care and privileges of a beloved child, in Christ. You read in verse 6 that Jesus is called the "firstborn." Then realize what Paul wrote in Colossians 1:18, that he is not merely the firstborn *over* creation, but that in his resurrection he is the firstborn *of* a new creation to which we belong by faith. Paul writes in Romans 8:29 that we were "predestined to be conformed to the image of his Son, in order that he might be the firstborn among many brothers." Jesus is the prototype of a new race in his resurrection, the firstborn to whom we are brothers and sisters.

Finally, verse 9 speaks of God anointing his enthroned Son "with the oil of gladness beyond your companions." We are among the companions of whom God speaks. By his righteousness Christ gains a kingdom, and we are members of that kingdom; we will reign with him, as his blessed companions, forever and ever. His joy and his righteousness are the blessings he gives to his royal subjects. This is what the prophet Isaiah foretold, speaking of the anointed Jesus Christ and the work he would come to do:

> The Spirit of the Lord God is upon me, because the Lord has anointed me to bring good news to the poor . . . to grant to those who mourn in Zion—to give them a beautiful headdress instead of ashes, the oil of gladness instead

of mourning, the garment of praise instead of a faint spirit; that they may be called oaks of righteousness, the planting of the LORD, that he may be glorified. (Isa. 61:1–3)

Beauty for ashes, gladness for mourning, praise instead of despair, a righteous people displaying the glory of the Lord—all this is the bounty of our righteous king, God's firstborn Son and our elder-born brother, his blessings to all who trust in him.

4

THE REIGNING LORD

Hebrews 1:10–14

You, Lord, laid the foundation of the earth in the beginning, and
the heavens are the work of your hands; they will perish, but you
remain; they will all wear out like a garment, like a robe you will
roll them up. (Heb. 1:10–12)

No chapter in the entire New Testament sets forth the divinity of Jesus Christ so thoroughly and fervently as this first chapter of the Book of Hebrews. Other chapters are notable for their portrayal of Christ's deity, such as John 1 and Colossians 1. But for the sheer weight of testimony to the divine nature of Christ, there is nothing in all of Scripture like the barrage of Old Testament verses applied to him in Hebrews 1.

THE DEITY OF CHRIST

From the very beginning, Hebrews 1 brings Christ into the closest relationship with God and his work. He is called "heir of all things, through whom also he created the world . . . the radiance of the glory of God and the exact imprint of his nature, and he upholds the universe by the word of his power" (vv. 2–3). In verse 6 we see the angels worshiping him, and by the testimony of the angels themselves, only God is to be worshiped (Rev. 19:10). But if there is any doubt left that the Son is God, this is dispelled utterly in verse 8, which says to him, "Your throne, O God, is forever and ever." This is a great trinitarian passage, for the Son is addressed as "God," and yet it also says that his God has exalted him: "Therefore God, your God, has anointed you with the oil of gladness beyond your companions."

With such a testimony, it is impossible to see how the authority of Scripture can be maintained while the deity of Christ is denied. Verse 10, which begins our present passage, is the climax of this whole presentation. Here the Holy Spirit, speaking through the writer of Hebrews, informs us of these words which are spoken by the Father to the Son: "You, Lord, laid the foundation of the earth in the beginning, and the heavens are the work of your hands; they will perish, but you remain; they will all wear out like a garment, like a robe you will roll them up, like a garment they will be changed. But you are the same, and your years will have no end."

It is traditional, when speaking of the attributes of God, to distinguish between his communicable and incommunicable attributes. Some of his attributes God can and does communicate to us, such as goodness, mercy, and holiness, to name a few. But other attributes are part and parcel of God's deity, and cannot be communicated to mortal creatures. In these verses, it is divine incommunicable attributes that are ascribed to the Son— attributes like eternity, omnipotence, and immutability. Indeed, we are deliberately reminded of Genesis 1:1—"In the beginning, God created the heavens and the earth." Here that work of creation is ascribed to the Lord Jesus Christ, with all the implications of divinity that accompany it.

We also observe here a striking contrast between the creation and the Son of God. Heaven and earth, we are told, will perish. The great works of God in creation will come to an end—the majesty of the mountains, the roaring of the waterfall, the beauty of the valley—all these will run their course and ultimately perish. Indeed, like an old set of clothes, they are even now wearing out. Stars are using up their hydrogen; matter is converted to energy and there is loss. Ours is a dying universe with its end in sight.

If this is true of God's creation, how much more of man's work! The tallest skyscraper will fall; the dams will burst; the greatest achievements will be forgotten. All this will happen not merely in the long-running course of time, with its decay, but suddenly, by God's Son when he comes to end history and judge the world. He will "roll it up like a robe," exchanging it at his desire for a new garment. The apostle Peter writes of this: "But the day of the Lord will come like a thief, and then the heavens will pass away with a roar, and the heavenly bodies will be burned up and dissolved, and the earth and the works that are done on it will be exposed" (2 Peter 3:10).

As Paul writes, "The present form of this world is passing away" (1 Cor. 7:31). But of God's Son we read the opposite: "They will perish, but you remain; they will all wear out like a garment. . . . But you are the same, and your years will have no end" (Heb. 1:11–12).

It is hard to imagine a more emphatic portrayal of Christ's divinity, a mighty Lord and God who is worthy of our faith.

PSALM 102: LAMENT AND REJOICING

Whenever we see an Old Testament citation, it is good to look back at the passage in its original context, because the New Testament writer often has that in mind as well. This is especially true of Hebrews 1:10–12, which is a lengthy citation from Psalm 102, which has this subtitle: "A Prayer of one afflicted, when he is faint and pours out his complaint before the Lord."

In the first half of that psalm, the writer laments the decaying nature of life, the weakness and ultimately the failure of all created things, and especially of human nature. He writes, "For my days pass away like smoke, and my bones burn like a furnace. My heart is struck down like grass and has withered. . . . Because of my loud groaning my bones cling to my flesh. . . . I lie awake; I am like a lonely sparrow on the housetop. All the day my enemies taunt me; those who deride me use my name for a curse. For I eat ashes like bread and mingle tears with my drink" (Ps. 102:3–9). In particular, the writer sees his mortality as a result of man's alienation from God on account of sin: ". . . because of your indignation and anger; for you have taken me up and thrown me down. My days are like an evening shadow; I wither away like grass" (Ps. 102:10–11). Man's mutability, weakness, and mortality on account of sin make up the content of this lament.

These are cries that will find themselves on the lips of everyone who lives on this earth for any length of time. Our days do pass away like smoke, and our bones do give way. Every one of us must reckon with the fact that death awaits us; even as we live we "wither away like grass," here today and gone tomorrow. The psalmist seems to be motivated by the destruction of Jerusalem at the hands of the Babylonians; in the bitterness of defeat he eats ashes and mingles his drink with tears. And while we live, we too will know the taunts and the oppression of enemies we are too weak to oppose.

But in the second half of the psalm, the lamenting man lifts up his eyes to see God and there he finds a great hope: "But you, O LORD, are enthroned forever.... You will arise and have pity on Zion.... For the LORD builds up Zion; he appears in his glory" (Ps. 102:12–16). Though all is lost in this life, though hardship and even death await, though the worst calamity brings destruction, the man who trusts the Lord sees him in his eternal reign of power, his unchanging and unchangeable character, and there he finds hope. For as God said in Isaiah 51:6, "The heavens vanish like smoke, the earth will wear out like a garment, and they who dwell in it will die in like manner; but my salvation will be forever, and my righteousness will never be dismayed." Despite all we may lose in this life, through faith in God we receive a salvation that is eternal and secure.

That is how Psalm 102 goes, and with the words of our passage in Hebrews 1 it approaches its end, remembering that God created all things and endures long beyond their end: "They will perish, but you remain; they will all wear out like a garment.... But you are the same, and your years will have no end."

One purpose in Hebrews 1 is to show Christ's superiority to the angels, and therefore the superiority of the new covenant to the old. That contrast is inescapable in light of these verses. If these things are true of the Son, then he is worthy of all our trust. We would be foolish in the extreme not to turn for our salvation to such a mighty Savior.

FATHER TO SON

In Psalm 102, these words are addressed to Yahweh, the personal, covenant name of the Lord in the Old Testament. What is striking about their repetition in Hebrews 1 is that here they are spoken by God to Jesus, the Son. It is God who addresses him as "Lord," which is equivalent to the Old Testament "Yahweh" or "Jehovah."

Indeed, in the light of the New Testament we must see both halves of Psalm 102 as applying to our Lord Jesus Christ. *He* is the afflicted man pouring out his lament before his Father. It is *his* voice, as he faces and then takes up the cross, that we hear crying out, "For my days pass away like smoke, and my bones burn like a furnace. My heart is struck down like grass and has withered. . . . All the day my enemies taunt me" (Ps. 102:3–4, 8). Jesus, in his humanity, knew what it was to have his days cut short, to die too young, afflicted and despised by men, and abandoned by even his friends. Crucified in shame, he died a cursed death, with all the bitterness and darkness a man can experience.

The second half of the psalm constitutes heaven's response to the anguished cry of the Savior. Yes, as man he was cursed and rejected and died on the cross, but as resurrected and exalted Son, God says to him: "But you, O Lord, are enthroned forever" (Ps. 102:12). Yes, the world may have crucified you, but I have enthroned you! "They will perish, but you will remain; they will all wear out like a garment. You will change them like a robe, and they will pass away, but you are the same, and your years have no end" (Ps. 102:26–27). Arthur Pink comments:

> *This* was God's answer to the plaint of Christ's being "cut off" in the midst of His days. . . . As man, in resurrection, He received "life for evermore." Do we really grasp this? For [almost two thousand] years since the Cross, men have been born, have lived, and then died. Statesmen, emperors, and kings have appeared on the scene and then passed away. But there is one glorious Man who spans the centuries, who in His own humanity bridges those [two millennia]. He has not died, nor even grown old: He is "the same yesterday, and today, and forever!" [Heb. 13:8].[1]

Seated at God's Right Hand

Psalm 102 is a wonderful portrait of what the resurrection and ascension of Christ are all about. We can see why the writer of Hebrews turned his thoughts to that great psalm. But in verse 13 we find yet another great psalm, the last of the Old Testament citations used to uphold the supremacy of Christ in Hebrews 1. Verse 13 shows us the opening words of Psalm 110:

---

1. A. W. Pink, *An Exposition of Hebrews* (Grand Rapids: Baker, 1954), 73–74.

"And to which of the angels has he ever said, 'Sit at my right hand until I make your enemies a footstool for your feet'?"

If the words of Psalm 102 are God's verbal reply to the cross, in this quotation from Psalm 110 we see God's action that accompanied those words. This enthronement is in keeping with what was said in Hebrews 1:3: "After making purification for sins, he sat down at the right hand of the Majesty on high."

Psalm 110 is the most frequently quoted psalm in the New Testament, because of what it tells us about where Christ went when he departed this earth in glory, and what he is doing now. The imagery of him seated comes from the oriental court, where the king sat upon his throne while his vassals and servants stood before him to show their deference and his supremacy. This is the picture the Bible gives us of God's throne room in passages like Revelation 7, where the angels and elders and living creatures stand before the enthroned sovereign God, worshiping him and ready to do his will. To be told, "Sit at my right hand," signifies a singular honor and dignity. It shows rank and power and authority in the kingdom.

The fact that Jesus is seated on the throne of God does not mean that he is inactive. Rather, he is attentively concerned with the affairs of his flock. Being seated, he wields authority over and for the sake of the church. Just perusing through the Book of Acts you will see how active the ascended and seated Christ was on behalf of the early church. He sent forth his Spirit to empower his human messengers and to bring many others to faith, as he did on the day of Pentecost in Acts 2. When Stephen, the first martyr, was facing the bloodthirsty mob, he cried out, "Behold, I see the heavens opened, and the Son of Man standing at the right hand of God" (Acts 7:56). Jesus stood to receive his own into the heavenly courts.

When the zealous persecutor, Saul of Tarsus, was heading to Damascus to harass the believers there, the risen Jesus appeared to him in all his glory, saying, "Saul, Saul, why are you persecuting me?" (9:4). Indeed, he commands angels and sends them for the service of his people, as was the case when Peter was rescued from Herod's prison by an angel (12:6–10). This is what the writer of Hebrews tells us about angels in verse 14: "Are they not all ministering spirits sent out to serve for the sake of those who are to inherit salvation?" The angels are servants who are sent; the risen Christ is the Lord who sends.

What a comfort it is to know that our Lord is so busy on our behalf from his heavenly seat of divine authority. We may never know when he has sent angels to minister to us in time of need, to thwart spiritual antagonists, and to strengthen us in times of weakness. Like the chariots of fire that surrounded the prophet Elisha, how many times do we receive unseen help from those ministering spirits that Christ sends to us?

We also know that Jesus sends the Holy Spirit to teach us of him, to enlighten our minds in the knowledge of God, to renew our wills, and to guide us in paths of righteousness. We know that Jesus intercedes for us with the Father, ensuring our acceptance in God's presence, sanctifying our petitions, and pleading our every cause from his seat of honor and favor and authority at God's right hand. Christ is exceedingly busy on our behalf! He who "upholds the universe by the word of his power," as we are told in verse 3, also upholds our faith by his prayers for us. As he said to his disciple Peter before his time of weakness: "Simon, Simon, behold, Satan demanded to have you, that he might sift you like wheat, but I have prayed for you that your faith may not fail" (Luke 22:31–32).

Every Enemy Defeated

Hebrews says that Christ will sit at God's right hand "until I make your enemies a footstool for your feet." In ancient times, a victorious general would place his foot upon the throat of a defeated foe, as Joshua had his commanders do to the captured kings of Canaan (Josh. 10:24). Who, then, are Jesus' enemies? The apostle Paul writes in 1 Corinthians: "Then comes the end, when he delivers the kingdom to God the Father after destroying every rule and every authority and power. For he must reign until he has put all his enemies under his feet. The last enemy to be destroyed is death" (1 Cor. 15:24–26).

The curse of the law, sin, Satan, the worldly powers, death, the grave—these are Christ's enemies. During his earthly ministry he advanced into the ranks of his enemy, casting out demons, purifying leprosy, bringing healing to the sick, exposing hypocrisy, opposing false teaching, humbling the proud, cleansing the temple of moneychangers, and all the while calling sinners to faith and repentance. It is especially in the extension of the gospel that he now overcomes his foes as men and women come to saving faith in him. In the end, he will have no enemies left standing, as the Book of Revelation tells us: "Then Death and Hades were thrown into the lake of fire" (Rev. 20:14). "He will wipe away every tear from [his people's] eyes, and death shall be no more, neither shall there be mourning nor crying nor pain anymore, for the former things have passed away" (Rev. 21:4).

Christ our Lord sits enthroned at God's right hand until his enemies become his footstool. This is the goal of his activity, after which he will present his triumph to God the Father. And then he will reign forever and ever, as proclaimed by the voices in heaven: "The kingdom of the world has become the kingdom of our Lord and of his Christ, and he shall reign forever and ever" (Rev. 11:15).

A Sufficient Savior

Thus concludes the sevenfold exposition of the supremacy and deity of Jesus Christ, going back to verse 4—seven Old Testament passages that prove his superiority to angels. How fitting that this portrait concludes with Jesus seated at God's right hand, for that is where he is now, reigning as Lord over and on behalf of his bride the church. He is a sufficient Savior, worthy of our trust and praise.

In these verses we see three divine attributes applied to Jesus Christ: eternity, omnipotent power, and immutability. Each of these attributes gives us compelling reasons to trust him as our Savior.

Ours is a Savior who was there from eternity, when the worlds were born. "You, Lord, laid the foundation of the earth in the beginning, and the heavens are the work of your hands" (v. 10). Here is a rock on which we can stand assured. And yet he came into this world as one of us; he took up humanity that he might make a place for man in eternal heaven. Even now he opens a door for all who would come to God through him.

Furthermore, our reigning Lord wields omnipotent might, overcoming all the enemies that oppose his reign, enemies that also enslave and afflict us. And yet it was through the greatest weakness that he lifted the heaviest burden, even the weight of our sins. It was because he submitted to the cross in all its agony and shame that God raised him to the position of glory and authority. On the cross Jesus showed his worthiness to reign in might forever, and therefore God has crowned him Lord of all. From God's right hand he is able to help us in time of need and save us unto eternal life.

Finally, our Savior is immutable—that is, unchanging and unchangeable: "You are the same, and your years will have no end" (Heb. 1:12). "Jesus Christ is the same yesterday and today and forever" (Heb. 13:8), and therefore we may always turn to him with confidence for salvation. He is never going to change his mind about us or lose his power to save us.

If all this is true, what can a soul need in time or eternity that cannot be found in Christ? Do you need pardon for your sin? See him exalted and know that God has accepted the sacrifice of his blood on your behalf. Do you need reconciliation to God? There he is at God's right hand, interceding for you and offering his own perfect work as the ground of your acceptance. Do you need newness of life—a new heart, a new strength to follow him? From his heavenly throne he sends mighty resources—even angels to your aid. Better yet, he sends his Holy Spirit to work within you with his own power.

Do you have troubles? Difficult decisions to make? Choices that worry you or problems that cause you fear and anxiety? Christ is enthroned in power, a Savior who cares for you with wisdom and love, with power and a grand purpose for your future. The practical value of this truth is immense, for it leads us to trust him and glorify him with our blood-purchased lives. Do you fear death? He is reigning now until even that last enemy shall be conquered. Because he reigns victorious, death will have no hold on you, but only ushers you into the courts of glory.

What is there you might need but that the risen and reigning Lord and Savior is the answer? There is nothing you might face, nothing you might lack, nothing you might need in all your weakness and sin and human frailty, that is not found abundantly in him who loves you and gave himself for you and now reigns forever as Savior and Lord, who remains the same and whose years shall have no end.

5

PAY ATTENTION!

Hebrews 2:1–4

Therefore we must pay much closer attention to what we have heard, lest we drift away from it. (Heb. 2:1)

e are living in a time when truth does not seem to count for much. The intellectual climate is summed up by the popular bumper sticker, "My karma ran over my dogma." In other words, "Don't get hung up on matters of doctrine or truth. Feeling good is what really matters." That may sound tolerant and attractive, but it is a far cry from the sentiment of the biblical writers, to whom such an attitude is a recipe for disaster.

To the apostles, as to the prophets before them, and as to the Lord Jesus Christ, matters of truth are of the highest priority. What we believe about Jesus is the most important thing, determining both our eternal destiny and our usefulness to God in this world. The apostle John wrote, "Whoever believes in him is not condemned, but whoever does not believe is condemned already, because he has not believed in the name of the only Son of God" (John 3:18). It is through belief in the truth that God saves us and then works in our hearts to make us holy. F. F. Bruce thus writes: "The truth and teaching of the Gospel must not be held lightly; they are of supreme moment, they are matters of life and death, and must be cherished and obeyed at all costs. The danger of drifting away from them, and so losing them, cannot be treated too gravely."[1]

A DANGER: DRIFTING AWAY

It is to this matter that the writer of Hebrews now turns in the first verse of chapter 2, "We must pay much closer attention to what we have heard, lest we drift away from it." This is the first of five major warnings in Hebrews, all of which deal with the danger of falling away from faith in Christ and therefore from salvation. The Book of Hebrews is a sermon on the theme "Do not fall away." These Hebrew Christians were being persecuted by the Jewish community around them, and the apostolic writer urgently warns them not to renounce Jesus Christ under pressure.

The author focuses on the danger of "drifting away" from the message they had heard. The Greek word here is a nautical term, *pararreō*, describing a ship at sail that has drifted off course, or a ship in harbor that has slipped its moorings. In other contexts it is used to describe something that slips from our minds, or even a ring that slips off a finger. One of the key ideas here is that this drifting away is something that happens largely unnoticed. While it is happening the changes are imperceptible; only later do its consequences become clear. This is a grave danger, against which we must respond with careful attention.

Some years ago, when my family was vacationing in Hawaii, my brother and I went snorkeling in a bay that was breathtaking in its beauty, with its coral reef and multicolored fish. Before we entered the water, our guide warned us against straying beyond a certain point because of the strong current that would pull us out to sea. He concluded with stories of people who had failed to pay attention and had been pulled out by the current, only to have their bodies wash up on other islands miles away. It was an effective deterrent, to say the least! This is what the writer of Hebrews wanted for his teaching. There is a current to this present evil age, pulling strongly out from the safe harbor of salvation in Christ. We do not have to actively betray Jesus

---

1. F. F. Bruce: *The Epistle to the Hebrews*, rev. ed., New International Commentary on the New Testament (Grand Rapids: Eerdmans, 1990), 60.

or renounce our faith. Simply by not paying attention, by becoming preoccupied with the sights and sounds of this world, we can be easily drawn out
until we are swept away forever.

Do you realize that? Do you realize that if you do not pay attention to
your spiritual condition it will deteriorate on its own? Do you realize, given
the corrupt nature of this world and of your heart, that you naturally become
dull and then deadened spiritually, steadily believing the lies of this evil age?
Without giving heed to the spiritual resources God provides, your heart will
revert to greed, pride, avarice, sensuality, and malice—all those characteristics that define our natural state in sin and lead to destruction.

The Book of Hebrews is notable for confronting us with the reality of
apostasy. To be sure, the Bible teaches the eternal security of all true believers in Jesus Christ. Jesus taught: "I give them eternal life, and they will never
perish, and no one will snatch them out of my hand" (John 10:28). Yet it is
also true that not all who give profession of faith are true believers. Judas
Iscariot is one infamous example. He walked with Jesus for three years.
Apparently the other disciples never suspected he was a fraud until he had
betrayed our Lord. Another excellent example is Paul's one-time companion Demas. At the end of Colossians and Philemon, Paul adds his name to
the list of his close companions. But in 2 Timothy we read these sober words:
"Demas, in love with this present world, has deserted me" (2 Tim. 4:10).
Here are the cases of a disciple of Jesus and a fellow-laborer with the apostle Paul. If they could fall away, we can, too.

We are secure through faith in Jesus Christ. But like a good tree, true faith
is revealed by its fruit (Matt. 7:17–19). Therefore Peter tells us to "be all the
more diligent to make your calling and election sure" (2 Peter 1:10). "Examine yourselves," Paul adds, "to see whether you are in the faith" (2 Cor. 13:5).
We must therefore persevere and use the resources God gives us to bear fruit
and thus not to drift away.

A Command: Pay Attention!

Mindful of the danger of apostasy, the author of Hebrews gives the accompanying command: "Therefore we must pay much closer attention to what
we have heard" (Heb. 2:1). "What we have heard" is the message of salvation
in God's Son, as the preceding chapter declared.

The Greek word for "pay attention," *prosechō*, is another term with nautical implications; it was used to denote holding to a course or securing an anchor. There is a danger, the writer argues, and there is also a remedy. To avoid drifting off course you hold the wheel of the ship in line; to avoid slipping out with the current you make fast the anchor.

Drifting away happens on its own without much effort on our part, but staying on course is quite the opposite. It requires constant diligence! C. S. Lewis was typically perceptive when he wrote, "We have to be continually reminded of what we believe. Neither this belief nor any other will automatically remain alive in your mind. It must be fed. And as a matter of fact, if you examined a hundred people who had lost their faith in Christianity, I wonder how many of them would turn out to have been reasoned out of it by honest argument? Do not most people simply drift away?"[2] In the matter of our belief, as in all other matters, Christianity requires hard work; the New Testament describes the life of faith as a fight, a race, and a field in which a farmer labors. Paul says in various places: "I press on . . . I follow after . . . I strive . . . I fight."

When it comes to the past tense of our salvation—to what is already finished and secure, namely, our justification through faith in Christ—there is no place for our works. We receive forgiveness of our sins not by our work but by Christ's work. Faith is, first, essentially passive; we do not act but receive, resting upon Christ's saving action on our behalf. But when it comes to the present tense of our salvation—that which is worked out progressively, namely, our sanctification—this is extremely active. Martyn Lloyd-Jones explains it well: "In the matter of our righteousness and justification we can never say too often that we do nothing, we can do nothing, it is entirely the work of Christ. But once we are saved and given this new life, then the progressive work of sanctification does not call for passivity, and we are exhorted to activity."[3]

J. C. Ryle, in his masterpiece on the Christian life, a book titled simply *Holiness*, added this:

2. C. S. Lewis, *Mere Christianity* (New York: Macmillan, 1952), 119–20.
3. D. Martyn Lloyd-Jones, *The Life of Peace* (Grand Rapids: Baker, 1992), 89.

I will never shrink from declaring my belief that there are no "spiritual gains without pains." I should as soon expect a farmer to prosper in business who contented himself with sowing his fields and never looking at them till harvest, as expect a believer to attain much holiness who was not diligent about his Bible-reading, his prayers, and the use of his Sundays.[4]

SANCTIFIED BY THE TRUTH

The particular means of security and sanctification the writer of Hebrews wants us to concentrate on is the gospel message, or, to put it more generally, God's saving revelation culminating in Christ. To use the metaphor of verse 1, God's Word is the anchor that secures our salvation, and it is the rudder by which we safely steer the ship of our souls.

This is a principle we vitally need today. People are looking for power from God to change their lives and assure them of salvation. Yet many Christians seem intent on using every method except the one highlighted for us all through the Bible, including this very passage: diligent study and understanding of the Word of God. Many people seek to come close to God through some intense emotional experience. Others follow disciplines, rituals, or special formulas that are guaranteed to make them more godly or secure. But look at the emphasis of the writer of Hebrews: "We must pay much closer attention to what we have heard," that is, to the Word of God.

We must remember and organize our thoughts around the Bible's message every day of our lives. We need to remember humanity's fall in sin and the corruption that remains within us. We need to recall what the Bible teaches about God's character—his faithfulness and power, his wisdom and love. We need to be told about his holiness and what an offense our sin is to him. Then we must look to the cross and see God's mercy so wondrously displayed, remembering that we have been purchased as a new and holy people, never more to dwell in sin. We need daily to ground our identity (1) in God's adoption of us as his own beloved children, (2) in Christ's blood that was shed to purchase us from sin, and (3) in our destiny as coheirs with him and as saints called to glory, but also as pilgrims sojourning through an alien

4. J. C. Ryle, *Holiness* (Darlington, U.K.: Evangelical Press, 1979), 21.

50

and dying world. In sum, we need to "pay closer attention" to the message of God's Word. It is like a firm anchor to hold us fast in salvation, like a compass to guide us safely .

This is a principle emphasized by Jesus himself. "If you abide in my word, you are truly my disciples," he said, "and you will know the truth, and the truth will set you free" (John 8:32–33). Praying to his Father on the night of his arrest, Jesus made it one of his chief requests that God's Word would lead his people to holiness: "Sanctify them in the truth," he prayed. "Your word is truth" (John 17:17).

The apostle Paul gave this principle similar emphasis. His great exposition of Christian doctrine in the Book of Romans turns to its application in the twelfth chapter. He begins by exhorting Christians to offer their lives to God in gratitude for his mercy. But how are we to live for God? Paul writes of the transforming effect of God's Word for those who "pay careful attention" to it: "Do not be conformed to this world, but be transformed by the renewal of your mind, that by testing you may discern what is the will of God, what is good and acceptable and perfect" (Rom. 12:2).

Donald Grey Barnhouse sums up this message in words that are pointed but true: "It is the Word of God that can establish the Christian and give him strength to overcome the old forces and to live the new. It can never be done in any other way. . . . You cannot find even one Christian on this earth who has developed into strength of wisdom and witness in the Lord who has attained it by any other means than study and meditation in the Word of God."[5] If we want to hold fast to Christ and advance in the faith, we must become people of the Book—the Bible—giving careful attention to its message all the days of our lives.

Two Reasons to Pay Attention

Hebrews 2:1 is the key verse in this passage, supplying both a warning and a command. Verses 2–4 provide support, making clear why this exhortation should be taken so seriously. In these verses we see both a negative and a positive commendation of the New Testament message in Christ.

---

5. Donald Grey Barnhouse, *Exposition of Bible Doctrines Taking the Epistle to the Romans as a Point of Departure*, 10 vols. (Grand Rapids: Baker, 1952), 1:137–38.

First there is negative support: "For since the message declared by angels proved to be reliable and every transgression or disobedience received a just retribution, how shall we escape if we neglect such a great salvation?" (Heb. 2:2–3a). This is an argument from the lesser to the greater. The old covenant had to be taken most seriously, even though—as we saw in Hebrews 1—it was spoken by angels and is subordinate to the new covenant. It was a valid and binding covenant, and "every transgression or disobedience received a just retribution."

The Old Testament, as the first readers of Hebrews well knew, is rife with examples. Korah, Dathan, and Abiram rebelled against Moses and were swallowed up into the earth (Num. 16:32). Aaron's sons Nadab and Abihu were consumed by fire (Lev. 10:2). And the whole generation of Israelites who did not trust the Lord were made to wander forty years in the wilderness and then to die. These are examples just from the exodus of those who disobeyed the old covenant and were severely punished.

If all that is true of the old covenant, which is the lesser revelation and lesser salvation, the writer then asks, How shall we escape if we neglect the greater salvation of the new covenant?

These words should dispel the common notion that the new covenant, or the New Testament, is an easier law than the old covenant. "God tried being legalistic in the Old Testament," the argument goes, "but since that didn't work, he changed his mind. In the New Testament he decided just to love us." First of all, this misunderstands the Old Testament, which presents not only a holy God but also a loving God to Israel. More importantly, it denies the point of our passage, which is that the stakes actually go up in the new covenant. There is a greater salvation, and the obligation to receive it in faith is more stringent. If we think the New Testament represents God rejecting judgment and embracing an undiscriminating love for everyone, we can be corrected merely by remembering the woes Jesus pronounced on the Pharisees. Of Capernaum, where many of his miracles were performed, Jesus said: "And you, Capernaum, will you be exalted to heaven? You will be brought down to Hades. For if the mighty works done in you had been done in Sodom, it would have remained until this day. But I tell you that it will be more tolerable on the day of judgment for the land of Sodom than for you" (Matt. 11:23–24).

If anything, Jesus' presentation of the law of Moses serves to bring its every nuance and spiritual demand into view. In the Sermon on the Mount he taught, "You have heard that it was said to those of old, 'You shall not murder; and whoever murders will be liable to judgment.' But I say to you that everyone who is angry with his brother will be liable to judgment; whoever insults his brother will be liable to the council" (Matt. 5:21–22). One after another, Jesus presents Old Testament laws in terms of their inner, higher, and spiritual demands. So did Jesus lower the demands of the law? According to him, "I have not come to abolish them but to fulfill them" (Matt. 5:17).

On the night of his arrest, Jesus said, "A new commandment I give to you, that you love one another" (John 13:34). People sometimes assume this means that God is willing to settle for less in the new covenant than in the old. Back in the Old Testament, they say, people wearied themselves obeying all kinds of rules and regulations. In the easier new covenant, all you have to do is love. That's it. Just love.

But of course, the command to love is vastly more difficult than the outward demands of the Old Testament law. It is easy to wash your hands. But washing your heart of anger, malice, and self-interest is another matter altogether. Therefore, the law's condemnation—always intended to drive sinners to God's grace in the gospel—is more intense in the light of Christ's coming. "This is the judgment," Jesus declared: "The light has come into the world, and people loved the darkness rather than the light because their deeds were evil" (John 3:19). Therefore it is most urgent for us to attend to and receive and hold fast the revelation that has come to us in Jesus Christ.

In the second half of verse 3 and then in verse 4, the revelation in Christ is positively commended. The writer says of this salvation, "It was declared at first by the Lord, and it was attested to us by those who heard, while God also bore witness by signs and wonders and various miracles and by gifts of the Holy Spirit distributed according to his will."

The gospel has come to us from the Lord himself. This is not the musing of some airy philosopher, the diatribe of some earthly despot, or the notions of some sentimental guru. Rather, this is a message that has come through God's own Son, who came from heaven to earth to be our Savior. This is what we saw in the opening verses of this letter: "Long ago, at many times and in many ways, God spoke to our fathers by the prophets, but in these last days he has spoken to us by his Son" (Heb. 1:1–2).

This message demands our attention because it was declared by the Lord himself. It declares a salvation that he gives as a free gift to all who believe. What a contrast there is between this gospel and every supposed gospel offered by this world! In every religion of man, people have to feed the god they serve. But Christ Jesus says, "I am the bread of life; whoever comes to me shall not hunger, and whoever believes in me shall never thirst" (John 6:35). In every human message of salvation, you carry the burden on your shoulders, and the false gods you serve weigh down upon your back. But in his gospel God says: "I have made you and I will carry you; I will sustain you and I will rescue you" (Isa. 46:4 NIV).

Furthermore, the writer adds, we know that this message really is of the Lord because it was attested to in the ministry of the apostles by "signs and wonders and various miracles and by gifts of the Holy Spirit distributed according to his will" (Heb. 2:4b). One of the greatest wonders that attests to the divine origin of the gospel is the very fact of the apostles' witness. These were men who knew for sure whether or not the gospel was true. Peter and John, for instance, were at the open tomb on the morning of the resurrection (see John 20:4–9). They knew whether or not Jesus really was raised. This means that they would have been aware if their message was false. What did they gain from preaching the gospel? The answer is nothing more than a life of persecution, poverty, and trial, with the likelihood of martyrdom staring them in the face the whole time. Peter was martyred, as were all of the original apostles except John. Acts 5 records them being threatened and then beaten by the Sanhedrin for teaching the Christian gospel. How did they respond? Acts 5:41 tells us, "They left . . . rejoicing that they were counted worthy to suffer dishonor for the name," and immediately resumed their preaching.

The wonder of the apostles' faith is a definite proof of the divine origin of the Christian message. Other signs and wonders and miracles and spiritual gifts fill the Book of Acts, and through them God gave his confirmation to the apostolic teaching. It is a message like no other, given by the Lord Jesus Christ, and witnessed to by the Holy Spirit.

Because of what God did in the apostolic age, we do not need signs and wonders today to prove the gospel. The writer of Hebrews speaks of this attestation in the past, not the present, tense: "God *bore* witness" by these signs and wonders. We have already been given all the proof we need to believe the gospel, namely, that it was given by the Lord himself and fully attested in the ministry of the apostles.

A MODERN MIRACLE

"We must pay much closer attention to what we have heard," the writer of Hebrews exhorts, "lest we drift away from it." These words are as relevant today as when first written. We should fear to be separated from the anchor of God's Word, or to have any other hand on the wheel of our lives than the Captain of our salvation, who speaks in the Bible. To drift away is ultimately to invite the judgment God will inflict on those who neglect his saving message in Jesus Christ.

The writer of Hebrews says God attested to the gospel in the apostolic age by signs and wonders and miracles. We are not to go seeking after signs and wonders, but there is a miracle that happens today in the lives of those who hold fast to the message of God's Word. It is the miracle of a changed life— a changed mind and a changed heart, changed attitudes and changed behaviors—changed into the likeness of God's Son, Jesus Christ. This is the wonder by which God commends his Word to the world today—Christian people enlightened in truth, purified in holiness, settled in peace, and energized in love. This is the life eternal that begins today in the lives of those who believe. As God does this in you, through his Word, he will use the miracle of your life to commend his message in Christ to others.

This is God's "karma," which runs over the dogma of this world's unbelief, so that many may believe and be saved, no longer neglecting so great a salvation, and thus escaping the wrath that is to come on all who disbelieve.

6

His Story

Hebrews 2:5—9

But we see him who for a little while was made lower than the angels, namely Jesus, crowned with glory and honor because of the suffering of death, so that by the grace of God he might taste death for everyone. (Heb. 2:9)

Several years ago I had the privilege of addressing a group of college students, many of whom were not believers, during Easter week. I set before them the death and resurrection of Jesus Christ as the only true answer to the problems of the world. Going through various solutions mankind pursued in the last century, things like education and social reengineering and income redistribution, I showed how each of these has failed and must fail because of the unresolved problem of sin in the human heart. At the end, one young man stood up and asked me, "If the death and resurrection of Jesus is the solution to the problems of this world, and if he has already died and been raised again, then why are the problems all still here?"

That is an excellent question, dealing with the relationship of the present world to the saving work of Jesus Christ. It is to this question that the writer of Hebrews turns as he continues to exhort his first-century readers. He has been talking about Christ's superiority to the angels. In demonstrating that point he has made much of the risen Lord Jesus' present reign at God's right hand, with all authority and dominion. Now he anticipates an objection to his line of argument. His readers, after all, were facing the prospect of violent persecution; how could this be happening, people might wonder, if Christ is now enthroned in power? Our present passage offers a remarkable solution to this problem, providing a sweeping view of all of history as it is centered on the death and resurrection and exaltation of Jesus Christ.

THE PROBLEM OF HISTORY: DOMINION LOST

Chapter 1 left off with Christ exalted in heaven, about to overthrow all his enemies. In verse 13 the writer asks, "To which of the angels has [God] ever said, 'Sit at my right hand until I make your enemies a footstool for your feet'?" Now he picks up that theme again, looking forward to the time when Christ's reign is consummated. He writes, "It was not to angels that God subjected the world to come, of which we are speaking" (Heb. 2:5).

"The world to come" is the time when Christ's lordship will be consummated over all, when all the promises and prophecies of blessing are fulfilled in his final reign. In one sense that consummation has already been secured, as Christ now reigns at God's right hand. This is what Jesus emphasized prior to his ascension, as the basis for the Great Commission: "All authority in heaven and on earth has been given to me" (Matt. 28:18). He is in control of his spiritual kingdom and reigns now over the world, and especially in the lives of those who call him Lord.

Here, then, is the situation: Christ is presently reigning over his new kingdom and new humanity, yet at the same time the readers of this epistle, like us, find themselves still subject to the conditions of the old reality. This is the apparent problem, and, as he has done before, the writer of Hebrews approaches it by means of a citation from the Psalms. His use of the Old Testament demonstrates that what is happening now is part of God's predetermined and prerevealed plan for history. In this case he quotes Psalm 8, which he sees fulfilled in the life and achievement of Jesus Christ: "It has been testified somewhere, 'What is man, that you are mindful of him, or the son of man, that you care for him? You made him for a little while lower than the angels; you have crowned him with glory and honor, putting everything in subjection under his feet'" (Heb. 2:6–8).

The author introduces this passage by saying, "It has been testified somewhere." The point is not that he is uncertain of its location; rather, it is enough for him that God has said it in Holy Scripture.

Psalm 8 gives praise to God for his majesty as revealed in creation. "O Lord, our Lord," David begins, "how majestic is your name in all the earth!" (v. 1). In comparison, he then reflects upon man's insignificance and marvels at God's care for his creature. "What is man that you are mindful of him, and the son of man that you care for him?" (Ps. 8:4). J. J. Stewart Perowne describes the psalmist's sentiment: "As the poet gazes on into the liquid depths of that starry sky there comes upon him with overwhelming force the sense of his own insignificance. In sight of all that vastness, before all that evidence of creative power, how insignificant is man!"[1]

Nonetheless, God's goodness to humanity is another cause for wonder. Psalm 8 continues, "You have made him a little lower than the heavenly beings, and crowned him with glory and honor. You have given him dominion over the works of your hands; you have put all things under his feet" (Ps. 8:5–6). This is a poetic reflection on what God did in the creation of men and women in his image. His image is manifested in us in part through the dominion God granted man over the garden paradise. We see this in Genesis 1:26, which reads, "Then God said, 'Let us make man in our image, after our likeness. And let them have dominion over the fish of the sea and over the birds of the heavens and over the livestock and over all the earth and over every creeping thing that creeps on the earth.'"

In verse 8 of Hebrews 2, the author points out how thorough mankind's dominion was: "Now in putting everything in subjection to him, he left nothing outside his control." Such was the lordship man was given over all the creation. Yet, the writer points out, this is not the situation we currently enjoy: "At present, we do not yet see everything in subjection to him." Here is a statement of the problem of our race—the problem of dominion lost. What God intended for man in creation is not what we see at present.

What an understatement! As we look around, the Bible says, it certainly doesn't appear as if man has everything under control! If God placed every-

1. J. J. Stewart Perowne, *The Book of Psalms* (Grand Rapids: Zondervan, 1966), 150.

thing under man's feet, then something has gone awry. If we begin making a list of those things in this world very evidently not under man's control, it quickly becomes quite large. Man is at the mercy of weather; his food supply even today is greatly influenced by forces outside his control. Mankind is starving, bleeding, crying, and suffering all over the globe. Hurricanes, droughts, tornadoes, and floods beat against man with unmastered fury. Man may enjoy a large degree of influence over nature and the animal creation, but he does not rule them. Indeed, man is not able to control his own self—his own passions or even his own thoughts. A quick look at the newspaper will display this in terms of international, civic, and individual crises that abound on every side. "At present, we do not yet see everything in subjection to him." That is an announcement of the problem that is extremely well backed up by the evidence.

The second and third chapters of Genesis tell us how things went wrong. God had given Adam, the representative of our race, the command not to eat of the tree of the knowledge of good and evil. He was not to seek autonomy from God; though lord of the garden, he was to acknowledge his own subjection to the Creator. God then attached a threat of punishment: "In the day that you eat of it you shall surely die" (Gen. 2:17).

Genesis 3 tells the horrible tale of what happened. The serpent deceived the woman, telling her that God gave the command to Adam only to keep them from their rightful destiny. It is always the devil's aim to persuade us that God really is not good, despite the abundant evidence of his generosity. So it was in the garden. Speaking of God's command against eating the forbidden fruit, Satan said to her, "You will not surely die. For God knows that when you eat of it your eyes will be opened, and you will be like God, knowing good and evil" (Gen. 3:4–5). Aided by Eve, Adam ate the forbidden fruit. He did come to know good and evil: he knew the good he had forfeited and the evil he had gained by rebelling against God. Adam did not become like God, but like the devil whom he had obeyed. Matthew Henry observes:

> Now, when it was too late, they saw the folly of eating forbidden fruit. They saw the happiness they had fallen from, and the misery they had fallen into. They saw a loving God provoked, his grace and favor forfeited, his likeness and image lost, dominion over the creatures gone. They saw their natures corrupted and depraved. . . . They saw themselves disrobed of all their orna-

ments and ensigns of honor, degraded from their dignity and disgraced in the highest degree, laid open to the contempt and reproach of heaven and earth, and their own consciences.[2]

Thus man—created by God as his image-bearer, crowned with glory and honor and dominion—became subject to God's curse even to the point of death. That curse marks mankind even now, with all its frustration and futility. Far from reigning over the creation, each and every one of us instead will return to the dust from which we came.

This is the problem of mankind: *Paradise lost*, and with it the dominion and blessing offered by God. This is the problem of history—the basic problem set forth at the beginning of the Bible—the answer to which is unfolded in all the rest of Scripture. God's creation of mankind, recorded in Genesis 1:26 and poetically celebrated in Psalm 8, has been spoiled by Adam's sin and the resulting curse of death. "At present," the writer says, "we do not yet see everything in subjection to him."

THE SOLUTION OF HISTORY: JESUS CROWNED

When we see that man's fall into sin and death is the great problem of history, it is easier to see the focus of God's redemptive work in the achievement of Jesus Christ. How we define a problem always determines the nature of its solution, and so it is with the solution that Jesus Christ brought for the problem of this world.

So how do people identify the problem of this world, and what solutions do they envision? Is the problem that people are ignorant? Is it that people who are basically good are simply not enlightened with the right philosophy and culture needed to form a successful society? If that is the problem, then education is the logical solution. Or is the problem that people have had bad childhood experiences, that dysfunctional environments have warped otherwise healthy creatures? If that is the problem, then social reengineering is the most appropriate solution. Or, again, is poverty the problem? Is it true that people's basic needs are not being met, so they never

2. Matthew Henry, *Commentary on the Whole Bible*, 6 vols. (New York: Fleming H. Revell, n.d.), 1:25–26.

get the chance to develop high-order skills that will make them model citizens? If so, then surely income redistribution is a good remedy.

But what if man's problem runs deeper? What if the problem of this world is that man is in bondage to sin and under the curse of death? What if man's problem is that since Adam's fall we are sinners by nature, condemned by God and unable to walk in righteousness and peace? In that case, a more radical solution is called for, a solution far beyond the reach of man himself. God must send a Savior to take away the curse of sin and to break forever the power of sin.

This is the Bible's assessment of man's problem, in Hebrews as well as in Genesis 3. Man was created in glory and honor and dominion, but has fallen from that estate. The resources needed for the recovery of Paradise are now beyond the reach of his guilty and cursed hands. According to the Bible, there is only one solution to this problem, the remedy that comes not from man but from God, not from the earth but from heaven. The apostle Paul writes: "For while we were still weak, at the right time Christ died for the ungodly. . . . God shows his love for us in that while we were still sinners, Christ died for us" (Rom. 5:6–8).

This is also what the writer to the Hebrews is saying. "At present," he says of man, "we do not yet see everything in subjection to him. But we see him who for a little while was made lower than the angels, namely Jesus, crowned with glory and honor" (vv. 8–9). On one hand there is man, captured in the darkness of his Paradise lost. Then onto the stage God sends his own Son, the New Man and Second Adam. He is the answer both to man's problem and to the problem of history. He is the great, the last, the only hope of a dying race; in him is the fulfillment not only of man's promised destiny but of God's plan as set forth in Psalm 8. History has become *his story*. Jesus is the new Adam of the new creation; what Adam lost he has regained. All who are found in him through faith will partake of the new humanity's reclaimed glory and honor and dominion. "We see Jesus." This is the aim of the book of Hebrews from start to finish, to show us Jesus as the Answer, the One who reclaims what mankind was created to be and to do.

HIS STORY: HUMILIATION, GLORIFICATION, TRIUMPH

From the perspective of the Bible, history is about man's fall from blessing and dominion through sin, and about Jesus Christ as the answer from

God, the redeemer of those lost in sin, and the forerunner of the new creation in which God's original purpose is brought to glorious fulfillment. At the center of history is the story of Jesus Christ, and the writer of Hebrews sees that story outlined in the words of Psalm 8, as he records them in verse 9: "But we see him who for a little while was made lower than the angels, namely Jesus, crowned with glory and honor because of the suffering of death, so that by the grace of God he might taste death for everyone."

Jesus' life and story can be organized into three distinct phases, the first two of which are set forth here: his humiliation and exaltation to the right hand of God.

First is Jesus' humiliation, which appears here with the words "who . . . was made lower than the angels" (Heb. 2:9). We should remember that Jesus was the second person of the Godhead before his birth at Bethlehem. He is eternally God the Son. His existence before the incarnation was one of perfect glory, yet he took up mortal flesh for the sake of his redeeming work, humbling himself beneath the angels as a man. The nadir of his humiliation came at the cross, where our Lord died a death that was shameful before men and cursed before God. Bearing the guilt of our sins, he was afflicted with the whole of God's wrath.

Hebrews 2:9 speaks of Jesus' "suffering of death, so that by the grace of God he might taste death for everyone." Jesus' death was not like the death of any other man, for he was not merely man but also God. He was not a sinner, but the spotless Lamb of God. By his death Jesus took God's curse against sin upon himself—the very curse that had ruined mankind. In the fall, man suffered death; but Christ came into the world as God and man that he might take that death upon himself and thus deliver us out of death and into life. As Paul writes in 2 Corinthians 5:21, God "made him to be sin who knew no sin, so that in him we might become the righteousness of God," and thus be reconciled to our Maker. That is the significance of the humiliation of Jesus Christ.

In response to Christ's obedience unto death, God raised him from the dead and exalted him to his right hand. This is the second phase of Christ's history. He is, verse 9 says, "crowned with glory and honor because of the suffering of death." In raising Christ from the dead, God the Father honored Jesus' perfect obedience, vindicated his cause, accepted his sacrifice, and established his reign over the new humanity of which he is both Lord and forerunner, the firstfruits of God's harvest. Death was not the victor over Jesus Christ, but rather the victim. Even now the Lord Jesus reigns in this second and present phase of his great and saving history, bestowing eternal life through the gospel on all who come to faith in him. Thus Paul wrote in 2 Timothy 1:10 that Jesus "abolished death and brought life and immortality to light through the gospel."

LORD OF THE AGE TO COME

That is what is going on in this world right now, and it sets up the answer to the question with which I began: "Why is this world still such a mess?" If Christ's death and resurrection is the solution to this world's ultimate problem, and if he has died and has been raised again, then why do we still see these problems? The answer is that there is a third act to Jesus' saving ministry that remains yet to come. His story is not yet complete, and in its culmination the history of this world comes to its glorious climax.

Jesus suffered humiliation for us and then God exalted him on high. But there is a third stage yet to come. The writer of Hebrews had it in mind at the beginning of this passage when he wrote, "It was not to angels that God subjected the world to come" (Heb. 2:5).

Does Christ reign now? Yes, but not visibly so. In this sense, the words applied to mankind also apply to him now: "At present, we do not yet see everything in subjection to him" (v. 8). Not every knee is now bowed before Jesus; not every tongue confesses him Lord of all. Yet Christ does reign spiritually over this age. He is advancing against his enemies with the sword of the gospel in his mighty hand. He is leading his own out of this present evil age, a people set apart to himself, who inherit eternal life even in the midst of a realm of death, who belong not to this world but to the world that is yet to come.

Let me put this another way. Christ the answer has come and achieved salvation. But the problem of this world still remains most evident. Here, then, is the final answer and it is coming soon—Christ is coming again with glory to consummate his reign, to triumph over all his enemies—sin and death and the devil and this present evil world—all of which will be placed under his feet and destroyed, making way for the new creation in holiness and light. Already this coming triumph is working in the lives of his people as they turn away from sin, in the life of the church as it receives more and more new believers, and even in the secular culture as Christians live as salt and light to extend Christ's reign.

This raises a vital question: To which age do you belong? In which age have you placed your hopes and dreams, your treasure and your salvation? If your trust is in this world, in this age, then you will suffer its fate when Christ comes in glory to separate his own from those lost in the guilt of their sin.

The old world, in which we now live, is the one that is tangible to our senses, to our sight and our touch and to our whole mortal existence. But when Jesus Christ was crowned on high, this present age lost its claim on all who trust in him, even though it grinds forward toward its pre-appointed end. The age to come, the age of the glory of Christ, is appointed to take the place of this passing world, and through faith in Christ we are made citizens of that new creation.

To the eyes of the world it is indeed true: "We do not yet see everything in subjection to him." But the eyes of our faith see Jesus crowned with glory and honor, reigning over the history which points to him and leads to his soon return, when every eye will see him. This is the "already/not yet" of the Christian life. Everything is *already* ours in Christ, though *not yet* realized in our experience. But by faith we see Jesus and spiritually partake of all the blessings of his coming reign.

Let us, then, ensure that we do not belong to this judged and passing world, that we escape the guilt of Adam's failure and our own sin through faith in Christ. Let us not look back upon this present evil age with longing, but back only to the cross with gratitude, where Christ suffered death for us and broke the teeth of this present evil age. And let us look forward to the day of triumph, when Christ will come again in glory, the King coming to reign in righteousness, peace, and joy forevermore. His history has become our hope. So we say, with the writer of Hebrews, "Yes, we see the world as it is, we see and feel and lament this reign of sin and death. Yes, we see it—but that is not all we see. We see Jesus, now crowned with glory and honor, because he suffered death, so that by the grace of God he might taste death for all who trust in him."

Come, Lord Jesus, Come.

7

PERFECT THROUGH SUFFERING

Hebrews 2:10–13

*For it was fitting that he, for whom and by whom all things exist,
in bringing many sons to glory, should make the founder of their
salvation perfect through suffering.* (Heb. 2:10)

he Book of Hebrews provides some of the most powerful
descriptions of our Lord Jesus Christ. So far we have seen him
as "heir of all things" and "the radiance of the glory of God"
(1:2–3). From the beginning he is identified as the Son of God, and throughout chapter 1 he is held forth in his present glory and might. Christians are
so used to seeing Jesus depicted in his earthly life as meek and mild that we
rarely think of Jesus as he lives now, "crowned with glory and honor" (Heb.
2:9) and reigning with power in heaven for us.

OUR ELDER BROTHER

Hebrews 2:10–13 tells us two great things about Jesus Christ: he is the
elder brother of all the redeemed and the pioneer of our salvation. Verse 10
speaks of God "bringing many sons to glory," that is, fellow sons with Christ.

Verse 11 tells us that "he who sanctifies and those who are sanctified all have one origin," or as the New International Version puts it, "are of the same family." It goes on to say that Jesus "is not ashamed to call them brothers." In verse 12 Jesus promises to declare God's name to "my brothers." Finally, in verse 13 he identifies us as "the children God has given me."

Jesus is the elder brother of every Christian. This is not an image that everyone finds attractive. I, for instance, am the younger of two boys. In my upbringing, an older brother was more an object of competition than an object of trust. An elder brother often exercises the father's authority over the younger children. I remember the day my father departed for a year-long tour of duty in the Vietnam War. I will never forget hearing the words I had known were coming, but dreaded with all my being. My dad said, "Jimmy, while I'm gone, you're the man of the house." You might observe that my name is not Jimmy!

But the Lord Jesus is the best of elder brothers. He is a source of inspiration for younger members of God's family, a source of help and salvation for spiritual siblings he loves with sacrificial care. In the Roman world, the elder brother was the sole heir, receiving the whole of the father's estate. Jesus has entered into his inheritance as God's firstborn Son, and we are coheirs with and in him (Rom. 8:17).

The most important blessing we gain by having Jesus as our elder brother is entry into the family of God. He is not only the elder brother, but he is also the natural-born Son of God. By grace we are adopted into the family to which Jesus belongs as the rightful Son. We are not his brothers and sisters because we are children of God; rather, we are children of God because we are his brothers and sisters. Ephesians 1:5 says, "[God] predestined us for adoption through Jesus Christ." Hugh Martin explains: "We find sonship in him: for he is the Son. The adopted sons have this privilege in the eternal Son. To bring saved men into a filial relation to God required a Saviour standing in that relationship himself. Hence when the fullness of the time was come, God sent forth his Son that we might obtain the adoption of sons."[1] We are adopted in Christ, and he then remakes our spiritual DNA by pouring the Holy Spirit into our hearts to make us real members of the family.

1. Hugh Martin, *Christ for Us* (Edinburgh: Banner of Truth, 1998), 218.

It is sometimes said that God is the father of all people. This is true only in the most general sense, since God is the Creator of all. But God is not in a fatherly relationship with unreconciled sinners; they are rebels against him, and his wrath abides on them (see Rom. 1:18). God has created a new family, a new humanity, a new and redeemed people through the Second Adam, who is the resurrected Jesus Christ. Paul wrote of this in Ephesians, referring to how God has taken both Jew and Gentile and created a new race through faith in Jesus Christ. Jesus died and rose again "so that he might create in himself one new man in place of the two, so making peace, and might reconcile us both to God in one body through the cross, thereby killing the hostility" (Eph. 2:15–16).

You should think of yourself this way if you are a Christian. You are not foremost a white person or a black person or a brown person, but a new creature in the new humanity created by the resurrection of Jesus Christ. That is why it is the Christian community that is best able to transcend the barriers of human existence, for we are one in Christ and no longer what we were before. Surely, each of us will have associations that serve to define us in this life—race, economic class, occupation, place of origin. But our union with Christ transcends all of these. In him we find our hearts more closely knit with other believers, regardless of fleshly differences, than we do with old friends from home, colleagues from work, or people who drive the same model car and live in the same kind of house.

It follows, then, that our attitudes, our aspirations, our motives, and our actions should not be derived from the world around us—the unbelieving and rebellious human race into which we were born—but from our new association in the resurrection family of God, into which we are born again in Christ.

The Family Traits

With Jesus as our elder brother, we are children of God. Hebrews 2 says two things about this new family. First, it is a brotherhood of those destined for glory. God, in Christ, is "bringing many sons to glory" (v. 10). This is the goal of the Christian life, the destination for which we are headed. God created man to share in his glory. The problem is that mankind, created in the glory of God's image, had that legacy shattered by the entrance of sin. God's intent in his redeemed children is that what once was lost should be regained and brought to perfection. Romans 8:29 tells us we were chosen for salvation, so that we would be "conformed to the image of his Son, in order that he might be the firstborn among many brothers."

The second description of God's new family makes essentially the same point. Verse 11 tells us that "he who sanctifies [or makes holy] and those who are sanctified [made holy] all have one origin." If we are saved, that means we have been born again, as John puts it, "born, not of blood nor of the will of the flesh nor of the will of man, but of God" (John 1:13). Jesus is God's Son, and we, his brothers, are born again of God.

Every family has distinguishing characteristics. In some families it is brains; in others it is wealth; in still others it is sloth or dishonesty or violence. So what is the defining trait of God's family? Holiness. This means that Christians are to be about the business of becoming holy. Ephesians 1:4 says, "[God] chose us in [Christ] before the foundation of the world, that we should be holy and blameless before him."

How few Christians have this perspective! Francis Schaeffer once defined the basic aspiration of people today, including evangelical Christians, as material affluence and enough personal peace to enjoy it. But what we see in this passage is something far greater, a higher and more wonderful destiny and calling. We were reborn in Christ as his fellow brothers and sisters for the glory that is his in the heavenly realms, and the holiness that distinguishes God and his children.

This is what the Christian life is about—growth in holiness. This involves the progressive removal of the old man, leaving sin behind us, while we are putting on the new man. We call this process *sanctification*, and it is our calling and our destiny and our duty. Paul said in Ephesians 4:21–24: "[You] were taught in him, as the truth is in Jesus, to put off your old self, which belongs to your former manner of life and is corrupt through deceitful desires, and to be renewed in the spirit of your minds, and to put on the new self, created after the likeness of God in true righteousness and holiness."

Life is not about climbing up the corporate ladder, amassing money, or accumulating fun experiences. It is about growing in holiness; this is why God allows us to go through trials, since they tend to further our reliance on him and pursuit of holiness. All of us want to know God's will for our life; Paul answers in 1 Thessalonians 4:3, "This is the will of God, your sanctification."

Jesus is not ashamed to call us brothers because our salvation is unto holiness. In order to make us holy, he took up our nature, so that we might share in his nature and his inheritance. He became like us so that we might become like him. He came to where we were to take us to where he came from so that we might become like him in his glory.

If you are a Christian, this is something you cannot avoid, nor should you want to. You are set apart to God, and he treats you differently from those who are not his children. As the writer of Hebrews will later point out, fathers discipline only their own children; therefore, God's chastening hand in our lives assures us that we are his children. There is a different process at work in the lives of Christians compared to others, and a far different destiny awaiting at the end. Martyn Lloyd-Jones thus observes:

> If God is your Father you must be special, you cannot help it. If the divine nature is in you, and has entered into you through the Holy Spirit, you cannot be like anybody else; you must be different. And that is what we are told about the Christian everywhere in the Bible, that Christ dwells in his heart richly through His mighty power in the depths of his personality, teaching him His will. "It is God who works in you both to will and to do."[2]

Jesus Christ is our elder brother, who leads us as fellow children into his family. God the Father then undertakes the duty of making us worthy sons and daughters. "Behold," Jesus says, "I and the children God has given me" (Heb. 2:13).

THE PIONEER OF OUR SALVATION

There is a second description given to Jesus in this passage, and it is, if anything, even more striking than the first one. Verse 10 speaks of him as "the founder of their salvation" or, in the NIV, "the author of their salvation." The Greek word here is *archēgos*, which is perhaps best translated as "forerunner" or "pioneer." F. F. Bruce explains:

2. D. Martyn Lloyd-Jones, *Expositions on the Sermon on the Mount*, 2 vols. (Grand Rapids: Eerdmans, 1959), 1:319.

He is the Savior who blazed the trail of salvation along which alone God's "many sons" could be brought to glory. Man, created by God for his glory, was prevented by sin from attaining that glory until the Son of Man came and opened up by his death a new way by which humanity might reach the goal for which it was made. As his people's representative and forerunner he has now entered into the presence of God to secure their entry there.[3]

The idea of a pioneer is familiar to any student of American history. Our nation's progress was plotted by the heroism and tenacity of men and women who headed west in covered wagons in the face of great hardship and danger. Of all the American pioneers, none were greater than Meriwether Lewis and William Clark, who opened up the way from coast to coast as they searched for a Northwest Passage.

Lewis and Clark headed west with a small band of men and a few supplies, but their resources of skill, courage, and determination saw them through to success. The greatest achievement of the expedition was crossing the Rocky Mountains, a terrifying and treacherous barrier that none of their fellow countrymen had ever dared to face.

This idea of a pioneer is appropriate to the work of Jesus Christ for our salvation. Like those stalwart settlers who followed Lewis and Clark into the fertile West, we follow a path blazed only by Jesus Christ, who leads us into the promised land of salvation and eternal life. He has gone where we could not go; by his own resources of righteousness and truth and an all-conquering life, he has opened up the way to heaven for us. This is what he explained to his first disciples just before leaving them to take up his cross: "In my Father's house are many rooms. If it were not so, would I have told you that I go to prepare a place for you? And if I go and prepare a place for you, I will come again and will take you to myself, that where I am you may be also. And you know the way to where I am going" (John 14:2–4). When they asked him what that way was, Jesus replied with the immortal words, "I am the way, and the truth, and the life" (John 14:6). Similarly, the writer of Hebrews identified Jesus as the way, the pioneer and trailblazer whom we must trust and follow.

3. F. F. Bruce, *The Epistle to the Hebrews*, rev. ed. (Grand Rapids: Eerdmans, 1990), 80.

MADE PERFECT THROUGH SUFFERING

The first chapters of the Bible tell us the sense in which we should understand this. If Jesus is our trailblazer, what was the wilderness, or the barrier, that he traversed and opened for us? The answer is given in Genesis 3, which recalls mankind's fall into sin and the curse of God's wrath: "The LORD God sent [Adam] out from the garden of Eden to work the ground from which he was taken. He drove out the man, and at the east of the garden of Eden he placed the cherubim and a flaming sword that turned every way to guard the way to the tree of life" (Gen. 3:23–24).

Israel's religious ritual was intended to remind the people of this problem, while also pointing forward to its solution. With regard to the tabernacle—the place where he would meet with man—God directed that its curtains be adorned with the image of cherubim. Cherubim are not the cute, cuddly figures often portrayed today, but are high angelic beings of awe and might. Their presence at the tabernacle recalled the barrier that stands between holy God and sinful man.

The rites that took place in the tabernacle made this point, while also revealing God's solution to the problem. Each year on Yom Kippur, the day of atonement, the high priest entered the innermost sanctum, the holy of holies, where God dwelt in his holiness. There the high priest was confronted with the ark of the covenant, containing within it the tablets of the Ten Commandments. Above the ark were two gold statues of cherubim, with their wings swept upward and their eyes focused downward upon the law of God.

This was a barrier far higher and more deadly than any range of mountains, for it signified God's holy wrath against sin. The eyes of God and his angels looked down at the just requirements of the law, and then upon the high priest as he represented the sinful nation. And the courts of God rang out, "The wages of sin is death" (Rom. 6:23).

While no mere man could solve this problem, God could. Therefore, he provided an atonement cover for the ark, called the mercy seat, where the priest could spread the blood of the sacrifice. This opened the way, for now God looked down and saw the blood of a fitting sacrifice rather than a broken law. His justice was satisfied, his wrath was turned away, and the way was opened up for sinners to dwell in peace before God's presence.

This is the wilderness through which Jesus opened a way for us; by his cross he broke through the desert of God's curse and wrath. The apostle Paul made this connection in Romans 3:25: "God put [Christ] forward as a propitiation." The word for propitiation is the same word, *hilastērion*, used for the mercy seat on the Old Testament ark of the covenant.

This is what the writer of Hebrews is getting at when he says that Christ was made "perfect through suffering" (v. 10). People sometimes balk at the idea of God's Son having to be made perfect, since he was without spot or blemish from the first. But he was perfected not in character but in his office as Christ. Bruce explains: "The perfect Son of God has become his people's perfect Savior, opening up their way to God; and in order to become that, he must endure suffering and death."[4] The language of "perfecting" also has the connotation of "consecrating"; priests in the temple "perfected" or "consecrated" themselves for service before God on behalf of the people, cleansing their bodies and donning priestly clothes. Likewise, as William Lane points out, Jesus "was fully equipped for his office. God qualified Jesus to come before him in priestly action. He perfected him as a priest of his people through his sufferings, which permitted him to accomplish his redemptive mission."[5]

The writer of Hebrews here begins a theme that will dominate much of this book. Jesus, the true high priest to whom all the others pointed, offered his own life and gave his own blood to open the way for sinners to come to God. Hebrews 9:12 tells us, "He entered once for all into the holy places, not by means of the blood of goats and calves but by means of his own blood, thus securing an eternal redemption." "Therefore," the writer exhorts, "since we have confidence to enter the holy places by the blood of Jesus, by the new and living way that he opened for us through the curtain, that is, through his flesh, and since we have a great priest over the house of God, let us draw near" (Heb. 10:19–22).

FITTING FOR GOD

The opening verse of our passage makes the marvelous statement that all of this "was fitting." What a wonderful statement this is—it was fitting for

---

4. Ibid., 80.
5. William L. Lane, *Hebrews 1–8*, Word Biblical Commentary 47a (Dallas: Word, 1991), 57–58.

God to do this, it was appropriate to his glorious character. For here is a gospel, a way of salvation, that brings glory to God and draws our hearts to worship him and him alone.

Yet there are people today who say the opposite thing altogether. They say, "It is unworthy of God to slay an innocent man." Or they say, "This religion of blood and suffering is inappropriate for a God of love. The idea of a God who slays his son is repulsive!" But we can never say this, when we realize it was all done for us, for the forgiveness of our sins, to reconcile us to God through the crucified and risen Son of God. Such criticism fails to recognize the height and the depth, the length and the width of the love of God that is in Jesus Christ. Saint Augustine wrote, "The cross was a pulpit, in which Christ preached his love to the world."[6] Here is God's love revealed in infinite degree; here is the extent to which he was willing to go for his own purposes to be accomplished. Why? "For God so loved the world, that he gave his only Son, that whoever believes in him should not perish but have eternal life" (John 3:16). John Murray said this truth elevates us to "the summit of amazement." He writes, "What love for men that the Father should execute upon his own Son the full toll of holy wrath, so that we should never taste it! This was John's amazement when he wrote: 'This is love, not that we loved God, but that he loved us, and sent his Son to be the propitiation for our sins' (1 John 4:10)."[7]

Not Ashamed

This explains why Jesus is not ashamed to call us brothers. He is not ashamed because our salvation brings glory to God his Father. He is not ashamed because he took up our humanity that we might see and even share in his glory. He is not ashamed because we are so beloved to him that he died for us, so that by the power of God's resurrection he might live with us forever. Even now he is bringing many sons to glory, children of God through union with himself.

As was his custom, the writer of Hebrews proves this point with Old Testament citations. The first is from Psalm 22, which so accurately anticipates Jesus' death on the cross. These words come after the suffering, when the psalmist was sure of deliverance, just as Jesus praised God after his resur-

---

6. Cited in Thomas Watson, *A Body of Divinity* (Edinburgh: Banner of Truth, 1958), 175.
7. John Murray, *Collected Writings*, 4 vols. (Edinburgh: Banner of Truth, 1977), 2:147.

rection from the dead: "I will tell of your name to my brothers; in the midst of the congregation I will sing your praise" (Heb. 2:12). This reminds us that Jesus is the true singer of the Psalms; they were written first and foremost for him, and it is always with him in mind that we sing them most truly. But this psalm also makes an important theological point: Christ died and rose again not merely to save us but also to make us worshipers of his Father. This is fulfilled in our churches today; literally, Hebrews 2:12 concludes, "I will sing hymns in the church."

Verse 13 presents two verses from the eighth chapter of Isaiah (17–18). The prophet had exhorted the people to trust the Lord but had been rejected by his own evil generation. However, God had promised him sons who would follow in the faith, pointing ultimately to a virgin who would be with child. In light of those promises, Isaiah cried out, "I will put my trust in him. . . . I and the children God has given me." By putting these words in the mouth of our Lord Jesus Christ, the Holy Spirit is telling us that like Isaiah's children we are the testimony to God's faithfulness in this present generation. We are children of God given to Jesus Christ, called to testify among this present generation to the reality of salvation that comes through Jesus Christ.

If it was fitting for God to send his Son to die on a cross, how fitting it is for us to be his witnesses in our generation. How fitting it is for us to bear the scorn of the world the way Jesus did, by the power of the Holy Spirit. How fitting it is for us to sing his praises out of the fullness of our hearts, and to declare his name not only before our brothers, but before all the world as he brings countless others into his and our family.

Christ is not ashamed to call us his brothers, and he has sent his gospel to us to declare open the way to God. Are we ashamed of him? Are we ashamed to tell the world? The apostle Paul wrote, "Do not be ashamed of the testimony about our Lord . . . but share in suffering for the gospel by the power of God, who saved us and called us to a holy calling." Of himself, he adds, "I am not ashamed, for I know whom I have believed, and I am convinced that he is able to guard until that Day what has been entrusted to me" (2 Tim. 1:8–12).

May we also be unashamed in our testimony to Christ and his gospel, for through our witness he will bring many other sons to glory—both men and women—to the praise of his name.

8

ABLE TO HELP

Hebrews 2:14—18

For because he himself has suffered when tempted, he is able to help those who are being tempted. (Heb. 2:18)

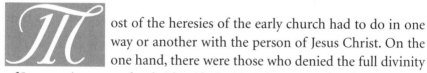ost of the heresies of the early church had to do in one way or another with the person of Jesus Christ. On the one hand, there were those who denied the full divinity of Jesus, a view most closely identified with Arius, a preacher from Alexandria in Egypt. The Arians held that however great Jesus was, he was still less than the eternal and almighty God. On the other hand were the Docetists, so called for the Greek word *dokeō*, which means "to seem" or "to appear." These held that while the divine Christ may have appeared as a man, he nonetheless was not. It would have been unworthy for the divine to take up flesh, they argued, much less to die in shame and weakness upon a cross.

The first church council at Nicaea, meeting in A.D. 325, dealt with such matters. It specifically condemned Arianism as a heresy, affirming Christ's full divinity and his full humanity. The Nicene Creed described our Lord Jesus Christ as "God of God, Light of Light, very God of very God, begotten, not made, being of one substance with the Father . . . and [he] was made man." More recently, the Westminster Shorter Catechism speaks of the eternal Son of God becoming man with these words: "Christ, the Son of God, became man, by taking to himself a true body and a reasonable soul, being conceived by the power of the Holy Ghost in the womb of the Virgin Mary, and born of her yet without sin" (Q/A 22).

Both aspects of this ancient controversy have already been answered in the Letter to the Hebrews. Christ's full divinity featured prominently in chapter 1, where verse 8 said of Jesus: "Your throne, O God, is forever and ever." This is about as clear a statement of deity as you can find. Chapter 2 speaks very deliberately to the other side of the equation. Hebrews 2:10–13 showed how thoroughly Jesus identified himself with mankind, making himself of one family with those he saves and even equipping himself for office by means of suffering. Hebrews 2:14–18 goes on to give proof-texts that are and have been devastating to any who would deny the full humanity of Jesus Christ. Verse 14 tells us that he "partook of . . . flesh and blood," while verse 17 says he was "made like his brothers in every respect." The One who is fully God—the very Son of the very God of heaven—both suffered and was tempted as a man, as we see in verse 18.

This is the great theme of these verses before us: the full humanity of Jesus Christ in his work as divine Savior. Assuming this truth, the writer of Hebrews draws forth its implications, making clear the reasons why God's Son became man and also detailing the final results of that work begun by his humble birth in the Bethlehem stable. The author highlights here three great aspects of Christ's saving work: first, he broke the devil's hold and liberated captive humanity; second, he made propitiation for God's holy wrath against our sin; and third, he became a merciful and compassionate minister who is able to help us who now are suffering under the trial of temptation.

DEATH DEFEATED

The passage begins by telling us: "Since therefore the children share in flesh and blood, he himself likewise partook of the same things, that through death he might destroy the one who has the power of death, that is, the devil, and deliver all those who through fear of death were subject to lifelong slavery. For surely it is not angels that he helps, but he helps the offspring of Abraham" (Heb. 2:14–16). This is the reason Christ came into the world as a man. His purpose is defined by two key verbs. The first is "to destroy." Jesus came to destroy the power of a tyrant who held mankind in slavery, namely, the devil. The second verb is "to deliver." Like Moses in the exodus, Jesus came to set his people free. This was the purpose of the incarnation. These verses also show the means by which he gained this victory: through his death.

Altogether this is a wonderfully succinct statement of Jesus' mission in this world. If someone asks, "Why did Jesus come into the world?" here is the answer: he came to die, that he might overthrow Satan's dominion, and set captive humanity free.

Several great statements are made here, beginning with a description of man's condition under sin. The writer of Hebrews says that all men "through fear of death were subject to lifelong slavery" (v. 15). He names our great oppressor, the devil, and says he "has the power of death." When the devil seduced our first parents into sin, he brought them under the curse of death. God had made this the punishment for disobedience, as seen in Genesis 2:17: "Of the tree of the knowledge of good and evil you shall not eat, for in the day that you eat of it you shall surely die." Ever since, the devil and his minions have tormented man by means of the fear of death. This now is the plight of our race, so that William Lane is surely right when he comments: "Hopeless subjection to death characterizes earthly existence apart from the intervention of God. Moreover, the presence of death makes itself felt in the experience of anxiety."[1]

The fear of death is something mankind still faces today. How much of our busyness, or our frenzy for entertainment, is mainly an attempt to divert our gaze from the shadow death casts across our lives? Death is not merely an event that awaits us, but a power that rules us now, the leaven of futility that permeates all our achievements and denies our souls peace and contentment.

This, then, is a clear statement of the problem our Lord Jesus came to solve. It is from this that he saves us—not merely from unhappiness or dysfunction or failure in life. What we need to be saved from is far greater, the comprehensive reign of death because of sin—a reign that now holds us in bondage through fear, that at the end of our lives afflicts us with the experience of death, and that beyond the grave sees us damned before the judgment throne of the holy God. Death is the problem from which we must be saved. Death is the rod of Satan's rule and the source of his laughter at our expense.

---

1. William L. Lane, *Hebrews 1–8*, Word Biblical Commentary 47a (Dallas: Word Books, 1991), 61.

Death is also what Christ overcomes by his saving work. He breaks the devil's power and sets us free by means of his own death on the cross. Taking our sins upon himself, Jesus endured the wrath of God that we deserve. At the cross, Jesus "abolished death and brought life and immortality to light" (2 Tim. 1:10). Jesus is the champion from heaven who has defeated our hellish foe by his victory on the cross.

Are you held in bondage by the spectre of death's reality? Though you must face death, are you free from the chains of its fear, knowing that for you death is the doorway to eternal life in glory? If you have relied on Jesus, you have been set free from death's sting. This is what Jesus did on the cross—he gave you freedom from the fear of death. Now, through faith in Christ, you can exult in his victory with the words of the apostle Paul: " 'Death is swallowed up in victory. O death, where is your victory? O death, where is your sting?' The sting of death is sin, and the power of sin is the law. But thanks be to God, who gives us the victory through our Lord Jesus Christ" (1 Cor. 15:54–57). John Calvin therefore exhorts us: "It is from this fear that Christ has released us, by undergoing our curse, and thus taking away what was fearful in death. Although we must still meet death, let us nevertheless be calm and serene in living and dying, when we have Christ going before us."[2]

Propitiation Made

Whenever we talk about Christ's death on the cross, we need to understand that there are two parties to whom his work was directed—both the sinner and God. This is why Paul writes, "For there is one God, and there is one mediator between God and men, the man Christ Jesus" (1 Tim. 2:5).

We have already seen one reason why Jesus became man, namely, to die and thus to free us from death. In that sense, we are the objects of his saving work. But there is also God the Father to be considered, who in his holiness cannot accept people who have stained themselves with sin, who are corrupted as an entire race and as individuals. Verse 17 deals with that aspect of Christ's death of which God is the object: "He had to be made like his brothers in every respect, so that he might become a merciful and faithful high priest in the service of God, to make propitiation for the sins of the people."

2. John Calvin, *New Testament Commentaries*, 12 vols. (Grand Rapids: Eerdmans, 1994), 12:31.

I mentioned earlier that controversies over Christ's divine and human natures have caused some of the key battles in church history. This verse gives a classic explanation as to why the Christ had to become fully man; namely, so that he might perform priestly service before God on man's behalf and thus propitiate—that is, turn aside—God's wrath against our sin.

The classic explanation of this doctrine was given by Anselm of Canterbury some nine hundred years ago in his towering work *Cur Deus Homo*, which means "Why God Became Man." Speaking of the payment that must be made for our sins, Anselm wrote: "It could not have been done unless man paid what was owing to God for sin. But the debt was so great that, while man alone owed it, only God could pay it, so that the same person must be both man and God. Thus it was necessary for God to take manhood into the unity of his person, so that he who in his own nature ought to pay and could not should be in a person who could."[3]

This is what the writer of Hebrews gets at in verse 17: "He had to be made like his brothers in every respect, so that he might become a merciful and faithful high priest." The Old Testament priests represented God before man, which was why they were garbed with glory and honor (Ex. 28:2). Their priestly apparel gleamed, to portray the righteousness of God before the people. But just as importantly, the priest represented man before God. This is why the high priest wore an ephod of gold, upon which were fastened twelve stones, bearing the names of the twelve tribes of Israel (Ex. 28:9–12).

Christ became man so that he might bear our names upon his shoulders. The true high priest, he is garbed in his own perfect righteousness, which he presents on our behalf. He went forth as our minister and representative, offering his precious blood—his divine and infinitely valuable life, which alone could atone for the sins of the world—to pay the debt of our sin. His work was one of propitiation, turning aside God's wrath from our sin.

This is why Jesus was born into this world, so that by his death as both God and man he might break the hold of death and set us free, while making propitiation to the holy wrath of God against our sins. As one of our great Christmas carols puts it: "Good Christian men, rejoice with heart and soul and voice; now ye need not fear the grave: Jesus Christ was born to save."

---

3. Anselm of Canterbury, *Why God Became Man*, in Eugene R. Fairweather, *A Scholastic Miscellany: Anselm to Ockham* (Philadelphia: Westminster, 1961), 176.

ABLE TO HELP

I said there are three reasons why God the Son had to become a man. The first was to free us from slavery to death, while the second was to propitiate God's just wrath. But there is a third reason given in this passage, set forth in verse 18: "Because he himself has suffered when tempted, he is able to help those who are being tempted."

When I was on the faculty of the United States Military Academy, I spent one summer with the counseling center during the training of new cadets, affectionately known as Beast Barracks. It is a grueling time of physical and psychological challenges, under which not a few young men and women begin to crack, which is why the Academy provides counselors. I was one of several officers who oversaw the center, but the counseling was done mainly by older cadets who had been through the brutal weeks of that first summer at West Point. The cadets had recently been through it themselves, and therefore were best equipped to help new cadets who were tempted to quit, go home, or otherwise fall into despair.

In the same manner, Jesus is ideally suited to help us in our struggle with temptation to sin and despair, because he has been through it all himself. Here again is a great proof of Christ's full humanity, that "he himself has suffered when tempted." We naturally think of Jesus' temptations in the wilderness at the hands of the devil. There Jesus was afflicted with great hunger and the temptation to accept the crown without the cross. Surely those were great temptations, and Jesus overcame them. But we mustn't overlook the whole range of temptations to which he was exposed during all his earthly existence, temptations that would have interacted with every aspect of his human nature. Because of them, Jesus knows exactly what we are going through. He knows what it is to be tempted because he experienced it himself. Our high priest has real sympathy and compassion for what we are going through.

Some people object that Jesus does not know the full human experience because he was not a sinner. Without the experience of sin's corruption, they say, he cannot have full sympathy with us. The answer to this is that far from Jesus knowing less than we do about temptation because he never fell into sin, the opposite is the case. Jesus knows far more about temptation than we do because he endured far beyond the point where the strongest of us gives in to the trial. B. F. Westcott is surely right when he observes: "Sympathy with the sinner in his trial does not depend on the experience of sin but on the experience of the strength of the temptation to sin, which only the sinless can know in its full intensity. He who falls yields before the last strain."[4]

Jesus has real and knowledgeable sympathy with those who are tempted. Therefore, the Scripture says, he is able to help. What a wonderful combination we have before us. On the one hand we have One who is mighty to save. In this respect, Jesus is not "just like us." He is the Redeemer and we are the sinners in so great a need for a champion. And yet his work is hardly impersonal or mechanical; it is heartfelt and sensitive. He was like us in his experience of pain and suffering and temptation. He felt nails as they were driven into his hands and his feet so that he might rescue us from the power of death. Thus there is a quality of mercy to Christ's work that is intimate, personal, and knowing. It calls us to love him as an intimate Savior, the God who has gone to such lengths to know us in our trials, to have the fellowship of our suffering even as he calls us into the fellowship of his.

What all this means is that Jesus is able. He is able to understand what you are going through. He is able to hear you with a sympathetic and merciful heart when you cry out. What an encouragement that is for you in all sorts of trials and temptations to turn to the Lord in prayer.

Most importantly, Jesus is able to deliver you. You can trust him, therefore, knowing that death will not bring you harm but will bring you to Jesus. You can also trust him for today, for your present temptations and struggles. He is able to help us, by praying for us at the throne of his Father in heaven and by sending the Holy Spirit into our hearts, giving us strength that is of him. This is why Paul said, "It is no longer I who live, but Christ who lives in me. And the life I now live in the flesh I live by faith in the Son of God, who loved me and gave himself for me" (Gal. 2:20). Despite all of Paul's many trials, it was with knowledge of Christ's present power that he could declare: "I can do all things through him who strengthens me" (Phil. 4:13).

4. B. F. Westcott, *The Epistle to the Hebrews* (London: Macmillan, 1903), 59.

LIKE YOU, FOR YOU, WITH YOU

Jesus Christ, God's own Son, became like us to be a total Savior, sufficient for the whole range of our need. How hollow, then, ring the world's complaints against our God. People are saying all the time today, lamenting in this world of woe, "Where is God? Why doesn't he do something?" Meanwhile, he has done everything, indeed, more than ever we could ask or imagine. God has entered into our world. He has walked through the dust of this earth. He who is life has wept before the grave, and he who is the Bread of Life has felt the aching of hunger in his belly. Is there anything more lovely in all of Scripture than the scenes of Jesus supping with the weak and the weary, the sinners and the publicans? He has taken the thorns that afflict this sin-scarred world and woven them into a crown to be pressed upon his head. And he has stretched open his arms in love, that the hands that wove creation might be nailed to a wooden cross. Then he rose from the dead, conquering all that would conquer us, setting us free to live in peace and joy before the face of God.

All that God has done, in the redeeming work of Jesus Christ, was done not for angels but for you. It was *like you* that he became, and it was *for you* that he died. It is *with you* that he sympathizes now, knowing well your struggle. He is able—but are you willing? That is the only question that remains. The hymn "Come, Thou Long-Expected Jesus" tells us the only answer that makes any sense, namely, that we should trust him to be this kind of Savior for us:[5]

Come, thou long-expected Jesus,
   born to set thy people free;
from our fears and sins release us;
   let us find our rest in thee. . . .

Come to earth to taste our sadness,
   he whose glories knew no end;
by his life he brings us gladness,
   our Redeemer, Shepherd, Friend.

5. Charles Wesley, "Come, Thou Long-Expected Jesus," stanza 1, 1744; stanza 3 copyright © 1978 by Mark E. Hunt. Used by permission.

9

THE GREAT APOSTLE

Hebrews 3:1—6

Therefore, holy brothers, you who share in a heavenly calling,
consider Jesus, the apostle and high priest of our confession.
(Heb. 3:1)

*T*he Book of Hebrews was written to exhort Christians under fire to stand firm in their faith in Jesus Christ. The opening passage of chapter 3 exemplifies that thrust, both beginning and ending with an exhortation to endurance. It begins by encouraging us to fix our thoughts on Jesus Christ and concludes by exhorting us to hold on to our courage and hope.

Verse 1 could very well belong to the previous chapter, which concluded by stressing that Jesus, having overcome sin and temptation, is able to help those who are being tempted. "Therefore," the writer concludes, "consider Jesus." Since Jesus is the One who conquered death and the devil and sin, the author reasons, "make him the conscious object of your faith." He calls his readers "holy brothers" and those "who share in a heavenly calling," and identifies them as both the recipients of Christ's work and those who are thus obliged to live for him.

CHRIST GREATER THAN MOSES

This exhortation receives further support starting with the description of Jesus in verse 1 as "the apostle and high priest of our confession." An apostle is one who is sent to represent God before men, and to speak and act on his behalf; a high priest represents men before God and offers a sacrifice for their sins. Moses was the only Old Testament figure to fulfill both of these functions, and as such he pointed forward to Jesus, whom we proclaim as *the* apostle and high priest of our confession.

Chapter 1 established Jesus' superiority over the angels, and now in chapter 3 we are told of his supremacy over Moses. The writer says he "was faithful to him who appointed him, just as Moses also was faithful in all God's house" (v. 2). Jesus is a figure who can be compared with Moses, the greatest prophet of the Old Testament and Judaism's greatest priestly figure. Both Jesus and Moses share the greatest accolade that could be given, namely, that they were faithful.

Not only is Jesus compared favorably with Moses, but he is even superior. This is what verse 3 tells us: "Jesus has been counted worthy of more glory than Moses—as much more glory as the builder of a house has more honor than the house itself." The point here is obvious, that these Hebrew Christians should not fall back from the new covenant in Christ to the old covenant of Judaism. Jesus is superior to the greatest old covenant hero, through whom the old covenant was given, and therefore his new covenant is also superior.

This passage is noteworthy in giving us a New Testament perspective on Moses' ministry, and thus on the Old Testament as a whole. Moses was a faithful servant in the house. But Christ is the Son and heir who builds the house for God. This means that Moses' ministry was not in conflict with Christ's, but Moses was a servant whose labor was part of Christ's ultimate work. Verse 5 tells us this was especially true of Moses' work as a prophet; he testified "to the things that were to be spoken later," that is, in the time of Jesus Christ.

We are reminded of Jesus' conflicts with the Pharisees, who accused him of violating the law of Moses by healing on the Sabbath. But Moses, the lawgiver, was Jesus' servant, and the law was Jesus' law. Jesus is the fulfillment of the law and its true teacher. This is what Jesus was doing in the Sermon on the Mount. "Do not think that I have come to abolish the Law or the Prophets," he taught. "I have not come to abolish them but to fulfill them" (Matt. 5:17). Jesus pointed out that Moses had foretold his ministry and directed people to trust in him. In John 5, Jesus told the Pharisees: "Do not think that I will accuse you to the Father. There is one who accuses you: Moses, on whom you have set your hope. If you believed Moses, you would believe me; for he wrote of me" (John 5:45–46).

Moses' work and message spoke of things to come. Moses was a servant whose work furthered the house-building project of God's Son and heir. Indeed, everything in the Mosaic administration points forward to Jesus Christ. The tabernacle spoke of God dwelling with man, which is what Christ did. The year of jubilee, in which slaves were released and land was returned to its original owners, spoke of the great day of deliverance that was to come in Christ. Jesus is called Immanuel, which is "God with us." The apostle John explains, "The Word became flesh and dwelt among us, and we have seen his glory, glory as of the only Son from the Father, full of grace and truth" (John 1:14). The sacrifices of lambs and bulls and goats spoke of his great atoning work on the cross. This is a point the writer of Hebrews will emphasize often in this letter, that the rituals of the law were "a shadow of the good things to come" (10:1).

Paul looks back on the way Moses brought manna from heaven and caused water to flow from a rock. He remembers that Israel "drank from the spiritual Rock that followed them, and the Rock was Christ" (1 Cor. 10:4). In John 6 Jesus taught, "It was not Moses who gave you the bread from heaven, but my Father gives you the true bread from heaven. For the bread of God is he who comes down from heaven and gives life to the world. . . . I am the bread of life" (John 6:32–35). Later, when Jesus was transfigured in glory on the mount before the disciples, Moses was there, with Elijah, discussing the exodus of which Moses' deliverance was but a foretype—Christ's death on the cross to deliver us from the Egypt of bondage to our sins (Luke 9:30–31).

Moses presented Israel with pictures or types of the Messiah to come, shadows that were cast backward into the Old Testament by the light of Christ and were fulfilled in his long-awaited coming. So what Jesus said is true: Moses testified about him. It was of Jesus that Moses spoke, for instance, in Deuteronomy 18:15: "The LORD your God will raise up for you a prophet like me from among you, from your brothers—it is to him you shall listen." This being the case, if Moses could write to the Jewish Christians, he would tell them the very thing emphasized by the writer of Hebrews: that they should hold fast to Christ in faith. In fact, Moses did write such a letter; he wrote the first five books in the Old Testament, and their ultimate purpose was to point to Jesus Christ as the Savior of his people, the apostle and high priest of our confession.

GOD'S HOUSE

These statements describe Moses as faithful as a servant in God's house, over which Jesus is builder and Lord. What are we to understand by "God's house"? Some commentators take this to be the tabernacle or tent of meeting in which Moses served so faithfully, while others point to Israel as a whole as God's household in which Moses served. Both are true. Verse 6 especially emphasizes the latter, saying, "And we are his house."

The house Jesus is building and in which Moses served is the people of God. This tells us there is a basic continuity between Old Testament Israel and the New Testament church. There are differences, since the old covenant looks forward to Christ with national Israel, and the new covenant looks back on Christ with the transnational church. But despite differences based on their redemptive-historical setting, Israel and the church are one. This passage exposes the error of dispensationalism, which sees Israel and the church as fundamentally different peoples in God's economy. The house in which Moses served is the house over which Jesus is Lord. The New Testament represents the fulfilling of what was promised and hoped for in the Old. For instance, the fulfillment of the tabernacle and temple typology is the church, which is God's house, built not by men or by means of purely human labor, but built by Christ and the power of his gospel (see also Eph. 2:19–22 and 1 Peter 2:9–10). To change metaphors, old covenant Israel is the bud of which the new covenant church is the flower.

If this is what Christians are—God's house—then we should ask, For what reason does one build a house? We might say that one builds a house for his glory. That certainly is in view here, and a majestic estate certainly does show the riches and the skill and artistry of the one who can afford to build it. But the main reason one builds a house is to live in it. What a marvelous truth this is, that God has redeemed us that we might be his own dwelling place (see also Rev. 21:3).

This emphasizes that God indwells his people. This is true of Christians individually. The title of Henry Scougal's classic book, *The Life of God in the Soul of Man*, provides an excellent description of what salvation is about. If you have come to God through Christ, then he is living in you, working in you to will and to act according to his good purpose, by means of the Holy Spirit. Jesus said of the Spirit he would send to his followers: "He lives with you and will be in you" (John 14:17 NIV).

While we must emphasize that individual application, the description here is mainly corporate. We are together God's house; he dwells among us as well as in us. In 2 Corinthians 6:16 Paul says, "For we are the temple of the living God; as God said, 'I will make my dwelling among them and walk among them, and I will be their God, and they shall be my people.'" He used this point to argue that the church is called to be holy, because God is holy. In another well-known verse, Peter said, "You yourselves like living stones are being built up as a spiritual house, to be a holy priesthood, to offer spiritual sacrifices acceptable to God through Jesus Christ" (1 Peter 2:5). The church is the holy temple where the holy God dwells in spirit, is worshiped and served.

This gives us vital information about the church. In building a house you first lay the cornerstone, which establishes the lines and angles for the whole. Then comes the foundation, which will support the structure that is built upon it. Paul tells us in Ephesians 2:19–22 that the church is such a house. Christ is the cornerstone and the apostles are the foundation. Their teaching, as it is recorded in the Bible, tells us how the church is established and how it grows. Since the apostles are the foundation, a Christian is one who receives and believes the apostolic testimony in the New Testament and builds his life on it, as that foundation rests on Christ himself.

People today tend not to take the church very seriously. We are rugged individualists and think we can go it alone. But the corporate community of saints is the household of God. If this does not transform our view of the church, then nothing will. We see that the church is not a human institution but a divine building which God erects and in which God himself dwells. To be part of the church is to have historical roots in the people of God and spiritual connectedness to others now, in past ages, and in generations to come. Christians know and study church history the way others research a family genealogy. Loving Christ causes us to love and serve his church and the people who make it up.

The Old Testament reveals a geography of salvation—if you wanted to know God, you could not look just anywhere. God is everywhere, yet he specially disclosed himself in a particular place, among his people in Israel, and especially at Jerusalem in the temple. If you wanted to find God, you had to go there, where God's house was, the way the queen of Sheba went to Jerusalem in Solomon's time. Today, if you want to learn about God, you should go to a church where his Word is taught. Though God is everywhere, it is still in his house where he especially reveals himself to those who come in faith.

This is one reason why Christians need to be members of a faithful church. Christian growth and discipleship take place in the church, in God's household, and not as a solo endeavor. This also says much about evangelism. If you want to bring others to God, you should bring them to the church, where God speaks through his Word with authority and power. Christian worship takes place most especially in the church, for when his people gather, God promises to meet with them (see Matt. 18:20). Thus the writer of Hebrews later exhorts his readers not to neglect meeting together (Heb. 10:25), for the gathering of God's people is God's own dwelling.

There is therefore no greater privilege than membership in the church. There is no greater calling than the Christian's calling to offer his gifts and talents, time and money to the work of the church. A Christian who gives all his energy to his job, uses her talents only for personal gain, who spends his money all on himself, neglecting the work of the church which will last forever, is simply a fool. Such a person does not realize that the church is the body, the temple, the bride of the exalted Jesus Christ, who even now reigns on high and soon will come to rule on earth forever. In the end it is what Christ is doing through the church that will matter most, will most shine in glory, and will have been most worth the offering of our lives. Therefore a Christian who is not involved in a ministry of the church, who does not pray regularly for the church's work, who is taking from but never giving to the church, should ask himself if he really understands what this life is about and if he is living for the things of eternity.

Consider Jesus

The Book of Hebrews is a letter of exhortation, and it includes a great many commands and conditional statements, one of which ends this passage. The author writes in verse 6: "And we are his house if indeed we hold fast our confidence and our boasting in our hope."

Christians sometimes are unnerved by these kinds of statements, often because they have experience with a legalistic theology that denies the believer's security in Christ. But since these conditional statements are in the Bible, they are appropriate, and even necessary. The point of this statement is to encourage faith in the face of trouble. The writer is saying, "Since you are the house God is building, this demands that you stand firm in your faith."

There is no conflict between the teaching that all true believers are safe in the hands of God and the teaching that emphasizes that Christians must persevere in faith. All true Christians will continue in the faith until they are gathered to God. But it is also true that true Christian faith is proved only by steadfastness under trial. We are saved by faith alone, but the test of our faith comes through our willingness to persevere under difficulty and persecution. Those who do not persevere, like Paul's one-time companion Demas (2 Tim. 4:10), and those who betray Jesus to this world, like Judas Iscariot, reveal by their actions that they never truly possessed saving faith and never truly were saved.

If you are a Christian, God will call you to show courage before the world, holding fast to your hope in Jesus Christ. But where does courage come from? The Bible's answer is that it comes from God, from our knowledge of him and his salvation, and from the Holy Spirit he sends to his children as they trust in him.

Let me put this differently: courage comes from seeing. On countless battlefields, the hearts of soldiers have been cheered by the sight of the flag waving still. What they saw reminded them of the home to which they hoped to return as heroes, and the cause for which they came. Seeing the flag waving, they knew that victory was at hand. This is what the gospel does for Christians, as it bears God's promise "that neither death nor life, nor angels nor rulers, nor things present nor things to come, nor powers . . . will be able to separate us from the love of God in Christ Jesus our Lord" (Rom. 8:38–39).

Knowing that God's saving work is sure, and that our treasure is safe in heaven, gives us boldness for this fleeting life with its trials and temptations.

It is well documented that the great commanders of history inspired terrific bravery by their simple presence, just by letting their soldiers set their eyes upon them. Alexander, Caesar, Napoleon, Patton—all had this aura of invincibility that produced undaunted courage in the hearts of those who saw them amidst the fray. This is what the eyes of our faith see when we fix them upon Jesus Christ, who is the captain of our salvation. Napoleon, probably military history's greatest conqueror, used to have his generals come into his tent and look into his eyes before they went out to lead the troops in battle; likewise our faith is to behold the face of Christ, and his brow once crowned with thorns but now with the laurel wreath of heaven. Napoleon, like most of the other great conquerors of this world, was ultimately defeated. Even those who never lost a battle in life, like Alexander the Great, nonetheless were defeated by death. But Christ is victor over every foe. When he went into the grave, even death became his captive. Now he lives and reigns forever, placing every enemy under his feet. Let us fix our eyes on him, then, and we will find strength for every battle, hope for every trial.

The original recipients of Hebrews were facing great persecution for their faith, perhaps even the threat of death. This is something Christians experience today as well. The remedy for fear of persecution is to see Jesus Christ enthroned. Hebrews 2:9 reminded us, "We see him who for a little while was made lower than the angels, namely Jesus, crowned with glory and honor because of the suffering of death." This was the sight that filled the eyes of Stephen, the first martyr. The Book of Acts tells us that as they were gathering to stone him, "he, full of the Holy Spirit, gazed into heaven and saw the glory of God, and Jesus standing at the right hand of God. And he said, 'Behold, I see the heavens opened, and the Son of Man standing at the right hand of God' " (Acts 7:55–56). With that sight he held on to his courage, and with the hope of salvation he even found grace to ask for his killers' forgiveness.

Persecution is one source of temptation, but people also fall away because they are enticed by the allure of the world and its pleasures. If we know our hearts, we will not underestimate this threat of worldliness to our faith. The answer here, too, is found in our passage: "Consider Jesus." Seeing Jesus in heaven as our forerunner and knowing ourselves coheirs with him, we anticipate a glorious treasure there, the hope of glory with him forever. He is our boast, not our jobs, our money, or our pedigree—not anything in this world that can be so easily taken from us. Psalm 16:11 says, "You make known to me the path of life; in your presence there is fullness of joy; at your right hand are pleasures forevermore." A love for the things of God and a keen anticipation of heaven are the greatest antidotes to worldliness.

Perhaps the most deadly temptations come from our own feeling of unworthiness, our discouragement because of sin, and the accusations of Satan that plague our weak conscience. We sin and the devil tells us, "How can you call yourself a Christian? Isn't it true that you have no part of Christ? Why don't you give up the façade?" Do you hear that voice, do you feel the sting of that accusation? Then consider Jesus. The Scripture says of him, "A bruised reed he will not break, and a faintly burning wick he will not quench" (Isa. 42:3).

Let Jesus Christ be your banner, the source of all your confidence. Fix your thoughts on Jesus, contemplate the sufficiency of his work for you, and reflect upon the love that bore your sins. And when Satan levels his accusing finger at you, saying, "You are a great sinner," you then can say, "Yes, I am a great sinner. But Jesus Christ is a greater Savior." Everything in this passage leads us to consider him. He is the great apostle sent by God to bring us salvation; he will not fail. He is the great high priest who reconciles us to God; nothing now shall separate us. He is the master architect and builder, constructing God's house for his own glory and dwelling. And we are that house. He will not be thwarted; he will not be overcome. The house he builds on the rock of his gospel will not be dashed by any storm. So we draw our courage and our confidence and our hope from him. And there we are safe, to the praise of his name.

PART 2

Warnings against Falling Away

10

A WARNING AGAINST UNBELIEF

Hebrews 3:7–12

Take care, brothers, lest there be in any of you an evil, unbelieving heart, leading you to fall away from the living God. (Heb. 3:12)

One of the hallmarks of Hebrews is its very high view of Scripture. As the writer exhorts his Jewish Christian audience to remain faithful to Christ in the midst of suffering, this high view of Scripture plays an important role. Over and over he appeals to Old Testament citations, expecting his readers to take the Bible as authoritative and binding. So sure is he of his readers' estimate of Scripture that he expects them to endure persecution because of its teaching.

The writer grounds his view of Scripture on direct claims to the divine authorship of the Bible. In the opening verse of the book he tells us that "God spoke to our fathers by the prophets" (Heb. 1:1). He acknowledges human instrumentation, but emphasizes divine authorship. Now, in Hebrews 3:7, he writes, "Therefore, as the Holy Spirit says." This is consistent with the broader biblical testimony that the Bible is the product of the Holy Spirit who has taken the things of God and given them to us through human writers. The classic statement to this effect occurs in 2 Peter 1:21: "No prophecy was ever produced by the will of man, but men spoke from

God as they were carried along by the Holy Spirit." The Holy Spirit has given God's Word through the Scriptures and now speaks to us by applying that Word to our hearts.

Furthermore, Hebrews 3:7–8 illustrates the abiding relevance and authority of the Scriptures: "Therefore, as the Holy Spirit says, 'Today, if you hear his voice, do not harden your hearts as in the rebellion.'" To show that God's Word is "living and active," as he will say in Hebrews 4:12, the writer emphasizes its relevance "today." In the Scriptures, he says, the Holy Spirit of God "speaks"—and we should note the present tense of this verb. The events described in this passage took place during the exodus. Many years later the psalmist showed their applicability to his own time, probably during the reign of David. "Today, if you hear God's voice," he says in Psalm 95:7. The writer of Hebrews picks up the same message, showing that God still speaks "today" in his own time a thousand years later. It was equally valid in his own era, equally authoritative and equally relevant, because it was from God, who never changes. So, too, do these same words apply to us two thousand years after the Book of Hebrews was written: "Today, if you hear his voice, do not harden your hearts." Such are the timelessness and authority of this book, which bears to us the very voice of God.

Israel's Testing in the Wilderness

Although this passage is timeless in its relevance, it points us back to a specific series of events that happened in history, namely, the revolts against Moses during Israel's sojourn in the desert. The writer of Hebrews directs his readers' attention to this situation as a terrible example of what it means to turn away from faith in God.

The previous passage concluded with an exhortation: "We are [God's] house if indeed we hold fast our confidence and our boasting in our hope" (v. 6). Picking that up in verses 7–9, the author now confronts us with an example of what the opposite looks like, a warning from the time of the exodus: "Today, if you hear his voice, do not harden your hearts as in the rebellion, on the day of testing in the wilderness, where your fathers put me to the test and saw my works."

The scenario recalled here is described in the Book of Exodus. The people of Israel had been delivered from their bondage in Egypt with a great display of God's power. Pharaoh had pursued them, but the Lord made a passage for them through the Red Sea, which then swallowed up the Egyptian army. All this is related in Exodus 13 and 14. In chapter 16 the people arrived in the desert across from the sea and immediately began complaining: "The whole congregation of the people of Israel grumbled against Moses and Aaron in the wilderness, and the people of Israel said to them, 'Would that we had died by the hand of the LORD in the land of Egypt, when we sat by the meat pots and ate bread to the full, for you have brought us out into this wilderness to kill this whole assembly with hunger'" (Ex. 16:2–3).

This is an expression of ingratitude and unbelief that we may find hard to fathom, until we realize that we demonstrate a similar attitude on far less pretense than starvation and thirst in a desert wilderness. Instead of trusting the Lord to supply their needs, something he had shown himself both willing and able to do, the Israelites complained against him. Even when the Lord graciously sent manna from heaven, the miraculous bread that rained down to earth, the people continued to complain and engage in petty disobedience, until they again confronted Moses in rebellion.

Exodus 17 begins, "All the congregation of the people of Israel moved on from the wilderness of Sin by stages, according to the commandment of the LORD." The writer of Hebrews tells us in verse 8 that this was a time of testing. God had delivered his people and now was testing their allegiance to him with these difficult travels in the desert. We see how miserably the Israelites failed:

> Therefore the people quarreled with Moses and said, "Give us water to drink." And Moses said to them, "Why do you quarrel with me? Why do you test the LORD?" But the people thirsted there for water, and the people grumbled against Moses and said, "Why did you bring us up out of Egypt, to kill us and our children and our livestock with thirst?" So Moses cried to the LORD, "What shall I do with this people? They are almost ready to stone me." (Ex. 17:2–4)

Again, God was gracious and he sent Moses to strike the rock with his staff, and water came out from the rock to provide for the people. Moses then named the place Massah and Meribah, which mean "testing" and "rebellion," the two words we see used in verse 8 of Hebrews 3 to signify God's displeasure at his unbelieving people.

The other Old Testament passage reflected here is Numbers 14, which records Israel's greatest revolt against the Lord. In chapter 13 God sent out one scout from each of the tribes, twelve in all, to spy out the Promised Land in preparation for the nation's entry. The scouts came back and delivered a sobering report: "We came to the land to which you sent us. It flows with milk and honey. . . . However, the people who dwell in the land are strong, and the cities are fortified and very large. . . . We are not able to go up against the people, for they are stronger than we are" (Num. 13:27–31). Only two of the spies, Joshua and Caleb, urged otherwise. Joshua pleaded with the people, "Do not rebel against the LORD. And do not fear the people of the land . . . the LORD is with us; do not fear them" (Num. 14:8–9). Nonetheless, Numbers 14 records a general revolt against the Lord's rule. The people cried out that the very God who had delivered them from Egypt now sought to kill them in Canaan. They refused to obey, refused to go forth into the Promised Land, and even set out to stone Joshua and Caleb, who had stood up against their unbelief.

It was at this moment that the glory cloud of the Lord appeared at the tabernacle, and thus ensued one of the most sobering moments in all of Scripture. "How long will this people despise me?" the Lord bellowed at Moses. "How long will they not believe in me, in spite of all the signs that I have done among them?" (Num. 14:11). Moses pleaded with the Lord for the lives of his people, arguing that if God struck down the Israelites now his name would be scandalized among the nations. Moses begged God to glorify himself by forgiving the people: "Please pardon the iniquity of this people, according to the greatness of your steadfast love, just as you have forgiven this people, from Egypt until now" (v. 19).

God did spare them, but he also punished them, as recorded in Hebrews 3:11. Quoting Psalm 95:11, the author recalls God's terrible words, "As I swore in my wrath, 'They shall not enter my rest.'" The nation of Israel would enter the Promised Land, but none of this generation would be left when that happened. Instead, they would wander forty years in the desert. Only when the last of the rebellious adults had died, leaving only Joshua and Caleb, who trusted the Lord, were their children permitted to enter into the land.

OUR TESTING IN THE WILDERNESS

What is the relationship between those distant events and the trials being endured by those early Jewish Christians, or by us today? The writer of Hebrews demonstrates an understanding of the Christian life that is common to the New Testament, comparing the exodus to the present life of faith. Like the Israelites, every man or woman who has come to salvation in Christ has been delivered by God from the house of bondage—in our case, the slavery that was our bondage to sin. Also, like Israel of old, we are headed toward a land of promise. We journey to cross the Jordan River, which is rightly compared to our passage through death, after which we enter into our heavenly inheritance. Additionally—and here is the point that is so relevant to our passage—just as the Israelites endured a passage of testing in the desert, so too is this present life a time of testing.

This is the time in the wilderness, the time of difficulty and often of sorrow and pain. We are not now living in the Promised Land but in the wilderness, and the sooner we realize this, the better. This helps answer questions like "Why does God allow things to go wrong in my life?" or "Why are things so hard?" The answer is that today is the day of testing, and the day of our rest is yet to come.

Every Christian is sure to be tested in this life; trials will manifest the reality of our faith, or the lack thereof. As A. W. Pink writes:

> Testings reveal the state of our hearts—a crisis neither makes nor mars a man, but it does *manifest* him. While all is smooth sailing we appear to be getting along nicely. But are we? Are our minds stayed upon the Lord, or are we, instead, complacently resting in His temporal mercies? When the storm breaks, it is not so much that we fail under it, as that our habitual lack of leaning upon God, of daily walking in dependency upon Him, is made evident.[1]

KNOWING GOD'S WAYS

We saw the difference between Joshua and Caleb's testimony and that of the ten unbelieving spies. Similarly, our profession of faith will be either proved or disproved by our response to trials. Jonathan Edwards wrote, "Tri-

---

1. A. W. Pink, *An Exposition of Hebrews* (Grand Rapids: Baker, 1954), 169.

als . . . have a tendency to distinguish between true religion and false, and to cause the difference between them evidently to appear."[2] Knowing this is crucial to the exhortation that epitomizes these verses: "Do not harden your hearts." Isn't that a temptation? Things go badly, you experience trouble, you become afraid, and how easy it is to blame God, to complain, to doubt his power and love and care. But do not follow the Israelites' example: remember God's saving works which demonstrate that he does care, that he will deliver you. Make it your goal to glorify God through faith before a watching world, even and especially in the context of difficulties and trials.

A complaining spirit is always an indicator of unbelief, as we plainly see from this Old Testament example. If we grumble about God's handling of our affairs, it must surely be because we doubt his wisdom or his goodness, or even his power to lead and protect us—in short, his worthiness to be trusted as our God. Douglas Wilson explains, "Complaint is the flag of ingratitude, and it waves above the center of unbelieving hearts—'when they knew God, they glorified him not as God, neither were thankful' (Rom. 1:21, KJV)."[3] The apostle Paul warned the Philippians about this attitude, writing, "Do all things without grumbling or questioning" (Phil. 2:14), and "Do not be anxious about anything, but in everything by prayer and supplication with thanksgiving let your requests be made known to God" (Phil. 4:6).

Complaining is a symptom of a deeper spiritual problem. If we grumble and complain, if we rebel and revolt, it indicates a very poor knowledge of God. Indeed, this was exactly the Lord's diagnosis of Israel, as we see in verse 10: "They always go astray in their heart; they have not known my ways." This was the same complaint God made through the prophet Isaiah: "The ox knows its owner, and the donkey its master's crib, but Israel does not know, my people do not understand" (Isa. 1:3).

How remarkable that these Israelites did not know God after all they had seen and heard and received from his hand! How could they not have known his ways? The point is that while they had enjoyed God's works, they had not reflected on him. They were interested in what God did for them, but not in God himself. We are reminded of Jesus' great prayer to the Father in

2. Jonathan Edwards, *The Religious Affections* (Edinburgh: Banner of Truth, 1986), 21.
3. Douglas Jones and Douglas Wilson, *Angels in the Architecture* (Moscow, Idaho: Canon Press, 1999), 80.

John 17, where our Lord said, "This is eternal life, that they know you the only true God, and Jesus Christ whom you have sent" (John 17:3). Salvation is not a matter of knowing God's blessings—after all, many people who do not know God know his blessings—but it is a matter of knowing him, understanding his character and his ways, and more and more trusting him in all things.

If you are not growing in your knowledge of God, your understanding and appreciation of his ways, let this be a warning to you. We are to be students of God's character, learning what God is like through the circumstances of our lives and especially through the Bible, and growing in our love for him. How is God manifesting his power and grace? Can we look back and discern his once-hidden wisdom, his goodness, his patience, his holiness and love? This is the way to worship him, and indeed, the way to keep our sinful hearts from hardening.

Let me put it another way. What should you be looking for when you read your Bible? There is nothing more important than for you to study God himself. "What does this Scripture tell me about God, about his character, and about his ways?" "How can I know him better and trust him more?" The study of the attributes of God is one of the most vital of all subjects, for to know God is to trust him and to worship him with both awe and gratitude. Charles Spurgeon was right when he said of the study of God: "It is a subject so vast, that all our thoughts are lost in its immensity; so deep, that our pride is drowned in its infinity. . . . But while the subject humbles the mind, it also expands it. Nothing will so enlarge the intellect, nothing so magnify the whole soul of man, as a devout, earnest, continuing investigation of the great subject of the Deity."[4]

When God is filling our thoughts, we learn to rejoice even in our trials. Indeed, we discern that trials are given to draw us nearer to him. Donald Grey Barnhouse observed this, saying: "How wonderful that when we are blinded by tears, we can nevertheless see our God. In fact, our tears become crystal lenses through which He is magnified; and in the midst of suffering we realize the greatness of His power and the tenderness of His love."[5]

---

4. Charles Haddon Spurgeon, *The New Park Street Pulpit*, vol. 1, 1855 (Pasadena, Tex.: Pilgrim Publications, 1975), 1.

5. Donald Grey Barnhouse, *Expositions of Bible Doctrines Taking the Epistle to the Romans as a Point of Departure*, 10 vols. (Grand Rapids: Baker, 1956), 4:89.

If you want the gifts while having no real interest in the Giver, then you will not persevere through the trials of this life, when circumstances turn against you and God's blessings are seen only with eyes of faith. If you resent the challenges God sends, then when the hot sun beats upon your back, when your throat becomes dry and weary, what was said of those ancient Israelites will be said of you as well: "They always go astray in their heart; they have not known my ways. . . . They shall not enter my rest" (Heb. 3:10–11).

Israel complained all through their forty years in the desert, never learning God's ways despite mercy after mercy. Over and again they complained and rebelled about the same old things. All the while God's pillar of fire guided them, the manna fell from heaven, water came forth from the rock, and even their clothes and shoes did not wear out as the Lord cared for them. Still, as the writer of Hebrews summarizes in verses 9–11: "Your fathers put me to the test and saw my works for forty years. Therefore I was provoked with that generation, and said, 'They always go astray in their heart; they have not known my ways.' As I swore in my wrath, 'They shall not enter my rest.'"

We are well advised, therefore, to heed the exhortation with which our passage concludes: "Take care, brothers, lest there be in any of you an evil, unbelieving heart, leading you to fall away from the living God" (v. 12).

JESUS' PATH THROUGH THE DESERT

Verse 1 of chapter 3 told us to fix our thoughts on Jesus, our apostle and high priest. The Israelites should have fixed their thoughts on Moses, who served as their mediator before God. They should have focused on him in their trials, or rather God's saving work revealed through his ministry. After all the great and mighty works they had seen, Moses was worthy of their trust; he was a fitting object of contemplation in their trials.

But if the Israelites were condemned for forgetting Moses, how much greater will be the charge against those who forsake Jesus Christ, a far greater mediator and God's own Son. As the writer of Hebrews put it: "How shall we escape if we neglect such a great salvation" (Heb. 2:3) as that revealed in Jesus Christ?

When we read the account of Jesus' life, we find him, too, sent into the wilderness for a period of trial. Matthew 4:1 tells us, "Jesus was led up by the

Spirit into the wilderness to be tempted by the devil." How significant that he went there for *forty* days—the very number of years Israel was tested and yet failed (Num. 13:25). When we study the devil's temptations against Jesus, we find that they correspond to the failures of Israel. Jesus did not complain about lack of food, but satisfied himself with faith in God. Whereas Israel tried the Lord God, Jesus (the true Israel of faith) replied to Satan, "It is written, 'You shall not put the Lord your God to the test' " (Matt. 4:7). Whereas Israel rebelled, Christ refused to turn his heart away from God. He reproved the devil, "You shall worship the Lord your God and him only shall you serve" (Matt. 4:10). In the wilderness of his temptation, Jesus walked in Israel's steps, succeeding where they had failed.

What this means is that Jesus has walked ahead of us to clear the way. He has blazed the trail of victory through perfect obedience for our salvation. Though we often fail, he did not. Through faith in Christ our failures are hidden in his victory; our faithlessness is garbed in his obedience. His righteousness is presented on our behalf, and now his power is made available to us in the Holy Spirit. This is why Paul insisted, "It is no longer I who live, but Christ who lives in me. And the life I now live in the flesh I live by faith in the Son of God, who loved me and gave himself for me" (Gal. 2:20).

Will we make it through this desert life safe across Jordan to the Promised Land ahead? We will if we trust ourselves to Jesus, relying on the strength he gives to all his pilgrim people. He is the shepherd of his flock, and if we follow him, looking to him in faith and relying on his provision, we will find "goodness and mercy . . . all the days of [our lives]," and "shall dwell in the house of the LORD forever" (Ps. 23:6).

11

SALVATION LOST

Hebrews 3:12—19

For who were those who heard and yet rebelled? Was it not all
those who left Egypt led by Moses? And with whom was he pro-
voked for forty years? Was it not with those who sinned, whose
bodies fell in the wilderness? And to whom did he swear that they
would not enter his rest, but to those who were disobedient? So we
see that they were unable to enter because of unbelief.
(Heb. 3:16–19)

The writer of the Book of Hebrews was a pastor. His concern in writing this grand exposition was a pastoral one, and we see this most clearly in passages like the one we consider in this chapter. Here he expresses concern that, as he says in verse 13, "none of you may be hardened by the deceitfulness of sin." His purpose is not merely to set forth doctrine, valuable though that is, but to apply his teaching and to bring it to bear with force upon his precious readers so they will persevere in faith through hard times. The thought of losing even one of this flock through unbelief is enough to motivate his strong exhortations.

This emphasis accounts for the repetition of the writer's chief theme in Hebrews 3: "Today, if you hear his voice, do not harden your hearts as in the rebellion" (Heb. 3:15; cf. 3:7–8). The rebellion he speaks of is that recorded in Exodus 17 and Numbers 14, when the Israelites refused to trust the Lord during their desert trials, after Moses had led them out from slavery in Egypt.

After their deliverance from Egypt and passage through the Red Sea, God directed the Israelites on difficult journeys in the desert that were intended to test their faith in him. Those trials are analogous to this present life, when Christians will undergo hardships and temptations that similarly reveal the quality of our faith. The Israelites, wearied by hunger and danger and fatigue, failed to trust in God's Word as given through Moses. Drawing from that example, the writer of Hebrews warns his readers not to fail, especially when we have the risen and exalted Jesus Christ as our leader through this world.

REBELLION AGAINST GOD

The writer of Hebrews continues this argument, teaching us three lessons from that generation of Israelites. The first is that *a good beginning does not ensure a good ending*. We see this in verse 16: "Who were those who heard and yet rebelled? Was it not all those who left Egypt led by Moses?" These people had seen the great miracles in Egypt, and especially the parting of the Red Sea. Yet when they experienced hardship, they turned away!

Even the most impressive of beginnings does not ensure perseverance in faith. Here we see how little we can rely upon emotional experiences that we had at the inception of our Christian life. Many people rely on a particularly emotional event in the past—a time when they prayed a certain prayer, or a revival when they walked down to the altar. But none of us will ever have an experience as vivid as that which this generation of Israelites had, yet their good beginning still could not take the place of daily trusting in the Lord in a long walk of faith.

Some will object that this conflicts with the Bible's teaching of eternal security. The Bible tells us that all who genuinely trust in Christ can be confident in his complete sufficiency as our Savior. Jesus said of his own, "I give them eternal life, and they will never perish, and no one will snatch them out of my hand" (John 10:28). But we need to remember that Judas was in his company at that time, and because he lacked faith, the promise was not for him. If we want assurance of our salvation, then our faith must persevere under trial. If we want to "make [our] calling and election sure" (2 Peter 1:10), then we must bear the fruit that salvation requires.

The Israelites in the exodus were safe so long as they walked with God in faith. The same will be true for us; as we trust in Jesus, we can be sure of our salvation. But this warns us against any complacency in our faith. James Boice sums up the Bible's teaching on perseverance:

> Some people talk as though it is not necessary for a Christian to persevere in this hope, on the grounds that since God perseveres with us, our perseverance is unnecessary. We are saved, and will be saved, regardless of what we do. This is not taught in the Bible. It is true that God perseveres. It is true that once he has begun a good work in us he will keep on performing it until the day of Jesus Christ (Phil. 1:6). But simply because he perseveres, we too will persevere.[1]

How terrible it is to read that *all* of those Moses led out of Egypt rebelled against the Lord. We do know of at least two exceptions, Joshua and Caleb, yet this sweeping statement could be made. Even after so great a beginning as the exodus, the entire body who experienced it went on to rebel against the Lord. How greatly this stark fact argues against any complacency on our part.

Second, we learn here *how dreadful it is to become hard-hearted toward God*. Warning us soberly of unbelief, the writer of Hebrews says, "Today, if you hear his voice, do not harden your hearts as in the rebellion" (Heb. 3:15).

The meaning of the terminology is obvious. A hardened heart is the opposite of a tender heart, one that is easily penetrated by the Word of God, is easily impressed by its teaching, is moved by God's love, and is touched and won over by God's great redemptive works. It is a dreadful thing to be hardened in heart toward God, for then his Word sits upon the heart without penetrating, until before long it is plucked away, never to be grasped, never to be loved and believed. This is how Jesus described it in his parable of the four soils (Matt. 13:4, 19). Perhaps the most frightening example in the Bible is that of Pharaoh. Despite the most forceful demonstrations of God's power and the clearest expressions of God's will, Pharaoh would not yield but stub-

---

1. James Montgomery Boice, *Genesis*, 3 vols. (Grand Rapids: Baker, 1998), 2:517.

bornly resisted to the point of his own destruction. How terrible that these Israelites, the very people who saw Pharaoh's example and escaped from his oppressive rule, followed his example! They, too, were hard in heart after all that God had done; they complained against him in every difficulty and accused God of meaning them harm despite his many great demonstrations of love.

We see, then, why such a heart is called evil or sinful in verse 12, for it turns away from the living God. In verse 17 those who would not believe are described as "those who sinned," and in verse 18 we are told that they disobeyed. This shows that sin is disobedience; it is failure to listen to and obey God's Word. In the accounts of this generation in Exodus and Numbers, we read of one sin after another. And yet the great sin the writer of Hebrews focuses on is the sin of unbelief.

There is an important insight here, namely, that unbelief is at the root of all sin. Specific sins are like rotten fruit hanging on a bad tree. But this is not the real problem; it is not the disease, but just the symptom. If we are greedy or hateful or selfish or dishonest, that is just evidence of dead and rotten things deeper inside. Bad fruit grows on a bad tree, just as sin grows from our sinful, corrupt nature. But deeper still, there is a root system to every tree; that is most important of all. Unbelief is the root system that feeds the whole rotten tree of sin.

By contrast, it is believing God that causes us to obey him. Noah is a good example. He believed when God foretold the flood, and it was because of his belief that Noah went ahead and built the ark. On the other hand, because the Israelites had never come to know God and had not believed his promises, they rebelled against him and sinned in the desert. The issue of faith versus unbelief is at the core of every spiritual issue.

Notice that lack of evidence is not the cause of unbelief. These Israelites had all the evidence anyone could ever want, but because their hearts were hard the evidence did not produce faith. Likewise, people today do not reject Jesus Christ on philosophical grounds but on moral grounds. They reject God's Word because they have a greater love for sin, and their love for sin requires hardness to God's Word. The philosophy comes later; it is only the fruit of hardness to God's Word and love for sin. This is what we find with this generation of Israelites: a hardening of heart that the writer earnestly desires us to avoid.

Third, the writer of Hebrews forces us to face *the reality of God's wrath against sin.* In verse 17 we learn that God was "provoked" with those who sinned in disbelief. In verse 18 we read that because of their attitude God swore that they would never enter his rest. In both instances, we see God's wrath against sin.

Many people today consider wrath to be an inappropriate response for God to make toward sin. God should be more like us, they think: he shouldn't take sin so seriously. But, unlike us, God is perfectly holy and therefore his wrath burns against sin.

When we speak of God's wrath, we do not mean God throws a temper tantrum in anger; rather, God's wrath is his deliberate response in judgment toward sin and sinners. As J. I. Packer explains, "This is *righteous* anger— the *right* reaction of moral perfection in the Creator towards moral perversity in the creature. So far from the manifestation of God's wrath in punishing sin being morally doubtful, the thing that would be morally doubtful would be for Him *not* to show His wrath in this way."[2]

Because of their unbelief and subsequent sin, this entire generation of Israelites, the very people God had redeemed out of Pharaoh's grasp, died in the wilderness. "And with whom was he provoked for forty years?" the writer of Hebrews asks. "Was it not with those who sinned, whose bodies fell in the wilderness?" It is God's own nature that requires this kind of response to sin. Leon Morris observes, "The Bible is clear that God is not impassive or indifferent in the face of human sin. He is a 'consuming fire' (12:29), and his inevitable reaction to sin is wrath. . . . God does care, and he did not allow the sinning Israelites to enter the rest."[3]

We often hear that God punishes the sin but not the sinner, but look at the contrary evidence here. It was not unbelief that died and left its bones upon the desert sands; it was the unbelievers themselves. So also will God cast unbelieving sinners into the fires of hell—not merely their sin but the unrepentant sinners themselves.

God's wrath was deliberate, not erratic; persistent, not fleeting. One commentator begins with the number of adult males we are told departed from Egypt, which was 603,550 (Num. 1:46), then adds in a likely number of adult

---

2. J. I. Packer, *Knowing God* (Downers Grove, Ill.: InterVarsity, 1979), 166.
3. Leon Morris, *Hebrews* (Grand Rapids: Zondervan, 1981), 34.

women, and calculates that on average 90 Israelite adults died every day for forty years, until the entire generation was gone. Daily they were reminded of what we so often forget, that "the wages of sin is death" (Rom. 6:23).[4]

This raises an obvious question: "Does this mean that all these Israelites suffered God's eternal wrath, that they not only died in the desert but also all went to hell?" On the one hand, the death of these unbelieving Israelites is certainly meant to point to God's wrath in the greater judgment that will send men and women into hell forever. On the other hand, it is not stated in the Bible that these Israelites were condemned to eternal damnation. Their problem was unbelief, and unbelief is what causes salvation to be lost—the opportunity to enter into God's rest is forfeited by lack of faith. Any individuals who did not repent and trust themselves to God during those forty years must certainly have died without salvation. However, we may hope that many of them repented, believed, and thus have been forgiven. After all, during the long sojourn years of their punishment, the Israelites had God in their midst, they had the ministry of Moses and Aaron, and they had the sacrifices of the tabernacle through which God's grace was daily offered to them. Nevertheless, their lost opportunity to enter the Promised Land furnishes a dramatic warning against the perils of unbelief.

A REMEDY FOR UNBELIEF

Surely, Israel's example alone is enough to alarm us with regard to the matter of unbelief. It is with this in mind that, with perhaps a new earnestness and sense of urgency, we turn to the remedy for unbelief contained in this passage. This remedy comes in the form of two exhortations, one that relates to ourselves and one that relates to others. First, the writer warns, "Take care, brothers," a command that is rightly taken as "Watch out" (Heb. 3:12). To this he adds, "Exhort one another every day" (Heb. 3:13).

This is an excellent instruction for us today. We are to exert a watchful guard over our own hearts and come alongside others in the church to exhort them to do likewise. John Calvin explains why this is so needful:

---

4. Simon J. Kistemaker, *Thessalonians, the Pastorals and Hebrews* (Grand Rapids: Baker, 1984), 93.

As by nature we are prone to fall into evil, we have need of various helps to help us in the fear of God. Unless our faith is repeatedly encouraged, it lies dormant; unless it is warmed, it grows cold; unless it is aroused, it gets numb. [The writer of Hebrews] therefore wishes them to stimulate one another by mutual encouragement, so that Satan will not steal into their hearts and by his falsehoods lead them away from God.[5]

The Greek word for "exhort" is *parakaleō*. The prefix *para* means "to come alongside," and the verb *kaleō* means "to call out." The picture, then, is that we are to come alongside one another daily, exhorting one another in the practice of Christian faith.

Christianity is not an individual but a team endeavor. So if we do not know the nature of our fellow believers' struggles, and if we do not share ours with them, then we will never be able to follow through with this command. The result, in that case, will be that people among us will fall prey to sin. Therefore we are commanded to be watchful for just these things in the body of Christ, thereby ensuring that none of us falls away because of sin's deceitfulness. As long as it is "today"—that is, this present age of testing, with opportunities and dangers like the ones the Israelites faced—we must watch out and exhort one another daily in the things of the faith.

Specifically, we must watch for the "deceitfulness" of sin. The Bible attaches this label to a number of things. It speaks often of false teachers who would lead us astray by their deceit. Paul warns against them, saying, "For such persons do not serve our Lord Christ, but their own appetites, and by smooth talk and flattery they deceive the hearts of the naïve" (Rom. 16:18). Colossians 2:8 says the same thing about worldly philosophies, and Proverbs 12:5 tells us that "the counsels of the wicked are deceitful." Certainly, then, we must exert a watchful care against enticing but misleading teachings that deceive the mind.

But it gets worse, for the Bible goes on to say that our very hearts are deceitful. Jeremiah 17:9 is the most famous verse to this effect: "The heart is deceitful above all things, and desperately sick; who can understand it?" In Ephesians 4:22, Paul tells us that our very human nature, apart from God's saving work, is "corrupt through deceitful desires." That gets quite a bit closer

5. John Calvin, *New Testament Commentaries*, 12 vols. (Grand Rapids: Eerdmans, 1994), 12:41.

to home—I cannot even trust my heart, the Bible says. My desires are not trustworthy. And the wise man comes to realize that this is so—that the things we long for are often foolish and vain, if not outright idolatrous— and therefore he seeks the scrutiny and exhortation of brothers and sisters in the Lord.

More threatening still is the presence of a personal deceiver loose in the world. The Bible tells us that the devil is a great deceiver who beguiles men and women into folly and unbelief, as he beguiled Eve in the garden. He even masquerades as an angel of light (2 Cor. 11:14). And then there is sin itself, which has as one of its main qualities that it is deceitful. We must not toy with sin, or we will be drawn in and ensnared.

Consider the case of a man who is tempted to leave his wife and children for another woman. The sin seems so alluring; she is so much more wonderful than the plain old wife he has grown tired of. And she admires him so; she plays to his ego where his wife only nags him. She would be better for him despite the broken taboos; he will be better off and happier with the adulteress. People will understand; they will get over it; his children will ultimately be glad for him.

It is all, however, a great deceit. It will not be more wonderful, for the problem with his marriage is his own heart, and he will soon get tired of his new lover as well. She admires him now but will think less of him when he loses his job, his reputation, his money, and his self-respect. His children will not get over it, but will bear scars and brokenness all the days of their lives. Sin says it will be better and he will be happy, but it is a deceit. He is stepping forward into misery and ruin, bringing disgrace upon himself and, if he is a Christian, scandal upon the church and even the name of Jesus Christ.

Sin advertises pleasure but delivers pain. The problem is that our hearts are so willing to be deceived. Combine this with the reality that sin is deceitful in its very nature, and you see why we have so great a need of godly fellowship, of exhortation, and of warning at the very first stages of temptation. We need help being watchful over the spiritually dangerous circumstances that we face—jobs or family ties or relationships or specific temptations that by their very nature are hostile to Christian faith. Therefore, we must exhort one another, lest some of us should fall prey to sin's deception, even to the hardening of our hearts against God.

We must realize that sin is not merely something we do. Sin is a power, an enemy army, like a pack of wolves surrounding the flock and darting in to pick off likely targets. Therefore, as Simon Kistemaker writes, "Believers have a corporate and an individual responsibility to care for the spiritual well-being of their fellow men. They must consider this responsibility a holy obligation and exhibit utter faithfulness."[6]

From deception grows hardness of heart—such was the fate of the Israelites who came under God's wrath. Christian fellowship, including prayer, Bible study, and meaningful friendship, is a great bulwark against sin's deception; in such company the arguments of sin lose their force, and we are strengthened in faith and obedience. Our goal is to persevere to the end and enter into God's rest, and our strategy is mutual watchfulness. What a worthy cause that is! It is worth inconvenience. It is worth giving up some leisure time. It is worth real sacrifice and will repay the dividends of eternal life.

In his great allegory of the Christian life, *The Pilgrim's Progress*, John Bunyan shows his understanding of the importance of godly fellowship. At one point in the journey to the Celestial City, Bunyan's hero—a man named Christian—finds companionship with a fellow believer named Hopeful. Bunyan writes, "They entered a brotherly covenant and agreed to be companions." What a wonderful statement! It is reminiscent of the description of the godly men of King Asa's generation, as told in 2 Chronicles 15:12, "They entered into a covenant to seek the LORD, the God of their fathers, with all their heart and with all their soul."

In such fashion Christian and Hopeful journeyed together, and their companionship was very profitable. Soon they came across another traveler, a man named By-ends from the town of Fair-speech. Pooling their discernment, Christian and Hopeful realized that this was a man to avoid. Next, they encountered a group led by Mr. Hold-the-world, who tried to tempt them into seeking dishonest gain, and together they reproved him. Next came Demas who called to them to depart from the way, promising a place filled with riches of the world. This time, Hopeful was deceived and wanted to go take a look. But Christian warned him, "I have heard of this place. . . . The treasure is a snare to those that seek it." He exhorted Hopeful, "Let us

---

6. Kistemaker, *Hebrews*, 98.

not go a step closer. Let us keep on our way," and the two companions went forward safely on the pilgrimage. Later, they came to Doubting Castle, where they were thrown into a terrible dungeon. Here it was Christian who faltered, falling prey to the Giant Despair's temptation to kill himself as the only escape. This time it was Hopeful who kept his faith, recalling God's commandments. With his help, Christian found the key, called Promise, that opened the door to let them escape Doubting Castle.[7] This is the kind of help we are to give one another, each of us in our weakness and doubt being helped by the strength and faith of our brother, each helping the other in turn so that together we may endure.

CONFIDENCE TO ENDURE

We saw earlier that a good beginning is not enough, that we must persevere through hardship to the end, holding fast and trusting Jesus Christ for our salvation. The author says this again in his summary in verse 14: "For we share in Christ, if indeed we hold our original confidence firm to the end." It is perseverance that tests and proves and demonstrates the fact that we are truly joined to Jesus Christ.

Note, however, what it is we are to hold until the end: "our original confidence" (Heb. 3:14). Of what are we to be confident? Not our own works or strength, but the power for salvation that is in Jesus Christ. It is our "original" confidence, namely, the very message of the gospel that saved us in the first place. This is what we need to persevere to the end. The gospel is not merely a message we need to hear only once, at the beginning of the Christian life. The gospel that makes us Christians—the good news of our crucified and risen Lord—also keeps us in the faith. So let us diligently and obediently proclaim the gospel to one another, that none of us might be hardened by sin's deceitfulness.

"Take care, brothers," says our author, "lest there be in any of you an evil, unbelieving heart, leading you to fall away from the living God." What does this involve? I think one of our great hymns, "Blest Be the Tie That Binds," puts it well:

---

7. John Bunyan, *The Pilgrim's Progress* (Nashville: Thomas Nelson, 1999), 85–100.

Before the Father's throne
    we pour our ardent prayers;
our fears, our hopes, our aims are one,
    our comforts and our cares.

We share our mutual woes,
    our mutual burdens bear,
and often for each other flows
    the sympathizing tear.[8]

Those are not merely words for us to sing, but words to live together in the church. And so may we all be found faithful to the end, that this great salvation should not be lost by us, and that in due time we may all enter into God's rest.

---

8. John Fawcett, "Blest Be the Tie That Binds," 1782.

12

THE SABBATH REST

Hebrews 4:1–5

*Therefore, while the promise of entering his rest still stands, let us
fear lest any of you should seem to have failed to reach it.*
(Heb. 4:1)

One of the striking characteristics of the Book of Hebrews is the
distinctive view of history it sets forth. We have been encountering this in the long exhortation that began in chapter 3 and continues through chapter 4. This exhortation centers around the writer's use
of Psalm 95, with the key verse, "Today, if you hear his voice, do not harden
your hearts."

The key term is "Today," which the writer says applies to his first-century
readers just as it did to David's readers a thousand years before, and just as
it did to the exodus generation he is referring to. "Today" is the time when
the promise that all believers will enter God's rest is still open and available.
"Today," in that sense, is our time as much as it was theirs.

The backdrop, as we have seen in previous studies, is the exodus wanderings of Israel in the wilderness. That generation failed the test; they complained and disobeyed God, not turning to him in faith. As a result, they did

not enter into God's rest—that is, into the Promised Land. The author of Hebrews now emphasizes: "You need to realize that you are in a similar situation. Your trials are like their trials; how you respond to them will determine whether or not you will enter into God's salvation."

This is the view of salvation history in the Book of Hebrews. As far as salvation is concerned, we are in essentially the same historical setting as the Israelites. This is especially true when it comes to those early Christians who first received this letter. Like them, we are living after the death and resurrection of Jesus Christ, after he ascended into heaven and took up the seat of authority there, and before the time of his second coming, when the opportunity for salvation will be gone and the harvest finally gathered. Therefore, how we now respond to the gospel "today" is the most decisive element in our lives.

THEREFORE TAKE HEED

It is in this context that we read the words of verse 1: "Therefore, while the promise of entering his rest still stands, let us fear lest any of you should seem to have failed to reach it." The Greek text literally says, "Let us be afraid." The point is to say: "Therefore, let us be alarmed at the prospect, given this decisive age of opportunity and testing, that any of you should not press on to salvation."

We see a couple of emphases here that are central to the overall message of this book. First is the demand for perseverance under trial. That is what the author means by saying "lest any of you should seem to have failed to reach it." The metaphor is an athletic one, and the idea is that of finishing the race. Perseverance is an essential element of the Christian life. Indeed, running the race to the end is the hallmark of genuine, saving faith, while falling away is the mark of a spurious faith that does not lead to salvation.

The second emphasis is that of corporate or mutual responsibility. We saw this a few verses earlier: "Exhort one another every day, as long as it is called 'today,' that none of you may be hardened by the deceitfulness of sin" (3:13). Here we have the same point of view: "Let us fear lest any of you should seem to have failed to reach it." Notice that the subject of the sentence is plural—it is "us" who must be careful—while the object is singular—lest anyone fall away. This is the attitude we need in the church today, one that says: "Yes, I *am* my brother's keeper. I have a stake in the spiritual affairs of others here and a responsibility not merely for my own salvation, but for theirs as well." This is not an invitation for destructive meddling but for the mutual building up that is to define life in the church. So important is this to the life of the church that the apostle James concluded his epistle on this very note: "Whoever brings back a sinner from his wandering will save his soul from death and will cover a multitude of sins" (James 5:20).

Simon Kistemaker is right when he observes, "We ought to take careful note of members who may be drifting from the truth in doctrine or conduct and then pray with them and for them. We are constantly looking for spiritual stragglers."[1] Reading these words, I cannot help but recall my days as an officer in the United States Army. Early every morning all the units would be out doing physical fitness training, hundreds of little units running in formation, often for long periods of time and until the men were utterly exhausted. You could tell everything you needed to know about the morale and the leadership and even the combat effectiveness of a unit by the way they ran in formation. A good unit was all together, even if they had to slow the pace a little bit. There was mutual encouragement going on. If a man fell out—and that is the very language in verse 1—if a man was exhausted or dispirited and lagged behind, a good unit would turn around to retrieve him, to exhort and bring back his determination. Not being a particularly gifted long-distance runner, I can remember times when I thought I could go no further, but was virtually carried by the encouragement of my fellow soldiers until my legs regained their strength. That is what it is like to be part of a real team.

The opposite was true of lesser outfits. In poor units you would see soldiers straggling way behind, falling out and even quitting altogether, while the main column went on oblivious. Soldiers who would have persevered in more cohesive outfits fell by the wayside—they fell short.

That is what the writer of Hebrews wants us to avoid, especially since the stakes are so much higher in the matter of salvation. A good church, therefore, will not be defined by the size of its building, nor by the number of people attending or the amount of money raised. Rather, by God's standard, a quality church will be one that leaves no stragglers to lag behind or perish

---

1. Simon J. Kistemaker, *Thessalonians, the Pastorals and Hebrews* (Grand Rapids: Baker, 1984), 104.

in unbelief. The kind of church the writer of Hebrews is looking for is one where the *dis*couraged are propelled forward by *en*couragement, where the weak find strength in the care of others, and those in danger of being deceived are recalled to the truth in a spirit of love.

SALVATION AS REST

The matter the writer of Hebrews has in mind here is nothing less than the eternal salvation of our souls. He has been referring to this with a term we have not yet discussed in detail. Consistently, and drawing his terminology from Psalm 95, he describes salvation as the "rest" offered by God.

What does he mean by this kind of language? The first way to answer is by looking at the context, namely, the exodus of God's people from Egypt to the Promised Land. As one commentator explains: "The concept of rest in the context of the promise to the Exodus generation had the connotation of entrance into Canaan (the Promised Land), where Israel would experience relief from turmoil and security from their enemies."[2]

In what sense does this apply to the readers of Hebrews? The writer does not mean that they will lead lives of material riches and temporal peace, since this letter was written to those facing persecution, with all the deprivation and danger that implies. The New Testament does not promise believers that they will be free from strife in this world. In fact, Jesus said, "In the world you will have tribulation" (John 16:33).

Obviously, then, the meaning is spiritual. It is our souls that will be supplied and kept safe. Surely this is what Jesus had in mind in his great Bread of Life discourse, recorded in John 6: "I am the bread of life; whoever comes to me shall not hunger, and whoever believes in me shall never thirst. . . . This is the will of him who sent me, that I should lose nothing of all that he has given me, but raise it up at the last day" (John 6:35, 39).

Jesus offers our souls the same benefits offered to Israel in the Promised Land: bountiful provision and complete security. Indeed, the language Moses used for the Promised Land may be directly applied to our spiritual blessings in Jesus Christ: "A land flowing with milk and honey. . . . A land of hills and valleys, which drinks water by the rain from heaven, a land that

2. William L. Lane, *Hebrews 1–8* (Dallas: Word Books, 1991), 98.

the LORD your God cares for. The eyes of the LORD your God are always upon it, from the beginning of the year to the end of the year" (Deut. 11:9–12).

Christians experience trials of all sorts, just as Israel's faith was challenged on the way to the Promised Land. But Paul could write of God's salvation rest words that God's faithful people have always found true: "My God will supply every need of yours according to his riches in glory in Christ Jesus" (Phil. 4:19).

GOD'S SABBATH REST

All of that is clearly implied by the reference to the exodus wandering and the offer of rest. The writer emphasizes this by repeating the quote from Psalm 95 in verses 3 and 5: "They shall not enter my rest." The point is not just to reiterate the failure of the unbelieving Israelites, but to emphasize the reality of the rest that was provided and remains offered to this day.

In the latter part of verse 3 and in verse 4, however, the writer of Hebrews adds another Old Testament reference to expand his definition of the salvation rest. Here the citation is from the creation account at the beginning of Genesis: "And God rested on the seventh day from all his works" (see Gen. 2:2). The point here, and it is a weighty one indeed, is that the rest God offers to us in salvation is nothing less than the very rest he himself has enjoyed since the completion of his creation work.

We remember from Genesis 1 that God labored for six days, each day adding more to his creation wonder. Then on the seventh day God rested. This rest was not a temporary state, but God's abiding condition. The first day was concluded with these words: "There was evening and there was morning, the first day" (Gen. 1:5). That phrase was repeated for each of God's six working days. This pattern, however, does not continue into the seventh day. Unlike the other days, this Sabbath day of rest does not end; it is not brought to completion, but goes on forever.

When we say that God rested, we do not mean that he went on vacation or removed his care from our world. The picture is rather that after having made and ordered and subdued the creation according to his desired plan, his control was so absolute, his sovereignty so unquestioned, that God enthroned himself without effective opposition. His reign is one of rest—that is, of absolute supremacy and unassailable sovereignty—so much so that he exerts all his rule from the position of rest. It is the kind of rest possible to a God who could say, "I am God, and there is no other; I am God, and there is none like me, declaring the end from the beginning and from ancient times things not yet done, saying, 'My counsel shall stand'" (Isa. 46:9–10). So when we think of God's Sabbath rest, we should immediately think of his utter, uncontested sovereign rule.

To enter God's eternal Sabbath rest, therefore, means to enter into saving relationship with such a God. When God becomes our Savior, we become part of that kingdom in which he so utterly and sovereignly rules over us and for us. His work in our lives is established, even as the writer of Hebrews says of God's work in creation, "His works were finished from the foundation of the world" (Heb. 4:3).

This means that if you have put your faith in this saving God, if you have trusted his gospel in Jesus Christ, you now can rest. You can stop worrying about whether or not you will have a place in heaven. You can stop fretting about whether you will endure as a Christian. You can stop being afraid of what the world will do to you. You can face the prospect of loss in this life, of suffering, and even of death, for ours is the God of the Sabbath, who established his purposes forever from the beginning. Through faith in him you enter into his rest. He is the God who says to us, "For I know the plans I have for you, declares the LORD, plans for wholeness and not for evil, to give you a future and a hope" (Jer. 29:11). So you can rest in his saving purpose for you.

Anyone who has been a soldier knows what it means to be in field operations and then to be sent behind the lines for a period of rest. On the front lines you are constantly dirty, your food supply is inconsistent, and what you get to eat is bland. Most difficult of all is the constant vigilance, the need to be always alert to danger, which is seldom far away. I vividly recall what it was like to be pulled out for rest, taking my first shower in days, eating hot and freshly-cooked meals. But best of all was the sense of peace, the opportunity to sleep long and deeply, the rest of security and provision.

This is what we enter spiritually by faith, and what we forfeit by unbelief. Jesus calls out, "Come to me, all who labor and are heavy laden, and I will give you rest. Take my yoke upon you, and learn from me, for I am gentle and lowly in heart, and you will find rest for your souls. For my yoke is easy, and my burden is light" (Matt. 11:28–30). He offers rest from the burden of your sins, which he takes onto his back and puts away at the cross, and rest from the troubles of this world. Yes, you will have them in this life, Jesus said, but "take heart; I have overcome the world" (John 16:33).

Salvation rest is living in God's presence, feeling the warmth of his love, trusting the strength of his hands to hold us forever. It is saying with the apostle Paul: "For I am sure that neither death nor life, nor angels nor rulers, nor things present nor things to come, nor powers, nor height nor depth, nor anything else in all creation, will be able to separate us from the love of God that is in Christ Jesus our Lord" (Rom. 8:38–39).

HEARING AND BELIEVING: THE WAY INTO GOD'S REST

Hearing the offer of such a rest, we can understand the urgency with which the writer of Hebrews speaks about faith in Jesus Christ. The question is: How can I enter into this wonderful rest? The answer is, By trusting the Lord Jesus Christ for salvation. Verse 3 tells us, "We who have believed enter that rest." Who are the people who are saved, the people of God who enter into his rest and enjoy a saving relationship with him? It is those who believe the message of the gospel they have heard.

We must embrace God's offer of salvation personally through faith. This is the writer's point in verse 2: "For good news came to us just as to them, but the message they heard did not benefit them, because they were not united by faith with those who listened." It is not enough simply to come to church, any more than it was enough to have been a member of Israel during the exodus. It is not enough to hear the gospel or even to understand it, to explain it to others or even to appreciate the wonder and beauty of the gospel. Unless you receive the gospel in faith, you will not enter into God's rest; you will not be saved. Indeed, if you hear the gospel and do not combine the hearing with believing, if you do not respond to it by confessing yourself a sinner and casting yourself upon Christ for salvation, that gospel, which verse 12 describes as "sharper than any two-edged sword," will become the source of damnation instead of your salvation. To all who hear but do not believe, regardless of anything else they do, God says, "As I swore in my wrath, 'They shall not enter my rest'" (Heb. 4:3).

If you have been attending church, listening to the gospel as it is preached, perhaps enjoying the music and the lovely setting, but have not personally put your trust in Christ, you are in great peril. Do not delude yourself by thinking you are in a neutral or even a promising situation, for you are not. Until you receive Christ as your Savior, you are a rebel against the gospel you have heard, you are excluded from God's rest, and are under his wrath. You must believe the gospel and rest upon Christ's saving work for you.

An illustration of the rest that faith brings comes from John G. Paton, a pioneer missionary to the New Hebrides islands. Paton set about the work of translating the Bible into the native language, which until then had no written form. Before long he encountered the problem that the language had no word for faith, which, given the Bible's message, was some problem indeed. But one day Paton observed a hunting expedition. As the hunters came back from their exertions, he watched as they threw themselves into chairs and cried out, "My, it is good to stretch yourself out here and rest." Paton jumped to his feet and wrote the words down; they provided his translation for the word "faith" in the native Bible.[3] By faith, the weary sinner stretches out to rest on Jesus Christ, upheld by his gospel. We might substitute Paton's translation into various verses from the Bible: "Stretch yourself out on the Lord Jesus, and you will be saved" (Acts 16:31). "For God so loved the world that he gave his one and only Son, that whoever stretches out on him shall not perish but have eternal life" (John 3:16).

What this means is that you must rely for your salvation not on what you have done or might do—which can lead only to condemnation because of sin and failure—but on what Jesus has done. Hebrews 4:10 puts it this way: "Whoever has entered God's rest has also rested from his works as God did from his." You no longer trust your own works but rest upon God and his finished work of salvation.

What a difference it makes to rest upon the Lord Jesus and thereby to enter God's rest. This brings peace with God and produces inward joy. That is all the more reason to trust in the Lord during this present day of opportunity, when the promise of entering God's rest still stands. For it will not profit any of us to hear without believing, without stretching out on him who came to save, calling us into God's eternal Sabbath rest.

---

3. See James Montgomery Boice, *The Gospel of John* (Grand Rapids: Zondervan, 1967), 195.

13

ENTERING GOD'S REST

Hebrews 4:6—11

So then, there remains a Sabbath rest for the people of God, for
whoever has entered God's rest has also rested from his works as
God did from his. (Heb. 4:9–10)

*H*eaven is like first base in a Little League baseball game. It
is said that the hardest challenge in sports is hitting a baseball, and after you do there are nine devils out there trying to keep you from safely reaching first. To many young boys and girls,
reaching first base is a distant goal, a high calling not unlike Israel's thoughts
of the Promised Land.

I use this comparison without making light in any way of the heavenly
rest that waits for all believers in Christ. I realize that the Christian life is
considerably harder than Little League and that the stakes are so much higher.
But what draws me to this comparison is the presence of two figures on the
Little League scene: a father and his child.

It is not the child alone who labors to reach first base. There was a father
who dreamt of seeing and cheering on, perhaps when those first steps were
taken or even before. There was a father who conveyed his own love of the

game, who told stories and first kindled the passion for line drives and stolen bases. He came home early from work when he could; he stood in the blazing heat or drizzling rain, throwing soft pitches one after another. There is a father who sits on rusty bleachers agonizing with his child over every pitch. Finally, when after long strife that little boy or little girl puts wood on the ball, races toward first, and plants foot on the bag while the umpire screams, "Safe!" it is toward the father that the child's beaming face turns, as they together bask in the sheer joy of what has been gained. "Did you see my son?" he cries with delight. "Did you see my little girl?"

This is why first base is like heaven—not merely because of the toil that precedes it, but also because of the satisfaction we will share with our heavenly Father when we finally arrive.

THE REST THAT REMAINS

It is ultimately heaven that is on the mind of the writer of Hebrews as he urges his readers to enter into the rest of God through faith in Christ. The term "rest" occurs five times in this passage (Heb. 4:6–11). It first occurred in 3:11, where he quoted Psalm 95 with reference to the faithless generation of Israel during the exodus: "As I swore in my wrath, 'They shall not enter my rest.'" There "rest" referred to entry into the Promised Land of Canaan, the land of prosperity and security. For several paragraphs, the writer of Hebrews has been exhorting us not to follow the example of that exodus generation that complained against God, accused him of failing to provide, and refused to place their trust in him. As a result, they did not enter the Promised Land, but died in the desert between Egypt and Canaan.

As this argument develops, the author anticipates an objection. His readers might naturally wonder, "Yes, that faithless generation did not enter the rest in Canaan, but their children did under Joshua. Why, then, do you keep talking about a 'rest' that still remains?" The writer responds:

> Since therefore it remains for some to enter it, and those who formerly received the good news failed to enter because of disobedience, again he appoints a certain day, "Today," saying through David so long afterward, in the words already quoted, "Today, if you hear his voice, do not harden your

hearts." For if Joshua had given them rest, God would not have spoken of another day later on. So then, there remains a Sabbath rest for the people of God. (Heb. 4:6–9)

The last verse of that passage (v. 9) makes clear that our salvation rest is something that is ultimately future; it is something that still remains for the people of God to enter. As great as Israel's rest in Canaan was, it was not the ultimate rest that God intended for his people. It was outward. It was physical and symbolic; rather than fulfilling God's rest it symbolized the rest that was to come. John Calvin explains: "This is not the final rest to which the faithful aspire, and which is our common possession with the faithful of that age. It is certain that they looked higher than that earthly land; indeed the land of Canaan was only thought of as of value for the reason that it was the type and the symbol of our spiritual inheritance."[1]

REALIZED ESCHATOLOGY

To understand what Hebrews means by a rest that remains, it helps to understand a theological concept known as *realized eschatology*. *Eschatos* is the Greek word for "last," and eschatology means "last things" or "with reference to the end." When we say that Hebrews holds a "realized" eschatology, we mean that the writer emphasizes our present possession of things that God has promised. Although those blessings will be fully received at the end of history, we already begin to realize their benefits now by faith.

For instance, we have already seen how Christ "destroyed" Satan by dying on the cross (Heb. 2:14). Some might argue that Satan is not yet removed from the scene; he is still a raging lion who torments us. Nevertheless, his doom is sealed and even now we experience freedom from slavery to him. This reality—which will be consummated at the end—is conveyed to us now by faith.

Another example of realized eschatology is the rest offered to God's people. On the one hand, we now enter that rest by faith: "We who have believed enter that rest" (Heb. 4:3). Note the present tense. Through faith we know the certainty of salvation and come into communion with the living God,

---

1. John Calvin, *New Testament Commentaries*, 12 vols. (Grand Rapids: Eerdmans, 1994), 12:48.

which is what eternal life is all about. Instead of laboring in futility to earn forgiveness of sins and acceptance with God, we *rest* upon the finished work of Jesus Christ. Even in this present life of toil, our faith rests on him and his saving power. This is what we mean by a "realized eschatology": the things of heaven, the things of the future which are promised us by God, are made real to us now through faith, so that we live by a strength that is not of us but of God. A major burden of this entire epistle is to encourage its early readers, with all their trials and weakness, that by faith they can be sure of what they hope for and certain of what they do not see (Heb. 11:1).

As strong as that emphasis is, however, it is important that we do not overstate the case. Israel in Canaan had a foretaste of God's rest; that is what the Promised Land signified. But they were in fact surrounded by real enemies; their need for labor and warfare was very great. The Book of Joshua tells of their successes and failures; it is a book of war and not of peace. The Canaan rest pointed to a greater salvation, of which it gave a foretaste but not the fulfillment.

This same understanding applies to the Christian life. How wonderful it is that we rest upon our Lord Jesus Christ. We lay our burdens upon him, we bring to him our tears and our fears, and we find real rest in him. Yet what we long for is the day when there will be no more tears, when there will be nothing to fear, and when God's promised rest is brought to full consummation in glory. Isaiah says of that day: "The ransomed of the LORD shall return and come to Zion with singing; everlasting joy shall be upon their heads; they shall obtain gladness and joy, and sorrow and sighing shall flee away" (Isa. 35:10).

But this is not our present experience. This present life compares to the wilderness journey, to the time of trial and testing, and not to the Promised Land itself. "There remains," the writer of Hebrews reminds us, "a Sabbath rest for the people of God." Though we have very real blessings in this present life, what we now experience is not all there is for the believer, and we rightly long for a greater rest to come.

FROM SABBATH TO LORD'S DAY

This brings us to another matter that is of real importance for the Christian, namely, the relationship of the Old Testament Sabbath to the Christian church. There are two basic views on the Sabbath, both of which draw from this passage in Hebrews. What makes Hebrews of special interest is a change in terminology that takes place in these verses. All through this exhortation, the writer has been using the Greek word *katapausis* for the idea of rest, which in the Greek translation of the Old Testament stood for rest in the land of Canaan. In verse 4 he expands his idea of rest by referring to God's rest in creation, so that his readers will start linking that geographical rest to the weekly Sabbath-rest of Israel. Now, in verse 9, the writer pointedly changes the word he uses for rest. Here he uses *apoleipetai*, combined with the word *sabbatismos*, a construction that designated the rest of the Sabbath day. It is because of this change of terminology that many English versions use the translation "a Sabbath-rest."

Clearly, the New Testament readers are being directed toward the Sabbath day, but the question is how this fits in the new covenant dispensation. There are two views. The first is that with the coming of Jesus Christ and the end of the old covenant, the Sabbath ordinance no longer exists and the fourth commandment does not continue in force. This is a view widely held among evangelicals today, and draws the support of such writers as Ray Stedman, D. A. Carson, and Andrew Lincoln.

This argument holds that since the Old Testament Sabbath, like Joshua's entry into Canaan, is a symbol that points to the greater Sabbath that came in Jesus Christ, it no longer holds force. The reality has come; the symbol has been fulfilled. The fourth commandment reads, "Remember the Sabbath day, to keep it holy. Six days you shall labor, and do all your work, but the seventh day is a Sabbath to the Lord your God" (Ex. 20:8–10). According to Ray Stedman, in the new covenant this refers to "that cessation from labor which God enjoys and which he invites believers to share . . . [it is] dependence on God to be at work through us."[2] That being the case, Sabbath-keeping no longer consists of observing a special day, but sabbath-keeping "is achieved when the heart rests on the great promise of God to be working through a believer in the normal affairs of living."[3] Those who make this argument also point to Paul's admonition in Colossians 2:16–17: "Therefore let no one pass judgment on you in questions of food and drink, or with

2. Ray Stedman, *Hebrews* (Downers Grove, Ill.: InterVarsity, 1992), 58.
3. Ibid.

regard to a festival or a new moon or a Sabbath. These are a shadow of the things to come, but the substance belongs to Christ." Based on these arguments, the view that is perhaps dominant today holds that the Sabbath command is exhausted with the coming of Christ and thus has no binding control on Christian practice.

As compelling as that position is, there are some significant problems with it. These are pointed out by those who differ, among whom are John Owen, A. W. Pink, and Richard Gaffin. First, they note that the Sabbath is instituted as one of the Ten Commandments. They then observe that all of the other nine commandments remain in force in the New Testament. For instance, children are admonished to obey their parents, and in making that admonition Paul explicitly references the fifth commandment (Eph. 6:1–3). More obvious examples have to do with murder, adultery, and blasphemy; no one denies that these are prohibited as much in the New Testament as in the Old. Isn't it peculiar, therefore, for only one of the commandments to be abrogated, especially when no such abrogation is stated in the New Testament?

Another problem is more telling. Those who argue against a Christian Sabbath note that the Sabbath was a sign pointing to something that now has come. When the reality comes, the sign passes away. This is the very argument that Hebrews will make about the sacrificial system of the Old Testament. Since the true Lamb of God has come and shed his blood for sins once-for-all, there is no longer any need to sacrifice bulls and goats and lambs. Indeed, to do so is to deny the reality and sufficiency of Christ's work.

But when it comes to the Sabbath, the very point of verse 9 is that the reality to which it points *has not yet come*: "There remains a Sabbath rest for the people of God." In other words, there is still a valid need for and benefit from the sign of the Sabbath rest. Yes, Hebrews teaches a realized eschatology in which we have a great part of its possession now as we trust in the Lord Jesus and rest on him. But this realized eschatology is not yet fully realized. There is something still to come, and the Sabbath points not to what has already come in Christ but to what has yet to come in fulfillment as part of his future work.

As is often the case, the concerns of both sides are worth listening to. People opposed to the idea of a Christian Sabbath are concerned that we not fall into either a legalistic or a mechanical approach to our worship. It is certainly true that with the coming of Christ we have passed from the administration of law to that of grace. But this does not do away with the Ten Commandments. We still must reckon with the realities of God's moral obligations, one of which deals with observing a full day of rest out of dependence on God. What then was the point of Paul's admonition to the Colossians (Col. 2:16–17)? In context with the whole New Testament, it seems that Paul was correcting those whose faith consisted of little more than keeping a calendar of special days.

It is as a concrete expression of faith in the sovereign resting God that the idea of a weekly Sabbath has particular value. Even Ray Stedman, who opposes the Sabbath, can still write:

> This does not mean that we cannot learn many helpful lessons on rest by studying the regulations for keeping the sabbath day found in the Old Testament. Nor that we no longer need time for quiet meditation and cessation from physical labor. Our bodies are yet unredeemed and need rest and restoration at frequent intervals. But we are no longer bound by heavy limitations to keep a precise day of the week.[4]

Citations like this show that among Bible believers, even opponents of the Sabbath end up advocating what amounts to Sabbath-keeping. The reason for this is obvious. Everyone agrees that Sabbath-keeping amounts to dependence upon God. But how you can possibly say that you actually depend on the Lord, that you are looking ultimately to him for provision, and not to your boss or to the work of your own hands, if in fact you labor without ceasing every day of the week, if you observe no regular pattern of rest? We have freedom to follow God's own pattern of labor and rest precisely because we are not left to our own devices. If I were to examine your weekly schedule, would it be clear that you are a person who depends upon the living God? If you find it impossible to set aside one full day a week (and surely this is the pattern we find in Scripture, not to mention the example of Jesus, who regularly assigned long portions of time to prayer and communion with the Father) to worship and draw near to God, then your claims to dependence on him are surely called into question.

4. Ibid., 59.

A recent television commercial for an overnight parcel service began with great fanfare and the rolling of drums to herald a big announcement: "We now offer full service on Sundays. Now you can work unhindered seven days a week!" I could not help but think of the mud-pits of Egypt, in which the slave population of Israel labored day after day, without a Sabbath rest. I found it depressing that today we celebrate our willing return to the very kind of slavery from which the people of Israel were delivered in the exodus. Surely Christians will avoid such a view of life.

At a minimum, Christians need to set aside time not only to worship God but also to enjoy him and his bounty, to rest upon him and experience at least a partial taste of that Sabbath rest that is to come. And while we are admonished by the apostle Paul not to set stock in particular days or calendars, surely we will find ourselves worshiping together with the people of God on a regular schedule, so that our normal practice will be to set apart Sunday as the Lord's Day, for both his worship and our enjoyment of the rest he has promised and now gives, at least in part. Few things are more profitable for Christians than to set apart the Lord's Day for true rest and enjoyment of God's provision, as well as for the worship he so surely is due.

Some will object that this seems legalistic. One use of the law is to reveal God's character; the fourth commandment does this like all the others. The second use of the law is to condemn sin and drive us to the cross for salvation. All of us, no doubt, have sins under the fourth commandment which, like the others, can be forgiven through Christ. Third—and this is my emphasis here—the law is a fitting guide for living our lives. In this respect, the fourth commandment is an apt example of what James meant when he spoke in his epistle of the "law of liberty" (James 1:25). Having been forgiven by Christ and now living by the power of God's grace, for us to live according to his commandments is the path of blessing and true freedom. In the case of the fourth commandment the freedom is from working without ceasing to a life of worship and rest.

Entering God's Rest

All of that hard interpretive work puts us in a good position to make sense of the last two verses in our passage, which tell us: "Whoever has entered God's rest has also rested from his works as God did from his. Let us therefore strive to enter that rest, so that no one may fall by the same sort of disobedience" (Heb. 4:10–11). At first glance, this seems contradictory. Verse 10 tells us that entering God's rest means resting from our work as he did from his. The very next verse tells us to get busy working for that rest; we are to make every effort to enter it and not fall away, as the Israelites did in the wilderness.

In fact, there is no problem here at all. The overarching model for this whole exhortation is the exodus wanderings of Israel. They had left the bondage of Egypt, but had not yet entered into the land of rest. We, too, are to press onward through our difficulties, not complaining against God or hardening our hearts against him, but relying on him in this present day of testing. We are to strive with the resources of his rest. In contrast to the unfaithful Israelites, who failed to trust the provision of God's grace, we follow and strive because our faith receives the benefits of God's saving work in Jesus Christ. Appreciating the reality of our present challenge—here is the difference between a realized and an overrealized eschatology, the latter of which forgets our present pilgrim status—we eagerly draw forth on every resource of grace that God provides.

Now is the day of our labor, the day when we do work. We rest our burdens on Jesus Christ, and he sends his Holy Spirit to help us shoulder the load. But the same Savior who offers us rest is also the Lord who commands, "If anyone would come after me, let him deny himself and take up his cross daily and follow me" (Luke 9:23). Our final day of rest is yet to come. It awaits us in heaven. God worked for six days and then he rested; now is the time when we work, after which we too will rest. This is what verse 10 emphasizes, pointing to the rest that is yet to come.

So understand that your labor now is not in vain. Your struggle, born of faith, fueled by God's Holy Spirit as he works in you, is not for nothing. We are storing treasure up in heaven. As the angel proclaimed to the prophet Daniel: "Those who are wise shall shine like the brightness of the sky above; and those who turn many to righteousness, like the stars forever and ever" (Dan. 12:3).

All of this brings me back to the subject of little boys and girls and the trials of Little League. Yes, it is they who swing the bat; but it was the father's hands which taught them how to grip it, his strong hands gently wrapping around their little ones until they got it right. His voice patiently gave instruction, coached them, encouraged them, inspired them. And when they get that first base hit, it is his voice that rejoices with them, saying to them as our heavenly Father will say to us on that great day, "Well done, my child. Well done."

Now is the day of our trouble and our toil. Now is the time of tears, of wrestling with sin, of witnessing to those around us, many of whom will scorn and abuse us. But if we do it all with our eyes looking up to heaven, gazing toward our home, trusting our heavenly Father, and asking him to find pleasure in our meager works, then we can be sure that he will. And in the day of our rest, we too will find joy in them forever.

14

GOD'S LIVING WORD

Hebrews 4:12—13

For the word of God is living and active, sharper than any two-edged sword, piercing to the division of soul and of spirit, of joints and of marrow, and discerning the thoughts and intentions of the heart. (Heb. 4:12)

One of the great reformations in the Old Testament began quite by accident. Josiah, the young king of Judah, had ordered Hilkiah the high priest to make repairs on the dilapidated temple in Jerusalem. Josiah seems to have been motivated by sincere religious devotion, and he was surely bothered by the way the run-down state of the building symbolized the spiritual malaise of the nation. Sprucing up the building, however, could offer only surface improvements, but inside the temple workers found something that promised to do much more. Hilkiah informed Josiah's secretary of momentous news from the construction site: "I have found the Book of the Law in the house of the LORD" (2 Kings 22:8).

Although this seemed to happen by accident, there was obviously a great providence at work. Josiah had sought to bless God by fixing the temple, and God blessed Josiah in return by placing in his hands the most powerful force in the world for reformation and revival, for hope and joy, for peace and salvation. The Lord had returned to Jerusalem that which had been lost, the very Word of God, which Hebrews tells us "is living and active, sharper than any two-edged sword, piercing to the division of soul and of spirit, of joints and of marrow" (Heb. 4:12).

Josiah began reading the Bible the workers had found, and soon he tore his clothes to lament what had been absent from Israel's life for so long. He gathered the most godly people around God's Word to study it. Then they put into practice the things they read in the Scriptures, and the result was a renewal of the covenant with God and the restoration of the blessings that come through faith in him. What Josiah and Jerusalem learned so many years ago is something the godly have been learning ever since. It is what the apostle Peter wrote about in his first epistle: "You have been born again, not of perishable seed but of imperishable, through the living and abiding word of God; for 'All flesh is like grass and all its glory like the flower of grass. The grass withers, and the flower falls, but the word of the Lord remains forever'" (1 Peter 1:23–25).

GOD'S LIVING WORD

This view of the Scriptures features prominently in the Letter to the Hebrews. In the long exhortation that runs through chapters 3 and 4, the writer implores his readers to hold fast to their faith under hardship. He boldly insists that a failure to believe the message of Jesus Christ is to forfeit the great salvation rest that God has offered. Consistently, he backs up such statements with the authority of the Word of God. All through this exhortation he has grounded his arguments on citations from the Old Testament, specifically from Psalm 95.

This psalm was written by King David about one thousand years before the writing of Hebrews. David was also interested in exhorting his readers, and he did so by reflecting on the unbelief of the exodus generation, which had led to their destruction some four hundred years earlier. Drawing on that example, David wrote, "Today, if you hear his voice, do not harden your hearts, as at Meribah, as on the day at Massah in the wilderness, when your fathers put me to the test" (Ps. 95:7–9). It is these words that the writer of Hebrews applies to his own generation. In doing so he assumes—indeed, he boldly asserts—that the words written by David not only have relevance, but also have authority over those who read them in his own time.

These readers were experiencing the beginnings of persecution; perhaps they were losing their jobs or even their property because of their faith in Christ. His argument to them is this: "Why should you sacrifice your labor, your worldly goods, and even your lives for the sake of Jesus? Because those words spoken by David are not just old news, irrelevant spiritual musings. They are the very Word of God, living and active even today, and in them your own destiny is bound up through either belief or unbelief." That is the point being summed up by the opening words from Hebrews 4:12: "For the word of God is living and active."

How can this be? How can David's words, which after all are the words of a man, be living and active? The reason is seen all through this book: *because they are also the words of God.* We saw this emphasis in the very first verse of this letter, in which the writer described the whole revelatory process with these words: "God spoke . . . by the prophets." This is what makes the Bible the Word of God. All through Hebrews the writer introduces Old Testament citations with "as God has said," or "as the Holy Spirit says." In verse 7 of chapter 4 he writes: "Again [God] appoints a certain day, 'Today,' saying through David so long afterward." The words spoken through the man David and written down on paper with some sort of writing implement, are not first and foremost to be thought of as David's own words, the words of man, but as the Word of God.

Here we need to be very careful not to deemphasize or even deny the human authorship of the Bible. The Bible was composed by some forty different human authors. They were real men; these were their real thoughts; these books deal with their actual circumstances and are colored by their own experiences and interests. To lose sight of this would be to lose much of their value.

How, then, is the Bible the Word of God? That question was important to the apostles, for they regarded the Old Testament writers as authoritative for their own readers. Perhaps the best-known statement is the one Paul made in his second letter to Timothy: "All Scripture is breathed out by God and profitable for teaching, for reproof, for correction, and for training in righteousness, that the man of God may be competent, equipped for every good work" (2 Tim. 3:16–17). The words of the Bible are not the *inspired* words of men, arising from their own spiritual insight, but they are *expired, out-breathed words* from God's very mouth given through them.

This is what makes the Bible so profitable to us, as Paul emphasizes. Through his Word God himself teaches us, rebukes and corrects us, trains us in righteousness and equips us for every good work. When you come to God's Word in faith—when you open up your heart and mind to the teachings of the Bible, either as it is preached or in your own reading of it—that Word comes alive within you because it is sent by God himself for that purpose. He lives and acts in you through his living and active Word. Therefore, as Martin Luther said, "Let the man who would hear God speak read Holy Scripture."[1] The Puritan Thomas Watson adds, "By reading other books the heart may be warmed, but by reading this book it is transformed."[2]

Paul gives us a very clear description; he tells us *that* Scripture is God's out-breathed Word, but he doesn't tell us *how* this is so. Fortunately, Peter gives us more insight: "No prophecy of Scripture comes from someone's own interpretation. For no prophecy was ever produced by the will of man, but men spoke from God as they were carried along by the Holy Spirit" (2 Peter 1:20–21).

By prophecy, Peter does not merely mean future prediction, but the whole prophetic revelation of God's teaching. The first thing he says is that prophecy does not reflect the prophet's own ideas. It is not his own interpretation that is written, nor did the thoughts originate with him, but with God. The key statement is in verse 21: "Men spoke from God as they were carried along by the Holy Spirit." Yes, it was men who spoke and wrote, but what they said came from God as the Holy Spirit carried them along in their work.

This is why we can say that the Word of God is "living and active." While there are differences in our cultural, social, and historical settings, compared to the original readers, and our understanding of a particular passage may and should reflect those differences, nonetheless we should read the Bible as God's Word to *us*. It is not merely relevant, but authoritative and bind-

---

1. Martin Luther, *What Luther Says*, comp. Ewald M. Plass (St. Louis: Concordia, 1959), 61.
2. Thomas Watson, *A Body of Divinity* (Edinburgh: Banner of Truth, 1958), 29.

ing on us as it was on them. It is timeless and living precisely because it is the Word of the eternal and living God. Therefore, Peter writes of the Bible: "You will do well to pay attention as to a lamp shining in a dark place" (2 Peter 1:19).

GOD'S LIFE-IMPARTING WORD

Another great evidence that the Bible is living and active has to do with its content and purpose. The Bible does not merely relate interesting facts and beliefs from our religious tradition. No, the Bible has one overarching theme: God's work in history for the salvation of sinful people. This is what the Bible records—what God has done to forgive our sins, so that we who are dead in trespasses might be brought to life in Christ. As Paul wrote to young Timothy, the purpose of the Bible is "to make you wise for salvation through faith in Christ Jesus" (2 Tim. 3:15). The Bible's message is God's work of salvation through Jesus Christ, and its purpose is actually to bring that salvation to individuals who receive that message and believe.

God's Word is living and active in the same way that Jesus' words were living and actives when he stood before the tomb of his dead friend and cried, "Lazarus, come out!" (John 11:43). At Jesus' word the dead man came to life and took off his graveclothes. So also for the Word of God as we have it in the Bible; not only is it alive but it is active in imparting life to us. It makes alive those who are spiritually dead.

The Christian apologist Ravi Zacharias tells the story of a drive he took with an evangelist in the nation of Lebanon. Lebanon was then occupied by the Syrian army, and their control was quite repressive. He and the pastor were driving in a van that was loaded with boxes of Bibles that they were transporting to another city where an effort was being made to reach lost sinners. Zacharias tells of his great anxiety as they stopped at a military checkpoint and a Syrian soldier stuck his rifle in their faces. "What is in this van?" the soldier demanded. Zacharias was horrified when the evangelist replied, "Oh, nothing but boxes of dynamite!" Then, handing the shocked soldier one of the Bibles, the bold pastor explained. "Here is what I am talking about. Read this and it will break into your life with God's own power." And so it does! The Word of God is living and active—spiritual dynamite sent by God into a world of darkness with power to overcome every stronghold of sin and human opposition.

GOD'S PENETRATING WORD

The writer of Hebrews has more to tell us about God's Word, continuing with an explanation of how it does its work. The Word of God is "sharper than any two-edged sword, piercing to the division of soul and of spirit, of joints and of marrow, and discerning the thoughts and intentions of the heart" (Heb. 4:12).

The image of the Word as a sword is often found in Scripture. In his description of the armor of God, Paul speaks of "the sword of the Spirit, which is the word of God" (Eph. 6:17). In his vision of the exalted Lord Jesus Christ, John tells us, "from his mouth came a sharp two-edged sword" (Rev. 1:16). As the ensuing letters to the seven churches illustrate, that sword is obviously his Word. Furthermore, it is a double-edged sword, equally fit to save or to judge.

What this image describes is the penetrating or piercing power of God's Word: "piercing to the division of soul and of spirit, of joints and of marrow" (Heb. 4:12). The point is not that a separation takes place between a man's physical and his spiritual natures. As Philip Hughes explains, "Our author is not concerned to provide here a psychological or anatomical analysis of the human constitution, but rather to describe in graphic terms the penetration of God's word to the innermost depth of man's personality."[3] The Word penetrates against all opposition so as to grip the whole man and not just any one aspect of his person.

Furthermore, we are told what the Word does once it gets inside: "discerning the thoughts and intentions of the heart" (Heb. 4:12). How often people think they are judging the Bible when just the opposite is true! The Word of God penetrates within, and its presence makes clear our true thoughts and attitudes. Many people affect to be good and even religious, but when the Word of God comes to them, they respond with hostility and repulsion. Their attitude to the Bible shows their true attitude toward God.

---

3. Philip E. Hughes, *A Commentary on the Epistle to the Hebrews* (Grand Rapids: Eerdmans, 1977), 165.

God's Word comes into us and it discerns, assessing our attitude toward the one who sent it. But when accompanied by the regenerating work of the Holy Spirit, it does more: it convicts us of our rebellion against God and subdues us; it leads us as sheep to the Good Shepherd. This is how we are born again. We hear God speaking, we read in Scripture of the perfect demands of the law as well as God's sure judgment, we realize our peril, we surrender ourselves and fall before the Lord in conviction of sin. Then in the Bible we learn of a Savior who has taken our sins away by dying on a cross for us, and we rejoice, we race forward to embrace him, we worship him and follow him.

John Newton was a man who was penetrated and captured by the Word of God. Raised in a Christian home in the mid-eighteenth century, he left home and joined the British navy. There he entered deeply into the ways of sin, and eventually he deserted to live in Africa. He chose that place because there his lusts could have the most opportunity for satisfaction. In the years that followed he became a slave trader, but was also abused by those who gained power over him and was even kept in chains. Physically wrecked, he escaped toward the sea and found his way aboard a British merchant vessel. Due to his knowledge of navigation he became a ship's mate. However, when the captain showed trust in him, he broke into the ship's supply of rum and became drunk—so drunk that when the captain returned and struck him on the head he fell overboard. If one of the crew had not rescued him, he would have drowned.

As the ship was nearing Scotland on the way home, it ran into a storm and was blown off course. For days the storm blew and water came into the floundering vessel. Newton spent countless hours down in the hold working the pumps, in desperate fear for his life. There his mind turned to Bible verses his mother had taught him before she died when he was six years old. The Word of God came alive within him, convicted his thoughts and attitudes, and brought him to repentance, and he cast himself on Jesus Christ for forgiveness and salvation.

The ship ultimately did make it safely to port, and Newton entered into the study of theology and became a notable Puritan minister. We know him best for his hymns, especially "Amazing Grace!"

Amazing grace!—how sweet the sound—
   that saved a wretch like me!
I once was lost, but now am found,
   was blind, but now I see.[4]

That is what God does through his Word—he saves wretches, he finds the lost, he takes those who are blind and makes them to see. God's Word is living and active, it pierces and discerns and judges, all for the great work of salvation that is its message and its purpose.

Newton's is a great example, but our own time is filled with other great ones. In the most unlikely ways, hardened sinners come to hear the Word of God, and it brings them to spiritual life through faith in Christ. Recent years have brought all sorts of amazing stories of new life for those who were lost: KGB officers once steeped in the ways of terror; Muslims locked deep within the lands of Islam; wealthy movie stars or media personalities ensnared by godless humanism. High and low, educated and dull, east and west, they are reached by the living and active Word of God.

Someone might object, saying, "I have encountered God's Word, but it has not affected me. I have not trusted Jesus Christ, I have not given my allegiance to God." Those things are, of course, precisely what the rebel wants to avoid; he sets up every conceivable roadblock, he turns away from the Word and pushes it away from himself. He avoids Christian teaching if at all he can; if his radio dial lands on a station with gospel preaching he cannot reach out fast enough to turn the dial.

But what these verses say is still true. God's living Word has found you, it has penetrated, it has discerned your thoughts and attitudes, and you stand judged by it. It is a double-edged sword, standing above you not with the blade that gives life, but with the blade that renders condemnation unto death. It tells you now to repent, to confess and surrender yourself to the God who freely forgives. Jesus came not to condemn the world but to save it. And yet he said, "The one who rejects me and does not receive my words has a judge; the word that I have spoken will judge him on the last day" (John 12:48).

4. John Newton, "Amazing Grace!" 1779.

God's All-Sufficient Word

We have seen how God's Word is living and active, as well as its penetrating power to bring our thoughts and attitudes into judgment so that we surrender to him. The final point we learn here is the sufficiency of God's Word for our every need in the things of faith and godliness.

We see this in verse 12, where a comparison is made between God's Word and worldly weapons. It is "sharper than any two-edged sword." Not only is God's Word a sword, but when compared with other weapons, it is sharper. Philip Hughes observes, "As the instrument of God's mighty acts it is more powerful and penetrating than the keenest instrument devised by man."[5] Since God's Word is "living and active," it is effective in a way no other weapon can be.

Another evidence God's Word is sufficient for our needs is found in verse 13: "No creature is hidden from his sight, but all are naked and exposed to the eyes of him to whom we must give account." God's Word is living and active, it penetrates and probes, and furthermore *nothing can escape it.* Interestingly, the writer of Hebrews here compares God's Word to God's eyes. It uncovers every heart, every act, every intention, every thought and desire and brings them before the penetrating gaze of the living God.

Yet we are living in a time when many Christians, even evangelicals who once were singularly known and even derided for their devotion to the Word, are losing confidence in the Bible's effectiveness. Yes, it is inspired; yes, it is useful; but it must be augmented by human means or wisdom or methods. Our evangelism now relies on manipulative psychological ploys, our spiritual growth depends on techniques and programs and store-bought gimmicks, our worship reflects the glitter of Hollywood entertainment. Far different is the message of the writer of Hebrews, who says that nothing is able to escape the revealing, energetic Word of God. Therefore, it alone is sufficient for our every need.

This was also the teaching of the apostle Paul. Do we need worldly methods and devices to do the work of the church? Paul wrote, "For though we walk in the flesh, we are not waging war according to the flesh. For the weapons of our warfare are not of the flesh but have divine power

5. Hughes, *Hebrews,* 164.

141

to destroy strongholds. We destroy arguments and every lofty opinion raised against the knowledge of God, and take every thought captive to obey Christ" (2 Cor. 10:3–5).

Consider what power is made available to us by the Word of God, and what an incentive this is to use it in our witness and in our own lives. It is sufficient for our every need. What better thing could we possibly do for the salvation of souls than to proclaim and explain God's Word? It alone conveys God's own power to convict and to save, to cut away the heart of stone and bring to life a new heart of flesh.

Consider the matter of our sanctification, that is, our own growth in holiness. What could be more effective than to shine the light of God's Word upon our lives, into our minds and hearts? This is what Paul emphasized, saying in Romans 12:2, "Do not be conformed to this world, but be transformed by the renewal of your mind." This is how Jesus prayed for our holiness, in John 17:17: "Sanctify them in the truth; your word is truth." Our passage says God's Word "discerns the thoughts and intentions of the heart." What a blessing it is to have that happen now: to be taught by him, rebuked and inspired by him, to be molded in obedience to God during this life, knowing that in the life to come he is the one, as verse 13 concludes, "to whom we must give account."

Consider the matter of Christian comfort. Do you sorrow or suffer? Are you tempted and tried? Do you want assurance of salvation and the peace that comes with it? Then turn to the Bible, which speaks of a God who is totally sufficient for your salvation, who is able and willing to save you and to keep you. "He who did not spare his own Son," it tells us, "but gave him up for us all, how will he not also with him graciously give us all things?" (Rom. 8:32).

Finally, let me ask you this: do you want to make a difference in this life? Then commit yourself to the Word of God, bring yourself into its life-changing light, and share it with the world by every means you can. This is what godly men and women have done all through history, people like King Josiah who recovered God's Word and restored a whole nation through it. For to his Word God has assigned great promises:

> For as the rain and the snow come down from heaven and do not return there but water the earth, making it bring forth and sprout, giving seed to the sower

and bread to the eater, so shall my word be that goes out from my mouth; it shall not return to me empty, but it shall accomplish that which I purpose, and shall succeed in the thing for which I sent it. (Isa. 55:10–11)

Therefore any work that relies on God's Word may be sure to have his blessing, to achieve his purpose, and to bring him glory even as it brings his power for salvation.

15

THE THRONE OF GRACE

Hebrews 4:14–16

*Let us then with confidence draw near to the throne of grace, that
we may receive mercy and find grace to help in time of need.*
(Heb. 4:16)

he Christian life is like a sailing vessel. This illustration help-
fully relates the requirements of following Jesus Christ with the
resources he gives to do them. God's commands are like the rudder that determines the ship's direction. Important as that is, however, the
ship does not have power to move until a strong wind comes and fills the
sails. In the Christian life, that strong wind consists of the resources that are
found in the gospel.[1]

The writer of Hebrews is concerned with relating requirements and
resources because he writes not just as a theologian but as a pastor. He later
describes his letter as "my word of exhortation" (Heb. 13:22). Exhort his readers he does, often sternly and always urgently, but he also is careful to explain
the reasons for his commands, as well as to offer the resources to do them.

---

1. I am indebted to Michael S. Horton for this illustration.

The end of Hebrews 4 concludes the long exhortation that began in chapter 3, in which the author charges his readers to press on in the faith, not hardening their hearts in the face of difficulties. To meet this requirement, so far he has articulated two key resources. First, he mentioned Christian fellowship and encouragement. This is needed, he says, so "that none of you may be hardened by the deceitfulness of sin" (Heb. 3:13). Another key resource is the Word of God, which imparts life to us and stirs us up in the faith (Heb. 4:12–13). The pastor now directs us to a third resource: prayer, through which we come before God's very throne to receive the mercy and grace we need to press on.

If the Christian life is like a sailing vessel, then the requirements in the Book of Hebrews are like the rudder that points and directs our lives. The commands are essential; without them we would founder upon the shoals and sink. However, as vital as they are, they do not actually move the ship. They provide no power to press ahead. For this we need the great resources that are ours in Christ—resources like fellowship, God's Word, and prayer. These are the wind that puts air into our sails and gives us power to move along the course God has charted. In Hebrews 4:14–16 the writer reminds us that we may approach God with confidence because of the redeeming ministry of the risen and ascended Lord Jesus Christ, our great high priest. The message here has three points, which we may set forth as *a requirement, a reason,* and *a resource.*

A Requirement: Hold Firmly to the Faith

The writer begins this passage by restating the requirement that this letter continually stresses, namely, the command to persevere in the Christian faith. He writes, "Let us hold fast our confession" (v. 14). This is not only a necessary requirement, but also an extremely difficult thing to do.

A young Christian woman once told me how a colleague at work had belittled Christianity as an escape from the difficulties of real life, an easy route chosen by the weak. "An escape!" she replied. "An escape! You try to live as a Christian, you try to wage war against the desires of the flesh, you try to live as an alien in a strange land, and then you come and tell me that Christianity is the easy way!" She was right! If what you are looking for is a lazy man's detour through life, if you are looking to avoid serious challenges and to follow the well-worn lanes, then Christianity is not for you. This was Jesus' teaching: "For the gate is wide and the way is easy that leads to destruction, and those who enter by it are many. For the gate is narrow and the way is hard that leads to life, and those who find it are few" (Matt. 7:13–14).

This is the stark reality of the Christian faith. To follow Christ is to seek treasures not here on this earth, not here in this life, but treasures in heaven. Christians, of course, acknowledge earthly blessings and enjoy them in good measure. But we are people who have set our hearts on the heavenly rest. We have stepped onto the spiritual battleground, with enemies like the flesh, the world, and the devil. We accept that this is the time of our labor, the time of sacrifice and willing self-denial for the sake of our discipleship to Christ; the day of reward will wait until the life that is to come.

In verse 14 the writer says it is "our confession" that we must hold fast. The early church employed theological formulas to express the faithful's confession, like the Apostles' Creed. This reminds us that there is truth content to our profession of faith and that this content is vitally important. Some people say that they are against creeds, but creeds are simply summaries of biblical teaching. The Latin word *credo* means, "I believe." It matters what we believe; there is content we cannot let go of without letting go of salvation in Christ: things like who Jesus is and what he has done to save us from our sins. J. C. Ryle explained:

> A religion without doctrine or dogma is a thing which many are fond of talking of in the present day. It sounds very fine at first. It looks very pretty at a distance. But the moment we sit down to examine and consider it, we shall find it a simple impossibility. We might as well talk of a body without bones and sinews. No man will ever be anything or do anything in religion, unless he believes something. . . . No one ever fights earnestly against the world, the flesh and the devil, unless he has engraven on his heart certain great principles which he believes.[2]

So it is for our Christian confession, to which we are required to hold fast as if our lives depend upon it—for they do.

2. J. C. Ryle, *Holiness* (Darlington, U.K.: Evangelical Press, 1979), 56.

A Reason: Christ's Ministry as High Priest

The writer of Hebrews goes on to give us a reason for our perseverance, and it is a doctrinal point he gives. What is it that motivates Christian people to enter into a life of struggle and strife, holding fast to the confession? The reason is set forth in verse 14: "Since then we have a great high priest who has passed through the heavens, Jesus, the Son of God, let us hold fast our confession."

The reason behind our perseverance is the person and work of Jesus Christ, who as the Son of God and as our great high priest has secured our salvation ahead of us. Jesus and his saving work are set forth here as the antidote mainly to fear: fear of failure, fear of falling away, and even the fear of drawing near to God that paralyzes so many Christians.

Many Christians struggle in their relationship with God, especially when it comes to prayer. The reason for this is felt by the writer of Hebrews, and it is expressed in what he has said in the preceding verse: "No creature is hidden from his sight, but all are naked and exposed to the eyes of him to whom we must give account" (Heb. 4:13).

Anyone with any spiritual awareness is made very uneasy by the thought of God's searching gaze. Remember the scene in the garden after Adam and Eve had first sinned. In their original state, before they fell into sin, they were "naked and were not ashamed" (Gen. 2:25). With no sin to condemn them, they delighted in the gaze of their loving Creator. But after the fall, they hid their shame even from one another, pathetically sewing on fig leaves for garments. Even more, they dreaded the presence of God, fleeing and hiding from him as he approached.

This is how many Christians feel in their relationship with God. The thought of his gaze chills their bones. They are willing to do anything but deal with God himself, skulking around the edges of his light rather than drawing near to him. They struggle to pray and seldom do unless forced by circumstances. It is this paralyzing fear that the writer of Hebrews now addresses. As Philip Hughes explains: "Sinners are no longer commanded to keep their distance in fear and trembling, but on the contrary are now invited to *draw near*, and to do so *with confidence.*"[3]

---

3. Philip E. Hughes, *A Commentary on the Epistle to the Hebrews* (Grand Rapids: Eerdmans, 1977), 173–74.

The reason for this change is the saving work of Jesus Christ to reconcile sinners to God. In particular, two aspects of that work come into view here: He has made propitiation for us in the heavenly tabernacle, and he now ministers on high with sympathy for our weakness.

When God discovered Adam and Eve's sin, he punished them by barring them from the garden and cursing them. But God then took the initiative in restoring them to fellowship with himself. Genesis 3:21 tells us, "The LORD God made for Adam and for his wife garments of skins and clothed them." God sacrificed an animal in their place and clothed them with the garment of the innocent substitute he had provided. That is a wonderful picture of what God has done for us in Jesus Christ, the Lamb of God who takes away our sin and whose perfect righteousness is imputed to us.

When the writer of Hebrews speaks of Jesus as our high priest—and with this passage his priesthood becomes the dominant theme in this letter—what he emphasizes is Christ's atoning work by dying upon the cross. He sets up a comparison between, on one hand, what Jesus did by dying and rising from the dead and then ascending into heaven and, on the other, the ceremonial office performed by Israel's high priest.

Once a year, the high priest entered the inner sanctum of the tabernacle to make atonement for the sins of the people. First offering a sacrifice for his own sins and then cleansing himself with water, the high priest—and he alone—one day a year and that day only—entered into the very presence of God. There in the holy of holies he saw the ark of the covenant, with the golden angels on top with their upswept wings, gazing down upon the two tablets of the Ten Commandments, God's law, which the people had broken by their sins. To avoid punishment, the high priest brought blood from the animal sacrifice, which he sprinkled upon the mercy seat, the tray for the blood which interposed between God's piercing gaze and the tablets of the law. When the blood was offered, God's wrath was propitiated, that is, it was turned away from the people's sin.

Israel's priests pointed forward to Jesus, the great high priest. He is great because of his divine nature. He is the Son of God, and his shed blood is sufficient to satisfy God's wrath forever. He is great because his sacrifice achieved a finished atonement, unlike the ones offered by Aaron, which had to be repeated daily. He is great because he is not a sinful man going into the holy of holies only once a year, and needing to come back again the next. Instead, he has gone through the heavens into the true tabernacle, the heavenly throne room of God, and offered his shed blood once-for-all. This is the contrast implicit in verse 14. Unlike Aaron, who was denied entry into the Promised Land because of his sin, and unlike the high priests who followed Aaron who were themselves sinners and could not offer the true sacrifice, Jesus has entered the land of rest, heaven itself, and has finished our redemption.

Because Jesus is our high priest, we are reconciled to God. This means that we can approach him freely. We do not have to hide from him; we do not have to flee like Adam in the garden; the veil barring us from God's presence is torn because of the sacrifice of Christ upon the cross. We may now, as the writer of Hebrews so greatly wants us to see, approach boldly into the presence of God that once was barred by our sin.

The mercy seat was the place where sinners might approach the holy God in safety and with confidence. This is what God said to Moses in the wilderness: "There I will meet with you, and from above the mercy seat, from between the two cherubim that are on the ark of the testimony, I will speak with you" (Ex. 25:22). This is where we meet safely and peacefully with the Lord our God, at the place made safe by the blood offered by our high priest, Jesus Christ.

The second aspect of Christ's priestly ministry is the sympathy he bears for us in heaven. Hebrews 4:15 tells us, "For we do not have a high priest who is unable to sympathize with our weaknesses, but one who in every respect has been tempted as we are, yet without sin." This is a point the author has made before, so it must be an important one. The Lord you serve, the Savior to whom you look, is not aloof from your trials, but feels them with intimate acquaintance. He is not disinterested or cold to what you are going through; he came to this earth and took up our human nature precisely so that he might now be able to have a fellow feeling with us. Therefore, he is eminently able to represent you before the throne of his heavenly Father, pleading your cause, securing your place, and procuring the spiritual resources you need.

That is the reason you must not give up, because Christ is there in heaven bearing human flesh, having endured what you are going through now—and more—yet without himself falling into sin. His righteousness represents you before God's throne and grants you access to the Father; his prayers plead for your sustenance and intercede on behalf of your needs. "Here am

I, and the children God has given me," Jesus declared upon his arrival in heaven (Heb. 2:13 NIV). He has opened the way for you, established your place where he is, and now he prays for your spiritual provision and protection to the Father who is certain to receive his every petition.

Jesus explained all this to his first disciples in the upper room on the night of his arrest. They did not fully understand as he spoke of what was to come, but they picked up enough to know that he was leaving. Jesus comforted them, saying, "Let not your hearts be troubled. Believe in God; believe also in me. In my Father's house are many rooms. If it were not so, would I have told you that I go to prepare a place for you? And if I go and prepare a place for you, I will come again and will take you to myself, that where I am you may be also" (John 14:1–3).

Yes, there would be hardships and troubles. The writer of Hebrews has assured us of this by comparing our earthly pilgrimage to Israel's journey through the wilderness to the Promised Land. But Jesus assured his disciples: "I will not leave you as orphans. . . . Because I live, you also will live" (John 14:18–19). What a great reason this is for hope, and what strength it gives to persevere!

A Resource: The Throne of Grace

Our *requirement* is to hold firmly to the faith we profess. Our *reason* to strive on is the high-priestly ministry of our Lord Jesus Christ. His ministry reconciles us to God and opens heaven's treasure chest of grace. This makes possible the great *resource* of prayer, to which the writer now turns: "Let us then with confidence draw near to the throne of grace, that we may receive mercy and find grace to help in time of need" (Heb. 4:16).

What does it mean to approach the throne of grace? It means to come to God in prayer on the basis of Christ's high-priestly ministry; that is, his propitiating sacrifice and present intercession. The language here is striking and clear. By telling us to come before God's throne, the author reminds us that it is the place where blood has been offered for us, the mercy seat where God calls sinners to meet with him. But we are also reminded that it is to a king that we come; we come to the royal throne of the King of kings.

In a great sermon on this text, Charles Haddon Spurgeon worked out some of the implications for our own approach to God in prayer. The first is that we must come in *lowly reverence*. If we show great respect in the courts of earthly majesty—in the White House, for example, or Buckingham Palace—then surely we will come with even greater reverence before the throne of heaven. There is no place for pride or vanity here, and if our eyes could see what really is before us spiritually, we would tremble at its awesome majesty. Spurgeon writes, "His throne is a great white throne, unspotted, and clear as crystal.... Familiarity there may be, but let it not be unhallowed. Boldness there should be, but let it not be impertinent."[4]

Second, we should come with *great joy*. Why? Because of the favor that has been extended to us in so high a privilege. What have we merited but rejection from God's presence and incarceration in his prison? Instead, we find ourselves received as favored children, invited to bring all our requests to the King of heaven.

Next, our prayers should include *enlarged expectations*, as befitting the power and goodness of the King to whom we come. Combined with this must be *submission to his wisdom and will*. As the apostle Paul reminds us, he is "able to do far more abundantly than all that we ask or think, according to the power at work within us" (Eph. 3:20). We honor him when we come with great and large requests, but also with contentment in his sovereign will. By faith, we gladly accept what he pleases to give, in the manner he chooses to give it, knowing that he is wise far above us and that he works out all things for our good (Rom. 8:28).

Finally, and this is the special point being made by the writer of Hebrews, we should come to God *with confidence*. We come knowing that we will be favorably received, knowing that we can speak freely, knowing that this is a throne of grace toward us. Why? Because of the High Priest who has gone ahead, securing access for us by his blood and interceding prayers.

We cannot overestimate the importance of such confidence. Many Christians struggle with prayer. We tremble as with stage fright, as if the light from God's throne exposed us in naked shame, when in fact it reveals the radiant robes that have been draped around us, the righteousness of Christ given to all who trust in him. This is the key to prayer—to praying often, to praying openly, to praying boldly and freely and with gladness of heart—to know

---

4. Charles Haddon Spurgeon, "The Throne of Grace," in *The Metropolitan Tabernacle Pulpit*, 63 vols. (Pasadena, Tex.: Pilgrim Publications, 1975), 17:855.

that we come clothed in the righteousness of Jesus Christ, invited by his own saving ministry, purchased by his precious blood, and anticipated by his sympathetic intercession. This is the secret to lively and happy prayer.

Yes, it is a throne to which you come, but that throne is a throne of grace. This means that when you come, your sins are covered by the blood of Christ, and that your faults are looked upon with compassion. Your stumbling prayers are not criticized, but are received with kindness. Moreover, Jesus' priestly ministry secures the Holy Spirit's help. The apostle Paul writes in Romans 8:26, "Likewise the Spirit helps us in our weakness. For we do not know what to pray for as we ought, but the Spirit himself intercedes for us with groanings too deep for words." God's Spirit helps us to pray, and he graciously interprets our prayers in the ears of the heavenly Father.

Furthermore, because it is a throne of grace to which we come, God is ready to grant our requests. He is glad to provide our needs, to give us strength to persevere through trials. He says, "My grace is sufficient for you, for my power is made perfect in weakness" (2 Cor. 12:9). So we are not afraid to ask of God, we who are so needy in this life. Why do we come? One commentator explains, "Man needs mercy for past failure, and grace for present and future work. . . . Mercy is to be 'taken' as it is extended to man in his weakness; grace is to be 'sought' by man according to his necessity."[5] And so, as Hebrews exhorts, "Let us then with confidence draw near to the throne of grace, that we may receive mercy and find grace to help in time of need" (Heb. 4:16).

A PLACE FOR YOU

God requires us to persevere in faith through the trials of this Christian life. He gives us a great reason to press on—the saving work of our great high priest, who is able to save us to the uttermost. He has gone ahead of us to open the doors and unlock the treasures of God's mercy and grace. Prayer is a great resource God gives us, one that we must not neglect if we are to grow strong in the faith and persevere through difficulties. Prayer brings us to a throne of power and authority, but also a throne of grace to all who are in Christ. Therefore, let us draw near to God with reverence, with joy, with

5. B. F. Westcott, *The Epistle to the Hebrews* (London: Macmillan, 1903), 109.

great expectations, and especially with the confidence that belongs to the sons and daughters of the King of heaven and earth. Spurgeon provides us a fitting conclusion, about the difference God's grace makes for us:

> I could not say to you, "Pray," not even to you saints, unless it were a throne of grace, much less could I talk of prayer to you sinners; but now I will say this to every sinner here, though he should think himself to be the worst sinner that ever lived, cry unto the Lord and seek him while he may be found. A throne of grace is a place fitted for you: go to your knees, by simple faith go to your Savior, for he, he it is who is the throne of grace.[6]

---

6. Spurgeon, "The Throne of Grace," 860.

16

APPOINTED AS PRIEST

Hebrews 5:1—6

So also Christ did not exalt himself to be made a high priest, but was appointed by him who said to him, "You are my Son, today I have begotten you." (Heb. 5:5)

*T*he Book of Hebrews stands out among the other epistles of the New Testament in its single-minded attention to the person and work of Jesus Christ. Paul's epistles take a somewhat different approach. In Romans, Paul begins with man's condition in sin. In other epistles he begins with problems that have arisen or concerns that are on his mind. Both of Peter's letters begin with praise to God the Father, and John's first epistle begins with a statement of his own apostolic mission and message.

From its very first verse, however, Hebrews is single-minded in its focus on Jesus Christ. Chapter 1 begins with a grand statement of who he is and what he has done. The rest of the book dwells upon his supremacy and utter sufficiency as our Savior. He is greater than angels, greater than Moses, greater than Joshua, and greater than Aaron the high priest. The writer's whole approach seems to be this: "If you only comprehend who Christ is and what he has done, this will make you persevere in the faith against all difficulties." If we get Christ straight, he argues, everything else will come into focus and we will hold fast to the end.

Hebrews stands out not only because of its singular concern with the person and work of our Lord, but also because of its detailed presentation of Christ in his office as high priest. John Calvin rightly observes: "There is, indeed, no book in Holy Scripture which speaks so clearly of the priesthood of Christ, which so highly exalts the virtue and dignity of that only true sacrifice which He offered by His death . . . and, in a word, so fully explains that Christ is the end of the Law."[1]

It would be overstating the case to say that Christ's priestly ministry appears only in this book of the New Testament, for this office is more than implied in other epistles, particularly whenever his sacrificial death is in view. But in this book, which so directly addresses the matter of Christian perseverance, it is the priestly ministry of Jesus Christ that appears as our main source of motivation and comfort. Indeed, only in Hebrews is the title of high priest specifically ascribed to Jesus. Already, we have encountered Christ as high priest in our study of Hebrews, but in the fifth chapter this becomes the main focus of our concern.

Hebrews 5:1–10 forms one unit of thought, focusing on the similarity between the high priesthood of Aaron in the old covenant and the high priesthood of Jesus Christ in the new covenant. The teaching presented here lays a foundation for what is to come. Later chapters focus at length on the differences between Christ and Aaron, and especially the supremacy of Christ's priesthood. But first we must comprehend the basic continuity between Christ and Aaron. To that end, Hebrews 5:1–10 sets forth first the qualifications of a high priest, then the requirement that priests be appointed by God, and finally how both of these are fulfilled in Christ. In this study we will consider the first six verses, and especially Christ's appointment as high priest for our salvation.

QUALIFICATIONS OF A PRIEST

The writer of Hebrews begins by explaining the qualifications of a high priest. We might see this as a job description, setting forth the conditions necessary for this employment, the nature of the work, and lastly the purpose of a high priest.

1. John Calvin, *New Testament Commentaries*, 12 vols. (Grand Rapids: Eerdmans, 1994), 12:1.

155

Verse 1 tells us, "Every high priest chosen from among men is appointed to act on behalf of men in relation to God, to offer gifts and sacrifices for sins." The word "men" is used twice in close proximity, with obvious emphasis. The high priest is taken out of mankind to act on behalf of mankind in things pertaining to God. The condition of entering the high priesthood, then, is to be human, because the nature of the work is to represent other humans through the offering of "gifts and sacrifices." The purpose of this calling and work is all too clear, namely, to deal with the problem of sin. The high priest is appointed by God to represent sinners before God by means of atoning gifts and sacrifices. Particularly in view is the annual sin offering on the day of atonement, which summed up the whole priestly enterprise.

A key idea here is that of representation: the priest had to be a human in order to represent other humans, because it is humans who stand condemned before God for sin. Philip Hughes writes, "The high priest was something far more than a cultic or liturgical specialist. His office was concerned, above all, with the radical problem of human sinfulness and the need of the people for reconciliation with God."[2] The priest was a mediator, not only representing the sinful people before God, but actually bringing them back into fellowship with God through his work on their behalf.

A priest had to be human to represent other humans, but he also had to be human in order to identify with them: "He can deal gently with the ignorant and wayward, since he himself is beset with weakness. Because of this he is obligated to offer sacrifice for his own sins just as he does for those of the people" (Heb. 5:2–3).

The human priests of Israel were able to deal gently with the sinful people because they were in the same boat. They were sinners, as was demonstrated by the offerings they made for their own sins. The writer of Hebrews has been keen to remind us that Jesus did not have any sins or failures (see Heb. 4:15), but also that he is able to sympathize with us nonetheless, because of his personal acquaintance with temptation and human weakness. Hebrews 5:2 says the high priest must be "beset with weakness." The Greek text literally puts it, "since he is *clad with*

2. Philip E. Hughes, *A Commentary on the Epistle to the Hebrews* (Grand Rapids: Eerdmans, 1977), 176.

weakness." Although Jesus had no sins, he put on human frailty, and thus is able to treat sinners with understanding and without harshness.

Moreover, the priest deals gently with "the ignorant and wayward" (Heb. 5:2). Surely this includes every believer. It is in our ignorance and waywardness that we sin against God. This also seems to recall the Old Testament distinction between, on one hand, those who sin in ignorance and weakness and, on the other, those who commit high-handed or openly rebellious sins (see Num. 15:22–31; Lev. 22:14–16; and Ps. 95:7–11). The difference today would be between believers who, despite their faith in Christ as Savior, still struggle with sin, and those who reject the gospel and sin without repentance. Sinning believers are forgiven through the saving work of Jesus. But unrepentant, unbelieving sinners have no one to bear their sins but themselves. How wonderful that "the ignorant and wayward" find a compassionate high priest who will gently lead them into God's grace.

JESUS' QUALIFICATION AS HIGH PRIEST

The obvious point of all this is that Jesus qualifies for such a priestly ministry. What particularly qualifies him is his full humanity, both in nature and in experience.

The New Testament often emphasizes the divine nature of Jesus Christ. He is the Son of God—not merely a man like the rest of us, but God in the flesh. The writer of Hebrews made this point quite clearly in chapter 1. The emphasis here, however, is on the human nature of Jesus. Indeed, the main reason the divine Savior, the Messiah, had to become man was to fulfill this priestly role. He must be one of us in order to represent us, and he must have shared our experience to identify with us in our trials.

How can God's Son represent and identify with us? The first answer is the incarnation, when the second person of the Trinity took up human flesh to undertake our cause. Hebrews 2:14 says, "Since therefore the children share in flesh and blood, he himself likewise partook of the same things, that through death he might destroy the one who has the power of death, that is, the devil." As we saw when studying that text, Jesus' death on the cross counted for men because it was men who owed God the debt, and in Christ it was a man who paid it. It was his divine nature that made Christ's blood infinitely valuable and able to propitiate God's wrath, but it was in his human nature that he offered it for us. If it had been angels he came to save, then he would have come as an angel; since he came to be the Savior of men, it was as man that he came. Hebrews 2:17 sums this all up: "Therefore he had to be made like his brothers in every respect, so that he might become a merciful and faithful high priest in the service of God, to make propitiation for the sins of the people." The incarnation stands behind the atonement. It was because Jesus became man that he represented men while dying on the cross.

What about the matter of identifying with us in our weakness? This has been a major emphasis of the writer of Hebrews, a key aspect of Christ's high-priestly ministry. Hebrews 2:10 told us this: "For it was fitting that he, for whom and by whom all things exist, in bringing many sons to glory, should make the founder of their salvation perfect through suffering." Jesus had to become perfect for this office not because there was some deficiency in him beforehand, but because a priest has to identify with what people are going through. "For we do not have a high priest who is unable to sympathize with our weaknesses, but one who in every respect has been tempted as we are, yet without sin" (Heb. 4:15).

As we read the Gospels, we find that Jesus was indeed familiar with the problems of this world, with the difficulties of living among a sinful race, the weakness of human nature, and even the horror of human mortality. He stood weeping before the tomb of his friend Lazarus, just as you weep over your beloved dead; he shed blood-tinged drops of sweat while contemplating his own death, just as you wring your heart over trouble and pain; he was himself abused and tortured; he died and was laid in a grave. Indeed, the cup of death and want and lonely pain, from which we sip only in part, he drank to the very dregs. He has been through the human experience, and he identifies with what we are going through.

Read the Gospels—Jesus' birth from the maid Mary, his life among men, and his cursed death before God—and you will see that he is abundantly fit both to represent and identify with us. All this is summed up in Hebrews 2:11, which tells us, "For he who sanctifies and those who are sanctified all have one origin. That is why he is not ashamed to call them brothers." Jesus has become our brother, in terms of both shared human nature and shared human experience, and thus he is fully qualified to be our great high priest.

Realize the implications of this. Early on the writer took pains to show us that Christ is now enthroned at God's right hand with power and authority. Now we see that it is our high priest who sits upon the throne. He is there first to represent us, so that his perfect righteousness might gain sinners like us entry into God's kingdom and family. Second, the enthroned Lord identifies with our struggles; he deals gently with us now in our ignorance and weakness. Our high priest does not merely have good intentions; he has power and authority to secure our place in heaven and help us now through the Spirit he sends.

Jesus himself anticipated the significance of all this. John 17 records his prayer before he submitted himself to be arrested and then crucified. It is known as Christ's high-priestly prayer. In it he spoke about his coming exaltation as prophet, priest, and king, and about the implications for those who trust in him. First he spoke of his coming enthronement as king: "Father, the hour has come; glorify your Son that the Son may glorify you. . . . I glorified you on earth, having accomplished the work that you gave me to do. And now, Father, glorify me in your own presence with the glory that I had with you before the world existed" (John 17:1, 4–5).

Next he spoke of his successful prophetic ministry, which led to the faith of believers in him: "I have manifested your name to the people whom you gave me out of the world. . . . For I have given them the words that you gave me, and they have received them" (John 17:6, 8).

Then he prayed as high priest, securing God's favor and power for all who trust in him: "I am praying for them. I am not praying for the world but for those whom you have given me, for they are yours. . . . And I am no longer in the world, but they are in the world, and I am coming to you. Holy Father, keep them in your name" (John 17:9, 11).

This is how Jesus prayed before he entered heaven in glory. Now that he is enthroned there for us, that same priestly ministry guarantees God's favor and power for our salvation, even the eternal life that is made available to us now through faith in him.

APPOINTED AS PRIEST

Jesus Christ meets the qualifications to be our mediator and high priest. But someone may be qualified for a position without actually having the authority to hold it. Qualification is a prerequisite, but there must be an appointment to the office if the work is to be acceptable and binding. In verses 4–6 we see that Jesus is not only qualified to be our high priest, but that God has also appointed him to this office.

This matter of appointment is important for two reasons. The first is that it determines the way the office is carried out. Verses 4 and 5 make this point: "No one takes this honor for himself, but only when called by God, just as Aaron was. So also Christ did not exalt himself to be made a high priest." A true priest is not one who has acted to elevate himself in the eyes of men or of God. A true priest is motivated solely by a desire to honor God and serve men, without concern for personal advancement.

This ought to be true of ministers of the gospel. Few things are worse than ministers who put themselves forward for prestigious posts, seeking praise and even worldly riches. Simon Kistemaker rightly comments, "Anyone inducted into sacred office must be called by God. If this is not the case, he is an affront to God and a provocation to his people."[3]

The office of priest was greatly honored in Israel, as it ought to have been. Similarly, the New Testament urges that ministers of the gospel are worthy of respect (1 Thess. 5:12–13; 1 Tim. 5:17). But praise and honor are always a danger to sinful men, which is why Peter admonished the elders, "Shepherd the flock of God that is among you, exercising oversight, not under compulsion, but willingly, as God would have you; not for shameful gain, but eagerly; not domineering over those in your charge, but being examples to the flock" (1 Peter 5:2–3).

What is true for the human office of priest or minister is especially true for the messianic office of priest that Christ assumed. If one thing is clear from his life and death, it is that he came not seeking glory for himself but to do the will of his Father in heaven. "If I glorify myself," he said, "my glory is nothing. It is my Father who glorifies me" (John 8:54). Philip Hughes observes, "In assuming the office of savior and high priest, so far was the Son from exalting and glorifying himself that he accepted it knowing full well that it meant for him the experience of the darkest depths of humiliation, rejection, agony and death."[4]

This is an important reason why this office comes only by appointment, but the second reason is, if anything, more important. The high priest must

---

3. Simon J. Kistemaker, *Thessalonians, the Pastorals and Hebrews* (Grand Rapids: Baker, 1984), 134.
4. Hughes, *Hebrews*, 180.

be appointed by God, not only so that he will serve selflessly, but also so that we might know that God himself has authorized his ministry in this capacity. On what basis do we believe that Christ's death atoned for our sins? Because God appointed him to this task, and thus has accepted Christ's work in this holy office. When Jesus entered the heavenlies, bearing his own blood as the sacrifice for our sins, why does that have any relevance for us? Certainly, he is qualified, but that is not enough. He represents us because God has appointed him as our high priest. Moreover, why should God listen to Christ's prayers for us? Surely he loves his Son, and Christ is sympathetic. But God accepts Christ's intercession because he appointed him to this very work; as our high priest, Christ fulfills God's own will and appointment for our salvation.

Therefore, it is important for the writer of Hebrews to prove that Jesus was in fact appointed to this office, which he does by citing two Old Testament verses. The first is Psalm 2:7, which says, "You are my Son; today I have begotten you." The second is Psalm 110:4, "You are a priest forever, after the order of Melchizedek."

The first quote already appeared in Hebrews 1:5. The burden of this verse is not the establishment of Christ's nature as Son of God, but his public declaration and confirmation as Son and heir. As Paul explains in Romans 1:4, Jesus "was declared to be the Son of God in power according to the Spirit of holiness by his resurrection from the dead." The resurrection and ascension were the fulfillment of this Old Testament citation and the occasion of his appointment to enter heaven as Son, heir, and high priest.

The second citation is more enigmatic, for here we encounter the first of nine references in Hebrews to Melchizedek, who first appeared in the story of Abraham (Gen. 14). There, Melchizedek was described as king of Salem (probably Jerusalem) and "a priest of God Most High." After his victory over the eastern lords, Abraham came and offered a sacrifice to this priest-king, who prefigured Jesus Christ. A thousand years after Abraham, Melchizedek's name surfaces again in Psalm 110, and with no real explanation. This is a messianic psalm; it begins with the Christ being enthroned. Verse 4 simply informs us that the Messiah will also be a priest in the order of Melchizedek.

After Psalm 110, Melchizedek never appears again in Scripture until the Book of Hebrews, where he serves as a type of Christ as a priest-king, and as an eternal priest who serves on the basis of his own indestructible life. We will speak about this later in considerable detail. Indeed, the writer of Hebrews himself concludes that it is not yet time to discuss the matter in full. Hebrews 5:11 says, "About this we have much to say, and it is hard to explain, since you have become dull of hearing."

There will be more to come about Melchizedek, but here the point is clear. These two Old Testament passages show that Christ "did not exalt himself to be made a high priest" (Heb. 5:5), but was appointed by God's own oath. The complete citation in Psalm 110:4 makes this point even clearer. David wrote, "The LORD has sworn and will not change his mind, 'You are a priest forever after the order of Melchizedek.'" God's appointment of Christ as high priest is an oath that can never be changed or rescinded.

All this has a tremendous impact on our assurance of salvation. The writer of Hebrews has long been discussing the matter of our perseverance. He compares his readers' situation to Israel's in the desert, when many fell away through disobedience, unbelief, and rebellion. Surely this causes us to ask, "How will I fare in the years ahead? Will I persevere through my own struggles and temptations?" It is an excellent question. Who is to say that believers will make it to the end—and we must if we are to be saved.

The answer to this question, and to our need of assurance, is the appointment of Jesus Christ as our high priest. He has already completed the work of dying for our sins. He has gone into heaven to offer his sacrificial blood for our sake. There he now sits enthroned as a priest who ministers on our behalf, praying for us, interceding with the Father, and sending the heavenly manna needed to feed and tend our faith. What good news this is! James Boice sums up the point for us: "The reason the saints will persevere is that Jesus has done everything necessary for their salvation. Since he has made a perfect atonement for their sin and since God has sworn to accept Jesus' work, the believer can be as certain that he or she will be in heaven as that Jesus himself will be there."[5]

This leaves only one question to be asked. Is he your high priest? Did he die for you? Have you confessed your sin and trusted him as your Savior? Is he now in heaven pleading your cause with his own blood? If the answer is

5. James Montgomery Boice, *Psalms*, 3 vols. (Grand Rapids: Baker, 1998), 3:902.

no, then you are not reconciled to God, you are not free from condemnation, you are clothed not in the righteousness of Christ but in your sins before the holy God.

But if you have trusted Jesus Christ, then you have peace that rests upon his work and God's Word, even God's sacred oath: "The LORD has sworn and will not change his mind: 'You are a priest forever'" (Ps. 110:4). In these words is our full assurance of salvation, for Christ has taken our names into the heavens with him, so that in due time, we might follow him into realms of glory.

When you come to Christ in faith, you have come also, as the writer of Hebrews says in his twelfth chapter, "to innumerable angels in festal gathering, and to the assembly of the firstborn who are enrolled in heaven" (Heb. 12:22–23). And you can be sure that one of those names is yours.

17

THE SOURCE OF OUR SALVATION

Hebrews 5:7–10

Although he was a son, he learned obedience through what he suffered. And being made perfect, he became the source of eternal salvation to all who obey him. (Heb. 5:8–9)

*I*n the eleventh canon of the sixth session of the Council of Trent, written in January of 1547, the Roman Catholic Church officially condemned the Protestant doctrine of justification by faith alone. If anyone says, it reads, "that men are justified, either by the sole imputation of the justice of Christ, or by the sole remission of sins," to the exclusion of the grace and charity that are at work within them, "let them be anathema."[1] This language, which grounds our justification on a righteousness in us, caused the Protestant Reformers to conclude that Rome had abandoned and even condemned the gospel. What the Council of Trent cursed was precisely what the Reformers taught as central to the whole Christian religion, the teaching that, as John Calvin put it, "it is entirely by the intervention of Christ's righteousness that we obtain justification before

---

1. See Philip Schaff, *The Creeds of Christendom*, vol. 2, *The Greek and Latin Creeds* (Grand Rapids: Baker, 1993), 113.

God. This is equivalent to saying that man is not just in himself, but that the righteousness of Christ is communicated to him by imputation, while he is strictly deserving of punishment."[2]

What troubled the Roman Catholics, and other opponents of the Reformation, was the idea that people who are still sinners can be declared righteous by a God who is just. To say we are justified by faith in Christ alone, even while we are still actually sinful, they complained, amounts to a legal fiction. It is unworthy of God, they argued, and unreasonable for us to expect that God can or will declare us just until we actually are innocent and pure. It is for this reason that justification by faith alone, as taught by the Reformers, was pronounced accursed by Rome—an anathema that is still very much in force.[3]

All this begs a question that is vital to our grasp of the gospel. On what basis does God declare someone just and accept him or her as worthy of fellowship with him? Or to put it differently, what is the ground of my standing with God; what is the source of my salvation? This is a vital issue, because for anyone who realizes that he is a sinner, that his guilt has placed him under God's holy wrath, this is the question of all questions.

The Bible addresses this matter thoroughly and clearly. Our present text looks it squarely in the eye and gives us a straight answer. Speaking of Jesus Christ, it says, "He became the source of eternal salvation to all who obey him" (Heb. 5:9). To understand this verse, we need to answer three questions: first, *what* does salvation require? second, *how* did Jesus become the source of what salvation requires? and finally, for *whom* is Jesus the source of eternal salvation?

WHAT SALVATION REQUIRES

What does salvation require? Another way of asking this is to say, "What is necessary for someone to enjoy eternal fellowship with God?" The Bible's answer is that to have fellowship with God one must possess perfect righteousness, attaining the perfect standards set forth in God's

2. John Calvin, quoted in R. C. Sproul, *Faith Alone* (Grand Rapids: Baker, 1995), 93.
3. See *Catechism of the Catholic Church* (New York: Doubleday, 1995), paragraph 1995, which insists that "justification involves the *sanctification* of [one's] whole being."

law. We might consider this in both a positive and a negative sense. Positively, one must perfectly manifest the holiness set forth in God's law. Negatively, one must not be blemished with any guilt or corruption, any transgression of that law.

Jesus often addressed this concern during his earthly ministry. When the rich young ruler approached Jesus and asked, "Teacher, what good deed must I do to have eternal life?" Jesus replied, "If you would enter life, keep the commandments" (Matt. 19:16–17). An expert in the law asked Jesus the same question: "Teacher, what shall I do to inherit eternal life?" "What is written in the Law?" Jesus replied. The man answered: "You shall love the Lord your God with all your heart and with all your soul and with all your strength and with all your mind, and your neighbor as yourself." "You have answered correctly," Jesus replied. "Do this and you will live" (Luke 10:25–28).

The basis of salvation, then, is righteousness. And to be righteous before God is to perfectly keep his law, to uphold his standards, both in thought and deed, with hands and heart. Both the rich young ruler and the teacher of the law got this part right. Where they went wrong was in claiming they had actually achieved it. For that reason Jesus sternly rebuffed them both. Nonetheless, the clear standard is that given in the law and repeated in the New Testament: "You shall be holy, for I am holy" (1 Peter 1:16).

Jesus' parable of the wedding banquet makes this point quite clearly. A man who tried to infiltrate into the king's feast was discovered and removed. "When the king came in to look at the guests, he saw there a man who had no wedding garment. And he said to him, 'Friend, how did you get in here without a wedding garment?' And he was speechless. Then the king said to the attendants, 'Bind him hand and foot and cast him into the outer darkness. In that place there will be weeping and gnashing of teeth'" (Matt. 22:11–13).

God requires us to be clothed in perfect righteousness. This is a great problem for us, indeed, a worse one than we tend to recognize. Our problem is not merely that we are morally flawed, but that we are morally corrupt through and through; not that our garments are slightly less than pearly white, but that they are horribly soiled. People find this hard to stomach today, but the Scripture plainly teaches it. Paul states it clearly: "None is righteous, no, not one" (Rom. 3:10).

People don't like to hear this, but when they stand before God they will not be able to deny it. This is exactly the picture we have in the Bible. Adam and Eve hid from God and tried to cover themselves after they had sinned. Job spoke boldly to God until the clouds parted and God appeared. Then he could only say: "I had heard of you by the hearing of the ear, but now my eye sees you; therefore I despise myself, and repent in dust and ashes" (Job 42:5–6). The great prophet Isaiah cried, "Woe to me! For I am lost!" when he stood before the vision of God in his holiness (Isa. 6:5). The same was true for the apostle John: when he saw the risen and exalted Jesus Christ in Revelation 1:17, he fell down as though dead.

Man is unrighteous, and yet righteousness is required for salvation. We can see, therefore, what the complaint against the doctrine of justification by faith alone is all about. It is right to say that we cannot stand upon any legal fiction; without a solid righteousness before God, not just words but reality, we must surely be condemned.

ROME'S TEACHING OF INFUSED RIGHTEOUSNESS

If righteousness is the requirement for salvation, the basis for fellowship with God, then where does our righteousness come from? This is the next and obvious question. What righteousness will commend us before the great white throne of God's perfect justice? The Roman Catholic answer, and that of many others who deny justification by faith alone, is that it must be a righteousness *within you*. If asked, "Why should you be allowed to enter into God's holy heaven?" they answer, "Because I have become righteous."

I point out the Roman Catholic teaching not to engage in intramural sparring, but to throw light on this grave issue by means of a clear contrast. It is sometimes wrongly claimed that Catholicism teaches self-righteousness, but this too is anathematized by Rome. Roman Catholics are quick to admit that no one becomes righteous without God's help through Jesus Christ. And yet that very way of putting it shows the difference between their teaching and justification by faith alone. God *helps* you to become righteous, without Christ you never *could* be righteous, and yet they nonetheless insist that the ground of your entrance into heaven is

167

your own righteousness.[4] Through a combination of the sacraments of baptism, penance, and the mass, your sins are removed and God's grace is preserved and strengthened until you pass from this life and into death.

Of course, when you die you cannot go directly to heaven. The reason is that you are not yet righteous enough to please God, as you and especially those close to you know perfectly well. Thus there must be purgatory, a teaching that finds no support in the Scripture, but is made necessary by this system of doctrine. Since I must become perfectly righteous and pure, and since I know I do not attain this in life, then it is the fires of purgatory that I trust to burn away my remaining iniquity, perhaps over several hundred or maybe several thousand years.[5]

This is the good news according to the Roman Catholic Church. Jesus is the source of salvation only in that his death makes this program possible. Were it not for him, there would be no hope at all for sinners. But now, by his grace, after a lifetime in the church and many lifetimes in the minihell of purgatory, you can hope to stand before God not on the basis of some legal fiction, but on the basis of your own personal righteousness. The technical theological term for this process is *infused righteousness.* Sinners get into heaven after they have achieved perfect holiness in purgatory, on the basis of the righteousness infused into them by Christ, through the church and its all-important priesthood and sacraments, and with the help of Mary and the saints.

4. See *The Canons and Decrees of the Council of Trent,* sixth session, chapter VII: "Justification . . . is not remission of sins merely, but also the sanctification and renewal of the inward man, through the voluntary reception of the grace, and of the gifts, whereby man [from] unjust becomes just, and [from] an enemy a friend, that so he may be an heir according to the hope of life everlasting. . . . The formal cause is the justice of God, not that whereby he himself is just, but that whereby he maketh us just, that, to wit, with which *we*, being endowed by him, are renewed in the spirit of our mind, and we are not only reputed, but are truly called, and are just, receiving justice within us, each according to his own measure." While justification is possible for us only because "the merits of the Passion of our Lord Jesus Christ are communicated" to us, "yet is this done in the said justification of the impious, when . . . the charity of God is poured forth, by the Holy Spirit, in the hearts of those that are justified, and is inherent therein: whence, man, through Jesus Christ, in whom he is ingrafted, receives, in the said justification, together with the remission of sins, all these [gifts] infused at once, faith, hope, and charity" (Schaff, *The Creeds of Christendom,* 2:94–96).

5. See *Catechism of the Catholic Church,* paragraph 1030, where purgatory is needed "to achieve the holiness necessary to enter the joy of heaven." (See also *Catechism,* paragraph 1054.) The catechism justifies the doctrine of purgatory by reference to Roman Catholic tradition and to the Apocryphal book 2 Maccabees 12:45 (see *Catechism,* paragraphs 1031–32).

According to Rome, the righteousness you need is found in you after the process of justification has finally tossed you onto heaven's shore. This may be good news, but it is not very good news. Furthermore, it is a far cry from what the writer of Hebrews meant when he said that Jesus Christ, by his obedience, "became the source of eternal salvation" (Heb. 5:9).

THE RIGHTEOUSNESS OF CHRIST

Hebrews says that Christ became the source of our salvation. The first thing we should notice is the verb "became." Until something happened, until something was attained, Christ was not the source of our salvation, the basis for our entry into heaven. So what did Jesus do that enabled him to become the source of eternal salvation? The writer tells us: "In the days of his flesh, Jesus offered up prayers and supplications, with loud cries and tears, to him who was able to save him from death, and he was heard because of his reverence. Although he was a son, he learned obedience through what he suffered. And being made perfect, he became the source of eternal salvation to all who obey him" (Heb. 5:7–9).

These verses set forth Christ's actual attainment of righteousness, his full achievement of the holiness expressed in the law of God, during his days in the flesh on this earth. In this respect, we need to understand the *context* in which Christ fulfilled the law, the *obedience* by which he fulfilled the law, and the *result* of his fulfilling the law in perfect righteousness.

What was the context for Jesus' attainment of righteousness? Jesus attained righteousness "in the days of his flesh" (Heb. 5:7). One commentator observes, "These moving words express how intensely Jesus entered the human condition, which wrung from him his prayers and entreaties, cries and tears."[6]

"Flesh" is a fairly comprehensive term, depicting human weakness, subjection to danger and want and temptation, as well as obligation to the law of God. John tells us, "The Word became flesh and dwelt among us" (John 1:14). In other words, the context in which Christ fulfilled all righteousness was no different from that in which you and I are compelled to live, except that Jesus was sinless and his pilgrimage through his world was if anything more arduous than ours.

6. William L. Lane, *Hebrews 1–8* (Dallas: Word, 1991), 119.

This is the very point that is made in the opening scenes of Christ's public ministry, starting with his baptism and then his temptation in the wilderness. John the Baptist had been calling sinners to be baptized for repentance. But when Jesus appeared, John was appalled at the idea of baptizing him, for here was One without sin, indeed, the One he had foretold who would be so much greater than himself. Matthew's Gospel tells us: "Jesus came from Galilee to the Jordan to John, to be baptized by him. John would have prevented him, saying, 'I need to be baptized by you, and do you come to me?' But Jesus answered him, 'Let it be so now, for thus it is fitting for us to fulfill all righteousness'" (Matt. 3:13–15).

How important this was for our salvation! Jesus placed himself in the path where sinners walk; he was, as Isaiah foretold, "numbered with the transgressors" (Isa. 53:12), in order that he might fulfill all righteousness precisely where we have so miserably failed.

Immediately after Jesus was baptized, and then publicly acclaimed by the voice from heaven and the Spirit descending as a dove, he was led out into the wilderness to be tested. We have been talking about the wilderness throughout our studies of Hebrews. The wilderness is where we live, the place of testing before the Land of Promise. This is what it meant for Jesus to be in the flesh, that he was in the wilderness where Israel had so badly failed, and where you and I likewise struggle with sin. But in the desert, with pain and hunger and temptation, Jesus fulfilled all righteousness so that he might be the source of our salvation. This was the context of his obedience.

What can we say about the *obedience* by which Christ fulfilled the law? Our passage says Jesus "offered up prayers and supplications, with loud cries and tears" (Heb. 5:7). In the desert Jesus ate nothing for forty days—the very number of years Israel was tested and failed, grumbling and revolting over the manna God sent them from heaven. But when the devil tempted Jesus over just this issue, our Lord replied, "Man shall not live by bread alone, but by every word that comes from the mouth of God" (Matt. 4:4). Jesus stood up to all of Satan's trials, no doubt often praying and crying out to God for help. He did not sin in thought, word, or deed, under temptations graver than any we will ever know. God heard him not merely because he was his only Son, but also "because of his reverence" (Heb. 5:7).

Back in verse 3 of this chapter we were told that the high priests of Israel offered sacrifices for their own sins. Only then did God hear their prayers and receive their ministry. But Jesus did not call to the Father on the basis of the blood of bulls and goats; his whole life, and especially his obedience in the events surrounding his terrible death, was the sacrificial offering that consecrated him as our high priest. William Lane writes, "Jesus learned experientially what obedience entails through his passion in order to achieve salvation and to become fully qualified for his office as eternal high priest."[7] His prayers and ministry are received by God because of his constant reverence and perfect obedience.

If there is one thing the New Testament emphasizes about the life of Jesus Christ, it is this: he obeyed God perfectly in all things, never entering into sin, never failing his Father and never falling under the condemnation of the law. This is what was prophesied before his coming. Isaiah said, "Righteousness shall be the belt of his waist, and faithfulness the belt of his loins" (Isa. 11:5). Jesus claimed this quite openly, demanding from his accusers: "Which of you convicts me of sin?" (John 8:46). They could not. Even when they brought him before Pontius Pilate, the callous despot was forced to admit his innocence: "I find no guilt in him" (John 18:38). Even in the hour of his death, those who looked on were stunned by what they saw: "When the centurion saw what had taken place, he praised God, saying, "Certainly this man was innocent!'" (Luke 23:47). Therefore Peter could say, "He committed no sin, neither was deceit found in his mouth" (1 Peter 2:22). The apostle Paul summed up his atoning death, writing: "For our sake [God] made him to be sin who knew no sin, so that in him we might become the righteousness of God" (2 Cor. 5:21).

Our passage emphasizes that it was in the midst of pain and struggle, in the shadow of death, that Jesus learned obedience. Two episodes especially come to mind: first, his anguish in the Garden of Gethsemane, where he anticipated the wrath of God upon the cross, and second, his death by crucifixion. In the garden Jesus prayed with tears and great anguish. "My soul is very sorrowful, even to death" (Matt. 26:38), he said to the disciples. Great was his struggle on that dreadful night: "He fell on his face and prayed." In the context of the greatest dread imaginable, Jesus prayed, "My Father, if it be possible, let this cup pass from me; nev-

7. Ibid., 121.

ertheless, not as I will, but as you will" (v. 39). This was reverent submission like no other, and for it God has received Jesus as our high priest.

On the cross Jesus cried out to the One who could save him: "My God, my God, why have you forsaken me?" (Matt. 27:46). "Father, into your hands I commit my spirit" (Luke 23:46). Jesus fulfilled all righteousness to the very end, crying out to the Father, trusting in him, and fulfilling the law once for all. His obedience opened up the way for sinners to enter into salvation, as was vividly represented when the veil separating the holy of holies was torn from top to bottom. "For their sake I consecrate myself," he said, "that they also may be sanctified" (John 17:19). Thus he fulfilled all righteousness and became the source of our eternal salvation.

This is the *result* of Christ's obedience: "Being made perfect, he became the source of eternal salvation to all who obey him, being designated by God a high priest after the order of Melchizedek" (Heb. 5:9–10). We saw before that righteousness is the source of salvation, and by his perfect life and sacrificial death the words of the apostle Paul are abundantly true: Jesus Christ is "our wisdom and our righteousness and sanctification and redemption" (1 Cor. 1:30). Now the way to God that was closed by sin is opened by Christ's righteousness. John Calvin writes, "He became the Author of our salvation because He made us just in the sight of God, when He remedied the disobedience of Adam by a contrary act of obedience."[8]

With this in mind, let me return to the questions I asked earlier. On what basis do you hope to stand before the throne of God? What will you give as an answer to God's question, "Why should you enter my holy heaven?" Surely the answer is not your own righteousness—either now or hereafter. Surely the only answer we can give is the one put so well in the words of the hymn "Rock of Ages":[9]

> Nothing in my hand I bring,
> > simply to thy cross I cling;
> Naked, come to thee for dress;
> > helpless, look to thee for grace;
> Foul, I to the Fountain fly;
> > wash me, Savior, or I die.

8. John Calvin, *New Testament Commentaries*, 12 vols. (Grand Rapids: Eerdmans, 1994), 12:66.
9. Augustus M. Toplady, "Rock of Ages, Cleft for Me," 1776.

This is what we mean by justification by faith alone. Our faith does not make us righteous; rather, faith lays hold of the righteousness of another, even our Lord Jesus Christ, who became perfect as our Savior and high priest, the source of our eternal life. Again, the hymn puts it well:

Not the labors of my hands
  can fulfill thy law's demands;
Could my zeal no respite know,
  could my tears forever flow;
All for sin could not atone;
  thou must save and thou alone.

Is this a legal fiction? Is it dishonoring to God's holy justice for us to say, "My only comfort in life and death is the righteousness of Christ alone"? It would be a legal fiction, I admit, were I to claim that faith itself justifies us. But what secures forgiveness and life eternal for sinners like us is Christ's perfect righteousness, received by faith alone. And this is no breach of justice, but rather the gift of righteousness from the God of grace, and to him is all the glory. It is this righteousness of Christ, not infused into us after a tortuous process, but imputed to us by God's decree through faith alone, of which the apostle Paul speaks in Philippians 3. Far from claiming any merits of his own, Paul said: "I . . . count them as rubbish, in order that I may gain Christ and be found in him, not having a righteousness of my own that comes from the law, but that which comes through faith in Christ—the righteousness from God that depends on faith" (Phil. 3:8–9).

There will indeed be a time when believers are not merely reckoned righteous but are finally made perfectly holy. This is a work taking place now, through the process of our sanctification, by which those who have been justified by God are being made holy in practical ways. God will himself perfect this work through the resurrection and not through any flames of purgatory. I, for one, greatly look forward to that day, but for now I can stand before God, though I am myself a very great sinner, clothed in the righteous robes of Jesus Christ. This is no legal fraud, but the actual righteousness attained for us by our precious Savior, who has thus become the source of our eternal salvation.

Righteousness Received through Faith

One question remains: "For whom is Christ the source of salvation?" The answer is clear: "He became the source of eternal salvation to all who obey him" (Heb. 5:9). What does it mean to obey Jesus Christ unto salvation? He himself gave the answer in John 6: "Then they said to him, 'What must we do, to be doing the works of God?' Jesus answered them, 'This is the work of God, that you believe in him whom he has sent'" (John 6:28–29).

If you do not trust in Jesus Christ, the good news is bad news for you. As Jesus himself taught, "Whoever believes in the Son has eternal life; whoever does not obey the Son shall not see life, but the wrath of God remains on him" (John 3:36). If you trust in his saving work, Christ will become your Savior. His sacrifice will pay the debt of your sins, and his will be the righteousness in which you are clothed before the throne of God.

But do not think all of this is easy. If you are to obey Jesus Christ, then you have to own up to some things and repudiate some others. You will have to confess that God is right to condemn you for your sins, and for your own total lack of righteousness. You will have to confess that you are not and cannot be righteous in and of yourself, because of the sin that is within you. Then you must reach out to Jesus Christ, by faith laying hold of his free offer of salvation, trusting his righteous life and sacrificial death for your only salvation.

Not only must you confess your need of Christ's blood and righteousness, but you must also repudiate your works, stained with sin as they are and altogether unable to save. You will have to repudiate your religious attainments, your faith in church-going, your proper upbringing, or your status in the world—your trust in anything except the saving work of Jesus Christ. Indeed, you will have to repudiate the world and all its sinful pleasures, what the apostle John describes as "the desires of the flesh and the desires of the eyes and pride in possessions" (1 John 2:16). Turning from sin is not the means of your salvation, but it is a necessary result of it, for there is no fellowship between light and darkness.

But when you have let go of all these, you will have gained everything if your hands are gripped firmly to the cross of Jesus Christ, where the righteous Son of God died for sinners, and became the sure source of eternal salvation for all who trust in him.

18

FROM MILK TO MEAT

Hebrews 5:11—6:3

For though by this time you ought to be teachers, you need some-
one to teach you again the basic principles of the oracles of God.
You need milk, not solid food. (Heb. 5:12)

*T*here is an old adage that expresses how people feel when a
preacher gets a little more personal than they would prefer.
When he is speaking in general terms, then he is preaching, of
which people heartily approve. But when he gets personal, when he actually speaks to areas of real sin and worldliness in people's own actual lives—
that, they say, is not preaching but meddling.

As we move to the end of Hebrews 5 and into chapter 6, the writer has def-
initely begun to meddle. The passage from Hebrews 5:11–6:3 comes as a
parenthesis; that is, it forms a break in the natural flow of the argument. This
parenthesis is a fairly long one and it serves as the third major exhortation in
this letter of exhortations. The first of these occurred in chapter 2, where we
learned of the danger of drifting away: "Therefore we must pay much closer
attention to what we have heard, lest we drift away from it" (Heb. 2:1).

The second major exhortation ran from 3:6 to the end of chapter 4. There the emphasis was on the citation from Psalm 95: "Today, if you hear his voice, do not harden your hearts." We are diligently to protect our hearts and those of others around us, so that we are not hardened against God's Word by the deceitfulness of sin (Heb. 3:12).

With that long exhortation over, the writer of Hebrews began his extensive instruction on the high priesthood of Jesus Christ, beginning in chapter 5. No sooner does he begin to explain this, however, than he realizes that he has a pedagogical problem on his hands. This is what he writes in verse 11: "About this we have much to say"—namely, about the priesthood of Jesus Christ according to the order of Melchizedek—"and it is hard to explain, since you have become dull of hearing." That being the case, our writer turns aside to deal with the matter of his readers' immaturity and lack of spiritual commitment. Until he has corrected this, there is no point proceeding into deeper matters of the faith.

The exhortation he begins here is short, but intense. Indeed, it is perhaps the most severe warning that appears anywhere in the pages of the New Testament. The writer of Hebrews deals first with immaturity and then with the danger of outright apostasy, or falling away from the faith altogether, before concluding with encouragement that is based on the security of God's promise. In this study, we will consider the beginning of this exhortation, from Hebrews 5:11 to 6:3.

Childish Faith

The author of Hebrews begins with a reproof that explains why he cannot proceed with his exposition: "About this we have much to say, and it is hard to explain, since you have become dull of hearing. For though by this time you ought to be teachers, you need someone to teach you again the basic principles of the oracles of God. You need milk, not solid food" (Heb. 5:11–12).

This is one of the passages that indicates that the readers of this epistle were not recent converts or new believers. "By this time you ought to be teachers," he says. He does not mean by this that they should all be ordained ministers, but that they ought to be able to instruct others in the faith, whereas in fact they haven't yet grasped the most elementary truths of God's Word.

The recipients of this letter were like many Christians today who think that theology is a waste of time. What difference does it make, people ask, whether God is a Trinity or not, whether Christ's righteousness comes by imputation or by infusion, and whether regeneration comes before faith or after? What is important, they say, is that we get along with each other. Then they cite passages commending a *childlike* faith, as if that were the same as a *childish* faith, that is, one that is indifferent to or ignorant of the Word of God.

This attitude is so prevalent today that perhaps the majority of profess-ing believers try to nourish themselves on the weak diet of milk alone. Not that there is anything wrong with milk. It is just that those who are no longer babies require a stronger diet if they are to grow. Yet we are living in a time when most church members are immensely ignorant of the Bible and its doctrines. Evangelicals heartily agree that the Bible is true, but they simply don't take time to learn what it teaches. Recent surveys show that most pro-fessing Christians cannot, for instance, list half of the Ten Commandments, cite the names of the four Gospels, or articulate what is meant by the term "justification." They do not know who Abraham was or what Paul wrote in the Book of Romans. Asked if the Bible says, "God helps those who help themselves," 80 percent of self-described "evangelical Christians" agreed (actually, it was Benjamin Franklin). Pollster George Gallup summarizes the situation today, citing "the glaring lack of knowledge about the Bible, basic doctrines, and the traditions of one's church . . . [and] the superficiality of faith, with many people not knowing what they believe, or why."[1] No won-der, then, that the secular culture is unimpressed by teachings in which we ourselves are so disinterested.

The writer of Hebrews minces no words regarding the importance of understanding what the Bible teaches. Using a comparison that the apostle Paul also uses in 1 Corinthians 3:1–2, he writes, "You need milk, not solid food, for everyone who lives on milk is unskilled in the word of righteous-ness, since he is a child. But solid food is for the mature, for those who have their powers of discernment trained by constant practice to distinguish good from evil" (Heb. 5:12–14).

---

1. George Gallup Jr. and D. Michael Lindsay, *Surveying the Religious Landscape: Trends in U.S. Beliefs* (Harrisburg, Pa.: Morehouse, 1999), 4.

The hallmark of spiritual infants, he says, is that they are "unskilled in the word of righteousness," or as the New International Version puts it, "not acquainted with the teaching about righteousness." This could refer to moral rectitude, our need for righteous conduct, but it more likely refers to the righteousness that comes from God in the gospel through the work of Jesus Christ and is received by faith. This is what he was writing about before launching into this reproof. In Hebrews 5:8–10 he wrote about Christ's obedience that perfected him for the role of Savior. By means of his righteousness, Christ became "the source of eternal salvation" and was consecrated as our high priest.

The point is that these perpetual infants were not able to articulate the basis of their salvation. They formed a community identified with Jesus Christ, but they didn't grasp how the Christian faith works. Perhaps that doesn't matter, as people say, so long as you are saved. But the writer shows just what the problem is: "But solid food is for the mature, for those who have their powers of discernment trained by constant practice to distinguish good from evil" (Heb. 5:14).

Does it matter whether or not you become mature in the faith? Yes! Immature believers are easily led astray, which has been the writer's concern all through this epistle. In Ephesians 4:14 the apostle Paul expresses a similar concern for that church, where spiritual infants are "tossed to and fro by the waves and carried about by every wind of doctrine, by human cunning, by craftiness in deceitful schemes." Those who do not progress in the truths of the faith are tossed back and forth, particularly when faced with deceivers and their false schemes, as we always will be.

Many observers of the church today point to a false antithesis between the heart and the mind that has led to anti-intellectualism among evangelicals: If you care about theology, then you must be spiritually cold and unloving. The result, laments Os Guinness, is that "we are people with a true, sometimes a deep experience of God. But we are no longer a people of truth."[2] In another assessment, *The Scandal of the Evangelical Mind*, church historian Mark Noll begins by saying, "The scandal of the evangelical mind is that there is not much of an evangelical mind. . . . Unlike

2. Os Guinness, *Fit Bodies, Fat Minds* (Grand Rapids: Baker, 1994), 38.

their spiritual ancestors, modern evangelicals have not pursued comprehensive thinking under God or sought a mind shaped to its furthest reaches by Christian perspective."[3]

In other words, theology bores today's Christians, which is another way of saying we are bored with God himself, except as he feeds our consumer needs. The writer of Hebrews points out the price we pay for this. Perpetually infant Christians are unable to distinguish between genuine and ungenuine expressions of the faith, between the sound and the dangerous, between the Spirit of God and the spirit of the age. In recent years, this has been demonstrated by vast hordes of shallow Christians, who chase after one or another of the bizarre movements emphasizing strange experiences or quick riches, but which have no discernible connection with the "teaching of righteousness" that is in Jesus Christ.

THE MARKS OF IMMATURITY

What does an infant believer look like? Hebrews 5:11–14 shows us three marks of milk-drinking Christians, who cannot handle meat. First, they are shallow in their understanding. Does this describe you? One way to answer is to ask what you give your mind to and what you find interesting. In my pastoral work I often find it to be a good diagnostic question to ask for the names of books a person has read in the previous six months. The point is not to promote my own approved reading list, but to see whether the person is fixated on himself, her own wants or search for experiences, or whether he is interested in the character of God, the treasures of the gospel, or the challenges of representing Jesus Christ in the world.

If you say, "So long as I love Jesus, it doesn't matter what else I believe," then you will never grow in your faith, in your character, or in your usefulness to God. Furthermore, there is no subject more worthy, no study more beneficial to us, than the study of God and his saving works. Baby believers know little or nothing of this, instead remaining fixed on their own little problems, their own petty kingdoms, little imagining the great and noble themes of eternity.

3. Mark A. Noll, *The Scandal of the Evangelical Mind* (Grand Rapids: Eerdmans, 1994), 3–4.

The first sign of an infant faith is shallowness, and the second is that such Christians are of little use to others in the things of the faith. "By this time you ought to be teachers," writes the author of Hebrews. In chapter 3 he spoke of the great need for spiritual exhortation, lest some be hardened by sin's deceitfulness. This requires Christians to be aware of spiritual reality, attuned to danger, and ready to employ the resources of the faith.

Many people assume that they can leave all the spiritual instruction to the ordained ministers. But whatever your situation in life, your responsibilities require that you grow in understanding of Christian teaching. A husband, for instance, cannot possibly provide the redeeming encouragement his wife needs and the Bible requires, much less raise his children in the fear and admonition of the Lord, without a mature grasp of biblical teaching. If you are a father—or hope to be one someday—what will you do when your teenagers, and then college-age children come home with questions they learned from unbelieving teachers and friends? You need to start growing now, before it is too late.

What about women? The apostle Paul writes with scorn about "weak women" who are unable to stand in the truth (2 Tim. 3:6–7); he expects older women to be a source of wisdom and instruction for those who are younger, as he describes in Titus 2. Indeed, every Christian is to be able "to make a defense to anyone who asks you for a reason for the hope that is in you," as Peter says in his first epistle (3:15), and the need is greater now than ever.

The third mark of the toothless, infant believer is an inability to discern the sound from the unsound. In contrast, the mature have trained themselves "to distinguish good from evil," an expression that seems to include both teaching and moral choices.

In each of these cases, that of the shallow, the useless, and undiscerning, there is one simple remedy. Apply yourself to the truth, train your mind, getting the ABCs of the faith right, and then advance toward a deep and profound grasp of biblical truth.

The Basics of the Faith

The writer of Hebrews proceeds to put forth an interesting set of subjects that compose, as he says, "the elementary doctrine of Christ," and also "the foundation" for all other matters of the faith (Heb. 6:1).

The early church employed creedal formulations as a means of preparing converts for baptism. These basic summaries were foundational for any profession of faith. It is likely that the list of items in 6:1–2 served that kind of function. We must admit, however, looking at these items, that their meaning is not transparently obvious to us: "Therefore let us leave the elementary doctrine of Christ and go on to maturity, not laying again a foundation of repentance from dead works and of faith toward God, and of instruction about washings, the laying on of hands, the resurrection of the dead, and eternal judgment."

The point is not to abandon these truths, but to establish them as a sure foundation for later building. There seem to be three sets of two items each, all of which comprise the elementary or foundational truths. The first is this couplet: "repentance from dead works and . . . faith toward God." This is straightforward. The movement from unbelief into Christianity begins with awareness of, conviction over, and then repentance from acts that lead to death. Dead works are sinful deeds that stand under God's condemnation (see Rom. 6:19–21), as well as vain religious exercises.

Coupled with repentance is faith in God for forgiveness and salvation. That is the great theme of this whole letter: holding fast to the way of salvation offered by God through faith in Christ. True repentence always leads to saving faith; we turn from our sinful allegiances and to God who offers forgiveness and new life. Put together, this most basic layer of the foundation corresponds to the doctrine of justification.

How important it is to understand this doctrine rightly, apart from which all our understanding must be fatally flawed. Jesus Christ came to fulfill the law and die in our place for the atonement of our sins; believers are declared just through his righteousness received by faith alone. This is the first layer of all Christian teaching. Thomas Watson was right when he wrote: "Justification is the very hinge and pillar of Christianity. An error about justification is dangerous, like a defect in a foundation. Justification by Christ is a spring of the water of life. To have the poison of corrupt doctrine cast into this spring is damnable."[4]

The next pair is a bit more difficult to understand: "instruction about washings, the laying on of hands." We would expect a list of fundamentals

4. Thomas Watson, *A Body of Divinity* (Edinburgh: Banner of Truth, 1958), 226.

181

to include instruction regarding baptism, particularly since most of these catechisms took place in the context of that sacrament. It is also evident that in the early apostolic church, baptism and the laying on of hands were closely related; laying on the hands signified the coming of the Holy Spirit, which was linked with the inception of the Christian life, symbolized by baptism.[5] That seems to be the reason for their coupling here.

There are some difficulties, however, beginning with the fact that the writer of Hebrews does not use the ordinary word for baptism, and also that he writes here in the plural. Instead of the normal word for Christian baptism, *baptisma*, he uses *baptismōn*, which more generally describes washings or ablutions. A survey of the various religious movements in first-century Judaism will find a great variety of teaching on the matter of ceremonial washings. There were those of the Old Testament pertaining to priestly consecration; the Dead Sea Scrolls have revealed great interest in washings among the Essenes at Qumran. There were also the baptisms of repentance like those performed by John the Baptist, over which there was sufficient confusion among Christians for it to be mentioned in Acts 18:25.

Meanwhile, the laying on of hands in the New Testament era was associated with blessing, healing, and especially ordination for office. In general, hands were laid on to signify the coming of the Holy Spirit. Taken together, washings and laying on of hands have to do with our empowerment for the Christian life; that is, they point us to sanctification. We see something similar in Romans 6:2–4, where Paul teaches on baptism as an incentive to the godly life.

The final pair that finishes off this list of Christian basics is "the resurrection of the dead, and eternal judgment." If the first couplet deals with justification, and the second with sanctification, it makes sense that the collection finishes off with a pair that deals with the matter of glorification—that is, the destiny of believers after death. Essential to the Christian hope is the resurrection that awaits us after the grave, the hope of glory. Indeed, all the dead will be raised in the great day of judgment; those who are in Christ will be received with joy while all who reject him are condemned forever in their sins.

5. F. F. Bruce, *Hebrews*, New International Commentary on the New Testament (Grand Rapids: Eerdmans, 1990), 142 n. 27.

This summary of the Christian faith constitutes the minimum creed, the foundation that must be laid if one is to build safely and fruitfully: justification, the act of God's grace by which sinners are declared righteous through the blood of Christ; sanctification, the process by which believers grow in holiness; and finally, glorification, the great hope of all who look to Jesus Christ and the day when we will be transformed in glory and received into the heavenly city for an eternity with God.

SANCTIFIED BY THE TRUTH

The single-minded aim of the writer of Hebrews all through this epistle has been that through faith in Jesus Christ we must persevere until the end. "Therefore let us leave the elementary doctrine of Christ and go on to maturity," he begins chapter 6, and he pledges in verse 3, "And this we will do if God permits." That is his great desire, to lead his readers into a mature understanding of Jesus Christ and his saving work so that their faith may endure to the end.

The writer of Hebrews understood perfectly well what Jesus meant in his great high-priestly prayer: "Sanctify them in the truth; your word is truth" (John 17:17). I wonder, however, if you realize this as well. You may reply, "But what really matters is that I love Jesus; what matters is my heart!" Perhaps, but if the heart is the sanctuary of the soul, the mind is the vestibule of the heart. Truth must enter through the mind. The question is: what will shape what you think and believe, what will control what goes on in your heart? What Paul wrote to the early church is a matter of equal urgency for us: "Do not be conformed to this world, but be transformed by the renewal of your mind, that by testing you may discern what is the will of God, what is good and acceptable and perfect" (Rom. 12:2).

This is an absolute imperative for every Christian who wants to grow, who wants to honor God with his or her life, and who wants to be of use to other believers and to the work of the gospel in this world. John MacArthur writes, "Having the knowledge of God's Word control our minds is the key to righteous living. What controls your thoughts will control your behavior.... Knowledge of God's Word will lead to 'all spiritual wisdom and understanding'" (Col. 1:9).[6]

6. John MacArthur Jr., *Colossians and Philemon* (Chicago: Moody, 1992), 29–30.

The key to perseverance and endurance is not some fleeting emotional experience, not this formula or that program—these are the mark of the immature, tossing back and forth on the passing waves. Not so the wise, or the mature, who do not build on shifting sand but upon the rock that is God's Word. That is what Jesus himself taught: "Everyone then who hears these words of mine and does them will be like a wise man who built his house on the rock. And the rain fell, and the floods came, and the winds blew and beat on that house, but it did not fall, because it had been founded on the rock" (Matt. 7:24–25).

That is where you want to be found, firm and secure upon the rock that is the Word of our Lord. Yes, the winds will roar and the rains will beat against you. But standing and building upon that rock, not as infants living on milk alone but as men and women of the faith nourished by the whole counsel of God that is meat indeed, you will prevail until the end.

19

ONCE ENLIGHTENED

Hebrews 6:4–8

*For it is impossible to restore again to repentance those who have
once been enlightened, who have tasted the heavenly gift, and
have shared in the Holy Spirit, and have tasted the goodness of
the word of God and the powers of the age to come if they then
fall away.* (Heb. 6:4–6a)

*O*ne of America's great commanders in the Second World War,
General George S. Patton, was well known for cultivating
the spirit of the attack in his soldiers. Particularly in the later
months of 1944, the swift advance of his troops stunned the German
defenders and played a large role in the collapse of Adolf Hitler's forces.
Patton's primary directive was that if at all possible one should attack,
for in battle the greatest security is found in advancing against
the enemy.

The writer of the Book of Hebrews would have appreciated Patton's spirit
because this was the very attitude he wanted to instill in his readers. All
through this letter he has been advocating an advance in the Christian life.
Patton once expressed as his reason for always pressing the attack, "I don't

like paying for the same real estate twice." The writer of Hebrews wants us to advance because it is the only way to be sure of salvation and endure to the end.

This has been the point of the writer's third major exhortation, beginning at verse 11 of chapter 5. The author chides his readers for their lack of diligence and progress. "By this time you ought to be teachers" (Heb. 5:12), he said, yet they had barely progressed beyond spiritual infancy. Now, starting at Hebrews 6:4, he goes on to give the most urgent reason for their growth in the faith, namely, the real and terrible danger of apostasy: "We desire each one of you to show the same earnestness to have the full assurance of hope until the end" (Heb. 6:11). Andrew Murray grasps his line of reasoning clearly when he writes:

> The argument is one of unspeakable solemnity. . . . In commerce, in study, in war, it is so often said: there is no safety but in advance. To stand still is to go back. To cease effort is to lose ground. To slacken the pace, before the goal is reached, is to lose the race. . . . The whole point of the argument from the case of those who fall away is—*Let us press on to perfection.*[1]

This passage is one of the most sober in all of Scripture, as well as one of the most fiercely contested, and we need to take careful stock of what it says. There are two main issues: first, who or what kind of person is described as falling away; and second, why the situation of apostasy is so very terrible. We will conclude by looking at some obvious implications of this teaching.

ONCE ENLIGHTENED

This passage presents one basic assertion: "For it is impossible to restore again to repentance those who have once been enlightened, who have tasted the heavenly gift, and have shared in the Holy Spirit, and have tasted the goodness of the word of God and the powers of the age to come, if they then fall away" (Heb. 6:4–6a).

One of the problems in dealing with this text is deciding just who or what is being described. There are three main answers, each of which depends

---

1. Andrew Murray, *The Holiest of All: An Exposition of the Epistle to the Hebrews* (Grand Rapids: Revell, 1993), 207.

upon the interpretation of what these descriptions portray. But before addressing these, we can make two important observations. The first is that the writer of Hebrews is not describing his readers themselves. I say this because he shifts here from his consistent use of the first and second persons to the third person. In both the passages before and after these verses, he speaks of "us" and "you." But here he shifts to the third person: now it is "those who have been enlightened." This tells us that he is not speaking directly of his readers' situation, an observation that is confirmed by verse 9: "In your case, beloved, we feel sure of better things."

Second, we should nevertheless avoid describing this as a hypothetical situation. A number of translations give this impression by using the term "if." This does not appear in the Greek text, which is best rendered not by the phrase "if they fall away," but "those who have fallen away." This situation of apostasy is very real, a very terrible possibility that must be earnestly avoided. It is something that does happen and will happen to real people. Indeed, it may be that there are particular people in view here who have fallen away and can no longer be restored.

We are now in a position to address the three main views regarding the identity of the people who fall away. The first is that these descriptions depict real salvation, that is, individuals who have been converted and have possessed a true and saving faith in Christ. The reason for this view is evident when we see just how strong the statements are. These people "have once been enlightened." This seems to indicate conversion, just as the rest of the terms seem to construct a thorough picture of regenerate and believing persons. They are people who have "tasted the heavenly gift . . . shared in the Holy Spirit . . . tasted the goodness of the word of God and the powers of the age to come." John Wesley, the great Methodist leader, made much of these verses, writing, "Must not every unprejudiced person see, the expressions here used are so strong and clear, that they cannot, without gross and palpable wrestling, be understood of any but true believers?"[2] People who hold this interpretation cite these verses as a key proof against the assurance of salvation or eternal security. Wesley was typical of many others when he wrote: "On this authority, I believe a

2. John Wesley, "Predestination Calmly Considered," from *The Complete Works of John Wesley*, 14 vols. (Peabody, Mass.: Hendrickson, 1984), 10:248.

saint may fall away; that one who is holy or righteous in the judgment of God himself may nevertheless so fall from God as to perish everlastingly."[3]

This is a compelling argument, but it is one that has very serious problems. The first is that this interpretation directly contradicts the many passages that do teach the eternal security of those who are born again and possess genuine saving faith. A key principle of biblical interpretation is that since God is the ultimate author of all the Bible, and since God is infallible and true, there can be no basic inconsistency in Scripture. This means that when faced with difficult passages, we must interpret them in light of clearer ones. That is important here because Wesley's view flatly denies statements like the one Jesus made in John 10:28–29: "I give them eternal life, and they will never perish, and no one will snatch them out of my hand. My Father, who has given them to me, is greater than all, and no one is able to snatch them out of the Father's hand." There are many other statements to this effect, like those in John 6:36–40, Romans 8:38–39, and Philippians 1:6, which tells us that "he who began a good work in you will bring it to completion at the day of Jesus Christ."

The second reason why Wesley's view cannot be accurate comes from this very chapter of Hebrews. We need to interpret any given passage not only in light of the whole teaching of Scripture, but also in context with what the particular writer is saying. In this case, the writer concludes this chapter with a bold statement of assurance for those who have truly received the gospel. Perhaps mindful of the false conclusion some may draw, in verse 17 he writes of "the unchangeable character of [God's] purpose" with regard to "the heirs of the promise." The point is that what stands behind all human activity is God's sovereign ordination and promise. The author concludes by writing of God's covenant promise to Abraham: "God desired to show [that] . . . we who have fled for refuge might have strong encouragement to hold fast to the hope set before us. We have this as a sure and steadfast anchor of the soul" (Heb. 6:17–19). These are hardly the words of someone who wants to convey a fundamental insecurity to those who have trusted in Christ! The original readers of Hebrews, on the basis of this conclusion of chapter 6, could well recite Paul's great statement of his own

---

3. John Wesley, "The Perseverance of the Saints," from *The Complete Works of John Wesley*, 10:340.

assurance: "For I know whom I have believed, and I am convinced that he is able to guard until that Day what has been entrusted to me" (2 Tim. 1:12).

The second major view of our text is that its language describes participation in the sacramental life of the church. According to this view, "once enlightened" refers to baptism. There is evidence that this terminology was used as early as the second century A.D. "Tasting the heavenly gift" speaks of the Lord's Supper, while "sharing in the Holy Spirit" speaks of the laying on of hands. "Tasting the goodness of the word of God" would correspond to preaching in the church, while "the powers of the age to come" would indicate the signs and wonders that accompanied the original preaching of the gospel, and which the writer of Hebrews already mentioned in chapter 2. This is a compelling picture, and it is one that could apply to those who never truly come to saving faith in Christ, but enjoy these extraordinary privileges through their affiliation with the church.

I am not hostile to this interpretation and think the language surely suggests contact with the means of grace found in the church. But I think it far more likely that these word pictures make direct reference not to the sacraments but to the experience of God's people in the exodus. This is the third major view and the one that best handles the text.

The Book of Hebrews contains five major exhortations, of which this is part of the third. Each of the other four makes explicit reference to an Old Testament situation. The lengthy exhortation in chapters 3 and 4 draws out the exodus as a basic counter-model for the Christian life, and it is extremely likely that this remains on the writer's mind in chapter 6.

This argument was lucidly made in an article in the *Westminster Theological Journal* by Dave Mathewson.[4] Mathewson reminds us that this epistle was written to show that the old covenant both pointed to and was fulfilled by the coming of Jesus Christ. That, along with the readers' familiarity with the Old Testament, is why the writer consistently draws from Old Testament texts and situations to make points about Christianity. This is his uniform method, and there is no reason to think he has departed from it in this passage which, like the others, derives its imagery from the life of Israel and looks back on the exodus as the general backdrop.

---

4. Dave Mathewson, "Reading Hebrews 6:4–6 in Light of the Old Testament," *Westminster Theological Journal* 61, 2 (Fall 1999): 209–26.

With this in mind, we can see that the author offers terminology his original Hebrew-Christian readers would connect with the exodus symbolism. Under this view, "once enlightened" probably refers to the pillar of light that guided the twelve tribes through the desert. The writer of Hebrews does not mean that these Christians literally saw the cloud of fire, but rather they experienced what it signified. He gets at the same idea later in the epistle by writing that they have received "the knowledge of the truth" (10:26) to guide them in this life. The same sort of connection can easily be made with each item in the list, such as the manna Israel ate in the desert, the Word of God that came through Moses, and the astonishing works of power that won Israel's deliverance from Egypt. According to Geerhardus Vos, this is consistent with the writer's overall bias toward "the *phenomenal* aspect of religion," a point Vos considers vital to the proper understanding of Hebrews 6:4–6. Vos explains that the view of religion in the Book of Hebrews "lies almost entirely in the sphere of consciousness. This may be contrasted with Paul's conception, which represents much of religion as lying *beneath* consciousness."[5]

What is the point of all this? As we saw back in chapters 3 and 4, the great majority of those who left Egypt with Moses did not enter the Promised Land but rebelled against the Lord, providing as great and terrible a portrait of apostasy as appears in all of Scripture. The warning, therefore, is that, like those who left Egypt as part of Israel, we may have a very real experience of the phenomena of God's saving power through our participation in the church. By virtue of our affiliation with the people of God, by being in their midst, we can have the very great privileges described in our text and yet not actually enter into salvation. We will be enlightened with knowledge, we will encounter and perhaps benefit from real spiritual power, and we may be influenced and blessed in many ways. That was the very situation with those who left Egypt in the exodus, but who fell away under hardship into rebellion and were judged by God so that they died in the desert. As we saw earlier in our studies, this is as stark a portrait of eternal despair as appears in all the Scripture. How could this happen? It can happen to us if our hearts are hard toward God, despite our great privileges.

5. Geerhardus Vos, *The Teaching of the Epistle to the Hebrews* (Phillipsburg, N.J.: P&R, 1956), 28.

Whether we take this description as pointing to the sacraments and means of grace in the church or to Israel in the desert (and the two are so closely related that they may both be in view), the point is the same. This passage describes professors of faith who are within the church community—church members, as we would say today—who experience the benefits of God's blessing in the church without ever personally committing themselves to faith in Christ. They are like those people Jesus spoke about in the Sermon on the Mount:

> Not everyone who says to me, "Lord, Lord," will enter the kingdom of heaven, but the one who does the will of my Father who is in heaven. On that day many will say to me, "Lord, Lord, did we not prophesy in your name, and cast out demons in your name, and do many mighty works in your name?" And then will I declare to them, "I never knew you; depart from me, you workers of lawlessness." (Matt. 7:21–23)

THE TERRIBLE REALITY OF APOSTASY

This is who these people are, those who have a personal but nonetheless secondary or indirect experience of Christianity. They may serve, they may preach, they may handle the powers of the age to come, but they are not really Christ's own. About such people the following assertion is made: "It is impossible to restore [them] . . . if they then fall away" (Heb. 6:4, 6).

These are sober words indeed. The statement "it is impossible" is unavoidable; indeed, as the first word in this whole passage it is greatly emphasized. This means that people in the church can "fall away" by repudiating Christ, and that "it is impossible to restore [them] again to repentance" (Heb. 6:4). Those who have come to a true knowledge of the gospel, who have experienced the phenomena of salvation by means of their participation in the church, but who ultimately turn their back on Jesus Christ, cannot afterward be restored to repentance. That is the unavoidable statement of this passage.

How do people "fall away"? They fall away by doing what the Israelites did in the desert: by removing their trust in the Lord, repudiating his authority and the salvation he offers, and denying him worship. The verb here is in the aorist tense, which in the Greek normally signifies a completed past

191

action. So we have a decisive break that happened and is now accomplished. In the case of these Hebrew Christians, it is likely that apostasy would mean a return to Judaism and therefore a denial of the saving significance of Christ's life and death, an action that was ominous in its terrible finality.

We see why it is impossible to restore such a person: "They are crucifying once again the Son of God to their own harm and holding him up to contempt" (Heb. 6:6). To reject Christ after having come to knowledge of the gospel is to say, as the Pharisees did, that he should be put away, that he is guilty as charged, a threat and enemy worthy of death. To repudiate Christ is, in effect, to take up hammer and nails and beat them into his hands and feet, to make common cause with those who crucified him, to mock him like the soldiers who laughed and sneered, "He saved others; he cannot save himself" (Mark 15:31).

Interestingly, the writer here shifts to the present tense ("are crucifying"); this represents a present and persistent state of affairs. What happened in the past has led to a present state of the heart analogous to the attitude of those who crucified Jesus in the first place, and that present state makes a future return impossible.

It is tempting to conclude that what is being said here is that people who are rejecting Christ cannot be saved because they are not repenting. But this is a point so obvious that it hardly bears emphasis. Instead, the point is that the people described here are not able to repent and return to faith in Jesus unto salvation because of the hardening effect of their apostasy.

We always want to leave room for the sovereign power of God, remembering Jesus' words to his disciples: "With man this is impossible, but with God all things are possible" (Matt. 19:26). In fact, that is a vital distinction for understanding this text. Again, a translation issue clears things up a bit. The Greek text does not say, "It is impossible for those who . . . fall away, to be brought back to repentance," as the New International Version reads. Rather, as the English Standard Version more accurately puts it, "It is impossible to restore again . . . [those who] fall away." *We* are not able to restore them, but that doesn't mean that *God* cannot. Indeed, as long as the gospel goes forth, we should never despair of its power to save anyone. The point here is not to deny apostasy as a real and terrible situation, or to soften the writer's statement that true apostates are in a dreadful spiritual state. Rather, the point is that we should never stop reaching out to others with the gospel, even if they seem to have fallen away in the manner described by this passage.

Certainly, it is dire to think of a professing Christian repudiating the Lord. But we have the example of Peter as one who did deny Jesus and yet came back to faith and was made the leading apostle. Set against him is the example of Judas Iscariot, who after long years in Jesus' company—having presumably evangelized others and performed miracles in his name (see Luke 10, for instance)—came to the decisive moment of apostasy that resulted in his great betrayal. At that point Judas was lost, and despite his evident mourning over what he had done, there was nothing left but death and eternal damnation.

What is the difference between Peter and Judas? One failed in his fidelity to Christ, as Christians will and often do, while the other decisively repudiated him. One did not live up to the cross, while the other despised it. This seems to be the distinction Paul had in mind in 2 Timothy 2, where he wrote: "If we deny him, he also will deny us; if we are faithless, he remains faithful—for he cannot deny himself" (vv. 12–13). It may be hard to discern the difference between these two, but the difference is a very great one indeed.

There is one way to positively identify those who belong to Christ, but it requires time. We see this in Hebrews 6:7–8, which provides an illustration that makes the matter much clearer: "For land that has drunk the rain that often falls on it, and produces a crop useful to those for whose sake it is cultivated, receives a blessing from God. But if it bears thorns and thistles, it is worthless and near to being cursed, and its end is to be burned."

What matters is not whether or not rain falls upon the ground, for God sends rain on the good and the evil (Matt. 5:45), just as he does his saving Word. It is the presence of fruit that ultimately tells the tale. Similarly, Jesus said, "A healthy tree cannot bear bad fruit, nor can a diseased tree bear good fruit. Every tree that does not bear good fruit is cut down and thrown into the fire. Thus you will recognize them by their fruits" (Matt. 7:18–20).

Truly regenerate, genuine believers can do terrible things, as Peter showed when he betrayed our Lord three times. The record of the church has revealed this over and over again. But a good tree—that is, one that is truly connected to Christ and has the Holy Spirit at work within—will necessarily go on to bear good fruit. It cannot do otherwise. The bad tree simply lacks the power to bear lasting fruit unto God, however well watered it may be, however real its second-hand experience of salvation by virtue of affiliation with the church. Particularly under trial or hardship, it produces only thorns and thistles, and thus it is, as we read here, "worthless and near to being cursed, and its end is to be burned" (Heb. 6:8).

IMPLICATIONS OF THIS TEACHING

Vital implications flow from this text. The first has to do with the nature of true and saving faith in Jesus Christ. Mere knowledge of the gospel is never enough. Understanding and even intellectually affirming Christian teaching is insufficient for salvation. As important as doctrine is, as important as knowledge of Scripture is, it is personal knowledge of and trust in Christ that alone constitute saving faith.

What does that say about your faith? Let me warn you that the church is no place for playing games, much less for indecision and loitering. When you hear the gospel and understand what is taught, you incur an obligation to God to press on to saving faith. Hebrews shows that it is very dangerous to toy with such knowledge; by delaying you run the risk of a terrible fate. Furthermore, if you are not willing to turn to Christ for salvation today, what makes you think it will be any different tomorrow? It will be harder to embrace Christ later if you delay now. Therefore, as Paul wrote, "Now is the favorable time; behold, now is the day of salvation" (2 Cor. 6:2).

A second implication is that the test of our faith is the fruit that we bear. Surely that is how this passage fits into the context of the overall letter. The author has been exhorting his readers to press on to maturity, and now he warns them that a failure to do so calls into question the reality of their conversion. How do we know someone is truly converted? We know not merely because he has made a profession of faith but because the power of the gospel bears fruit under trial.

We always have to be careful here, and admit our own inability to read the hearts of men and women. Nevertheless, this is an implication we have to take seriously. If you are content with merely drinking in the rain, but not concerned to honor God in your life, if you are unable or unwilling to hold fast to God and praise his name in times of trouble, then that is a very alarming sign that ought to provoke fundamental reflection regarding the state of your soul.

194

One class of people described by the statements in verses 4–5, people who have knowledge and an experience of spiritual reality, is children who grow up in the church. How easy it is for them to reproduce verses and slogans they have been hearing all their lives, either to keep their parents happy or to merit their praise. But we must look for fruit in their lives, fruit issuing forth from their profession of faith. We must challenge them to give evidence of a heart commitment, to grow and advance in the faith, which is their only safety. I have noticed that if an adult is a truly vile and blasphemous hater of Christ and Christianity, it is often someone who was raised in the church and whose rock-hard heart is described by this passage. Let us therefore pray diligently for our children and set an example not of spiritual hypocrisy but of real and attractive faith.

Our passage ought furthermore to cause us to reflect upon what passes for evangelism in our time, and especially upon revivalism. The goal, it often seems, is simply to place people's names on a list, to increase the size of the congregation in the name of eternal security, to pat ourselves on the back and move on to the next "convert." When such people later repudiate Christ, whom they have never really known, they are left far worse off than they were before. Surely this passage tells us that evangelism and discipleship can never be separated, just as conversion is manifested and proved only by the bearing of spiritual fruit.

CAN I BE SURE?

This leads to a final consideration: what does this passage say about the idea of eternal security and assurance of salvation? The first answer is that it ought to make our statements more careful and sober. The picture here is a somber one. It depicts professing believers, probably church members, who are not really saved but fall away into a hopeless state. Therefore, as Andrew Murray puts it, "My assurance of salvation is not something I can carry with me as a railway ticket or a bank note, to be used, as occasion calls. . . . My assurance of salvation is alone to be found in the living fellowship with the living Jesus in love and obedience."[6]

6. Murray, *Holiest of All*, 209.

It is for this reason that Reformed theology has traditionally and wisely shunned use of the term "eternal security," but has instead emphasized the "perseverance of the saints," which is the emphasis of the writer of Hebrews. Iain Murray notes the distinction by telling of a Calvinist who was surprised to find one of Wesley's preachers in agreement with this teaching. The Calvinist stated that he did not think they taught the perseverance of the saints. The Wesleyan replied, "O Sir, you have been misinformed; it is the perseverance of *sinners* we doubt."[7] He was right—it is the saints who persevere, those who trust and walk with God are safe and secure.

Where, then, do you look for assurance? You can and should look to the unchanging character of God and the certainty of his promises. You can and should look to the once-for-all work of Jesus Christ which is sufficient for all your need. Do not look to yourself, to the strength of your faith, to the protection of various spiritual disciplines or methodologies, however useful they may be. It is not yourself or any regimen that depends on human strength that assures your salvation, but God, who said, "'I will never leave you nor forsake you.' So we can confidently say, 'The Lord is my helper; I will not fear.'" That is the writer's own conclusion in 13:5–6. In assurance, as in all else, "Salvation belongs to the LORD" (Jonah 2:9).

Assurance is something that comes from the knowledge of God and of his promises, and is thus the result of the exercise of faith. The same is true of security; it is through faith alone that we are ever secure. Security comes from trusting in Jesus Christ, from persevering to the end in the power of the Lord. Perhaps the best statement of this is found in Philippians 3:12, where Paul writes, "I press on to take hold of that for which Christ Jesus took hold of me" (NIV).

Therefore, like General Patton's soldiers, do not stand still but take up the offensive. Press onward in faith, which is the way of perseverance and the route to hope and joy in the Lord. If you stumble or fall, call out to the Lord who is rich in mercy; he will lift you up. This is the best way to give thanks to God for his great gift of salvation, the way to honor him before the eyes of this world and to make your life worthwhile as you bear fruit—real fruit that will last forever and be a blessing to many.

---

7. Iain Murray, *Wesley and Men Who Followed* (Carlisle, Pa.: Banner of Truth, 2003), 66.

20

DILIGENT TO THE END

Hebrews 6:9–12

And we desire each one of you to show the same earnestness to have the full assurance of hope until the end, so that you may not be sluggish, but imitators of those who through faith and patience inherit the promises. (Heb. 6:11–12)

*I*t is usually not difficult to get Christians to fear for their salvation. If a preacher says, as the New Testament does, that the ungodly shall not inherit the kingdom of heaven, he can be sure that many of his hearers will spend sleepless nights. If he suggests that some in the church may be false believers, as Jesus and the writer of Hebrews insist there are, then he can be sure to cause quite a disturbance in the pews.

There is a reason for this. Although true believers can be sure of their salvation, they are nonetheless in real and great danger. We live in a world that is perilous to faith in Christ. The writer of Hebrews has described it as a harbor where the current pulls hard out to sea, and if we are not anchored firmly we can be dragged away (2:1). Believers also have to contend with opposition from strong and crafty spiritual powers. The apostle Peter writes, "Be sober-minded; be watchful. Your adversary the devil prowls around like a roaring lion, seeking someone to devour" (1 Peter 5:8). In addition to dangers around us, believers gaze inward and invariably find much that is opposed to God. Our faith seems weak and our love for the world strong. Therefore, while we know that true believers are kept safe by God's power (1 Peter 1:5), the Christian life takes place within the context of grave danger. While the New Testament speaks of assurance, this is why it never allows for sloth or complacency.

Assurance of salvation is something we can have and should strive for, but it comes only through the active exercise of faith in Christ. J. C. Ryle was right when he said, "I bless God that our salvation in no wise depends on our own works. . . . But I never would have any believer for a moment forget that our *sense of salvation* depends much on the manner of our living."[1] That being the case, it is axiomatic that the only way Christians can have joy in our salvation and full assurance of hope is through practical godliness that flows from our relationship with Christ.

This issue of confidence in salvation is on the mind of the writer of Hebrews. He has issued very severe warnings, and now he comforts his readers with grounds for their assurance: "Though we speak in this way, yet in your case, beloved," and here he is referring to his prior words regarding the danger of apostasy, "we feel sure of better things—things that belong to salvation" (Heb. 6:9). This is the writer's confidence regarding their salvation, which is followed by his fervent longing for them to press on to the full assurance of faith.

CONFIDENT OF BETTER THINGS

It is the duty of every pastor to know the spiritual condition of his congregation. The writer of Hebrews has repeatedly demonstrated a close understanding of his flock. He knows that they are "dull of hearing," that though they have been in the faith long enough to be teachers, they are still spiritual children, and that as a result they have a hard time telling good from evil (Heb. 5:11–12). So concerned is this pastor for the state of his flock that he warns them of the real danger of falling away altogether if they are slothful about their faith in Christ (6:4–6).

1. J. C. Ryle, *Holiness* (Darlington, U.K.: Evangelical Press, 1979), 115–16.

This pastor also knows that his words will shake up his congregation, perhaps a little too well. So now he seeks to calm their fears as well as to assure them of his affection. He addresses them here as "beloved," which shows the tenderness of his pastoral devotion to them. Furthermore, despite the warnings, he tells them he is not without encouragement for their spiritual condition; he is at least persuaded that theirs is a genuine and not a spurious faith. In verses 9 and 10 he gives two reasons for his confidence: first, what he believes about them, and second, what he knows about God.

His first sign of confidence is that he has observed in his congregation the things that accompany salvation. He describes qualities that are not the cause of salvation, but that accompany it. Where there is salvation, these characteristics will invariably be found. "God is not so unjust as to overlook your work and the love that you showed for his sake in serving the saints, as you still do" (Heb. 6:10).

First he mentions their work. This points back to the contrast he drew between the field that produces a bad crop and that which produces a good and useful crop (Heb. 6:7–8). He is able to say that he sees real spiritual fruit in the lives of his readers. This is something that accompanies salvation, and so it encourages him about their faith.

This matter of bearing fruit is a serious one. Are your faith in Jesus Christ and your relationship with him exerting an influence upon your character, so that you find yourself thinking and responding in a way that is less worldly and more godly? If not, then you should be concerned and should turn to God for grace.

Paul writes, "The fruit of the Spirit is love, joy, peace, patience, kindness, goodness, faithfulness, gentleness, self-control" (Gal. 5:22). So do you find hatred giving way to love and peace? Is envy being conquered by joy, insatiable craving by gentleness and self-control? These are things we can discern about our own lives and which gauge our spiritual condition. Certainly the fruit of the Spirit includes things we should earnestly pray for and seek to cultivate as God works in us through his Holy Spirit.

Spiritual fruit is important, but it seems that the writer of Hebrews especially had in mind particular works his readers had demonstrated in times past and would demonstrate again in the future. He chronicles these works in chapter 10:

But recall the former days when, after you were enlightened, you endured a hard struggle with sufferings, sometimes being publicly exposed to reproach and affliction, and sometimes being partners with those so treated. For you had compassion on those in prison, and you joyfully accepted the plundering of your property, since you knew that you yourselves had a better possession and an abiding one. (Heb. 10:32–34)

This good crop of works points to real and saving faith; such works are not the cause of salvation but they surely accompany it. In particular, the writer of Hebrews focuses on the ministry his readers have shown to one another in the church as a good sign of real spiritual life. He writes of "the love that you showed for his sake in serving the saints, as you still do" (Heb. 6:10).

How do you show your love to God? You show it by coming to church to worship him. You show it by making time in your day to read Scripture and pray, and by taking a stand for him in the circumstances of your life. But, most tangibly, Christians show their love for God by their loving ministry to other Christians. The apostle John put it this way: "We love because he first loved us. If anyone says, 'I love God,' and hates his brother, he is a liar; for he who does not love his brother whom he has seen cannot love God whom he has not seen. And this commandment we have from him: whoever loves God must also love his brother" (1 John 4:19–21).

This is why the writer of Hebrews is excited to see that his people are busy helping one another. The Greek word here is *diakoneō*, from which we derive the word "deacon." Diaconal ministries are those that address the physical or temporal needs of the congregation and community, such as housing, financial assistance, and visitation of the sick. This is an important part of life in the church and a vital way in which we show our love to Christ. We remember that Jesus foretold that on the day of judgment he will say to his own:

"Come, you who are blessed by my Father, inherit the kingdom prepared for you from the foundation of the world. For I was hungry and you gave me food, I was thirsty and you gave me drink, I was a stranger and you welcomed me, I was naked and you clothed me, I was sick and you visited me, I was in prison and you came to me." Then the righteous will answer him, saying, "Lord, when did we see you hungry and feed you, or thirsty and give you drink? And when did we see you a stranger and welcome you, or naked and clothe you? And when did we see you sick or in prison and visit you?" And the King will answer them, "Truly, I say to you, as you did it to one of the least of these my brothers, you did it to me." (Matt. 25:34–40)

It is for this reason that practical love demonstrated in a congregation is a good sign of its spirituality. If we have come to know God and his love for us, if we have responded with gratitude and love toward him, that love will find expression as we sacrificially give of ourselves for the sake of our fellow Christians.

All of this together forms the first reason why the writer of Hebrews has confidence about the salvation of his readers. He sees in them things that accompany salvation and draws the conclusion that there must be real spiritual life. Where there is smoke, we say, there is fire; so also, where there is fruit there must be life.

God Is Not Unjust

The second basis of the writer's confidence has to do with God himself: "God is not so unjust as to overlook your work and the love that you showed for his sake in serving the saints, as you still do" (Heb. 6:10).

Some people read this and erroneously conclude that it teaches some kind of works-righteousness. Roman Catholic apologists cite these words to support the doctrine of the meritorious character of good works unto justification. We know from many other passages, however, that such a view is alien to the Bible. Paul says emphatically in Ephesians 2, "By grace you have been saved through faith. And this is not your own doing; it is the gift of God, not a result of works, so that no one may boast" (vv. 8–9). John Calvin sums up how we should approach Hebrews 6:10 by noting: "The apostle is not referring expressly here to the cause of our salvation, and therefore no conclusion should be drawn from this passage about the merits of works. . . . It is clear everywhere in Scripture that there is no other fount of salvation but the free mercy of God."[2] The point here would therefore seem to be similar to that of the apostle Paul when he wrote: "He who began a good work in you will bring it to completion at the day of Jesus Christ" (Phil. 1:6). Since this work in you is God's work, he will surely bring it to completion.

2. John Calvin, *New Testament Commentaries*, 12 vols. (Grand Rapids: Eerdmans, 1994), 12:79.

There is probably something else at work here, too. Christians are often tempted to think that God disregards their condition, and takes no notice of their perseverance and works of faith. Like the Israelites, we often murmur in our hearts, "My way is hidden from the LORD, and my right is disregarded by my God" (Isa. 40:27).

The point of Hebrews 6:10 is that God does regard our condition and treasures every petition of prayer, every deed of love, and every act of fidelity. With regard to the idea of rewards, the Scriptures teach that God will reward us for what we do in this life. Having been saved by grace alone, apart from works, we are now called to works. God, like any loving father, will reward the works we do for him. A. W. Pink sums up the matter: "What God rewards is only what He Himself has wrought in us: it is the Father's recognition of the Spirit's fruit. . . . It may look now as though God places little value on sincere obedience to Him, that in this world the man who lives for self gains more than he who lives for Christ; yet, in a soon-coming day it shall appear far otherwise."[3]

What a wonderful contrast this presents. On the one hand, the Scripture assures us that in Christ God forgets our every sin. Psalm 103 tells us: "As far as the east is from the west, so far does he remove our transgressions from us" (v. 12). In chapter 8, the writer of Hebrews will remind us of God's great promise in forming the new covenant in Christ: "For I will be merciful toward their iniquities, and I will remember their sins no more" (v. 12). That is marvelous enough, but consider what is said to us here in Hebrews 6, that though God forgets our every sin, he remembers every act of love we ever express to him. What a marvelous grace this is, and what great love the God of heaven has revealed for us. There is no greater incentive for us to turn our hearts from the world and its pleasures and give them to him who loves us so.

A PASTOR'S DESIRE

That is the confidence this pastor has for the salvation of his flock, both the evidence of those things that accompany salvation and the faithfulness of God to all who are his own. This leads the writer to open his own heart

---

3. A. W. Pink, *An Exposition of Hebrews* (Grand Rapids: Baker, 1954), 327.

to express his fervent wish and desire: "We desire each one of you to show the same earnestness to have the full assurance of hope until the end, so that you may not be sluggish, but imitators of those who through faith and patience inherit the promises" (Heb. 6:11–12).

First, the author wants his readers to press onward in the Christian life, which is the duty of the Christian and the only way of salvation. As we noted in our last study, security in salvation comes only through perseverance in the faith, which is itself the result of God's preserving grace.

But there is something more that the writer of Hebrews has in mind. Yes, he worries for his readers' salvation and urges them to make their profession of faith sure; yet he also entrusts them into the hands of God. That being the case, he turns his thoughts to their present state. He wants them each to show diligence in the faith so that, literally, their "hope might be filled up" (Heb. 6:11). The New International Version puts it, "to make your hope sure," and the English Standard Version has "to have the full assurance of hope." But the verb here is to "fill up," so the meaning is that he wants them to have and know the fullness of the hope that ought to be theirs through faith.

This is every true pastor's fervent desire for his flock, that his people would not press forward grudgingly, but would know the full assurance of their salvation, and therefore the joy and the peace that are provided for them in Christ. I am reminded here of Paul's pastoral prayer for the Ephesians, where he prayed that they "may know what is the hope to which he has called you, what are the riches of his glorious inheritance in the saints, and what is the immeasurable greatness of his power toward us who believe" (Eph. 1:18–19). This is what diligence in the faith provides: an increasing awareness and possession of the riches that are ours in Jesus Christ, with ever-increasing joy in the Lord.

A WELL-WORN PATH TO GLORY

What, then, is the plan for this diligence? We see it in verse 12, which argues that we must not become lazy or swoon into a dull or sluggish faith. Instead, "[Be] imitators of those who through faith and patience inherit the promises."

By imitation, the writer certainly does not mean that we simply go through the motions like robots, but that we look to the examples in the faith that

203

have walked before us. His point is that we should learn what faith and patience are all about through the lives of other Christians. The writer of Hebrews plants here an idea that will blossom into full life in chapter 11, where we have the hall of the heroes of the faith. But, starting in Hebrews 6:13, he gives us a foretaste by means of the example of Abraham.

Abraham is one who waited for the fulfillment of God's promise, in his case the promise of a son. When Abraham grew impatient and stopped trusting God, he acted foolishly. The great example is the child he fathered through his wife's maidservant Hagar, which stands as a living reminder of the folly of impatience and unbelief. Ultimately Abraham trusted God's promise, and his wife, though elderly and barren, gave birth not to just any son but to a son who would carry the blessing of God into the future. We are to reflect upon and profit from such examples in Scripture, imitating what is of faith and shunning the path of unbelief. Abraham shows us that however foolish it may seem to the flesh, we are never mistaken in placing our patient trust in the promises of God.

It is for this reason that we need to reflect on what we read in the stories of the Bible. What do they say about our own situation, about the blessings that come through long-suffering and patient reliance on the Lord? Let me add that this is why reading Christian biography is always profitable. In chapter 13 the writer of Hebrews comments that "Jesus Christ is the same yesterday and today and forever" (v. 8). This is not simply a statement about the ontological being of Christ, but also an affirmation that faith in him is the same from one generation to the next. Therefore, when we read about Christ's sufficiency in the life of an earlier Christian, or when we hear about how Christ gave someone power to overcome temptation or to persevere through great trial, we can know that he will be the same toward us. Yes, circumstances vary, and needs are somewhat different, but the living Savior never changes. If he has delivered others, he will deliver us, and for the same reason—because of his overflowing love and for the honor of his holy name. He is the same yesterday and today and forever. We can learn to follow him, to rely on him, and to find grace in him from the examples of others who walked before us.

Because of this, what wonderful communion we have with all the saints in Jesus Christ. We each are like a mountain climber who ascends a great peak, gazes out upon the glorious vista, and marvels at the glories before him and the difficulties required to arrive at the place. But he looks down at the rock before him and discovers the name of a previous climber carved into the rock. Even more, he recognizes the name of his father or a beloved mentor, and he realizes that he stands at the same spot where the one who inspired him received his own inspiration.

What a glorious thing it is to realize that we are not the first to take on the challenge of the godly life. What wonderful communion we have with other saints to realize that we share with them our deepest spiritual longings as well as our trials and satisfactions.

If you have long been a student of the Bible, then you know the fellowship you have with its heroes. You find yourself struggling to leave behind the pleasures and treasures of this sinful world and then as a result encounter the reproach of God's people. Then you realize that this is just what Moses endured, and you enter into fellowship with him. You engage in lonely service, unnoticed by those around you, and you recall young David's experience tending his father Jesse's flocks in the fields. You find yourself surrounded by a pagan culture, struggling to be useful in the world while not becoming of it, and you think of Daniel. You read his account in the Bible, and your heart draws close to him with thanks for the example that he set. You come to a trial of some sort; perhaps it is a thorn in the flesh. You cry out to God time and again, and he tells you, "My grace is sufficient for you, for my power is made perfect in weakness." Then you realize that you are sharing the very experience of the apostle Paul in 2 Corinthians 12. Or perhaps while being persecuted by an unjust authority, you find grace to stand fast, and your mind turns to the fourth chapter of Acts where Peter and John rejoiced to have been "counted worthy to suffer dishonor for the name" (Acts 5:41). Someday we will see them, and we will have much to talk about, all the saints in the Lord who have fought this good fight of the faith! But even now, on the peaks and in the valleys of our lives as believers, we see evidence of their prior passing, and we are encouraged to remember that their faith and patience have earned them a share in all that God has promised.

If that is true of the merely human figures of the Bible, how much more true is it of our Lord Jesus Christ who, although God, entered into our very struggle so as to lead us through this barren world to a paradise with him in heaven. Hebrews 4:15 tells us that Jesus came into this world in part because he wanted to gain sympathy for us in our weakness. He wanted to know us intimately, to experience for himself the pains and trials of human life. Therefore, in all our trials and sorrows, our chief aspiration should be to have fellowship with him, to draw near to his heart, to know him through obedience, following the example that he set. This was what the apostle Paul set down as his own chief ambition: "I [want to] know him and the power of his resurrection, and [to] share his sufferings, becoming like him in his death, that by any means possible I may attain the resurrection from the dead" (Phil. 3:10–11).

What Paul had realized—and this changed everything in his life—is that in every valley and on every peak he traveled he saw marks of Jesus' prior passage. It was a path Jesus walked so that he could leave a trail for us, so that he could open the once-barred way to heaven, and so that he could encourage us with strength along the way. "Jesus was here" is etched into the rock of every trial, tribulation, and sorrow we ever can know. So, Paul reasoned, if Jesus wanted to love me and know me like that, then I want to love him and know him in his sorrows as well, because I see that the path that leads to the cross takes me to the light of an open tomb, the dawn of a new creation in the glory of Christ.

"[Be] imitators of those who through faith and patience inherit the promises," says our author (Heb. 6:12). This is great advice with regard to all those who walked before us in faith. How much more is it true with regard to our Savior himself. Through faith in him, with patient endurance on the trail he blazed before us, we will inherit all that God has promised in him. And we will come to know him, to be his disciples, and to know forever the reality of his love, which is the greatest gift of all.

21

AN ANCHOR FOR THE SOUL

Hebrews 6:13–20

We have this as a sure and steadfast anchor of the soul, a hope that enters into the inner place behind the curtain. (Heb. 6:19)

*E*ncouragement is one of friendship's greatest treasures. Most of us can remember significant turning points that came by means of some encouragement at a crucial time. Perhaps it was a coach who spent extra time developing your potential, or a teacher who said you had a gift for writing, or a parent who understood that you were about to give up and came with the words you needed to hear.

Encouragement comes in many forms. Hebrews 6:13–20 brings two types of encouragement. The first is a heartening example that shows how perseverance led to hope and blessing. Seeing someone who walked before us and found success always encourages us to follow in those same footsteps. The second form of encouragement is perhaps the best kind: the assurance of ultimate success. In business, confidence of success leads people to commit their talents and their fortunes. In war, confidence of victory communicates the spirit of bold attack. In sports, we hear of teams that simply would not give up because they knew they ultimately would prevail. The same is true in the way of faith. The writer of Hebrews encourages his readers with both of these sources of encouragement: an example to follow and the assurance that faith in Christ is certain of success.

THE EXAMPLE OF ABRAHAM

The example is that of the patriarch Abraham, who lived roughly four thousand years ago. Abraham is a pivotal figure of the Old Testament, his story spanning fourteen chapters in the Book of Genesis, from chapters 12 to 25. It was with Abraham that God established his covenant, and it was to Abraham that God made the promises in which we Christians find our hope. This is why Abraham is called our father in the faith (Rom. 4:11); in both Romans and Galatians, the apostle Paul makes the strongest of connections between Abraham's experience and our salvation. Galatians 3:29 tells us, "If you are Christ's, then you are Abraham's offspring, heirs according to promise." So this is a very important example and precedent for us.

It is no surprise, then, that the writer of Hebrews turns to the record of Abraham for the encouragement of his readers. Here is as great an example of God's grace as appears in all of Scripture. Abraham was the son of an idolater, living in a godless land, and yet God came to him with the call of divine grace: "Now the LORD said to Abram, 'Go from your country and your kindred and your father's house to the land that I will show you. And I will make of you a great nation, and I will bless you and make your name great, so that you will be a blessing. . . . In you all the families of the earth shall be blessed'" (Gen. 12:1–3).

These were very great promises to Abram, promises he did not deserve and could not bring to fulfillment on his own, but which he was to receive by faith. God promised Abram a homeland and a vast host of descendants— blessings for all the nations of the earth. Yet if there was ever a man who needed faith, it was this Abram, as he was called then. His name meant father of a people, yet he was seventy-five years old when he set out for the land of promise, childless and a pilgrim. His elderly wife, Sarai, was barren and beyond any hope of giving him children. It is no wonder that Abram complained to God: "O Lord GOD, what will you give me, for I continue childless, and the heir of my house is Eliezer of Damascus? . . . Behold, you have given me no offspring, and a member of my household will be my heir" (Gen. 15:2–3).

Abram needed encouragement to believe, as we do, and so the Lord renewed the promise of land and seed, as beautifully told in Genesis:

> And behold, the word of the LORD came to him: "This man shall not be your heir; your very own son shall be your heir." And he brought him outside and said, "Look toward heaven, and number the stars, if you are able to number them." Then he said to him, "So shall your offspring be." And he believed the LORD, and he counted it to him as righteousness. And he said to him, "I am the LORD who brought you out from Ur of the Chaldeans to give you this land to possess." (Gen. 15:4–7)

With such great encouragement, Abram looked upon the future in faith; he trusted the word of the Lord and his promise of salvation, and by faith he was reckoned as righteous, because he believed God.

The story of Abram's life is that of perseverance leading to greater and greater faith. Early on he was barely able to follow, often doubtful and sometimes angry. Abram doubted God's promise, and so he had an illegitimate child through his wife's maidservant Hagar. Again God came to him, in Genesis 17, to reaffirm the promise of a child, born not of unbelieving stratagems but born of divine grace in fulfillment of the promise. God changed his name from Abram to Abraham, from "father of a nation" to "father of many nations." He also changed Sarai's name to Sarah, which means "princess," and gave the visible sign of circumcision as a sign of his covenant.

All through Abraham's life, despite the weakness of his faith, God encouraged him so that his faith persevered and grew. He learned to trust God, and finally he received the child of promise, Isaac. His example should encourage us, for like Abraham our patient endurance will see the fruit of salvation. This is what the writer of Hebrews points out in verse 15: "Thus Abraham, having patiently waited, obtained the promise."

Verses 13–15 recall a specific episode late in Abraham's life. God had promised a son through the womb of barren Sarah. In Genesis 21 we learn that God brought her womb to life, after she was more than ninety years old, and Isaac was born. God gave the child of promise through a barren womb to demonstrate that salvation is by grace alone, by God's saving power and not by the will or ability of man. Yet this fulfillment led to a greater test of Abraham's faith. In Genesis 22 God commanded him to offer up this very son

Isaac as a sacrifice. Abraham would have to offer this precious son's life, the child of the promise, as an expression of absolute confidence in God. Not knowing how God would deliver him, but trusting his Word completely and demonstrating the kind of faith long years of perseverance had produced, Abraham prepared to offer Isaac's life. Here is what happened:

> The angel of the LORD called to him from heaven and said, "Abraham, Abraham!" And he said, "Here am I." He said, "Do not lay your hand on the boy or do anything to him, for now I know that you fear God, seeing you have not withheld your son, your only son, from me." And Abraham lifted up his eyes and looked, and behold, behind him was a ram, caught in a thicket by his horns. And Abraham went and took the ram and offered it up as a burnt offering instead of his son. So Abraham called the name of that place, "The LORD will provide"; as it is said to this day, "On the mount of the LORD it shall be provided." (Gen. 22:11–14)

After this God renewed the promise given so many times before. In response to Abraham's great faith the angel brought this message from heaven: "By myself I have sworn, declares the LORD, because you have done this and have not withheld your son, your only son, I will surely bless you, and I will surely multiply your offspring as the stars of heaven and as the sand that is on the seashore" (Gen. 22:16–17).

Hebrews 6:14 is a direct citation from this passage: "Surely I will bless you and multiply you." The emphasis here is on the assurance of the promise, particularly as it appears in the original language: "I will certainly and greatly bless you." The writer of Hebrews adds, "And thus Abraham, having patiently waited, obtained the promise" (Heb. 6:15).

The point is that by persevering in the faith, despite great obstacles, and despite many causes for doubt and unbelief, Abraham received God's promise. This is the encouragement the writer of Hebrews wants us to hear, using the example of Abraham. We have many reasons to doubt, we are tired of trusting God for the things we do not have, and we are weary of looking to the future. Therefore the writer says, in effect, "Look to this example as encouragement to press onward in faith toward God."

It is noteworthy that in chapter 11 the writer of Hebrews observes that Abraham never did receive all that was promised to him in this life. Instead, he looked to the kingdom that lies beyond the grave: "By faith he went to live in the land of promise, as in a foreign land, living in tents with Isaac and Jacob, heirs with him of the same promise. . . . These all died in faith, not having received the things promised, but having seen them and greeted them from afar" (Heb. 11:9–13).

Abraham did receive the son who was promised, Isaac, through whom all the promises would later come true, namely, through Isaac's descendant. It is in Christ that the seed of Abraham brings blessing to all the nations, gathering children of faith as numerous as the stars in the sky. Hence the apostle Paul could write, "For all the promises of God find their Yes in him," that is, in Christ (2 Cor. 1:20). Through Isaac, Abraham was looking forward to Christ, in whom all the things promised would be received. As Jesus said in John 8:56, "Your father Abraham rejoiced that he would see my day. He saw it and was glad." Abraham did not receive all the blessings he longed for during his earthly life. He did not, for instance, gain possession of all the Promised Land. But he did receive the promise of every blessing God had for him, and with the promise he received assurance and certainty of all that someday would be his.

GOD'S OATH AND PROMISE

Abraham's whole life of faith was directed toward receiving God's promise. Genesis 12 begins his story with a promise from God: "I will make of you a great nation, and I will bless you and make your name great, so that you will be a blessing. . . . In you all the families of the earth shall be blessed" (Gen. 12:2–3). In Genesis 15, after Abram had persevered for a while in faith, God reiterated that promise and gave the added assurance of a covenant. Again, after more endurance, God returned with the promise and added the sign of circumcision, and changed Abram's name to Abraham (Gen. 17). After a whole life of perseverance in faith, Abraham received the ultimate version of this one promise, in Genesis 22, where God swore an oath by himself, securing the promise as tightly as possible. This is what the writer of Hebrews emphasizes:

> For people swear by something greater than themselves, and in all their disputes an oath is final for confirmation. So when God desired to show more

211

convincingly to the heirs of the promise the unchangeable character of his purpose, he guaranteed it with an oath, so that by two unchangeable things, in which it is impossible for God to lie, we who have fled for refuge might have strong encouragement to hold fast to the hope set before us. (Heb. 6:16–18)

This tells us three things, the first of which is that by swearing by himself God gave his promise an especially solemn character. To show this, the writer of Hebrews reminds us how men use oaths. Men swear by something greater than themselves, typically by God, thereby inviting the wrath of that greater power should they violate the oath. This, the writer says, "is final for confirmation," or as the New International Version says, it "puts an end to all argument," ensuring the intent of the one who so swears. God, however, stands beneath no one and no thing; there is nothing greater than he, no higher name than his own, so that if God is to swear an oath he must do so by his own name. In doing so, God placed his own dignity and character on the line when it came to the fulfillment of this promise to Abraham. That is the ultimate surety for a promise. God sealed his intent "by two unchangeable things," namely, his promise and his oath to go along with it. The promise is therefore especially solemn, certain, and inviolable.

The second thing this passage tells us is why God would do such a thing: because "God desired to show more convincingly to the heirs of the promise the unchangeable character of his purpose" (Heb. 6:17). God did not swear an oath to Abraham to make his purpose unchanging, but to let Abraham know with absolute certainty that it was so. This is an astonishing condescension from God. God does not need to swear; in the Gospels, for instance, Jesus chastised the Jews of his day who used oaths because their word could not be trusted (Matt. 5:33–37). God does not need oaths because he is infallibly trustworthy, and yet here he swore an oath to accommodate the weakness of our faith. He swore by himself so that Abraham would not fall prey to doubt or unbelief ever again.

This is how the passage fits into the flow of the writer's thought. His purpose is to exhort the Hebrew Christians to persevere in the faith despite their great hardship. In the preceding verses, he chastised them for their lack of maturity and growth (5:11–6:3), warned them of the danger of falling away (6:4–8), and encouraged them with good signs he had seen among them

(6:9–12). Now, using the example of Abraham's perseverance, he informs them of a key principle, that growth in assurance comes through perseverance. Abraham, by waiting patiently, received certainty with regard to the promise, and the same will be true for us.

Abraham's life of faith was long and weary, and it took place in the face of great doubts and obstacles. Abraham sometimes showed heroic faith, but at other times was cowardly. But he persevered—that is the main point. He pressed on. He did not abandon his faith in God, even though he often failed to apply it or to honor God as he should. But he pressed onward, and by persevering he obtained a firmer and firmer grip on God's promise. Again and again he received a growing assurance of blessing and salvation, an increasing possession of what God had promised.

What does this mean for us, but that assurance of salvation, confidence in God's promise, and an increased grasp of spiritual blessings will come as we press forward in the faith? For all our doubt and weakness and failure, we have an example to follow in Abraham: "Abraham, having patiently waited, obtained the promise" (Heb. 6:15).

It is noteworthy that the verb used here, *epitynchanō*, is not the ordinary verb for "receive" or "obtain"; it has the particular connotation of "arriving at" or "reaching." The sense is that the promise had been there all along, but by persevering patiently amidst all sorts of doubts and obstacles, with great encouragement from God, Abraham finally "got it." This is what will happen for us if we press on in the faith, as God works in ways seen and unseen, expected and unexpected, to bring us to confident assurance, and the firm receipt of his certain promise.

HOPE FOR US

Our passage says three things about God's oath to Abraham. The first is that God's oath made the promise solemn and inviolable. The second is that God did this to encourage the faith of Abraham by making the certainty known. But there is one more thing here of vital importance to all of us. Verses 17–19 tell us: "So when God desired to show more convincingly to the heirs of the promise the unchangeable character of his purpose, he guaranteed it with an oath, so that by two unchangeable things, in which it is impossible for God to lie, we who have fled for refuge might have strong encouragement to hold fast to the hope set before us. We have this as a sure and steadfast anchor of the soul."

God gave this promise, then, not merely for Abraham's sake but also for ours. "God desired ... [that] we ... might have strong encouragement" (Heb. 6:17–18). This inviolable promise, secured by an oath, "two unchangeable things, in which it is impossible for God to lie," is the foundation of our own assurance and hope.

How can this be, when the promise and oath were not given to us but to Abraham so long ago? The answer is that while Abraham was the recipient of this great promise, we are its objects. It has reference to us. When God took Abraham out beneath the dark sky and pointed to the countless specks of light, he was pointing to us. God promised Abraham descendants as numerous as the stars in the sky, and in Christ Jesus we are those descendants, we are those of the nations blessed through him. This is best explained by the apostle Paul: "Now the promises were made to Abraham and to his offspring. It does not say, 'And to offsprings,' referring to many, but referring to one, 'And to your offspring,' who is Christ. ... In Christ Jesus you are all sons of God, through faith. ... If you are Christ's, then you are Abraham's offspring, heirs according to promise" (Gal. 3:16, 26, 29).

Through faith in Christ—who is the promised offspring of grace, in whom all the promises are received, obtained, and fulfilled—we like Abraham become God's children and heirs with him of all the blessings of salvation. This means that when you put your faith in Jesus Christ for salvation—for forgiveness of sin and adoption into God's family—you can be certain of that salvation. You can be sure because God promised a vast starry host of spiritual descendants to Abraham through his one special descendant, Jesus Christ. In receiving you through faith, God is honoring his promise not merely to you but also to his own Son, Jesus, and fulfilling the inviolable promise sworn by an oath upon himself, given to Abraham so long ago.

The result of this is hope for us. How greatly people need hope today, but how few actually have hope! This is something even secular authorities are pointing out today. Armand Nicholi Jr., professor of psychiatry at Harvard Medical School and editor of *The Harvard Guide to Psychiatry*, notes the explosive increase in depression today. As of 1996, he tells us, about 11 million Americans were receiving treatment for depression and in that year 250,000 people attempted to take their own lives. What can account for such huge figures in a society with few external threats and unprecedented material abundance? Nicholi argues that it is a crisis of hope: "Our culture has forsaken its spiritual roots, [and] we live in an overtly secular society without even the pretense of spiritual values. Many young people today feel that their cultures fail to provide answers to questions of purpose and meaning and destiny. We fail, they feel, to provide some reason for hope. The consequence is that we are now in a cultural crisis and living in what is being called 'The Age of Despair.'"[1]

But people have always needed hope to persevere. This is why the writer of Hebrews so emphasizes the Christian's hope. God wanted us to "have strong encouragement to hold fast to the hope set before us. We have this as a sure and steadfast anchor of the soul" (Heb. 6:18–19). God wanted us to have a sure hope, so he gave his oath to his promise of a great salvation. Just as an anchor holds a ship secure despite great storms and tossing seas, so this hope, tethered to us by God's unchangeable, oath-bound promise, holds our hearts fast to Jesus Christ and the salvation that is ours in him. The Puritan Samuel Rutherford thus remarks: "Our hope is not hung upon such an untwisted thread as, 'I imagine so,' or 'It is likely'; but the cable, the strong rope of our fastened anchor, is the oath and promise of Him who is eternal verity. Our salvation is fastened with God's own hand, and Christ's own strength, to the strong stake of God's unchangeable nature."[2]

The writer of Hebrews describes believers as those "who have fled for refuge" (v. 18) to God. It is not certain exactly what he has in mind. He may be thinking back to the Old Testament cities of refuge, where those fleeing the wrath of God's law could find safety (Deut. 4:42; 19:5; Josh. 20:9). Similarly, we seek escape from God's judgment on our sins. But the writer could also be returning to the persecution his readers had earlier experienced, which included the loss of their homes (Heb. 10:34). All Christians flee to God for refuge from the trials of life in a fallen world—from death, sorrow, and futility. These are things non-Christians contend with, only without real hope. Lacking refuge, the unbelieving world falls prey to despair. Believers flee not only from despair but also to hope. We remember that Christian in

1. Armand Nicholi Jr., "Hope in a Secular Age," in *Finding God at Harvard: Spiritual Journeys of Thinking Christians*, ed. Kelly Monroe (Grand Rapids: Zondervan, 1996), 112–13.
2. Samuel Rutherford, *Letters*, quoted in J. C. Ryle, *Holiness* (Darlington, U.K.: Evangelical Press, 1979), 120.

The Pilgrim's Progress fled not only from the City of Destruction but also to the Celestial City. Philip Hughes writes, "For every Christian . . . to flee for refuge is to turn to Christ and in him to find salvation and security."[3]

AN ANCHOR FOR THE SOUL

Anchors are a clear and familiar image of security, yet there is something special about this anchor in Hebrews 6:19. Every other anchor goes down into the sea, but this one goes up into heaven. The anchor of a ship goes down beneath the waves to a place unseen to hold us secure, but this anchor of our hope goes up to a place where by faith we can see "into the inner place behind the curtain" (Heb. 6:19).

What a powerful portrayal of Christian hope, which is like no other hope in this world. For others, hope is mere wishing; it is wanting but not having. And the failure of mere wishful thinking leads so many people into the despair of depression. Christians, too, want many things. We want blessing, we want peace, we want security, and we want heaven. But unlike the hope of the world, which goes nowhere and has no anchor, our hope in Christ goes before us into heaven, where it is anchored in the unchanging character of God and the oath he has sworn. Our hope goes where we cannot yet go ourselves. It goes into heaven, where Christ is now. And there he sets the anchor of our hope with his own pierced hand, so that our hope of salvation is attached by the finished work of Christ to the secure foundation of the unchangeable character of God.

Our anchor of hope is secure because "Jesus has gone as a forerunner on our behalf" into heaven, "having become a high priest forever after the order of Melchizedek" (Heb. 6:20). Jesus came into the world to become our Savior, to blaze a trail through the barrier of sin by his perfect life and atoning death. He then went up into heaven to reign as our high priest—not a temporary priest like the Levites in Israel, but "a high priest forever after the order of Melchizedek." We will examine Melchizedek more thoroughly in our next study, but for now the point is that Christ will never be replaced in his heavenly mission for us. He will never fail, and never die.

---

3. Philip E. Hughes, *A Commentary on the Epistle to the Hebrews* (Grand Rapids: Eerdmans, 1977), 234.

Jesus came to earth to live and die for us, and when he returned to heaven, it also was for our sake, to affix the anchor of our hope "sure and steadfast" in the inner sanctum of heaven itself. In the great promises of God, secured in Christ, we therefore have a cable of salvation that nothing can break or destroy, so that we can be certain of arriving safe in the harbor of heaven.

"Forerunner" is yet another of the nautical terms used in Hebrews. The particular word here, *prodromos*, is one that appears nowhere else in Scripture, but has to do with a familiar scene in the ancient world. Louis Talbot explains:

> The Greek harbors were often cut off from the sea by sandbars, over which the larger ships dared not pass till the full tide came in. Therefore, a lighter vessel, a "forerunner," took the anchor and dropped it in the harbor. From that moment the ship was safe from the storm, although it had to wait for the tide, before it could enter the harbor. . . . The entrance of the small vessel into the harbor, the forerunner carrying the ship's anchor, was the pledge that the ship would safely enter the harbor when the tide was full. And because Christ, our "forerunner," has entered heaven itself, having torn asunder everything that separates the redeemed sinner from the very presence of God, He Himself is the Pledge that we, too, shall one day enter the harbor of our souls and the very presence of God, in the New Jerusalem.[4]

Can unforeseen circumstances break the line to this great anchor? Can the work of men, the temptations of the devil, or the hostility of the world sever a cord forged and emplaced by God himself? Can your sin break the line to this great anchor? The answer to all of these is No. God is greater than them all, and his oath shall overrule every opposition. Believers are saved and we are safe because of God's oath-bound promise, secured and made fast by the finished work of Jesus Christ.

What encouragement we have as we follow Christ as pilgrims in this barren world! Is this hope yours? Have you trusted Jesus Christ for your salvation? If not, then what is your hope? How will it hold up on the solemn day of God's judgment? If you have trusted in Christ, then yours

4. Louis Talbot, *Studies in the Epistle to the Hebrews*, 23.

is a hope nothing can break, a hope that encourages you indeed, an anchor for your soul in the storms of this life. As the hymn puts it,

> Who trusts in God, a strong abode
> in heaven and earth possesses;
> who looks in love to Christ above,
> no fear his heart oppresses.
> In you alone, dear Lord, we own
> sweet hope and consolation:
> our shield from foes, our balm for woes,
> our great and sure salvation.[5]

---

5. Joachim Magdeburg, "Who Trusts in God, a Strong Abode," 1572; trans. Benjamin H. Kennedy, 1863.

PART 3

Our Great High Priest

22

MELCHIZEDEK

Hebrews 7:1—10

*He is first, by translation of his name, king of righteousness, and
then he is also king of Salem, that is, king of peace. He is without
father or mother or genealogy, having neither beginning of days
nor end of life, but resembling the Son of God he continues a
priest forever. (Heb. 7:2–3)*

Comparison is a potent form of description. If we were to compare a public figure to George Washington, we would be emphasizing his integrity and patriotism. A comparison to Abraham Lincoln would evoke thoughts of visionary leadership, while Martin Luther King Jr. recalls moral courage and commitment to reconciliation. On the other hand, the name of Benedict Arnold has long stood for treasonous self-interest, and Richard Nixon's name will forever be associated with abuse of power and public disgrace. By means of a comparison, we can say much with only a few words.

The Book of Hebrews describes the high-priestly office of our Lord Jesus Christ by comparing him to a historical figure. Unlike the people I have named—people who are well known and have reams of material written about them—the writer of Hebrews uses one of the most mysterious and obscure figures in all the Old Testament. He writes in Hebrews 6:20 that Christ has "become a high priest forever after the order of Melchizedek." This comparison has been made three times already in the Book of Hebrews. It has been lingering, awaiting explanation, since it first occurred in 5:6. The writer draws this comparison from Psalm 110:4, where David used it to describe the coming Messiah: "The LORD has sworn and will not change his mind, 'You are a priest forever after the order of Melchizedek.'"

WHO IS MELCHIZEDEK?

Melchizedek appears only briefly in the Book of Genesis (Gen. 14:18–20). The patriarch Abraham encountered him after his military victory over the coalition of kings from the east. Melchizedek blessed him, and in return Abraham gave him a tithe of the spoils.

> After his return from the defeat of Chedorlaomer and the kings who were with him, the king of Sodom went out to meet him at the Valley of Shaveh (that is, the King's Valley). And Melchizedek king of Salem brought out bread and wine. (He was priest of God Most High.) And he blessed him and said, "Blessed be Abram by God Most High, Possessor of heaven and earth; and blessed be God Most High, who has delivered your enemies into your hand!" (Gen. 14:17–20)

The question that has puzzled interpreters through the centuries and still perplexes today is: "Who was Melchizedek?" Given the godless depravity of the Canaanites in the time of Abraham, how did this great spiritual figure arise? And why is nothing more said about him?

As to Melchizedek's identity there have been various views. Some have said that he was Shem, the son of Noah and Abraham's ancestor, and others that he was an angelic or otherwise celestial being. The problem with both of these views is that there is nothing in the text to support them.

Still others argue that Melchizedek is the preincarnate Christ. But the description in Hebrews 7 rules this out. If this great figure were Christ himself in preincarnate appearance (and this happened at various times in the Old Testament), then it is hard to see how he can be described as "*resem-*

bling the Son of God," as he is in verse 3. Nor would it make sense for Jesus' priesthood to be described as in the "order of Melchizedek." Melchizedek is set forth as a type of Christ, and a type is *some other* person who symbolizes and anticipates the one who is to come.

We must conclude, therefore, that we know very little about the person of Melchizedek, except that, apart from the line of Abraham, he kept pure religion as he had received it handed down from the time of the flood. He was a most extraordinary man, but a man nonetheless, and one of whom the Bible intentionally tells us only what it wants us to know. John Calvin said of him: "Amid the corruptions of the world, he alone, in that land, was an upright and sincere cultivator and guardian of religion."[1]

Melchizedek reminds us that it is possible to follow and honor God in a godless world. The writer of Hebrews highlights four things for us to note about this Melchizedek.

The first is that Melchizedek was both king and priest (Heb. 7:1). In Old Testament Israel, the kingly and the priestly offices were kept strictly separate. There was a separation of power not unlike the United States Constitution's checks and balances between the executive, legislative, and judicial branches. Because of this separation, no one man could utterly dominate Israel's civic life. Yet Melchizedek not only combines these vital offices, but is manifestly worthy of them both.

Second, Melchizedek met Abraham when he returned from his victory, and he blessed him. We remember that God had long promised blessing to Abraham, although to the eyes of the world he must not have seemed very important. But here we see this priestly figure confirming his blessedness in the most public manner after the great victory over the kings of the east, a time when Abraham was probably more in the limelight than at any other during his entire life. Martin Luther saw it this way: "Melchizedek presents Abraham to the entire world and declares that only with him, in his house and family, are the church, the kingdom of heaven, salvation, forgiveness of sins, and the divine blessing."[2]

1. John Calvin, *Genesis* (Carlisle, Pa.: Banner of Truth Trust, 1965), 388.
2. Martin Luther, *Luther's Works*, vol. 2, *Lectures on Genesis Chapters 6–14*, ed. Jaroslav Pelikan and Daniel E. Poellot (St. Louis: Concordia, 1960), 389.

One thing that stands out in the Genesis account but does not explicitly appear in Hebrews is that Melchizedek brought bread and wine to Abraham. Roman Catholic teachers have long seen this as a vindication of their view of the priesthood and the eucharistic mass, a view that the Protestant Reformers roundly condemned. Many Protestant commentators conclude that the bread and wine are a mere coincidence, having nothing to do with the comparison between Melchizedek and Christ, particularly since this is overlooked in Hebrews. However, the Holy Spirit, inspiring Moses as he wrote the Book of Genesis, surely knew that in the light of the completed Scriptures a sacramental connection would be made by this appearance of the bread and the wine. I believe, therefore, that this is part of what the writer of Hebrews intended when he noted that Melchizedek blessed Abraham. He not only spoke the blessing, but also spiritually ministered to Abraham's need. Jonathan Edwards puts it well: "The bread and the wine signified the same blessings of the covenant of grace that the bread and wine do in the sacrament of the Lord's supper. . . . Melchizedek's coming to meet him with such a seal of the covenant of grace, on the occasion of this victory, evinces, that it was a pledge of God's fulfillment of the same covenant."[3]

As far as the Roman Catholic priesthood is concerned, this passage offers no support at all. Instead of some merely human priesthood exercising sacramental powers, Melchizedek represents the messianic priesthood of the Son of God, based on the power of his sacrificial death and resurrection life.

Third, the writer of Hebrews considers Melchizedek's name and title: "He is first, by translation of his name, king of righteousness, and then he is also king of Salem, that is, king of peace" (Heb. 7:2). The name Melchizedek consists of the Hebrew word *melek,* which means "king," combined with *tsedeq,* which means "righteous." Such a name speaks volumes about the man. In the midst of the extreme depravity of the Canaanites, in contrast with the despicable worship and gross immorality of men like the king of Sodom, this man exercised his kingly rule for

---

3. Jonathan Edwards, "A History of the Work of Redemption," in *Works* (Peabody, Mass.: Hendrickson, 1998), 1:544.

the extension of righteousness. This indicates an upright and holy life, sharply in contrast with the unrighteous kings all around him.

Melchizedek's title was "king of Salem." Traditionally Salem has been identified with Jerusalem, and with good reason. For one thing, Jerusalem means "city of Salem," so it would be natural for this title to signify its king. For another, we know from Psalm 76:2 that Salem and Zion are linked in the Old Testament. What is particularly striking is that Salem comes from the Hebrew word *shalom*, which means peace, indeed, divine and comprehensive peace. In a godless, warring region, here was a king of righteousness who ruled the city of peace.

Fourth, Melchizedek's appearance has one especially noteworthy feature. The writer of Hebrews observes: "He is without father or mother or genealogy, having neither beginning of days nor end of life, but resembling the Son of God he continues a priest forever" (v. 3). This statement leads many to suppose Melchizedek to be some sort of celestial being, or even the preincarnate Christ. But what is in view here is not Melchizedek himself as being without beginning or end, but Melchizedek as presented in Scripture. Quite in contrast to nearly everybody else of consequence in the Book of Genesis, Melchizedek is not accompanied by a genealogy, but appears without any introduction or conclusion. He has no mother or father. The writer of Hebrews, following a long rabbinic tradition of interpreting passages like this, sees as much significance in what the text omits as in what it says. A. W. Pink explains: "The silence of the Old Testament Scriptures concerning his parentage has a designed significance. The entire omission was ordered by the Holy Spirit . . . in order to present a perfect type of the Lord Jesus."[4] F. F. Bruce notes this about the biblical portrayal: "In the only record which Scripture provides of Melchizedek . . . he appears as a living man, king of Salem and priest of God Most High; and as such he disappears. In all this—in the silences as well as in the statements—he is a fitting type of Christ. . . . Melchizedek remains a priest continually for the duration of his appearance in the biblical narrative."[5]

4. Arthur W. Pink, *Gleanings in Genesis* (Chicago: Moody, 1981), 160.
5. F. F. Bruce, *The Epistle to the Hebrews,* rev. ed. (Grand Rapids: Eerdmans, 1990), 160.

Melchizedek as a Type of Jesus Christ

When we consider this whole description, we see how well Melchizedek serves as a type for the high-priestly ministry of the Lord Jesus Christ. If we look at the four emphases in our passage about Melchizedek, we see how wonderfully they depict Christ as high priest over the church.

First, we noted that Melchizedek was both king and priest. Since earthly kings were righteous only in part, and often were not righteous at all, they were not entrusted with the priestly office. But Jesus Christ, who like Melchizedek is a king of righteousness and peace, is thoroughly qualified for such a trust. Exalted in heaven, he is both king and priest for us, and therefore the one mediator for our whole salvation. Having offered the sacrifice of his blood, shed on the cross for the atonement of our sins, and having won God's help by his intercessory prayers, he also possesses royal power to subdue our hearts, govern his flock and kingdom, and defend his own people against every enemy. As the writer of Hebrews will go on to observe, this king and priest of the order of Melchizedek is "able to save [us] to the uttermost" (Heb. 7:25).

Second, in Melchizedek's going out to bless Abraham in the presence of the Canaanites, we see a wonderful type of Christ's ministry to us. When our battle is over, the risen Jesus Christ will bless us before the eyes of this world. Indeed, in the sacrament of the Lord's Supper, he proclaims us blessed even now from the throne of heaven. Like Abraham, we are despised by the world. Our blessing is hidden to sight, and no one realizes that we hold the promises of God. But Christ acknowledges us as God's own, and the day will come when every eye will see it.

His blessing helps us inwardly as well as outwardly. Melchizedek's bread and wine spoke of the body and blood of Christ, sacrificed on the cross for us, as the source of spiritual blessing to all who believe, and thus he brought bodily and spiritual refreshment to Abraham. So too Christ now ministers to us from that same source, by means of his Holy Spirit. Paul sums this up by saying, "Christ redeemed us ... so that in Christ Jesus the blessing of Abraham might come to the Gentiles, so that we might receive the promised Spirit through faith" (Gal. 3:13–14).

Third, we saw the meaning of Melchizedek's name and titles, "king of righteousness" and "king of peace." How well these apply to our Lord Jesus, and how important it is for us to note the order in which they come. It is only as Jesus achieved righteousness by his life, and secured that righteousness for us by his death on the cross, that peace with God is available to sinners. He offers us peace because he first achieved the righteousness we lack and need. Charles Spurgeon rightly remarked, "Note well the order of these two, and the dependence of the one upon the other; for there could be no true peace that was not grounded upon righteousness; and out of righteousness peace is sure to spring up."[6]

It is because Jesus came to set up a reign of righteousness that he was such a disappointment to those who sought military might or national pride, but not righteousness. Underestimating their sin and forgetting God's perfect holiness, they thought of their need as political or military, not spiritual. This is why the crowds shouted for Barabbas, the violent insurgent, and then cried, "Crucify him," when it came to Jesus. Because he came to establish righteousness first, and then peace, Christ ascended not an earthly throne, not a warhorse, but the cross. There they nailed the sign saying "King of the Jews." But they might well have written "Melchizedek": King of Righteousness to reign over the city of peace. Spurgeon comments: "He knew that he could not be King of peace to us till, first of all, he had woven a perfect righteousness in the loom of his life, and dyed it in his own heart's blood in his death."[7]

Finally, Melchizedek shows us that when Christ was raised from the dead and ascended on high, he took up an eternal priesthood, becoming a priest for our salvation forever. Because he lives forever, there will never be a time when this great priest cannot show forth his blood that was shed for you, when his prayers will not pour forth effectual blessing upon your life. When you die and are presented before God's throne, he will be there, pointing to the wounds he earned upon the cross, charging your debt to the account he has already paid. His priesthood is eternal, never-ending, securing eternal life to give to you.

6. Charles Haddon Spurgeon, *The Metropolitan Tabernacle Pulpit*, 63 vols. (Pasadena, Tex.: Pilgrim Publications, 1975), 30:162.
7. Ibid., 164.

A BETTER PRIESTHOOD

The writer of Hebrews had a pressing concern to show the supremacy of Christ's priesthood over that of Aaron and the Levites under the old covenant. In Hebrews 7:4–10 he proceeds to the priesthood of Melchizedek, which is such a model of Christ's, to make this point.

The writer presents three arguments related to Melchizedek to show the supremacy of Christ's priesthood. The first is that Abraham paid a tithe to Melchizedek: "See how great this man was to whom Abraham the patriarch gave a tenth of the spoils!" (Heb. 7:4). A few verses later, the writer employs customary Old Testament logic to observe that "one might even say that Levi himself, who receives tithes, paid tithes through Abraham, for he was still in the loins of his ancestor when Melchizedek met him" (Heb. 7:9–10). If the Levites, through Abraham, paid a tithe to Melchizedek, then his must be the superior priesthood.

Second, Melchizedek's priesthood must be greater because he blessed Abraham, and "it is beyond dispute that the inferior is blessed by the superior" (Heb. 7:7). On that basis, the priesthood represented by Melchizedek must be greater than the one to come from Abraham.

Third, as he symbolized immortal life, Melchizedek represented a better priesthood than did the mortal Levites. Verse 8 argues, "In the one case tithes are received by mortal men, but in the other case, by one of whom it is testified that he lives." To be a priest in Israel one had to demonstrate the proper lineage; in books like Chronicles and Ezra we see just how carefully such records were kept. The reason for this was that it was a priesthood of dying men, none of whom were able to secure salvation, so proper succession was essential. Melchizedek, however, stands for a greater priesthood—that of the living priest Jesus Christ who, according to Hebrews 7:16, "has become a priest, not on the basis of a legal requirement concerning bodily descent, but by the power of an indestructible life."

One of the great concerns of this letter is that these Hebrew Christians under persecution not renounce Christianity in favor of a return to Judaism. The point, therefore, is that Christ is superior to Judaism. Indeed, the law of Moses with its priesthood stands upon the greater foundation of the gospel of Christ, represented by Melchizedek who blessed Abraham. To renounce Christ, therefore, is to renounce all that the old covenant stood upon, the source from which even Abraham received his blessing.

This helps us to understand the relationship between the old covenant in Moses and the new covenant in Christ. Through Melchizedek, salvation in Christ was made known before the coming of the law and the old covenant. The new covenant in Christ, therefore, is not an innovation. It is not God's reaction to the supposed failure of his first attempt through Moses. It is not different in character from the way of salvation that is described in every period of the Bible after the fall.

The new covenant is called "new" not because it is different but because it brought to fulfillment all that had been represented and anticipated for so long. Indeed, it was in Christ that Abraham saw his hope. As Jesus said to the Pharisees, "Your father Abraham rejoiced that he would see my day. He saw it and was glad" (John 8:56). Jesus may have had Melchizedek particularly in mind when he said that. How glad Abraham must have been to see the one who represented the source of every spiritual blessing, holding forth the bread and wine that spoke of Christ's saving work to come!

SO GREAT A SAVIOR

It was essential that the Hebrew Christians who received this letter not turn back from Christ to Moses, from the gospel to the law, for both Moses and the law themselves looked to Christ. That is why the original readers must not turn away, despite great hardships, but must hold fast to Christ alone.

This passage also proclaims great reasons to us today, reasons why we must honor Jesus Christ, turn to him, and trust him for our salvation. The first of these is the excellency of Christ.

I noted earlier that comparison is an economical way of describing a person, and in the sketch of Melchizedek we see the outlines of the Messiah. Who else but Jesus Christ fulfills what Melchizedek prefigures? Who else fills in the beautiful portrait first sketched by this holy man? Who else can be both priest and king, ruling in hearts even as he upholds the heavens by his mighty Word? Who but Jesus Christ combines such lofty power with meekness of spirit? Who else lives forever by the power of his own divine and eternal life? In whom else can we find such perfect righteousness and peace?

229

If you want to see righteousness portrayed, then read the story of Jesus' life. If you want to see peace, then look at the effect of his presence. Look at those who received his grace. Look at the storm he calmed and the demons he cast out and the sicknesses he healed. Jesus is our righteousness and our peace.

The second reason to turn to Jesus Christ is his ministry as portrayed in these verses. He is the One who offers the blessing of God, the One who distributes spiritual nourishment, as Melchizedek did in blessing and feeding Abraham. True blessing, both now and forever, comes only through acknowledging Jesus Christ as Savior and Lord. Jesus taught, "I am the bread of life; whoever comes to me shall not hunger, and whoever believes in me shall never thirst" (John 6:35).

Finally, you must come to Jesus Christ, because apart from his righteousness there will never be peace for you. Peace is what you are seeking, the comprehensive peace that comes only from God. Through entertainment, ambition, materialism, romance, and sensuality, people seek desperately to quiet the restless voice within. But without righteousness there is never peace: not in our homes, not in our workplaces, not in our hearts. Where sin reigns there never is and never can be peace.

But Jesus is our Melchizedek. He is our King of Righteousness, cleansing us from our sin by his blood and clothing us in the royal robes of his perfect obedience. That is why his is the city of peace, where those who find righteousness in him shall dwell forever in peace with him. He says, "Peace I leave with you; my peace I give to you. . . . Let not your hearts be troubled, neither let them be afraid" (John 14:27). He is our righteousness, and he gives us peace. Forever and ever he will reign as the righteous king over his eternal city of peace. The Bible tells us: "He will dwell with them, and they will be his people, and God himself will be with them as their God. He will wipe away every tear from their eyes, and death shall be no more, neither shall there be mourning nor crying nor pain anymore" (Rev. 21:3–4).

23

A BETTER HOPE

Hebrews 7:11—19

*For it is witnessed of him, "You are a priest forever, after the order
of Melchizedek." On the one hand, a former commandment is set
aside because of its weakness and uselessness (for the law made
nothing perfect); but on the other hand, a better hope is introduced, through which we draw near to God. (Heb. 7:17–19)*

One of the main purposes of the Book of Hebrews is to bring the
old covenant in Moses and the new covenant in Christ into proper
relationship. The reason for this was the danger that the original
readers would slip back into their former religion, either to escape persecution or because of a faulty understanding. All through this letter the writer
emphasizes the superiority of Christ and the new covenant he inaugurated.

A covenant establishes the terms for a relationship; biblical covenants are
established and administered by God to bring mankind into a specified relationship with him. When Christ came, he brought a new covenant—a new
administration by which we relate to God. Speaking of this, the apostle Paul
emphasized, "The old has passed away; behold, the new has come" (2 Cor.
5:17). To fall from Christ back into Judaism, therefore, was not merely to

231

regress into former ways, but to fall back into an administration that was no longer valid, having been fulfilled and replaced by the coming of Christ.

In the discussion of Christ's superior priesthood, this new covenant involves the replacement of the old covenant priesthood—that is, the priesthood of Aaron and the tribe of Levi—with the new priesthood of Christ. By comparing these two we not only see how this change of priesthood effected a new administration of salvation, but we also come into a deeper understanding of what Christ has done and now is doing, and thus what it means to be a Christian living under the new covenant.

We will look at three things in this study: first, we will note that with Christ's coming there are a new priesthood and a new law; second, we will observe how and why the new covenant offers a better hope than that offered in the Old; and third, from the difference between the old covenant and the new, we will draw some conclusions about what it means for us to live under this new covenant brought into history by the saving work of Jesus Christ.

A NEW PRIESTHOOD, A NEW LAW

Why is there a new administration or way of salvation? Hebrews 7:11–19 argues that since Christ is a new kind of priest, he represents a new law or covenant administration: "Now if perfection had been attainable through the Levitical priesthood (for under it the people received the law), what further need would there have been for another priest to arise after the order of Melchizedek, rather than one named after the order of Aaron?" (Heb. 7:11).

The word translated as "perfection" (Greek, *teleiōsis*) could equally be rendered as "completion." It is used here to refer to salvation, for perfection or completion is the condition in which people are made acceptable to God. The point is that the need for a new priesthood indicates that the old priesthood could not itself accomplish the salvation to which it pointed. The very fact that there was another priesthood testifies that the old priesthood was imperfect and transitory.

This argument assumes that the Levitical priesthood and the Old Testament law as an administration of salvation were inseparably linked. This linkage is made clear in verse 11, which says of the Levitical priesthood that "under it the people received the law." The priesthood, with its sacrifices, was the means under the old covenant by which sinful people were reconciled to God; the law served as an agent of their priestly ministry. One commentator explains:

> The priesthood and the tabernacle with its sacrifices were the means God employed to render the sinful people acceptable to himself. They constituted the shadow of Jesus in the Old Testament. Then the law was given with its sharp demands to awaken the people to their true condition so that they might avail themselves of the sacrifices. . . . The law was a teacher to lead to Christ (represented in Israel by the tabernacle and its priesthood).[1]

The Old Testament priests pointed forward to Christ's death on the cross for the salvation of sinners; his death brought an end to their function and thus to the law as a way of salvation.

The writer makes three points to establish this teaching. The first is that since Jesus Christ is not a member of the tribe of Levi (the only tribe authorized for priestly office in the old covenant), but is rather a member of the tribe of Judah, the coming of his priesthood constitutes a new order of priests altogether: "For the one of whom these things are spoken belonged to another tribe, from which no one has ever served at the altar. For it is evident that our Lord was descended from Judah, and in connection with that tribe Moses said nothing about priests" (Heb. 7:13–14). The priesthood revealed and established by the coming of Christ is therefore different from that established under Moses. There has been a change of priesthood in Christ.

The second point is that all this did not happen without advance warning. It was precisely this change of priesthood that David foretold when he wrote of the Messiah, "You are a priest forever after the order of Melchizedek" (Ps. 110:4). David lived under the old covenant, under the law and the Levitical priesthood, but even then—through the inspiration of the Holy Spirit—he announced a new order of priest that would come in the future. It was in the Messiah, he wrote, that God promised this new kind of priest. Therefore, long before the coming of Christ, the old order was recognized as transitional, temporary, and insufficient.

1. Ray Stedman, *Hebrews* (Downers Grove, Ill.: InterVarsity, 1992), 82.

Third, the coming of a new priesthood signals the arrival of a new way of salvation. The author writes in verse 12, "For when there is a change in the priesthood, there is necessarily a change in the law as well." By the term "law" he does not mean the Ten Commandments—that is, the moral law of God. God's moral law never changes, because he does not change and the moral law reflects his character. This is why Jesus said, "Do not think that I have come to abolish the Law or the Prophets; I have not come to abolish them but to fulfill them" (Matt. 5:17). In the Sermon on the Mount Jesus went on not only to affirm the Ten Commandments, but also to insist upon their sharpest application, their highest and most heartfelt expression. Therefore, when we speak of the law as God's moral requirements, we must say that they are not set aside in the coming of Christ, but rather established and reaffirmed. Every Christian should be able to say with the psalmist, "Oh, how I love your law!" (Ps. 119:97).

The writer of Hebrews has another meaning here, namely, the Mosaic law as an administration of the covenant of grace—that is, as a system of salvation. This is what he means when he writes, "For when there is a change in the priesthood, there is necessarily a change in the law as well" (Heb. 7:12). A new order of priesthood and a new kind of priest usher in a new administration of salvation, a new law.

A Better Priest, a Better Hope

Why is the new law of the new priest—that is, the new administration of salvation brought by the coming of Christ—better than the old one? The difference has to do with the priest himself and with the authority by which he holds the priestly office, and therefore with the nature of his ministry. The author describes Jesus Christ as One "who has become a priest, not on the basis of a legal requirement concerning bodily descent, but by the power of an indestructible life. For it is witnessed of him, 'You are a priest forever, after the order of Melchizedek'" (Heb. 7:16–17).

The priesthood was an office of great honor and privilege under the old covenant. The priests alone labored in God's temple and not in the fields or the army or the marketplace. They touched and handled the mysteries of God, serving as mediators who interacted with the Lord. What was it, then, that made a Levite a priest instead of a Benjamite or a son of Reuben or

Naphtali? What secured this great privilege for this one tribe? The regulation of the law and that alone. A priest didn't have to have a sterling character or superlative accomplishments. It wasn't his education, his training, or his spiritual devotion. He got the job because the law said so. It was the law that made him a priest, and as a priest it was the law that he relied upon for his ministry.

The nature of the Levite's authority determined the kind of ministry he offered. He held his priesthood on the basis of the external code, and the external code is what his ministry offered. The law operated by way of the priesthood. If you went to the Old Testament priest and asked how he intended to draw you near to God, he would speak of the commandments and the rituals of the ceremonial law. How much better, then, is the priesthood of Christ. Jesus rests his priesthood on a different basis: his own indestructible life, which is the power he therefore has for his ministry as high priest in the order of Melchizedek.

When you ask Jesus what he offers to draw you near to God, he answers with his shed blood that fulfilled the law and with his offer of spiritual rebirth unto eternal life. This was the contrast Jesus himself proclaimed during his earthly ministry. At the temple, in the presence of the Levitical priests, he cried out: "If anyone thirsts, let him come to me and drink. Whoever believes in me, as the Scripture has said, 'Out of his heart will flow rivers of living water'" (John 7:37–38). By this Jesus meant the Holy Spirit that he would send from his priestly throne in heaven. This is the difference between the old covenant and the new covenant in Christ. The old covenant administered salvation through the outward commandment; the new administers salvation through the transforming power of life. "I came that they may have life," Jesus said, "and have it abundantly" (John 10:10).

The Messiah, represented prior to the law by the figure of Melchizedek, and identified under the law by David in Psalm 110, would establish a new and eternal priesthood. His priesthood is an eternal one, not merely or even essentially in terms of its unlimited duration, but in the character of its life. This priesthood rests upon and advances not merely the power of the outward commandment and ritual, but the inward power of eternal life—unquenchable life from heaven that is of God himself and lasts forever. Andrew Murray writes: "When God speaks to His Son, 'Thou art Priest for ever,' it not only means that the priesthood will never cease, but it points to what is the root and cause of this; it roots in the life and strength of God."[2]

Jesus manifested the power of an unconquerable and indestructible life when he died for our sins and rose again from the grave. It is because of him that Paul could write, "Death is swallowed up in victory" (1 Cor. 15:54). Philip Hughes therefore writes of Christ's eternal priesthood: "He who died once for us now lives, never again to die. The crown has followed the cross, and it is this power of an indestructible life which guarantees that he is indeed our priest forever."[3]

When Jesus died on the cross, he fulfilled the intent of the old priesthood, accomplishing the full atonement it anticipated, and therefore its order was set aside. Then, rising from the dead and ascending to the right hand of God the Father in heaven, he established a new and eternal priesthood that is able to accomplish all that the old priesthood could not. His heavenly ministry, in the power of eternal life, sends forth that life by the Holy Spirit, to change us and draw us near to God.

THE TWO COVENANTS

The writer of Hebrews is greatly concerned to rightly relate the old covenant to the new, mainly because of the danger that Christians would fall back to their former ways and forfeit salvation. From the beginning, the author has advanced this theme by pointing out the supremacy of Christ. In chapters 1 and 2 he showed Christ's supremacy to the angels, through whom the old covenant was given; in chapter 3 he moved on to Christ's supremacy over Moses, and in chapter 4 to his supremacy over Joshua. Now in chapter 7 he advances his main argument: the supremacy of Christ's priesthood over the earlier priesthood of Aaron and the Levites.

The centerpiece of this argument is the citation from Psalm 110:4, "The LORD has sworn and will not change his mind, 'You are a priest forever after the order of Melchizedek.'" Melchizedek was the priest and king who

2. Andrew Murray, *The Holiest of All: An Exposition of the Epistle to the Hebrews* (Grand Rapids: Revell, 1993), 260.

3. Philip E. Hughes, *A Commentary on the Epistle to the Hebrews* (Grand Rapids: Eerdmans, 1977), 264.

met Abraham, blessing him and receiving from him the tithe. This was the point of Hebrews 7:1–10, that since the Old Testament priests came from Abraham, Abraham's homage to Melchizedek shows the latter's supremacy. Melchizedek represented Christ, both by ministering to Abraham the bread and wine that speak of his saving work, and by representing an eternal priesthood based not on his lineage but on his righteousness and life. From Melchizedek, representing Jesus Christ some four thousand years ago, even the Old Testament priests received their blessing in Abraham. This is one way of showing the supremacy of the new covenant over the old.

Our present passage advances that argument a step further, as the writer of Hebrews continues to explain the difference between the two administrations: "On the one hand, a former commandment is set aside because of its weakness and uselessness (for the law made nothing perfect); but on the other hand, a better hope is introduced, through which we draw near to God" (Heb. 7:18–19). These verses say something negative about the old administration and something positive about the new one. This is not to say that the old covenant was wrong. In the flow of God's redemptive history, it was necessary and good. The negative point that the writer of Hebrews makes is simply that as an administration of salvation, the law could not bring about what it sought. The goal of every priesthood is to draw people to God, but the old covenant could not do this. This was its weakness, and why it demanded another covenant to come.

The same is true today. An outward code, a system of rules, may point us in the right direction (and the moral law of God certainly does that). However, it offers no power, no change of heart, to motivate us along that change of course, and no impetus to move along the new azimuth. For this we need power, a new disposition or attitude, which the law cannot convey, but which comes only by the Holy Spirit as he is poured out on us by our heavenly high priest.

Donald Grey Barnhouse explained this by using the example of a lion in the zoo:

> Take the eleventh chapter of Isaiah, which says that the lion shall lie down with the lamb, and read it to the lions in the zoological garden. Tell the lion that God's Word says that he is to lie down with the lamb. The lion will roar

and say that he is tired of horse meat and would like to have some lamb. But he wants it to devour—not as a companion. In order to turn the lion from his natural appetite for flesh, it will be necessary to change his nature. Only then will the eleventh chapter of Isaiah come into its fulfillment. And in order to make mankind (corrupt in all his thoughts and ways and deeds) live up to the requirements of the [law], the miracle of regeneration will be necessary which plants within him the new nature, the life of Christ.[4]

The prophet Jeremiah wrote about this long before, in the ruins of Old Testament Jerusalem. The problem with the old covenant, he said, was not the law. As Paul would later insist, "The law is holy, and the commandment is holy and righteous and good" (Rom. 7:12). The problem was that the people were not able to keep the law; they broke the covenant because of the wickedness of their sinful nature. Therefore God promised a new covenant: "The days are coming, declares the LORD, when I will make a new covenant with the house of Israel and the house of Judah, not like the covenant that I made with their fathers on the day when I took them by the hand to bring them out of the land of Egypt, my covenant that they broke, though I was their husband, declares the LORD" (Jer. 31:31–32).

How will the new covenant differ from the old? The difference is not the grace of God, for the old covenant was also a covenant of grace; it took place in the context of the exodus deliverance. God says he even took Israel for his bride, a magnificent statement of grace. Jeremiah explains the difference when he says of the new covenant: "I will put my law within them, and I will write it on their hearts" (v. 33). Because of the inward work of the Holy Spirit, Christ's ministry offers "a better hope . . . through which we draw near to God" (Heb. 7:19).

What is the difference between the old covenant and the new? The old covenant worked externally by the law, and therefore was unable to empower the people to uphold their end of the relationship; under the administration of the new covenant comes the miracle of regeneration—new hearts to make a new people eager to do God's will. This was never offered under the old covenant, which explains its weakness, its uselessness for actually working salvation.

4. Donald Grey Barnhouse, *Exposition of Bible Doctrines Taking the Epistle to the Romans as a Point of Departure*, 10 vols. (Grand Rapids: Eerdmans, 1953), 2:282.

This is the very comparison the apostle Paul used in 2 Corinthians 3, where he contrasted the law versus the Spirit, and spoke of the transforming power of the spiritual ministry of the exalted Jesus Christ. Paul points out that under the old covenant only Moses actually went in to God. Moses alone went into the tabernacle where God dwelt. When he came out, his face was radiant with the glory of God. There was an outward glow on the face of the prototype Old Testament priest. The people saw only fleeting glimpses of God's glory, for Moses covered himself with a veil to hide the fact that the radiance was fading. In great and marvelous contrast stands life in the new covenant. In Christ, it is not merely Moses but all the people who enter into personal relationship with God; the glory we receive from God is not an outward glory but the inward glory of being transformed into God's own likeness. Paul concludes: "Now the Lord is the Spirit, and where the Spirit of the Lord is, there is freedom. And we all, with unveiled face, beholding the glory of the Lord, are being transformed into the same image from one degree of glory to another. For this comes from the Lord who is the Spirit" (2 Cor. 3:17–18).

This is the better hope of the new covenant in Christ, which Paul describes as "freedom," and the writer of Hebrews speaks of as "drawing near to God." This is our freedom as Christians—not to presume upon God's grace through loose living or by flirting with sin, but the freedom to draw near to God by his Spirit. It is the freedom to fellowship with God himself, which was always the goal of the priesthood, but is accomplished only by the heavenly ministry of our great high priest, Jesus Christ, through the Holy Spirit. This is a much better way, a much better hope, than any Old Testament saint ever knew.

DRAWING NEAR TO GOD

We tend to underappreciate the present high-priestly ministry of our Lord Jesus Christ and its significance to our lives. How impoverishing it is to our spiritual vibrancy that we think of his ministry as past tense only, little recognizing the great resources available to us now through our everlasting union with him by faith.

When we think of Jesus as high priest, many of us think only of him fulfilling the ministry of Aaron and the Levites. We think of Christ offering his perfect righteousness and precious blood to atone for our sins. This is a glorious work that is done once for all; we rightly look to it for forgiveness of sins and reconciliation with God.

Yet this was not the final priesthood; the priesthood typified by Aaron has given way to that of Melchizedek. Christ now is a living high priest, offering us life and the power we need to receive salvation, and then helping us to press on in the faith. He sends the very life of God to renew us inwardly, so Paul could say, "Though our outer nature is wasting away, our inner nature is being renewed day by day" (2 Cor. 4:16). As we trust in Christ, the Spirit of God works to change our affections from the things of the world to those of heaven, from unrighteousness to the righteousness that pleases God.

An emphasis on the present ministry of the Spirit has always been a hallmark of the Protestant faith. This is why, for instance, we reject the Roman Catholic mass, which tragically shows Christ as crucified still, an ongoing sacrifice, always the priest of Aaron and never of Melchizedek. This is why Roman Catholic crosses portray the body of Christ still there, whereas Protestants have always insisted that he is no longer on the cross. Jesus is now in heaven, victorious, no longer laboring for what Aaron sought, but now ministering like Melchizedek. The crosses we display are bare, and when we receive the sacrament of communion, we look to a risen Christ who is no longer dying. It is from an exalted and glorified high priest that we receive a better hope: the living Spirit of God to renew us, restore us, lead us, and empower us in newness of life.

Since our high priest is exalted in heaven with power to transform us, the Christian life is not a matter of outward performance, but of drawing near to God by the Holy Spirit. Jesus has opened the way for us, so that we no longer relate to God through an external code, but in a living relationship through faith in Jesus Christ. By the Spirit we also are able to fulfill the righteousness represented in the law, since by the Spirit we have both the power and the desire to keep it (see Rom. 8:2–4). It was for this that Christ came. Whereas the law "made nothing perfect," through the life Christ gives "a better hope is introduced, through which we draw near to God" (Heb. 7:19).

This is Christ's goal and desire, the end of his labor—not only to see us justified and forgiven of our sins, but actually led into relationship with God through the Holy Spirit, who gives us power to stop being law-breakers and instead to be law-keepers through faith in Christ.

This leads to very practical questions: Do you live in fellowship with God? Through God's Spirit do you know and relate to him? Do you talk with God in prayer? Does his voice speak to your mind and your heart as you receive his Word in the Scriptures? Are you living in new obedience by his power, with evidence of his fruit growing in your life? This is the true Christian life, and everything short of it is a counterfeit. The Christian life is life in the Spirit of God, obeying and drawing near to God in spirit and truth. This is not mysticism. It is not irrational, nor does it depend on emotions. Rather, it is the life of spiritual communion with God himself as he takes the Word he has given and writes it on our hearts and minds, on the tablets of our very souls, through the Holy Spirit as we trust in Christ as our Savior and Lord.

Many Christians seem more comfortable with an Old Testament spirituality than with new covenant life. We would rather gaze upon God's work in some other person, like the Israelites staring at Moses. We are fascinated with our favorite preachers or musicians, glorying in them as spiritual celebrities. But we do not worship God and find our whole portion in him, to whom Christ brings us by his present ministry of the Spirit. Yet this is the goal of the better hope, the end for which Christ died and rose again, that we would "draw near to God" through him.

How, then, do you get the Spirit? You get the Spirit not by seeking after supposedly spiritual experiences, but by fixing your eyes on Jesus Christ and turning to him in faith, who died for the forgiveness of your sins, fulfilling the priesthood of Aaron, and who now lives forever as the eternal priest in the order of Melchizedek to grant you eternal life. What we most need is something the external code can never impart and we ourselves cannot produce by any fleshly means, yet Jesus gives it to all who come to God through faith in him: a new heart, a new attitude, a new power for godliness and newness of life for the glory of God, all of which come through faith in Christ as he is offered in the gospel, as Christ responds to our faith with the ministry of the Holy Spirit.

Charles Wesley wrote a hymn to direct the eyes of our faith to the living Savior, Jesus Christ, whose redeeming ministry is always what we really need. It provides us the best news we could ever receive:

> I know that my Redeemer lives,
> and ever prays for me;
> a token of his love he gives,
> a pledge of liberty.
>
> I find him lifting up my head;
> he brings salvation near;
> his presence makes me free indeed
> and he will soon appear.[5]

5. Charles Wesley, "I Know That My Redeemer Lives," 1742.

24

BECAUSE HE LIVES

Hebrews 7:20–25

*This makes Jesus the guarantor of a better covenant. . . . Conse-
quently, he is able to save to the uttermost those who draw near to
God through him, since he always lives to make intercession for
them.* (Heb. 7:22, 25)

here are two great issues in life, the first of which is, "What do
we do with sin?" How do we handle the things others have done
to us? More importantly, what are we to do with the things we
have done to others, things done in violence or anger or envy or greed? How
do we deal with sins done to us and sins we have done to others?

Many people today offer a therapeutic solution. First, sin is reclassified
as dysfunction. Our society does this with violators ranging from child
molesters to murderers, from gossips to adulterers. Instead of transgressions
of a divine moral law, these are viewed as unfortunate though often under-
standable choices.

Second, we blame our behavior on external forces. It was our childhood,
or the environment in which we have to live or work. The remedy to wrong-
doing under this approach is rehabilitation. What we need, people say, is not

forgiveness and redemption—that would be to assign blame. We need therapy or a changed environment. More and more, however, our generation is feeling the futility of this approach—its failure to deal with the reality of evil, the failure of mere denial and therapy to wash away the guilt of our sin. Despite its advertisements, the therapeutic model has not brought and cannot bring peace to the earth, on either the individual or the national level.

The first great issue in life—the problem of sins we have committed—deals with the past. The second great issue of life deals with the present and the future. It is the problem of our weakness and inward corruption. This is not just the outward reality of sin but the inward problem that is its source. On the surface we are able to make some changes—changes to our waistline, our resumé, and our lifestyle. But when it comes to our hearts, to who we really are, to our attitudes and affections and character, we find that change is quite a bit harder. Indeed, it is beyond our grasp. We buy new outfits and advance to higher positions, we grow a bit older and learn a few life lessons, but from year to year we are basically the same person. When it comes to a real and substantial and lasting change of heart, within ourselves we simply lack the power and the resources.

This is the backdrop against which we should read these verses from the Letter to the Hebrews. In contrast with every salvation that this world has to offer, Jesus Christ "is able to save to the uttermost those who draw near to God through him" (Heb. 7:25). The reason for the success of his salvation—his ability to deal with both our outward sins and our inward condition—is that he lives forever with power to save. Because he lives, he has a permanent priesthood, always interceding for his own, and thus he is able completely to save those who trust in him.

The Guarantee of Our Salvation

The writer of Hebrews declares the total sufficiency of salvation in Christ by noting that the permanence of Jesus' priestly ministry guarantees our relationship to God. The author of Hebrews gets at this by means of his continued exposition of Psalm 110:4, which is the basis of all his teaching in this chapter: "The LORD has sworn and will not change his mind, 'You are a priest forever.'" He has already squeezed this verse hard enough to get almost all the juice out of it, and so far it has been very nourishing indeed. Psalm 110 is a Davidic psalm that speaks of the messianic king who would come to save his people. In his prior exposition of this verse, the writer of Hebrews focused on the link between Jesus Christ and Melchizedek. Melchizedek was the priest and king who ministered to Abraham and received his tithe, appearing in the Book of Genesis without any record of birth or death, parents or genealogy. Melchizedek was a type of the Messiah. As David wrote, "You are a priest forever after the order of Melchizedek" (Ps. 110:4). In contrast to the priests of Aaron's order—that is, the priests of Old Testament Israel—Melchizedek represented Jesus' priesthood as established "not on the basis of a legal requirement concerning bodily descent, but by the power of an indestructible life" (Heb. 7:16).

Our present passage goes on to elaborate another difference between the Old Testament priests and the priestly office of Jesus Christ. Here the difference deals with the nature of his ordination to ministry: "And it was not without an oath. For those who formerly became priests were made such without an oath, but this one was made a priest with an oath by the one who said to him: 'The Lord has sworn and will not change his mind, "You are a priest forever."'" This makes Jesus the guarantor of a better covenant" (Heb. 7:20–22).

In what manner, then, does God's oath make Jesus' priesthood the guarantee of a better covenant? To answer, we should observe that this is not the first time we have heard the writer of Hebrews refer to an oath from God. In 6:13–14 he pointed out that Abraham's promise of blessing was secured by a divine oath: "By myself I have sworn, declares the LORD, . . . I will surely bless you, and I will surely multiply your offspring as the stars of heaven and as the sand that is on the seashore" (Gen. 22:16–17). God did not give the oath because *he* needed it, but in order to give *us* every surety that he will do what he has promised. He said, "By myself I have sworn." Speaking of that oath-bound promise, which belongs to everyone who shares the faith of Abraham, the writer of Hebrews observed, "We have this as a sure and steadfast anchor of the soul" (6:19).

In chapter 7, Hebrews refers to another of God's oaths, an oath regarding the Messiah: "The Lord has sworn and will not change his mind, 'You are a priest forever'" (Heb. 7:21; Ps. 110:4). Both of these oaths have reference to God's dealings with Abraham. In the one case God promised to bless Abraham, and in the other he promised the Messiah that he would be a priest in the order of the priest-king Melchizedek. It stands to reason that these two oaths, so closely related in terms of God's covenant to Abraham, serve similar functions—namely, to give assurance to those who look to God with the faith of Abraham.

These oaths serve as seals of God's promised salvation. The oath to Abraham sealed God's intention to bless him; God swore by himself that he would do it. Similarly, the oath to the promised Messiah sealed the means by which God would accomplish that intention, the sending of a Savior to accomplish what God had promised. This is precisely the point made in verse 22: "This makes Jesus the guarantor of a better covenant." It is by means of his priesthood that God's promises are accomplished.

God's oath to the Messiah, that is, to Jesus Christ, given through King David in Psalm 110 almost one thousand years before his coming, guarantees the covenant with Abraham, through which we also are saved. A covenant is a binding arrangement, with stipulated conditions and promised benefits upon their fulfillment. God's covenant with Abraham was his promise to bless him with salvation, along with all who look to God in faith as Abraham did. The oath of Psalm 110 seals this covenant because it guarantees the One who would bring it to pass: the Savior who would bear Abraham's and our sins upon the cross, and who then would rise again, ascending to heaven to secure the blessings God had promised. As one commentator explains: "The divine oath verifies the absolute reliability of the priesthood of Christ, upon which the hopes of the Christian community are anchored. The achievement of its purpose is assured."[1]

The Greek word for "guarantor" or "surety" appears in the New Testament only in Hebrews 7:22. The word is *engyos,* and it was used in ancient legal documents for "one who stands security." The *engyos* offered his goods or even himself as security to ensure what was promised. This helps us grasp the writer's point, namely, that as long as Jesus lives, the covenant of our salvation is secured by him.

This is not the only time God offered a surety to his covenants. After the flood, God sealed his promise to Noah with the surety of the rainbow: "I have set my bow in the cloud, and it shall be a sign of the covenant between me and the earth" (Gen. 9:13). As long as there are rainbows in

---

1. William L. Lane, *Hebrews 1–8*, Word Biblical Commentary 48a (Dallas: Word, 1991), 187.

the sky, we can be sure there will never be a judgment that comes by such a flood. Likewise, in Jeremiah 31:35–36 God sealed his promise to Israel by saying that only if the sun by day and the moon and stars by night should vanish from the sky, only then would their descendants cease to be a nation before him.

It is hard to imagine an end to rainbows, or to the sun, moon, and stars. But it is conceivable. By comparison, we see how much greater is the oath establishing Jesus as the surety of God's covenant promise. As long as Jesus lives, the covenant will stand—and he lives forever. He is the very Son of the living God, the One who died and yet death could not hold him. As Jesus said in the Book of Revelation, "I am the first and the last, and the living one. I died, and behold I am alive forevermore" (Rev. 1:17–18).

Jesus is the One whom God the Father exalted to the heavens according to the promise "You are a priest forever." Therefore, God sees Jesus Christ in heaven, the second person of the Trinity and the eternal Son, in the humanity he took up in the virgin birth, and God is visually reminded of the oath he made. He sees his own appointed surety, the security he himself established to seal the covenant of our salvation. Therefore, because Jesus lives, we too will live.

The strength of God's oath explains how it is that we have "a better covenant" (Heb. 7:22). The contrast is between the new covenant in Christ and the old covenant in Moses. In the old era, priests did not live forever. They were mere men, and their ministry did not have a divine oath that guaranteed permanency. This is why there was a procedure for passing on the office by blood descent.

The priests were the ones who mediated with God, offering prayers and sacrifices. Some were better than others. There were godly priests, like Zadok, who served in the time of David. The problem was that even the best priests always died, and then it was on to someone else. If you lived in the time of the prophet Malachi, who wrote of impure priests who offered sacrifices that were defiled, then things were not so good.

All of this is changed in the new covenant in Jesus Christ, which relies upon a priest who not only pleases God in all things, but also lives forever and will always guarantee our relationship with God. This is the assurance of our salvation in him. There is no stipulation for passing on his priesthood, because there is no need. As Hebrews emphasizes: "The former priests were many in number, because they were prevented by death from continuing in office, but he holds his priesthood permanently, because he continues forever" (Heb. 7:23–24).

This means that if you have come to Jesus Christ for salvation, then you have come to a living priest who offered his blood for your sins and now reigns in heaven to secure your future. This is your assurance of eternal salvation. God established him as the guarantee of the covenant, of his promise of eternal life, and he lives forever. As Jesus said to his disciples, "Because I live, you also will live" (John 14:19).

ABLE TO SAVE

The oath given to Jesus Christ through King David utterly and completely seals and guarantees the salvation that is in him. But how does his priestly ministry actually save us? Hebrews answers: "He holds his priesthood permanently, because he continues forever. Consequently, he is able to save to the uttermost those who draw near to God through him, since he always lives to make intercession for them" (Heb. 7:24–25).

The word "consequently" at the beginning of verse 25 links together the permanent priesthood of Christ and the intercession of Christ. We have made much of Jesus' permanent presence in heaven as our surety, but he is not just sitting there. He is active in his intercession for us.

To intercede is to approach on behalf of others, and this is what Jesus does for us at the throne of the heavenly Father. He represents us and pleads our cause. Indeed, in verse 25, "to save" is linked with "to intercede." Intercession is the means by which Jesus so thoroughly saves us, gaining us complete divine favor and every resource we need for our salvation. Andrew Murray writes: "Without ceasing there streams forth from Him to the Father the prayer of His love for every one and every need of those that belong to Him; His very person and presence is that prayer, so closely and inseparably is He identified with those He calls His brethren."[2]

Whenever we think of intercession in heaven, there are two great errors we must avoid. The first and greater error is to think that Jesus is an insuf-

---

2. Andrew Murray, *The Holiest of All: An Exposition of the Epistle to the Hebrews* (Grand Rapids: Revell, 1993), 272.

ficient intercessor, that he is somehow disinterested or incompetent. This is the grave error of those who would turn to others (such as deceased relatives, or saints, or the virgin Mary) for their intercession. Philip Hughes rightly says: "To rely upon angels or saints or any other finite beings for their intercessions is not only futile; it also betrays a failure of confidence in the adequacy of Christ as our intercessor, and it is to honor the creature rather than him who is our Creator and Redeemer."[3] Jesus is "able to save to the uttermost" through his intercession; to turn to any other is to deny this and impugn God's Word.

Another error is to infer from Jesus' intercession that the Father sits in hostility toward us, and is only begrudgingly placated by the labors of his Son. It is true that we are worthy of God's complete disdain. But never let us forget that Jesus here fulfills the office to which the Father appointed him. We are saved because the Son does the will of his Father for us, opening the way for our full reconciliation as God's beloved children. It is God himself who "so loved the world that he gave his only Son" (John 3:16).

LIVING TO INTERCEDE

Earlier we observed that there are two great matters for which the world has no effective solution. The first is the problem of our sin. Despite all our efforts, we are utterly unable to make things right with one another. We may cry "Peace, peace," but there is no peace. This is true on the human level, but when we bring God into the picture—when we consider that our sins have offended the unchanging and perfect justice of heaven—things become not only worse but utterly hopeless, so far as our own resources are concerned.

The same is true when it comes to our weakness. Not only are we unable to make right, we are unable to be or to do right. Our hearts are corrupt; as the Scripture says of us, "in their paths are ruin and misery, and the way of peace they have not known" (Rom. 3:16–17). Despite all our therapy, despite all our attempts to deny or forget the reality of our sin, we are simply unable to bring salvation.

3. Philip E. Hughes, *A Commentary on the Epistle to the Hebrews* (Grand Rapids: Eerdmans, 1977), 270.

I point out these categories—guilt and weakness—because they are precisely the dimensions of our need for which Jesus' intercession makes provision. While we are utterly unable to save ourselves, "he is able to save to the uttermost those who draw near to God through him" (Heb. 7:25).

We need our guilt removed, and this is permanently accomplished by Jesus' intercession. The apostle John tells us, "If anybody does sin, we have an advocate with the Father, Jesus Christ the righteous. He is the propitiation for our sins" (1 John 2:1–2). Jesus speaks to the Father in our defense, John says, on the basis of his death on the cross. We have seen that when God the Father sees our Lord Jesus Christ in heaven, he sees his own appointed surety which guarantees the covenant of grace. But John reminds us of what God sees in Jesus. He sees the marks on his hands and feet, and the wound in his side where the soldier stuck the spear, and he sees that the debt of our sin has been paid. God sees that the Good Shepherd has loved his sheep by laying down his life for them. How, then, will God condemn us now? As Paul answered in Romans 8:34: "Who is to condemn? Christ Jesus is the one who died—more than that, who was raised—who is at the right hand of God, who indeed is interceding for us." Therefore, as Paul earlier had explained, there is now "no condemnation for those who are in Christ Jesus" (Rom. 8:1).

You may ask, How can Christ speak for me in the filthiness of my sins, with my record of failure and infidelity? The answer is that Jesus need not speak at all. He needs only to identify you as one of his own. He needs only to direct his pierced hand toward you and, if he speaks at all, to say, "Father, this is one of my own, who comes to you through my shed blood for his salvation." Your sins are dealt with completely, to the uttermost, because Jesus intercedes for you with the remedy of his cross.

The spiritual value of this teaching is enormous. We try to deal with guilt by doing things on our level, by confessing or fasting or praying or doing good works. Of course we are to confess our sins. First John 1:9 says, "If we confess our sins, he is faithful and just to forgive us our sins and to cleanse us from all unrighteousness." We are in relationship with Christ, and he wants us to come to him with our sins, hating and mourning our iniquity. But our confession cannot actually remove our sin. What removes our sin is not something we do but what he did once for all on the cross, an all-sufficient redemption that now is on display in heaven and will be forever.

If you are a child of God through faith in Christ, his wounds effectually intercede for your sins day and night, every day of every year, without end forever. The answer to the guilt of our sin is Jesus Christ, who died to take our punishment and now lives to intercede for us.

When we turn to the other great problem we face, our terrible weakness, the intercession of Jesus Christ is equally effective. It was Christ's intercession that upheld the faith of Simon Peter when he denied our Lord three times. "Simon, Simon," Jesus told him in advance, "Satan demanded to have you, that he might sift you like wheat, but I have prayed for you that your faith may not fail" (Luke 22:31–32). As Jesus prayed for the disciples in the Garden of Gethsemane, surely he prays now for us at the right hand of God: "Holy Father, protect them by the power of your name" (John 17:11 NIV).

What about our difficulty in prayer? Many of us struggle with prayer because we are spiritually weak. Here, too, Jesus intercedes on our behalf, sending the Spirit to our aid. Paul writes, "The Spirit helps us in our weakness. For we do not know what to pray for as we ought, but the Spirit himself intercedes for us with groanings too deep for words" (Rom. 8:26). Therefore we can have confidence in prayer despite our weakness.

BECAUSE HE LIVES

Christianity is radically different from every other religion and every other solution to life in this world. All the other philosophies or religions have one thing in common: they rely on the performance, the work, or the power of man. Whether the hope is education or social action, New Age mysticism or some other solution, salvation depends on what you do and how well you do it. The answer is found in having the right technique or desire. What sets Christianity apart is a living Savior, who not only puts away our sin forever but sends us power from heaven. What matters most for Christians, therefore, is not what we are doing, not the spiritual power we are supposedly working up, but the wholly effective and powerful ministry of Jesus Christ, who lives and ministers forever as our great high priest.

If you will believe that because Jesus lives you have everything you need not only to remain in the faith but to bear abundant fruit, it will change your entire life. You will be freed from the bondage of performance religion. You will have the peace that comes from laying your burden on him, trusting him in his time to give you power for newness of life. Believing this will give you a new fervor in prayer, because you will know you are praying to a living Lord, who is ministering now for you in heaven. "Because he continues forever . . . he is able to save to the uttermost those who draw near to God through him, since he always lives to make intercession for them." Therefore, speak to your soul, as Charles Wesley's hymn advises, and proclaim to it an all-sufficient Savior in the crucified, risen, and ascended Jesus Christ:

Arise, my soul, arise,
    shake off your guilty fears;
the bleeding Sacrifice
    in my behalf appears:
before the throne my Surety stands,
    before the throne my Surety stands,
my name is written on his hands.

He ever lives above,
    for me to intercede,
his all-redeeming love,
    his precious blood to plead;
his blood atoned for every race,
    his blood atoned for every race,
and sprinkles now the throne of grace.

Five bleeding wounds he bears,
    received on Calvary;
they pour effectual prayers,
    they strongly plead for me.
"Forgive him, O forgive," they cry,
    "forgive him, O forgive," they cry,
"nor let that ransomed sinner die!"[4]

4. Charles Wesley, "Arise, My Soul, Arise," 1742.

25

PERFECTLY FITTING

Hebrews 7:26–28

*For it was indeed fitting that we should have such a high priest,
holy, innocent, unstained, separated from sinners, and exalted
above the heavens.* (Heb. 7:26)

s we conclude the seventh chapter of Hebrews, we come to
one of several crescendos in this majestic epistle. "Crescendo"
is a musical notation calling for a gradual increase in power
until a climax is reached. In this chapter the writer of Hebrews has been
building his argument up to the point of summation and integration that
we find in the last three verses.

When people speak of the great chapters in the Bible, they don't often
refer to the seventh chapter of Hebrews. All Scripture is God-breathed and
profitable, yet there are certain chapters which rise to special heights, pas-
torally, doctrinally, or doxologically. Psalm 23 beautifully expresses our
relationship as sheep to the Shepherd of our souls: "The LORD is my shepherd; I shall not want" (Ps. 23:1). Another great chapter is Romans 8, which
serves as an exclamation point on the doctrine of grace that the apostle
Paul so deliberately laid out in that book. When it comes to doxology—

that is, to the praise of God—what is more perfect than Psalm 19, which begins, "The heavens declare the glory of God, and the sky above proclaims his handiwork"!

I would like to make the case for the inclusion of Hebrews 7 on the list of great chapters. The subject matter here is Christology, our understanding of Christ and his work, and the chapter is like a doctrinal staircase climbing ever higher until the great summary statement in verses 26–28.

Hebrews 7 begins with Melchizedek as a type of Jesus Christ. Melchizedek shows us the excellency of Jesus—he is both king and priest, a bearer of righteousness and peace, and one who reigns and serves forever. We see there the ministry of Christ, for as Melchizedek met Abraham after his battles, to acclaim him and invite him to receive bread and wine, so also Christ says to us, "Come to me, all who labor and are heavy laden, and I will give you rest" (Matt. 11:28).

The exposition moves forward in verses 11–19 to show that Jesus is a better hope than that offered in the old covenant. When he appears as a new priest, he also brings a new and better administration of salvation. Possessing an indestructible life, he is able to give life, so that we might have a better and firmer hope.

Then in verses 20–25 the writer of Hebrews informs us of the implications of Jesus' eternal and permanent priesthood. Because he lives forever, he is the guarantee of God's covenant. Reigning forever in heaven, he assures our salvation, always interceding for us with the Father, so that "he is able to save to the uttermost those who draw near to God through him" (Heb. 7:25).

This is all wonderfully thorough Christology, but now we reach the climax, the summation of this exposition that is one of the high points of the entire epistle. Drawing together all that has been said about the person and work of Jesus Christ as our heavenly high priest, the writer of Hebrews concludes, "It was indeed fitting that we should have such a high priest" (Heb. 7:26). That is the point, isn't it? Not just that he is admirable, not merely that he is worthy in an abstract sort of way, but, as the New International Version renders this verse, "Such a high priest meets our need." He is perfectly fitting for us, in terms of both his person and his work, perfectly suited for our predicament and perfectly able to save us to the uttermost.

Fitting in His Person

Hebrews 7:26 begins with these words, "It was indeed fitting that we should have such a high priest." A better translation would be, "Such a high priest was fitted to us." The point is that Jesus as high priest is perfectly fitted for the predicament in which we find ourselves; he is appropriate in every way to be the Savior of sinful humankind.

Perhaps an ideal way of entry into this discussion is that provided by the medieval scholar Herveus. He pointed out that when you are discussing a sacrifice, there are four things you must take into account: "Namely, what is offered, to whom it is offered, by whom it is offered, and for whom it is offered."[1] Our passage starts with two of these already understood, namely, those *for whom* the sacrifice is offered—sinful man under condemnation of the law—as well as the One *to whom* it is offered—the holy God who must do right as judge of the universe. Those two points clearly describe our predicament, our unworthiness and condemnation in the presence of God. What remains is *what* is offered and *by whom*. It is in this respect that Jesus Christ is perfectly fitted to be our high priest in terms of the sacrifice he offers and of the high priest he is in offering it. John Owen explains: "Unholy sinners stand in need of a holy priest and a holy sacrifice. What we do not have in ourselves we must have in him, or we will not be accepted by the holy God, who has such pure eyes that he cannot look on sin. Such a high priest is the Lord Christ."[2]

Hebrews 7:26 sets Jesus forth as a high priest who is fitted to our need in that he offers himself. There are five things said about Jesus in this verse, beginning with a triplet of adjectives: holy, innocent, and unstained. These are related concepts all of which point to the perfection of Christ's person. Philip Hughes organizes these terms as, first, pertaining to God (holy); second, pertaining to other people (blameless); and third, pertaining to himself (pure).[3] William Lane sees them as pertaining first to the religious qualification of a priest—the word "holy" might be rendered as "devout." This deals not with how Jesus appears before men, but how he appears before

---

1. Quoted in Philip E. Hughes, *A Commentary on the Epistle to the Hebrews* (Grand Rapids: Eerdmans, 1977), 278.
2. John Owen, *Hebrews* (Wheaton, Ill.: Crossway, 1988), 178.
3. Hughes, *Hebrews*, 271.

God. Next comes the moral qualification of a priest: he is blameless, never having done wrong to his fellow men, sinless both in action and in motivation. Finally comes the cultic, we might say professional, qualification of a priest: he is pure, and thus undefiled for priestly service. Jesus our high priest is not merely pure in an external way, the way the Pharisees thought of purity by merely washing the outside, but he was pure throughout, outwardly and inwardly. Holy, blameless, pure—this is how Jesus qualifies in his person. "Taken together," Lane concludes, "these three adjectives describe the sinlessness of the high priest."[4] Jesus is everything we are not, so he can stand before God on our behalf.

The verse goes on to provide two participial phrases as a couplet: "separated from sinners, and exalted above the heavens." In what sense was Jesus set apart from sinners? Owen answers:

> He was not set apart from them in his nature, for God sent his own Son "in the likeness of sinful men" (Rom. 8:3). He was not set apart from men during his ministry on earth. He did not live apart from everyone in a desert. He spoke with tax collectors and prostitutes, and the hypocritical Pharisees rebuked him for this. Being set apart from sinners declares what Christ is, his state and condition. He is holy and undefiled. . . . He was separate from sin, in its nature, causes, and effects. He had to be like this for our benefit. He became the middle person between God and sinners and had to be separate from those sinners in the thing he stood in their place for.[5]

Jesus underwent all manner of temptation, but he is separate from sin. He is in a different category from sinful man, because he overcame temptation and emerged sinless. You see the importance of this for us. If we need Jesus to represent us because we are sinners, then it is vital that he be without sin, "separated from sinners."

Lastly, we read that Jesus was "exalted above the heavens." The point is not that Jesus has been elevated to some place higher than heaven, but rather that he is now higher than every other heavenly being, seated at the right hand of God with authority and power forever. Having seen

---

4. William L. Lane, *Hebrews 1–8* (Dallas: Word Books, 1991), 192.
5. Owen, *Hebrews*, 179.

his religious, moral, and ceremonial perfection, we now are reminded that his person is in heaven, where he is needed on our behalf.

In all these respects, Jesus was fitted according to our need. He is all that we are not, but need to be, and so he offered himself for us. Verse 27 says, "He offered up himself," and it was with reference to our sin that he was fitted to be our sin-bearing sacrifice and holy high priest. Because Jesus is untouched by sin, he is able to lay down his life in the place of sinners, so that we will be forgiven by God.

WHERE IS THE LAMB?

The late James Montgomery Boice had a favorite sermon, the title of which corresponds to the second issue presented in this passage. The sermon's title was "Where Is the Lamb?" The quote comes from Genesis 22:7, where it was spoken by Isaac, Abraham's son, whom God had directed Abraham to sacrifice atop Mount Moriah. "Take your son, your only son Isaac, whom you love," God commanded him, "and go to the land of Moriah, and offer him there as a burnt offering on one of the mountains of which I shall tell you" (Gen. 22:2). Isaac did not yet know that he was the one to be sacrificed. As they drew near to the site, he took note of the materials, the kindling and the knife and the fire, but noticed the lack of a sacrificial lamb. "My father!" he inquired. "Behold, the fire and the wood, but where is the lamb for a burnt offering?" (Gen. 22:7). Where is the lamb? Abraham, trusting God despite his great anxiety, answered, "God will provide for himself the lamb for a burnt offering, my son."

That is just what happened. As Abraham raised the knife to plunge it into young Isaac, an angel appeared saying, "Abraham, Abraham! . . . Do not lay your hand on the boy, for now I know that you fear God, seeing you have not withheld your son, your only son, from me" (Gen. 22:11–12). Looking up, Abraham saw a ram that God had provided. He offered it as his sacrifice in Isaac's place and named the site "The LORD will provide" (Gen. 22:13–14).

As Boice pointed out in his sermon, Isaac's question might well be the theme verse for the entire Old Testament, along with Abraham's reply: "Where is the lamb?" "The LORD will provide." This is the story of the Old Testament, the story of God's people up until the actual coming of Jesus Christ. Early in the Bible we learn that man is sinful before God and must either be judged or have another lay down for him an atoning sacrifice. We see this as early as Genesis 3, where Adam and Eve, having fallen into sin against God, were clothed by God with the skins of innocent animals (v. 21). They must have been horrified to see death taking place for the very first time, right before their eyes, an awful indicator of the wages of sin that is death (Rom. 6:23).

Apparently Adam and Eve learned from the example, because they taught their son Abel to approach God only on the basis of a blood sacrifice. Abel was received by God when he sacrificed lambs; his brother Cain, however, was rejected because he sought to worship God through the works of his sin-smeared hands.

But surely Adam and Eve must have known that animals could never atone for the sin of man. Animals are lower, beneath man in the order of God's creation, so their blood could not suffice to take the place of human beings. Furthermore, God had promised that the One who would truly deliver them would be the seed of Eve's own body (Gen. 3:15). Thus he would bear true humanity. This must have puzzled them, and yet they clearly believed God and were forgiven. The question that remained was, "Where is the lamb?"

In the time of Moses things became clearer. To release Israel out of Egypt, God broke Pharaoh's will by slaying the firstborn in all the land. Only the Israelites escaped this judgment, having marked their doors with the blood of a lamb. God told them: "Kill the Passover lamb. . . . For the LORD will pass through to strike the Egyptians, and when he sees the blood on the lintel and on the two doorposts, the LORD will pass over the door and will not allow the destroyer to enter your houses to strike you" (Ex. 12:21, 23). The Israelites must have realized that it was not the value of the lambs' blood that protected them and must have wondered, "Where is the true lamb?"

Later yet, when God was angry with his people for their sins, Moses tried to offer himself as a sacrifice in their place, to placate God's wrath against the people. But God refused to accept Moses' offer. Why? Because Moses was not able to atone for anyone else's sin. He was a sinner himself and thus needed an atonement for his own sin before God. But if not even Moses could make atonement, who could do better? "Where is the lamb?"

When Israel's priesthood was established, the death of animals was institutionalized, with lambs and goats and rams offered and sacrificed almost continually. Hebrews 7:27 mentions that the priests had to offer sacrifices over and again for their own sins, not to mention those of the people. As we will read in chapter 9, the blood of animals could only make the outside ceremonially clean, but could do nothing to cleanse the inner man; it could not actually remove the stain of guilt. "Where, then, is the lamb?" This is the obvious question.

This question and theme connects the entire Old Testament. Abraham offered his son Isaac as a sacrifice atop Mount Moriah. Second Chronicles 3:1 tells us that it was there that Solomon later built the temple. Upon the very rock where Abraham made his altar and raised his knife above the breast of his son, the offerings of Israel were made, century after century, pointing forward to the true sacrifice that would be made on nearby Mount Calvary. It was God's Son then. Unlike when Abraham sought to offer his only son, his beloved son Isaac, there was no angel to stay the hand of God when the hammers drove the nails into Jesus' hands and feet. Had Abraham been there watching while the Son of God was crucified for our sins, had he returned to see what the Lord provided in his own time upon the mount, surely he would have echoed the angel's words to him: "Now I know that you love me," he would have prayed with thanks to God, "seeing you have not withheld your Son, your only Son, from me."

The answer to this question, Where is the lamb? and to the whole anxious anticipation of the Old Testament, is Jesus Christ. He is, as John the Baptist announced, "the Lamb of God, who takes away the sin of the world!" (John 1:29). Jesus rode into Jerusalem on what we call Palm Sunday, but it was also the day the Passover lambs were driven in for slaughter, a vivid scene associating Jesus with these sacrificial lambs. Then, in the midst of the Passover feast, as the thousands of lambs were being actually slaughtered, the soldiers' hammers nailed our Lord Jesus to the cross, there to die for us. The symbolism is obvious, as Paul writes in 1 Corinthians 5:7: "Christ, our Passover lamb, has been sacrificed." He is the true Lamb.

Hebrews 7 tells us why Jesus alone is qualified to serve in this capacity. In his person he is perfectly fitted to our need, suited to our predicament, because he is "holy, innocent, unstained, separated from sinners," and now "exalted above the heavens." Because of who and what he is, Jesus Christ is able to be the Lamb whose blood was sacrificed for the sins of all his people.

FITTING IN HIS WORK

As we learned from Herveus, there are four things to consider in any sacrifice. There are those for whom it is offered, namely sinners, as well as the one to whom it is offered, that is, our righteous and holy God and Judge. As we have seen, Jesus meets our need with regard to the next part, the sacrifice that is offered. All that is left now is the one who offers the sacrifice, and in this, too, Jesus alone is fitted for our need. Hebrews 7:27–28 deals with Jesus' work as the priest who offers the sacrifice to God. In his priestly work, he alone meets our need.

Verse 27 contrasts Jesus' priestly work with that of the Old Testament priests of Israel: "He has no need, like those high priests, to offer sacrifices daily, first for his own sins and then for those of the people." The Old Testament high priests were really not able to meet our need. They were like someone who is hired for a job, who is given the right tools, and who works hard but simply lacks the ability or skill. Sculptors need artistic ability; scientists need mathematical prowess; athletes need speed and strength and grace. Priests need holiness. The reason is the nature of their work, namely, to bring pure offerings before a holy God.

The Old Testament priests showed their inability here, both in that they had to offer sacrifices for their own sins, and also in that their work was never finished. The insufficiency of any one sacrifice was illustrated by the need for more sacrifices later. In the greatest possible contrast, Hebrews 7:27 speaks of Jesus' fully sufficient sacrifice: "He did this once for all when he offered up himself." Whereas the Old Testament priests were sinners, he is holy; while their sacrifices were insufficient, his is sufficient; while the old priests were not able to meet the need of sinners, he is able once for all to reconcile us to God. Just as Jesus was perfectly fitting in his person, so is he also in his work. He fully meets our need, having been fitted by his perfection to our weakness and sin.

WHERE IS THE PRIEST?

All of this suggests another question begged by the Old Testament. Not only must the people have asked, "Where is the lamb?" but also, "Where is the priest?" Just as God's people before the time of Christ must have realized the inability of sheep and goats to atone for human sin, so also they must have realized that the mortal priests, sinners like themselves, were not qualified for the work of offering the true sacrifice before God.

Exodus 28 tells us about the special garments made for the high priest. There were a breastplate and an ephod, a robe with a tunic, a turban and a sash. These were made of gold and the finest linen, corresponding to the decorations of the tabernacle, and thus showing that the priest belonged in the presence of God. The priestly garb showed the resplendence of holiness. Going before God, a priest needed to appear righteous and holy, and his garments served that purpose.

The very need for this outerwear, however, vividly showed that those high priests lacked the holiness they needed. This is why they needed garments to put on. We know how this works today: if you need to wear the right clothes to be confident, then you really are not confident. The priests needed holiness to be confident before God, and these clothes showed that they had no basis for such confidence in themselves.

Indeed, the accounts of the high priests from the Old Testament remind me of a children's pageant. One child comes out as a sunflower, waving at her parents from behind the cardboard outfit. Another comes out as the sun, still another as clouds, and then little cardboard raindrops. In the same manner, Exodus tells us about the holy garments worn by the high priest. There was even a gold plate affixed to the high priest's turban, that read "Holy to the Lord" (28:36). He represented something that he very evidently was not himself; that was why he needed the costume. John Calvin observes, "What was required for the proper discharge of the office was lacking in the priests of the Law. . . . The external adornment of the high priest showed this defect . . . because the reality was absent."[6] Gazing upon all this, the spiritually perceptive person must have asked, "Where, oh, where, is the true priest we need?"

If we had been there on the day of atonement, which the writer of Hebrews has especially in mind, we would have seen many reasons not to have confidence in the old covenant priesthood. All of this is laid out in Leviticus 16. First, the high priest had to cleanse himself with water—not a very positive beginning if he is to have God's favor. Then he put on the garments we have already described, which testified to his own inadequacy. Next the high priest

6. John Calvin, *New Testament Commentaries*, 12 vols. (Grand Rapids: Eerdmans, 1994), 12:102.

took two goats, placing his hands on the one that would be the scapegoat, thus transferring the sins of the people to it, and then sacrificing the other as a sin offering for the people. This was supposed to remove their sins and turn away God's wrath. Then the high priest had to sacrifice an animal for himself—a very bad sign. This must have been disconcerting for those relying upon his ministry. As Calvin asks, "How could he have appeased God for others when God was rightly angry with him himself?"[7]

Only then would the high priest advance toward God's presence with the sacrificial blood, trembling at the thought of actually standing before such holiness. As he went forward, the bells that were woven into his outfit were ringing, and as he advanced beyond the curtains, every ear was tuned to hear them still, as proof that the high priest had not been struck dead before God's holy throne.[8] This whole procedure would do anything but encourage trust in such a priest. The people must have gazed on in dismay, asking, "Where is the true high priest?"

The writer of Hebrews mentions that the high priest made sacrifice for his own sin every day, and then made sacrifices for others. It seems that the author is including here the practice contemporary to his own time, when the high priests offered daily sacrifices simply because of their important position and out of anxiety for their sin and failure. Obviously, these were not priests who could really bring the people near to God. So, "Where is the priest?"

Hebrews answers by contrasting the old priesthood of the law with that of Jesus Christ: "For the law appoints men in their weakness as high priests, but the word of the oath, which came later than the law, appoints a Son who has been made perfect forever" (Heb. 7:28). The law appointed men who were weak. The oath, which came later than the law and therefore indicated the former priesthood's temporary status, appointed God's Son, who is perfect as high priest forever. William Barclay summarizes the point: "The Levitical High Priest was a sinful man offering animal sacrifices for a sinful people; Jesus was the sinless Son of God offering himself for the sin of all men. . . . Because he was what he was, the sinless Son of God, he was equipped for his office as no human High Priest could ever be."[9]

---

7. Ibid, 103.
8. See Ecclesiasticus 45:9.
9. William Barclay, *The Letter to the Hebrews* (Louisville: Westminster/John Knox, 1976), 85.

"Where is the true priest?" Jesus Christ is the One to whom all the priests beforehand pointed: the One who is holy, blameless, and pure; the One who is qualified to sacrifice "once for all" with the offering of his own blood; the One who is able to redeem us from sin and reconcile us to God.

FITTING TO WORSHIP

Jesus is perfectly fitting to deliver us from our predicament in sin and weakness. He is fitting in his person and fitting in his work. But Jesus Christ is also fit for our worship.

The things we are taught in this passage are also the things essential to true worship. Where does true worship begin? It begins with an awareness of our need. This passage says that Jesus meets our need and we must admit that need—the need for forgiveness, the need for reconciliation with God, the need for eternal life. Without confessing that need you may come to church but you will never really worship God. Until you abase yourself before him, acknowledging your need for mercy and grace—admitting that unless God will save you, you cannot be saved—until then you will only worship yourself and your fine religious attainments.

The other thing we need for true worship is the awareness that in Jesus Christ God has met our need. Our word "worship" comes from the older word "worth-ship." To worship someone or something is to acclaim its worth. And when you realize that Jesus Christ is not just some fine moral teacher, not some guru among a crowd of religious figures, but the very Savior you need, the only solution to your predicament, the only lamb able to bear your sin before God, and the only priest able to offer that sacrifice to God—when you realize that, then you will truly worship him. Indeed, if you do not worship Jesus Christ, then you do not understand either your need or the sufficiency of his saving work. If you do not worship Jesus Christ, then you are not saved, because he alone meets our need, is fitted to our predicament, as sinners confronted by a holy God.

That is what the redeemed do in heaven: they worship the true Lamb, the Lamb who was slain. The apostle John opens a window to this in the Book of Revelation, where he saw a Lamb that was slain upon the throne of heaven. And then he heard this song in heavenly joy: "Worthy are you . . . for you were slain, and by your blood you ransomed people for God from every tribe and language and people and nation, and you have made them a kingdom and priests to our God, and they shall reign on the earth" (Rev. 5:9–10).

This is the song that all the redeemed will sing in heaven. What is more, the song tells us that even those who once were sinners have now been made priests themselves to serve before God, because they are washed forever by the blood of the Lamb.

No matter who you are, no matter what you have done, the High Priest and Lamb of God, Jesus Christ, is perfectly fitting to your need. If you will admit that need—not just for a little help, but for an atoning sacrifice to take away your sin—and if you will bring that need to him, then he will take away your sin and open for you the door to heaven. And you will serve with him, in the beauty of holiness, both now and forevermore.

26

A SUPERIOR MINISTRY

Hebrews 8:1—6

*Christ has obtained a ministry that is as much more excellent
than the old as the covenant he mediates is better, since it is
enacted on better promises.* (Heb. 8:6)

*I*n 1517 a great discovery was made in the city of Wittenberg
in Saxon Germany. The man who made it was an Augustinian
monk named Martin Luther. Luther had been a troubled soul,
earnestly seeking to be right with God. His search resulted in what the
Book of Hebrews would describe as a change of covenant. What he found
was nothing less than the gospel of Jesus Christ, a superior covenant and
a superior ministry that would sweep across Germany and ultimately the
whole world.

A covenant is an agreement or contract established for relating to someone; it is the terms of a relationship. Marriage is a covenant, establishing
how a husband and wife will relate to one another in matrimony. Every religious system seeks to do the same, setting forth how a man is to relate to
God. Luther had been seeking God according to the varied means of the
Roman Catholic system of religion. He had tried confession, he had tried

the relics of saints, he had tried works of penance. Luther had labored to be accepted by God through every device of a religious system built on works and sacramental grace. But none of these really worked, he found. They could not overcome the reality of his sin and of God's judgment; they could not truly bring him to God.

What Luther discovered was a different covenant, a different way of salvation and fellowship with God. He found it in the pages of the Bible, where the apostles of Jesus recorded the teachings of this new covenant. What Luther found was a way of justification—that is, of forgiveness and pardon and acceptance with God—that is not by works but is by God's grace alone, through faith alone, in Christ alone. One of his biographers says that Luther "was like a man climbing in the darkness a winding staircase in the steeple of an ancient cathedral. In the blackness he reached out to steady himself, and his hand laid hold of a rope. He was startled to hear the clanging of a bell."[1]

That bell rang loudly in Luther's Wittenberg, just as it had rung in the first century A.D. when that same covenant, that same way of salvation, was first proclaimed in the name of Jesus Christ. The analogy between Roman Catholicism and the Judaism against which the author of Hebrews was writing is imperfect. But in the matter of how a sinner comes to God, the comparison is valid and profound. In both cases, the way of salvation taught in the Bible had been corrupted by worldliness and human reasoning. Both demanded works for justification with God. This is what so troubled Luther; he realized that all his works were hopelessly stained by sin. But the bigger problem with both Catholicism and Judaism was not the works they demanded, but the grace that they offered. In both Rome and Jerusalem, grace relied upon an earthly priesthood of imperfect men, whose ministry fell short of a sinner's true needs. Luther found that a grace that depends upon men is no grace at all. In great contrast to an imperfect priesthood of sinful men on earth—either in Jerusalem or in Rome—the writer of Hebrews points to the perfect priesthood of the Son of God in heaven—a superior ministry that is able to do what none other can: actually save sinners once for all and forever.

1. Roland H. Bainton, *Here I Stand: A Life of Martin Luther* (New York: Penguin, 1955), 64.

This is the truth that changed Wittenberg and launched the Protestant Reformation. It is the truth that lifts our eyes from earth to heaven, from our works of weakness to God's works of power, from man's enslaving religion to Christ's liberating salvation. It is the truth that turned the tongues of Wittenberg loose in song. One hymn expressed this superior ministry in these words:

> Thy work alone, O Christ,
>   can ease this weight of sin;
> thy blood alone, O Lamb of God,
>   can give me peace within. . . .
>
> . . . 'Tis he who saveth me,
>   and freely pardon gives;
> I love because he loveth me,
> I live because he lives.[2]

SUCH A HIGH PRIEST

Like the hymn writer, the writer of Hebrews wants us to focus not on any earthly ministry—not on ourselves and not on an earthly priest—but on Jesus Christ in heaven. It is his person and work that we have been exalting since our author began expounding Christ's priestly office at the beginning of chapter 7. It was Christ who brought joy to Wittenberg, as to the first recipients of this letter. And it is to Christ that the author draws our attention in verse 1: "The point in what we are saying is this: we have such a high priest."

The final section of Hebrews 7 served as the climax of a crescendo that had been building all through that great chapter. Hebrews 7 leads us upward in our understanding of Christ's ministry as heavenly high priest. Now, at the beginning of chapter 8, we are on a plateau, regrouping and ordering ourselves for the next climb up to a higher level still. The chief point the author wants us to grasp before moving onward is the superiority of Christ's priestly ministry in heaven. There are five features of Christ's high-priestly ministry that demonstrate its superiority, beginning with his perfection as high priest.

---

2. Horatius Bonar, "Not What My Hands Have Done," 1861.

Chapter 7 concludes by saying that Christ "has been made perfect" (v. 28). Now Hebrews 8 begins by saying, "We have such a high priest," that is, a perfect one. Whereas the earthly priests of Israel were imperfect, Christ is perfect. This speaks both to his sinless person and to his work on earth that accomplished all that was needed for him to be high priest forever. Jesus was perfect in his person from the start to the finish of his earthly life, but in his work he *became* perfect. Verse 3 reminds us that a priest must have a sacrifice to enter the sanctuary; since Jesus is in the true sanctuary of heaven, his perfect sacrifice has been received and accepted so as perfectly to establish his priestly ministry.

The writer of Hebrews has emphasized Jesus' becoming perfect or becoming complete several times, so this is obviously an important matter to him (see 2:10; 5:9; and 7:28). By taking up human flesh, by living under the law and perfectly fulfilling it, by sharing in our sufferings and sorrows, experientially "learn[ing] obedience through what he suffered" (Heb. 5:8), and then by offering himself in our place as the spotless Lamb of God, Christ completed or perfected the work needed to qualify him as our high priest. In this he is superior to any earthly priest. Earthly priests can share our suffering, but cannot transcend it; while they are able to sympathize with our weakness, they are likewise under sin's ruthless grip. Jesus alone has shared in our humanity while adding the power of his own divine nature, so that his work is superior. In a word, it is perfect.

This is why our Lord left heaven in the first place, to make himself perfect for his return to heaven as our great high priest. Philip Hughes articulates this well, speaking of Jesus' descent from heaven in the incarnation and his return to heaven in the ascension:

> He left as the Son of God. He returned both as Son of God and also, by reason of the incarnation, as Son of man. He left as Lord. He returned both as Lord and also as Minister on our behalf in the presence of the Father. He left as King. He returned both as King and also as High Priest and Intercessor for those whom he is not ashamed to call his brethren (Heb. 2:11). He left as Sovereign. He returned also as Savior.[3]

3. Philip E. Hughes, *A Commentary on the Epistle to the Hebrews* (Grand Rapids: Eerdmans, 1977), 283.

By coming to earth and by his work as God's Servant and our substitute, Christ established a ministry that is superior in every way to any other system of approach to God. He alone is able to meet our need as sinners before God's holy throne.

PRIEST AND KING

The second feature demonstrating that Christ's ministry is superior is that he is both priest and king. We have such a high priest, we read, "who is seated at the right hand of the throne of the Majesty in heaven" (Heb. 8:1). In other words, Jesus has taken his royal place at heaven's throne. This was never true in Israel; the men who ruled as king were not the men who served before the Lord as priests.

It is hard for us to appreciate the significance of this until we grasp the central role of the kings in Israel's history. One of the Old Testament's main history books is called "The Book of Kings." It is essentially the record of what kind of king ruled from one generation to the next; as the king went, so the kingdom went.

We know how important a leader's character is in our own time: the moral example of a school principal, a mayor, or even more so of a president. This was particularly true when it came to an Old Testament king, who not only set the tone for the nation, but also led the people in their service to God.

Imagine the anxiety, therefore, when one king died and was replaced by another. Asa was a godly king who brought blessing, but also became proud later in his life. When he died, all eyes turned to Jehoshaphat, his son. How relieved the godly people were to learn that this new king was himself a most godly man, a man who walked before God and brought blessing to the nation. Jehoshaphat's reign saw victory and prosperity. But after a long reign, the time came for Jehoshaphat to die. Unfortunately, the great mistake of his career was to ally himself with Ahab, the king of Israel and one of the Bible's most notorious villains, and to marry his son and successor to one of Ahab's daughters. The Bible says of Jehoshaphat's son: "He walked in the way of the kings of Israel, as the house of Ahab had done, for the daughter of Ahab was his wife. And he did what was evil in the sight of the Lord" (2 Kings 8:18). What an unmitigated disaster this was! All that had been gained by Jehoshaphat now was lost.

The character of a king has consequences for his kingdom. What a blessing it is, then, to find that the One who ascends to the throne over us, the One who comes to play such a pivotal role on our behalf, the King who single-handedly determines God's attitude toward all his kingdom, is none other than our great high priest, Jesus Christ. His kingdom is an everlasting kingdom, and he will reign forever and ever. That is good news for us, because we need not fear a change in regime. With him as our king forever, we will be forever blessed.

He Sat Down

The third item that draws attention to the superiority of Christ's priestly ministry comes through the words, "We have such a high priest, one *who is seated*" (Heb. 8:1). This is the second time such a statement has been made in this letter, the first time having occurred in 1:3, which said, "After making purification for sins, he sat down at the right hand of the Majesty on high."

There is a contrast here with the Levitical priests of the Old Testament, who never sat down inside the tabernacle. There were no seats there, so they were not invited to do so. Furthermore, the symbolism here has to do with the finished work of Christ versus the unfinished and therefore ongoing sacrifice of those earthly priests. Their work was not finished, their sacrifice was not sufficient, their atonement was not actual but only pointed forward to the better one to come. That is why they did not sit down. But Christ's work is finished. His sacrifice of himself is sufficient to reconcile us to God, and his atonement actually takes away our sin forever. This is why he entered into the heavenly sanctuary, completed his sacrifice once for all, and then sat down at God's right hand to signify that all is finished.

It was this reality that animated worship in Martin Luther's Wittenberg as well as doctrine. Chief among his reforms was the rejection of the Roman Catholic mass, which taught an ongoing sacrificial offering. Like the Levites, the Catholic priests labored week after week, performing the mass as the continual offering of Christ's blood. They did not, as it were, sit down. Every week the poor sinners filed into Catholic cathedrals, as they do today, anxious to have their sins covered for the time being, but knowing there would always be a need for more and more sacrifice. This is exactly what the Jewish priests offered—perpetual sacrifices of goats and bulls and sheep, ever seeking and never finding rest and peace with God. What a joy it was for Luther's generation to learn that Christ in heaven has won that peace, has offered the final sacrifice, and does not participate in the ongoing charade of the mass. He offered his blood once for all and then sat down. His gospel, proclaimed by the Reformers as by the writer of Hebrews, sets us free from spiritual bondage, from endlessly striving after God's favor. Isaac Watts puts it best in his hymn:

Not all the blood of beasts
    on Jewish altars slain,
could give the guilty conscience peace,
    or wash away the stain:

But Christ, the heavenly Lamb,
    takes all our sins away,
a sacrifice of nobler name
    and richer blood than they.[4]

He sat down, his work accomplished once for all, a superior ministry that offers final, eternal peace to weary sinners now forgiven and accepted by God in heaven. There is nothing more for him to do to win us salvation, nothing more for us to do but rest with joy in him. It is finished.

REIGNING WITH POWER

The fourth evidence of the superiority of Christ's priestly ministry is the power with which he presently reigns. Hebrews 8:1 says he sits at the right hand of the Majesty in heaven, that is, of God the Father himself. That is a seat of power and authority, which he exercises for our blessing. Matthew Henry explains: "This authority he exercises for the glory of his Father, for his own honour, and for the happiness of all who belong to him; and he will by his almighty power bring every one of them in their own order to the right hand of God in heaven, as members of his mystical body, that where he is they may be also."[5]

---

4. Isaac Watts, "Not All the Blood of Beasts," 1709.
5. Matthew Henry, *Commentary on the Whole Bible*, 6 vols. (New York: Fleming H. Revell, n.d.), 6:742.

This is where our assurance is grounded—that Christ is seated in heaven for us. He is there as our forerunner; since we are in him, we are seated in heaven. He guarantees our place. This is what Paul was getting at in Ephesians 2 where he spoke of the blessings that are ours through faith in Jesus: "[God] raised us up with [Christ] and seated us with him in the heavenly realms in Christ Jesus" (Eph. 2:6). Paul could say that in the past tense—that we have already been raised and seated with Christ—because Jesus is there for us; in him we shall be there too and even are represented there now. Thus we find full assurance of salvation in Christ who is seated in heaven. Because of his authority in heaven Jesus is confident of our salvation, saying in John's Gospel: "I shall lose nothing of all that [the Father] has given me, but raise it up on the last day" (John 6:39).

We, too, can be confident of our salvation because we are in Christ, who is seated in heaven, and also because Christ is in us, working with power. The Christ who is at work in us is the One who has been crucified; dead to sin's influence, he is victorious over sin. He is alive with resurrection power and is reigning with authority and power. The Westminster Shorter Catechism explains that Jesus fulfills his office as king "in subduing us to himself, in ruling and defending us, and in restraining and conquering all his and our enemies" (Q/A 26). He has power to win our hearts, to rule us, to govern us, to shape and change us, and to protect us in our pilgrim quest through a dark and dangerous world. Therefore we are not afraid, since Christ's superior ministry wins our salvation and guarantees it from the throne at God's right hand.

Serving in the True Tabernacle

The fifth and final feature of Christ's superiority is laid out at the end of verse 2, which says that our high priest is "a minister in the holy places, in the true tent that the Lord set up, not man." This theme is picked up in verses 4–5, which expand the idea: "Now if he were on earth, he would not be a priest at all, since there are priests who offer gifts according to the law. They serve a copy and shadow of the heavenly things. For when Moses was about to erect the tent, he was instructed by God, saying, 'See that you make everything according to the pattern that was shown you on the mountain.'"

This statement fends off a criticism that was leveled against Christians by the Jewish community, namely, that Christians had no priest. This might seem to be a sign of inferiority, in comparison with the earthly priesthood of Judaism. But the writer of Hebrews insists that this is not a sign of weakness, but rather of Christianity's superiority. We do have a priest—but not on the earth. Indeed, the earthly priesthood is nothing more than a "copy and shadow" of the true priestly ministry in heaven, which is the priesthood of Jesus Christ.

To say that Christ serves in the true tabernacle is not to say that the Israelite temple service was false. The contrast is between the true—that is, the final, the real, the ultimate—and the "copy and shadow" that was on earth. It is not true versus false, but true versus temporary and illustrative.

To say that Moses was required to make everything according to the pattern shown to him does not mean that the earthly tabernacle described in Exodus physically depicts heaven, but that its elements symbolize the realities of Christ's coming ministry in heaven. Christ's ministry is not inferior but superior, because it is the real, the final ministry that was pictured by the old. Now that the new has come, the old must give way.

Many of the original readers of Hebrews must have been cast out and barred from the religious life of their native culture. Verse 5 clues us that this letter was written before the fall of Jerusalem in A.D. 70, and thus at a time when the priestly service in the temple was still active, because the text says "they serve" at a sanctuary. That is in the present tense. It must have been a burden to be denied access to the great temple in Jerusalem, where Jesus himself had stood and taught. In response to that burden, the writer assures his readers that they have the reality and the substance of what on earth is only typical and temporary, that the real sanctuary is not on the earth but in heaven, where the true and real high priest, Jesus Christ, serves on their behalf.

There is a point here for us, too. Jesus is not still a pilgrim on his way. The cross is no longer before him. He has no more trials, no more foes, no more work to be done. He has arrived at his appointed destination, and there he ministers for us until he comes again to bring history to a close. Jesus is there in heaven, the true tabernacle where God himself dwells, and it is the goal of his superior ministry to bring us to where he is, near to God in heaven. It is his work to do all these things for those he saved, and he will do it. He is himself, as he said in John 14:6, "the way, and the truth, and the life." When we come to Jesus, he brings us to God, to heaven, and to eternal life. He brings us home because he knows the way and has opened it for us.

A Superior Salvation

All of these are evidence that Jesus Christ has a superior ministry—superior to the earthly and ineffective ministry of Israel's priests, superior to the works-religion that so tormented Martin Luther, and superior to all the earthly means by which men try to present themselves to God today.

Hebrews 8:6 wraps this up by saying that Jesus' ministry is superior because his covenant is superior, having better promises. We will consider those promises in our next study. But we have seen plenty already to tell us that this *is* a better covenant—a better way of salvation—better than anything we have ever known before. It is superior because Jesus is superior, because his work actually saves us. He doesn't give us the chance to be saved, to save ourselves, or to be saved by others if we are fortunate. He saves us. He wins our salvation by his perfect and finished work, a work so finished that he sat down. He applies that salvation to us with his power and authority, ruling over us and in us and for us so that his kingdom will be established. And he awaits us in heaven, not merely passively, seeing if we will make it. No, he draws us to himself by his divine power. "I will not leave you as orphans; I will come to you," he says (John 14:18). Such is our complete and sure salvation if we trust in Jesus Christ. His ministry is superior in every way, because he saves us to the uttermost.

The recovery of this gospel—which speaks of our sufficient Savior in Jesus Christ—has always brought joy to the church. We will never have the joy of salvation if we are relying on our own works. But when we rely completely on Christ—both his perfect offering for us and his present ministry on our behalf—we have a joy that nothing can take away. This is what Martin Luther discovered and transmitted to multitudes. He found a ministry that was superior to the exercises and fastings and confessings of his former life, to the taking of masses and abusing of himself, to constant laboring and seeking to ascend to a heaven that is an infinity away. There is a superior ministry to all of that, the perfect ministry of Jesus Christ. He asks you only to look to him, trust in his Word, and be saved.

What about fear? Many Christians are afraid because of weakness, awareness of guilt, uncertainty for tomorrow. Do you fear those things? Then look to Jesus, who is seated for you in heaven. He has undertaken your cause, and he extends his power to ensure that you will come to where he is. In that respect, our passage anticipates what the writer of Hebrews will say in chapter 13: "[God] has said, 'I will never leave you nor forsake you.' So we can confidently say, 'The Lord is my helper; I will not fear; what can man do to me?'" (vv. 5–6).

27

THE NEW COVENANT

Hebrews 8:6—13

For this is the covenant that I will make with the house of Israel
after those days, declares the Lord: I will put my laws into their
minds, and write them on their hearts, and I will be their God,
and they shall be my people. (Heb. 8:10)

One of the unfortunate innovations of recent times is the no-fault divorce. A couple meets, starts dating, gets married, and moves in together (not necessarily in that order). And as man has found since time immemorial, it is then that real life sets in. A real relationship has to be worked out; it is then that faults are recognized and magnified, and getting along becomes less than easy. In so many cases today, failure leads to frustration and misery. Hence, the no-fault divorce. The point is not that no one is to blame, but that everyone is to blame. Instead of trying to untie the convoluted knot and thus prolonging the agony, the knot is simply cut. There is no blame, no fault, no hassle. That is just the way it goes, an apparent inevitability in a world where breaking promises is so much easier than breaking habits. There are few tragedies, I think, that so sadly testify to the despair that grips our time as the no-fault divorce.

Divorce is something that happens in the Bible, too. The Bible recognizes grounds for divorce, namely infidelity and abandonment (see Matt. 19:9 and 1 Cor. 7:15). But divorce is never "no-fault," nor is it ever "no big deal." It is always a big deal, and the result is always lamentable. "I hate divorce," God says in Malachi 2:16 (NIV), just as he always hates the breaking of faith.

It is especially a tragedy when someone is forced into an unwanted divorce. Usually this happens because a spouse has been unfaithful and rejects his or her partner. It may surprise you to learn that this very thing has happened to God. The old covenant was shattered because of Israel's infidelity, her worship of other gods, and rejection of the Lord. The old covenant was a marriage agreement between God and his people, like that between a man and a woman today. Jeremiah 3:8 explains what happened: "For all the adulteries of that faithless one, Israel, I had sent her away with a decree of divorce." God knows what it is like to be a rejected lover, to be forced into an unwanted divorce.

Marriage begins with the exchange of vows: "I take thee to be my wedded wife, for richer or poorer, in joy and in sorrow, in sickness and health, so long as we both shall live." Yet when someone is faced with the infidelity of a partner, he or she is not able to keep his own wedding vows. That is one of many tragedies in divorce. When faced with rejection, we are sometimes unable to change our spouse's heart or to erase the devastation of what has been done. If our spouse is unwilling to honor the marriage vow, all we can do is walk away from our own promise, with a broken vow, a broken heart.

But there is a difference between God and us: he is able to remake what has been broken. He is able to keep the promise he has made, no matter what. He vowed to his bride Israel, "I will take you to be my people, and I will be your God" (Ex. 6:7). And though they broke that marriage covenant, God had prepared a new covenant in which his promise would be fulfilled. That is what this teaching in Hebrews 8:6–13 is about: the new covenant that secures God's wedding vow to his people and better promises that actually secure a people for God forever.

A NEW COVENANT

The overall purpose of Hebrews is to warn Jewish Christians against falling back into Judaism. Having refused to accept Jesus as the promised Messiah,

Judaism was set aside as a valid way to God and to salvation. Our passage argues this by making a point about the new covenant that came in Christ and was promised even in the days of the old covenant. Verses 8–12 are a citation from Jeremiah 31, at the time of the fall of Jerusalem, when the old covenant was finally shattered. That great chapter promises not that the old covenant would be patched up and fixed, but that its aims would be accomplished through a new and different covenant.

"I will be your God, and you will be my people," was always the expression of the purpose of the covenant. Jeremiah 31 shows that a new covenant will come to bring that to pass; the writer of Hebrews points out that this proves the deficiency of the old covenant. Now that the promised new covenant has come, it would be the gravest folly to go back to the old one it supplanted: "Christ has obtained a ministry that is as much more excellent than the old as the covenant he mediates is better, since it is enacted on better promises. For if that first covenant had been faultless, there would have been no occasion to look for a second" (Heb. 8:6–7).

The point is reinforced in Hebrews 8:13, which points out that the old covenant religious system would soon be done away with altogether. It is possible that this reflects an awareness of the events of A.D. 70, which were perhaps about to take place, when the Romans conquered Jerusalem and destroyed the temple once and for all. The argument in Hebrews, however, is simply that the new covenant necessitates the abandonment of the old: "In speaking of a new covenant, he makes the first one obsolete. And what is becoming obsolete and growing old is ready to vanish away" (Heb. 8:13).

The middle verses, Hebrews 8:8–12, present the new covenant as foreseen in Jeremiah 31, and particularly the promises that make it better. A study of these promises helps us understand Christianity by way of contrast to the old covenant.

But first we need to understand what was wrong with the old covenant. This was not a no-fault divorce, and the blame is clearly assigned in our passage. It is sometimes said that the problem with the old covenant was that it was not a covenant of grace. But the old covenant was given amidst the greatest manifestation of grace in the entire Old Testament, namely the exodus. It was given "when I took them by the hand to bring them out of the land of Egypt" (Heb. 8:9). God saved Israel by grace. He led his people out of Egypt and only then brought them to Mount Sinai to receive his law. The problem was not a lack of grace in the old covenant.

What, then, was the problem? Verse 9 tells us plainly: "For they did not continue in my covenant, and so I showed no concern for them." The problem with the old covenant was the infidelity of the people. Read the Old Testament and you will find a continuous history of idolatry and faithlessness. Using the illustration of an adulterous wife, Jeremiah summarized this entire record by writing, "Lift up your eyes to the bare heights, and see! Where have you not been ravished? By the waysides you have sat awaiting lovers. . . . You have polluted the land with your vile whoredom" (Jer. 3:2).

Hebrews 8:9 shows the chilling cause-and-effect relationship so well displayed in the Old Testament: "They did not continue in my covenant, and so I showed no concern for them, declares the Lord." That is what happens when people reject God—he turns away from them. The result for Old Testament Israel was military defeat, the vast destruction of their society, and national enslavement. If salvation meant deliverance from slavery in Egypt, rejection of God meant a return to bondage in the form of the Babylonian captivity.

The same principle applies today. People think that rejecting God opens the door to freedom. They can do what they want without fetters or restriction. But this is not the case, because they are not free from the consequences of their sin. Western culture is a vast illustration of this principle: having rejected God, we now are left to deal with godlessness on a vast scale. "They did not continue in my covenant, and so I showed no concern for them, declares the Lord" (Heb. 8:9). This is the worst thing that could ever happen to any people, entailing both the withdrawal of God's special care and the visit of sin's terrible wages.

The blame for this broken covenant lay squarely on the unfaithful people. Yet the point of this passage is to show the inadequacy of that old covenant. Its main problem was not that it lacked grace, but that it was an external administration of salvation. That is, it did not convey to the people the inward power needed to fulfill its demands. It is in this respect that the new covenant is better, and is able to succeed where the old one failed. The new covenant works internally; it transforms those who come to God through it.

The First Promise: The Spirit's Transforming Work

The first great promise of the new covenant is stated in verse 10: "I will put my laws into their minds, and write them on their hearts." In the old covenant, God gave the people his law, but that covenant did not give them the ability to receive it, love it, or keep its demands. In Romans 8:3 Paul says the old covenant law was compromised by the weakness of human nature; this is why the relationship between God and his people broke down.

But in the new covenant, God makes provision for human weakness, promising not only to give the law but actually to place it within us. This points to the work of the Holy Spirit as Jesus sends him to his own.

Second Corinthians 3 provides a parallel to this promise in Hebrews 8. There Paul also contrasts the external work of the old covenant to the internal work of the new, using the same metaphor of tablets of stone in contrast to tablets of the heart, on which God has written. That chapter concludes with an explanation of how this takes place, namely, that believers in Christ "are being transformed into his likeness with ever-increasing glory, which comes from the Lord, who is the Spirit" (2 Cor. 3:18 NIV).

Every true Christian has personal acquaintance with this. If you possess eternal life through faith in Christ, you have experienced at least something of this. You start wanting to do things you never wanted to do before, while old pleasures seem disturbing. You find yourself eagerly attending church, praying, reading the Bible, serving others, while shunning evil more and more as Christ leads you and God writes his law upon your heart.

Hebrews 8:10 also tells us something important about saving faith: "I will put my laws into their minds and write them on their hearts." There is a progression here, beginning with the mind and moving to the heart. "I will place or give my law into their minds," God says. The point is that he will give us understanding of his Word. But that is not enough: "I will write my law on their hearts." In contrast to the old covenant administration, which was given externally on tablets of stone, the new covenant is applied by God to the hearts of men and women.

This tells us that faith takes place in both the mind—our thinking faculty—and in the heart, which includes our will and affections. First we have to understand truth, and then we have to embrace it, commit to it, and love it in our hearts. This is how saving faith works. Both the head and the heart are necessary. It is sometimes said that the heart is the sanctuary of the soul, and that is true. But the mind is the vestibule of the heart. Light shines through the mind and warms the heart.

People say, "I want heart religion, not head religion," but this is impossible. Certainly it is possible to have understanding in the mind that makes no impression on the heart. But such bare knowledge or even assent to truth does not constitute saving faith. Until knowledge pierces the heart, wins us to Jesus Christ, and begins to reshape our lives and our loves, then we have not known saving faith. It is equally wrong to pursue emotional warmth without understanding. If you say you have love for God, it must be in response to what God has revealed about himself, to the salvation he has revealed in his Word, and which most certainly has doctrinal or propositional content. Many people have religious emotionalism and yet are not saved because they have not known the God of the Bible.

The promise of God's inward work makes the new covenant a better covenant. God promises that he will work faithfulness into us. What the old covenant could not do—give us a heart to obey and glorify God—the new covenant can do. This means that if you have faith in Christ, if you are saved under this new covenant, God is doing this in you. "For it is God who works in you," Paul says, "both to will and to work for his good pleasure" (Phil. 2:13). Genuine, saving belief in Christ will always affect our will and our affections, or else it is not the faith that saves us by means of this new covenant.

Far from being a source of worry, this is a great encouragement. You may come before God and say, "Lord, I believe on Jesus, but I am not faithful. I am not trustworthy." But he says here that if you trust in him, if you walk with him by the blood of Jesus, he will make you faithful. He will work faithfulness into you; he will engrave it on your heart. We lament, "Lord, I love things that are wicked and find precious little attraction in holy and good things." But what a great promise we have here in the new covenant in Christ! He will reveal his law to your mind, he will give you understanding and then will write it upon your heart. He will change you so that you will increasingly reflect his character. Let this encourage every struggling Christian about the benefit that will come through the sincere and persistent study of God's Word.

Our passage promises that God will do this, without telling us how it happens. The apostle Paul, however, explains this very clearly: "Do not be conformed to this world, but be transformed by the renewal of your mind, that by testing you may discern what is the will of God, what is good and acceptable and perfect" (Rom. 12:2). God changes us by his Word, applying it to us, illuminating our hearts, and regenerating our will by the work of the Holy Spirit. It is by God's Word that he saves us and changes us.

Therefore, trusting in this great promise, what we are to do is become people of his Word. You say, "I cannot change my heart," and that is true. But you can give your mind to the Word of God, you can seek the light that shines forth from Scripture—and as your mind is transformed, God will shine that light into your heart, warming it to the things of God.

THE SECOND PROMISE: FORGIVENESS OF SINS

A second great promise actually comes third in the passage, but logically comes next: "I will be merciful toward their iniquities, and I will remember their sins no more" (Heb. 8:12). The reason this promise comes last is that it is the great and climactic promise and the basis for the superiority of the new covenant. As John Owen writes, "This is the great fundamental promise and grace of the new covenant. . . . The first thing that is necessary is the free pardon of sin."[1]

There are two parts to this promise, and both of them are wonderful good news. The first is that God will forgive our wickedness. This was foreseen by Jeremiah as he looked forward to the future when Jesus Christ would come and die upon the cross.

"I will be merciful toward their iniquities," God says. The word "merciful" (Greek, *hileōs*) is the root of the word that is used in the description of the mercy seat that sat atop the ark of the covenant. In Greek, it was called the *hilastērion*. This was the place where the blood of the sacrifice was brought by the high priest on the day of atonement. The high priest came into the holy of holies, the inner sanctum, where the golden cherubim rested atop the ark of the covenant. This was God's throne from which he looked down upon the broken Ten Commandments, which were kept in the ark. Before him came the high priest, representing all the sinful and wicked people. According to God's law he must be struck down immediately, except

---

1. John Owen, *Hebrews* (Wheaton, Ill.: Crossway, 1988), 189.

that he brought before him the blood of the sacrifice, shed for the sins of the people. The blood was poured upon the mercy seat, so that God looked down and no longer saw the law that was transgressed, but the blood that paid the debt of sin. We might well read the promise of verse 12, therefore, as saying, "I will be mercy-seated toward your iniquities."

This is how God forgives our sin, by the blood of a spotless sacrifice. In writing this, Jeremiah looked forward to the coming of the Messiah, Jesus Christ, who was identified by John the Baptist with these words: "Behold the Lamb of God, who takes away the sin of the world!" (John 1:29).

God is merciful toward our wickedness when we acknowledge our sin and put our faith in Christ's blood that was shed for us. This was signified in the Last Supper. Jesus took the cup of wine, gave thanks, and used it as a symbol for his sacrificial death. He told the disciples: "This cup that is poured out for you is the new covenant in my blood" (Luke 22:20). It is because of Jesus' death, received by faith, that God promises, "I will forgive their wickedness."

The second part of this promise is that God will remember our sins no more. How, we might well ask, is it possible for God to forget? How can God, on the one hand, know all things, be perfect in knowledge, and yet, on the other, forget the wicked things we have done? The answer is found in the prior statement. God's forgetting is based on his forgiving.

Scripture uses the language of the marketplace to describe how God forgives and forgets. You owe a debt to someone and you haven't paid it. The one thing you can count on is that he will not forget. The man you owe will remind you, probably every time you see him. But if someone else comes along and pays the debt for you, he in turn will no longer bother you about what was owed. He has forgotten your debt because he has received full payment. That is what has happened with God in his perfect justice toward the debt of our sin. It has been fully satisfied, fully paid, and God can declare that he remembers our sin no more.

What a difference this makes to our relationship with God. Many marriages are embittered by the remembrance of sin, despite claims to forgiveness. Sometimes it is something that happened years and years ago. Yet the husband or wife stills brings it up, still holds it before the other. "I have never forgotten what you said at such and such a time!" "I want you to know that I remember what you did that time long ago!" "Don't think I forget the time you let me down!" It is always there, like poison in the well of the relationship, making everything bitter and dead.

This is something that we will never hear from God. He has put away our sin. He has forgotten all the dreadful things we have done. That is what Psalm 103:12 celebrates: "As far as the east is from the west, so far does he remove our transgressions from us." How far is the east from the west? Infinitely far! This is the great promise of the new covenant in Jesus Christ. God has forgiven us and so our sin is no more!

This is the kind of grace that allows Christians to overcome sin and guilt in our own relationships, truly forgiving and putting away the sin because of the grace we have received through Jesus Christ. Many Christian marriages have been saved, and should be saved, because of the power of forgiveness through the blood of Jesus Christ.

THE CULMINATING PROMISE: "I WILL BE THEIR GOD"

The last promise culminates and results from the previous two: "I will be their God, and they shall be my people. And they shall not teach, each one his neighbor and each one his brother, saying, 'Know the Lord,' for they shall all know me, from the least of them to the greatest" (Heb. 8:10–11).

This promise also has two parts, the first of which is God's promise to be our God. Andrew Murray writes, "Personal, direct fellowship with God: this is the crowning blessing of the new covenant."[2] The condition of such fellowship is holiness, for God is holy—and he now promises to write his law on our hearts. The threat to such fellowship is our sin—and he has promised to forgive and forget it completely through Jesus Christ. Therefore, this crowning blessing can be given and received: "I will be their God, and they shall be my people."

This is the sealing of a marriage—one that had been broken by man but rests upon the unbreakable promise of God. Therefore, he replaces the old covenant with a new one, a covenant that deals both with our internal problem—a sinful nature—and our external problem—the guilt of our sin—so that he can keep his promise of old: "I will be your God" (Ex. 6:7). Instead

---

2. Andrew Murray, *The Holiest of All: An Exposition of the Epistle to the Hebrews* (Grand Rapids: Revell, 1993), 295.

of a no-fault divorce, or even a covenant broken by the acknowledged guilt of an adulterous spouse, God has overwhelmed our sin with the power of his grace. What we have here is nothing less than the reaffirmation of his wedding vow: "I will be your God."

The second part of this promise constitutes our responding vow to God, which he also promises: "They shall be my people. . . . They shall all know me, from the least of them to the greatest" (Heb. 8:10–11). This promises an affirmation from God's purchased and betrothed people, each of them and all of them, their acknowledgment that he is their Lord and God.

This is what God desires: an expression of fidelity, of marital commitment and intimacy, the loving cry of the faithful wife: "I know him—he is my Lord." What God desires from us, what he requires from us, he bestows upon us by grace in this new and better covenant. Not only will he say and fulfill his vow, but all his own will speak and faithfully fulfill their vows to him. Sadly, we know too little of this in our present experience, although God continues to work in us toward this end. But this is the scene with which the whole Bible comes to its culmination, the future day when all of this will fully come to pass: "I saw the holy city, new Jerusalem, coming down out of heaven from God, prepared as a bride adorned for her husband. And I heard a loud voice from the throne saying, 'Behold, the dwelling place of God is with man. He will dwell with them, and they will be his people, and God himself will be with them as their God'" (Rev. 21:2–3).

So Long As We Both Shall Live

One of my greatest joys as a gospel minister is to perform wedding ceremonies, establishing a covenant of marriage between a man and a woman. I always like to point out that the bride, in her joy, in all her shining white glory, is a wonderful picture of what it means to be a Christian. This is not just my idea, but it is the teaching of Scripture: "I will greatly rejoice in the Lord; my soul shall exult in my God, for he has clothed me with the garments of salvation; he has covered me with the robe of righteousness" (Isa. 61:10). Isaiah goes on to say that these garments are like those of a groom and a bride on their wedding day.

A bride purchases her gown and puts it on just for that one day. Afterwards, she will change into regular clothes, and her white wedding gown is put away. But here is the point: the way we see the bride for just one day is the way that God sees us every day of our lives in Jesus Christ. This is what this new covenant is all about—a love relationship sealed and consummated forever by the blood of Jesus and the ministry of the Holy Spirit. Because Jesus has woven your gown of righteousness and taken away your sin, what Isaiah says is true: "as the bridegroom rejoices over the bride, so shall your God rejoice over you" (Isa. 62:5).

He has given us a garment of salvation, a robe of righteousness, even the righteousness of Christ. And he is working in us the love and affection suitable for a bride to such a husband. There will be no divorce, for this covenant is made effectual by God himself. He says, "So long as we both shall live, I will be your God." And by his work within us, all God's people respond in love: "So long as we both shall live, we will be your people." We will know him and acknowledge him as Lord and God; we will follow him with minds renewed in truth, with hearts renewed in holiness—our affection drawn to him—and we will be to him forever a bride in shining white. He has promised it. He has accomplished it in Christ. And through faith in his Word it will be true in our lives.

28

THE EARTHLY SANCTUARY

Hebrews 9:1—10

By this the Holy Spirit indicates that the way into the holy places is not yet opened as long as the first section is still standing (which is symbolic for the present age). According to this arrangement, gifts and sacrifices are offered that cannot perfect the conscience of the worshiper, but deal only with food and drink and various washings, regulations for the body imposed until the time of reformation. (Heb. 9:8–10)

*I*n C. S. Lewis's classic fantasy *The Chronicles of Narnia,* four children discover an attic wardrobe that seems normal enough from the outside. But creeping inside, they discover an entire world that was hidden from their view, the world of Narnia with the White Witch and Aslan the lion-lord. What seemed mundane on the outside turned out to be filled with mystery.

The ancient people of Israel also had a normal-looking structure that contained things of great significance. It was the tabernacle God commanded them to build in the time of Moses. This tent structure did not seem like much from the outside. But once inside, one was confronted with holy things—indeed, with the holy God himself.

Hebrews was written to warn Jewish believers against reverting back to the now obsolete religion of Judaism. To make his case, the author compares the old covenant ways with new covenant Christianity. Along the way, we gain rich instruction about the person and work of Jesus Christ, and about our lives of faith through the lens of Old Testament forms and patterns. Hebrews 9 offers a particularly vivid example, as the writer turns our attention to Israel's tabernacle, which he says was an illustration of things to come.

THE HOLY PLACE

C. S. Lewis's *Narnia* books present basic ideas of the Christian religion through the characters and events of their story. Similarly, the Old Testament tabernacle contained items that symbolized great redemptive truths. It showed what must be done for sinners to approach God, and typified the blessings of our relationship with God. Hebrews 9 takes up two subjects, namely, the arrangement of the tabernacle and the priestly service that took place within it.

Beginning with the tabernacle itself, verse 1 calls it an earthly sanctuary for the old covenant, in contrast with the heavenly sanctuary of the new covenant. And verse 8 tells us that as long as this sanctuary stood (or by implication its counterpart the Jewish temple), it symbolized that access to God was barred. This greatly contrasts with the open way provided by the sacrifice and offering of Jesus Christ.

With regard to the tabernacle's arrangement, verses 1–5 remind us that it consisted of two tents or rooms. In fact, there were three areas of the tabernacle, if you also count the outer courtyard. The courtyard contained an altar on which the sacrifices were made and the bronze laver where priests were washed clean. Next, immediately within the tabernacle, was the outer chamber, which the writer of Hebrews identifies as the holy place. It was rectangular in shape, twenty cubits long, ten cubits wide, and ten cubits high.[1] He reminds the readers of the well-known furnishings of this room,

---

1. See Exodus 26. A cubit is about 18 inches, so that 10 cubits is roughly equivalent to 15 feet.

which are described in detail in the books of Exodus and Leviticus. Inside the first room were the lampstand, the table on which the showbread was arranged, and finally, the altar of incense.

The lampstand, also known as the menorah, had seven branches, three on either side of the main stem (Ex. 25:31–36). The priests in their rotation kept these lamps supplied with oil so that they burned continuously.

The next item was the table of showbread, so named for God's command in Exodus 25:30, "You shall set the bread of the Presence on the table before me regularly." Twelve loaves were placed on the table each Sabbath, to be eaten only by the priests serving in the tabernacle.

Finally, the golden altar of incense rested immediately in front of the veil separating the outer room from the inner sanctum (see Ex. 30:1–6). Every morning and evening, when the priests came into the holy place to keep the lampstand burning, they also refreshed the incense for this altar. The Old Testament makes it clear that this item was located in the outer room and not the holy of holies, as the writer of Hebrews must have known. In verse 4, however, he associates it with the inner sanctum because of the vital role the cloud of incense played in covering the high priest's approach as he passed through the curtain on the day of atonement.

The writer of Hebrews tells us that it was not the details of these items that concerned him: "Of these things we cannot now speak in detail" (Heb. 9:5). Still, we can make some general observations. The holy place was where the priests had fellowship with God on behalf of the people, symbolized by the bread—twelve loaves for twelve tribes—which the priests ate at the Lord's table. The light represented God's revelation of himself, his illuminating presence, and the incense altar symbolized the prayers of God's people.

We can also see how these tabernacle symbols each point to Jesus Christ. The opening chapter of John's Gospel tells us, "In him was life, and the life was the light of men. . . . The true light, which enlightens everyone, was coming into the world" (John 1:4, 9). In John 6, Jesus first feeds the multitudes with just a few loaves and then proclaims, "I am the bread of life; whoever comes to me shall not hunger, and whoever believes in me shall never thirst" (John 6:35). Similarly, it is Jesus' intercessory prayers that sustain us in God's presence, a point that has been strongly made by the writer of Hebrews. The whole picture is summed up by John 1:14, where the apostle writes, "The Word became flesh and dwelt among us [literally, 'tabernacled among us'], and we have seen his glory, glory as of the only Son from the Father, full of grace and truth." It is in Christ that we have fellowship with God, just as the priests of Israel had fellowship with God in and by means of the tabernacle.

INTO THE MOST HOLY PLACE

There was, however, a significant difference between fellowship with God in the tabernacle and our fellowship with God in Christ. This point is suggested in verse 3, where we read, "Behind the second curtain was a second section called the Most Holy Place." The priests served in God's presence in a limited way through the symbolic items in the holy place, but God himself dwelt in the next chamber, which was separated by a thick curtain or veil. This inner room of the tabernacle was the Most Holy Place, also known as the holy of holies. It was a cube in shape, ten cubits or fifteen feet on each side.

The writer of Hebrews tells us about this room as well. In this inner sanctum rested the ark of the covenant, the gold-paneled container which also served as the footstool of God's throne. On top of the ark were two golden cherubim, between which God's glory especially dwelt. In the ark were the two stone tablets of the Ten Commandments given by God to Moses. These tablets prescribed the terms of the covenant, and from them the ark derives its name. Also there were the jar containing manna from the wilderness sojourn and Aaron's staff, which God had caused to bloom when he identified Aaron as the specially chosen priest.

The writer's focus is not mainly on these items, but on what happened inside these rooms. On a regular basis, he says in verse 6, the priests entered the outer room to serve God, "but into the second only the high priest goes, and he but once a year, and not without taking blood, which he offers for himself and for the unintentional sins of the people" (Heb. 8:7). Every day the priests came into the outer room to serve God, worship him, have an indirect sort of fellowship with him before the candlelights and incense altar. But direct access to God himself was denied. The key item in this whole description is the second curtain, for it stood between the priests and God's presence. The whole time that they were in the holy place they were made aware of two things: the holy God's actual presence just on the other side of the curtain, and the barrier that kept them from seeing or entering into that holiest place. Andrew Murray writes:

The veil was the symbol of separation between a holy God and sinful man: they cannot dwell together. The tabernacle thus expressed the union of two apparently conflicting truths. God called man to come and worship and serve Him, and yet he might not come too near: the veil kept him at a distance.... Love calls the sinner near; righteousness keeps him back. The Holy One bids Israel build Him a house in which He will dwell, but forbids them entering His presence there.[2]

This frustrating tension was hardly alleviated by the one day of the year, the day of atonement, when the high priest actually did go into God's presence. Verse 7 tells us that only he entered, only on that one day, and only with blood from the sacrifice to cover his sins and those of the people. Far from minimizing the separation between the holy God and his unholy people, that one day emphasized it all the more. The day of atonement proclaimed that the way was in fact barred on any regular basis.

But the day of atonement also pointed forward to a day when the way would fully be opened: "By this the Holy Spirit indicates that the way into the holy places is not yet opened as long as the first section is still standing" (Heb. 9:8). The whole point of the tabernacle system of worship was on the one hand to show God's intent to have fellowship with his people, while on the other hand showing that the way for this was not yet open. The key phrase is "not yet." Therein is summed up the entire Old Testament religion. No, the way was not open to God; it was barred. But it was not simply not open, but not yet open—not yet, that is, until the time of Christ.

The writer of Hebrews conceives of these two rooms as a statement regarding worship and life in the two covenants. Life in the old covenant was life in the holy place. The priests were called to serve God. They had an indirect, mediated relationship with God, but they did not know him directly. They could not know him this way because their sin, though covered temporarily, was not yet removed. Year after year, the high priest took the sacrificial blood before God, so the people were not altogether rejected. But they could not and did not dwell in his direct presence.

In great contrast to this is life in the new covenant, symbolized by the Most Holy Place. By his own blood, the blood of the new covenant, Jesus

2. Andrew Murray, *The Holiest of All: An Exposition of the Epistle to the Hebrews* (Grand Rapids: Revell, 1993), 305.

Christ did what had not yet been done in the Old Testament. In him the way into the Most Holy Place is opened, and through faith in him we actually enter into direct fellowship with God.

The New Testament tells us that on the day Jesus died, the curtain that barred the way was actually torn in two. How astonished must the priests have been! They were serving in the temple while the Son of God was dying, actually paying the debt of our sin, shedding the blood that he would present to God for our forgiveness. Matthew tells us that at the very moment Jesus died, "the curtain of the temple was torn in two, from top to bottom" (Matt. 27:51). By divine action the inner sanctum was now wide open, showing that through faith in Christ believers might have direct fellowship with God. We are no longer consigned to outward forms without inward reality. In Christ Jesus, we now have direct access to the Father. We may come before him without fear, for our guilt is removed, our debt paid in full. God's desire to call us into communion with himself and not merely into service, like ancient Israel, has been brought to fruition by the precious blood of Christ.

COMMUNION WITH GOD

Verse 8 says, "The Holy Spirit indicates" this. On a first reading we might think that this simply refers to the Spirit's role in inspiring Scripture. The writer of Hebrews speaks this way on two other occasions (3:7; 10:15). However, that is not what is being said in this case. For one thing, there is no citation from the Old Testament found here. For another, the verb is not past tense but present tense. We see, therefore, a deliberate contrast. On the one hand, the old tabernacle *was showing* that the way was barred, because the curtain kept the priests from the holy of holies. Now the Holy Spirit *is showing* the opposite, that the way to God is finally open.

The linking of the Holy Spirit and the holy of holies in this passage is also deliberate. The character of God's Spirit is appropriate to his inner sanctum: the Spirit is "Holy." Furthermore, we recall that the tabernacle Jesus entered with his own blood was not on earth but in heaven. Verse 11 goes on to make this very point, calling it "the greater and more perfect tent (not made with hands, that is, not of this creation)." He died, he was raised from the dead, and then he ascended into heaven. That is where

Jesus presented his blood to God, just as the high priest of Israel presented the blood of the sacrifice on the mercy seat in the holy of holies.

We ask ourselves, therefore, what took place after Jesus ascended into heaven, and the answer is Pentecost. Jesus went into heaven as our high priest, offered his blood once for all, and sent his Holy Spirit into the world, fulfilling the ancient promise. Galatians 3:13–14 summarizes by saying, "Christ redeemed us from the curse of the law . . . so that in Christ Jesus the blessing of Abraham might come to the Gentiles, so that we might receive the promised Spirit through faith." In the old covenant, God wrote his law on tablets of stone; in the new covenant, he is writing it by his Holy Spirit upon our very hearts. The point of verse 8 is that the Holy Spirit's work proves we have access to God in the new covenant. Jesus Christ has torn away the veil and won us access to God by his blood. Now he sends his Spirit to enlighten our eyes and renew our hearts so that we might have fellowship with God. It was because of the Spirit that the apostle John could write, "Our fellowship is with the Father and with his Son Jesus Christ" (1 John 1:3).

This means that we have unrestricted access to God the Father through faith in Christ. Because of the finished work of Jesus Christ, our sins do not keep us from the holy God. It is true that sins still affect us. They will, for instance, keep us from enjoying our fellowship with God. But our access to God is secured forever through Jesus Christ because of his finished and sufficient work. The Spirit's work within us reminds us that we are now in fellowship with God and imparts to us the knowledge of his grace. As Paul explains in Romans 8:14–16: "All who are led by the Spirit of God are sons of God. For you did not receive the spirit of slavery to fall back into fear, but you have received the Spirit of adoption as sons, by whom we cry, 'Abba! Father!' The Spirit himself bears witness with our spirit that we are children of God."

A Higher Christian Life?

It is at this point that a significant error is made by some Christians, who see in the tabernacle two stages of the Christian life. There are select Christians, according to this teaching, who lead the higher life. These are also known as "spiritual Christians," and they dwell in the holy of holies. There are also those who lead a lower life, called "carnal Christians"; they know only the outer room, dimly lit and distant from God. Andrew Murray, a late-nineteenth-century writer I have sometimes quoted in these studies, is one who teaches this erroneous view:

> The two compartments of the tabernacle represent two degrees of nearness to God, two dispensations of God's grace, or two stages in the Christian life, a lower and a higher. . . . Many believers never in experience enter into this life of the inner sanctuary, the more complete and abiding nearness to God. They have, in the outer court, seen the altar, and received the pardon of sin; they have entered upon the service of God, they seek to do His will, but the joy of His presence as their abiding portion they know not.[3]

This is a plausible argument, partly because we know that there are growth and advancement in the Christian life. Furthermore, experience shows that many Christians fail to manifest the joy of the Lord as they should. But this is not the point of Hebrews, nor is such a two-stage theory taught in the Bible. The contrast in our passage is not between two types of Christians, higher and lower, but between the old covenant and the new covenant. While the first tabernacle and the old covenant religious system were still standing—that is, before they were superseded by Christ's entry into the new and heavenly tabernacle—the way to God was not yet disclosed. Now in Christ that way has been made known. The whole point of Hebrews is that a failure to move from the old covenant to the new covenant does not risk a lower state of salvation, but rather the loss of salvation altogether: "How shall we escape if we neglect such a great salvation?" (Heb. 2:3).

What higher-life teachers like Murray describe as the carnal Christian is in fact no Christian at all. To live outside the sphere of the Spirit of God, to bear no evidence of the Spirit's sanctifying presence and work, to display no reliance on or pleasure in your relationship with God through Jesus Christ is not to be a weak saved person but an unsaved person altogether. If you have not actually rested upon Jesus for your salvation, have not known his Spirit's presence changing your heart and molding your affections, enlightening you with the gospel and enflaming you with commitment to Christ—then you are not saved.

3. Ibid., 308–9.

On the other hand, anyone who has come into God's presence through faith in Christ, and has known the Spirit's work within, but yet finds himself slow and weak and dull in his struggle with sin, is not a lower-level Christian but a normal Christian. There is no such thing as a Christian who is not struggling with some issue of sin (see 1 John 1:8), and who is not daily dependent on God's grace. Paul said of himself, "Not that I have already obtained this or am already perfect, but I press on to make it my own, because Christ Jesus has made me his own" (Phil. 3:12). There is more to be grasped and enjoyed, more power and life in Christ, than any of us presently know.

Therefore, we see that the higher-life teachers err on both sides of the equation. There are no "carnal" Christians who have yet to pass through the veil into a personal relationship with God; such persons are not Christians at all. Likewise, there are no "spiritual" Christians for whom all struggle is gone in this life, who have entered into a stage of perfect sanctification. Indeed, the expectation of the latter stage is injurious to the Christian's spiritual life, for the struggle with sin and weakness is not a sign that we have not yet arrived as Christians. Rather, it is merely the reality of life this side of heaven, a life we are to live through faith as God's strength is made perfect in our weakness (2 Cor. 12:9). If anything, we are all carnal Christians, the word "carnal" meaning "fleshly." This is how Paul described himself, "The life I now live *in the flesh* I live by faith in the Son of God, who loved me and gave himself for me" (Gal. 2:20). Instead of seeking some higher spiritual plateau, our calling is simply to grow in grace as we learn more and more to trust and love the Lord our God.

A CLEAN CONSCIENCE

Verses 9 and 10 complete our survey of the earthly sanctuary and the whole system attached to it. Verse 9 tells us, "According to this arrangement, gifts and sacrifices are offered that cannot perfect the conscience of the worshiper."

As sinners we have an inner consciousness of guilt that keeps us from drawing near to God. Sin had that effect in the garden, when Adam and Eve fled from the voice of God, and it has that same effect on us. This was a great problem in the old covenant. The curtain in the tabernacle was a barrier erected by God. But there is another barrier within. Knowing our guilt, we naturally erect our own barrier against God—we dread drawing near to his presence, dread seeing him in his holiness or being seen by him in our sin.

The sacrifices of the Old Testament "cannot perfect the conscience of the worshiper" (Heb. 9:9). They were like all the other external rites, rules concerning food and drink and other outward ceremonies and regulations. This is the point of verse 10, which speaks of "regulations for the body imposed until the time of reformation." Until the time of the new order—the time foreseen by Jeremiah in his declaration of the new covenant (see Heb. 8)—this was all an outward show of an inward reality that had not yet come. The Israelites could sacrifice animals day after day—and they did—without having their consciences truly cleaned, without having peace about drawing near to God in his holiness. Until that happened, there could never be the fellowship between God and his people that the Lord desired. F. F. Bruce writes, "The really effective barrier to a man or woman's free access to God is an inward and not a material one; it exists in the conscience. It is only when the conscience is purified that one is set free to approach God without reservation and offer him acceptable service and worship."[4]

As the Old Testament priests drew nearer to the presence of God in the tabernacle, so too their fear and dread began to mount, because God looks upon the heart. Without a new heart, without a conscience that has been cleansed, man cannot come near to God.

The most awesome proof of this is what took place in Jerusalem after the death of Jesus Christ. We have already noted that immediately upon his death, the veil of the temple was rent in half, revealing that the way to God was open. But what did the priests do? Did they walk boldly through the way into God's presence that now was opened? Did they look upon Jesus as the true Lamb of God, who is now able to fulfill their fondest desire of drawing near to the Lord? Far from it! In the greatest of tragedies, they sewed up the veil again. With their own hands, they reestablished the barrier God himself had removed. What greater symbol could there be of the old covenant and its inability to bring sinners to God!

But Jesus has done what the sacrifices of the old covenant could not do. He did not merely cover our sins, but took them upon himself, removing them by his death on the cross. Think of the most terrible thing you have

---

4. F. F. Bruce, *The Epistle to the Hebrews,* rev. ed. (Grand Rapids: Eerdmans, 1990), 209.

ever done—the dark secret that haunts your nights, the great truth that if people really knew they would condemn you out of hand. God, who knows that secret and who does see that sin, has placed it upon his own Son so that you will not be condemned. This is the point of Paul's great statement in Colossians 2:13–14, "And you, who were dead in your trespasses and the uncircumcision of your flesh, God made alive together with him, having forgiven us all our trespasses, by canceling the record of debt that stood against us with its legal demands. This he set aside, nailing it to the cross." "Therefore," Paul concludes, "do not let anyone pass judgment on you" (v. 16). No, not Satan, not even yourself. You have been made clean by the blood of the Lamb.

This has the profound effect of removing our own inner barrier against the idea of drawing near to God. Hebrews 9 says that what the old arrangement could not do, Jesus has done through his own death: "perfect the conscience." Once we were guilty before God and hostile toward him in our thinking, in our will, and in our affections. We were utterly prejudiced against God, but now we are drawn to him by the Holy Spirit, who applies Christ's cleansing blood to our souls. The Puritan John Owen explains, "The Holy Spirit so persuades us that God loves us that our souls are filled with joy and comfort. This is his work and he does it effectively. To persuade a poor sinful soul that God in Jesus Christ loves him, delights in him, is well pleased with him and only has thoughts of kindness towards him is an inexpressible mercy."[5]

This is God's way of bringing us through the veil that was torn and into communion with himself in Christ. Relying on his love for us, inwardly cleansed by the saving work of Christ, we draw near to worship God and to have fellowship with him as his people.

JESUS THE WAY

John 14 tells of the conversation Jesus had with his disciples on the night of his arrest. He spoke to them about his departure to be with God, to go into heaven. Thomas responded, "Lord, we do not know where you are going. How can we know the way?" (John 14:5). If Thomas had understood better,

5. John Owen, *Communion with God* (Edinburgh: Banner of Truth, 1991), 181–82.

he might have comprehended the magnitude of what Jesus was saying. Jesus was going to God, doing what the high priest only dimly prefigured one day a year, and he was making a way for his disciples. "How can we know the way?" Thomas asked. Jesus replied, "I am the way" (John 14:6).

This is what the old covenant worship pointed to—the true sacrifice, the true priest who would open the way past the veil into the dwelling of God himself. This was God's intention from the first: "I will be their God, and they will be my people." It was with love that God called the people to himself at the tabernacle, but sin barred the way. Jesus opened the way by removing the barrier of our guilt and God's holy wrath on sin, dying on the cross in our place. He then sent God's love to us, removing the barrier within our hearts to enable us to come to God.

So let me ask you the question: What is it that is keeping you from God? Is it your sense of guilt, the feeling that you are dirty, that makes you uneasy in the presence of God? Then Jesus Christ is God's way to you and your way to God. "Behold, I have taken your iniquity away from you" (Zech. 3:4), he says, having given his own blood for your salvation. Now, by his Holy Spirit, he calls you into true fellowship with God unto newness of life.

The time of the new order has now come in the ministry of Jesus Christ. Once you were a sinner barred from God's presence and unwilling to come to him. But through faith in Jesus Christ, what Paul writes will be true: "You were washed, you were sanctified, you were justified in the name of the Lord Jesus Christ and by the Spirit of our God" (1 Cor. 6:11). And through faith in Christ you are now free to worship and live as a child of God forever. "My God is reconciled," says the hymn,

> his pardoning voice I hear;
> he owns me for his child,
> I can no longer fear;
> with confidence I now draw nigh,
> with confidence I now draw nigh,
> and "Father, Abba, Father!" cry.[6]

---

6. Charles Wesley, "Arise, My Soul, Arise," 1742.

29

THE BLOOD OF CHRIST

Hebrews 9:11—14

*For if the sprinkling of defiled persons with the blood of goats and
bulls and with the ashes of a heifer sanctifies for the purification
of the flesh, how much more will the blood of Christ, who through
the eternal Spirit offered himself without blemish to God, purify
our conscience from dead works to serve the living God.*
(Heb. 9:13–14)

he image of the blood of Jesus Christ is central to the message
of Christianity. If you skim through a hymnal, you will find
that this is so. We sing of being "washed in the blood," or "saved
by the blood of Jesus," and even exult in a "fountain filled with blood." To
critics of Christianity this seems bizarre and primitive. Bishop John Shelby
Spong, for instance, complains that this image of Jesus as crucified and
shedding his blood for our sins is so pervasive "that one can hardly view
Christianity apart from it."[1] He is right about that, but he therefore pro-
poses that we need a new kind of reformation—not one that recovers the

---

1. John Shelby Spong, *Why Christianity Must Change or Die* (San Francisco: HarperCollins,
1999), 84.

truths of the Bible, but one that jettisons the blood of Christ. "I would choose to loathe," he writes, "rather than to worship a deity who required the sacrifice of his son."[2]

People who share Spong's view will not think much of our present text, because if there is one passage in the Bible that exults in the blood of Jesus Christ it is this one. It shows why the crucifixion of Jesus Christ is not only necessary but also a source of great joy and power; it shows not a cruel and twisted heavenly tyrant, but a God of love who makes the most costly provision so that we can draw near to him.

For some time, the writer of Hebrews has been discussing the high-priestly ministry of the risen and exalted Jesus Christ. In chapter 7 he emphasized Jesus' present reign in heaven, where he now ministers with power for his own. Chapter 8 showed how this priestly ministry in heaven brings about the new covenant that was promised of old, a covenant relationship with God marked by the indwelling of the Holy Spirit and forgiveness of sin. Now in chapter 9 he comes to a theme at which he has hinted from time to time, namely, the atoning blood of Christ. Earlier, he wrote that this high priest made a sacrifice for sin once for all "when he offered up himself" (Heb. 7:27). He also noted that this high priest became man in order "to make propitiation for the sins of the people" (Heb. 2:17). These verses anticipated the theme to which we now turn, a theme that has inspired the loftiest heights of Christian praise:

> Oh! precious is the flow
> that makes me white as snow;
> no other fount I know,
> nothing but the blood of Jesus.[3]

As has been the case all through this epistle, the writer of Hebrews is interested in a comparison between Christianity and old covenant Israel. He has contrasted Jesus to Moses, Christ's priesthood to that of Aaron, the new covenant to the old covenant, and the heavenly tabernacle to the earthly tab-

---

2. Ibid., 95.
3. Robert Lowry, "Nothing but the Blood," 1876.

ernacle. All of these comparisons are summed up in the phrase "the good things that have come" (Heb. 9:11), as compared to the provisional and shadowy order of the earlier time.

Jesus Christ has brought in an entirely new order. Before was the time of shadows and types. But now that Christ has gone "through the greater and more perfect tent" (Heb. 9:11)—that is, into the tabernacle of heaven as our high priest—all the good things of the promised new order have been inaugurated. Verses 1–10 symbolized this new situation by comparing it to the tabernacle, with the curtain removed so that the holy of holies was laid bare to the sight of the priests in the outer room. Our access to God and the sending of the Holy Spirit are at the heart of this new order. But what is the power behind these staggering changes? Verse 12 answers: "He entered once for all into the holy places, not by means of the blood of goats and calves but by means of his own blood, thus securing an eternal redemption." The writer has three things to tell us about the blood of Christ: first, the superiority of Christ's blood; second, the power of Christ's blood; and finally, the purpose of Christ's blood, shed for us.

THE SUPERIORITY OF CHRIST'S BLOOD

The superiority of Christ's shed blood is evident from a comparison with the blood shed under the law of the old covenant: "The sprinkling of defiled persons with the blood of goats and bulls and with the ashes of a heifer sanctifies for the purification of the flesh" (Heb. 9:13). The point is not to show the failure of the animal blood that was shed and applied under the old covenant, but how effective it was. "The blood of goats and bulls and with the ashes of a heifer" has to do with the sacrifices prescribed for the cleansing of anyone declared unclean under the Old Testament law. "The blood of goats and bulls" is a general expression pointing to the whole sacrificial system for dealing with sin. The last phrase, "the ashes of a heifer," refers to a ritual described in Numbers 19 in which the ashes of a red heifer were mixed with water for the purification of those rendered unclean by contact with a dead body. Sin and death were the things that defiled; thus these sacrifices dealt with the two great problems that separated man from the holy and ever-living God.

These sacrifices provided a kind of solution to the problem. They did "sanctify" those who were unclean so that they could be restored to fellowship with God and Israelite society. Yet there was also something that they were unable to do: "Gifts and sacrifices are offered that cannot perfect the conscience of the worshiper" (Heb. 9:9). The blood of bulls and goats succeeded in restoring the unclean to ceremonial cleanliness and therefore to the religious life of the nation. But there was a better blood to which they pointed, a blood that in its shedding would actually cleanse the inner man, and therefore restore people to real fellowship with the holy God.

What we see here is called a "how much more" argument. The writer of Hebrews is showing the superiority of Christ's blood in that it is able to do much more than the old sacrifices could do. There are three reasons why Christ's blood is superior and truly purifying—able, as verse 12 says, to "secur[e] an eternal redemption" once and forever.

The first reason is that Christ's blood represents a better sacrifice. The old covenant required sacrificial animals to be without spot or blemish, and we see in verse 14 that Jesus offered himself "without blemish to God." The old covenant required obedience to the law, and Christ fulfilled those demands. At Mount Sinai God had told the Israelites, "Now therefore, if you will indeed obey my voice and keep my covenant, you shall be my treasured possession among all peoples" (Ex. 19:5). To this the people replied, "All that the LORD has spoken we will do" (v. 8), thus agreeing to these terms. But they did not keep them, and neither do we. Therefore Jesus came to fulfill the law with his own perfect obedience. He stood unblemished before God, able and willing to bear our sin, for he was himself acceptable to God.

Jesus not only rendered the obedience God required of us, but he also took upon himself the penalty due to our sins. How could one man, we ask, take the penalty for so many people? The answer is that he was more than a man; he was the very Son of God, with blood of infinite value. He redeemed us with the coin of his own precious blood, the blood of the only begotten Son of God. Goats and bulls and calves did not possess such worth, but pointed forward to the One of whom it could be said, "with his stripes we are healed . . . [for] the LORD has laid on him the iniquity of us all" (Isa. 53:5–6). Andrew Murray writes,

It was the life of God that dwelt in Him. That life gave His blood, each drop of it, an infinite value. The blood of a man is of more worth than that of a sheep. The blood of a king or a great general is counted of more value than hundreds of common soldiers. The blood of the Son of God!—it is in vain the mind seeks for some expression of its value; all we can say is, it is His own blood, the precious blood of the Son of God![4]

The second reason Christ's blood is superior is that it is God's appointed means of our salvation. We see this in the reference to "the blood of Christ" (v. 14). The Christ was the Anointed One, the Promised One, the Servant of the Most High God. He came into this world with a commission, an appointment. The angel told Joseph before he was born, "You shall call his name Jesus, for he will save his people from their sins" (Matt. 1:21). In the Garden of Gethsemane, Jesus could pray, "Father . . . I glorified you on earth, having accomplished the work that you gave me to do" (John 17:4). And then upon the cross he could cry out in satisfaction, "It is finished" (John 19:30), before giving up his spirit. The blood of bulls and goats was appointed by God for ceremonial cleansing, but the superior blood of Christ was appointed for actual and eternal redemption from sin. Here is the one way appointed by God, apart from which there is no salvation (Acts 4:12).

Third, Jesus offered his sacrifice "through the eternal Spirit" (Heb. 9:14). In other words, his sacrifice was offered up not merely bodily but in spirit. We should always remember that Christ's physical sufferings were nothing compared to the spiritual agony of his alienation from the Father as God's wrath poured down upon him in spirit. It was the spirit of Christ, not just the body of Christ, that drank up the penalty for sin; his infinite and divine spirit absorbed all the wrath of an infinitely holy God. Since his spirit is divine and is, as 7:16 says, "indestructible," he survived and emerged to enter into heaven as our perfect high priest.

Because it was a spiritual sacrifice, this blood is applied to us spiritually, whereas the blood of animals could be applied only to the flesh. The whole point of this passage is that Christ's blood applies to the heart, a spiritual sacrifice that is spiritually applied, actually restoring us to fellowship with

4. Andrew Murray, *The Holiest of All: An Exposition of the Epistle to the Hebrews* (Grand Rapids: Revell, 1993), 320.

God, who is spirit (John 4:24). Christ's blood was offered to "purify our conscience from dead works to serve the living God" (Heb. 9:14).

THE POWER OF CHRIST'S BLOOD

This leads to the second main point of this passage, that Christ's blood, being superior to that of bulls and goats, has power to cleanse the conscience of sinners.

We don't often think about our conscience as a serious problem when it comes to God. The problem is what he thinks about us, not what we think about ourselves. But even after God has accepted us in Christ, our unclean conscience can keep us far from God. Christ's intent as high priest is to bring us to God. Therefore, he not only reconciles God to us, but also cleanses our consciences so that we may enter into his service.

The conscience serves to tell us about ourselves. It communicates to us what we are. Charles Haddon Spurgeon, in his sermon on this text, pointed out three problems revealed by our conscience: a knowledge of past sinful acts; a knowledge of our sinful nature, with its thoughts and desires; and our ongoing contact with evil in this world. All of these conspire, unless cleansed, to keep us from serving the Lord. About the first of these, Spurgeon writes:

> Upon our consciences there rests, first of all, a sense of past sin. Even if a man wishes to serve God, yet until his conscience is purged, he feels a dread and terror of God which prevent his doing so. He has sinned, and God is just, and therefore he is ill at ease. . . . "God is angry with the wicked every day, if he turn not, he will whet his sword; he hath bent his bow, and made it ready"; and the sinner, knowing this, asks, "How can I serve this terrible God?" He is alarmed when he thinks of the Judge of all the earth; for it is before that Judge that he will soon have to take his trial.[5]

Christ's blood, however, possesses power to cleanse this great fear from our hearts, this great condemnation from our consciences. His death preaches to us that the debt has been paid for all our sin; an infinite atone-

---

5. Charles H. Spurgeon, *The Metropolitan Tabernacle Pulpit*, 63 vols. (Pasadena, Tex.: Pilgrim Publications, 1975), 31:438–39.

ment has been made to relieve us of the burden of so great a guilt. This is what causes Christians to sing about the shedding of Christ's innocent blood, for in it we see our own guilt washed away. Indeed, this is the theme of the song of heaven: "Worthy is the Lamb who was slain!" (Rev. 5:12).

There is no greater burden in this world than the guilt of our sin. Other burdens weary the feet or the back; this burden wearies the soul. People who abhor the idea of a blood-shedding God may write platitudes about the goodness of man. People may say that we are finding our destiny out of a Darwinian soup. Perhaps we are not yet what we might be, but we are certainly not guilty, they insist. But in a moral universe ruled by a holy God, such words will not wash away the reality of the things we have done.

If you come to recognize how your words have torn the hearts of others as knives tear the flesh; if you think for just a moment how your neglect of duty and selfish pursuit of gain have meant sorrow and woe for real people; if you merely ask how many men and women in this world have real cause to resent you, to wish you had never crossed their paths; if you take stock of God's holy and unyielding law and your incessant violation of it, then your conscience will speak against you about what you really are and deserve. You will crave a cleansing such as Christ alone can give.

How, then, can robes be washed in blood and come out white? The answer is that Christ's shed blood, representing the sacrifice of his perfect life upon the cross, is the cleansing agent provided by God for the stain of the guilt of our sin. For this reason, Christ's blood preaches forgiveness of sin: "Though your sins are like scarlet," it says, "they shall be as white as snow" (Isa. 1:18).

What about the second problem of the conscience, the awareness of sinful desires and thoughts, the knowledge not merely of our sinful deeds but also of our sinful nature? This, too, is cleansed by the blood of the Lamb. We feel unclean and this keeps us from God. Like Isaiah, we see the seraphim praising God in his temple, saying, "Holy, holy, holy is the Lord of hosts." At such a sight we cry, "Woe is me! For I am lost; for I am a man of unclean lips" (Isa. 6:5). But Jesus, like the angel in Isaiah's vision, flies to grasp a coal from the altar on which his own blood was shed and presses it to our lips. "Behold," he says, "your guilt is taken away, and your sin is atoned for" (v. 7). Our conscience tells us what we must think of ourselves, but the blood of Christ tells us what God thinks of us in Christ. Jesus stands there with basin and towel in hand and says, "You are clean" (John 13:10). Then, as our heavenly high priest, he sends his Holy Spirit to work within us, his blood having procured the resources of heaven, so that we are "being transformed into [Christ's] image from one degree of glory to another" (2 Cor. 3:18).

Finally, our conscience recoils as we walk through this world, brushing against all kinds of sin and evil, which bring defilement as contact with death did to the Israelites of old. Just as Israel's priests sprinkled the blood of bulls and goats upon the skin, we have in Christ a ready cleansing: "If we confess our sins," 1 John 1:9 tells us, "he is faithful and just to forgive us our sins and to cleanse us from all unrighteousness." We have cleansing through the blood of Jesus. His superior blood has power to do what no bull or goat could ever offer. As Isaac Watts writes:

> Jesus, my great High Priest,
>   offered his blood and died;
> my guilty conscience seeks
>   no sacrifice beside.
> His powerful blood did once atone
>   and now it pleads before the throne. . . .
> Behold my soul at freedom set;
>   my Surety paid the dreadful debt.[6]

The Purpose of Christ's Blood

What is the purpose for this grace that is offered in the blood of Jesus Christ? There are many reasons, of course: God's love and Christ's glory head the list. But one purpose is directly tied to the high-priestly office of our Lord and the tabernacle setting in which this passage fits: "How much more will the blood of Christ, who through the eternal Spirit offered himself without blemish to God, purify our conscience from dead works to serve the living God" (Heb. 9:14).

We are called into God's priestly service. As John wrote in his great doxology, "To him who loves us and has freed us from our sins by his blood and made us a kingdom, priests to his God and Father" (Rev. 1:5–6). And as Peter wrote, "You are a chosen race, a royal priesthood, a holy nation, a people for

---

6. Isaac Watts, "Jesus, My Great High Priest, 1709.

his own possession, that you may proclaim the excellencies of him who called you out of darkness into his marvelous light" (1 Peter 2:9). Again, it is what we see pictured in the worship scenes of heaven, as Revelation says of those who have washed their robes in the blood: "They are before the throne of God, and serve him day and night in his temple" (Rev. 7:15). This eternal service begins in the present life, which is our preparation for heaven and the beginning of that for which we are destined in glory.

When we consider the wonderful work of grace that has brought us salvation, the shedding of Christ's precious blood, we need to ask, "What is this for?" The purpose is not simply our own benefit. It is not merely that we should escape a deserved judgment, much less that we should have a nice, quiet, affluent Christian existence. The purpose is that the living God might have a fitting priesthood, for the service and praise of his glorious name. This cleansing in Christ's blood is not the end, but only the beginning for the Christian.

The Greek word "to serve" (*latreuein*) has a specifically priestly connotation. It is the service of the priests in the tabernacle we are called to perform, not outwardly but spiritually. The priests entered into the holy place to light the lampstand, and we too are to serve as light-bearers for all the world. They came and sent incense up before God's throne, and so, too, we are ministers of intercessory prayer with real access to the throne of God. Unlike the Old Testament priests, our service takes place with the veil torn asunder, with God's presence unhindered and our service readily accepted in Christ.

We were made and redeemed to serve God, and it is in the service of him that we discover our true freedom. Spurgeon says: "To serve the living God is necessary to the happiness of a living man: for this end we were made, and we miss the design of our making if we do not honor our Maker. 'Man's chief end is to glorify God, and enjoy Him forever.' If we miss that end we are ourselves terrible losers. The service of God is the element in which alone we can fully live."[7]

Hebrews 9:14 speaks of our cleansing from "dead works." This is what the world is busy about, works that if not sinful are certainly pointless and dead from the perspective of eternity. Building empires that will fall, buying things that do not satisfy or last, serving ambitions that are destined for the grave.

7. Spurgeon, *Metropolitan Tabernacle Pulpit*, 31:436–37.

How crushing such a life is for those made in the image of God! Humanity was fashioned for God and his pleasure. To neglect God, to refuse his service, to deny his presence and rule is to shrink into the dust. It is to be ruled by the flesh, as beasts rather than as the men and women God made in his image. Isn't this just what our secular, unbelieving society is discovering?

But not so the Christian. We are priests with a holy calling, a service of joy born of gratitude, for a God who loves us enough to have shed the precious blood of Christ. What we do for him will carry beyond the grave, lasting forever in heaven, where Christ reigns now as the priest upon the throne at the right hand of the living God.

CLEANSED BY THE BLOOD

Once "purified," we are "to serve the living God." To serve God is to be his vessel, to have him pour himself into us for the shining of his glory into the world, both now and forever. It is to grow toward him, in life and peace and joy.

But of course none of this is possible until we have first been cleansed by the blood of Jesus Christ—the precious blood of the Son of God that is superior to that of bulls and goats, that has power to cleanse the conscience, and that has the purpose of sanctifying us for God's own priestly service. Until then we may not serve the Lord, for he is a holy God and we must be kept as lepers outside the camp of Israel, as those defiled by death and unclean before his throne. What Joshua told Israel is also true for us, until we have turned to Christ's cleansing blood: "You are not able to serve the LORD, for he is a holy God. He is a jealous God" (Josh. 24:19). Therefore let us turn to Jesus, whose blood has all the power to cleanse us from our sins.

30

LAST WILL AND TESTAMENT

Hebrews 9:15–22

For where a will is involved, the death of the one who made it must be established. For a will takes effect only at death, since it is not in force as long as the one who made it is alive.
(Heb. 9:16–17)

One of the greatest speeches ever given was delivered by Mark Antony, who was consul of Rome in 44 B.C. The occasion was the funeral of Julius Caesar, who had ruled Rome until his assassination that year. The members of the senate who had killed Caesar, led by Marcus Brutus, forbade Antony from stirring up the crowds, but they did permit him to give the traditional funeral eulogy. We do not have the record of Antony's speech, but we do have William Shakespeare's immortalization in his play *Julius Caesar*. "Friends, Romans, countrymen," Antony began, "lend me your ears; I come to bury Caesar, not to praise him."

But praise Caesar he did. In the speech, Antony dealt with the main accusation against Caesar and the justification for his murder, namely, that he was ambitious and therefore dangerous to the nation. He recounted Caesar's triumphs for the sake of Rome, his compassion for the poor, and his refusal to accept the kingly crown when it was three times offered to him. "Was this ambition?" he asked. "Yet Brutus says he was ambitious; and Brutus is an honorable man." At that point the crowd started to go Antony's way, and the conspirators became increasingly alarmed. Then Antony struck the match that set the people aflame. "Here's a parchment with the seal of Caesar," he continued. "I found it in his closet; 'tis his will." If only the people knew what was in the will, he said, they would race forward to kiss dead Caesar's head. "We'll hear the will!" they cried. "Read it, Mark Antony."

Under Shakespeare's masterful hand, Antony gathered the mob around the corpse of Caesar to hear his last will and testament. He descended from the platform to stand in their midst. "If you have tears," he warned, "prepare to shed them now." Then pointing out the various wounds upon the body, he recited the names of the conspirators, assigning a wound to each and working the crowd into a fever pitch. Then, only then, Antony opened the will, under Caesar's seal: "To every Roman citizen he gives . . . seventy-five drachmas. . . . Moreover, he hath left you all his walks, his private arbors, and new-planted orchards, on this side Tiber; he hath left them you, and to your heirs forever—common pleasures, to walk abroad and recreate yourselves." At the news of such a magnificent will and testament, their own inheritance from Caesar, the crowd broke forth in mutiny, putting to flight the senate and its conspirators out of the gates of Rome.[1]

Few things stir up gratitude like a generous inheritance. History records that Caesar left each Roman citizen two and a half months of wages, and that used up only one quarter of his total wealth, the rest of which went to his adopted son and heir, Octavius. Scripture records another inheritance, also left for a vast host of beneficiaries. It is both freedom from the condemnation of sin and everlasting life. The One who left this last will and testament is Jesus Christ, God's own Son and heir, who died so that we might live. Mark Antony pointed out the wounds of Caesar, from which so many gold coins flowed for the people; we may point out the wounds of Christ, by which our eternal souls are redeemed, and through which flowed the blood that washes away our sins.

1. William Shakespeare, *Julius Caesar*, Act III, Scene II, 80–273.

MEDIATOR OF THE COVENANT

Hebrews 9 celebrates the superiority of the blood of Jesus Christ. It is superior because of his divine nature and his finished work of salvation. He is able to do what sacrificial bulls and goats could never do, namely, to remove our guilt and reconcile us to God. Hebrews 9:15 picks up on this reasoning, saying, "Therefore he is the mediator of a new covenant, so that those who are called may receive the promised eternal inheritance, since a death has occurred that redeems them from the transgressions committed under the first covenant." A mediator is someone who represents two different parties. In order to mediate between the holy God and sinful humans, Christ first had to die.

This reasoning starts with the understanding that the first covenant—the old covenant under Moses—required the obedience of the people. They had to fulfill its commands or be condemned. Its key words were expressed in the giving of the law, to which the people responded, "All that the LORD has spoken we will do" (Ex. 19:8). If they failed to do so, if they transgressed the law, the covenant demanded God's punishment on their sin.

One of the best ways to understand the terms of the old covenant is through a ceremony that took place on two hills in Samaria, Mount Ebal and Mount Gerizim, as described in Deuteronomy 27 and Joshua 8. There all the people of Israel were gathered in accordance with God's command. On Mount Ebal, half the people stood to read the curses for disobedience to God. The curse was read on all those who commit idolatry, and all the people said, "Amen!" Then came the curse for adultery, and the people said, "Amen!" On and on went the curses for sin: for murder, for false testimony, for moving a boundary stone, and in each case the people all cried, "Amen!" Finally, the curses concluded: "Cursed be anyone who does not confirm the words of this law by doing them" (Deut. 27:26). Then all the people said, "Amen."

On the other mountain, Mount Gerizim, blessings were read for obedience. One blessing after another would rain down in response to obedience to the law: victory in battle, plenteous harvests, an abundance of offspring. But this was the capstone: "The LORD will establish you as a people holy to himself, as he has sworn to you, if you keep the commandments of the LORD your God and walk in his ways" (Deut. 28:9). This was the condition of the old covenant for Israel as a nation. The rest of the Old Testament is the record of how well Israel did fulfilling it, and unfortunately their performance fell far short of the obedience needed to attain to God's blessings.

God had a claim on all the people who related to him by means of the old covenant. What is not so easy to see is why he then needed a mediator. A mediator serves to work things out between two parties; here there was nothing to work out, only a curse to be applied in punishment and wrath. God had entered into a conditional covenant with Israel. The people had broken those conditions and the punishment must now be executed.

This is how things look on the surface. But beneath the surface there was a problem, a tension, even a dilemma for almighty God. That problem was a prior covenant he had made, his covenant with Abraham, which did not depend on the obedience of God's people. Hebrews calls the Mosaic covenant the "first" covenant, but that is only in relationship to the new covenant in Christ. There was an earlier covenant, one established on the basis of a unilateral promise, in which God swore by himself, "I will establish my covenant between me and you and your offspring after you throughout their generations for an everlasting covenant, to be God to you and to your offspring after you" (Gen. 17:7).

It would be inexact to say that God's covenant with Abraham was unconditional, since it did impose on Abraham the duty of circumcising all males in his household, and it implied the obligation of faith. But an important characteristic of this covenant is that God alone guaranteed its fulfillment and blessings. There is no "if you do this," nor does Abraham make any promises as his part of this covenant. According to the conventions of the ancient world, God ratified his covenant with Abraham by walking alone through the severed pieces of animals. Normally, both parties would walk through the severed pieces—the point being, "Let what happened to these animals happen to me if I do not fulfill my part of this covenant." God walked through alone, signifying his willingness to take full and sole responsibility for fulfilling the promises he made to Abraham. If God did not fulfill his promise, he would himself be under the curse (Gen. 15:8–21). But Abraham's descendants, to whom God had promised blessing, were the very ones God was later bound to curse and punish under the old covenant, that is, the law covenant given through Moses. This is why a mediator was needed. Because of his sin, man needed a mediator. But because of his promise, God, too, needed a mediator. For if God cursed his people so that Abraham's offspring were cut off from salvation—as their failure under the Mosaic covenant obliged him to do—his own curse would fall upon himself.

We might therefore ask why God brought in the law covenant through Moses. Surely he knew that men are sinners and therefore unable to obey his holy law. Yet he imposed a covenant that demanded that very obedience as a condition of the blessing he had promised. So why did God do this? The answer is that the law establishes man's need for grace. Philip Hughes explains:

> The inability of man to keep [the law's] demands made unmistakably clear his guilty state before God. Man's great and radical need is justification; but the law can never justify the law-breaker. Despairing of his efforts to achieve righteousness by his works, man's only hope was to turn away from himself and to seek the refuge of faith in the pardoning grace which he had been promised. Thus "the law was our custodian until Christ came, that we might be justified by faith" (Gal. 3:23).[2]

In other words, God gave the law with Christ in mind, so that salvation would come by grace alone. As Paul says in Romans 11:32, "For God has consigned all to disobedience, that he may have mercy on all." This mercy comes to us as our inheritance through the death of Christ.

Only the death of Christ could release sinners from the curse of the law, and it was to offer that pardoning grace that he came. Christ offered his innocent life, a life of infinite value since it is divine, to pay the debt of our sin. Paul writes, "Christ redeemed us from the curse of the law by becoming a curse for us—for it is written, 'Cursed is everyone who is hanged on a tree'" (Gal. 3:13). Therefore, God's just wrath is satisfied; he may now look upon us with blessing and peace without compromising his own nature. Christ has enabled God to fulfill his own promise of blessing, as Paul goes on to say: he redeemed us "so that in Christ Jesus the blessing of Abraham might come to the Gentiles, so that we might receive the promised Spirit through faith" (Gal. 3:14).

2. Philip E. Hughes, *A Commentary on the Epistle to the Hebrews* (Grand Rapids: Eerdmans, 1977), 366.

Hebrews 9:15 shows the result of Christ's death on the cross: "Therefore he is the mediator of a new covenant, so that those who are called may receive the promised eternal inheritance." The new covenant has the closest connection with God's covenant with Abraham. Indeed, it secures the eternal inheritance God promised to Abraham: "I will be your God and the God of your descendants after you." Abraham's descendants are spiritual. As Paul points out in Galatians, they are those who, like Abraham, trust in God: "If you are Christ's, then you are Abraham's offspring, heirs according to promise" (Gal. 3:29).

Christ's Will and Testament

It is at this point that the idea of a will is introduced to this discussion. The Greek word for will (*diathēkē*) is also the word for covenant. This is the standard New Testament word to translate the Hebrew word for covenant, *berith*. A covenant is a solemn arrangement, the stipulated terms for a relationship between two parties. But *diathēkē* was also the Greek word for a last will and testament, and the writer of Hebrews capitalizes on this word play. This is the only time the word is used in this sense in the New Testament, yet it is because of this passage that the two halves of the Bible are known as the Old and New Testaments.

The writer's point is that the new covenant may be viewed as a last will and testament, particularly in that its benefits are disbursed only in the event of the death of the one who made it: "A will takes effect only at death, since it is not in force as long as the one who made it is alive" (Heb. 9:17).

We all know how a will works. Someone lives out his years and accumulates a certain amount of wealth. Some of it is in money, some may be in stocks or bonds, or other portions may be in property or in possessions. The purpose of the will is to make an arrangement for the distribution of this wealth after death. It was by dying, therefore, that Jesus made all the riches that are found in him available to us, specifically, the blessings of his covenant obedience. When we are joined to him in faith, therefore, we are made heirs of this great inheritance.

This connects with one of the great messages of the Book of Hebrews, that in Christ we have privileges of membership in God's family. The writer's idea of salvation is that of Jesus revealing God's redemption to sinners and then declaring before the court of heaven, "Behold, I and the children God has given me" (Heb. 2:13). In Hebrews 9 we see that this includes an inheritance. As Paul reasons in Romans 8:16–17, "We are children of God, and if children, then heirs—heirs of God and fellow heirs with Christ, provided we suffer with him in order that we may also be glorified with him."

See just how amazing this promise is. As heirs of Christ we inherit all the blessings that he has in God. What does this mean in this life? It means that God watches over us with loving care, as he watched over Jesus. It means he sends his Holy Spirit to empower us in godliness, as he sent the Spirit to Christ. It means that we have eternal life, the life of heaven, working within us so that we are being motivated by a new and holy power. It means that God has become our Father, and we are his own children in this world. He takes a fatherly interest in us. He is molding us, challenging us, teaching us, and yes, disciplining us toward the harvest of righteousness that he desires (Heb. 12:11).

As great as our inheritance is in this life, it is far greater in death. Then we inherit Christ's resurrection life, a place in heaven, and a home with God forever and ever. Indeed, we will inherit his perfect holiness. The apostle John marvels: "See what kind of love the Father has given to us, that we should be called children of God; and so we are. . . . Beloved, we are God's children now, and what we will be has not yet appeared; but we know that when he appears we will be like him, because we shall see him as he is" (1 John 3:1–2).

MY BLOOD OF THE COVENANT

The writer of Hebrews next turns again to the example of the old covenant: "Therefore not even the first covenant was inaugurated without blood" (Heb. 9:18). The word "therefore" refers back to verse 15, Christ having died as a ransom for those who sinned under the first covenant. God gave the old covenant with Christ in mind, and this is proved by these verses: under the law all of us are condemned, but God gave the law with Jesus Christ in mind, that he might be our Savior to the glory of God's wondrous grace.

Verses 19 to 21 amplify the relationship between Christ's work and the old covenant:

> For when every commandment of the law had been declared by Moses to all
> the people, he took the blood of calves and goats, with water and scarlet wool

and hyssop, and sprinkled both the book itself and all the people, saying, "This is the blood of the covenant that God commanded for you." And in the same way he sprinkled with the blood both the tent and all the vessels used in worship. (Heb. 9:19–21)

These verses recount the ratification of the old covenant when it was first given through Moses. Exodus 24 tells us that Moses began by reciting the whole law, after which the people replied, "All the words that the LORD has spoken we will do" (Ex. 24:3). We have already observed how fateful those words were, given the fact that they would not be fulfilled. The next morning, however, Moses got up and offered sacrifices to the Lord:

> Moses took half of the blood and put it in basins, and half of the blood he threw against the altar. Then he took the Book of the Covenant and read it in the hearing of the people. And they said, "All that the LORD has spoken we will do, and we will be obedient." And Moses took the blood and threw it on the people and said, "Behold the blood of the covenant that the LORD has made with you in accordance with all these words." (Ex. 24:6–8)

As Hebrews 9:21–22 go on to observe, just about everything was sprinkled by blood. Death was the penalty for breaking the covenant. Ray Stedman writes of this blood, "It was meant to impress on them that sin cannot be set aside, even by a loving God, without a death occurring. His judicial sentence, 'the soul who sins is the one who will die' (Eze. 18:4), must be carried out."[3] The point was that the mark of death was upon this covenant and all its ordinances and stipulations.

The blood of the covenant showed the penalty for breaking the covenant, but it also pointed forward to Christ and the new covenant in him. "Without the shedding of blood there is no forgiveness of sins," the writer observes (Heb. 9:22). But it is therefore true that *with* the shedding of blood—that is, with the death of a suitable sacrifice—forgiveness may be received. Stedman continues, "By sprinkling the blood of an animal on the people, Moses is saying that God would accept that substitution as a temporary reprieve until the true Substitute should come."[4]

---

3. Ray Stedman, *Hebrews* (Downers Grove, Ill.: InterVarsity 1992), 100.
4. Ibid.

The new covenant brings forgiveness in Christ: "He is the mediator of a new covenant . . . since a death has occurred that redeems them from the transgressions committed under the first covenant" (Heb. 9:15). Jesus Christ is the true substitute who came to bring true forgiveness for sins. When he instituted the sacrament of the Lord's Supper on the night of his arrest, Jesus made an explicit link between his own death and the blood that Moses sprinkled on the people under that first covenant. Holding the cup, he said, "This is my blood of the covenant, which is poured out for many" (Mark 14:24). The blood that Moses sprinkled represented Christ's precious blood. "This is *my* blood of the covenant," Jesus said, and it is this blood that he applies to cleanse those who come to him in faith.

Without the shedding of blood there is no forgiveness. This is the uniform testimony of Scripture. This is what made Abel's sacrifice better than Cain's. Cain brought the work of his hands, but Abel brought the blood of a sacrifice, and he alone was received (Gen. 4:3–4). Without the shedding of blood there is no forgiveness. Let us get this into our heads, that once we have sinned against God there is no way for the sin to be put away, except by the shedding of blood. But the price for our redemption is one that we cannot pay ourselves and yet survive. What we need is someone to pay it for us, a substitute, in whom is the power of eternal life. Andrew Murray writes:

> God is willing to receive man back again to His fellowship, to admit him to His heart and His love, to make a covenant with him, to give full assurance of all this; but—not without blood. Even His own Son, the Almighty and All-perfect One, the gift of His eternal love, even He could only redeem us, and enter the Father's presence, in submission to the word, not without blood. But, blessed be God, the blood of the Son of God, in which there was the life of the Eternal Spirit, has been given, and has wrought an eternal redemption! He did, indeed, bear our sins and take them away. He put away sin by the sacrifice of Himself. . . . There can be no fellowship with God, but in the blood, in the death, of His blessed Son.[5]

5. Andrew Murray, *The Holiest of All: An Exposition of the Epistle to the Hebrews* (Grand Rapids: Revell, 1993), 336–37.

This means that all those who were saved under the old covenant were saved by the new covenant, even when they were living under the old administration. By faith, they trusted in the blood of the sacrifices, and through them they trusted in the blood of Christ. Perhaps the best example of this is Psalm 51:7, where King David cries, "Purge me with hyssop, and I shall be clean; wash me, and I shall be whiter than snow." Hyssop was the plant that Moses and the priests used to make the brush for sprinkling the sacrificial blood. David was saying, in effect, sprinkle on my sin the blood of Jesus Christ, and I will be cleansed whiter than snow. This is also why it is not at all morbid to sing the words of William Cowper's great hymn:

> There is a fountain filled with blood,
>   drawn from Immanuel's veins;
> And sinners plunged beneath that flood
>   lose all their guilty stains.[6]

This is simply the truth of the Bible, that without the shedding of blood there is no forgiveness; without the application of that blood to our souls by faith, there is no cleansing for our sins or our guilty conscience. Unless you have obeyed God without sin—and not one of us has—then you require this very blood if you are to be forgiven and loved by God. What you must do is confess your sins, trust in Christ's saving work, and you will be cleansed before God, whiter than snow.

HEIRS OF GOD

Three observations from this passage demand our attention. First, could it possibly be clearer that salvation is the gift of God? We are not men and women who have received our blessings from God the old-fashioned way, by earning it. Indeed, we have received it by an older way. We have received salvation as a gift, as an inheritance that is freely given. An inheritance is not earned; it is the free gift of a loving benefactor. Indeed, this is what saving faith is about: simply receiving God's gift in Christ, like the citizens of Rome

---

6. William Cowper, "There Is a Fountain Filled with Blood," 1771.

who rejoiced at the reading of Caesar's will. Faith has its palms open to receive, not outstretched to grasp or clenched to achieve. We receive salvation as a gift, as heirs who gain the privilege by accepting a gift from our gracious God and Savior.

Second, what a gift we receive by the new covenant in Jesus Christ: fellowship with God! How exciting it is to realize that as Christ's heirs we receive all that he received from the Father. But the greatest gift of all is always the Father himself. Our God is not an over-busy Father who sends down gifts but does not share himself. No, his greatest gift is himself: "I will be your God, and you will be my people."

If you trust in Jesus, your sins will be forgiven, you will escape the penalty for your sins committed against the law, and you will enter into heaven, with riches untold. But all that is really so little compared to this: you will gain God himself. You may say with the psalmist, "God is the strength of my heart and my portion forever" (Ps. 73:26). You will know fellowship with the infinite, the holy, the transcendent God who is a consuming fire. Your life will have passion, meaning, purpose, joy, and peace and wonder unbounded—for all of these are found in the worship of and the knowledge of and fellowship with the Lord God Almighty, the God who is light and love. "I will be their God, and they shall be my people. And they shall not teach, each one his neighbor and each one his brother, saying, 'Know the Lord,' for they shall all know me, from the least of them to the greatest" (Heb. 8:10–11).

Finally, there can be only one reaction to so amazing a gift, and that is overwhelming gratitude. If the people of Rome could celebrate two and a half months' wages, and if they could cry out, "Most noble Caesar! O royal Caesar!" because of a mere mortal's last will and testament, what shall we say of the gift of Christ? If they could be filled with zeal to rise up and drive out through the gates of their city the treacherous villains who caused Caesar's death, what must be the result of our receiving the free gift of eternity, of God himself? Surely this inheritance, purchased with the freely offered death of Jesus Christ, God's only Son and spotless Lamb, ought to lift our voices with hearts aglow in praise. And we ought to rise up against the enemies that put him to death—namely, our sins—and drive them with holy zeal beyond the gates of our hearts, outside the limits of our lives.

If we have inherited from Jesus Christ, the King of kings, we will begin to act like princes and princesses, royal children of the God of light. We will worship him who secured such blessings, and the God who is their author, with all that we have—even with our very lives. As Isaac Watts put it in his wonderful hymn: "Love so amazing, so divine, demands my soul, my life, my all."[7]

7. Isaac Watts, "When I Survey the Wondrous Cross," 1707.

31

ONCE FOR ALL

Hebrews 9:23–28

And just as it is appointed for man to die once, and after that comes judgment, so Christ, having been offered once to bear the sins of many, will appear a second time, not to deal with sin but to save those who are eagerly waiting for him. (Heb. 9:27–28)

hat was the pivotal moment in human history? The way a person answers that question tells me a great deal. If he replies that it was Gutenberg's invention of the printing press, or the beginning of the Enlightenment, that probably means he thinks history is defined by the progress of ideas. If he answers that the key moment was the publication of Darwin's *Origin of Species*, that indicates that he supports the abandonment of supernaturalism for rigorous naturalism. If he says it was the development of Athenian democracy, or the signing of Magna Carta, or more recently the French Revolution or the American Declaration of Independence, that shows his belief in the primacy of politics.

The ancient Greeks would have refused to answer such a question at all, considering the question to be illegitimate. The Greeks did not believe that there could be a turning point to history, because history is circular. To them, the individual soul was not immortal. After death the individual ceased to exist. What lasted forever was the march of time, the circular process of history. This way of thinking has seen a recent resurgence in Western culture, especially in literature and films that celebrate "the circle of life."

One of the most influential books ever written attacked this philosophy of history head-on. The book was *The City of God,* and the writer was the Christian theologian Augustine of Hippo. Saint Augustine wrote his book to refute the charge that the rise of Christianity had caused the fall of Rome. He achieved his purpose admirably, and along the way articulated the Christian and biblical view of history. Augustine began by noting that there is one event in history that is unrepeatable by its very nature, namely, the death of the Son of God for the forgiveness of our sins. By its nature, this event could happen only once. From this insight he went on to develop a Christian view of history that is linear; he said that history has a start, a central turning point, and a definite conclusion. According to Augustine's presentation of the Bible, history finds its consummation in the day of judgment, when the City of Man and the City of God are finally separated. The decisive point of history was the death of Christ, upon which everything turns.

CHRIST'S ENTRY INTO HEAVEN

Hebrews 9 also presents a philosophy of history, one that is very much in accord with Augustine's *City of God.* Hebrews 9:23–28 provides a point of entry by recounting Christ's return into heaven after his death and resurrection. We must always remember that Christ's ascension is linked to the cross; it is all part of one integrated work in his first coming. Jesus was born of a woman in order to be a fitting representative for man. He was made perfect under the law, so that he would have an accomplished righteousness to offer up to God. Both of these truths have frequently been emphasized in the Book of Hebrews (e.g., 2:10–18; 5:9; 7:28). Jesus died on the cross to bear our sins, was raised from the dead by the Father in acceptance of that sacrifice, and finally ascended into heaven to reign forever as priest and king and to send the Holy Spirit for the salvation of his people. All of this forms one integrated work, centered on the cross.

Hebrews 9:23–28 focuses on the culminating event of that whole work, namely, Christ's entry into heaven, having offered his own blood for our sin.

"It was necessary," the writer begins, "for the copies of the heavenly things to be purified with these rites" (Heb. 9:23). This refers to the procedures in the earthly tabernacle under the old covenant, as described in Hebrews 9:18–22, which we learn here are "copies of the heavenly things." "But the heavenly things themselves," the writer continues, had to be purified "with better sacrifices than these. For Christ has entered, not into holy places made with hands, which are copies of the true things, but into heaven itself, now to appear in the presence of God on our behalf" (Heb. 9:23–24).

The writer of Hebrews wants us to consider the implications of Christ's return into heaven as Redeemer and High Priest, having shed his blood upon the cross. Regarding this pivotal event, he has two points to make: the need for a better sacrifice than that of bulls and goats, and Christ's application of that better blood to "the true things . . . in heaven itself . . . in the presence of God" (Heb. 9:24).

All through this chapter we have seen the need for a blood that is better than that of bulls and goats. Hebrews 9:9 states that the animal sacrifices "cannot perfect the conscience of the worshiper." Verse 14 adds that, by contrast, the blood of Christ is able to "purify our conscience from dead works to serve the living God." The blood of the animal sacrifices, on which the old covenant depended, was symbolic of the true sacrifice to come. It stands to reason, therefore, that in the true sanctuary of heaven, where God himself dwells, it would be the true blood that would be necessary. The old covenant was provisional and symbolic of a true reality that now has come. Therefore, the actual work of redemption done by Christ is performed with his own blood that successfully procures our salvation.

That point is readily understood, but the next one is not so easy. What does it mean that Christ has purified the heavenly things themselves with his better sacrifice? The commentators offer a number of views regarding "the heavenly things themselves" (Heb. 9:23). One compelling proposal comes from F. F. Bruce, who connects the cleansing of the heavenly sanctuary with the cleansing of our consciences, a theme that dominates this chapter. He argues that heaven does not need to be cleansed since it is not defiled. He also points out that the New Testament frequently describes believers together as God's spiritual house (see 1 Peter 2:5 and Eph. 2:22). It is therefore the inward cleansing of believers that is in view here, he says, by the ongoing work of the Holy Spirit. Concerning believers, Bruce says, "It is they who need inward cleansing, not only that their approach to God may be free from defilement, but that they may be a fit habitation for him."[1]

Those things are true, but they do not adequately explain what the writer of Hebrews is talking about here. Verse 24 is clearly discussing Christ's entry into heaven. Furthermore, the writer of Hebrews has stated that Israel's tabernacle was an earthly version of the heavenly reality. This does not mean that there are an actual lampstand and table of showbread and altar of incense in heaven, but rather that those things symbolized features of God's relationship with man. The same is true of the ark of the covenant. The ark represented man's status before God. When the high priest entered into the holy of holies, he encountered the ark, with its two golden angels, between which God symbolically dwelt. Beneath God's gaze were the tablets of the Ten Commandments. This represents man's great problem. Our first problem is not our relationships with other people, not our jobs, and not our finances. Our problem is that we are transgressors of God's holy law and that we stand in judgment before his holy throne. We are in jeopardy of eternal damnation. This is the heavenly reality symbolized by the "earthly copy" that was the ark of the covenant.

What, then, was the significance of the application of the blood, which was sprinkled on everything in the tabernacle? The furnishings in the earthly tabernacle spoke of the great privileges arising from our fellowship with God. But since we have fallen into sin, we are not worthy of these privileges. The lampstand spoke of God's revealing light, though sinners are not worthy of any revelation save that of God's wrath. The table of showbread spoke of intimate fellowship with the living God. But the very thought of sitting down to table with sinners is repugnant to God's holy character. The incense altar spoke of the privilege of access in prayer, but man in sin deserves no such access.

Without the blood, apart from a sacrifice, everything in the tabernacle speaks to privileges that sinners must be denied. There could only be the piercing gaze of God, the tablets of the law open before him while the sinner stands condemned.

1. F. F. Bruce, *The Epistle to the Hebrews*, rev. ed., New International Commentary on the New Testament (Grand Rapids: Eerdmans, 1990), 229.

You see, therefore, what the blood accomplished. For when you apply the blood of the sacrifice—the sacrifice that has borne the sin in the sinner's place, the sacrifice that has satisfied God's justice and turned his wrath aside—the whole situation is changed. Now when God turns to the lampstand and sees the sprinkled blood, he gladly shines forth his light to the sinner. Why? Because the blood speaks of the way he has provided through Jesus Christ, the forgiveness of sins through the blood. The same is true of the table of bread; God receives and feeds us because the blood of the Lamb has been applied. The same is true with regard to full and open access to God in prayer, symbolized by the altar of incense. Because of the blood, for us God's throne is a throne of grace, and our prayers are received as those of dear children. "Without the shedding of blood there is no forgiveness of sins" (Heb. 9:22). But with the blood, applied to every aspect of our relationship with the God who lives in heaven, there are forgiveness, acceptance, blessing, light, and life.

The cleansing blood provides us with a relationship with God in this life and secures for us a place in heaven. Without the blood, even the angels would hardly tolerate our presence there, so wretched is the thought of sin to holy hearts. But the blood of Christ has made heaven a home for us, and as Peter indicates in his first epistle, we have become a source of wonder and joy to the eyes of angels (1 Peter 1:12). No longer the condemned, we are now the redeemed—fellow children of the firstborn of the new creation.

This cleansing of heaven for us by the blood of Christ is the turning point of history. This is what verse 26 means when it says that Christ "appeared once for all at the end of the ages." That expression marks this as the decisive point of history, when God's redemptive plan comes into full focus as the climax of all history. Before Christ went into the heavens, having died on the cross and been raised from the dead, there was no way for sinners to have fellowship with the holy God. It had been promised and symbolized, that is true. That is what Old Testament Israel was all about. But when our great high priest entered into heaven with his own saving blood, everything changed forever for those who come to God through him. His appearing there for us is the definitive act of history so far as the salvation of sinners is concerned.

THE FINALITY OF DEATH AND JUDGMENT

A right view of history is important to our writer, and to make things perfectly clear, he relates the history of God's redemptive work to the personal history of every person born on earth: "Just as it is appointed for man to die once, and after that comes judgment, so Christ, having been offered once to bear the sins of many . . ." (Heb. 9:27–28). There is a relationship between the personal history of every individual and God's redemptive history that centers on the death of Christ. Indeed, the latter is fitted to the needs of the former, and therefore they are similarly arranged.

The point verse 27 makes is important. People want to know—or at least they should want to know—what happens after they die. Are they disintegrated into nothing, or absorbed into a great impersonal cosmic sea? That was the general view of the ancient Greeks. At best their hope was a vague "if." As the Roman historian Tacitus wrote in eulogy of a man he admired: "If there be any habitation for the spirits of just men, if great souls perish not with the body, mayest thou rest in peace." "If" was all he could hope for. Marcus Aurelius, the philosopher-emperor of Rome, could think only of a spark from man's soul returning to be lost forever in God.[2] People who look to the Eastern tradition of reincarnation have a hope that is hardly better. They think of souls returning to the earth for near-endless toil in one life after another, until finally they merit the reward of oblivion.

The Christian answer to this question could not be more different. What happens after we die? The answer is in Hebrews 9:27: "It is appointed for man to die once, and after that comes judgment." Therefore, there are no multiplications of a person's life. There is this life and death, and no others, after which comes judgment before God's holy throne. There is a resurrection for both the just and the unjust. All will die, and after death come to stand before God to be measured according to the perfect standard of God's holy law.

This rules out the many "second-chance" theories that are occasionally popular in Christian circles. People like to think that even if we deny Christ in this life and then die in our sins, we can have another chance when we see him after death. Not so, says this passage. After death is judgment. As Jesus

2. Cited in William Barclay, *The Letter to the Hebrews* (Philadelphia: Westminster, 1976), 111.

warned, "Unless you believe that I am he you will die in your sins" (John 8:24). Indeed, the great gospel verses in John 3 make it plain that those who refuse Jesus Christ will perish: "Whoever believes in him is not condemned, but whoever does not believe is condemned already, because he has not believed in the name of the only Son of God" (John 3:18).

If you have not reckoned on this reality, if you have not made provision for your coming judgment, a judgment that is as near to you as your death, the date of which you do not know, let this warning apply to you. Ahead of you is death, but that is not the end. It leads to judgment, a judgment in which sinners cannot stand. Jesus taught about the judgment of unforgiven sinners, saying, "These will go away into eternal punishment" (Matt. 25:46). But Jesus has made provision for the forgiveness we need. He has died in our place on the cross, taking up our sins, and then appeared before God in heaven with the marks still on his hands and feet, his blood bearing testimony to his redeeming work for all who look to him in faith. If you trust in Jesus Christ, you have no fear of judgment to come, for Christ has exhausted the fury your sins have deserved. For you, judgment will be an open door to life everlasting, a portal to eternity as beloved children of God.

ONCE FOR ALL

The particular point our writer has in mind, however, is to show that Christ's death—his shedding of blood, and his appearance in heaven as Redeemer of his own—is a once-for-all event that changes everything. Since Christ died to remove our sin, this need happen only once. His blood is sufficient to the task, so there is no need for a repetition. Not only does this need to happen only once, but it can happen only once. This was the point Saint Augustine made. Christ died to satisfy the justice of God, and now that justice is satisfied. He died to pay the debt, and that debt having been paid, God's perfect justice can never come back for more. The accounts are settled. It is finished. The debt is paid. Israel's high priest came into the sanctuary with sacrificial blood once per year, as a sign of the inadequacy of that animal blood. But it is absurd to expect the same when the blood is that of the priceless Son of God, the true Lamb who exhausts and ends the sacrifices once for all.

This has profound implications for our spiritual lives. It is, sadly, a very common experience today for Christians to supposedly experience conversion over and over. Some Christians are even baptized repeatedly. The reason is that they feel an ongoing need to deal with the guilt of their sin. They come to Christ, perhaps at a revival meeting which emphasized the importance of a personal decision, answering a call to come to the altar. There they gave their hearts to Jesus, pledging faith to him and enmity to sin. The emphasis was on their action, their decision. In the evening, as they lay their heads down to sleep, there were a joy and a peace they had never known before, the joy of the redeemed and the peace of the forgiven. In the morning, however, they awoke in the world and not in heaven. How much easier it would be were that not so! They awoke still as sinners, perhaps to their great alarm. Though truly saved, and though God had given them the new birth, they found that they still sinned. Yes, often the Lord gives grace for an immediate deliverance from particular sins, and this is a great encouragement to the new believer. But total deliverance from all of sin's power, total escape from our sinful nature, comes only at death, and not at conversion. This is why Hebrews so strongly warns believers to avoid the snares of sin (see 3:13; 12:1); were sin no longer a problem, such warnings would not have been needed.

But the weak believer discovers the continuing reality of sin, to his alarm. With clawing fear he contemplates a judgment he now is more keenly aware of than ever before. Over and over again he seeks forgiveness out of the resources of his own capacity to believe and repent, a capacity that is limited and insufficient to the task. Whole lives are spent like this, seeking a conversion that will finally stick, seeking an experience that will do the job, seeking a passion that will cleanse them once-for-all.

If we were saved by our faith, it would not be "once-for-all," because our faith itself is not reliable or permanent. We wax and wane, sometimes weak and sometimes strong. "Once-for-all" is not an expression used for us—for our faith or for our repentance. You have not sinned for the last time, I am sorry to say. You have not experienced your last doubt, or shed your last tear for sin and failure.

But the good news of the gospel is that you are not saved by your faith, but by Christ. What cannot be said about you can be said of him. His death saves you, and that was once-for-all. His entry into heaven to minister for you there saves you, upholds your weak and wavering faith, and that is once-for-all. What is not once-for-all for you is once-for-all for him. Where, then, is peace to be found, a peace that lasts, a peace that is once-for-all? It is not in us, but in Christ. Yes, we must receive him by faith, but it is not upon our faith that salvation relies, but upon him, of whom it can be said, "once-for-all."

From our own works we will never derive peace, hope, or joy. The Scripture says that God has "no variation or shadow due to change" (James 1:17), but that cannot be said of us. But once-for-all our Lord Jesus Christ appeared before God, and there he remains, bearing the marks of his once-for-all sacrifice. Because he is there, our forgiveness is once-for-all, and God's love for us is sure forever. Christ does not have to die over and over. He does not have to bring his blood back and forth to God, because "he has appeared once for all at the end of the ages to put away sin by the sacrifice of himself" (Heb. 9:26). Therefore, we need not seek forgiveness over and over, but may rest our hearts in Christ and then get busy serving his cause in the world.

HOPE FOR THOSE WAITING

Let me conclude by making two observations that surely are central to the writer's intent for this passage. First, in the death of Christ and in his ascension into heaven something definitive has happened. It is a definitive work with a definitive result: "to bear the sins of many" (Heb. 9:28).

This passage contains a statement of means and ends for all of history. The means is the appearance of Jesus Christ as the decisive intervention that changes all things. This was the import of his first coming: Christ was sacrificed . . . to appear for us in God's presence. That twofold work—Christ's death for our forgiveness and Christ's life for our salvation—is the focus of all redemptive history. Paul writes in Romans 6:10, "The death he died he died to sin, once for all, but the life he lives he lives to God." Christ died definitively and he lives definitively, securing our salvation by his eternal testimony to his once-for-all work of redemption. Together, his death and his eternal life in heaven are the means of our salvation: "For Christ has entered, not into holy places made with hands, which are copies of the true things, but into heaven itself, now to appear in the presence of God on our behalf" (Heb. 9:24).

Verse 26 then expresses the end toward which this all is directed: "to put away sin." Verse 28 says it again: "to bear the sins of many." Christ has taken away our sin. His work was directed to that end, and it is done once-for-all and forever. This was the designed intention of the saving work of Christ, all of which is now declared in the past tense. He was sacrificed . . . he entered heaven to appear for us. It is a definitive work, accomplished, secure, and finished. Yes, we still have to contend with sin; it is defeated but not removed. Therefore we eagerly await Christ's return to save us from this struggle. But while we wait, we are secure forever in him. This is why we can sing about this struggle with such confidence and hope:

> When darkness veils his lovely face,
>   I rest on his unchanging grace;
> in every high and stormy gale,
>   my anchor holds within the veil.
> On Christ, the solid rock, I stand;
>   all other ground is sinking sand.[3]

That leads to my second observation, namely, that although Christ's death and appearance in heaven for us is the turning point of history, it is not the end of history: "Christ . . . will appear a second time, not to deal with sin but to save those who are eagerly waiting for him" (Heb. 9:28).

What remains, then, but the extension of this gospel, the ingathering of the redeemed through faith in Christ? History had a beginning in the creation of all things. History has a problem, namely, man's fall into sin and condemnation. History has a focal turning point that answers our every need: the first coming of Christ, with his death, resurrection, and ascension into heaven as our Savior. History also has its culmination: the return of Christ not in weakness but in glory, "not to deal with sin but to save those who are eagerly waiting for him" (Heb. 9:28). What a great hope this provides to all who believe, but struggle in this world. The great Puritan John Owen writes,

> Faith in the second coming of Christ is sufficient to support the souls of believers, and to give them satisfactory consolation in all difficulties, trials, and distresses. All true believers do live in a waiting, longing expectation of the coming of Christ. It is one of the most distinguishing charac-

3. Edward Mote, "My Hope Is Built on Nothing Less," 1834.

teristics of a sincere believer so to do. . . . At the second appearance of Christ there will be an end of the business about sin, both on his part and ours.[4]

Judgment is inevitable, but sin is not. We will not have to put up with sin forever. It is not simply the way things are or always will be. It has been dealt with, and even as we war against it still, we know a victor's crown lies not far ahead.

What matters, then, is really only one thing. Are you in Christ? Did he die for you? When he entered heaven to appear before God as the guarantee of salvation and intercessor for his people, was your name among that number? The way to know for sure is to put your trust in him. If we have trusted him, then we have a peace and a joy that must bear fruit within our lives. We are waiting for him, but not idly. We are waiting for him, and while we wait, we serve him and we worship him with all our lives, bearing witness to a lost and guilty world. This is the worship of those who have joy and hope, awaiting the great day when salvation comes in the return of Christ.

4. John Owen, *An Exposition of the Epistle to the Hebrews*, 7 vols. (Edinburgh: Banner of Truth, 1991), 6:417.

32

THE BODY OF CHRIST

Hebrews 10:1—10

Consequently, when Christ came into the world, he said, "Sacrifices and offerings you have not desired, but a body have you prepared for me; in burnt offerings and sin offerings you have taken no pleasure. Then I said, 'Behold, I have come to do your will, O God, as it is written of me in the scroll of the book.'"
(Heb. 10:5–7)

I understand dating, now that I am married. When I got to college, I understood high school perfectly. I also know what it is like to start your first job, fresh out of college, eager to succeed. I know the joys and pitfalls. It is a pity, however, that I did not understand them when I was going through them. I suppose that years from now I will understand parenting, but right now, with a house full of little children, I'm feeling a little rough around the edges. It seems that we never really understand something until we no longer need to, until we can look back with the enhanced vision of hindsight.

A similar phenomenon is set forth at the beginning of Hebrews 10. The writer of Hebrews is looking back on life under the law in old covenant Israel, with insights that really were not possible to those who were in it. His concern, as it has been all through this epistle, is that his fledgling Christian community have a proper perspective on Judaism—a new covenant perspective—and thereby resist the temptation and persecution that were seeking to draw them back into former ways.

As we have often found, the writer's observations about the old covenant offer useful reflections on our present life in the new covenant. Likewise, it turns out that my reflections on dating offer insights for my marriage. My first-job experiences have something to say about my present work. My memories of childhood might shine some light into the uncharted regions of parenthood. In the same way, reflections on old covenant life can offer us insights into our lives as Christians.

UNDERSTANDING THE OLD TESTAMENT

In our last study we received a history lesson dealing with the significance of Christ's once-for-all sacrifice. Hebrews 10 opens up with another redemptive-history lesson: "The law has but a shadow of the good things to come instead of the true form of these realities" (Heb. 10:1). A relationship is established here, a sequence between the old covenant, the new covenant, and the good things that are still to come at the end of redemptive history. The writer of Hebrews says that the law was no more than a shadow of the heavenly realities. By shadow he means a sketchy outline. We might think of a person who stands in front of an object and blocks the sun's rays. The shadow is the outline cast back behind the person. In a similar way, the reality in Christ cast its shadow back into the old dispensation, but only in a bare sketch.

The main emphasis here has to do with the roughness of the picture available to the Old Testament saints. John Calvin explains that the things of the law "were like the rough outlines which are the foreshadowing of the living picture. Before they put on the true colours with paint artists usually draw an outline in pencil of the representation which they intend."[1] Such was the shadow that was the law in the old covenant.

This statement sets up some important observations for interpreting the Old Testament in light of the New. First of all, this passage affirms a basic

---

1. John Calvin, *New Testament Commentaries*, 12 vols. (Grand Rapids: Eerdmans, 1994), 12:132.

continuity between the Old and New Testaments. Some Christians deny this; they maintain that only the New Testament is valid for us. This view is found particularly within the older forms of dispensational theology, although this excess is generally corrected by dispensationalists today. Because of this logic, some people reject such vital portions of Scripture as the Ten Commandments, and even the Lord's Prayer, since it was taught to Jews under the law. This interpretation led to the proliferation of Bible editions featuring only the New Testament, along with the Psalms and Proverbs.

Our passage emphasizes a basic unity, however. The Old Testament is the reality in Christ projected backward, redemptively speaking. Old Testament saints were saved by the blood of Christ, to which the animal sacrifices merely pointed.

In most English translations, the shadow of the law is contrasted with "the true form" of these realities, as the English Standard Version puts verse 1, or with "the realities themselves," as the New International Version renders it. In the original Greek text, the word is *eikona*, which is a form of the word *eikōn*. Greek lexicons translate this as "image" or "likeness." This is the same word Paul uses of Christ in Colossians 1:15: "He is the *image* of the invisible God." The King James Version does a much better job translating Hebrews 10:1, rendering it as "the very image" rather than "the realities."

This brings out what Calvin was getting at in his example of the painting. There is the reality, which awaits us in the last days. There is the true image, the detailed picture of that reality represented in Christ. He is the "way and the truth" (John 14:6); in him we now have the true likeness of heavenly things. But we are not yet in heaven. Cast back from Christ is his shadow in the law. It is a rough outline, but with real continuity with things to come. This image depends on a real unity between the testaments, while also explaining the difference between the two.

Another thing we want to observe about the Old Testament is that its subject matter is Christ. To be sure, it is Christ in shadow form through various types and representatives in the Old Testament. But the subject is Christ nonetheless. Any time we interpret the Old Testament with results opposed to the gospel, or that have no relevance to Christ and his saving work, we have forgotten this vital principle and wrongly understood the Old Testament. Jesus himself emphasized this after his resurrection, as he taught the disciples on the road to Emmaus: "Beginning with Moses and all the

Prophets, he interpreted to them in all the Scriptures the things concerning himself" (Luke 24:27). Christ is not found only in selected Old Testament passages, but "in all the Scriptures." This must have been quite a sermon to hear, but we needn't think there is anything Christ unfolded to the Emmaus disciples that is not equally available to us in the Old Testament. Moreover, for forty days prior to his ascension into heaven, Jesus taught the apostles from the Old Testament, and the redemptive-historical approach they learned from him appears throughout the New Testament.

Our passage in Hebrews informs us, however, that the pictures of Christ in the Old Testament will be rough ones. We should not be surprised if each type of Christ, each prophetic anticipation, and each promise made in the old covenant provides only rough outlines and not a point-by-point correspondence. The old covenant was a shadow, and by its very nature a shadow is better understood when the reality is there to be seen. A rough draft is better filled in by those who have the final version to consult. It is for this reason that the Christian with the New Testament is able to give the proper interpretation of the Old Testament. Indeed, like a married man looking back on dating, Christians have a better understanding of the Old Testament than did those who lived under it, and certainly a better one than unbelieving interpreters of the Old Testament today. Because we have Christ, whom the Old Testament foreshadowed, we have "the word of the prophets made more certain" (2 Peter 1:19 NIV).

Everything we have said about interpreting the Old Testament has bearing on the Old Testament religious system. If the law was a shadow, a rough outline, then its sacrifices cannot be expected to function adequately. Anyone who relied upon the mechanics of Old Testament animal sacrifice would be horribly let down by the actual results. They did not, as Hebrews 10:1 puts it, "make perfect those who draw near."

This was all made clear by the simple fact that the sacrifices were "continually offered every year" (Heb. 10:1). The fact that nothing had been done to remove the guilt of the people made perfectly clear the need for a more real system of atonement. After all, these were dumb and unwilling animals that were being sacrificed for the willing, volitional sins of spirit-bearing human beings.

Indeed, Hebrews 10:3 makes the telling remark that far from removing sin, the Old Testament system of atonement was "a reminder of sin every year." The sacrifices pointed not to themselves as a solution, but away from themselves. Their main teaching was not what they could do but what they could not do. William Barclay explains this with a simple analogy: "A man is ill. A bottle of medicine is prescribed for him. If that medicine effects a cure, every time he looks at the bottle thereafter, he will say, 'That is what gave me back my health.' On the other hand, if the medicine is ineffective, every time he looks at the bottle he will be reminded that he is ill and that the recommended cure was useless."[2]

In just that sense we must see the Old Testament as a question demanding an answer, as a cry awaiting its comfort, as a hunger awaiting the bread of life. "How long, O Lord?" was a cry on the lips of many a prophet; it was the collective longing of that covenant that was the shadow of better things to come.

Indeed, Barclay's illustration really doesn't go far enough. The ongoing sacrifices not only showed their own futility, but dramatized the greater danger. They daily proclaimed, as every lamb and goat was slain, "This is what will happen to you unless a better atonement can be found." They were a reminder not only of sin and of failure, but of the judgment that must come as a result.

A Telling Contrast

Hebrews 10:5–7 also makes a point about the insufficiency of the Old Testament sacrifices to achieve God's will. Once again, the writer draws from the Psalms, this time from Psalm 40: "Consequently, when Christ came into the world, he said, 'Sacrifices and offerings you have not desired, but a body have you prepared for me; in burnt offerings and sin offerings you have taken no pleasure. Then I said, "Behold, I have come to do your will, O God, as it is written of me in the scroll of the book"'" (Heb. 10:5–7; cf. Ps. 40:6–8).

There are several ways we can look at the assertion that this psalm came from the mouth of Jesus. For one, we might observe that Psalm 40 was spoken by King David, who was a major type of Christ in the Old Testament. The Old Testament contains numerous types of Christ as part of his shadow in that covenant. Some types were institutions like the temple. Others were

---

2. William Barclay, *The Letter to the Hebrews* (Louisville: Westminster/John Knox, 1976), 113.

particular rituals like those of the sacrificial system. Other types were people, and prominent among them was David, from whose line Jesus would actually be born. The point here is that David's statements in Psalm 40 could not really be made by David himself: "Sacrifices and offerings you have not desired, but a body have you prepared for me." It is hard to see how that applies to David, a man under the old covenant. Therefore, this must have been a statement that anticipated the mission of Christ, whose shadow is found in these verses. This is the view of John Calvin, who sees Psalm 40 as a foretelling of Christ's coming to fulfill the law. Another reason Psalm 40 can be attributed to the lips of Jesus is that its content corresponds to the incarnation. The writer of Hebrews says, "When Christ came into the world, he said, . . . 'a body have you prepared for me.'"

Hebrews 10:5–7 employs a contrast between that which God does not desire and that which he does. God does not desire sacrifices and offerings, but rather the doing of his will. In what sense, however, can we say that God does not desire sacrifices and offerings, when he was the One who established these very ordinances as the way to draw near to him in the old covenant? One way to resolve this difficulty is to recall the many prophetic passages expressing God's displeasure with sacrificial ritual. These warnings do not condemn the sacrifices themselves, but the hypocrisy of those who simply went through the motions without any heart involvement. A good example of this comes from Psalm 51, where David cries, "For you will not delight in sacrifice, or I would give it; you will not be pleased with a burnt offering. The sacrifices of God are a broken spirit; a broken and contrite heart, O God, you will not despise" (Ps. 51:16–17). The same might be said today about people who just go through the motions of worship. As Jesus taught the woman by the well, "The true worshipers will worship the Father in spirit and truth, for the Father is seeking such people to worship him" (John 4:23).

But there is a more fundamental point being made. Perhaps the best Old Testament example comes from the ministry of Samuel in his confrontation with wicked King Saul. Saul had disobeyed an explicit command of God not to take captive any livestock from his enemies. When Samuel challenged him for this, Saul offered to sacrifice a few of his contraband animals to God, paying him off, as it were, according to the letter of the Levitical system. Samuel's stinging rebuke is famous: "Has the LORD as great delight in burnt offerings and sacrifices, as in obeying the voice of the Lord? Behold, to obey is better than sacrifice, and to listen than the fat of rams" (1 Sam. 15:22).

With these words, Samuel stripped Saul of the kingship, giving it instead to David, the unknown youth, who was a "man after [God's] own heart" (1 Sam. 13:14). Samuel's point, and the point of our passage, is that even though God established the sacrifices of animals, these were not God's true desire. They were not a statement of the solution, but of the problem. What God desires from us is obedience, not sacrifices to cover our disobedience. The sacrifices showed the constant presence and horrid nature of sin. Every time a lamb's breast was opened and blood flowed down the altar, this point was made. This was not what God desired; this was hardly an expression of what makes his holy heart glad! No, what gladdens God is heart-obedience from his people bought with his love.

Another classic expression of this comes from Micah 6, where the prophet asks if sacrifices are really what God wants. He answers: "Will the Lord be pleased with thousands of rams, with ten thousands of rivers of oil? . . . He has told you, O man, what is good; and what does the Lord require of you but to do justice, and to love kindness, and to walk humbly with your God?" (Mic. 6:6–8). Here is the telling contrast between Christ and the Old Testament system, as the writer of Hebrews conveys it: "Sacrifices and offerings you have not desired, but a body have you prepared for me; in burnt offerings and sin offerings you have taken no pleasure. Then I said, 'Behold, I have come to do your will, O God, as it is written of me in the scroll of the book'" (Heb. 10:5–7).

Obedience pleases God. He is satisfied by a heart eager to do his will, by a life expressing the character of God set forth in the Ten Commandments, or as Jesus summarized them: "You shall love the Lord your God with all your heart and with all your soul and with all your mind. This is the great and first commandment. And a second is like it: You shall love your neighbor as yourself" (Matt. 22:37–39). This is what God wants, and only this satisfies him.

The Body of Christ

In addition to the contrast between what does and what does not please God, Hebrews 10:1–10 contrasts the animal sacrifices and the self-sacrifice of Christ. An animal sacrifice was valuable in that blood was shed and a life taken, and thus it signified the terrible wages of human sin. But they were not of sufficient value to satisfy God. In this regard, F. F. Bruce surely penetrates the author's thinking when he observes: "Our author's contrast is . . . between the involuntary sacrifice of dumb animals and 'sacrifice into which obedience enters, the sacrifice of a rational and spiritual being, which is not passive in death, but in dying makes the will of God its own.'"[3]

This reflection adds to what we have already observed about Jesus Christ and the superior, utterly sufficient value of his sacrificial death. In an earlier study we noted its value because of his divine life; the value of this blood was that of the Son of God. Furthermore, we noted its value in that Christ was a spotless Lamb, without blemish or defect from sin. But to this is added even more worth, namely, that Christ's sacrifice represents that which is most precious to God above all other things, the doing of his will.

"A body have you prepared for me . . . I have come to do your will, O God," our passage attributes to Christ (Heb. 10:5–7), and this is the sacrifice that pleases God. In that respect, can there have been in the entire course of time a more precious moment to the heart of God than when his only Son offered up to God his will by dying on the cross? Matthew's Gospel tells us about the terrible events on the night of his arrest, when Jesus went alone into the Garden of Gethsemane to pray, to ready himself for the terrible physical ordeal ahead, and the even more terrible spiritual ordeal of God's holy wrath poured out against sin. Matthew records the scene: "Going a little farther he fell on his face and prayed, saying, 'My Father, if it be possible, let this cup pass from me; nevertheless, not as I will, but as you will'" (Matt. 26:39).

"To obey is better than sacrifice," Samuel had said. But who had ever obeyed like this? Who had ever perfectly fulfilled the Father's will, both in terms of the moral law and in terms of the work he was given to do? "Behold," Jesus could say to God all his days, but especially in the days of his passion, "I have come to do your will, O God." Everything written of him in the book, as verse 7 puts it—that is, all the law of God that expressed the character of Christ—he did. But this refers especially to those many shadows of Christ, the prophecies that laid out the terrible path of obedience that led to the cross. Isaiah 42:1 said, "Behold my servant, whom I uphold, my chosen, in

---

3. F. F. Bruce, *The Epistle to the Hebrews,* rev. ed. (Grand Rapids: Eerdmans, 1990), 241, quoting J. Denney, *The Death of Christ* (London, 1951), 131.

whom my soul delights; I have put my Spirit upon him; he will bring forth justice to the nations." This is what we find in the life of Jesus. But even more important are words like those recorded in Psalm 22, which spoke in grisly terms of the cross that he would bear for our sins, in perfect obedience to the will of God: "I am poured out like water, and all my bones are out of joint; my heart is like wax; it is melted within my breast. . . . I can count all my bones—they stare and gloat over me; they divide my garments among them, and for my clothing they cast lots" (Ps. 22:14–18).

People complain about the doctrine of predestination that it makes of us mere puppets, without willing obedience. But this is not true. There was never a man whose life was so scripted for him as Jesus; his life was not only predestined but also prerecorded in minute details. Yet his obedience to that script was anything but mechanical. Here was the divine Son of God in the flesh, the freest of all men ever born. And yet that freedom bore fruit in the most careful conformity to God's will for him, as set forth in the Scriptures, predestined and prerecorded. "Behold," he says to God's great joy, "I have come to do your will." God was pleased with this in a way that no millions of sheep or goats could ever approach. F. F. Bruce puts it well: "Wholehearted obedience is the sacrifice which God really desires, the sacrifice which he received in perfection from his Servant-Son when he came into the world. . . . The psalmist's words, 'I have come to do your will, O God,' sum up the whole tenor of our Lord's life and ministry, and express the essence of that true sacrifice that God desires."[4]

The better sacrifice that the Old Testament demanded, lest the knife should fall upon us and not on some sheep and goats and bulls, the sacrifice that pleases God and wins his acceptance, is the sacrifice of Christ. "Sacrifices and offerings you have not desired"—that was a statement of the problem. But Jesus answers, "A body have you prepared for me. . . . I have come to do your will, O God." Jesus offers to God on our behalf a sacrifice that involved real and costly obedience in fulfillment of the perfect demands of God's law.

It is significant that the writer of Hebrews links Christ's incarnation with his sacrificial death: "A body have you prepared for me" (Heb. 10:5). Because God desires obedience, he prepared a body for his Son, the eternal Word—

---

4. Ibid., 240, 242.

a body in which he could live in the world, honor God, and die in obedience to his command. Athanasius, the great church father, said, "As the Word who is immortal and the Father's Son it was not possible for him to die, and this is the reason why he assumed a body capable of dying. . . . When he offered his own temple and bodily instrument as a substitute for the life of all, he fulfilled in death all that was required."[5]

In other words, that little baby boy we sing about on Christmas was born for the sake of the cross. The manger was the beginning, and the cross was the destination. This is why the angel told Joseph, "You shall call his name Jesus, for he will save his people from their sins" (Matt. 1:21). God prepared a body for the eternal Son, so that in it he could obey the Father with joy all of his days. Jesus said to his disciples, "My food is to do the will of him who sent me and to accomplish his work" (John 4:34). And it was when that body, prepared for him by God, was crucified for the sins of his people, that he finally could rest from that labor of love. Only after the cross did Jesus say, "It is finished" (John 19:30), giving up his spirit into the hands of a happy God.

A New and Living Way

All of this is why Jesus did not need any animal sacrifices when he appeared in the true sanctuary that is heaven. He had done God's will and he entered on his own merits. This, of course, is something we cannot say about ourselves. We do not enter on our own merits, but on his merits, his blood having washed away our sin. This is how our passage ends, with the observation that "he abolishes the first," that is, the old covenant system, "to establish the second" (Heb. 10:9), that is, the new and living way opened up by his own perfect obedience to the will of God. It was this that tore the veil in the temple, opening up the way to God: a perfect man who rendered the obedience that pleases God, so that all who come by means of him may enter freely. He has set aside the law, with all its ordinances, as the way to God. He is "the door of the sheep" (John 10:7) by the offering of his own obedient life.

Hebrews 10:10 concludes our passage with this very emphasis: "By that will we have been sanctified through the offering of the body of Jesus Christ once for all." God is holy, his heaven is holy, his standards and requirements

5. Athanasius, *De Incarnatione* 9, 44, 17.

are holy as well. Hebrews 12:14 therefore rightly says, "Without holiness no one will see the Lord" (NIV). Through faith in Christ we are made holy, because his body was offered up for us once for all. We are no longer like the rest of the world in the sight of God. We are no longer what we previously were to him. We are holy, because Christ has won God's pleasure with the perfect obedience of his own life.

How, then, shall we live, having been made holy unto God by the saving work of Christ? The apostle Paul answered very plainly at the end of his great exposition of God's saving mercy: "I appeal to you therefore, brothers, by the mercies of God, to present your bodies as a living sacrifice, holy and acceptable to God, which is your spiritual worship" (Rom. 12:1).

Surely this is how we must worship our God, who has saved us with such a gospel. The Bible always defines true worship in the terms that were set for Jesus in Psalm 40, recounted in Hebrews 10:5–7: "Sacrifices and offerings you have not desired, but a body have you prepared for me; in burnt offerings and sin offerings you have taken no pleasure. Then I said, 'Behold, I have come to do your will, O God.'" This is what our bodies and our lives are now for, to be living sacrifices, offered freely by redeemed image-bearers of God who long to please their Lord and Savior.

What do you give the God who has everything? What will you give him out of gratitude for so great a salvation? He already has everything in all creation! If you want to please God (and what could be more worthwhile in all of life?), if you want to give him pleasure (and who is more worthy of our worship?), then you will do his will, as it is written in his Book, in the name of Jesus Christ, who loved you and gave himself for your sins.

33

A GREAT CONCLUSION

Hebrews 10:11—18

*The Holy Spirit also bears witness to us; for after saying, "This is
the covenant that I will make with them after those days, declares
the Lord: I will put my laws on their hearts, and write them on
their minds," then he adds, "I will remember their sins and their
lawless deeds no more." Where there is forgiveness of these, there
is no longer any offering for sin.* (Heb. 10:15–18)

Some of the most memorable passages in all the Bible are those that
serve as conclusions to great doctrinal portions of Scripture. Probably the two most famous come from Paul's Letter to the Romans.
In chapter 8 Paul sums up his systematic exposition of the doctrine of salvation with a great and well-loved statement of Christian assurance: "For I
am sure that neither death nor life, nor angels nor rulers, nor things present nor things to come, nor powers, nor height nor depth, nor anything else
in all creation, will be able to separate us from the love of God in Christ Jesus
our Lord" (Rom. 8:38–39). From that high plateau Paul then goes upward
into the doctrine of God and his sovereignty in chapters 9–11, climaxing
with this great conclusion: "Oh, the depth of the riches and wisdom and

knowledge of God! How unsearchable are his judgments and how inscrutable his ways! . . . For from him and through him and to him are all things. To him be glory forever. Amen" (Rom. 11:33–36).

Perhaps Hebrews 10 lacks the sheer eloquence of those great conclusions. In fact, the absence of that kind of rhetorical flourish is one of many indicators that the apostle Paul did not write Hebrews. Yet we have in this passage another great conclusion. If it is not great in its prose, then it is great in its ideas, great in terms of the magnitude and significance of the argument it brings to a close.

A GREAT STATEMENT

The central doctrinal section of Hebrews began in chapter 7. In this lengthy exposition the writer has compared Christ and his priestly work to the whole sacrificial system of the old covenant. He showed that Christ is superior as priest to Aaron and his successors and better when compared to Melchizedek, who came before. He showed in chapter 8 that Christ's covenant is better than the old one in Moses, and in chapter 9 that Christ's blood is better than that of the animal sacrifices of the Old Testament. John Calvin rightly observes: "There is, indeed, no book in Holy Scripture which speaks so clearly of the priesthood of Christ, which so highly exalts the virtue and dignity of that only true sacrifice which He offered by His death, which so abundantly deals with the use of ceremonies as well as their abrogation, and, in a word, so fully explains that Christ is the end of the Law."[1]

In concluding this great argument, our present verses drive home the lesson the writer has been hoping to teach, namely, that while the old covenant offered no real solution for sin, Christ's priestly work in the new covenant successfully and sufficiently solves this great problem of all mankind:

> Every priest stands daily at his service, offering repeatedly the same sacrifices, which can never take away sins. But when Christ had offered for all time a single sacrifice for sins, he sat down at the right hand of God, waiting from

1. John Calvin, *New Testament Commentaries*, 12 vols. (Grand Rapids: Eerdmans, 1994), 12:1.

that time until his enemies should be made a footstool for his feet. For by a single offering he has perfected for all time those who are being sanctified. (Heb. 10:11–14)

These verses may not have all the eloquence of Romans 8, or the soaring prose of Paul's doxology in Romans 11, but they deliver the most wonderful good news ever heard by the ears of men. Indeed, all of redemptive history, from the time when God clothed guilty Adam and Eve with the skins of the slain animal at the gate of the garden; to Abraham receiving a ram to be slain in the place of his son Isaac upon Mount Moriah; to the Israelites in the time of Moses, spreading the lamb's blood on their doorposts lest the angel of death should come in; to generation after generation of Israel, with the priests slaying thousands and millions of lambs and goats and bulls, sacrifices the writer of Hebrews insists could never have atoned for one human sin—all of that history had craned its neck to hear words such as these, had waited with bated breath, had cried with bitter tears, "How long, O Lord, how long!" to hear words like these. Where is the lamb? Where is the true sacrifice? Where is the real atonement that will not merely place an ill-fitting lid on the boiling cauldron of sin, but actually exhaust the fury of God's wrath and justice against it? Where is, as John the Baptist said upon spying the Lord Jesus Christ, "the Lamb of God, who takes away the sin of the world" (John 1:29)? Hebrews 10:11–14 proclaims the one true sacrifice that takes away our sins and makes us holy.

The primary purpose that motivated this letter was to warn the Hebrew Christians not to fall back into the ways of the old covenant. They were experiencing persecution—either from the Jewish community or the Roman authorities, or both—and the pressure made a denial of Christ in favor of Judaism a tempting option. But these verses sum up the whole of his revulsion at such a thought. What? he might say, return to a religion, a priesthood, a covenant, that despite all the labor, all the activity, all the blood and sweat and tears "can never take away sins" (Heb. 10:11)? It is unimaginable folly, despite the worldly pain of persecution for the sake of Christ, to go from forgiveness and peace and real access to God, back to the old situation of sin and its dreadful alienation. By his one and finished sacrifice, Christ has put away sin and made holy all who hold fast to him. No earthly prize is of such value; no worldly sacrifice is too great for such gain.

This was an overwhelming argument for the first-century Hebrew Christian, fretfully wondering if fidelity to Christ was worth the cost. But it speaks just as powerfully to people today, fretfully considering the claims of Christ and the cost of discipleship. Whether we are on the doorstep of faith or the exit ramp of unbelief, what we find in these verses is equally significant. What do verses 11–14 tell us, but that in Christ we have not mere religion, but salvation? We do not have ritual and tradition, but spiritual reality and power. We have not warm sentiments, not moral self-help, but the forgiveness of our sins by the work of the Savior, and power for holiness from a heavenly Lord.

Here is the great statement that makes this a great conclusion: Jesus Christ has done upon the cross what no priest of Israel could ever have done, and what no worldly religion can ever achieve today. For both the Hebrew Christian in danger of abandoning Christ and today's fence-sitting doubter in danger of passing by the one and true salvation, these verses sound a clanging gospel bell: there are a true sacrifice for our forgiveness and a priest reigning in heaven to make us into what we were created to be. If we hear and believe, we gain the right to sing the gospel hymn with joy:

My God is reconciled;
   his pardoning voice I hear;
he owns me for his child,
   I can no longer fear;
with confidence I now draw nigh,
   with confidence I now draw nigh,
and "Father, Abba, Father!" cry.[2]

A GREAT TRANSITION

Hebrews 10:11–18 is not only a conclusion, but also a transitional passage, setting the stage for the outstanding applications that follow in the rest of this epistle. It does this through the use of an expression we have encountered numerous times already, the phrase "made perfect." This phrase occurs in verse 14 for the seventh out of nine times in the Book of Hebrews: "By a

2. Charles Wesley, "Arise, My Soul, Arise," 1742.

single offering he has *perfected* for all time those who are being sanctified." In earlier chapters it mainly referred to Jesus Christ. In Hebrews 2:10 we read that "it was fitting that he . . . in bringing many sons to glory, should make the founder of their salvation perfect through suffering." As we observed at the time, the point is not that Jesus was ever less than perfect in his person, but rather that the experiences of his life and death perfected him— prepared him or qualified him—for his office and work as Redeemer. Hebrews 5:8–9 elaborates on this same point, stating, "Although he was a son, he learned obedience through what he suffered. And being made perfect, he became the source of eternal salvation to all who obey him."

These statements regarding the perfecting of Jesus Christ present the main doctrinal point of Hebrews, namely, his perfect and unique fitness to put away our sins, both as perfect sacrifice and as perfect priest. Once this point has been made, the writer of Hebrews then uses the same phrase, "made perfect," in reference to what God intends for believers. Indeed, the last four uses of this expression, beginning in chapter 10, all refer to believers. Hebrews 10:1 complains that the old covenant "can never, by the same sacrifices that are continually offered every year, make perfect those who draw near." Verse 14 says that Christ, by his one sacrifice, "has perfected for all time those who are being sanctified." Later on we will consider the great statement of Christian worship that is found in Hebrews 12:18–24, in which believers in heaven are described as "the spirits of the righteous made perfect" (Heb. 12:23).

This is what unfolds in the flow of Hebrews. Christ was made perfect in his role as Savior and High Priest for the church in order to sit at God's right hand—this is the first half—so that we would be made perfect in him for our role as worshiping priests in heaven before the very throne of God— this is the second half. This is the macrostructure of redemption as taught in the Book of Hebrews.

A GREAT REALITY

It is important that we understand the concepts and the terms in this passage. The Greek word translated as "made perfect" (*teteleiōken*) might also be rendered as "made complete," "finished," or "made fitting." This is how it was used in reference to Jesus. When applied to us, it is used almost synonymously with the idea of sanctification. We see this conjunction of ideas in Hebrews 10:14, where believers are "made perfect" and "are being made holy."

The basic meaning of holiness is "set apart." Things that are made holy are taken out of a profane category and placed into a sacred or holy category. This was undoubtedly on the writer's mind because of the priestly context. Just as the vessels of the temple were holy, set apart for sacred service, so too believers are set apart for the service of God.

In this sense, holiness emphasizes status or position. It is not our character, not our intrinsic holiness that sets us apart for God and to God. Far from it! Verse 10 emphasizes that we "have been sanctified" or "made holy" by the cross. We have received this status and holy position by the work of Christ.

But holiness also carries the idea of conformity to God's character. Holy things are to be kept pure; their purity is fitting for their holy status. If we, therefore, have been made holy by Christ, God's purpose is that we will now conform to his holy character. This is put very strikingly by the apostle Paul in Romans 8:29, where he states that we were saved, even predestined, "to be conformed to the image of [God's] Son."

Another way to get at this is to follow the tenses of the verbs in Hebrews 10. We have here the past, the present, and the future. First, there was a past completed action: "When Christ had offered for all time a single sacrifice for sins, he sat down at the right hand of God" (Heb. 10:12). The verbs "offered" and "sat down" occur in the past tense. They are in the Greek aorist tense, which here signifies a completed past action.

Verse 14 tells us the effect of Christ's work and uses a different tense, the perfect tense: "By a single offering he has perfected" us. The perfect tense signifies a completed past action that has an ongoing effect into the present and future. Something of vital significance has happened, and its effects continue now and forever. Here the effect is that we have been made perfect. Finally, we have a present participle: "those who are being sanctified." This signifies a present activity that continues into the future.

Putting these verbs together, we have an event that took place in the past, that is finished and completed—the sacrificial death of Christ, along with his subsequent resurrection and enthronement as heavenly high priest. This has implications and results that come forward to us—we have been made perfect in his perfection. Finally, there is a present process—we are therefore being made holy. That is to say, we are being transformed into what we have been made.

The key to all of this is the perfect tense and the statement "he has perfected" us. The perfect tense is vital to Christianity as to no other religion. No other faith rests upon the present power of past events, namely, the death, resurrection, and ascension of the Lord Jesus Christ. This is why Christianity alone is good news. It is a gospel because it presents news of great events that changed everything once and for all. What has happened to Christ makes our salvation possible and real. If Christ's death has not happened, we are damned in our sins; but if it has happened—and it has!—we who believe are saved with great joy, secure in him forever.

This has important implications for our view of the Christian life. Our sanctification has a once-for-all as well as an ongoing sense. It is "already" as well as "not yet." A popular Christian bumper sticker says, "I'm not perfect, just forgiven," but in an important sense this is not true! In the eyes of God you have been made perfect because you are in Christ; you are a beneficiary of his perfection. Of course, there is a process that is not yet complete, but a Christian's sanctification is so certain of achievement that it is now viewed as accomplished: "You have been made perfect."

The present tense of Christianity is always linked to and rests upon the past tense of Christ's finished work. Christianity says to believers, "Because he died you have died in him. Because he arose, you are alive in him. Because he is made perfect, you are made perfect in him." As Paul wrote to the Ephesians, "[God] raised us up with him and seated us with him in the heavenly places in Christ Jesus" (Eph. 2:6).

These realities, however, are not abstracted from our present life. What we have been made in the heavenlies is not unrelated to what we must become on the earth. The Christian rule is this: we are to be what we are in Christ. Since we have been made perfect in Christ, we are now becoming holy in practical ways. Holiness is our established destiny, and so it is becoming our present reality. If this cannot be said of us as individuals, our claim to be in Christ at all is challenged.

To return to the thought world of Hebrews, we think of Israel's high priest wearing a golden plate on his turban that read "Holy to the LORD." That same designation has been applied to us by Jesus Christ. We are perfect, fit, complete. This is our identity, our destiny, our reality. It is the spiritual gravity of every Christian's life to which we are being pulled and shaped and sometimes shoved by the Spirit of God living within us. We cannot escape it, and if we do, that simply bears testimony that we are not in Christ at all. Those who possess faith in Christ simply cannot go on living as they did before. We are different because of what has happened—not by a power that is from us, but a power that is from heaven, where Christ reigns for us and in us.

Hebrews 10:15–17 looks back on the new covenant, already examined in chapter 8, to highlight both the external and the internal, the objective and the subjective aspects of our salvation: "And the Holy Spirit also bears witness to us; for after saying, 'This is the covenant that I will make with them after those days, declares the Lord: I will put my laws on their hearts, and write them on their minds,' then he adds, 'I will remember their sins and their lawless deeds no more'" (Heb. 10:15–17). God has forgiven our sins (v. 17)—this relates to justification. It is external and objective. He has put his law in our hearts and written it upon our minds (v. 16)—this is sanctification, and it is internal and subjective. Salvation is a definitive act of God whereby he forgives our sins forever and accepts us in Christ. But it is also a lifelong process of deliverance from the power of sin and the coming of new life that is "after the likeness of God in true righteousness and holiness" (Eph. 4:24).

I can think of nothing more thrilling than this, that I will become perfect, "like God in true holiness." I will become perfect as the creature God intended me to be. I will become perfect in the bearing of his image in conformity to Christ. I will be perfect in fruit, perfect in worship, and perfect in thought, word, and deed. It is staggering to my mind, so foreign is this to my actual present experience! And yet this, because of what Christ has done for me, is my reality, and not what is now seen in me. This is what is true and real for all believers in Christ. We will be perfect in glory—the glory that comes from him and reflects back to the praise of his name. The very thought of this should create in us a great appetite for practical holiness, with dread of and loathing for sin. If we have grasped only a portion of this truth, if we have laid hold of a fragment of our true identity in Christ, we will no longer live as we have.

A Great Comparison

These great truths are all focused on the one great comparison that is driven home in the Book of Hebrews. By now we are familiar with it: a comparison between Israel's priests and the perfect high priest, Jesus Christ. There in all his futility stands the priest of the old covenant, day after day offering the same sacrifices over and over, reminding us of, but unable to repair, the terrible problem of sin. Hebrews 10:11 sounds the familiar refrain that the old priests and their sacrifices "can never take away sins." The entire picture is one of futility, fatigue, and frustration. The greatest possible contrast is presented when we then consider the effectual work of the true high priest, Jesus Christ: "But when Christ had offered for all time a single sacrifice for sins, he sat down at the right hand of God, waiting from that time until his enemies should be made a footstool for his feet. For by a single offering he has perfected for all time those who are being sanctified" (Heb. 10:12–14).

One commentator puts the contrast in these striking terms:

> The priest of the Old Testament stands timid and uneasy in the holy place, anxiously performing his awful service there, and hastening to depart when the service is done, as from a place where he has no free access, can never feel at home; whereas Christ sits down in everlasting rest and blessedness at the right hand of Majesty in the holy of holies, His work accomplished, and He awaiting its reward.[3]

Christ's sacrifice was not offered over and over, but once for all, and in this we see the sufficiency of his blood for the forgiveness of our sins. The resulting situation could not stand in greater contrast with that of the old covenant priests. William Barclay writes: "The priests stand offering sacrifice; Christ sits at the right hand of God. Theirs is the position of a servant; his is the position of a monarch. Jesus is the king come home, his task accomplished and his victory won."[4] And Andrew Murray rightly exclaims, "The once of Christ's work is the secret of its being forever: the more clear the acceptance of that divine once for all, the

---

3. Franz Delitzsch, *Commentary on the Epistle to the Hebrews*, 2 vols. (Edinburgh: Clark, 1877), 2:161.
4. William Barclay, *The Letter to the Hebrews* (Philadelphia: Westminster, 1976), 118.

more sure the experience of that divine forever. . . . His forever is one of victory, and of the blessed expectation of its full manifestation."[5]

Christ is seated in the heavens. His work is accomplished, established, inevitable. Our author is wrapping up all his great ideas, here returning to the theme in chapter 1, that Christ has been exalted with almighty power as he rules over history for the church.

Christ is seated and enthroned, in a position of rest like that of God on the seventh day of creation. It is a rest of sovereignty, of omnipotent rule, control, and confidence. This has the most horrible implications for Christ's enemies: for the devil and the demons, and also for every sinner who rejects his claims. He is "waiting from that time until his enemies should be made a footstool for his feet" (Heb. 10:13). Unbelievers may deny him, mock him, and exult in their apparent freedom from his lordly rule. But all the while he sits enthroned, with history racing toward the judgment over which he will reign supreme.

Meanwhile, this has wonderful and life-transforming implications for all who trust in him. Verse 12 tells us he is seated; verse 13 adds that he is waiting as this present age runs its course; and verse 14 tells us why he can afford to wait: "By a single offering he has perfected for all time those who are being sanctified." Verse 18 concludes our passage, indeed, the whole great doctrinal portion of the Book of Hebrews, with the same great idea. Where sins have been forgiven, "there is no longer any offering for sin." There is no longer any labor for the Savior, and no longer any threat to the salvation of those who look to him in faith. Jesus can rest enthroned, waiting for the day of his final triumph; we, too, can rest through faith in him, as we await his return in glory.

A GREAT CONCLUSION

This is the great conclusion to the main doctrinal instruction of the Book of Hebrews. From here we will move forward to the wealth of applications in the final chapters, including the examples of faith in chapter 11. We are far from finished with the Book of Hebrews. Yet here we stand at the conclusion of this great doctrinal teaching. How then shall we conclude our own reflections on these matters?

5. Andrew Murray, *The Holiest of All: An Exposition of the Epistle to the Hebrews* (Grand Rapids: Revell, 1993), 360–61.

There can be only one answer, and that is to draw our thoughts and our hearts, our whole spiritual orientation, upward to where Jesus Christ sits now enthroned, reigning with power for our salvation, having accomplished everything needed for us to be saved. He is at the center of it all, above it all; he is the meaning of everything we have considered in the Book of Hebrews. The tabernacle and temple were about him and his work. The priests and the rituals of the Old Testament served only to point to him. The blood that was shed year after year and day after day spoke only of his blood, shed once for all upon the cross. The veil that was torn invites our gaze into the heavens, where now our Savior sits at rest, reigning for his own, securing us for himself forever, and ruling our hearts by the Spirit he sends. Everything points to him; everything is found in and with him; everything for us comes from him and draws us to him as his people, his own reward for obedience to the will of the Father.

This is the great conclusion we must draw from the teaching of Hebrews. It must be the profession of our faith. And Christ must be the great affection of our hearts. To know him and serve him, to grow in his likeness, must become the great ambition of all our lives.

PART 4

Exhortations to and Examples of Faith

34

HOW SHOULD WE THEN LIVE?

Hebrews 10:19–25

*Since we have a great priest over the house of God, let us draw
near with a true heart in full assurance of faith, with our hearts
sprinkled clean from an evil conscience and our bodies washed
with pure water.* (Heb. 10:21–22)

*J*n 1976 Francis Schaeffer wrote a significant book titled *How
Should We Then Live?* His purpose was to show how ideas as they
have been embraced or discarded have shaped the rise and
decline of Western culture. In his opening chapter he writes: "What [peo-
ple] are in their thought world determines how they act. . . . The results of
their thought world flow through their fingers or from their tongues into
the external world. This is true of Michelangelo's chisel, and it is true of a
dictator's sword."[1]

This is exactly how the New Testament presents matters. The reason so
much of the Bible is devoted to doctrine—statements regarding what we
must know and believe—is that the consequences of these truths are utterly
definitive. We are living in a time that says it matters not so much what we

---

1. Francis A. Schaeffer, *How Should We Then Live?* (Old Tappan, N.J.: Fleming Revell, 1976), 19.

believe as how we believe it, that is, with sincerity and tolerance for other views that are diametrically opposed. Quite in contrast, the apostles demanded fidelity to the truths God revealed through them and through the prophets before them. The apostle Paul therefore begins his Letter to the Galatians by writing, "Even if we or an angel from heaven should preach to you a gospel contrary to the one we preached to you, let him be accursed" (Gal. 1:8). Truth is of central importance and is definitive for salvation. To deny truth with even the best of apparent intentions is to rebelliously reject God and suffer eternal condemnation.

"How should we then live?" Schaeffer asked in his book, and he answered by saying that our manner of living must be consistent with our professed faith. This is a view strongly espoused by the writer of Hebrews. He has devoted nine and a half chapters to the proclamation of truth regarding the person and work of Jesus Christ. Now, in the transition from doctrine to application he says, "Therefore, brothers." We should always take note of the Bible's "therefores," because they provide the link between cause and effect. "Therefore," the writer of Hebrews says by way of transition, what we believe must transfer into our life and actions.

Two Definitive Possessions

Verses 19–21 summarize all that has been taught in the great doctrinal sections of Hebrews by identifying two definitive possessions. There are two things we have, the writer says, because of Christ's person and work.

The first of these possessions has to do with access to God through Jesus Christ: "Therefore, brothers, since we have confidence to enter the holy places by the blood of Jesus, by the new and living way that he opened for us through the curtain, that is, through his flesh" (vv. 19–20). The key concept here is "confidence to enter by the blood of Jesus." This confidence is something believers have and must know that they have in order to lead productive, godly lives. People who trust in Jesus Christ stand before an open door, with free and open access to God, and with their sins atoned for by his blood. It is by his blood that we come, or as verse 20 puts it, by his body, which refers to the whole of his earthly achievement in life and in death on the cross. Surely that access to God makes a most important impact on how we should think and live.

Francis Schaeffer writes, "The central message of biblical Christianity is the possibility of men and women approaching God through the work of Christ."[2] This is our possession, and it is, verse 20 tells us, something new. It is a new way Jesus has opened. We possess what the Old Testament saints did not, namely, the right to enter through the holy place and into the presence of God. Jesus has opened it by his life and by his death, so that we have free access to God through him.

Furthermore, it is a living way because Jesus lives forever to secure this access. He is, in this sense, the veil through which we are invited to pass in order to draw near to God by his life and death. Christ's work as priest and as sacrifice has produced a new situation that did not exist before, but it will exist forever as he reigns eternally in heaven.

Our second great possession is directly linked to the first: "we have a great priest over the house of God" (Heb. 10:21). We have two things: confidence to enter and a great high priest. The point is that the one who opened and secured the way for us into God's presence is there himself. He is there as our priest, representing us and pleading effectually for our acceptance, securing and sending to us the Holy Spirit so that we are fitted and empowered to be worshipers and priests before his throne. Because our high priest is there, we can know that we belong there, too, and can thus approach with confidence.

A LIFE OF WORSHIP

It is because of our great possessions in Christ that Christians have an obligation to live a certain way. This was Francis Schaeffer's argument, and it is the point now offered by the writer of Hebrews. In lovely symmetry he sets forth a threefold manner of life as our reasonable response to Christ's saving ministry to us. Three times in Hebrews 10:22–25 the writer says, "Let us." Together these exhortations present a life pattern that every believer is to make his or her own.

The first of these comes in Hebrews 10:22, which calls us to a life of worship: "Let us draw near with a true heart in full assurance of faith, with our hearts sprinkled clean from an evil conscience and our bodies washed with

2. Ibid., 245.

pure water." Because we have confidence to approach God's throne, and because we have a great priest over the house of God, let us in fact draw near to God.

This, of course, exhorts us to prayer. If we are to lead fruitful lives, we must draw near to God in our minds and hearts. This links up with an early exhortation that our writer/pastor gave as an intended encouragement to his readers: "Let us then with confidence draw near to the throne of grace, that we may receive mercy and find grace to help in time of need" (Heb. 4:16).

More broadly, the writer exhorts us to a life of worship. Worship is both our highest privilege and our most central duty. We were made to worship God, and he demands our worship (see Ex. 20:3–4). Worship is most beneficial for us. In worship we find the freedom to be what we were meant to be. Musicians feel this way about music, runners feel this way about racing, and Christians feel this way about worship: it is the activity in which they find themselves. Worship is therefore essential to our spiritual health and well-being. Martyn Lloyd-Jones explains: "It is only when I am near to God in Christ that I know my sins are forgiven. I feel his love, I know I am his child and I enjoy the priceless blessings of peace with God and peace within and peace with others. I am aware of his love and I am given a joy that the world can neither give nor take away."[3]

By worship, I certainly mean coming to church, gathering together with God's people for corporate worship as a body. This is certainly on the writer's mind, since he says in verses 24–25: "Let us consider how to stir up one another to love and good works, not neglecting to meet together." But of course worship is also more than our corporate gatherings; worship is our whole response to the mercy of God. This is what Paul meant in Romans 12:1, "I appeal to you therefore, brothers, by the mercies of God, to present your bodies as a living sacrifice, holy and acceptable to God, which is your spiritual worship."

Hebrews 10:22 presents a compact how-to for drawing near to God in worship. In this single verse the writer sets forth four guidelines for worship, beginning with sincerity: "let us draw near with a true heart." A true heart functions as it is supposed to. It relates to God adoringly, with right affec-

3. D. Martyn Lloyd-Jones, *Tried and Triumphant* (Grand Rapids: Baker, 1994), 212–13.

tions and priorities. Second, he tells us to worship "in full assurance of faith." We might say that full assurance is what is in the heart that is true. The sincere, believing heart is filled with assurance in God, through unwavering trust in him and his promises.

Next, the writer of Hebrews tells us to draw near to God "with our hearts sprinkled clean from an evil conscience." This is a matter of great importance to him; he frequently complained that the old covenant sacrifices failed at this very point, being unable to cleanse the conscience. By sprinkling he refers to the blood of Christ, which alone sets free the sinner's guilty conscience. Through his blood we know that our sins are removed and our hearts are set free from the burden of guilt.

Fourth, we must worship having "our bodies washed with pure water." Most commentators see this as a reference to baptism, and it is hard to deny the connection. However, surely John Calvin is right to see the point not in baptism itself, but in that which baptism symbolizes: the spiritual renewal that is the work of the Holy Spirit. Calvin would have us remember the words of Ezekiel 36:25–26, which are necessary for us to worship God as we should: "I will sprinkle clean water on you, and you shall be clean from all your uncleannesses, and from all your idols I will cleanse you. And I will give you a new heart, and a new spirit I will put within you. And I will remove the heart of stone from your flesh and give you a heart of flesh."[4]

These guidelines apply to all seven days of the week, but it is helpful if we consider how they bear on our coming together on Sunday to worship God in church. Yes, all our lives are worship, but how we worship when we gather together in God's name is especially important. Verse 22 tells us we are to come to the worship service with a true heart; that is, with undivided affection and intent to worship him. God is worthy, and we must come to worship him, and not merely to seek some personal benefits. Second, we must come with the assurance and confidence of acceptance that comes from genuine faith in his saving work. Third, we must be able to deal with our own sinfulness, our guilt from things we have done and the sinfulness we bring into the sanctuary. This is why we should read the law and confess our sins, affirm our faith and hear God's word of pardon in our services of worship. Such elements of worship do not make up a pointless liturgy, but provide

4. John Calvin, *New Testament Commentaries*, 12 vols. (Grand Rapids: Eerdmans, 1994), 12:142.

the biblical way by which sinners come to God. Finally, we must come believing and relying upon the work of the Holy Spirit, trusting him to cleanse and renew our hearts as we come to the Father in Christ's name. If you are not benefiting from worship—as you must to grow in Christ—and if you doubt that God is blessed by your worship, you might consider the words of Hebrews 10:22 and its instruction on worship.

A LIFE OF TRUTH

Christians are called to a life of worship, but we are also called to a life of truth. "Let us," says the writer of Hebrews for a second time, "hold fast the confession of our hope without wavering, for he who promised is faithful" (Heb. 10:23). This is the second of the three exhortations: that we must hold firm to the gospel hope in an unbelieving world. The Greek word for "confession" (*homologia*) here means a public and doctrinal confession, and it is in this manner that we must uphold the truth.

Evangelical Christianity in today's affluent Western culture is noteworthy for its cavalier treatment of truth. We readily trade our doctrines in order to get along with others, to create a more impressive sense of unity. But we are literally surrounded by a global Christianity that suffers gladly for the truth. All around the world today our brothers and sisters in Christ are valiantly taking their stand upon the hope that we profess.

By writing of "the confession of our hope," the author speaks of the substance of our faith. All around the globe Christians are publicly professing the content of their faith, and often suffering real persecution as a result. In places like Sudan, Laos, and China, there would be no Christianity without valor for truth, and the unswerving confession of true believers has led to a vast expansion of the church.

Western Christians are surrounded not only geographically, but also historically, by those who have been unswerving in their devotion to the content of our hope. In the early church, Christians were tortured to death for their refusal to compromise with the cult of Caesar. They would not bow and say, "Caesar is Lord." They would not rationalize any betrayal, but gladly died for their faith. In the English Reformation, the Protestant martyrs were burned to death for what many today would think are petty theological distinctions, but which were in fact necessary doctrines for the hope that they professed. Revelation 12:11 shows such faithful believers in heaven, where the angel says of them, "They have conquered by the blood of the Lamb and by the word of their testimony, for they loved not their lives even unto death."

Unswerving devotion to Christ and his gospel is obviously a matter of special importance to the writer of Hebrews, and he is determined to thwart any idea of compromise among his readers. They were not to compromise with those who called them back into the former ways of Judaism, but were firmly to take their stand for Christ. It was unpopular and costly then, and it is the same today for us. But it is essential for our salvation.

This point is made repeatedly in this letter. In 3:6 the author wrote that we are Christ's house "if indeed we hold fast our confidence and our boasting in our hope." In 3:14 he said, "We share in Christ, if indeed we hold our original confidence firm to the end." In 4:14 he added, "Since then we have a great high priest who has passed through the heavens, Jesus, the Son of God, let us hold fast our confession." Our confession must not waver. We have every reason to hold fast, for, as verse 23 concludes, "he who promised is faithful."

Francis Schaeffer's book *How Should We Then Live?* is important with regard to just this point. We are tempted to separate our theological convictions from how we live. What other generations of Christians willingly died for, we consider needless points of doctrine. All the time today we hear that theology doesn't matter so long as we are living good lives. But that is a false and dangerous position, and one that leads us away from God and back to the world. Schaeffer wrote his book to remind us that "as a man thinketh, so he is. . . . The inner thought world determines the outward action."[5]

Nothing is more important than what ideas we believe; nothing so shapes the way that we will live, and nothing is more important to the Christian life than the content of the faith we profess. Therefore, we are not to be silent, nor to compromise the truth we have received, but to hold unswervingly to the gospel truths and promises that give us our hope. "He who promised is faithful," says our writer, and we, as a result, can be faithful to him.

5. Schaeffer, *How Should We Then Live?* 19–20.

A LIFE OF LOVING COMMUNITY

The third and last exhortation is found in Hebrews 10:24–25: "And let us consider how to stir up one another to love and good works, not neglecting to meet together, as is the habit of some, but encouraging one another, and all the more as you see the Day drawing near."

Here is a summons to a life of loving community. William Lane describes it as "continued care for one another that finds an expression in love, good works, and the mutual encouragement that active participation in the gatherings of the community makes possible."[6] This is not an invitation for us to be judgmental busybodies, making the lives of others a burden. But it does mandate that we take a lively interest in the affairs of other believers. As the writer says, "Let us consider how to stir up one another to love and good works." We are to study and implement schemes that motivate one another in godly living.

This means that no Christian can be an individualist. We *are* our brothers' keeper. We must give thought to how we can be of help to other believers. We must consider the impact of our actions on the faith of others, often surrendering personal freedoms so as not to offend the weak (see Rom. 14:13–16). This alone provides an excellent reason to come to church and other Christian gatherings: that we may be of benefit to others, encouraging them and taking a care that they are standing firm as the day of the Lord approaches. This also provides a mandate for the types of practical ministries that help our churches make a powerful impact on people's lives: men's groups, women's groups, youth ministries, college ministries, single adult ministries, marriage retreats, and more.

A study of the verbs in these two verses offers a practical primer on how to be a good and helpful member of the church, filled as it always is with people who are struggling in one way or another. First comes the verb "consider," which has to do with our thinking. We are accustomed to think only of ourselves, but our thoughts are better given to others. Is someone doubting? Is he discouraged? Is she tempted? Without needless prying, we should give thought to the condition of those around us. If we

6. William L. Lane, *Hebrews 9–13*, Word Biblical Commentary (Dallas: Word Books, 1991), 289.

are not doing this, then we are nothing more than takers, consumers of religion who are of little use for the eternal destiny of other people.

The next term, "stir up," means to incite or provoke or stimulate. The way we live and talk and act should be provocative to other Christians, in the best sense of the word. They should be reminded of spiritual truth because of what we are saying and how we are living. The result of our example and conversation should be love and good works in the lives of other believers. Let me ask you, then, if the way you handle yourself provokes others to take seriously what the Bible teaches. Does your counsel cut against the grain of worldly logic and press home the claims and promises of God? Does your behavior set a helpful model for weak or new believers? If not, you are not making the impact you should for Christ's work in the church.

Finally, we are to "encourage" one another. This requires us to come alongside other people with words and actions that will strengthen them in Christ. Encouragement may mean bearing a load for them, it may mean prayer, companionship, or sharing your own conviction that God is faithful based on your experience of his loving care.

The writer of Hebrews made this same point in chapter 3, "Exhort one another every day, as long as it is called 'today,' that none of you may be hardened by the deceitfulness of sin" (3:13). We little consider how threatened each of us is by sin, which is deceptive in its very character. Like climbers roped together on a steep mountain, like soldiers teamed together on a battlefield, we must keep track of one another. We must work together if we are to reach our objective safely.

One of the essential means by which Christ guides and protects his people is the active participation of other believers in their lives. The day of Christ's return is fast approaching, and it will be a day of judgment for all who fall away. Remembering this, let us give sober reflection not merely to our own affairs but to the spiritual concerns of our brothers and sisters in Christ.

THESE THREE REMAIN

"How should we then live?" We are answering this question in light of our great possessions in Christ, who has opened the way to heaven and ministers to us as heavenly high priest forever. This is the kind of passage we should check ourselves against from time to time, both individually and as a church. In these verses we have encountered three exhortations that correspond to the great triad of the Christian life set forth by the apostle Paul: "Now faith, hope, and love abide, these three" (1 Cor. 13:13).

These three abiding graces coincide with the three exhortations of Hebrews 10:22–25. First comes faith, which is the burden of Hebrews 10:22, since faith secures for us a relationship with God: "Let us draw near with a true heart in full assurance of faith." People ask how to have a closer relationship with God. The answer is by faith. God has opened the way; he has accepted you in his love because of Jesus Christ. All that lacks is for you to believe that good news, to trust him and the promises in his Word. You must therefore give yourself to his Word. You must search the Scripture for its teaching and claims and promises, and then you must trust God for what he has said. It is this faith that must fill our hearts. Faith starts with the mind, but what the mind receives must be embraced by the heart; only then will you know a growing relationship with God and an ability to worship him "in spirit and truth" (John 4:24).

How should we then live? First comes faith, but, second, there is hope. The Christian lives by hope, drawing strength and stability from its anchor in the stormy seas of life. That is what Hebrews 10:23 is about: "Let us hold fast the confession of our hope without wavering, for he who promised is faithful." Geerhardus Vos explains why hope is so vital to the Christian experience:

> The Christian is a man . . . who lives with his heavenly destiny ever in full view. His outlook is not bounded by the present life and the present world. He sees that which is and that which is to come in their true proportions and in their proper perspective. The centre of gravity of his consciousness lies not in the present but in the future. Hope, not possession, is that which gives tone and colour to his life. His is the frame of mind of the heir who knows himself entitled to large treasures upon which he will enter at a definite point of time.[7]

In our study of Hebrews 6:19–20, we learned that our gospel hope is certified by the oath-bound promise of the holy God, the seal of which is affixed

---

7. Geerhardus Vos, *Grace and Glory* (Carlisle, Pa.: Banner of Truth, 1994), 142.

in heaven by the nail-scarred hand of the Lord Jesus Christ. If we will hold fast to those truths, we will then possess a hope that is an anchor for our very souls.

Faith brings us into relationship with God for a life of worship, while hope anchors us unswervingly to a future of unimaginable blessings. Last comes love, which Paul says is the greatest of these three. That is what we find in verses 24–25, in its exhortation that we "stir up one another to love and good works, not neglecting to meet together . . . encouraging one another."

Though love is the greatest, it is not the first of these graces. There is a progression at work here. First is faith, which unites us to Christ and brings us to God. The result of that faith is hope, which secures our hearts in the storms of this life. With hope we no longer fear for ourselves but are able to give loving encouragement to others. Hope therefore springs forth in love, the love of God that fills the hearts of all who hope in him. John rightly tells us, "We love because he first loved us." But he adds, "Whoever loves God must also love his brother" (1 John 4:19, 21).

How long are we to love? Hebrews 10:25 says we are to encourage one another "all the more as you see the Day drawing near." The day of Christ is fast approaching. It races toward us through either the end of history or our own deaths, both of which bring us into Christ's presence. How should we then live? If we want to please God, grow in grace, and help other believers, let this agenda of faith, hope, and love define the pattern of our lives for however much time is given to us to live on this earth.

35

A DREADFUL PUNISHMENT

Hebrews 10:26–31

For if we go on sinning deliberately after receiving the knowledge of the truth, there no longer remains a sacrifice for sins, but a fearful expectation of judgment, and a fury of fire that will consume the adversaries. (Heb. 10:26–27)

here are four major warnings in the Book of Hebrews. The first appeared in chapter 2, a warning against drifting away by failing to hold fast to the gospel. The second came in chapter 3 where the writer exhorted his readers that they must not turn away from God with an unbelieving heart. A similar warning appeared in chapter 6, where we read of the dire consequences of apostasy. Now in chapter 10 we encounter a fourth exhortation. All of these exhortations amount to the same thing. In them we see the concern that drove this whole epistle: that these Hebrew Christians, having heard and accepted the gospel of Jesus Christ, might turn away into unbelief. Those who deliberately reject Christ, the writer says, have "a fearful expectation of judgment, and a fury of fire that will consume the adversaries" (v. 27).

THE REALITY OF HELL

This passage makes very clear a teaching that is widely denied today, even by many who consider themselves evangelicals. That teaching has to do with both the reality and the nature of hell. It is not only that our generation does not like the idea of hell, but that it simply will not accept it. Ours is a humanistic age; we think of good mainly in human terms. According to this way of thinking, what is best for the greatest number of human beings is what is best ultimately. People who think this way would, on their own authority, banish the lake of fire of which Scripture so plainly speaks.

Perhaps the best discussion of this topic to come out in recent years is found in D. A. Carson's outstanding book *The Gagging of God*. Carson collects and analyzes various attempts to do away with hell, or at least to turn down the temperature on eternal punishment.

First, there are those who deny the idea of judgment altogether, as unworthy of a loving God. Clark Pinnock expresses this view passionately:

> I consider the concept of hell as endless torment in body and mind an outrageous doctrine, a theological and moral enormity, a bad doctrine of the tradition which needs to be changed. . . . Everlasting torment is intolerable from a moral point of view because it makes God into a blood-thirsty monster who maintains an everlasting Auschwitz for victims whom he does not even allow to die.[1]

Others, who find themselves unable to brush aside the biblical data in the way Pinnock does, are attracted to the idea of total destruction as opposed to everlasting torment. These people are called "annihilationists." They agree that God will punish the wicked, not eternally, not with everlasting torment, but with annihilation. The wicked will not suffer perpetually in hell but will simply cease to exist. Annihilationists point to the imagery of fire and observe that fire not only torments but consumes, so that what is burned is destroyed. This idea of destruction, they point out, is a strong theme in the Bible (see Phil. 3:19; 1 Thess. 5:3; 2 Thess. 1:9; 2 Peter 3:7).

Probably the best-known representative of this view is John Stott, who writes: "I find the concept [of eternal conscious punishment in hell] intol-

---

1. Clark Pinnock, cited in D. A. Carson, *The Gagging of God* (Grand Rapids: Zondervan, 1996), 519.

erable and do not understand how people can live with it without either cauterising their feelings or cracking under the strain." But, recognizing the folly of allowing our emotions to determine our creed, he adds, "as a committed Evangelical, my question must be—and is—not what does my heart tell me, but what does God's word say?"[2]

What, then, does the Bible say about hell? Hebrews 10:26–31 is of great help in dealing with this subject. First of all, we find an inescapable affirmation of the judgment of God. We may not like the idea of a God who judges. We might prefer a God who only loves, however foolish such a desire is. But the Bible plainly declares what we find in verse 30: "For we know him who said, 'Vengeance is mine; I will repay.' And again, 'The Lord will judge his people.'" Verse 27 tells us that those who deliberately reject God have "a fearful expectation of judgment, and a fury of fire that will consume the adversaries."

How do we reconcile the idea of divine wrath with a loving God? The answer is that God's wrath is not opposed to God's love; indeed, the two are inseparable. God has the same attitude toward sin that a mother has toward a fatal disease that threatens her home. J. I. Packer gives a helpful explanation:

> God's wrath in the Bible is never the capricious, self-indulgent, irritable, morally ignoble thing that human anger so often is. It is, instead, a right and necessary reaction to objective moral evil. God is only angry where anger is called for.... Would a God who did not react adversely to evil in His world be morally perfect? Surely not. But it is precisely this adverse reaction to evil, which is a necessary part of moral perfection, that the Bible has in view when it speaks of God's wrath.... This is *righteous* anger—the *right* reaction of moral perfection in the Creator towards moral perversity in the creature. So far from the manifestation of God's wrath in punishing sin being morally doubtful, the thing that would be morally doubtful would be for Him *not* to show His wrath in this way.[3]

What people who reject the idea of judgment and wrath really oppose is the very idea of God. It is not how he exerts his sovereignty, but his sover-

2. John Stott, cited in Carson, *Gagging of God,* 520.
3. J. I. Packer, *Knowing God* (Downers Grove, Ill.: InterVarsity, 1973), 136, 166.

eignty itself that humanistic man recoils against. If God is sovereign, if he is responsible for the disposition of all things, then he cannot be a God of love without being a God of wrath; he cannot be good as God without being just in his punishment of sin.

This explains why many evangelicals are attracted to the idea of annihilation. They cannot hold a biblical view of God without accepting the idea of divine wrath, and yet they cannot stomach the idea of everlasting punishment. They support their position with the biblical statements that employ the terms "consume" and "destroy." In Matthew 10:28 Jesus says, "Do not fear those who kill the body but cannot kill the soul. Rather fear him who can destroy both soul and body in hell." John Stott comments, "If to kill is to deprive the body of life, hell would seem to be the deprivation of both physical and spiritual life, that is, an extinction of being. . . . It would be strange," he adds, "if people who are said to suffer destruction are in fact not destroyed."[4]

This might be a compelling argument, and an attractive one, were it not ruled out by direct statements elsewhere in Scripture. In Matthew 18:8, for instance, Jesus speaks of the danger of being cast into "eternal fire." Hell's fire does not burn out, but is "eternal." In Mark 9:48, Jesus speaks of hell as a place where "their worm does not die and the fire is not quenched."

In Revelation 20, the scene of the great day of judgment, we receive further clarification. In verse 9 we find that fire will come down from heaven to "consume" the enemies of God's people. This seems to support annihilationism. But verse 10 goes on to say this: "The devil who had deceived them was thrown into the lake of fire and sulfur where the beast and the false prophet were, and they will be tormented day and night forever and ever." We might be comforted by saying that this refers to the devil and not to humans. But the devil is also one of God's creatures, and if a loving God is able to send the devil into perpetual suffering, then he is capable of doing the same to sinful human beings.

The scene in Revelation 20, however, does not stop with the devil. Verses 11–15 bring all humanity into the picture with these words:

4. Cited in Carson, *Gagging of God*, 520.

Then I saw a great white throne and him who was seated on it. From his presence earth and sky fled away, and no place was found for them. And I saw the dead, great and small, standing before the throne, and books were opened. Then another book was opened, which is the book of life. And the dead were judged by what was written in the books, according to what they had done. And the sea gave up the dead who were in it, Death and Hades gave up the dead who were in them, and they were judged, each one of them, according to what they had done. Then Death and Hades were thrown into the lake of fire. This is the second death, the lake of fire. And if anyone's name was not found written in the book of life, he was thrown into the lake of fire.

This is the very same lake of burning sulfur where the devil "will be tormented day and night for ever and ever."

The Bible depicts judgment and hell not merely as destruction but as everlasting punishment and torment for the enemies of God. Against this backdrop we see the urgency with which the writer of Hebrews speaks to this Christian community. Over against the reality of hell, we can see why he writes in verse 31: "It is a fearful thing to fall into the hands of the living God."

TRAMPLING THE GOSPEL

Our passage does not give a general statement regarding sin and its punishment, but rather a particular warning to these Jewish people who had professed faith in Jesus Christ. The writer's concern is the same that he voiced in the other exhortations, namely, that they would not turn away from God in rejection of the gospel. There was pressure for them to do this. They were experiencing persecution and temptation, just as we are tempted to repudiate Christ by opposition from the world, the flesh, and the devil. Therefore he warns them: "If we go on sinning deliberately after receiving the knowledge of the truth, there no longer remains a sacrifice for sins" (Heb. 10:26).

It is important to understand what the writer is talking about, and what he is not talking about. He speaks here of those who "go on sinning deliberately." This refers to a distinction made in the Old Testament between intentional and unintentional sins. Moses spoke of this often, such as in

Numbers 15:30: "The person who does anything with a high hand, whether he is native or a sojourner, reviles the LORD, and that person shall be cut off from among his people."

In Hebrews 10:26 the key Greek word is *hekousiōs*, which occurs only twice in the New Testament: here and in 1 Peter 5:2, where it means "without compulsion." In other Greek writings the noun form is used for those who serve as volunteers. What this verse describes is not believers who are struggling with sin, or even those who have besetting sins which plague their spiritual life and displease the Lord. Rather, this refers to those who reject God's authority to tell them what to do, and who flagrantly continue in their sin. Proverbs had this kind of person in mind when it described those "who forsake the paths of uprightness to walk in the ways of darkness, who rejoice in doing evil and delight in the perverseness of evil, men whose paths are crooked, and who are devious in their ways" (Prov. 2:13–15). Leon Morris comments with regard to our passage in Hebrews:

> It is clear that the writer has apostasy in mind. He is referring to people who "have received the knowledge of the truth." . . . The people in question, then, know what God has done in Christ; their acquaintance with Christian teaching is more than superficial. If, knowing this, they revert to an attitude of rejection, of continual sin, then there remains no sacrifice for sins. Such people have rejected the sacrifice of Christ, and the preceding argument has shown that there is no other.[5]

I had a pastoral situation some time ago that is instructive here. It involved a young woman who had been close to my wife and me while she was a student at the college where I taught. After she graduated, we maintained some contact, and it became clear after several years that this woman had fallen deeply into sin. At one point she visited our home and lamented this with tears. She attended church with us and went back to where she lived determined to do better. However, she soon fell in with an unbelieving crowd, and the next time I spoke with her she informed me that she had come to realize the falsehood of Christianity. Unable to answer her atheist friends, she began reading Nietzsche and other atheist philosophers, and rejected

---

5. Leon Morris, "Hebrews," in *Expositor's Bible Commentary*, 12 vols. (Grand Rapids: Zondervan, 1981), 12:106.

the faith. Needless to say, I was distressed by this news. So far as this went, our passage in Hebrews 10 presented a stark possibility to my soul, since her deliberate embrace of sin suggested "a fearful expectation of judgment" (Heb. 10:27).

Time passed, until I was asked to perform a wedding for a young man I had also known in those days. The wedding was in this woman's hometown, and she was invited. Sure enough, she was there at the wedding reception, sticking out like a sore thumb in this Christian crowd by the way she dressed and acted. Reluctantly, she approached me, and after a brief conversation she agreed to drive me to the airport that evening.

Along the way she recounted to me the various philosophies that had led her away from Christ, many of them advocating ideas the writer of Hebrews wanted his own flock to avoid. I was tired after the wedding and didn't think I could manage to keep straight the various Christian answers to each of these challenges. Instead, I simply asked her, "Tell me, which came first: your descent into sin or these philosophical convictions? Was it the philosophy that persuaded you of sin or the sin that persuaded you of the philosophy?" To my astonishment, she broke down at once into tears, admitting that atheism had gripped her only after she had fallen badly into sin. However, she insisted she was no longer a Christian but an apostate. She had betrayed the Lord. Even if she wanted to come back, she said, citing passages like the one before us here, her sins had damned her forever.

As our conversation progressed, now at the airport, I confronted her with a question at the heart of what our passage from Hebrews is all about. I asked her, "Have you renounced Jesus Christ? Can you do that now? Can you say that he is not the Son of God, that he did not die upon the cross for sinners? Do you now repudiate Jesus Christ? If you can do that, I will admit that you are damned."

I don't know which of us was more nervous. But she could not repudiate Jesus, and that evening I had the privilege to evangelize her all over again, starting with the cross where Jesus took the wrath of God in her place. She had been backslidden—badly so—but not apostate. As of this writing, she has repudiated her life of sin, is an active member in a Bible-believing church, and is growing steadily in the Lord.

THE HORROR OF APOSTASY

Sadly, this is not the way it always goes. There are apostates—not real Christians who fall away, but professing Christians who were never really saved and show this by their subsequent repudiation. As Hebrews 10:29 makes clear, there is a kind of person who mentally grasps the teaching of the gospel, and who knows and understands about Jesus, yet "has spurned the Son of God, and has profaned the blood of the covenant by which he was sanctified, and has outraged the Spirit of grace." Such an apostate is deserving of eternal punishment in hell, and is in fact consigned to that fate by his or her rejection of the only atoning sacrifice. People who rejected Moses' law died without mercy, says verse 28. What then will become of those who reject the grace of God? Only judgment and raging fire.

The formulation of Hebrews 10:29 makes clear that we are not talking about believers who struggle with sin. This statement of apostasy involves the flagrant rejection of three things: first, the person of Christ as Son of God ("one who has spurned the Son of God"); second, the saving work of Christ on the cross ("and has profaned the blood of the covenant by which he was sanctified"); third, the Holy Spirit who has brought the gospel near ("and has outraged the Spirit of grace"). That last item relates this statement to the words of Jesus in Matthew 12:32, where he speaks about the unforgivable sin against the Holy Spirit: "Whoever speaks against the Holy Spirit will not be forgiven, either in this age or in the age to come." The episode that occasioned that remark was the Pharisees' accusation that Jesus was of the devil because he cast out demons. Hebrews 10:29 makes clear that the sin involved—the unforgivable sin—is the willful repudiation of the gospel by those, like the Pharisees, who see it and understand what it means.

Recall the words of Clark Pinnock, who labeled any idea of eternal judgment an outrage against morality. But it is not an outrage for apostates to be damned. The outrage has to do with God sending his own precious Son into this world. He came not to judge us, though certainly we were already guilty. He came to save us. This is the kind of God we are talking about here— the God who "so loved the world that he gave his only Son, that whoever believes in him should not perish but have eternal life." That great statement of John 3:16 speaks of God's abounding love. That he should judge sinners is not the outrage; the outrage is that man, having received this gift from

God, should then despise it, should trample under foot the name of Jesus as God's Son, should treat as unholy his precious blood, and should insult the Spirit of God as he bears testimony to the gospel in this world.

This is the real outrage, one the Bible recognizes by the fact that John 3:16 leads to John 3:18: "Whoever does not believe is condemned already, because he has not believed in the name of the only Son of God." Surely A. W. Tozer was right when he said: "There will be only one text in hell, and it may be cut against the great walls of that terrible place—'True and righteous are thy judgments, O Lord!'"[6]

THE GIFT OF GOD'S LOVE

Hebrews 10:30–31 puts the exclamation point on the writer's warning about judgment: "For we know him who said, 'Vengeance is mine; I will repay.' And again, 'The Lord will judge his people.' It is a fearful thing to fall into the hands of the living God." If one thing proves the reality of Hebrews 10:31 it is the experience of Jesus Christ as he contemplated God's judgment. On the night of his arrest, Jesus went into the Garden of Gethsemane to pray, and it was the dreadful wrath of God that preyed upon his mind. Luke tells us how he prayed: "'Father, if you are willing, remove this cup from me. Nevertheless, not my will, but yours, be done.' . . . And being in an agony he prayed more earnestly; and his sweat became like great drops of blood falling down to the ground" (Luke 22:42–44). James Montgomery Boice comments: "This was not a man shrinking from mere physical death. . . . It was the horror of the holy, eternal Son of God as he faced the experience of being made sin for us and of bearing the wrath of separation from the love of God in our place. He was delivered up so that we might be spared. He bore the wrath of God so that we might never have to bear it."[7]

God has said that he will repay sin, visiting his vengeance on sinners. Hebrews 10:30 quotes two passages from Deuteronomy 32 that establish this judgment against sin. But it was in the death of his Son that God really proved it to the world, for it was God's wrath against our sin that Jesus bore upon

---

6. A. W. Tozer, *The Tozer Pulpit*, vol. 1, *Selections from His Pulpit Ministry* (Camp Hill, Pa.: Christian Publications, 1994), 89.

7. James Montgomery Boice, *Romans*, 4 vols. (Grand Rapids: Baker, 1992), 2:964.

that cross. What he experienced there was dreadful indeed. J. I. Packer describes it: "The physical pain, though great (for crucifixion remains the cruelest form of judicial execution that the world has ever known), was yet only a small part of the story; Jesus' chief sufferings were mental and spiritual, and what was packed into less than four hundred minutes was an eternity of agony—agony such that each minute was an eternity in itself."[8]

Is that dreadful? Yes it is. The point it makes is not that God is cruel, for it was God himself in the second person of the Son who bore that wrath. The point is not that God is morally objectionable, but that sin is morally repulsive. This is what we find hard to accept. This is lost on those who complain about God's wrath. Sin is terrible, and the cross of Christ declares it so to the world, even as it declares the holiness of God in letters of blood. For even when it was Jesus himself, the beloved Son of heaven, who bore our sin upon the cross, God the Father still poured out his wrath. This led J. C. Ryle to observe: "Terribly black must that guilt be for which nothing but the blood of the Son of God could make satisfaction. Heavy must that weight of human sin be which made Jesus groan and sweat drops of blood in agony at Gethsemane and cry at Golgotha, 'My God, My God, why hast Thou forsaken Me?' (Matt. 27:46)."[9]

The cross reveals the reality of sin as well as the reality of God's holy judgment upon it. But the cross reveals something else: the answer to the question about God's love. How can we call the God of the cross the God of love? Because the cross reveals how wide and long and high and deep is God's love. This is what it took for God to satisfy his holy justice, the full payment of the debt of sin. If this is what it took for God to love the world—the offering of his only Son, the only One who measured up to God's holy standards—then God was willing to do it. If the death of Christ was required for God to be reconciled to his creatures, then in that death we see the fullness of his love. "God so loved the world," and the death of Jesus was the provision of God's love for us.

Therefore, let us not trample Jesus Christ, God's Son, under our feet by unbelief. Let us not count as unholy that blood, precious in its value and saving in its virtue, that was shed for us. Let us not insult the Spirit of grace

8. Packer, *Knowing God,* 176.
9. J. C. Ryle, *Holiness* (Darlington, U.K.: Evangelical Press, 1979), 6.

who bears testimony to such love to our hearts. And if we do, should any of us repudiate this gospel of justice and love, then surely God will avenge, he will repay. And well he should. Even the thought of falling into his holy hands for justice, without the covering of Christ's blood received by faith, is dreadful. How terrible it will be for those who defy him today, but on that day will fall into his hands for condemnation.

36

IN A LITTLE WHILE

Hebrews 10:32–39

*For, "Yet a little while, and the coming one will come and will not
delay; but my righteous one shall live by faith, and if he shrinks
back, my soul has no pleasure in him." But we are not of those
who shrink back and are destroyed, but of those who have faith
and preserve their souls.* (Heb. 10:36–39)

One of the helpful things about studying a book of the Bible carefully is that you get a feel for the biblical author. As you follow along through the chapters, you gain insights into the way he thinks, into his relationship with his original audience, and even into his personality. This is particularly enjoyable in the case of the Book of Hebrews because we don't know who the author is. There is a greater sense of discovery than in the letters of Paul or Peter or John, all of whom we get to know quite well in the New Testament. The writer of Hebrews is the mystery man of the New Testament; when we considered the matter of authorship, I argued that there is no way to identify the writer, except to say he is probably not one of the other more familiar apostolic figures.

Here is what we have learned about the writer of Hebrews so far. First, he was a pastor. His attention was focused on the concerns of his flock. Furthermore, as our present passage makes particularly clear, he was intimately familiar with his readers. He knew their strengths and weaknesses. He knew the threats to their faith. He also knew the events that made up the particular history of this congregation. Second, he was single-minded and tenacious in his concern that they not shrink back and be destroyed. He understood that whatever might happen, this mattered above all else. Finally, he was versatile in his approach. He realized that some people need to be challenged, others encouraged, others warned, and still others inspired. If our writer was an associate of Paul, as there is good reason to believe, then he exemplified Paul's pastoral wisdom in 1 Thessalonians 5:14: "Admonish the idle, encourage the fainthearted, help the weak, be patient with them all."

A POWERFUL MEMORY

The writer of Hebrews places great stock in the use of historical examples. In chapter 11 he will make a tour de force through biblical history, but here in the last verses of chapter 10 he turns back to the history of this particular congregation.

Ours is a generation that foolishly thinks history is irrelevant. This is partly because we are self-centered, so we don't really care about anyone but ourselves. Many Christians are shaped in their thinking by secular ideas of progress or synthesis, and so think anything that happened before our own time is necessarily inferior. C. S. Lewis labeled this phenomenon "chronological snobbery." But the writer of Hebrews thought the past was an important resource for the present. He begins with a word that is one of three verbs that shape this passage. That word is "remember" or "recall": "Recall the former days when, after you were enlightened, you endured a hard struggle with sufferings" (Heb. 10:32).

The first thing we should notice is that the author does not "recall" his readers' attention to the "good old days" where faith seemed easy. It is not the times when things go well that really define our Christian lives. The really significant times, the periods that make up the highlights of our own histories, are those of trial and difficulty and danger.

This tells us something about how we should approach trials when they come. Things happen, circumstances suddenly change, a great problem arises, and we think something terrible has occurred. From one perspective we are bound to think this way in the face of sickness or job loss, the death of a loved one, or the sudden loss of a key leader. Of course we do not look forward to such things. But this passage reminds us that these are the occasions that make us rise up in our faith and character. It is when supports are stripped away that we find out what our faith is really made of. In this sense we should view trials as opportunities to glorify the Lord, as positive challenges to bring out and display our faith in God.

The times we will remember are the times of difficulty when God proved himself to our faith. These are the things our children will remember from their childhood in the church. Whenever we face real trouble, we should endeavor to mine out treasures for the future, which is just what the writer does. He wants his readers to remember what Christians can do through faith, what they had been able to do in an earlier trial, and how sufficient is God's grace for those who look to him in trouble: "You endured a hard struggle with sufferings, sometimes being publicly exposed to reproach and affliction, and sometimes being partners with those so treated. For you had compassion on those in prison, and you joyfully accepted the plundering of your property, since you knew that you yourselves had a better possession and an abiding one" (Heb. 10:32–34).

Notice the kinds of things God carried the Christians through by the power they received through simple faith in him. There was "a hard struggle" characterized by suffering. What is it that Christians fear about suffering? Most of all we fear that we will give in and that our faith will fail. But these Christians learned of God's sustaining grace. Having faced a hard struggle, Hebrews 10:32 says, "You endured."

In their earlier trial the recipients of the letter had been subjected to "reproach and affliction." This is the kind of thing that Christians in the West may soon experience. We worry that in response to insult and persecution we might deny our faith, or that we might be afraid to let people know we are Christians. But God enabled these believers to do the opposite, "being partners with those so treated" (Heb. 10:33). To this the writer adds that some were put into prison and many had their property confiscated. By faith his readers ministered to those afflicted and even accepted their own losses with joy. This, indeed, was the hallmark of the early church: not merely that they endured affliction, but they exhibited joy throughout it all. This is what faith requires; if we are not willing to endure affliction, then we simply cannot be Christians. Jesus taught: "If anyone would come after me, let him deny himself and take up his cross daily and follow me. For whoever would save his life will lose it, but whoever loses his life for my sake will save it" (Luke 9:23–24).

We are reminded here of Peter and John during the early days after the resurrection. The Sanhedrin called them in and demanded that they stop preaching the gospel in the city of Jerusalem. To drive the lesson home they had the apostles savagely flogged. Luke's description in Acts is all the more powerful for its matter-of-fact brevity: "They left the presence of the council, rejoicing that they were counted worthy to suffer dishonor for the name" (Acts 5:41).

This is what faith can do, and the lesson from the Hebrews' past is indeed a lesson of faith. Speaking of their confiscated property, he says, "You yourselves had a better possession and an abiding one" (Heb. 10:34). He might have written similarly about the threat of death: "You knew you had a better and lasting life." He might have said this about suffering, pointing to a "better and lasting comfort," and similarly about disgrace, since everyone who holds to Christ in faith has no less than eternal glory awaiting in store. This was Paul's perspective when he wrote, "I consider that the sufferings of this present time are not worth comparing with the glory that is to be revealed to us" (Rom. 8:18).

Early in our married life, my wife had a friend whose powerful faith during trials left a lasting imprint on our lives. One of her favorite sayings went very well with the thinking of the writer of Hebrews. "There are only three kinds of things that can happen to a Christian," she would say, "and all three of them are good. First, you can be blessed, and that of course is good. Second, you can die, and that takes you into the presence of Jesus. That is very good. Third, you can suffer, and the Lord uses that to make you more like Jesus, and that too is a very good thing." This is precisely how faith in Christ reasons, and it was this attitude that had empowered the Hebrew congregation in its prior success.

Hebrews 10:32–34 shows us that the goal of Christians in trials is that we stand firm. "You endured," the author says, with reference to the past. "Do not shrink back," he says as he turns to the present. This is what we are to do. Christians do not have to win the culture war, nor should we expect worldly triumphs. Our first goal is always to be true to the faith in this hostile world, standing on the solid rock of Christ.

The writer challenges the readers to remember what their forebears in the faith had done through faith. No doubt it was by remembering that their predecessors withstood their trials. The anti-Christian forces employed insult and persecution against them. But they would have thought of Jesus and the ridicule he received on the cross. They overcame their fear of suffering with a greater fear—the fear that they might fail to have fellowship in Christ's sufferings. This is the logic the world cannot understand—the logic that caused Jesus to take up the cross and that causes Christians to meet with him there.

This readiness to share in suffering has always confounded tyrants who tried to suppress the Christian faith. They put Christians in prison to isolate them, but other Christians just came to prison to keep them company. They confiscated their homes and possessions, seeking to break their spirits. But it was they, the persecutors of the church, whose spirits fell when the Christians responded with sacrificial sharing to provide for all the believers. This was the testimony of the wonderful Christian congregation in suffering, to whom the writer of Hebrews was writing. This was the display of faith by which Christians turned the ancient world upside down. In the words of the Puritan Jeremiah Burroughs, a man also familiar with persecution, "When a Christian can walk in the midst of fiery trials, without his garments being singed, and has comfort and joy in the midst of everything . . . it will convince men, when they see the power of grace in the midst of afflictions."[1]

"You May Receive"

These were all fine things for the Hebrew Christians to remember, particularly as they braced themselves for another round of trial, as the writer expected to happen. These verses show us the power of the past; yet if there is any one tense our writer thinks is all-important, it is the future.

1. Jeremiah Burroughs, *The Rare Jewel of Christian Contentment* (Edinburgh: Banner of Truth, 1964), 122.

There are three key verbs that structure this passage, the first of which relates to the past: "remember." The second occurs in Hebrews 10:36, and it relates to the future. What is in the Greek a single word is translated into English with the expression "you may receive." That is what the future holds for the Christian. If the present involves suffering, we are able to know that the future involves receiving. We look forward to receiving all that God has promised those who trust in him. Here is yet another way in which Christians are the true countercultural people today. Where the world says, "Buy now, pay later," the Christian says, "Sacrifice now, receive later."

The future orientation of the Christian faith is one of the great emphases of the Book of Hebrews, and here we see why that is. The knowledge of what is stored up for us empowers us in present trials. This is the point of the definition of faith in Hebrews 11:1, "Now faith is the assurance of things hoped for, the conviction of things not seen." We will see this lesson reinforced over and over in that great eleventh chapter.

This future orientation may be emphasized in the Book of Hebrews, but it is common to the entire Bible and its people. It is this that gives boldness to Christians. The circus performer, high upon a wire, is emboldened by the net beneath him. Likewise, Christians are brave in the sure knowledge of a glorious future. As Paul put it in 2 Corinthians 5:1: "We know that if the tent, which is our earthly home, is destroyed, we have a building from God, a house not made with hands, eternal in the heavens." Similarly, Peter began his first epistle to other Christians under trial by writing of "an inheritance that is imperishable, undefiled, and unfading, kept in heaven for you, who by God's power are being guarded" (1 Peter 1:4–5).

Because we are citizens of heaven even now, we are able to grasp things that are not yet real to our experience but are promised to those who trust in Christ. We bring future blessing into our present trouble as power to persevere. We rely on a future when, as Revelation 7:16–17 puts it, "They shall hunger no more, neither thirst anymore; the sun shall not strike them, nor any scorching heat. For the Lamb in the midst of the throne will be their shepherd, and he will guide them to springs of living water, and God will wipe away every tear from their eyes."

The writer of Hebrews especially locates our hope in the return of our Lord Jesus Christ. Verse 37 says, "Yet a little while, 'and the coming one will come and will not delay.'" But Jesus is present to us spiritually even now.

This has been the point of so much of this letter's teaching, that when Christ went to heaven, he did not become inaccessible to us, but even more accessible. He is bodily absent but spiritually present. Therefore, we wait for our king to return from a far country to reestablish his rule. We know for sure that he is coming, and we serve him while waiting, looking forward to the future with hope and joyful expectation.

Donald Grey Barnhouse emphasized that this is why Christians never simply tolerate their circumstances. We do not descend into stoic resignation, but rather are enlivened by a mighty hope:

> There is no thought of, "I can stand it." The pagan, in dull hopelessness, bows to the inevitable. The Christian accepts the suffering, knowing that God is bringing him through to glory; and from the hope of the past to the hope of the future, he sees the connection running through his suffering like a thread that binds all together. His life is like the turbulent rapids of a river, but he knows that the river comes from a still spring and is flowing to a calm ocean. In this knowledge, the Christian has settled peace.[2]

All of this being true, the only real danger to a Christian is that of abandoning the faith. "O death, where is your sting?" we say in Christ, but apart from Christ's resurrection, death is mortally ruinous. This explains the writer's urgency about the matter of perseverance in the faith. "For you have need of endurance," he says in verse 36, "so that when you have done the will of God you may receive what is promised."[3] Perseverance is the present tense of the Christian life, and it typically involves fierce struggle.

PERSEVERANCE OF THE SAINTS

Given a past marked by triumph and a future filled with hope, the writer of Hebrews constructs a present mandate for his Christian readers. What are we to do now? Are we to go on the offensive against the world, trying somehow to hasten Christ's return? Are we to go into hiding, desperately

---

2. Donald Grey Barnhouse, *Expositions of Bible Doctrines Taking the Epistle to the Romans as a Point of Departure*, 10 vols. (Grand Rapids: Eerdmans, 1959), 4:95.

3. "Endurance" is not a verb, but a noun. However, in the sentence construction it carries a verbal ideal. "You have need of endurance" is roughly equal to "You need to endure."

hoping to hold out by becoming invisible? The answer is found in the third verb that defines this passage: "Endure." "For you have need of endurance," the author writes, "so that when you have done the will of God you may receive what is promised" (v. 36).

"The perseverance of the saints" is one of the defining doctrines of Reformed theology. This doctrine teaches that while we are saved by grace alone, because of God's sovereign predestination, Christians must yet persevere until the end of their lives, or until Christ returns. Probably the clearest statement linking these two ideas of sovereign grace and the necessity to persevere comes in 2 Peter 1:10–11, where the apostle writes, "Therefore, brothers, be all the more diligent to make your calling and election sure, for if you practice these qualities you will never fall. For in this way there will be richly provided for you an entrance into the eternal kingdom of our Lord and Savior Jesus Christ."

Peter's point is not that we are to elect ourselves, as if we could, but rather to make sure that we are among God's elect people. How? By persevering in the faith, that is, by growing in grace through faith in Christ and continuing as Christians all through our lives. What are the qualities that mark a persevering Christian? In 2 Peter 1:5–7 the apostle had defined perseverance in terms of positive growth: "Make every effort to supplement your faith with virtue, and virtue with knowledge, and knowledge with self-control, and self-control with steadfastness, and steadfastness with godliness, and godliness with brotherly affection, and brotherly affection with love." This is the path along which Christians grow, and by which we persevere in faith through every kind of trouble.

The teaching that we must persevere and grow in faith should not be alarming to any Christian. Instead, it should simply remind us of the teaching of our Lord. Jesus said, "By this my Father is glorified, that you bear much fruit and so prove to be my disciples" (John 15:9). It is by bearing fruit that our salvation is proved. Arthur Pink puts this very simply: "No presumption is worse than entertaining the idea that I am bound for Heaven while I live like a child of Hell."[4] This is not in any way at odds with an emphasis on divine sovereignty and grace, but balances it biblically with

---

4. A. W. Pink, *An Exposition of Hebrews* (Grand Rapids: Baker, 1954), 33.

the call to spiritual responsibility. With that in mind, the Puritan Thomas Watson writes of the activity necessary to Christian perseverance:

> Christians do not arrive at perseverance when they sit still and do nothing. It is not with us as with passengers in a ship, who are carried to the end of their voyage while they sit still in the ship; or, as it is with noblemen, who have their rents brought in without their toil or labour; but we arrive at salvation in the use of means; as a man comes to the end of a race by running, to a victory by fighting.[5]

The same God who ordained the end of salvation for his elect also ordained the means by which we will get there, and that is perseverance in faith. Perseverance means acting in faith, and acting in faith means growing. We cannot sit still. To persevere, therefore, we must make use of the means of grace, especially by worshiping together, feeding upon God's Word, partaking of his sacraments, and communing with him in prayer. The bottom line to our perseverance is set forth in Hebrews 10:38: "My righteous one shall live by faith, and if he shrinks back, my soul has no pleasure in him." We must hold fast to Christ, come what may, looking to him at every step for the strength to endure and persevere.

YET A LITTLE WHILE

"Do not throw away your confidence, which has a great reward," writes our author (Heb. 10:35). He draws that confidence from the past, as water drawn up from a well. He also grasps it from the future, the way wonder is drawn from the stars above. In both past and future the confidence comes from the Lord who "is and who was and who is to come" (Rev. 1:8). In the past we find the gracious Lord who sustained us then and surely will sustain us now. We gain confidence from the future, because that same Savior is there in eternity, waiting ahead and coming for us in due time.

This is why Christians believe in the value of history, because history is *his story*. The past is defined by the victory of Christ at the cross and empty tomb; the future holds before us the victory of Christ in his glorious return

---

5. Thomas Watson, *A Body of Divinity* (Edinburgh: Banner of Truth, 1958), 280.

and eternal reign. But the present, with all its trials, is where we are now sustained by the power of that victorious Christ. Victory is not the absence of trial, nor the removal of all our worldly foes. Victorious Christianity is not merely something that takes place at political rallies, nor is it defined by rising sales of Christian products in the store. It is what happens when a grieving believer smiles through tears at a graveside, thinking of the resurrection morning. Victory comes when a follower of Christ shows love to an unpleasant neighbor because of the love of Christ for the world. Victory is gained today when persecuted believers, like this Hebrew Christian community in the Bible, stand firm before the mocking culture, refusing to abandon their creed. Victory is standing beside fellow believers in their persecution. It is singing hymns of joy while jobs or house or friends are lost.

"This is the victory that has overcome the world," wrote the apostle John, "our faith" (1 John 5:4). No matter what the world can do to the man or woman in Christ, we can sing for joy because of what tomorrow holds for us. "In all these things," Paul wrote, "we are more than conquerors through him who loved us." Why? "For I am sure that neither death nor life, nor angels nor rulers, nor things present nor things to come, nor powers, nor height nor depth, nor anything else in all creation, will be able to separate us from the love of God in Christ Jesus our Lord" (Rom. 8:37–39).

"We are not of those who shrink back and are destroyed," wrote the great pastor of the Epistle to the Hebrews, inspired with the confidence that comes from the Lord Jesus Christ, "but of those who have faith and preserve their souls" (Heb. 10:35). With what is ours in Christ, we have every reason for that kind of confidence, even in the worst of trials.

"You have need of endurance," God tells us. This is the bottom line for every Christian. But we do so knowing this: "Yet a little while, and the coming one will come and will not delay" (v. 37). The future is coming, and it brings to us the fullness of our salvation, a day without hunger or danger or tears. So we are not just sitting by idly, waiting for that future to happen. We are to live the future now, to be citizens of heaven even in the kingdom of this world. This is what our Lord Jesus did; this is what his cross is all about, the power of God to transform our earthly circumstances, to turn defeat into glorious victory. James Montgomery Boice wrote words that fitly conclude our study of Hebrews 10:

Victories in such sufferings are eternal in the same way that the victory of our Lord upon the cross is eternal. Our sufferings endure for a moment, but they achieve an eternal victory. They point to the truth and grace of God forever. I am convinced that in the farthest reaches of heaven, in what we would call billions of years from now, there will be angels who will look on everyone who has been redeemed by Jesus Christ and thrust into spiritual warfare by him, and they will say, "Look, there is another of God's saints, one who triumphed over evil by the Lord's power!" Revelation 12:11–12 describes how they will exclaim of our great victories over Satan: "They overcame him by the blood of the Lamb and by the word of their testimony; they did not love their lives so much as to shrink from death. Therefore rejoice, you heavens and you who dwell in them!" In achieving those eternal victories, we who love the Lord Jesus Christ will have indeed been more than conquerors.[6]

6. James Montgomery Boice, *Romans*, 4 vols. (Grand Rapids: Baker, 1992), 2:996.

37

What Is Faith?

Hebrews 11:1—3

Now faith is the assurance of things hoped for, the conviction of things not seen. For by it the people of old received their commendation. By faith we understand that the universe was created by the word of God, so that what is seen was not made out of things that are visible. (Heb. 11:1–3)

The Christian life is the life of faith. Faith is the issue on which the matter of salvation depends; it is the key that turns the lock on the door to eternal life. Faith is the channel by which we receive the benefits of Christ's saving work; it is the cup into which God pours his saving grace.

The eleventh chapter of Hebrews most clearly deals with the matter of faith, most carefully defines its nature, and most exhaustively describes its working. This chapter is to faith what the thirteenth chapter of 1 Corinthians is to love, which is why it is so treasured by God's people and so frequently studied. Hebrews 11 is the work of a master teacher and loving pastor who is convinced that the fate of his readers hinges on their faith. If they are to enter into eternal life, he knows, it will be through the possession and the exercise of faith, and in that alone. We see his concern in the verses that immediately precede this chapter, and are intimately connected to its purpose:

> You have need of endurance, so that when you have done the will of God you may receive what is promised. For, "Yet a little while, and the coming one will come and will not delay; but my righteous one shall live by faith, and if he shrinks back, my soul has no pleasure in him." But we are not of those who shrink back and are destroyed, but of those who have faith and preserve their souls. (Heb. 10:36–39)

It is through faith—by believing—that we are saved, and through want of faith that we are lost. John Owen tells us why in his commentary on Hebrews:

> It is faith alone which, from the beginning of the world, in all ages, under all dispensations of divine grace . . . hath been the only principle in the church of living unto God, of obtaining the promises, of inheriting life eternal; and doth continue so to be unto the consummation of all things. . . . Spiritual life is by faith; and victory; and perseverance; and salvation: so they were from the beginning.[1]

In this chapter, therefore, we will devote ourselves to a thorough study of faith, which the Westminster Confession calls "the alone instrument of our justification" (11.2). Hebrews 11 is an enjoyable chapter, presenting a brilliant series of examples and connecting us to some of the greatest episodes of the Old Testament. But it is also a chapter with a purpose. Its aim is that we would emulate the faith of these heroes of Scripture so that the salvation they received would be ours as well.

WHAT IS FAITH?

Hebrews 11:1 is an oft-quoted and oft-memorized definition of faith: "Now faith is the assurance of things hoped for, the conviction of things not seen." This is not a comprehensive definition of faith—there are impor-

---

1. John Owen, *An Exposition of the Epistle to the Hebrews*, 7 vols. (Edinburgh: Banner of Truth, 1991), 7:5.

tant truths about faith that are not mentioned here—but it serves as a well-crafted introduction to all that the writer of Hebrews wants us to consider in this chapter.

Verse 1 describes the environment in which faith exists and works. Faith takes place when things are hoped for but not yet possessed or manifested. In this respect, faith deals with the future. Paul spoke of the expectancy of faith in Romans 8: "Hope that is seen is not hope. For who hopes for what he sees? But if we hope for what we do not see, we wait for it with patience" (Rom. 8:24–25). Faith concerns unseen spiritual realities, things as they are in God's sight. Faith, therefore, relates to the things we do not yet have, to the things we hope for and do not see, to things that are promised by God but are so far unfulfilled in our actual experience.

Scholars translate Hebrews 11:1 in a variety of ways. The reason is that the key word in the opening clause, *hypostasis*, carries with it a number of shades of meaning. In the Septuagint, the Greek translation of the Old Testament commonly used by the apostles, *hypostasis* occurs twenty times to translate twelve different Hebrew words. The English Standard Version, along with the New American Standard and the New Revised Standard, renders it as "the assurance." The New International Version translates it as "being sure," while the King James Version has it as the "substance" of things hoped for. J. B. Phillips calls it "full confidence."

Philip Hughes's excellent commentary on Hebrews lists four main ways we may take *hypostasis*, all of which have something to offer. The first corresponds to the way it is used in Hebrews 1:3. There this same word describes God's substance or being: "[The Son] is the radiance of the glory of God and the exact imprint of his *nature*." This is the idea that comes across in the King James Version of 11:1: "Now faith is the *substance* of things hoped for." The point is, as Hughes says, that "faith lays hold of what is promised and therefore hoped for, as something real and solid, though as yet unseen."[2] By faith, therefore, we possess things that are hoped for; faith is the manner in which we hold them, and by faith they are real in our experience.

This is the idea of faith emphasized in the second half of verse 1, where we read that faith is "the conviction of things not seen." The key

---

2. Philip E. Hughes, *A Commentary on the Epistle to the Hebrews* (Grand Rapids: Eerdmans, 1977), 439.

Greek word here is *elenchos*, which the New International Version translates as "being certain" and which normally means proof or evidence or attestation of "things that are not yet seen." These things are not seen, but their proof and our conviction of them are realized through faith. One of the reasons many favor the translation of *hypostasis* as "substance" is that they see a parallel between the first and second halves of this verse: faith is the "substance of what we hope for and the evidence of things not seen."

Clearly, this idea is important to the writer's thought. He is going to make much of the example of Abraham, who lived as a pilgrim in the land of promise. Although others occupied and controlled that land during his lifetime, he nonetheless possessed it by faith. His faith gave evidence to him of what was promised but not yet seen. The same held true with regard to the promise of a son. God changed his name from Abram—father of a nation—to Abraham—father of many nations—by virtue of the promise he possessed by faith, though he was at that time still childless. This, then, is how faith functions: it makes real to us and gives us possession of things that are hoped for but are not yet part of our experience.

The second way we may take *hypostasis* is as a *foundation*. The construction of the word lends itself to this, combining the prefix "under" with the word for "standing." A *hypostasis* is something that stands under something else, as a foundation to a building. This is the way Saint Augustine understood our passage, that faith is the beginning which contains the certainty of the end. By faith we begin what we will ultimately conclude by possessing and seeing.

Third, *hypostasis* may be taken as *confidence* or *assurance*, which is how the majority of translations render it. This definition deals with what faith is, namely, a confidence or assurance in things hoped for but not yet seen. This is how the word is used in Hebrews 3:14, the other occasion where it appears in this letter: "we share in Christ, if indeed we hold our original *confidence* firm to the end." Faith, then, is our attitude toward our circumstances, particularly toward uncertainty and want. Paul wrote, "We walk by faith, not by sight" (2 Cor. 5:7). By faith we live as if things were other than they appear, because of what God has said.

Finally, this word may be rendered as *guarantee* or *attestation*. Faith, in this sense, is the title deed to things we do not possess but hope for in the

Lord. One commentator writes, "Faith is a guarantee of the heavenly realities for which we hope; not only does it render them certain for us, but it envisages them as rightfully belonging to us; it is, in itself, an objective assurance of our definite enjoyment of them. Consequently, faith 'takes possession by anticipation' of these heavenly blessings and is a genuine commencement of the divine life."[3] Faith is our guarantee that provides a foretaste of the spiritual blessings that ultimately we will know in full.

I have said that this word *hypostasis* can be taken in at least four ways, and so the question may arise as to which one is right. It seems that the writer of Hebrews deliberately chose a word that has a broad and rich array of meanings, all of which are to the point. Faith is the substance of things hoped for; it is the foundation upon which they are brought into being; it is a confident attitude toward those things God has promised; and it is the guarantee that gives us a sure possession even now.

What God Commends

When it comes to understanding and defining faith, there are two basic approaches we may safely take, or two basic questions for which we may find an answer. The first of these has to do with what faith *does* and the second addresses what faith *is*. If the question concerns what faith does, the answer is that it makes real to us things that are otherwise unreal to our experience; it presents to our hearts things that cannot be seen with our eyes. John Calvin writes eloquently on this point:

> The Spirit of God shows us hidden things, the knowledge of which cannot reach our senses. . . . We are told of the resurrection of the blessed, but meantime we are involved in corruption; we are declared to be just, and sin dwells within us; we hear that we are blessed, but meantime we are overwhelmed by untold miseries; we are promised an abundance of good things, but we are often hungry and thirsty; God proclaims that He will come to us immediately, but seems to be deaf to our cries. What would happen to us if we did not rely on our hope, and if our minds did not emerge above the world out of the midst of darkness through the shining Word of God

3. Ceslas Spicq, cited in ibid.

and by His Spirit? Faith is therefore rightly called the substance of things which are still the objects of hope and the evidence of things not seen.[4]

If that is what faith does, the answer to what faith is must be closely related—faith is confidence in those things that are not present to us but are promised in the Word of God. If we believe, we are acting upon things that are not yet manifest but which we accept as true.

Noah believed there would be a flood with no other evidence than the word of God. That was faith. Think of Abraham dwelling as a pilgrim long years on end, because he held his citizenship in the city to come. Or think of Moses going down in such worldly weakness to demand that Pharaoh release the tribes of Israel. These believers show us authentic models of faith. They display a confidence that translates into action despite all the contrary testimony of the world. The Chinese evangelist Watchman Nee is right to conclude: "Faith is always meeting a mountain, a mountain of evidence that seems to contradict God's Word, a mountain of apparent contradiction in the realm of tangible fact . . . and either faith or the mountain has to go. They cannot both stand."[5]

Those who put their faith in God and in his Word, and not in this world and the evidence it presents, are those whom God receives. This is the point stressed in verse 2, which indicates where the author of Hebrews is taking us in this chapter: "For by it the people of old received their commendation." What will follow in this chapter is the record of those men and women God commends in Scripture, starting in the Book of Genesis. What we are to note in each and every case is that the one thing that brought people God's commendation was their faith. Not their gifts, not their attainments, not their beauty, strength, or popularity—these are the things that bring people the commendation of the world. This, by the way, is why the men and women we will study in Hebrews 11 are unnoticed and unrecorded in the secular histories. What the world admires is power, wealth, worldly glory, fame. Thus you will find no great monuments to Abraham and the others, no tablets celebrating their lives in the libraries of ancient empires, because what they had is of no account to the world. But their faith in God, though

---

4. John Calvin, *New Testament Commentaries*, 12 vols. (Grand Rapids: Eerdmans, 1994), 12:157–58.
5. Watchman Nee, *The Normal Christian Life* (Wheaton, Ill.: Tyndale, 1977), 78–79.

scorned by men, made them great in the eyes of the Lord and brought them his commendation and approval. Here in this chapter we see God's record, his hall of fame. The obvious point, therefore, is that if we want God's favor, God's approval, God's commendation during these brief years of our own lives, then it will come only by the possession and exercise of faith.

FAITH PERCEIVING ITS CREATOR

The method our writer takes in this chapter is to follow the record of the Old Testament as it presents different men and women of faith. To that end, he begins with the opening chapter of Genesis, finding proof of his doctrine even in the creation of the world. "By faith," he says, "we understand that the universe was created by the word of God, so that what is seen was not made out of things that are visible" (Heb. 11:3). His point may seem obscure, but it is one that is especially germane to our times. The nature of the universe, the creation or beginning of all things, cannot be explained by evidence that is available to our eyes. Without faith we cannot even explain the world in which we exist.

Ours is a time committed to atheism—that is, to a view of the universe and history that excludes God. Nowhere is this lifeview more evident than in contemporary attempts to explain the origins of the universe. Undoubtedly the most popular answer today is the Big-Bang Theory, which says the universe was caused by a massive outward explosion of an incredibly dense mass. But that begs the question, "What caused the Big Bang?" This is a question scientists leave unanswered. Ravi Zacharias observes:

> We have an "ontologically haunted" universe—an uncaused reality that exists which is unlike any other physical reality that we know. This has to be something more than physical. . . . A strictly physical or natural explanation is not provable by the laws that govern a physical or natural universe. . . . Something beyond a physical reality is needed to explain this universe.[6]

Only faith provides an answer, both for the Christian and for the atheist. The non-Christian's faith is in the Big Bang. As Dallas Willard observes,

6. Ravi Zacharias, *Can Man Live without God?* (Dallas: Word, 1998), 192.

"'The bang' has stepped into a traditional role of God, which gives it a nimbus and seems to rule out the normal questions we would ask about any physical event."[7] For the materialist, the Big Bang has taken on divine qualities that rule out questions regarding its origin. But the Christian finds the answer not in this kind of scientific mysticism, but in the Word of God. According to Hebrews 11:3, "The universe was created by the word of God, so that what is seen was not made out of things that are visible." The universe was formed from nothing by the Word of God, who alone existed before creation.

Here the writer of Hebrews appeals to the Word of God as the object of our faith. If God's Word was capable of creating everything out of nothing, then surely that Word is a sufficient ground for our hope. Indeed, if God's Word was sufficient to bring all that is into existence, it is also sufficient to give me all that I need. I am without peace, but God promises me peace in his Word (Phil. 4:7), the same Word that made everything out of nothing. Surely God will make peace for me, and so I believe that Word. God's Word promises victory (1 John 5:4), but I feel defeated. Isn't that Word, which created galaxies, sufficient for my faith? The same holds true for life and joy and salvation; though we do not see them, we see God's Word, we remember its power, and we rest our hearts in it.

This is how we distinguish biblical faith from the popular notion of faith as a leap in the dark. Faith is not blind trust, wishful thinking, a mere manifestation of our positive attitude. We believe the Word of God because it is the Word of the God who made all things, and who, as Hebrews 1:3 tells us, "sustain[s them] by his powerful word" (NIV).

Our faith, therefore, feeds upon the Word, the way Jesus described when tempted by the devil: "Man shall not live by bread alone, but by every word that comes from the mouth of God" (Matt. 4:4). Our faith grows strong from the Word, rests secure in the Word, and bears fruit from the Word, which, as the writer of Hebrews has said, "is living and active" (Heb. 4:12). Ours is not a blind faith, but a faith that sees by the light of God's sure revelation. Faith says with the psalmist, "Your word is a lamp to my feet and a light to my path" (Ps. 119:105).

---

7. Cited in J. P. Moreland and Kai Nielsen, *Does God Exist?* (Nashville: Thomas Nelson, 1990), 197.

THE CENTRALITY OF FAITH

What are the practical implications of what this passage says about faith and its centrality to the Christian life?

First, if what we read here is true, then faith is how we receive the blessings of salvation. What are the unseen things that our faith grasps? There are our justification, the forgiveness of our sins, and the imputation of Christ's righteousness to us. There is only one way to receive and to know and then to grow into full assurance of our acceptance with God, and that is through faith in his Word. Romans 8:1 tells us, "There is therefore now no condemnation for those who are in Christ Jesus." God's acceptance, promised through his Word, overrules even the condemnation we feel for our sin. We receive this assurance by faith alone, trusting in God's Word that says, "Therefore, since we have been justified by faith, we have peace with God through our Lord Jesus Christ" (Rom. 5:1).

The apostle Paul begins Ephesians by praising "the God and Father of our Lord Jesus Christ, who has blessed us in Christ with every spiritual blessing in the heavenly places" (Eph. 1:3). He goes on to outline some of those blessings, namely, our election in Christ, our adoption as sons of God in Christ, our holiness in God's sight, our redemption through Christ's blood, and the forgiveness of our sins, all because of God's grace (Eph. 1:4–7). Now how do all these become real to us, how do they make a difference in our lives, how do they give us joy and hope and strength and love? The answer is by faith, which is receiving and being sure of them because of God's Word. All these things become ours through the channel of faith. What God asks us to do is believe the gospel of his Son and thereby be saved; only through faith can we know the benefits of what Christ has achieved for us.

Second, faith sustains us in the midst of trial and difficulty. We find an excellent example in the life of the apostle Paul. At the end of his life he told Timothy what happened to him at his trial before Caesar:

> At my first defense no one came to stand by me, but all deserted me. May it not be charged against them! But the Lord stood by me and strengthened me, so that through me the message might be fully proclaimed and all the Gentiles might hear it. So I was rescued from the lion's mouth. The Lord will rescue me from every evil deed and bring me safely into his heavenly kingdom. (2 Tim. 4:16–18)

The strength that sustained Paul came through faith in Christ and in God's Word. At the beginning of his long imprisonment for preaching the gospel, John Bunyan begged that if he might be more useful to God at liberty, the Lord would allow him to go free, but that if he would be more useful in prison, then God's will be done. Clearly, God thought him more useful in prison, because by faith that is where Bunyan wrote *The Pilgrim's Progress*, which has so blessed the church for hundreds of years. Only through faith do the people of God ever find strength and courage to stand up against the world and the trials of this life. This is the kind of Christianity our own world needs, the kind this world always needs, a Christianity made bold by the reality of faith.

Third, faith makes us pleasing to God and useful to others in this life. This is what we are going to find all through our studies of the biblical examples set before us in Hebrews 11. As verse 2 tells us, it is for faith that the ancients were commended by God. Faith is what got these men—Noah, Abraham, Moses—into the Bible. None of them was perfect or sinless, but all of them served the Lord by faith.

Writing about Moses, J. C. Ryle said: "In walking with God, a man will go just as far as he believes, and no further. His life will always be proportioned to his faith. His peace, his patience, his courage, his zeal, his works—all will be according to his faith."[8] Ryle then catalogs a number of great Christians such as John Wesley and George Whitefield and Robert Murray M'Cheyne, pointing out that it was faith that made them great. Some might say that it was prayer that strengthened them, to which Ryle replies, "Why did they pray so much? Simply because they had much faith. What is prayer, but faith speaking to God?" Others might account their success to diligence and labor, to which he responds, "What is Christian diligence, but faith at work?" Perhaps it was boldness, but "what is Christian boldness, but faith honestly doing its duty?" If, then, we desire to be pleasing to God and useful to those around us, Ryle commends to us faith: "Faith is the root of a real Christian's character. Let your root be right, and your fruit will soon abound. Your spiritual prosperity will always be according to your faith. He that believeth shall not

8. J. C. Ryle, *Holiness* (Durham, U.K.: Evangelical Press, 1979), 144.

only be saved, but shall never thirst, shall overcome, shall be established, shall walk firmly on the waters of this world and shall do great works."[9]

Therefore, let us pray with the disciples, "Lord, increase our faith!" (Luke 17:5). Nothing is more valuable to us, or more beneficial to others, than the faith that saves us through union with Christ, the faith that sustains us in the wilderness of this world, the faith that alone will make us pleasing to God and useful to his kingdom. If we believe in the supreme value of faith, then we will give our time, our effort, and our favor to those things that build up our faith, scorning all those things that stand opposed to it.

Of one thing we may be sure, God will not deny faith to those who seek it of him. "Ask," Jesus said, "and it will be given to you; seek, and you will find; knock, and it will be opened to you. For everyone who asks receives, and the one who seeks finds, and to the one who knocks it will be opened" (Matt. 7:7–8).

9. Ibid.

38

FAITH JUSTIFYING

Hebrews 11:4

*By faith Abel offered to God a more acceptable sacrifice than
Cain, through which he was commended as righteous, God commending him by accepting his gifts. And through his faith, though
he died, he still speaks.* (Heb. 11:4)

As we study this great eleventh chapter of Hebrews, we will discover the variety of things that faith does or accomplishes.
We often think of this chapter as focusing on the heroes of
the faith, on the people themselves, and certainly the writer of Hebrews does
draw upon the wonderful histories of the Old Testament and therefore on
its personalities. But ultimately it is not these men and women who are on
display, in all their variety of experience, but rather the one faith that shows
its various facets in their lives. Through these historical and biblical figures,
the author personifies the faith he is commending, and we thereby see all
the things faith does and the benefits it conveys.

In the previous chapter we saw two things that faith does. It makes present and real things that are future and unseen. By faith we presently lay hold
of our possessions in Christ. Moreover, faith sees the Creator behind the cre-

ation; by faith we understand who made and sustains the universe. As we proceed through this chapter, we are going to see more of the many things faith does. Faith pleases God; it does good works; it looks upon a heavenly city; it trusts God's promises; and it conquers over obstacles. This is what the apostle John had in mind at the end of his first epistle: "This is the victory that has overcome the world—our faith" (1 John 5:4).

CAIN AND ABEL

The first example of faith that the writer presents is that of Abel: "By faith Abel offered to God a more acceptable sacrifice than Cain." This refers to the episode recorded in Genesis 4:1–5:

> Now Adam knew Eve his wife, and she conceived and bore Cain, saying, "I have gotten a man with the help of the LORD." And again, she bore his brother Abel. Now Abel was a keeper of sheep, and Cain a worker of the ground. In the course of time Cain brought to the LORD an offering of the fruit of the ground, and Abel also brought of the firstborn of his flock and of their fat portions. And the LORD had regard for Abel and his offering, but for Cain and his offering he had no regard. So Cain was very angry, and his face fell.

Hebrews says that Abel's sacrifice was better than Cain's because of faith. There are two ways to understand this statement. The first is that because Abel was a man of faith and Cain was not, God accepted Abel's sacrifice while rejecting Cain's. The issue was not the sacrifices but the men themselves. John Calvin held this view: "The sacrifice of Abel was more acceptable than that of his brother only because it was sanctified by faith.... Where did his pleasing come from other than that he had a heart purified by faith?"[1]

You see the logic of this view, a logic we want to heartily endorse. God receives the man of faith and therefore his offering, rejecting the man who lacks faith. The apostle Paul spoke this way when he wrote in Romans 14:23, "Whatever does not proceed from faith is sin." And in Galatians 5:6 he wrote, "The only thing that counts is faith expressing itself through love" (NIV). According to that standard we see that because he lacked faith, whatever Cain offered had to be rejected, while faithful Abel's offering was received.

---

1. John Calvin, *New Testament Commentaries*, 12 vols. (Grand Rapids: Eerdmans, 1994), 12:160.

We want to affirm this way of thinking, but it does not seem to be a sufficient explanation for what we find in Genesis 4. The Old Testament text seems to emphasize the difference between the two offerings, and not merely between the two men. It wasn't that the two brothers brought the same offering, one that was received because of faith while the other was rejected for unbelief. No, the offerings were different, and in that difference we see the faith of one and the unbelief of the other.

We might begin by asking whether God had given commands or regulations at that time concerning the type of sacrifice his people were to offer him. "Just what," we ask, "had God revealed to these first children or to their parents, Adam and Eve?" The answer brings us back to the prior chapter, and specifically to Genesis 3:21.

Genesis 3 tells the tragic story of man's fall into sin. Verses 1–7 record how the serpent deceived the woman so that she ate the fruit from the forbidden tree, then how Adam ate it with her and joined her in transgressing God's commandment. Verses 8–13 relate God's confrontation of our first parents in that primordial sin, and their pathetic attempt to shift the blame even as they confessed their misdeed. In verses 14–19 come God's curses, first on the serpent, then on the woman, and finally on Adam. Then, in verse 21, we see God's action to deal with the problem of their sin, which we must consider central to God's message of salvation because it is his most direct response to sin: "The LORD God made for Adam and for his wife garments of skins and clothed them." God dealt with their sin by slaying an innocent animal, a spotless substitute. God had said that sin would produce death and here we see that it did—not the death of Adam and Eve, although death did come upon their race—but the death of a substitute that would shed its blood in their place and offer its own innocence to clothe their guilty stains. The great evangelist George Whitefield rightly connected this to Jesus and his death upon the cross:

> What were the coats that God made to put on our first parents, but types of the application of the merits of the righteousness of Jesus Christ to believers' hearts? We are told that those coats were made of skins of beasts. . . . Those beasts were slain in sacrifice, in commemoration of the great sacrifice, Jesus Christ, thereafter to be offered. And the skins of the beasts thus

slain, being put on Adam and Eve, they were hereby taught how their nakedness was to be covered with the righteousness of the Lamb of God.[2]

In this way, God revealed the manner by which sinful man was to approach him. Here he taught sinners what kind of sacrifice they ought to bring. This is how we must evaluate the fitness of Abel's versus Cain's offering: "Cain brought to the LORD an offering of the fruit of the ground" (Gen. 4:3). There must have been much to commend such an offering to Cain. Here was a portion of what arose from his own hard-fought labor. God had said to Adam in his curse, "By the sweat of your face you shall eat bread" (Gen. 3:19). So what Cain brought to God came only by hard labor, just as farming continues to demand today. Furthermore, it must have been beautiful, pleasing to the eye, and sweet to the taste.

What, then, was the problem with Cain's offering? It did not involve the shedding of blood. This was the key difference between Abel's offering and Cain's: Abel "brought of the firstborn of his flock and of their fat portions" (Gen. 4:4). In keeping with the pattern that God had established with his parents, and that had undoubtedly been taught to him by Adam and Eve, Abel brought a sacrifice that pointed forward to the atoning death of a spotless substitute. By faith Abel's sacrifice was better than Cain's, not just because Abel's faith made it better, but because by faith he offered the sacrifice God had established as the means by which he would accept sinful mankind.

THE ONE WAY

We learn several important lessons from this episode. First, we see that sinful man is justified, or accepted by God, only by faith in the blood of the sacrifice that God has provided. This is a doctrine the Book of Hebrews has repeatedly stressed. Chapter 9 spoke of the blood of Christ which opens up heaven for those who trust in him: "Christ [was] offered once to bear the sins of many" (Heb. 9:28). Similarly, Hebrews 7:27 tells us about the meaning of the cross: he sacrificed for our sins "once for all when he offered up himself."

2. George Whitefield, "The Lord Our Righteousness," sermon 14 in *Select Sermons of George Whitefield* (Edinburgh: Banner of Truth, 1958), 117.

This means that you cannot come to God any way you choose. You do not just say you believe in God and then decide for yourself how you will draw near to him. That was Cain's problem. He would decide the terms of his coming to God; he would offer a sacrifice according to his own devising. How bitter he was when God rejected him and his self-righteous worship.

There really are only two kinds of offerings, two ways to come to God— those that point to our own work, our own merits, our own righteousness, and those that point to Jesus Christ, crucified in our place to pay for sins. Unless we come to God confessing the guilt of our sin and our need for his grace, and embracing the gift of his own Son to die in our place, we reject the one way that he has provided. We then will be rejected, condemned for our sins, and made to suffer the eternal pains of hell. But people nonetheless persist in rejecting the way provided by God, especially in churches that deny or downplay the gospel. James M. Boice wrote of this in his commentary on Genesis: "That is the problem with so many 'good, religious people.' They come to God with their heightened sense of esthetics and want to be received by God because of their beautiful offerings. But God rejects them and their godless worship. There is no blood, no Christ and, hence, no true Christianity, however beautiful their service might be."[3]

We should offer our best to God. We should offer beautiful worship to him because he is deserving of our very best. There is no higher privilege than for us to do all we can to honor and bless his name. But this comes only after the blood, only after we have confessed our guilt and placed our faith in the blood of the sacrifice. Boice continues:

> If one comes first through faith in Christ and his shed blood, then he can present all the beautiful things he is capable of finding or creating. And God will be pleased by this, because the person does not trust these things for salvation but rather is offering them to God just because he loves him and wants to show affection. It is only on the basis of the sacrifice of Christ that one can come.[4]

You may say you are coming to God by any of a number of ways. You may say you are coming because of your sincere heart. You may say your religion

---

3. James Montgomery Boice, *Genesis*, vol. 1, *Creation and Fall* (Grand Rapids: Zondervan, 1982), 201.
4. Ibid., 202.

is based on your good works. You may trust sacraments or religious tradition or church membership. But apart from the blood of Jesus Christ all of these will be rejected, like Cain's offering, because you have not come by faith in the way God has provided. The apostle Peter said to the Sanhedrin, "There is salvation in no one else, for there is no other name under heaven given among men by which we must be saved" (Acts 4:12). Jesus taught, "I am the way, and the truth, and the life. No one comes to the Father except through me" (John 14:6). These passages refer not merely to some vague belief regarding Jesus Christ but to his atoning blood, to which Abel's sacrifice pointed and on which it relied, his substitutionary death in our place upon the cross. As Hebrews 9:22 tells us, "Without the shedding of blood there is no forgiveness of sins."

JUSTIFICATION BY FAITH

If there is any doubt about the importance the writer of Hebrews attaches to faith, Hebrews 11:4 removes any ambiguity. Here he tells us that it was by faith that Abel was declared to be righteous: "By faith . . . he was commended as righteous."

By faith Abel was declared righteous, or justified, by God. This is one of the great teachings of the Bible: the doctrine of justification by faith. This is why those early Hebrew Christians who first received this letter were exhorted not to abandon their faith, as they were tempted to do: because by faith in Christ alone are sinners justified by God. This doctrine is at the core of the gospel, the good news God offers us in Christ, because it declares exactly what we see in the case of Abel, how a sinner can be accepted and declared righteous by the holy God.

John 3:16 declares that "God so loved the world, that he gave his only Son, that whoever believes in him should not perish but have eternal life." By believing on Jesus Christ, by resting on his saving work for the forgiveness of our sins, by accepting God's Word and coming to him the one way he has provided, we are forgiven and are, as our text says, "declared righteous by faith." We are not righteous by works, which declare our supposed merit— that was Cain's mistake and the cause of his rejection—but by faith, which declares our need and our acceptance of God's gracious gift.

We find this truth emphasized in the Genesis account. Abel was a sinner, being the son of Adam and bearing sin's corruption in his fallen human nature. Yet when he came to God bearing the blood of a substitute, "the LORD had regard for Abel and his offering" (Gen. 4:4). The blood turned away God's wrath by speaking of the coming cross of Christ, and on that basis God received Abel with gladness. This acceptance was not available only to him; Cain could have been justified this same way. As God explained to a bitter Cain, "Why are you angry, and why has your face fallen? If you do well, will you not be accepted?" (Gen. 4:6–7).

Justification by faith makes the same claim to everyone reading these words. It is not just those who were born into Christian families, who have the right connections, who have the proper appearance or works or money to offer, but everyone may come in this way. That is why God said to Cain, "Why do you not come in the way I have graciously provided?" God offers each and every one of us salvation, forgiveness of sin, and restoration into fellowship with him by the sacrifice he has provided, even the blood of his own Son.

This point is forcefully made in the early chapters of Genesis. We have seen the first sacrifice, when God clothed Adam and Eve with the skins of innocent animals (Gen. 3:21). Although Adam did not die, his sin barred him from the Garden of Eden. Genesis 3:22–23 tells us he was no longer fit to dwell with and serve God there, to eat from the tree of life and live forever. But then verse 24 adds a remarkable detail: "[God] drove out the man, and at the east of the Garden of Eden he placed the cherubim and a flaming sword that turned every way to guard the way to the tree of life." East of Eden, into the curse-blasted world of sin went Adam and Eve, their way back barred by angels with flaming sword.

This imagery would become important later in Israel's history, in the time of Moses, when instructions were given for the construction of the tabernacle. The tabernacle was the place where people came to meet with God and where God dwelt in the midst of his people. At its center, in the holy of holies, rested the ark of the covenant, God's throne on the earth, where he kept the tablets of the Ten Commandments, his law.

The tabernacle was a movable structure made of wooden frames and curtains. The writer of Hebrews made a careful study of it in chapter 9. There was an outer court where sacrifices were offered and the priests were cleansed before entering. The outer room, called the holy place, was where the priests served. Finally, there was the inner sanctum, the holy of holies, where God himself dwelt, separated by a thick veil from sinful mankind. What is striking when we read the instructions in the Book of Exodus for the construction of the tabernacle is that the image of cherubim was to be worked into the curtains of the tabernacle: "You shall make the tabernacle with ten curtains of fine twined linen and blue and purple and scarlet yarns; you shall make them with cherubim skillfully worked into them" (Ex. 26:1). This detail evidently carried great significance because it is repeated four times in the Book of Exodus (26:1, 31; 36:8, 35). Just as the cherubim guarded the way to God in the garden with a fiery sword, so the symbolic cherubim on the curtains in the tabernacle kept sinners away.

We may infer from this that after their sin and expulsion from the garden, Adam and Eve still came to worship God at the entrance to Eden. It was to the guarded way between the cherubim that they came with sacrifices of blood. Likely, this is where Abel and Cain came, one with a sacrifice of blood and the other with an offering representing his works. Abel would have been like the later priests of Israel, able to come to the gate, to the holy place, to live and serve in God's reflected light, but barred from the inner sanctum by the guardian angels, just as the thick veil with the image of cherubim kept Israel's priests out of the holy of holies.

But that is not the end of the story. The Book of Exodus gave further instructions concerning the mercy seat, the atonement cover for the ark of the covenant within the holy of holies:

> You shall make a mercy seat of pure gold. Two cubits and a half shall be its length, and a cubit and a half its breadth. And you shall make two cherubim of gold; of hammered work shall you make them, on the two ends of the mercy seat. Make one cherub on the one end, and one cherub on the other end. Of one piece with the mercy seat shall you make the cherubim on its two ends. The cherubim shall spread out their wings above, overshadowing the mercy seat with their wings, their faces one to another; toward the mercy seat shall the faces of the cherubim be. And you shall put the mercy seat on the top of the ark, and in the ark you shall put the testimony that I shall give you. (Ex. 25:17–21)

Although no sinner could come directly into God's presence, just as neither Adam nor Abel could return to the garden, there was one day of the year, the day of atonement, when Israel's high priest could enter into the holy of holies. This one day prophesied an entire age to come. When the high priest came, he was confronted by the sight of the two cherubim. The atonement cover of the ark of the covenant thus graphically portrayed the gate to the garden. There two mighty angels faced each other, with wings upswept, casting down the shadow of their presence. Their eyes gazed downward to the ark which contained the tablets of the law of God, broken by sinners. They saw that man is barred from the garden and from the presence of God. Because he is a transgressor, man is under the sentence of death and therefore cannot enter back into life.

But on the day of atonement, the high priest came and poured the blood of the atoning sacrifice upon the mercy seat between the cherubim. And thus the way that was barred now was opened. This provides an important insight about the guardian cherubim: they not only kept shut the way to God without the atoning blood, but they also secured the way for the great day to come when the true sacrifice would open wide the gates to Paradise. That one day a year when the high priest came before the cherubim with a blood offering symbolized an entire age that would be opened by the true high priest with the true blood he himself had shed. God therefore said to Moses, concluding his commands for the mercy seat: "There I will meet with you, and from above the mercy seat, from between the two cherubim that are on the ark of the testimony, I will speak with you" (Ex. 25:22).

God met with his people between the cherubim—not in the garden, but at its gate. God met with them at the place where the blood was poured to cover the breaking of the law. Between the angels on the ark of the covenant sat the mercy seat. In Greek this is the *hilastērion*, the very term the apostle Paul used in Romans 3:25 to describe what God presented to us in the death of Jesus Christ. "God put [him] forward as a *hilastērion*," that is, a *mercy seat*. The English Standard Version precisely defines this as "a propitiation," and the New International Version gives the more general translation, "a sacrifice of atonement." The point is that what the angels were looking for all along was Christ, whose coming would end their watch, and therefore they guarded the way to God until his coming.

That great day for which the angels looked did come. The Gospels tell us about it. The day came when the curtain with its cherubim was not merely pulled aside temporarily but torn from top to bottom, removed altogether, the angels thus relieved of their ancient task. Matthew 27 tells us of the death of Christ: "Jesus cried out again with a loud voice and yielded up his spirit. And behold, the curtain of the temple was torn in two, from top to bottom" (vv. 50–51).

Finally, the true high priest had come to the gate between the cherubim, and there he offered his own blood once-for-all. The gate was opened, the angels went their way rejoicing, taking with them the sword of death. Now the way is open wide and secured by Christ himself, who is the way. Now it is to him that we come, not merely to the gate but into the garden to walk with God. Between the cherubim, Abel was declared righteous by faith, because he looked to the sacrifice to come. Now through faith in Christ every sinner can come to be accepted into fellowship with God and to receive everlasting life.

What Angels Longed to See

Hebrews 11:4 concludes by saying of Abel, "And through his faith, though he died, he still speaks." Faith bore testimony to Abel, that he was accounted righteous, and now Abel bears testimony about faith—about its value, its worth, and its power to justify those who trust in Christ.

Shortly after making his faithful offering, Abel was killed. Cain tried to silence his testimony; we learn in Genesis 4:8 that instead of repenting, Cain murdered his brother to put away the testimony about faith and the righteousness it brings. And yet the man of faith still speaks to us in the Word of God. Faith in God is never silenced, because God himself keeps alive the testimony of his faithful servants.

When I think of Abel, I often recall Peter's statement about the gospel: "Even angels long to look into these things" (1 Peter 1:12 NIV). Abel's faith spoke to those angels; it declared to them the wonder that sinners might come back to God, that those under the curse might meet with him at the place the angels guarded. What a wonder it was to the guardian cherubim when Abel by his sacrifice of faith was accepted and approved of God.

410

The same must have happened when Abel was killed: the first man to die, but also the first to appear in heaven. What an event that must have been! For the first time a sinner appeared in the holy courts of glory, cleansed and clothed in the righteousness of God's Son. How the angels must have marveled at this mystery of grace! G. Campbell Morgan writes:

> It was a great occasion when this first soul representing a fallen race appeared in the unsullied light of the home of the unfallen. He came by faith, ransomed by love, at the cost of sacrifice. As the Scripture declares that "the angels desire to look into" these things, this must indeed have been a mystery of life and love demanding their close attention, and not perchance, even fathomed by them, until the explanation . . . was wrought out upon the Cross of Calvary.[5]

Before the time of Jesus Christ, Abel—though dead—spoke of a sacrifice yet to come that would take away our sin, and of faith in the sacrifice that declares the sinner righteous. Now that Christ has come, Abel speaks of it still, with a voice that fully rejoices. Many of our hymns echo the words that Abel, though dead, must speak about his Savior. Horatius Bonar's words would be welcome and familiar to the lips of Abel, who brought a sacrifice of faith in the work of the Savior's blood:

Not what my hands have done
  can save my guilty soul;
not what my toiling flesh has borne
  can make my spirit whole. . . .

Thy work alone, O Christ,
  can ease this weight of sin;
thy blood alone, O Lamb of God,
  can give me peace within. . . .

No other work, save thine,
  no other blood will do;
no strength, save that which is divine,
  can bear me safely through. . . .

5. G. Campbell Morgan, *The Crises of the Christ* (Old Tappan, N.J.: Fleming Revell, 1903), 392.

I praise the God of grace;
   I trust his truth and might;
he calls me his, I call him mine,
   my God, my joy, my light.[6]

Thus speaks the voice of Abel. And so shall we, if we are justified by faith in that same blood, clothed in that same righteousness, and thus accepted into the love of God, just as Abel was before us.

6. Horatius Bonar, "Not What My Hands Have Done," 1861.

39

FAITH PLEASING GOD

Hebrews 11:5–6

> *By faith Enoch was taken up so that he should not see death, and*
> *he was not found, because God had taken him. Now before he*
> *was taken he was commended as having pleased God. And with-*
> *out faith it is impossible to please him, for whoever would draw*
> *near to God must believe that he exists and that he rewards those*
> *who seek him.* (Heb. 11:5–6)

he Westminster Shorter Catechism is famous for its first question, "What is the chief end of man?" and its answer, "The chief
end of man is to glorify God and enjoy Him forever." Of all the
people depicted in Scripture, apart from our Lord Jesus Christ, there is no
one whose description more closely attains this standard than that of Enoch,
the seventh in the line from Adam. So dear was this man to the heart of
God that he took Enoch to himself without demanding that he suffer the
pains of death. It is no surprise, therefore, to find Enoch in this procession
of heroes of the faith.

Interestingly, the account of Enoch's life in Genesis 5 makes no mention
of his faith. Yet his faith seems to motivate the statement of Hebrews 11:6,

413

that without faith it is impossible to please God. The idea is that we can be sure Enoch was a man of faith, because otherwise he never could have pleased God the way he did.

Hebrews 11 presents its heroes of the faith in chronological order as they are found in the Bible, yet several commentators point out that there is probably more at work than a historical progression. Specifically, it appears that there is also a topical progression to the points their stories make about the life of faith. That is especially true of the three men who lived before the great flood—Abel, Enoch, and Noah.

Andrew Murray, for example, describes them as Abel, the sacrifice of faith; Enoch, the walk of faith; and Noah, the work of faith.[1] Certainly that is a progression supported by the Bible: first we are brought into a right relationship with God by trusting the sacrifice he has provided in the blood of Christ; second, having been brought into relationship with God, we then walk with him by faith; and third, only then do we perform the works of faith, the practical good deeds that follow as a result of God's grace.

Arthur Pink sees these three figures combining to provide "an outline of the life of faith": "Abel is mentioned first not because he was born before Enoch and Noah, but because what is recorded of him in Genesis 4 illustrated and demonstrated where the life of faith begins. In like manner, Enoch is referred to next . . . because what was found in him . . . must precede that which was typified by the builder of the ark."[2] Pink's outline traces faith's worship in Abel, faith's walk in Enoch, and faith's witness in Noah.

It is hard to say whether the writer of Hebrews had this kind of explicit outline in mind, since he does not put it that way himself. It seems that he is mainly following the biblical order, with each portrait making a particular point about faith. However, it does seem that the Divine Author has placed them together in such a way as to build the progression of which Murray and Pink speak. Pink reminds us of the importance of a biblical ordering of the Christian life: "Witnessing and working ('service') is what are so much emphasized today. Yet dear reader, Heb. 11 does not begin with the example of Noah. No indeed. Noah was preceded by Enoch, and

---

1. Andrew Murray, *The Holiest of All* (Grand Rapids: Fleming Revell, 1993), 445–56.
2. Arthur W. Pink, *An Exposition of Hebrews* (Grand Rapids: Baker, 1954), 667–68.

for this reason: There can be no Divinely-acceptable witness or work unless and until there is a walking with God! . . . And this, in turn, must be preceded by Abel's worship of faith."[3]

Enoch, Who Walked with God

In the last chapter we saw that Abel was declared righteous by faith, since he came to God through the blood of Christ. Now we turn to the walk of faith with the life of Enoch. The Bible says very little about this man. All that we have comes from the genealogy in Genesis 5: "When Enoch had lived 65 years, he fathered Methuselah. Enoch walked with God after he fathered Methuselah 300 years and had other sons and daughters. Thus all the days of Enoch were 365 years. Enoch walked with God, and he was not, for God took him" (Gen. 5:21–24).

What we know about Enoch, therefore, is that he was the seventh patriarch in the line of Adam through Seth. When he was 65 he had a son named Methuselah. He lived a total of 365 years, after which he mysteriously departed from the earth without dying. Considering all the information we do not know about this man, this doesn't seem to be much of a biography. But the Bible tells us one vital fact that speaks volumes. Twice in these verses we are told, "Enoch walked with God." This wouldn't make a bad inscription on a gravestone. It tells us much about the character and the pattern of this man's life. Far more important than the job titles he held or his attainments in life was his walk with God.

What does it mean to walk with God? First, this speaks of a living relationship, a companionship between a man or woman and God. It implies personal knowledge, an ever-increasing understanding of the one with whom we walk. It implies agreement of mind and heart. The prophet Amos rightly asked, "Do two walk together, unless they have agreed to meet?" (Amos 3:3). There are an intimacy, a fellowship, and a joy of company between two who walk together. When it is God with whom we walk, there is a hierarchy, just as when the disciples walked with our Lord Jesus Christ. One is Lord; the other is disciple. One is teacher; the other is student. One is Father; the other is child.

3. Ibid., 668.

There can hardly be a more beautiful description of the Christian life than the idea of walking with God. The great Puritan Thomas Watson said:

> To walk with God is to walk by faith. We are said to draw nigh to God (Heb. 10:22) and . . . to have fellowship with him. "Our fellowship is with the Father" (1 Jn. 1:3). Thus we may take a turn with him every day by faith. . . . "They shall walk in the light of thy countenance" (Ps. 138:5). "Yea, they shall sing in the ways of the Lord." It is like walking among beds of spices, which send forth a fragrant perfume.[4]

Peter Lewis tells the story of a Chinese pastor who was imprisoned in a labor camp for his faith. His captors put him in charge of cleaning and emptying the contents of the camp latrine. Every day he would take the foul excrement out and distribute it in a field as fertilizer. The smell was so bad that the guards drew away and gave him plenty of space as he did his work. For that reason, the pastor came to love his lowly occupation, because in the resulting solitude he could talk and sing to God aloud, both of which were otherwise forbidden. He joyfully named the dung-heap in which he worked his garden and sang:

> I come to the garden alone,
> while the dew is still on the roses. . . .
> And he walks with me and he talks with me,
> and he tells me I am his own,
> and the joy we share as we tarry there,
> none other has ever known.[5]

This is what the Christian life is intended to be: a walk of faith, abiding fellowship with our loving God. His presence transforms even the worst circumstances into beds of roses, simply because he is there with us. What glory this is, that when God calls us to faith in him, he invites us to walk by his side! So every day—ordinary days, difficult days, joyful days—are days with God, a foretaste of heaven: to be with him, to know his love, to see his light and feel the warmth of his pleasure.

4. Thomas Watson, *A Body of Divinity* (Edinburgh: Banner of Truth, 1958), 53–54.
5. C. Austin Miles, "In the Garden," 1912.

Walking with God is its own destination, yet at the same time we are indeed going somewhere! We are growing in our knowledge of the infinite and divine; we are growing more like him in character as he guides us; we are realizing progress in spiritual things. This is the Christian life! It is not a bare knowledge of facts, or a grim recitation of doctrines. To be a Christian is to walk with God, to know him and to live in the light of his presence.

Interestingly, Hebrews 11:5–6 does not focus on the idea of "walking with God" but rather on "pleasing God." The explanation for this is that the writer of Hebrews is quoting from the Greek translation of the Old Testament (the Septuagint) and not from the Hebrew original. This Greek version, which so many apostolic writers used, is noted for its reluctance in using anthropomorphisms, that is, descriptions of God in human terms. The Bible speaks of God's arm or God's hand or the eyes of the Lord, all of which are anthropomorphisms. Literally, of course, God has no body and no hands, but his functions and activities are described in human terms for our benefit.

Because of its hostility to this way of speaking, the Septuagint often removed anthropomorphisms in its translation from Hebrew into Greek. The passage from Genesis 5 on Enoch's life provides a classic example. Instead of saying that he walked with God, the Septuagint says, "Enoch pleased God." Following that translation of Genesis 5, the writer of Hebrews comments that Enoch was pleasing to God and therefore must have lived by faith.

We need not be troubled by this human interference in the divine Word, for the New Testament, which is divinely inspired, sanctions this reasonable interpretation of Enoch's life. We may rightly take this idea of pleasing God as a working definition of what it means to walk with him. If we want to enjoy God's fellowship and to feel God's pleasure, it is going to result from obedience to his Word. Jesus talked about this with his disciples shortly before his departure. "Abide in me," he said, "and I in you. . . . If you keep my commandments, you will abide in my love, just as I have kept my Father's commandments and abide in his love" (John 15:4, 10). While walking with God involves more than simple obedience to his commands, obedience is necessary and integral to any life lived in fellowship with God.

Two Elements of Faith

The main point of our passage is yet another proof of the necessity of faith. Enoch pleased God and therefore was taken by God even before he died, which surely would have been impossible without faith. The writer goes on to point out two vital components of genuine faith: "Whoever would draw near to God must believe that he exists and that he rewards those who seek him" (Heb. 11:6).

The first of these statements points out that faith must have an object. Today we often hear about the power of faith without anything being said about the object or content of that faith. Mainly we are told to believe in ourselves, and it is true that self-confidence will help you accomplish many things. A baseball player is more likely to hit a fastball if he thinks he can. A salesman is more likely to close the deal if he believes in his ability to do so.

But the faith the writer of Hebrews is describing differs greatly from that. At first glance it may seem that he is asking people to believe only that God exists, to hold at least some abstract assent to the idea of God. On closer study, however, he is being much more specific. A literal translation of the Greek would read this way: "It is necessary for anyone who comes to God to believe that he is." This wording points to the confessional or doctrinal aspect of faith in a way the original Hebrew audience surely would have noticed. The wording here is reminiscent of the basic creed of Israel, called the Shema: "Hear, O Israel: The LORD our God, the LORD is one" (Deut. 6:4). The Shema was the great confessional statement of the Jewish faith, as it still is, and the original Hebrew readers would have understood this as a way of saying, "Anyone who comes to God needs to have straight just who God is."

At a minimum, the original Jewish-Christian audience could not help but see a connection to the great statement God made to Moses at the burning bush in Exodus 3:14. Having just been told to go down to Egypt and confront mighty Pharaoh, Moses asked God, "What is your name?" God answered him, saying, "I AM WHO I AM. . . . Say this to the people of Israel, 'I AM has sent me to you.'" Again, in the Greek translation used by the early church, the link is even more explicit. In the Septuagint, Exodus 3:14 says, "Tell them I am the one who exists." Pointedly using that very language, our writer says, "Whoever would draw near to God must believe that he exists."

Therefore, this first element of faith has to do with its content and doctrine. Faith must identify the God of the Bible, the Lord who spoke to Moses from the burning bush, as the one true God. Faith must be in him if it is to be saving faith. Over and over he says, "I am God, and there is no other" (Isa. 46:9). Faith must first agree with God's affirmation and turn to him as the only true God.

This element of faith also corresponds to the first of the Ten Commandments: "I am the LORD your God. . . . You shall have no other gods before me" (Ex. 20:2–3). This is a warning against all forms of idolatry, and especially philosophies and theologies that compete with the Bible. Whoever draws near to God, our passage says, must believe that the God of the Bible is the One and the true God, putting no others in his place.

First, then, we have the content or object of faith. Second comes the motivation of faith: "Whoever would draw near to God must believe that he exists *and that he rewards those who seek him*" (Heb. 11:6). We must believe not only that this is the true God, but also that we have to deal with him, that he is the Judge and Arbiter of our destiny and fortune.

As soon as we speak of God giving out rewards, some people get upset; they perceive a threat to the clear biblical teaching of salvation by grace alone. "If salvation is a matter of getting your reward, then we must be talking about works-salvation," they reason. However, that is very far from the case. This particular statement simply asserts the reality that God is the One who determines blessing versus condemnation. To have faith, we must realize and accept that we have to deal with this God, that his judgment about us is the vital one, and that we had better seek him; that is, that we had better gain his favor.

By calling this second element the motivation of faith, I mean that faith must turn to God as the One who saves; it must come to him seeking reward, seeking favor, seeking his grace. The alternative is to ignore him, to think that it doesn't matter what God thinks of us, what he intends for our future. This is what unbelief is all about. Few people deny the existence of God, but many deny the relevance of God, the need to seek him for salvation. This is demonstrably true in our own day. The vast majority of people agree that God must exist, yet they are not seeking him. Instead, they are serving other worldly gods as the source of the rewards they so highly covet.

This begs a vital question: "Do I have to deal with God? Do I need to pay attention to him, to listen as he speaks, to open my heart to a relationship with him, to let him change the way I live, to make him the great hope for the whole of my life? The answer, according to God's own revelation in the Bible, is Yes!

Although there are many reasons why we must come to God in faith, I will give just two. First, God tells us that he is a holy judge who will surely punish every sinner. God says that at the end of days he will bring everyone to stand before him for judgment. Revelation 20:12 paints the picture: "And I saw the dead, great and small, standing before the throne, and books were opened. . . . And the dead were judged by what was written in the books."

People deceive themselves that they will fare well on that day, since they are by their own assessment "basically good people." But the Bible renders a far different verdict, according to God's standard of perfect holiness. Romans 3:23 puts it directly: "All have sinned and fall short of the glory of God." Romans 6:23 tells us the consequences: "The wages of sin is death." Every person who stands guilty of sin—and that includes every one of us—is in dire peril of this condemnation. For this reason, we had better seek God, to find out how we might gain his favor.

This is one reason why we must deal with, as Francis Schaeffer put it, "the God who is there." A related and positive reason, and one we are confronted within the record of Enoch, is that there is a life after this one, with a God to be known and enjoyed with awe. There is a life after death, where God himself awaits us.

Perhaps the most interesting point about Enoch is one that we have not yet considered. Enoch never died. The writer of Hebrews puts it this way: "Enoch was taken up so that he should not see death, and he was not found, because God had taken him." One day this godly man was there and the next he could not be found. People looked for him, but he simply wasn't there. They may never have known what happened to Enoch, but we do. God took him out from this life and into the next without having to die. There are only two people of whom this is recorded: Enoch and the prophet Elijah, the latter of whom God swept up in a chariot of fire. The amount of speculation devoted to these matters has literally filled books, but these are the bare facts Scripture tells us, and further speculation is useless.

The point is that Enoch's record tells us of a life after death, and of God's ability to reward his own with everlasting life. Indeed, this is the way we should think about rewards from God—namely, what he himself said to Abraham: "I am your shield, your very great reward" (Gen. 15:1 NIV). What greater reward could we ever desire than God himself? F. F. Bruce rightly observes, "The reward desired by those who seek him is the joy of finding him; he himself proves to be their 'exceeding joy' (Ps. 43:4)."[6]

Our reward is the one Enoch received, namely, everlasting life with God—his free gift to all who turn to him in faith. Earlier I quoted Paul's statement in Romans 6:23, which begins with the first reason we should seek after God: "The wages of sin is death." But that sentence is completed with the second reason: "The free gift of God is eternal life in Christ Jesus our Lord." We see this gift in the experience of Enoch, the man who pleased God by faith, and that is the greatest motive for seeking the Lord. Just as in Abel we saw the power of Christ's death to restore us to God, so in Enoch we see the power of his resurrection life, the new life we too may enter by faith in him.

Seeking and Finding God

God is a rewarder of those who seek him. What, then, does it mean to seek God? It does not mean that we search him out the way a scientist seeks out knowledge. We are not left to follow an obscure trail of clues, eagerly seeking to piece together a workable theory. No, God is all around us; the evidence of his being is before our eyes this very second. The whole universe is a display, as Paul says, of "his eternal power and divine nature." God is, Paul concludes, "clearly perceived, ever since the creation of the world, in the things that have been made" (Rom. 1:20).

Seeking God therefore means seeking his favor, seeking a relationship with him. For sinners it means seeking forgiveness. It means coming to him, confessing that we are sinners, the way David did in Psalm 51: "Have mercy on me, O God, according to your steadfast love. . . . For I know my transgressions, and my sin is ever before me. . . . Purge me with hyssop, and I shall be clean; wash me, and I shall be whiter than snow" (Ps. 51:1–7). Hys-

---

6. F. F. Bruce, *The Epistle to the Hebrews* (Grand Rapids: Eerdmans, 1990), 287.

sop was a plant the priests used as a brush to sprinkle the sacrificial blood. "Purge me with hyssop" is David's way of saying that he was coming to God, seeking forgiveness through the blood of Christ, the Lamb of God who takes away the sin of all who come through faith in him.

But seeking God means more than seeking his favor and forgiveness, which he freely gives in Jesus Christ. It also involves a relationship with him. It means making him the God of your life: your King, your teacher, and your Lord. It means, as Enoch shows us, to walk with God and to offer your life for his pleasure. It means seeking that which is the chief end for our lives, the purpose for which we were made, namely the glory of God and the enjoyment of him.

Seeking God is just another expression for living by faith, which is what this great chapter in Hebrews is all about. Andrew Murray says this:

> Faith seeks for God; it believes that He is; it keeps the heart open towards Him; it bows in humility and hope for Him to make Himself known. To know God, to see God in everything and everywhere, in our daily life to be conscious of His presence so that we always walk with Him—this is the true nobility of man; this is the life that faith lives; this is the blessedness Jesus has now fully revealed in the rending of the veil. Faith can walk with God.[7]

What, then, will you find if you do seek after him? Enoch gives the answer. You will find life. Eternal life. That means a life that goes beyond the grave, a life in heaven. But it also means heaven in this life, in this world. It means the answer to the problem of death. God spared Enoch death because by faith he was pleasing to God. For us it means a similar triumph over death; it means that death will lose its sting. Death shall be an open door to the fullness of the life we begin here by faith. Death will mean the perfection of what here is only imperfectly attained, to walk with God, to rest in him, to delight in him, and to know his pleasure, which is faith's greatest reward.

This leaves but one last question: If you seek, can you be sure to find him? The answer is obvious, isn't it? Our passage says God "rewards those who seek him," not that you have to find him on your own. If you seek God, he

---

7. Murray, *Holiest of All*, 450.

will respond to your seeking. "No one can come to me," Jesus said, "unless the Father who sent me draws him. And I will raise him up at the last day" (John 6:44). This means that if you seek God, he has in fact been seeking you, and therefore you will find him. God is drawing you into the arms of his love for the purpose of the eternal life that comes through faith in Christ. Those who seek him he rewards with himself, and those who walk with him in this life he brings to himself in the next, conquering the grave, for a fellowship of joy that will last forever.

40

FAITH WORKING

Hebrews 11:7

By faith Noah, being warned by God concerning events as yet unseen, in reverent fear constructed an ark for the saving of his household. By this he condemned the world and became an heir of the righteousness that comes by faith. (Heb. 11:7)

Our study of Old Testament examples of faith in Hebrews 11 now brings us to the story of Noah, one of the great figures of human history. Noah shares a distinction with Adam, that every single human being today is one of his descendants, since God restarted the human race through his family after the great flood.

The flood from which Noah was saved is one of the great events in the history of our planet. It was an event brought on by the magnitude of humanity's sin. Genesis 6:5 says, "The LORD saw that the wickedness of man was great in the earth," so God expended his wrath in the destruction of our rebel race, saving only faithful Noah and his family. Not surprisingly, practically every religion and mythology, from Asia to North America, remembers Noah and the flood. A Sumerian tablet from 1600 B.C. tells how a king was warned about a destructive deluge and therefore built a great boat. In Akkadian there is the *Atrahasis* epic, which tells of a great flood that destroyed mankind after earlier attempts to curb its wickedness. Only Atrahasis and his family, who were warned by the creator-god Enki, escaped in the boat they were told to build. This saga seems to have provided the source material for the Babylonian epic *Gilgamesh*, which tells a similar story.[1] While these and other examples are corrupted by pagan ideas, they preserve a shared memory of this cataclysmic event.

Noah's name seems also to have passed down into one language after another. In ancient Sanskrit his name became Manu, based on the word *ma* for water. Thus the name is "Nu of the waters." This was passed on to ancient India, where Manu was the father of all peoples. Egyptian mythology named its water god Nu, and the mythical founder of the Germanic peoples was Mannus, from which we get the word "man."[2]

The events of Noah's life have great theological significance. The words "righteousness" and "grace" first appear in the Bible in his account. He gives us a great symbol of judgment in the flood. His ark provides a symbol of salvation (1 Peter 3:20). The rainbow remains an enduring symbol of the covenant—a reminder God put in the sky for himself, standing between us and God's judgment, just as Jesus now is "the guarantee of a better covenant" (Heb. 7:22).

Noah is perhaps best known today as a conservationist icon, a kind of Santa Claus for the environmental movement. The main thing associated with him is the animals he saved, but in Hebrews 11 it is faith for which he is remembered. Everything we have said about Noah proves that he was a very great and significant man, yet it was his faith that made him great in God's eyes. Indeed, Noah sums up everything we have learned about faith so far in Hebrews 11. Like Enoch he "walked with God" (Gen. 6:8–9); like Abel he was an heir of the righteousness that is by faith.

A MODEL FAITH

Hebrews 11:7 begins, "By faith Noah, being warned by God concerning events as yet unseen, in reverent fear constructed an ark for the saving of his

---

1. *New Bible Dictionary*, ed. J. D. Douglas et al., 2d ed. (Downers Grove, Ill.: InterVarsity, 1982), 382.
2. See James M. Boice, *Genesis*, 3 vols. (Grand Rapids: Zondervan, 1982), 1:258–59.

household." This tells us that Noah is an outstanding example of faith as being "certain of what we do not see" (Heb. 11:1 NIV). There were two things Noah believed that were unseen: the great flood that God had promised and the salvation that would come by means of the ark. The key verses describing this are Genesis 6:13–18:

> God said to Noah, "I have determined to make an end of all flesh, for the earth is filled with violence through them. Behold, I will destroy them with the earth. Make yourself an ark of gopher wood. Make rooms in the ark, and cover it inside and out with pitch. This is how you are to make it: the length of the ark 300 cubits, its breadth 50 cubits, and its height 30 cubits. Make a roof for the ark, and finish it to a cubit above, and set the door of the ark in its side. Make it with lower, second, and third decks. For behold, I will bring a flood of waters upon the earth to destroy all flesh in which is the breath of life under heaven. Everything that is on the earth shall die. But I will establish my covenant with you, and you shall come into the ark, you, your sons, your wife, and your sons' wives with you.

Genesis 6:3 tells us that God spoke these words to Noah 120 years before the flood. There had never been an event such as God described, or such a vessel. The ark Noah was told to build was stupendous in size—about the size of a modern battleship—and we can guess that Noah was to build it on dry ground, far from any ocean or sea. That is faith in things unseen! Even though he had not one shred of proof apart from God's Word, Noah nonetheless believed. This shows that faith in things unseen is the same as faith in God's Word, the same as faith in God's promises. We believe things apart from tangible evidence because God has so informed us and given his promise. We believe God himself, and that is faith in things unseen.

This kind of faith required Noah to stand alone in his generation. Apart from his immediate family members—and the strength of their faith is not at all clear—Noah alone trusted in the Lord. If we are going to live by faith and not by sight, that will often be true of us as well.

Noah also provides an excellent example of what we are told in Hebrews 11:6, that "without faith it is impossible to please [God]." We know that Noah pleased God because Genesis 6:9 says, "Noah was a righteous man, blameless in his generation. Noah walked with God." Like Enoch, Noah was an eminent man of faith, with much to say to us.

426

Because Noah is described as blameless, many people argue that he was justified or that he pleased God by his works. This fails to recognize what the preceding verse says: "Noah found favor in the eyes of the LORD" (Gen. 6:8). It isn't that he was blameless and thereby found grace with God, but that his blamelessness itself was the result of God's favor. Indeed, God's grace was the source of his faith, which in turn was the motivating power behind his works. Hebrews 11:7 insists that Noah did everything "by faith." Faith was the operating principle for all that Noah did or achieved. "By faith Noah ... constructed an ark for the saving of his household." He shows us that the same faith that brings us into a right relationship with God also moves us to actions that please God in practical works of obedience.

Indeed, what God demanded of Noah was far greater than what he asks of us. God required Noah to believe something that had never happened before, something totally unprecedented and seemingly unlikely. By contrast, God asks us to believe things that have already happened, namely, the death and resurrection of Jesus Christ—things that were done not in a corner but in the full light of history and recorded in the Bible. Similarly, God promised to do something for Noah that was difficult to imagine, that is, to save him through the flood by means of the ark. But God promises us something he has done countless times before, probably in the lives of people we know personally. He promises to forgive our sins through faith in Christ, to give us his Spirit and lead us into a new life. Some promises remain for the future, such as the resurrection from the dead. But even this lacks novelty, since it already happened to Jesus, who has gone before us in all things. Like Noah, we are saved by believing things that are not seen, and we please God only by believing his Word and trusting his promise.

FAITH AND WORKS

In addition to showing us a model faith that saved him and his family, Noah also demonstrates that faith always results in works: "By faith Noah, being warned by God concerning events as yet unseen, in reverent fear constructed an ark for the saving of his household" (Heb. 11:7).

People are often confused about the relationship between faith and works. The apostle Paul insists that we are declared righteous in Christ "apart from works" (Rom. 4:6). But the apostle James says that "faith by itself, if it does not have works, is dead" (James 2:17). James goes on to say, "Show me your faith apart from your works, and I will show you my faith by my works" (v. 18). This apparent contradiction has led many people to choose one versus the other. Martin Luther, for instance, a famous champion of Paul and of salvation by faith alone, derided James's letter, questioning its canonicity and labeling it "an epistle of straw."[3]

One of the most helpful expressions in sorting this out is a famous one from John Calvin. Calvin said, "We are saved by faith alone, but the faith that saves is never alone." True and saving faith is always accompanied by obedience, "which flows from faith like water from a fountain."[4]

Hebrews 11:7 tells us two things that proved Noah's faith, flowing forth naturally from that fountain. The first is one word in the Greek, but three in our English text: "in reverent fear." The Greek word is *eulabētheis*. F. F. Bruce translates it as "out of reverent regard."[5] B. F. Westcott renders it, "moved with pious care."[6] Philip Hughes puts it as "taking heed" with careful attentiveness.[7] The point is that Noah had reverence for God, which led to his attentive care to the details of what God commanded.

In Genesis 6:14–21 we read a summary of detailed instructions for building the ark. Undoubtedly Noah needed such details to do the job given him. But his faith is commended by his attentive care to all that God told him: "Noah did this; he did all that God commanded him" (Gen. 6:22).

The Puritans in seventeenth-century England were like Noah. The name "Puritan" was given to them by scoffers because of their care for studying and obeying God's Word in great detail. Then, as today, people think such reverent attentiveness to be narrow religion. They wrongly equate it with the attitude of the Pharisees, who made life difficult not with their biblical obedience, but with their man-made restrictions. Yet biblical obedience

---

3. *What Luther Said: A Practical In-Home Anthology for the Active Christian*, ed. Ewald M. Plass (St. Louis: Concordia, 1959), 988.

4. John Calvin, *Calvin's New Testament Commentaries*, 12 vols. (Grand Rapids: Eerdmans, 1994), 12:165.

5. F. F. Bruce, *The Epistle to the Hebrews* (Grand Rapids: Eerdmans, 1990), 286.

6. B. F. Westcott, *The Epistle to the Hebrews* (London: Macmillan, 1903), 358.

7. Philip E. Hughes, *A Commentary on the Epistle to the Hebrews* (Grand Rapids: Eerdmans, 1977), 463.

does not fetter you, or make you narrow. Rather, it liberates you to what is good and true and wholesome. This is why James speaks of "the law of liberty" (James 1:25). Studying and following through on God's Word will not shrink you but make you grow. Yet the path of obedience to Christ is a narrow one, one that speaks both yes and no, one that keeps us in the ark and out of the flood. Jesus taught: "For the gate is wide and the way is easy that leads to destruction, and those who enter by it are many. For the gate is narrow and the way is hard that leads to life, and those who find it are few" (Matt. 7:13–14).

This was Noah's manner of life, arising from his faith. But there is one great work that both flowed from his faith and served as its main evidence—Noah's ark. Hebrews 11:1 says that faith is the "conviction of things not seen," and Noah's ark was evidence that pointed to the flood long before anyone saw the raindrops falling.

Noah's ark provides a classic demonstration of the relationship of faith to works. Why did Noah build the ark? What caused this work? It was his faith. It was "by faith" that he built the ark. That is clearly the case, because unless he believed, it would have been lunacy to do something like this. Noah built the ark only because he truly believed that what God said about the flood was true, that the flood was going to come, and that unless he built the ark, he would be drowned with everyone else.

But what if Noah had not built the ark? What would we say about his faith? Imagine Noah insisting that he believed what God had said if he were not busy working on the ark! What would we say to a faith like that? We would say what James did—that such faith is useless and dead unless accompanied by works. If Noah did not even start working on the ark, chopping down trees and making diagrams, then the simple fact is that he could not have believed. But he did believe and therefore he built the ark. That is how faith and works fit together.

The same is true for us. We always act according to our beliefs, in keeping with our real convictions. If you believed there were a bomb in your room, you would run out of it right now. If we trust that it is necessary to repent and believe the good news to be saved, we will flee temptation and at least begin chopping at the trees of our sinful habits and building our faith. It took Noah 120 years to build the ark, and it will take a while for our sanctification. But if we believe, we will at least get to work now. There is no escaping the truth: faith and works are inseparable. As Alexander Maclaren put it, "If faith has any reality in us at all, it works. If it has no effect it has no existence."[8]

FAITH CONDEMNING THE WORLD

Hebrews 11:7 provides a stark comparison of faith and unbelief, as viewed through Noah and his unbelieving generation: "By this he condemned the world." Noah can be said to have condemned the world in several ways, but before he condemned the world, we can be sure the world condemned him. Ray Stedman says:

> We may rightly visualize the mockery and jeering which Noah must have daily faced as he built a huge ship. He was a hundred miles from the nearest ocean, with a ship many times too big for his own needs, and when he had finished, he filled it with animals! Had he lived in our day he would have been dubbed, "Nutty Noah!" Yet Jesus used "the days of Noah" as representative of the condition of the world before his own return, and indicated that his followers must be prepared to face the same kind of scornful hostility that Noah met day after day.[9]

The Christian life seems just as nutty to a self-absorbed age like our own. That anyone would deny himself, willingly sacrifice, and devote himself to holiness is mind-boggling to the world around us.

Noah's faith condemned the world, first of all through his witness. Second Peter 2:5 calls Noah a "herald of righteousness." Surely he would have explained his actions, why he was building the ark, to those who inquired and went on to laugh at him. He would have warned the world of a judgment to come and offered the way of safety in the ark. Likewise, we are to teach and explain the life we lead, the truth we believe, and the salvation we seek. And in its rejection of our message, the world is condemned for unbelief.

Noah's witness condemned the world, but we can also say his faith condemned the world. There it was before their eyes, evidence of God's Word,

8. Alexander Maclaren, *Expositions of Holy Scripture*, 11 vols. (Grand Rapids: Eerdmans, 1959), 10:116.
9. Ray Stedman, *Hebrews* (Downers Grove, Ill.: InterVarsity, 1992), 122.

430

which they rejected or ignored. Ignoring Noah comes to the fore in Jesus' description: "For as in those days before the flood they were eating and drinking, marrying and giving in marriage, until the day when Noah entered the ark, and they were unaware until the flood came and swept them all away, so will be the coming of the Son of Man" (Matt. 24:38–39). Just like today, the great mass of people paid no attention to spiritual matters; they were indifferent to God's Word as it was proclaimed, and Noah's faith condemned them for their unbelief.

John Calvin points out that Noah also condemned the world by his salvation: "The fact that Noah obeyed the command of God condemns by his example the obstinacy of the world, and the fact that he was miraculously saved from the midst of death is proof that the whole world, which God would doubtless have preserved had it not been unworthy of salvation, justly perished."[10] Noah's salvation proved that anyone could have been saved through trust in the Word of God. Noah's salvation certainly vindicated his faith and his testimony, once wickedly made sport of by the voices of the world. Alexander Maclaren pointedly remarks:

> No doubt there were plenty of witty and wise things said about him. . . .
> And then, one morning, the rain began, and continued, and for forty days
> it did not stop, and they began to think that perhaps, after all, there was
> some method in his madness. Noah got into his ark, and still it rained. . . .
> I wonder what [they] thought about it all then, with the water up to their
> knees. How their gibes and jests would die in their throats when it reached
> their lips![11]

FAITH INHERITING RIGHTEOUSNESS

This leaves one final statement about Noah, that he "became an heir of the righteousness that comes by faith" (Heb. 11:7). There are two key elements in this statement: inheritance and the righteousness that comes by faith.

Let me treat the second of these first. The apostle Paul follows a similar line of reasoning in Philippians 3, where he contrasts the righteousness of faith with the righteousness of the law. First he tells about his former

10. Calvin, *New Testament Commentaries*, 12:166.
11. Maclaren, *Expositions of Holy Scripture*, 10:119.

righteousness as a Pharisee: "If anyone else thinks he has reason for confidence in the flesh, I have more: circumcised on the eighth day, of the people of Israel, of the tribe of Benjamin, a Hebrew of Hebrews; as to the law, a Pharisee; as to zeal, a persecutor of the church; as to righteousness, under the law blameless" (Phil. 3:4–6). He then places these items onto a balance sheet, noting that the very things he once considered assets, so far as righteousness is concerned, he now understands as liabilities. Only one asset provides the righteousness God accepts—the righteousness that is by faith. He continues:

> But whatever gain I had, I counted as loss for the sake of Christ. Indeed, I count everything as loss because of the surpassing worth of knowing Christ Jesus my Lord. For his sake I have suffered the loss of all things and count them as rubbish, in order that I may gain Christ and be found in him, not having a righteousness of my own that comes from the law, but that which comes through faith in Christ, the righteousness from God that depends on faith. (Phil. 3:7–9)

The key statement is the last, that Paul wants not the righteousness of his own works under the law—which must be flawed at best and therefore useless—but the righteousness of Christ, which comes only through faith in him. Surely the writer of Hebrews is making the same point about Noah: although he did many good things, he sought not a limited and imperfect righteousness of his own, but the perfect righteousness from God that comes through faith.

This righteousness, we are told, came to Noah by means of inheritance. By faith he became an heir of righteousness. By faith he became a child of God. This is why it was so appropriate for him to act in a godly and righteous way—because by faith Noah was God's child and therefore destined to inherit his riches. Inheritance means that the source of the gift was not his own resources, but the one who granted the inheritance. This is how the righteousness of Christ comes to us: as an inheritance from God to his children and not from ourselves as an achievement. Furthermore, an inheritance is established by a fixed law and procedure. Paul speaks of this in Romans 4:16, where he says that our inheritance "depends on faith, in order that the promise may rest on grace." It is a gift, and a gift is received with open hands to the praise and the glory of the Giver himself.

This is what makes the righteousness of faith so secure. When we receive righteousness as an inheritance, by the open hands of faith, it is afterward possessed as a right. It is not something that has to be protected. Children do not hold their inheritance by conquest or by cunning, but as an unbreakable right inherent in their status as children of the father. In just that manner, our righteousness in Christ, received as an inheritance by faith, cannot be lost or taken away. It is as closely joined to us as a father's name is joined to his child who bears it. Ultimately, our inheritance is based upon the sovereign will of God and not upon our own will: "To all who did receive him, who believed in his name, he gave the right to become children of God, who were born, not of blood nor of the will of the flesh nor of the will of man, but of God" (John 1:12–13).

All that being true, how much more secure is this righteousness that comes by faith than any we might try to win for ourselves, a crown more steady than any we could have placed upon our own heads, perfect and completely acceptable in the sight of the Lord.

A MINISTRY OF SALVATION

Noah's faith meant salvation to some—namely, himself and his family— and condemnation to others, indeed to all the rest of the world, which fell under God's holy wrath. But the direct result of his faith was salvation, while condemnation was only an indirect consequence.

Hebrews 11:7 says that Noah's faith condemned the world. Christians are sometimes encouraged by statements like this to make it their job to condemn the world; they make it their ministry to point out how rotten it is, to fixate on the reigning sins and unite in hysteria over the latest debaucheries. But that does not seem to be the way Noah lived; he charted a different course for us.

Everything Noah did was calculated to save. He acted as an instrument of salvation, even though his faith indirectly condemned the world. He was an ambassador of the grace of God, and that is what every Christian is called to be.

Noah was "a herald of righteousness" (2 Peter 2:5). Surely that involved a condemnation of sin and a warning of judgment, but all of that was done in the shadow of the ark of salvation. That is where Noah's real effort went. His faith set him to work upon the ark. If the world would not seek its open door, then yes, it would be destroyed. But Noah directed his labor to salvation. Our labor must have this same influence: to commend and offer salvation to others, praying that God will grant them faith to believe and be saved. This is the labor of the Christian, by faith in the Word of God. Paul said this in 2 Corinthians 5:19–20: "In Christ God was reconciling the world to himself, not counting their trespasses against them, and entrusting to us the message of reconciliation. Therefore, we are ambassadors for Christ, God making his appeal through us. We implore you on behalf of Christ, be reconciled to God."

Believe, God says to the world through our faith, that a judgment is yet to come. And believe that in the cross of Christ—an ark as wide and long and high and deep as Noah's ever was—everyone who believes will find safety through the storm. Peter Lewis says it well:

> Christ Jesus is our ark now: big enough for the whole world, strong enough to withstand the shocks of life, the rising waters of death, and the upheavals of the last judgment. There is safety here in the Son of God, sent to be for us all the shelter, the salvation, that we so desperately needed; our ark and safe passage into the new world God has planned. From that ark we will emerge to inherit a new heaven and a new earth (Rev. 21:1).[12]

God asks simply that you believe, that you trust him, and through that faith he will do the rest in and through you, saving you and others from the wrath to come and carrying you to the wonderful salvation he has provided in Jesus Christ.

12. Peter Lewis, *God's Hall of Fame* (Ross-shire, U.K.: Christian Focus, 1999), 52.

41

Faith Looking Forward

Hebrews 11:8—10

By faith Abraham obeyed when he was called to go out to a place
that he was to receive as an inheritance. And he went out, not
knowing where he was going. By faith he went to live in the land
of promise, as in a foreign land, living in tents with Isaac and
Jacob, heirs with him of the same promise. For he was looking for-
ward to the city that has foundations, whose designer and builder
is God. (Heb. 11:8–10)

O f all the studies of the life of faith in Hebrews 11, the longest and most involved is that of Abraham, the patriarch of Israel. His is also one of the longer accounts in the Old Testament, running from chapters 12 to 25 in the Book of Genesis.

Abraham's significance can hardly be overestimated. It was through him that God gave the covenant of grace by which we are saved. Therefore, our salvation rests in part on God's faithfulness to Abraham. Paul gives Abraham the important designation "the father of all who believe" (Rom. 4:11). Thus we are saved as the spiritual offspring promised by God to Abraham, and his faith provides a model we are bound to follow. Therefore, Jesus responded to the Jews' boast that they were children of Abraham by saying, "If you were Abraham's children, you would be doing what Abraham did" (John 8:39).

In the New Testament, Abraham provides the example of faith par excellence. In the Old Testament, he is the first person to be specifically commended for his faith. Genesis 15:6 says, "[Abram] believed the LORD, and he counted it to him as righteousness." The apostle Paul particularly emphasizes Abraham as a model for faith. Paul's discussion of justification by faith in Romans 3 is followed in chapter 4 by a proof of his doctrine from the life of Abraham. The Book of Galatians also relies strongly on the precedent of Abraham's faith.

Given all this, we are not surprised that the writer of Hebrews pays so much attention to Abraham. Earlier, he appealed to Abraham's example, writing of his patient faith that received God's promise (Heb. 6:13–15). In chapter 11 the account of Abraham runs from verse 8 to verse 19, with four different statements that begin "by faith Abraham." We will consider his faith in four studies, beginning here with verses 8–10, a passage that opens with, "By faith Abraham obeyed when he was called. . . . And he went."

Faith Obeying God's Call

The story of Abraham begins after a brief biography of his father Terah at the end of Genesis 11. We learn of God's call to Abraham in Genesis 12:1: "Now the LORD said to Abram, 'Go from your country and your kindred and your father's house to the land that I will show you.'" Abraham's life of faith begins here for, as our passage says, by faith he "obeyed. . . . And he went out, not knowing where he was going" (Heb. 11:8). This was not only the beginning of Abraham's salvation, but an important beginning in the history of God's redemptive work.

We see in Abraham that faith acts in response to God's call. It is God's initiative that is emphasized at the beginning of Abraham's life of faith, God's sovereign grace that goes forth with his saving call.

It is important to realize that Abraham was saved not because there was something special about him, but by virtue of God's sovereign choice. Abraham was not singled out because of his faith, but because of God's grace. We might think that he was picked because he was a good man. But the Bible argues otherwise: "Listen to me, you who pursue righteousness, you who seek the LORD: look to the rock from which you were hewn, and to the quarry from which you were dug. Look to Abraham your father and to Sarah who bore you" (Isa. 51:1–2). Isaiah's point is that nothing in their ancestry commended them to God apart from God's gracious initiative.

Joshua 24:2–3 is even clearer: "Long ago, your fathers lived beyond the Euphrates, Terah, the father of Abraham and of Nahor; and they served other gods. Then I took your father Abraham from beyond the River and led him through all the land of Canaan, and made his offspring many." Abraham was not seeking God; he was a pagan idol-worshiper when God called him. What Paul wrote in Romans 3:11–12 was true of Abraham as well: "No one understands; no one seeks for God. All have turned aside; together they have become worthless; no one does good, not even one."

Abraham was saved, then, because God sought him. His faith was preceded by God's call and responded to God's call, a call that came by grace alone by God's sovereign choice. James M. Boice applies this example to us: "In the way God called Abraham, God calls all who become his children. God comes to us when we are hopelessly lost in sin and without knowledge of him (Eph. 2:1–7). This is a universal fact in the spiritual biography of Christians. And our response is nothing more than belief in God and in his promises."[1]

This is how Abraham's story begins: "By faith Abraham obeyed when he was called. . . . And he went." He was seventy-five years old, living in Ur, the land of his fathers, at that time a thriving locality. In Acts 7:2–3 Stephen tells us, "The God of glory appeared to our father Abraham when he was in Mesopotamia, before he lived in Haran, and said to him, 'Go out from your land and from your kindred and go into the land that I will show you.'"

The life of faith begins when God reveals himself to us. In Abraham's case it was apparently a divine visitation. For us it may be hearing God's Word preached, or opening and reading a Bible. It may begin by seeing something Christ-like in the life of another person. But in every case faith begins with God revealing himself to someone lost in sin, ignorant of and unconcerned about him.

---

1. James Montgomery Boice, *Ordinary Men Called by God* (Grand Rapids: Victor, 1982), 18.

We see here, too, what faith requires. Abraham had to leave his home, his family, his prospects for life, to go where God called him. So it is for everyone who would be saved. God calls us not merely to believe some abstract facts, but to obey his call and to follow him. Abraham's example shows us what real conversion looks like, namely, that there is a definitive change of life. Arthur Pink writes:

> The evidence of regeneration is found in a genuine conversion: it is that complete break from the old life, both inner and outer, which furnishes proof of the new birth. . . . The moment a man truly realizes that he has to do with God, there must be a radical change: "Therefore if any man be in Christ, he is a new creature; old things are passed away, behold, all things are become new" (2 Cor. 5:17).[2]

For Abraham this meant rising when called and going where he was commanded as a manifestation of his trust in God. Astonishingly, verse 8 tells us that he didn't even know where he was going. Abraham did not have a crystal-clear plan, a vision that mapped out where he would be in five or ten or fifty years. Rather, he met God, he heard God's call, and at great cost to himself and surely with much perplexity, he obeyed and went. Faith always demands decisive action and always manifests itself in obedience to God's command. Speaking of Abraham, James wrote about faith and works: "You see that faith was active along with his works, and faith was completed by his works" (James 2:22). As Pink says, "Faith and obedience can never be severed; as the sun and the light, fire and heat. . . . Obedience is faith's daughter."[3]

We begin the life of faith not knowing where we are going. At the beginning, most of us, Abraham included, could not handle an awareness of all that will happen in and to us, all that will be required, all we will give up and receive along the journey of faith. Like us, Abraham really didn't know what was in store, but he had met God and heard his call. He believed, and by faith he obeyed and went. That itself is more than flesh alone can ever do, and it shows that faith is a divine gift inspired and empowered by God himself.

Imagine what Abraham's friends and neighbors would have thought about him. As he was packing, they would surely have asked, "Where are you

---

2. A. W. Pink, *An Exposition of Hebrews* (Grand Rapids: Baker, 1954), 692.
3. Ibid., 695.

going?" To this he could only reply, "I do not know. I have been called by God to follow him." Imagine their response, and then realize that it will be no different for you. People will ask you, if you answer God's call in faith, "Why are you giving up the pleasures of sin? Why are you throwing your life away to serve where God calls you? Why are you obeying the Bible instead of doing what is popular?" You, like every believer since Abraham's time, must only reply—even if with much difficulty—"I have met God, and he has called me I know not where. I must obey, for I want to be saved by faith in him."

FAITH BELIEVING GOD'S PROMISE

The call to faith is always followed by the life of faith; the same principle by which we first are saved enables us to live as saved people. Thus we find this description of Abraham's life in the land of Canaan: "By faith he went to live in the land of promise, as in a foreign land, living in tents with Isaac and Jacob, heirs with him of the same promise" (Heb. 11:9).

We have seen how difficult it is to obey God's call. But many a Christian has learned how much easier it is at the beginning of the life of faith and how much harder it is to live that life of faith over a period of many, many years. Abraham began by obeying God's call, and he persevered by believing God's promise. God had promised him a land as his own inheritance, and Abraham's faith consisted of receiving that promise as he continued to obey and serve.

With fits and starts, Abraham finally arrived in the land of Canaan, which God had promised that he would possess. However, when Abraham got there, he found that it was inhabited by the Canaanites, an idolatrous people who did not know the Lord. By faith he lived there, not as its owner but as a stranger "in a foreign land" (Heb. 11:9). He lived as a sojourner, a resident alien, in the very land God had promised would be his own.

This presents a classic picture of the life of faith. We have great promises from God which belong to us now, but by and large have not yet been manifested in our experience. Abraham went to the land promised to him, but when he got there it did not yet belong to him. This shows us the "already–not yet" character of the life of faith. We possess the promises already, but they

439

are not yet consummated in our lifetime. This is what Hebrews 11 emphasizes from the beginning, that faith is the evidence, the possession, of things not yet seen.

By faith Abraham lived in the land that was not yet his own. As Stephen said, "[God] gave him no inheritance in it, not even a foot's length, but promised to give it to him as a possession and to his offspring after him, though he had no child" (Acts 7:5). Like us, Abraham received the promise by faith; he lived upon the promise since he had not yet received the reality. Even when he had children and began to see the future take its shape, he was "living in tents with Isaac and Jacob, heirs with him of the same promise" (Heb. 11:9). Even many years later, upon the death of his wife Sarah, Abraham had to purchase a plot of land in which to bury her—sure evidence that he was but a pilgrim in this land that God had promised would be his own.

Abraham's experience informs us that the life of faith is not one of receiving all God's promises in tangible form, but rather of believing them in the face of hardship, receiving them by faith, living as Abraham did out of confidence in and reliance on God. From beginning to end, the Christian life is one of faith and not of sight. Philip Hughes writes:

> He who begins by faith must continue by faith, for faith is the principle not only of initiation but also of perseverance. The life of faith did not cease for Abraham when he left Ur of the Chaldees behind him or when at length he set foot on the territory toward which he had directed his steps. Indeed, the situation into which he moved on his arrival in the land of promise was a more severe trial of his faith than was the call to leave home and kindred, and it was easier for him to live by faith as he journeyed toward a goal as yet unseen than to do so upon reaching this goal and finding that the fullness of all that had been promised was "not yet."[4]

Abraham's situation is well expressed by the salutation that begins the apostle Peter's first epistle. Peter was writing to early Christians who were "scattered" across Asia Minor. He thus began his letter with these words: "To God's elect, strangers in the world" (1 Peter 1:1 NIV). This description told them two things about themselves—the same two things shown to us in the

---

4. Philip E. Hughes, *A Commentary on the Epistle to the Hebrews* (Grand Rapids: Eerdmans, 1977), 468.

life of Abraham. The first is that we live this life in a world that is not our own, as pilgrims rather than possessors, as strangers living in an alien country. This means that Christians do not belong to this world but to another. As the apostle Paul writes: "Our citizenship is in heaven. And we eagerly await a Savior from there, the Lord Jesus Christ" (Phil. 3:20). Our allegiance belongs to another realm. This is what we pray in the Lord's Prayer: "Thy kingdom come, thy will be done on earth as it is in heaven." As strangers, our long-term interests are not attached to this present world, which we know is passing away. We do not find our comfort here, not because we are a difficult sort of people, but because our permanent home is elsewhere and we have a growing homesickness for the place where we belong.

Being a pilgrim means that we do not love the things of this world. Colossians 3:1–3 tells us, "If then you have been raised with Christ, seek the things that are above, where Christ is, seated at the right hand of God. Set your minds on things that are above, not on things that are on earth. For you have died, and your life is hidden with Christ in God." It is always good, therefore, for Christians to assess how tightly worldly things grip our hearts. We must take seriously what John writes in his first epistle: "Do not love the world or the things in the world. If anyone loves the world, the love of the Father is not in him. For all that is in the world—the desires of the flesh and the desires of the eyes and pride in possessions—is not from the Father but is from the world. And the world is passing away along with its desires, but whoever does the will of God abides forever" (1 John 2:15–17).

This is how Christians have lived in every generation. The Puritan Jeremiah Burroughs gave this helpful admonition:

> The Scripture tells us plainly that we must behave ourselves here as pilgrims and strangers (1 Pet. 2:11). Consider what your condition is, you are pilgrims and strangers; so do not think to satisfy yourselves here. . . . So let us not be troubled when we see that other men have great wealth, but we have not. Why? We are going away to another country; you are, as it were, only lodging here for a night. If you were to live a hundred years, in comparison to eternity it is not as much as a night, it is as though you were traveling, and had come to an inn.[5]

---

5. Jeremiah Burroughs, *The Rare Jewel of Christian Contentment* (Edinburgh: Banner of Truth, 1964), 95.

Therefore we are to live as those who expect to wake up soon in the realm of glory. That is where we belong in Christ. That is the other part of Peter's salutation that so well describes Abraham's position and ours. He writes to his readers not merely as strangers in the world, but as "those who are elect . . . according to the foreknowledge of God the Father, in the sanctification of the Spirit, for obedience to Jesus Christ and for sprinkling with his blood" (1 Peter 1:1–2). This is who we are, this tells us where we belong. We are God's chosen people, his elect and beloved children in Christ.

This means that though the world accounts you nothing, you are chosen of God. It is a hard truth that you do not fit in here, that the world is not likely to think much of you as you live by faith within its precincts. There is a reason why secular history records nothing of Abraham—because Abraham and what he represented were of no interest, of no appeal to the world. He was not a mighty king or a famous entertainer or a villainous rogue. These are the things that catch the eye of the world. And as you lead a quiet, godly life, you will not interest the world much either. You do not belong to it, but you do belong to God. He cherishes you, even if the world despises you—as it did our Lord Jesus Christ. God has set you apart for himself, he has sanctified you by the Holy Spirit, he has purchased you by the precious blood of Jesus to be his very own.

The reality of our pilgrimage is often difficult for us to bear. We grow impatient for more possessions, resentful that we cannot be like the others around us. The desire to put down real roots here in this world, a weariness with the pilgrimage of faith, leads many into spiritual difficulties. This is why we must live by faith as Abraham did. We live and feed our faith upon promises, delighting in God's boundless love for us, remembering our end which will be so different from that of this world. And while we wait, God gives us himself as our present comfort, our near companion, our saving help. As with the men of faith before him, Abraham did not make his pilgrimage alone in this world, for he walked with God. What God said to him in comfort, he also says to us: "I am your shield, your very great reward" (Gen. 15:1 NIV).

FAITH SEEING A CITY

Our passage concludes with one of the greatest statements of the life of faith, a statement that has inspired the hearts of countless believers.

Verse 10 tells us what kept Abraham going all those long years: "For he was looking forward to the city that has foundations, whose designer and builder is God."

It is easy for us to think of those who lived long ago as primitives, as men necessarily possessing a very feeble comprehension. But it is clear that Abraham had a highly developed sense of his spiritual position. What was it, we ask, that allowed this man to live so heroically in such difficulties? The answer is here: "He was looking forward to the city that has foundations."

Imagine how many times Abraham looked out from the flaps of his tent at some city or settlement in that land. He must have yearned for those comforts. He had a keen desire for the things offered in that land, dusty as it was—a longing to settle down, to live in peace and rest. But our text tells us plainly that by faith he lifted his eyes upward to better if distant things, to a city far surpassing anything set before his eyes—a city with foundations—designed and built not by Canaanite kings, but by the Lord of heaven.

There is an obvious comparison between the tents in which Abraham lived, dwellings without foundations, and the cities of Canaan with their earthly foundations, and finally the city to come, the City of God, with its eternal foundations. Abraham longed for foundations, but he chose the eternal instead of that which passes away. We can say the same about the splendor of those cities. They must have been impressive compared to Abraham's tents. But he compared them to the city of which God was the architect and builder, a city of speechless glory and infinite majesty. Abraham looked to what is to come, not contenting himself with the offerings of the world, not sacrificing his inheritance for the refuse of a dying humanity. Abraham's heart was in the city to come, and he placed his hopes there by faith in God.

Abraham applied to his situation what we often call an "eternal perspective." He considered his present in light of his future inheritance with God. This is how Christian faith is sustained in the midst of deprivation and trial. John MacArthur writes:

> The Christian . . . is willing to forsake the present glory, comfort, and satisfaction of this present world for the future glory that is his in Christ. In contrast to the "buy now—pay later" attitude prevalent in the world, the Christian is willing to pay now and receive it later. What makes Christians willing to make such sacrifices? Hope, based on faith that the future holds something

far better than the present. Paul writes in Romans 8:18, "I consider that the sufferings of this present time are not worthy to be compared with the glory that is to be revealed to us."[6]

An eternal perspective acquired from God's Word is essential for any consistent and persevering Christian life. A great picture of this is offered in John Bunyan's classic allegory, *The Pilgrim's Progress*. Bunyan's hero, Christian, had left his home like Abraham and started out on the way to an eternal city. Along the way, he encountered one hardship after another. On one occasion he wandered off the path and got lost; later he was tempted by men named Simple, Sloth, and Presumption. Then he was wearied by the Hill of Difficulty, almost to be driven back by the roar of lions along the way.

Finally, Christian came to House Beautiful, a way station where he could rest and be equipped for the harrowing trials ahead. He received many things there from godly helpers, and as he prepared to strike out again, they advised him to delay long enough to climb a mountain from which he could gaze far, far ahead. There, nestled in the Delectable Mountains, he could just see the Celestial City, the destination he sought. That vision gave vigor to his limbs and resolve to his heart. Ahead of him lay many dangers and trials: spiritual warfare with Apollyon, persecution in the town of Vanity Fair, a harrowing escape through the Valley of the Shadow of Death. Yet that one vision of the city of heaven—the city with foundations—did much to encourage him forward through a long journey of trials.

This is how Abraham lived by faith for long years, in a land not his own: "He was looking forward to the city that has foundations, whose designer and builder is God." If we are going to persevere in the Christian life, then we too must fix our eyes on that city. For that is our destination, our true home, though we know not what lies between it and us.

Like the apostle John in the Book of Revelation, we must by faith be taken away to "a great, high mountain" to see "the holy city Jerusalem coming down out of heaven from God" (Rev. 21:10). It shines, we are told, "having the glory of God, its radiance like a most rare jewel, like a jasper, clear as crystal" (v. 11). John tells us, "The city has no need of sun or moon to shine on it, for the glory of God gives it light, and its lamp

6. John A. MacArthur Jr., *Colossians and Philemon* (Chicago: Moody, 1992), 20.

is the Lamb" (v. 23). There flows the river of the water of life, beside which grows the tree of life. John's vision concludes with these words:

> The leaves of the tree were for the healing of the nations. No longer will there be anything accursed, but the throne of God and of the Lamb will be in it, and his servants will worship him. They will see his face, and his name will be on their foreheads. And night will be no more. They will need no light of lamp or sun, for the Lord God will be their light, and they will reign forever and ever. (Rev. 22:2–5)

This is the city to which we belong, if we have trusted in Christ, and are trusting in him now. That is where this journey leads us, difficult though it is; by faith we shall some day arrive at the gates of the city with foundations, there to see the glory of God. There we shall find entry if these final words are true of us: "Blessed are those who wash their robes, so that they may have the right to the tree of life and that they may enter the city by the gates" (Rev. 22:14).

That is where Christ leads us through faith in him. That is the inheritance finally received after a life begun by faith responding to God's call, a life pursued with the receipt of God's promise, a life sustained by the vision of God's city yet to come. And if that is true—and it is—then surely we must live now as citizens belonging to that city, as royal sons and daughters of heaven, where we will soon live forever.

42

FAITH IN THE PROMISE

Hebrews 11:11—12

By faith Sarah herself received power to conceive, even when she
was past the age, since she considered him faithful who had
promised. Therefore from one man, and him as good as dead,
were born descendants as many as the stars of heaven and as
many as the innumerable grains of sand by the seashore.
(Heb. 11:11–12)

n the world you will have tribulation." That is how our Lord
Jesus concluded his time with the disciples in the upper room
before heading out to the Garden of Gethsemane and his arrest
(John 16:33). Peter, who heard those words and learned the truth of them,
said in his first epistle, "Beloved, do not be surprised at the fiery trial when
it comes upon you to test you, as though something strange were happening to you" (1 Peter 4:12). This is something pastors learn very quickly, that
there are much trouble and sorrow in the world. And every one of us will
learn and experience this if we only live long enough.

It is important for us to realize the certainty of trouble when we are talking about faith, as does the eleventh chapter of Hebrews. Faith does not

sprout only in the soil of blessing, or grow only when the sun is shining. Christian faith is not like faith in our favorite sports team, which blossoms only in the midst of a winning streak, or like faith in other people, which so easily withers when they let us down. What makes Christian faith so different is that its object is truly and always worthy of our trust. Our faith is in God, and even in sorrows and trials we are to say by faith, "The LORD is my strength and my song; he has become my salvation" (Ps. 118:14).

ABRAM'S GREAT SORROW

Hebrews 11 continues with the life of Abraham as an example of faith, and brings to our attention God's remedy for the great sorrow of his life. Verse 11 says, "By faith Sarah herself received power to conceive, even when she was past the age, since she considered him faithful who had promised." This verse refers to the time when God came to Abraham with a promise of great blessing: "Fear not, Abram, I am your shield; your reward shall be very great" (Gen. 15:1). Imagine hearing such words from the Lord, and yet when Abram (as he then was called) heard them, instead of rejoicing he complained. "O Lord GOD," he said, "what will you give me, for I continue childless, and the heir of my house is Eliezer of Damascus? . . . Behold, you have given me no offspring, and a member of my household will be my heir" (vv. 2–3).

This scene encourages us that God does not dismiss us in anger when we complain to him despite the many great blessings he provides. Here Abram resembles us. He is the beneficiary of amazing grace, yet his heart is breaking because of the one thing dear to him that he does not have. The writer of Hebrews draws our attention to this circumstance so as to add more lines to his portrait of the life of faith.

Abram's sorrow was made especially poignant by his name, which means "father of many." Yet he was into his later years and had not fathered a single child. Long before, God had promised, "To your offspring I will give this land" (Gen. 12:7), but after decades Abram had no offspring. This would be a source of great consternation in our society, but in the Orient where Abram lived it was a galling humiliation. Donald Grey Barnhouse notes that Abram was a prominent man in a land that was a crossroads for travelers. He imagines a likely conversation with a merchant stopping by: "In the evening time the merchants would have come to Abram's tent to pay their respects. The questions would have followed a set pattern. 'How old are you? Who are you? How long have you been here?' When the trader had introduced himself, Abram would be forced to name himself: 'Abram, father of many.'" It must have happened a hundred times, a thousand times, and each time more galling than the time before. "Oh, father of many! Congratulations! And how many sons do you have?" And the answer was so humiliating to Abram: "None." And many a time there must have been the half-concealed snort of humor at the incongruity of the name and the fact that there were no children to back up such a name. Abram must have steeled himself for the question and the reply, and have hated the situation with great bitterness.[1]

This is the way great sorrow and longing often rears its head. It sours otherwise pleasant encounters. Single people find it hard to be in married company, sometimes shying away from the church for that reason alone. People like Abram and his wife, who cannot have children, often find the mere sound of children a constant reproach and burden. Men who think themselves failures cannot stand the success of others. Women who think themselves homely envy the beauty of those more blessed among their kind. On and on it goes, with life seeming like a parade of sadness and envy, heartbreak and discontent. However much we have, there is often something missing that embitters our existence. We know, therefore, what it is like to be in Abram's shoes, responding to God's grace with an angry, teary cry: "What can you give me, since I do not have this!"

The Bible responds to our cry of discontent directly, unabashedly making promises of great blessing. We find this in the case of Abram. Genesis 15 goes on to depict one of the most marvelous scenes in all of Scripture. First, God promised Abram that a son from his own body would be his heir. Abram had heard this before, and he was incredulous. Therefore, as he so often does, God appealed to another of Abram's senses, taking him outside under the canopy of stars. He said, "Look toward heaven, and number the stars, if you are able to number them. . . . So shall your offspring be" (Gen. 15:5). Imagine the scene! Abram was led by God out into the night to gaze upon the countless multitude of the stars as the measure of his coming blessing. How

---

1. Donald Grey Barnhouse, *Expositions of Bible Doctrine Taking the Epistle to the Romans as a Point of Departure*, 10 vols. (Grand Rapids: Eerdmans, 1954), 4:311–12.

overwhelming it must have been; indeed, we know that it was overwhelming enough to overpower his unbelief. The next verse tells us Abram's response, in what the apostle Paul uses as a paradigm for us all: "Abram believed the Lord, and he counted it to him as righteousness" (Gen. 15:6; Rom. 4:3).

The God of Promises

God relates to his children in this world largely through promises. In the Old Testament, the Israelites were a people looking beyond the horizon, looking for the promise yet to come, yet to be fulfilled. That great coming arrived in the person of Jesus Christ, and yet Christians, too, are waiting for things that are yet to come. The New Testament believer is also one who looks for that which is yet to come, for the promises yet to be fulfilled. As 2 Peter 1:4 says, "He has granted to us his precious and very great promises."

Abram's experience shows at least two reasons why God deals with us through promises. The first reason is to lift our eyes above the realm of our circumstances, even as he lifted Abram's eyes high into the heavens. All through our lives, God's promises lift our aspirations higher. On our own we would be content with some happy relationships; God wants us to have union with the Son of God. We aspire for earthly success; he intends for us heavenly glory. We would settle for health and wealth; yet he has everlasting life in store for us.

Such was the case with Abram. He wanted a son, but God intended that he would become the father of all the redeemed. Already God had told Abram that through him he would bless all the nations (Gen. 12:3). But Abram's appetite was shaped, as ours generally is, by his local and recent experience—by his felt needs, as they are called today. He just wanted the caravan leaders to think highly of him. He wanted to know the human joy of looking into the eyes of a son. He wanted respect; he wanted to fit in; he wanted to feel good. These are things we want, too. They are good things, as far as they go, but they fall far short of what God intends for us. Paul reminds us, "No eye has seen, nor ear heard, nor the heart of man imagined, what God has prepared for those who love him" (1 Cor. 2:9). To keep us from filling ourselves on lesser things, God leaves us in circumstances of want and also gives us promises of great blessing, far beyond our imagining.

The second reason God deals with us through promises is related to the first, and is also revealed in Abram's example. God is moving us along, directing us to our feet for a journey. Given a choice, we would all settle down in this life, in this world, this fleshly existence. Abram, we can be sure, would have been all too happy to raise a brood of sons alongside a good, clean well, with mud-baked bricks to form the walls of a sturdy house. But this world is not our home, it is not where God would settle us forever. Again, Paul tells us, "For the present form of this world is passing away" (1 Cor. 7:31). We were not meant for this place. Our souls were not created only for this life, so God uses the combination of want and promises to raise us to our feet and move us along the way.

When we realize that God deals with us through promises, and when we start looking for them, we soon begin to feel like Abram underneath the starry host. The promises of God are great beyond all reckoning. J. C. Ryle puts it well:

> There are "shalls" and "wills" in God's treasury for every condition. About God's infinite mercy and compassion; about His readiness to receive all who repent and believe; about His willingness to forgive, pardon and absolve the chief of sinners; about His power to change hearts and alter our corrupt nature; about the encouragements to pray and hear the gospel and draw near to the throne of grace; about strength for duty, comfort in trouble, guidance in perplexity, help in sickness, consolation in death, support under bereavement, happiness beyond the grave, reward in glory—about all these things there is an abundant supply of promises in the Word. No one can form an idea of its abundance unless he carefully searches the Scriptures, keeping the subject steadily in view. If anyone doubts it, I can only say, "Come and see." Like the Queen of Sheba at Solomon's court, you will soon say, "The half was not told me" (1 Ki. 10:7).[2]

FAITH THAT WAITS

Abram received God's great promise with faith, yet the years to come proved hard nonetheless. His wife particularly seems to have suffered from

---

2. J. C. Ryle, *Holiness: Its Nature, Hindrances, Difficulties, and Roots* (Durham, Eng.: Evangelical Press, 1979), 263.

her inability to bear children. In Genesis 16 we see how she responded: "Now Sarai, Abram's wife, had borne him no children. She had a female Egyptian servant whose name was Hagar. And Sarai said to Abram, 'Behold now, the LORD has prevented me from bearing children. Go in to my servant; it may be that I shall obtain children by her'" (vv. 1–2).

Abram slept with Hagar and she conceived, bearing him a son named Ishmael. This may have seemed like an answer to prayer—a blessing from God—but if so, the delusion was soon dispelled. The first result was turmoil within Abram's house, as Hagar and Sarai predictably launched a bitter war for pride of place and authority. This took place when Abram was eighty-six years old, ten years after his arrival in the land. The second problem emerged thirteen years later, when Abram was ninety-nine. God came to reaffirm the original promise and inform Abram that Ishmael would not be the son of blessing.

The problem with Sarai's suggestion and Abram's action was that it tried to achieve God's promise by man's power. Abram had grown weary over so many years, and his wife's discouragement wore away at his resolve. Finally, he gave up on the idea of such an elderly woman bearing a child—something humanly impossible—and decided to help things along by taking Hagar to his bed.

That is the kind of thing we are tempted to do. We have a great longing and trust that God intends to bless us according to his wisdom. But just to help him out, we take matters into our own hands, according to our wisdom, even employing sinful means to attain the ends we want. Tired of waiting for a husband, we give in to premarital sex in order to win a man's heart. Anxious to get that promotion we so richly deserve, we lie or take advantage of other people. We justify all this by saying it is faith, just as Abram and Sarai must have done, when in fact it is unbelief that is holding our hands. Doubting God's power for what seems impossible, we manipulate what is possible by our own devices.

This happens in churches, too. Eager to do God's work but unwilling to wait on his timetable, many churches go about it in man's way. Thus we use psychological manipulation to create the appearance of conversions, when in fact only God can convert the soul. Eager to fill the church—surely God wants that!—we resort to cheap marketing and other patently unbiblical measures. Though God says his Word is sufficient for all our needs, churches all too easily cast Sarai aside for the seemingly more fertile embrace of Hagar. Whenever churches do this, they (like Abram) bear illegitimate children who (like Ishmael) are denied the blessing of God.

Genesis 17 tells us of God's return to Abram, when Ishmael was thirteen years old. God challenged him, even while renewing the promise. He said, "I am God Almighty; walk before me, and be blameless, that I may make my covenant between me and you, and may multiply you greatly" (vv. 1–2). God was confronting Abram for his unbelief and sin. "I am God Almighty," he said, forcefully asserting his worthiness to be trusted absolutely, his omnipotent power to accomplish all that he had promised. "Walk before me, and be blameless," he then commanded, pressing his requirement of obedience. Both rebuking Abram's unbelief and encouraging him to new faith, God added, "I will make [or 'confirm'] my covenant . . . and multiply you greatly."

Abram was ninety-nine years old, but his success with Hagar showed that he could produce children. Therefore, it must have been a great encouragement to Abram, however astounding it might have been, when God declared that henceforth his name would be Abraham. Not Abram, the "father of many," but Abraham, "father of a people." Surely God intended this to be a sign of Abram's faith. Abram had stumbled in his faith, but God placed him back upon his feet with an even greater sign of blessing and a call to renewed trust.

Imagine aged Abram coming back from this meeting, setting his one and only child beside him and announcing that he had a new name. People would have whispered, "He finally couldn't take it anymore. It's going to be Abechad, 'father of one.'" How astonished they must have been when the man of faith announced, "My name is no longer Abram, father of many, but Abraham, father of a nation." This was the kind of absolute conviction and commitment that God demanded of Abraham, and demands of us as well.

The point is that faith must wait upon the Lord. Abram was seventy-five years old when he set out for Canaan, eighty-six when he gave in and had a child with Hagar, and ninety-nine when God set him back on his feet with a new promise and a new name. Faith receives God's promise and faith waits on him, often for very long periods.

The Psalms constantly extol this theme. Psalm 27 ends, "Wait for the Lord; be strong, and let your heart take courage; wait for the Lord!" (v. 14). Psalm 37 says, "Be still before the Lord and wait patiently for him. . . . Wait for the LORD and keep his way" (v. 7, 34). Psalm 130 puts it in words perhaps closest to our hearts: "I wait for the LORD, my soul waits, and in his word I hope; my soul waits for the Lord more than watchmen for the morning, more than watchmen for the morning" (vv. 5–6). Spurgeon comments: "This is a most divine precept, and requires much grace to carry it out. To hush the spirit, to be silent before the Lord, to wait in holy patience the time for clearing up the difficulties of Providence—this is what every gracious heart should aim at." Waiting on the Lord is difficult, but it is the sign of a wise and believing heart that trusts an omnipotent and gracious God. Spurgeon concludes, "Time is nothing to him, let it be nothing to thee. God is worth waiting for. . . . Wait in obedience as a servant, in hope as an heir, in expectation as a believer."[3]

To wait upon the Lord is to rely on him; it is to study and trust his attributes. It is, for instance, to know that he is faithful, often in ways we had never considered. It involves committing ourselves to his power, his goodness, and his wisdom, as all of these unite to superintend the affairs of our lives, not according to our plan but according to his. These are the things the Psalms talk about as they exhort us to wait upon the Lord. Psalm 27, for example, begins with words of comfort, based on who and what God is: "The LORD is my light and my salvation; whom shall I fear? The LORD is the stronghold of my life; of whom shall I be afraid?" (v. 1).

Faith waits upon the Lord. Arthur Pink says:

> Faith provides a firm standing-ground while I await the fulfillment of God's promises. Faith furnishes my heart with a sure support during the interval. Faith believes God and relies upon His veracity: as it does so, the heart is anchored and remains steady, no matter how fierce the storm nor how protracted the season of waiting. . . . Real faith issues in a confident and standing expectation of future things.[4]

Despite stumbling into unbelief and sin, Abraham sets a great example of waiting on the Lord in faith. The New International Version of Hebrews 11:11 rightly links Abraham's faith with Sarah's, saying, "By faith Abraham,

---

3. Charles Haddon Spurgeon, *A Treasury of David*, 3 vols. (Peabody, Mass.: Hendrickson, n.d.), 1:172, 178.

4. A. W. Pink, *An Exposition of Hebrews* (Grand Rapids: Baker, 1954), 650.

even though he was past age—and Sarah herself was barren—was enabled to become a father because he considered him faithful who had made the promise." Romans 4:20–21 gives another classic description of Abraham's waiting faith. Speaking of Abraham, Paul writes, "No distrust made him waver concerning the promise of God, but he grew strong in his faith as he gave glory to God, fully convinced that God was able to do what he had promised."

ALL OF GRACE

Hebrews 11:11 seems to have a specific episode from Abraham's life in mind, because it includes Sarah's faith that also received the promise. Indeed, there is some question as to who is the main subject of this verse, Abraham or Sarah. Different versions make one or the other the subject of this verse. The flow of thought makes Abraham the main subject, especially in connection with verse 12, yet it was together that this sorrowful pair found grace to trust in God and in his promise.

Abraham was ninety-nine when God renewed the promise, yet he did not have the child of promise. God had changed his name; he also changed the name of his wife from Sarai to Sarah, a name that means "princess," to indicate that his promise still dealt with her. Yes, Abraham would father a nation, but not through young slave girls he bought and brought to his bed. It would be through his legitimate wife, Sarah, despite her advanced age and barren womb. God said: "As for Sarai your wife, you shall not call her name Sarai, but Sarah shall be her name. I will bless her, and moreover, I will give you a son by her. I will bless her, and she shall become nations; kings of peoples shall come from her" (Gen. 17:15–16).

God's insistence that Abraham's offspring would be born through Sarah is a sign that salvation is by grace alone. God promised great blessing to Abraham in terms of offspring. We have mentioned the embarrassment he must have suffered in going so long without children, but there is another matter that is far more significant. Abraham's childlessness brought God's covenant into question—God's faithfulness and his plan of salvation. How would the world be blessed? How would the seed of salvation come? Would it be by natural means—by works—or by supernatural means—by grace alone? We find God's plain answer in his promise regarding Sarah. "She shall become nations," God said of this ninety-year-old, wrinkled woman. "Kings of peoples will come from her."

On the surface, this really was laughable. In fact, Abraham did laugh at the idea. In the verses that follow, we find that "Abraham fell on his face and laughed and said to himself, 'Shall a child be born to a man who is a hundred years old? Shall Sarah, who is ninety years old, bear a child?' . . . [But] God said, . . . 'Sarah your wife shall bear you a son, and you shall call his name Isaac. I will establish my covenant with him as an everlasting covenant for his offspring after him'" (Gen. 17:17–19).

This is how God has designed salvation to work: in a manner that confounds human expectation and leaves all the glory to him alone. In Genesis 18 God made the same promise again, this time in the presence of Sarah, and she laughed too (Gen. 18:12). But Genesis 21 tells us that Abraham went to her and she bore a son. They named him Isaac, which means "laughter." They no longer laughed in unbelief but cried tears of joy in renewed wonder at the power and faithfulness of the promise-keeping God.

Hebrews 11:12 tells us what can happen when faith waits upon God's promise: "Therefore from one man, and him as good as dead, were born descendants as many as the stars of heaven and as many as the innumerable grains of sand by the seashore." Fighting through their natural tendency to unbelief, Abraham and Sarah trusted the Lord. It is wonderful that Hebrews 11 says nothing about their unbelieving laughter and complaints—sins that were washed away by the blood of Christ—but speaks only about their faith, which God remembered. Believing God, they came together as husband and wife, and by the power of his grace God brought life from the dead womb, bringing a salvation that is all of grace.

In that manner, the barren womb signifies salvation by grace all through the Bible. Isaiah could boldly write, "Sing, O barren one, who did not bear; break forth into singing and cry aloud, you who have not been in labor! For the children of the desolate one will be more than the children of her who is married" (54:1).

This rose to a new level when another descendant of Abraham, indeed the special seed that God had in mind all along, was born not of the barren but of the virgin womb. The barren womb speaks of human failure and weakness and futility; the virgin womb speaks of a work that belongs to God alone, in which human works have no place at all—a rock cut not with human hands. God spoke to Joseph about a child from his virgin fiancée's womb: "She will bear a son, and you shall call his name Jesus, for he will save his people from their sins" (Matt. 1:21).

The virgin birth tells us that the means by which the gospel produces its ends are not natural or man-controlled; they are not things we can manipulate for our own success, or that rely upon us. The blessing God promised to Abraham could come about only if a barren and elderly woman could conceive and give birth. When it comes to Christ, we find that there will be salvation from our sins only if a virgin girl can do the same. That Sarah conceived and gave birth, and that Mary did the same, tells us that the salvation we trust is of God from first to last, and to the glory of his name alone. Therefore, let us trust ourselves to this God who gives life to the dead and produces blessing from the barren womb, even salvation through the virgin womb that bore our Lord Jesus Christ.

Surely this exhorts us to turn to God for the whole of our need, and with all of our longings, trusting his might and waiting upon him for all the precious promises we receive in Scripture. Jeremiah Burroughs exhorts: "Every time a godly man reads the Scriptures . . . and there meets with a promise, he ought to lay his hand upon it and say, This is part of my inheritance, it is mine, and I am to live upon it."[5]

Then let us realize that our greatest inheritance is God himself; his greatest promise is this: "I will be your God, and you will be my people." It is God himself that we receive as we rest upon his promises. And it is our hearts that he is seeking through this long and sometimes difficult life of faith as he calls us to wait upon him. Through the faith of Abraham, we too may receive the words of blessing: "Fear not, . . . I am your shield; your reward shall be very great" (Gen. 15:1).

5. Jeremiah Burroughs, *The Rare Jewel of Christian Contentment* (Edinburgh: Banner of Truth, 1964), 82–83.

43

FAITH SEEKING A HOME

Hebrews 11:13–16

These all died in faith, not having received the things promised,
but having seen them and greeted them from afar, and having
acknowledged that they were strangers and exiles on the earth.
For people who speak thus make it clear that they are seeking a
homeland. If they had been thinking of that land from which they
had gone out, they would have had opportunity to return. But as
it is, they desire a better country, that is, a heavenly one. There-
fore God is not ashamed to be called their God, for he has pre-
pared for them a city. (Heb. 11:13–16)

*T*he apostle Paul illustrated his teaching on the doctrine of justification by faith by appealing to the example of Abraham. He
pointed out that Abraham is the father of both believing Jews
and believing Gentiles in their faith. He describes him as "the father of all
who believe without being circumcised, so that righteousness would be
counted to them as well, and . . . the father of the circumcised who are not
merely circumcised but who also walk in the footsteps of the faith that our
father Abraham had before he was circumcised" (Rom. 4:11–12).

Paul's point is that neither circumcision nor uncircumcision matters as far as our standing with God is concerned, because Abraham was justified by faith alone before he was circumcised. What matters is walking in the footsteps of faith, footsteps laid out before us by our father in faith, Abraham. This makes our studies of the faith of Abraham something more than academic. If we are saved, he is our father in faith, and we are to walk in his steps. In his Romans commentary John Murray says, "To 'walk in the footsteps' is to march in file. Abraham is conceived of as the leader of the band and we walk, not abreast, but in file, following in the footsteps left by Abraham."[1]

Many people tend think of the Christian life only in terms of a past definitive event. We talk about having been born again, or "deciding for Jesus," as if that were the whole of the Christian life. But the idea of walking in faith shows that the Christian life is a pilgrimage with its destination not in this life, but only far off in the next. That is what our passage explores as we continue to study Abraham's faith. It presents us with three points: (1) the end of faith's journey; (2) faith leaving its worldly home; and (3) faith seeking a true and heavenly home with God.

THE END OF FAITH'S JOURNEY

Hebrews 11:13–16 looks upon faith as a pilgrimage. Verse 13 describes what the end of this life's journey looks like for a Christian: "These all died in faith, not having received the things promised, but having seen them and greeted them from afar." It is not certain whether "these all" refers to all the examples given from the beginning of Hebrews 11 (Abel, Enoch, Noah, etc.) or to Abraham and his immediate family. The context suggests only the latter, although these words could be said of every believer presented in the Bible. They died still believing, but not having all the things their faith set itself upon. They were looking for something not realized in this world, in this life. The promises they trusted were not fulfilled in their present earthly existence: "[They saw] them and greeted them from afar." Abraham was promised children, and he did live to see the promised son from the womb of Sarah. But *all* that God had promised—offspring like stars in the sky,

1. John Murray, *The Epistle to the Romans* (Grand Rapids: Wm. B. Eerdmans, 1968), 139.

and with them his possession of the land—did not occur in his earthly life. He died still hoping for all that he had longed for and journeyed toward in this life.

This verse might seem to express a tragedy. After all, Abraham and those with him spent their whole lives longing for things they were promised, longing to have a home of their own. They trusted God for this and believed the promises he gave them, yet they died without having received them. What a dismal story! What a poor commendation for the faith they represented! If this is what our faith is about, dying with only unfulfilled hopes, then surely we are, as Paul said, "of all people most to be pitied" (1 Cor. 15:19).

One thing this tells us, however, is that Christianity is not a religion focused on the earth and this present life. The Scriptures make this point over and over again. Paul says, "Set your minds on things that are above, not on things that are on earth" (Col. 3:2). Jesus taught, "Do not lay up for yourselves treasures on earth, where moth and rust destroy and where thieves break in and steal, but lay up for yourselves treasures in heaven, where neither moth nor rust destroys and where thieves do not break in and steal" (Matt. 6:19–20).

This directly confronts a view that is quite prevalent in our time: a packaged version of Christianity that offers mainly temporal benefits. It goes like this: "If you trust Jesus, you will do better at work, you will be a better husband or wife or parent, you will have less stress and lose weight." Certainly, Christianity does give us spiritual resources that transform this present life—resources like righteousness, peace, and joy. But how easily we forget that to be a Christian means to be persecuted in this world. Our blessings are spiritual rather than material (see Eph. 1:3). To be a Christian means living as an alien and a pilgrim; it means not being able to fit in with others who are slaves to sin; it means denying yourself and picking up your cross; it means a life of struggle and fellowship in the sufferings of Christ. The Christian life means peace with God, but war with the flesh, the world, and the devil. The primary blessings Christianity offers do not lie in this life at all, but in the life to come, in the resurrection from the dead. Indeed, even our present blessings, abundant and wonderful as they are, are located in heaven and are accessed by the exercise of faith.

It never crossed Paul's mind that to be a Christian meant happiness and health and wealth in this present life. Instead, he admitted that if we do not receive great blessings beyond the grave, we would be better off living like hedonists, enjoying the temporary pleasures of sin. "If the dead are not raised," he argued, "let us eat and drink, for tomorrow we die" (1 Cor. 15:32).

This is essentially how the world lives, but it is not the way of the Christian. The Christian realizes that even at the end of this life, the blessings we have hoped for will not yet have been received. We are pilgrims here, and our homeland, our rest, our treasure lies in the land across the grave. Hebrews 11:13 says, "These all died in faith, not having received the things promised, but having seen them and greeted them from afar." Christians are presently filled with joy because of the certainty of what lies ahead; by faith we greet and enjoy the things promised for the life to come.

It is obvious, therefore, that the Christian has a vastly different view of death than does the non-Christian. I mentioned the apostle Paul's emphasis on the life to come; that emphasis shaped his view of death. He wrote his Letter to the Philippians from a Roman jail, fully aware that he might be put to death. His attitude to all this was wonderfully straightforward: "For to me to live is Christ, and to die is gain" (Phil. 1:21). Paul lived in this world as a servant of Christ, with a longing for Christ, and therefore death became the means by which his heart's desire could be achieved. Paul was not suicidal; he was willing to live as long as the Lord intended. But far from fearing death, he saw it as the crowning moment of his faith.

Some years later Paul was back in jail for preaching the gospel, this time sure that death loomed near. He wrote to Timothy, "I have fought the good fight, I have finished the race, I have kept the faith. Henceforth there is laid up for me the crown of righteousness, which the Lord, the righteous judge, will award to me on that Day" (2 Tim. 4:7–8). Paul was not like the man of this world, who faced death looking backward, thinking about the good old days, about his glorious achievements, and wishing he could go back. For Paul this life was but a journey to what lies beyond death: a crown of righteousness and a home in glory with the Lord. No matter how full this life might have been, it was merely preparation for what is yet to come. In contrast to whatever wonders one might have experienced here, Paul could say, "What no eye has seen, nor ear heard, nor the heart of man imagined, . . . God has prepared for those who love him" (1 Cor. 2:9).

Paul's view of death was centered on the cross of Jesus Christ. It is because of the cross that Paul could say: "Death is swallowed up in victory. O death, where is your victory? O death, where is your sting?" (1 Cor. 15:54–55). This does not mean that death is no longer terrible, that it is no longer an enemy. It *is* an enemy, but one that Christ has vanquished by taking from us the guilt of our sin. This is what the next verses say: "The sting of death is sin, and the power of sin is the law. But thanks be to God, who gives us the victory through our Lord Jesus Christ" (1 Cor. 15:56–57).

The Westminster Shorter Catechism summarizes the Bible's teaching on what death does for a believer: "The souls of believers are at their death made perfect in holiness, and do immediately pass into glory, and their bodies, being still united to Christ, do rest in their graves till the resurrection" (Q/A 37). Similarly, Thomas Watson writes:

> A believer at death is freed from sin; he is not taken away in, but from his sins; he shall never have a vain, proud thought more; he shall never grieve the Spirit of God any more. . . . Death smites a believer as the angel did Peter, and made his chains fall off (Acts 12:7). Believers at death are made perfect in holiness. . . . Oh! what a blessed privilege is this, to be without spot or wrinkle; to be purer than the sunbeams; to be as free from sin as the angels! (Eph. 5:27). This makes a believer desirous to have his passport and to be gone; he would fain live in that pure air where no black vapours of sin arise.[2]

Verse 13 says that Abraham and the others "all died in faith," or as the New International Version puts it, they "were still living by faith when they died." What a difference faith makes for every child of God in the hour of death which, unless the Lord should come, all of us must someday face. Charles Spurgeon says:

> The grave—what is it? It is the bath in which the Christian puts on the clothes of his body to have them washed and cleansed. Death—what is it? It is the waiting room where we robe ourselves for immortality; it is the place where the body, like Esther, bathes itself in spices that it may be fit for the embrace of its Lord. Death is the gate of life; I will not fear to die, then.[3]

---

2. Thomas Watson, *A Body of Divinity* (Edinburgh: Banner of Truth, 1958), 296–97.
3. Charles Haddon Spurgeon, *Spurgeon's Sermons*, 10 vols. (Grand Rapids: Baker, n.d.), 1:229.

461

Abraham's approach to death is instructive. We see here that he never did receive the promise of owning the land during his lifetime. Genesis 23, however, tells us what he did when the time came to prepare for death. Sarah, his wife, finally died at a great old age, and Abraham mourned and wept over her. But then he did something he had never done before. He went to Ephron the Hittite, a nearby landowner, and bought the cave of Machpelah as the burial place for Sarah and later for himself. Obviously Abraham was well respected, because Ephron wanted to give him the land without making him pay. But Abraham insisted; he would own that one piece of Canaan outright. You see the point Abraham was making: in life he was a pilgrim in that land, but in death he would be an owner. His and Sarah's bodies would lie on land owned by him, because it was in death that he looked for the fulfillment of God's promise of a land and a home.

Abraham died in the faith. Spurgeon thinks on this and sees in his mind a mausoleum erected by God, not unlike Abraham's cave, in which lie the bodies of all his people. On it, Spurgeon sees inscribed the words of verse 13: "These all died in faith." He writes, "As for those who died without faith, they died indeed; but, as for his people, a glorious resurrection awaits them. They sleep in Jesus, and are blest, how kind their slumbers are."[4]

FAITH LEAVING A HOME

Our passage describes the life of faith as a pilgrimage in a foreign land, a journey through life to a home that awaits beyond the grave. Verses 13–15 make an important point about such a pilgrimage, namely that it requires that we first leave our prior home: Abraham and the others "acknowledged that they were strangers and exiles on the earth. For people who speak thus make it clear that they are seeking a homeland. If they had been thinking of that land from which they had gone out, they would have had opportunity to return."

Abraham and the others confessed themselves to be "strangers and exiles." This is a direct quote from Genesis 23:4. When Abraham went to the Hittites to buy his burial plot, he told them, "I am a sojourner and foreigner

---

4. Charles Haddon Spurgeon, "An Inscription for the Mausoleum of the Saints," *Metropolitan Tabernacle Pulpit*, 63 vols. (Pasadena, Tex.: Pilgrim Publications, 1973) 31:105.

among you." In the Greek, the writer of Hebrews renders this with two words, the first of which is *xenoi*, meaning "aliens." This was a pejorative term indicating outsiders. It is not the sort of word one wanted to have applied to oneself. It describes not merely a person from another place, but rather someone who doesn't fit in, who doesn't belong. In our society, aliens can assimilate, but the writer of Hebrews says that in this world Christians never do.

The other term is *parepidēmoi*, or sojourners. These are people who are passing through to a destination somewhere else. In Greek writings the term was applied to someone lodging temporarily in an inn, without a home in the place where he sojourned, even if he would be there for a while. That is what our text says about Abraham and those who follow him in faith. By admitting they are aliens and strangers, they "make it clear that they are seeking a homeland" (v. 14), namely, one in the world to come.

Since we all come from someplace, this requires the believer to leave home to answer God's call. Abraham was living in the land of his fathers when God called him to leave and go to the land of promise, there to live as an alien and stranger. Hebrews commends him for his faith in that he made no attempt to go back: "If they had been thinking of that land from which they had gone out, they would have had opportunity to return" (Heb. 11:15). Nothing stood between Abraham and his former home—nothing except his faith. The fact that he made no attempt to go back shows the strength and reality of that faith.

Practically the worst thing that can be said of someone who once professed faith in Christ is that he went back to the home he had left. Lot's wife was turned into a pillar of salt simply because she looked back on Sodom; her heart went back with her eyes, and God judged her for unbelief. The strongest charge laid against the Israelites in the exodus was that they complained about the hardships of their journey and longed to return to their former slavery in Egypt. They cried, "Oh that we had meat to eat! We remember the fish we ate in Egypt that cost nothing, the cucumbers, the melons, the leeks, the onions, and the garlic" (Num. 11:4–5). For this and many other sins God made a whole generation wander and die in the desert. It was for the same spiritual betrayal that Paul sadly reported the apostasy of one of his helpers: "Demas, in love with this present world, has deserted me" (2 Tim. 4:10). In contrast to these examples, people of faith are like Peter and James and John when

Jesus called them to be his disciples. Luke 5:11 tells us they "brought their boats to land, they left everything and followed him."

Whether or not we have really left this world, the place of our former allegiance, is determined not just by what we say, but by how we live. This teaching seems to have been stressed in the early church. One very early document, the Epistle to Diognetus, speaks in strong terms: "[Christians] dwell in their own countries, but only as sojourners. . . . Every foreign country is a homeland to them, and every homeland is foreign. . . . Their existence is on earth, but their citizenship is in heaven."[5] Jesus put this as a simple challenge: "Where your treasure is, there your heart will be also" (Matt. 6:21). And where your heart is, surely that is your home.

When Abraham left Ur, he no longer thought of himself in terms of his former home but of the home to which he was headed. Is that true of you? In what terms do you think of yourself? What establishes your identity? Is it your family background? Is it your race or social class or profession? Is it your earthly homeland or the school from which you graduated? If these are the sources of your identity and your desire, then they are still your home. You have not set your heart upon the city that is to come, the heavenly home to which God has called you. Your old allegiances will hold you back and discourage you from a true pilgrimage in faith before the Lord. This does not mean that Christians must physically change their place of residence, though that might be involved, but rather we must exchange our former hopes and dreams and affections in this world for new ones in Christ and in the world to come.

Christians are increasingly to think of themselves not in terms of the old categories, the old homeland, but in terms of where we are headed, in terms of him who calls us and those with whom we will spend eternity in heaven. What liberty we have for godliness when our hearts have left our earthly homes! What an ally in repudiating worldliness and sin and in putting on a heavenly character! If we will not leave behind our former home, we cannot advance to the heavenly place God has called us; if we will not leave, we simply show that we are not longing for a better country, a heavenly one. This is a sober test of our faith. As Jesus put it: "Whoever loves father or mother more than me is not worthy of me, and whoever loves son or daugh-

5. Cyril C. Richardson, ed., *Early Christian Fathers* (New York: Collier, 1970), 217.

ter more than me is not worthy of me. And whoever does not take his cross and follow me is not worthy of me. Whoever finds his life will lose it, and whoever loses his life for my sake will find it" (Matt. 10:37–39).

Faith Seeking a Home

Abraham willingly left everything, and in this he shows what faith requires. Faith leaves one home in search of another: "They desire a better country, that is, a heavenly one" (Heb. 11:16). This is not only the counterpart to the idea of living as a stranger and an alien, but it is also the rationale and motive. What makes people spend their lives as those passing through, except that they are headed somewhere dear to their hearts? Abraham lived as a pilgrim here because of his eagerness to have that which can be possessed only by faith and is achieved only in a world that is yet to come. His home was elsewhere, with God and the city God had prepared, so it was only natural for him to live the way he did.

Let me put this differently. We saw earlier how Christians view the matter of death. Death itself is terrible; it is not a good thing. But for those who trust the Lord, it becomes the gateway into life. If we believe that, then our view of death will change our view of life. It is not here that we will set our hearts, but beyond life's horizon. This new focus transforms our view of present trials and sorrows. A famous preacher expressed this attitude in a letter to a friend announcing the death of his beloved wife: "I have some of the best news to impart. One beloved by you has accomplished her warfare, has received an answer to her prayers, and everlasting joy rests upon her head. My dear wife, the source of my best earthly comfort for twenty years, departed on Tuesday."[6] It is not that this man felt no sadness at the loss of his wife, but that he understood what death meant for her. It meant finding and reaching the home and joy for which she long had sought. Christians by faith have seen better things in another place. Our treasure is there and so our heart follows. Therefore, we gladly accept the fact that we are sojourners here, because this tells us we have an inheritance there. As the well-loved hymn puts it, we will "cherish the old rugged cross, and exchange it someday for a crown."

---

6. Henry Venn, announcing the death of his wife—cited in J. C. Ryle, *Holiness* (Darlington, U.K.: Evangelical Press, 1979), 190.

Armed with this attitude, Christians do not find their rest here, settling for lesser riches. This is what John Bunyan conveyed in *The Pilgrim's Progress*, when Christian explained his departure to those who tried to keep him from leaving his home and were puzzled by his eagerness to depart a comfortable worldly life. Christian urged them to come with him: "Everything you forsake is not worthy of being compared with what I am seeking to enjoy (2 Cor. 4:18). If you will come with me, and hold steady, we will prosper. For where I go, there is enough and to spare (Luke 15:17). Come with me, and prove my words." One of the men replied: "What are the things you seek, since you leave all the world to find them?" Christian answered: "I seek an inheritance incorruptible, undefiled, that does not fade away (1 Pet. 1:4). It is reserved and safe in heaven (Heb. 11:16), to be given at the time appointed to them that diligently seek it."[7]

Abraham was such a man. His faith, too, sought a home—a heavenly city God had prepared for him. Every Christian knows something of the yearning that Abraham knew, living in tents in sight of the earthly city, looking upon its pleasures but lifting his eyes to the promises of God, forsaking the one so as to gain the other.

How wonderful, then, to read what verse 16 says in conclusion: "Therefore God is not ashamed to be called their God, for he has prepared for them a city." What could be more lovely than this: that God, the holy God and the God of grace, the sovereign God of all the world, is not ashamed of those who trust in him, who sojourn in this world longing for the home he has prepared? What Jesus said to the woman by the well is true of Abraham and all who walk in his steps: "The Father is seeking such people to worship him" (John 4:23).

All those long years Abraham identified himself not by the home he had left or by the place where he resided, but by the home he was seeking and the God who called him and gave the promises he believed. He and his sons were willing to be called men of God, not men of the world, and therefore God was willing to say, as we so often read in the Old Testament: "I am . . . the God of Abraham, the God of Isaac, and the God of Jacob" (Ex. 3:6). If we would walk in Abraham's steps, then we may insert our own names in that place. God eagerly says to us, "I will be your God, and

---

7. John Bunyan, *The Pilgrim's Progress* (Nashville: Thomas Nelson, 1999), 13.

you will be my people." To all who will hear he unashamedly says of us, "I am their God," if in return we will say to the world that we are his.

Two Deaths

Our passage speaks about dying in faith and receiving a home in place of the one we have left in this passing world. What a difference it makes in the hour of death to have a better home beyond the grave, a country and a city prepared for us by God himself! But what a tragedy death is for all whose only home is here, who have no home and no life except in this poor and dying world.

In 1899 two prominent men died, and the manner of their deaths well illustrates this difference. The first was Colonel Robert G. Ingersoll, for whom the Ingersoll lectures on immortality at Harvard University are named, and who gave his brilliant mind to the refutation of Christianity. Ingersoll died suddenly that year, leaving his unprepared family utterly devastated. So grief-stricken was his wife that she would not allow his body to be taken from their home until the health of the family required its removal. His remains then were cremated, and his funeral service was such a scene of dismay and despair that even the newspapers of the day commented upon it. Death came to this man and there was no hope, but only an irredeemable tragedy.

The other man who died that year was Dwight L. Moody, the great Christian evangelist. He had been declining for some time, and his family had gathered around his bed. On his last morning, his son heard him exclaim, "Earth is receding; heaven is opening; God is calling." "You are dreaming, Father," said his son. But Moody replied, "No, Will, this is no dream. I have been within the gates. I have seen the children's faces." Moody seemed to revive but then started to slip away again. "Is this death?" he was heard to say. "This is not bad; there is no valley. This is bliss. This is glorious." His daughter now had come and she began to pray for him to recover. "No, no, Emma," he said. "Don't pray for that. God is calling. This is my coronation day. I have been looking forward to it."

Moody died not long after that, his family confident of his entry into heaven. His funeral was a scene of triumph and great joy. Those in attendance sang hymns and exalted God. "Where, O death, is your victory? Where, O death, is your sting?" they exclaimed. Walking in Abraham's steps, the

Christian had found the home he had been seeking throughout his earthly sojourn. He had not been ashamed of God, and now God was not ashamed of him. He had lived for God in this world, leaving behind its pleasures and its glory, and God had prepared a city for him—"an inheritance," Peter says, "that is imperishable, undefiled, and unfading, kept in heaven" for him (1 Peter 1:4). "Now," he could say along with Paul, "there is laid up for me the crown of righteousness, which the Lord, the righteous judge, will award to me on that Day, and not only to me but also to all who have loved his appearing" (2 Tim. 4:8).

44

FAITH TESTED

Hebrews 11:17—19

*By faith Abraham, when he was tested, offered up Isaac, and he
who had received the promises was in the act of offering up his
only son, of whom it was said, "Through Isaac shall your offspring be named." He considered that God was able even to raise
him from the dead, from which, figuratively speaking, he did
receive him back. (Heb. 11:17–19)*

In Genesis 22 we read that God came to Abraham and tested
him. This marks the fifth time that Genesis records God appearing to Abraham. The first occurred in chapter 12, God's initial
call to Abraham. In chapter 15 God came and promised Abraham descendants like stars in the sky. Then in chapter 17 God came to redirect Abraham back to the path of faith he had departed in his encounter with Hagar.
And in chapter 18 the angel of the Lord appeared to Abraham and Sarah
to announce the birth of the child of promise, and to deal with the problem of sin in Sodom and Gomorrah. In the first of these encounters, God
called Abraham to faith; in the second and third encounters God strengthened his faith; in the fourth encounter God rewarded his faith. Now, in the

fifth and last of these significant encounters between Abraham and the Lord, that faith would be tested by the most difficult of commands.

The New Testament confirms that God tests the faith of his people. In 1 Peter 1 the apostle speaks of various trials and then adds, "These have come so that your faith—of greater worth than gold, which perishes even though refined by fire—may be proved genuine and may result in praise, glory and honor when Jesus Christ is revealed" (1 Peter 1:7). God's purpose is the strengthening of faith by trial, the proving of faith by means of tests that God himself provides.

ABRAHAM'S FAITH TESTED

God tested Abraham with the greatest trial imaginable: "[God] said, 'Take your son, your only son Isaac, whom you love, and go to the land of Moriah, and offer him there as a burnt offering on one of the mountains of which I shall tell you'" (Gen. 22:2).

In the first place, this was a trial of Abraham's devotion to the Lord. Devotion to God is at the heart of his law: "You shall love the LORD your God with all your heart and with all your soul and with all your might" (Deut. 6:5). The proof of love is always found in the willingness to sacrifice. God tested Abraham not merely by asking for a sacrifice, or even a great sacrifice, but the sacrifice of that which Abraham held most dear: his covenant heir, Isaac. The test of our Christian devotion always involves this, that we love not so much the gifts—great as they are—but the Giver himself above all. The question is always whether we are willing to make God first—indeed, whether we are willing to make him everything. John Owen writes: "God says to us, 'My son, give me your heart' (Prov. 23:26). And God commands us to love him with all our heart, soul, strength and mind (Luke 10:27). This is the response God wants from us in return for his love to us. . . . This is love, that God loves us first, and then we love him in response to his love."[1]

We might wonder if God has the right to demand such singular devotion. The answer is a resounding "Yes!" Arthur Pink explains:

1. John Owen, *Communion with God* (Edinburgh: Banner of Truth, 1994), 17–18.

The Lord has an absolute claim upon us, upon all that we have. As our Maker and Sovereign He has the right to demand from us anything He pleases, and whatsoever He requires we must yield. All that we have comes from Him, and must be held for Him, and at His disposal. . . . The bounty of God should encourage us to surrender freely whatever He calls for, for none ever lose by giving up anything to God.[2]

We can expect God to test our devotion to him in great or small ways. We will be challenged to sacrifice or subordinate our careers to his will. Or perhaps it will be a relationship that is dear to us, but that cannot abide with our higher devotion to Jesus Christ. It may be money; it may be a certain self-image or a lifestyle; it can be practically anything. God tests our faith in terms of our willingness to sacrifice for him, and in this manner he also protects us from the idolatry to which our hearts are so inherently prone. Even good things he has given us, such as Isaac, this child of God's promise, God demands that we place back into his hand, always holding everything as a trust on behalf of the Giver and Possessor of all things.

Second, this was a trial of Abraham's spiritual understanding. We see this in verses 17–18: "He who had received the promises was in the act of offering up his only son, of whom it was said, 'Through Isaac shall your offspring be named.'" God had made great and surpassing promises to Abraham—possession of the land, offspring like the sand on the seashore, all the nations blessed through him—all to be fulfilled through this very son Isaac, whom God now commanded him to sacrifice.

We can see how vexing this would have been. God's promise seemed to be pitted against God's command. If God was to be faithful to his promises to Abraham, then Isaac must live; but if God's command was to be obeyed, then Isaac must die. It seemed to be so inconsistent, so internally contradictory. None of us ever receive this particular command from God, since Abraham was fulfilling a unique role in history, but God may call us to obey him in a way that seems spiritually counterproductive to ourselves or our projects. Like Abraham we will have to summon up the spiritual understanding needed to obey God's Word.

2. A. W. Pink, *An Exposition of Hebrews* (Grand Rapids: Baker, 1954), 745.

Third, it was a trial of Abraham's knowledge of God and trust in him. I say this because of the horror of what was involved in this command. Abraham was to strike his own son dead. Furthermore, it was "his only son." This was not strictly true, for Isaac was not the only living son; the point is that he was the one child of the promise, the one heir of the covenant. William Lane writes, "When Abraham obeyed God's mandate to leave Ur, he simply gave up his past. But when he was summoned to Mount Moriah to deliver his own son to God, he was asked to surrender his future as well."[3]

Additionally, Genesis 22:2 reminds us of Abraham's deep love for this son: "Take your son, your only son Isaac, whom you love." This was godly and appropriate love, and no doubt an intimate and intense love from a father to his son and heir. The mere thought of plunging a knife into his chest must have been terrible for Abraham, much more so the act itself. Obedience required that Abraham know God and trust him with unshakable confidence.

A Great Problem for Faith

Abraham passed the test by obeying God. Hebrews 11:17 simply tells us, "By faith Abraham, when he was tested, offered up Isaac." The Genesis account is considerably fuller:

> So Abraham rose early in the morning, saddled his donkey, and took two of his young men with him, and his son Isaac. And he cut the wood for the burnt offering and arose and went to the place of which God had told him. On the third day Abraham lifted up his eyes and saw the place from afar. Then Abraham said to his young men, "Stay here with the donkey; I and the boy will go over there and worship and come again to you." And Abraham took the wood of the burnt offering and laid it on Isaac his son. And he took in his hand the fire and the knife. So they went both of them together. And Isaac said to his father Abraham, "My father!" And he said, "Here am I, my son." He said, "Behold, the fire and the wood, but where is the lamb for a burnt offering?" Abraham said, "God will provide for himself the lamb for a burnt offering, my son." So they went both of them together. When they came to the place of which God had told him, Abraham built the altar there and laid the wood

3. William L. Lane, *Hebrews 9–13* (Dallas: Word Books, 1991), 360.

in order and bound Isaac his son and laid him on the altar, on top of the wood. Then Abraham reached out his hand and took the knife to slaughter his son. (Gen. 22:3–10)

This remarkable account raises some significant questions. How does faith overcome the natural objections to this command? How does faith pass this kind of test? I want to offer four answers, beginning with this: faith kneels before God in humble submission.

Abraham must surely have had a long night before setting out with his son for the place of sacrifice. Surely he must have reflected on the staggering demand God had made, and also on God's right to make it. He must have thought about how much he loved Isaac, and also about his devotion to the Lord. While unable to reason through all the problems, he must have knelt before God, trusted him, and asked for grace to obey. It is worth pointing out that this greatest test occurred at the end of his life's journey of faith. Abraham's success here is the product of earlier and lesser trials, many of which he failed, as God honed and refined his character and his faith. Having received this command, Abraham must have reckoned that God's will was higher than his own will. "Thy will and not mine be done," he must have prayed, perhaps with tears at the thought of what that required. Abraham's faith humbly knelt before God and thus was able to obey God's command.

However much difficulty this test caused for Abraham, the account of it has tried the faith of many more people. Many people read these verses and recoil from the God who speaks in them. How could a good God ask a father to kill his son? Many therefore reject the Bible on the grounds of this supposedly twisted use of divine authority. Moralists reject God, but existentialists reject Abraham, finding his faith impossible to embrace. The classic example is Søren Kierkegaard, whose book *Fear and Trembling* demanded to know how Abraham could be sure it was really God speaking to him; how could a father really do what Abraham went ahead and did? Surely this is not the kind of faith a decent authentic existentialist wants to emulate today!

How would Abraham respond to that line of reasoning? Surely he would have replied that he was a creature before the Creator. Abraham worshiped God as God and therefore did not think to place himself in the position of judge of the Most High and Lord of heaven. Abraham's faith was rooted in conscious humility; his faith knelt before the throne of a God he would no longer dare to judge.

Occasionally I find myself talking with someone who is disturbed about a subject like this test of Abraham's faith, or God's hardening Pharaoh's heart in Exodus, or the Bible's teaching on the eternal bodily punishment of sinners in hell. Inevitably, from the person's perspective, what God is doing is a terrible thing. How can a good God do something that is so wrong?

From the perspective of their humanism, people with these questions are never going to receive an acceptable answer. Humanism is the belief, so ingrained in us all, that what is best for the greatest number of humans is ultimately the yardstick of all good. But God is not a humanist; he is a theist! God does not think that the greatest good for man is the greatest good. He thinks that the glory of his own name is paramount. He thinks that the manifestation of his justice and his holiness and, yes, his love is worth more than all the stars in the sky.

When it comes to such disturbing matters as the command God gave to Abraham, our humanism will never be satisfied. God does not intend to satisfy our humanism, but to drive us out from it. God is not going to satisfy our queries in judgment of him; God will not accept a position on the witness stand, while we presume to sit on the bench. It is only on our knees before a true God that we will receive and be able to accept satisfactory answers to questions like those regarding Abraham's test. Abraham was no longer a humanist; all his years exercising faith had taught him to kneel humbly before the Lord and put his trust in him.

In asking how Abraham resolved his problems and passed this test of faith, the second explanation is that the faith that receives God's promises must also obey God's commands. We see more than a hint of this in our Hebrews passage. Who obeyed God's command? "He who had received the promises" (Heb. 11:17).

The same faith that receives and relies upon God's Word in the promise is obligated to receive and obey God's Word in the command. It is the same God and the same Word. This is what Job said to his wife, when she urged him to complain about what God had allowed to happen to him: "Shall we receive good from God, and shall we not receive evil?" (Job 2:10). Faith accepts both promise and precept, commands and comforts, Christ as Lord as well as Christ as Savior, knowing that the one cannot be had without the other. Faith knows that the path of safety and of blessing is also the path of obedience. Arthur Pink writes, "Spiritual faith does not pick and choose: it fears God as well as loves Him."[4]

Some may object that in this case the promise and the command stand in stark opposition. The command can be obeyed only by undermining the promise. The answer to that objection is that the faith that obeys God's command leaves the means of the promise's fulfillment to God. If God has commanded it, then God knows what he is doing and is able to work it out for good. Indeed, this is one of the striking differences between the one who believes in God and the one who believes in self. Those who trust in God do not find their solace in being able to solve the puzzle by adding up their own mental arithmetic. The Christian finds peace when he knows what God has revealed and commanded; even without understanding, his faith accepts it as true because it comes from God.

In short, we believe that God knows better than we do. He has more and better information, even infinite data compared to our slim sample size. God also has an infinitely higher capacity for processing and ordering that information. Furthermore, God does all this without sin, whereas the Christian realizes that sin has infected all the circuit boards of his own mental computer. Thus the believer is glad to trust God when he has spoken, having in his Word an infinitely better and surer guide than even our own powers of reason.

The third explanation follows from this. On the one hand, faith obeys even without answers; but we also must observe that faith gains understanding through God's Word. God tested not only Abraham's devotion, but also his spiritual understanding. Part of the reason he was able to succeed in this test was the answers he found in what God had already revealed.

This, too, is something that Hebrews makes clear: "He considered that God was able even to raise him from the dead" (Heb. 11:19). This was not autonomous, unbelieving reason, but faithful reasoning from what God had revealed. This faith explains Abraham's willingness to take his beloved son's life. He believed that God could raise him back to life from the dead. This statement in Hebrews is not found in the Genesis account, but it is proved there. Genesis 22:5 tells us that when Abraham arrived at the appointed place

---

4. Pink, *Hebrews*, 748.

he said to his servants, "Stay here with the donkey; I and the boy will go over there and worship and come again to you." Notice what he said: "*We* will come back."

Where, then, did Abraham get the idea that if he killed his son God would raise him from the grave? First, he must have realized that God's promise required that Isaac be alive. If Isaac had to be alive and yet had to be killed, then God had to raise him from the dead. This logic makes sense, but surely there is something more. Remember the circumstances of Isaac's conception and birth, when Sarah was far beyond child-bearing age, all in a manner promised and predicted and produced by the power of God. All of this surely made clear to Abraham that God has power over life, and if he has power over life then he has power over death as well. This was the ultimate answer to Abraham's problem, as it is for all of our problems. With the knowledge of God's power to take and give life, Abraham was able to obey.

Abraham's understanding came from faithful reflection on what God had earlier revealed about himself. Abraham did not have the Bible, none of which had yet been written, but he did have personal experience with God. We do have the Bible, God's very Word and revelation, and our faith will find power to obey by learning and understanding God's ways through the study of his Word.

Finally, and surely this is the most significant explanation, Abraham was able to obey because he knew and trusted God. Because he had really come to know God, Abraham was able to trust him completely, to rely upon the Lord as his God, and to honor him by obeying. Philip Hughes explains:

> Because he enjoyed a proper relationship with God Abraham knew that God is altogether holy and just and loving and that he cannot be untrue to himself; and he realized that it was not for him, a sinful, finite creature, to query the word of his infinite Creator. . . . This trial, in fact, so far from shaking Abraham's faith, actually served to establish it, for through it the unchangeable character of God's purpose and the impossibility that God should prove false to his promise became more than ever the great motivating realities to him.[5]

5. Philip E. Hughes, *A Commentary on the Epistle to the Hebrews* (Grand Rapids: Eerdmans, 1977), 482.

476

This doesn't mean that it was easy for Abraham to obey. Abraham must have died a thousand deaths during the three days' march to the place where he would sacrifice the son he loved. But it does mean he was able to obey by faith, and it will mean that for you if you come to know God, to study and understand his attributes, to realize that because he is holy then all his motives are holy, and that because he is almighty nothing lies beyond his ability to save. Because God is good, as Paul wrote in Romans 8:28, "In all things God works for the good of those who love him" (NIV). "Abraham reasoned that God could raise the dead" (Heb. 11:19 NIV), and a God like that was worthy of his trust, as he is of our own.

THE PARABLE OF THE OFFERED SON

Verse 19 concludes by saying, "Figuratively speaking, he did receive him back." This tells us how the story ended. As they walked up the mount, Isaac asked his father about the lamb for the burnt offering. "Where is the lamb?" he asked. To this, Abraham gave a provocative answer: "God will provide for himself the lamb for a burnt offering, my son" (Gen. 22:8). This shows us how much Abraham was able to understand, even though he lived at such a primitive time in redemptive history.

Genesis tells us how God provided for Abraham. As his knife began the deadly arc that would end Isaac's life:

> The angel of the LORD called to him from heaven and said, "Abraham, Abraham!" And he said, "Here am I." He said, "Do not lay your hand on the boy or do anything to him, for now I know that you fear God, seeing you have not withheld your son, your only son, from me." And Abraham lifted up his eyes and looked, and behold, behind him was a ram, caught in a thicket by his horns. And Abraham went and took the ram and offered it up as a burnt offering instead of his son. So Abraham called the name of that place, "The LORD will provide"; as it is said to this day, "On the mount of the LORD it shall be provided." (Gen. 22:11–14)

It is on the basis of this account that Hebrews concludes, "Figuratively speaking, he did receive him back." Isaac did not die and have to be resurrected, but God spared his life and honored Abraham's faith.

Christians have long seen the episode atop Mount Moriah as a picture of God's provision of another sacrifice, the true sacrifice and Lamb of God. "Where is the lamb?" asked Isaac, just as the whole of the Old Testament asked that same question. Years later, in the Israelite priesthood, lamb after lamb was slain day after day at the temple. Yet all the while everyone knew that mere animals could not really take away sin. "Where is the true lamb?" the priests and people must often have asked. The answer was finally given by the last prophet of the old dispensation, John the Baptist, who saw Jesus walking along the Jordan and cried out, "Behold, the Lamb of God, who takes away the sin of the world!" (John 1:29).

It is interesting to note that the Greek text in Hebrews 11:19 does not say that Isaac's deliverance was "figuratively speaking" like a resurrection. The word it uses is "parable," so that verse 19 literally reads, "Abraham reasoned that God could raise the dead, and *as a parable*, he did receive Isaac back from death." Christians have long understood this to mean that Isaac's death illustrated and pointed forward to another death, the true death that takes away our sin.

Indeed, the parallels are striking. Abraham was a father asked to sacrifice his son. We noted earlier that the expression "one and only son" doesn't exactly fit here, although Isaac was singular as the child of promise. But perhaps the real purpose of the phrase is to point us to another Father who did give his one and only Son as a sacrifice. John 3:16 tells us, "For God so loved the world, that he gave his only Son, that whoever believes in him should not perish but have eternal life."

There is considerably more to this. Isaac carried wood for the offering on his back, just as Jesus Christ would later carry his cross to his own place of sacrifice. Abraham and Isaac's journey through the valley of the shadow of death totaled three days, and for three days Jesus Christ lay in the tomb before he, as Isaac prefigures, was raised by the power of God. Clement of Alexandria, writing in the second century A.D., sees Isaac's deliverance as "an intimation of the divinity of the Lord . . . for Jesus rose again after his burial, having suffered no harm, like Isaac released from sacrifice."[6] Indeed, some Christians see the ram in the thicket as a symbol of Christ's human

6. Cited in ibid., 485.

nature, offered up to death for us, and Isaac as a symbol of Christ's divine nature, which though taken to the place of death is not allowed to die.

These are interesting—indeed, more than provocative—parallels. But if we add them up, what does it mean for us? We considered earlier the revulsion people experience at the idea of a father being commanded to offer up his son to death. What, then, do we think of a Father who does this voluntarily, as God has done? If this repulses us, it is only because we have forgotten or denied the essential fact of our situation, that we are sinners before a holy God. Only by bowing before God will we ever make sense of a passage like this, but now we must add that we can grasp it only by confessing the guilt of our sin and our need of a lamb to die like this for us. We must be the ones who cry out, "Where is the lamb? Where is the lamb for me?"

If we will cry for the lamb in faith, we will discover in God's Word the amazing fact that God the Father gave his one and only Son out of love for us. Romans 3:25 tells us, "God presented him as a sacrifice of atonement, through faith in his blood" (NIV). Speaking of Jesus, Paul writes, "In him we have redemption through his blood, the forgiveness of our trespasses, according to the riches of his grace" (Eph. 1:7). As Paul also says, all of this is "to the praise of his glorious grace, with which he has blessed us in the Beloved" (Eph. 1:6).

The key to accepting God's Word is to realize that God's glory is higher than man's good. But here we find that in reality, for sinners, God's glory is also the source of our good, namely, our redemption in Christ's blood and the forgiveness of our sins. If this does not change our way of thinking about a Father offering up his Son, then I suppose nothing ever will. In the cross of Jesus Christ we find what Paul described as "what is the breadth and length and height and depth [of] the love of Christ that surpasses knowledge" (Eph. 3:18–19). That is the love that calls us to faith in God.

Therefore, whenever God tests our faith, trying our devotion to him, whenever God calls on us to say, "Your will be done," let us remember Jesus Christ, who faced his death on a cross for us with similar words. With blood-tinged drops of sweat upon his brow, Jesus prayed, "Father, if you are willing, remove this cup from me. Nevertheless, not my will, but yours, be done" (Luke 22:42).

How great was Abraham's joy upon the mount. He named it for what had happened there, calling the place "The LORD will provide." We look back with greater joy to another mount, where another Lamb was slain in our place, and we name it "The Lord has provided." Therefore, whenever God tests our faith, whenever he imposes his sovereign rights, we remember that he is a God who has purchased for us a free salvation, a full forgiveness, a costly redemption at the price of his own Son's life. As Peter Lewis wrote: "The faith of Abraham may inspire us but it is the faith of Jesus that saves us, the Son who 'humbled himself and became obedient unto death—even death on a cross' (Phil. 2:8). There is no atonement on Moriah but on Golgotha there is a once-for-all and perfect sacrifice for sin; it was what was done *there* that saves Abraham and Isaac and you and me."[7] It saves us, that is, if we turn to that Father and to his Son in faith, eager to receive what he has promised and willing to obey his Word, because we have come to know his love and trust his grace.

7. Peter Lewis, *God's Hall of Fame* (Ross-shire, U.K.: Christian Focus, 1999), 86.

45

FAITH TRUSTING GOD'S PLAN

Hebrews 11:20–22

*By faith Isaac invoked future blessings on Jacob and Esau. By
faith Jacob, when dying, blessed each of the sons of Joseph, bowing
in worship over the head of his staff. By faith Joseph, at the end of
his life, made mention of the exodus of the Israelites and gave
directions concerning his bones. (Heb. 11:20–22)*

hen God came to Abraham, he entered into covenant not only
with this one man, but also with all the generations that were
to come through Abraham: "I will establish my covenant
between me and you and your offspring after you throughout their generations for an everlasting covenant, to be God to you and to your offspring
after you" (Gen. 17:7). Therefore, when the record of Hebrews 11 moves past
Abraham, we do not encounter just random individuals, but the generations that came from him. Verses 20–22 consider the faith of the heirs of the
three generations that followed: Isaac, Jacob, and Joseph.

God not only made covenant with Abraham, but through promises and
prophecies he also revealed much of his plan to him:

> Behold, my covenant is with you, and you shall be the father of a multitude of nations. No longer shall your name be called Abram, but your name shall be Abraham, for I have made you the father of a multitude of nations. I will make you exceedingly fruitful, and I will make you into nations, and kings shall come from you. . . . And I will give to you and to your offspring after you the land of your sojournings, all the land of Canaan, for an everlasting possession, and I will be their God. (Gen. 17:4–8)

God also gave this particularly clear prophecy to Abraham: "Know for certain that your offspring will be sojourners in a land that is not theirs and will be servants there, and they will be afflicted for four hundred years. But I will bring judgment on the nation that they serve, and afterward they shall come out with great possessions . . . they shall come back here in the fourth generation" (Gen. 15:13–16).

For the men we will study in this chapter those events were still future; they lived in the shadow of God's plan, revealed through promises and prophecies. Despite all their difficulties and weakness, they trusted God and responded in faith to the plan he had revealed. The apostle Paul tells us that God has a plan according to which he "works all things according to the counsel of his will" (Eph. 1:11). In Ephesians 3:10–11 he adds that this eternal purpose is accomplished in Jesus Christ and is for the praise of the glory and wisdom of God. In the midst of the dangers and uncertainties of their world—a world essentially like our own—Isaac, Jacob, and Joseph realized something of God's plan and put their trust in him.

THREE PORTRAITS OF RIPENED FAITH

Having given a great deal of attention to Abraham, the writer of Hebrews summarizes the faith of three patriarchs who followed: Isaac his son, Jacob his grandson, and Joseph his great-grandson. To summarize their faith, he looks at each of these three at the end of their lives, offering portraits of ripened faith that confirm the statement made in Hebrews 11:13: "These all died in faith."

First we view Isaac, the child of promise born to Abraham and Sarah, who, though the younger half-brother of Ishmael, received the covenant blessing. When Abraham died, the Lord came to Isaac to confirm the covenant with him: "To you and to your offspring I will give all these lands, and I will establish the oath that I swore to Abraham your father. I will multiply your offspring as the stars of heaven and will give to your offspring all these lands. And in your offspring all the nations of the earth shall be blessed" (Gen. 26:3–4). This is a recapitulation of the promise God had made to Abraham before him.

As we read the account of Isaac in the Book of Genesis, he does not come across as the boldest man of faith. His life was mostly uneventful, while God blessed him richly. Most of the biblical material about him concerns the passing on of the blessing to his sons Jacob and Esau. This is what the writer of Hebrews focuses on in verse 20: "By faith Isaac invoked future blessings on Jacob and Esau."

Genesis 25 tells of the birth of these twin boys, Esau the older and Jacob the younger. They were born in answer to Isaac and Rebekah's prayer for her barrenness. During her pregnancy the Lord informed Rebekah that the younger son would receive the blessing (v. 23), so they knew from the start this much of God's plan. However, Isaac preferred Esau. Genesis 25:28 tells us in unflattering terms that Isaac liked him better because Esau was a skillful hunter and Isaac "had a taste for wild game" (NIV).

In one of the Bible's more famous episodes, Jacob tricked his aged and blind father Isaac into giving him the blessing instead of Esau. In this manner, the prophecy God had given was fulfilled and God's plan was upheld. Isaac had told Esau to kill some game and prepare his favorite dish, after which he would give him the blessing. But at his mother's urging, Jacob went to Isaac in his place, having covered himself with animal skins to present the feel and smell of Esau and having brought a meal like the one his father wanted. Isaac therefore gave Jacob the blessing he had intended for Jacob's twin.

When Esau returned to find that Jacob had stolen the blessing, he begged his father to undo what had happened. "Bless me, even me also, O father!" Esau cried (Gen. 27:34). But Isaac, apparently recognizing the working of God's plan, knew he could not undo what had been done. In giving such blessing as he had left to give, he informed Esau that he would indeed serve his younger brother. Some blessing! Apparently the writer of Hebrews has in mind this response to God's providential control when he writes, "By faith Isaac invoked future blessings on Jacob and Esau."

The Bible's account moves from Isaac to Jacob, and he too presents a less than sterling life-history. What Jacob did to gain his father's blessing became a life pattern. He tricked his father to steal Esau's blessing, and he went on to trick his father-in-law Laban out of great flocks in order to make himself rich. Jacob's grasping tendencies did not truly bless him, for with each self-reliant achievement he had to flee the anger of those whom he had wronged. Finally, this pattern brought him to the end of his prodigious mental resources. Beside the Jabbok River, God wrestled Jacob into submission, and the grasper was made a man of faith (see Gen. 32). God changed his name from Jacob to Israel, and thereafter he was a model believer. Hebrews 11:21 tells us about the end of his life, saying, "By faith Jacob, when dying, blessed each of the sons of Joseph, bowing in worship over the head of his staff."

Just as Isaac had blessed his sons Jacob and Esau, the time came for Jacob to pass on his blessing to the next generation. Years after the dramatic events by which Jacob was wrestled to faith, Jacob and his family had come to Egypt during a famine. After the amazing sequence of events recorded in Genesis 37–42, Joseph was serving in Egypt as prime minister to Pharaoh. Genesis 48 tells us of Jacob giving Joseph the blessing of the firstborn, and then passing on his blessing to Joseph's two sons, Manasseh and Ephraim.

Hebrews 11:21 really tells of two different episodes: the giving of the blessing and Jacob's request that Joseph promise to have him buried in the land of his fathers, a request we are told was made as he worshiped God while leaning on his staff. "Do not bury me in Egypt," he said, "but when I rest with my fathers, carry me out of Egypt and bury me where they are buried." "I will do as you say," Joseph answered. "'Swear to me,' he said. Then Joseph swore to him, and Israel worshiped as he leaned on the top of his staff" (Gen. 47:29–31 NIV).

This picture of Jacob worshiping God as he leaned on his staff, near the end of his strength, presents a beautiful picture of faith. It was fitting for Jacob to make this request in this way, for the staff was the sign of Jacob's pilgrimage. William Lane writes, "Jacob's final act of worship, leaning upon the top of his staff, was characteristic for one who lived his life as a stranger and a sojourner." We see why the writer of Hebrews chose this passage to summarize Jacob's life as a pilgrim believer "who, in the face of death, lays claim to the future through the exercise of faith in the realization of the promises of God."[1]

---

1. William L. Lane, *Hebrews 9–13* (Dallas: Word Books, 1991), 365.

Finally, we have Joseph, who by faith "at the end of his life, made mention of the exodus of the Israelites and gave directions concerning his bones" (Heb. 11:22). Out of all the exciting events of Joseph's life this seems a strange summary, but it fits the approach of viewing the patriarchs' faith at the time of death. Joseph's story is well known: betrayed by his brothers, he ended up a slave in Egypt. Trusting God, he was ultimately delivered and raised up to be prime minister to Pharaoh, with great power and wealth. When a famine struck Canaan, the family arrived as refugees, only to find their long-lost brother as the keeper of Egypt's grain. Jacob, who had mistakenly thought Joseph dead, rejoiced, and the covenant family came for what would turn out to be a very long stay in Egypt.

Earlier, we considered God's prophecy to Abraham, telling him of the events that were now transpiring in Egypt. His descendants would be aliens in another land, enslaved and mistreated for four hundred years, after which God would deliver them in a great exodus (Gen. 15:12–16). We know that this prophecy stayed in the family, because Joseph was aware of it and trusted what God had revealed about his plan. Therefore, as his own death approached, he exhorted the others to believe the promise of deliverance, and directed that his remains be taken out of Egypt when the exodus took place. Despite the fact that his palaces and great riches were all in Egypt, and even though his great achievements were there—the earthly monuments to his wisdom and skill in saving the nation from famine—Joseph knew that his future lay with the promises of God. To show this, and no doubt to encourage generations of enslaved Israelites about the exodus to come, Joseph directed that his bones be taken for burial in the tomb of Abraham and Isaac and Jacob in the Promised Land. If he could not live there in life, then he would go there in death, trusting in the God of the promise. John Calvin writes: "The fact that wealth, luxuries, and honours did not lead the holy man to forget the promise nor hold him back in Egypt, is a strong argument for faith."[2]

Faith Trusting God's Plan

These three brief descriptions, and the Genesis records to which they point, exemplify everything we have seen in this chapter on faith. Hebrews

2. John Calvin, *New Testament Commentaries*, 12 vols. (Grand Rapids: Eerdmans, 1994), 12:175.

11:1 says, "Now faith is the assurance of things hoped for, the conviction of things not seen." Surely this is what we find in the record of Isaac, Jacob, and Joseph, who trusted in things unseen, spiritual realities made tangible to them only by faith. Their faith *was* focused on spiritual realities. It was rooted not in things of this world, but in the things of heaven. In verses 9–10 the writer includes these patriarchs in the great statement about Abraham's faith: "By faith he went to live in the land of promise, as in a foreign land, living in tents with Isaac and Jacob, heirs with him of the same promise. For he was looking forward to the city that has foundations, whose designer and builder is God."

These three family members had varied experiences. But they all were looking to God for spiritual blessings while they lived like pilgrims in this world. In this way, they demonstrated that their citizenship was in heaven, and they each showed a concern to pass on a spiritual inheritance to their children. We will be diligent to do the same if we possess the same faith.

The faith of these men was first spiritual, but second, it was forward-looking, as the passing of the blessing demonstrates. None of these men experienced the fulfillment of the promises when they died, but were looking ahead to what God would do in the future. This is why they took the passing on of God's blessing so seriously. Isaac died believing that God's plan would play out through his descendants, ultimately leading to his own salvation in the coming of the Messiah. Joseph, especially, grounded his hope in a tangible understanding that though he was forced to live and serve in a foreign land, in the future God would provide a home for him, even in death.

Hebrews 11 also emphasizes how faith handles the prospect of death, and this is a third feature of the patriarchs' faith. It is obvious that these men trusted in God's resurrection, for they faced death with a calm serenity, Jacob worshiping God while resting on his staff. It is always a mark of Christian faith to approach death with a peace that comes from God. Christian poetry and hymnody abound in expressions of trust in God in the face of death, and of death as the entrance into life eternal, as in the lines of this Christian poem:

The pale horse stands and will not bide,
    the night has come and I must ride;
but not alone to unknown lands,

my Friend goes with me, holding hands.
I've fought the fight; I've run the race;
   I now shall see him face to face,
who called me to him long ago
   and bade me trust and follow. . . .
I'll mount and ride, no more to roam,
   the pale horse bears me to my home.[3]

Fourth and finally, the faith of all three patriarchs was firmly fixed upon the Word of God, and therefore upon the plan God revealed through it. They received God's revelation in faith, and in his plan they saw that they were joined to his grand redemptive purpose, stretching back in history through Abraham and those before him, and reaching forward toward eternity future. They saw that by the grace of God they played a part in that plan, and that they were links connecting others to God's true Promised Land. In the promises and prophecies of God's Word, they saw the substance of things to come just as we must, and they knew how to face the present as well as the future, which is what faith does for the believer.

God's Unfailing Plan

If understanding God's plan was essential to these patriarchs, and if they are spoken of in Hebrews 11 as models for our faith, then the plan of God must be of great importance to every Christian. Abraham and his descendants knew some things about what God had in store, and what they knew, they trusted. We have the whole Bible, which tells us far more, and what we have we too must trust.

The Bible shows that God's plan centers on the work of Jesus Christ for the salvation of sinners. It is in Christ that these promises to Abraham have come true. The apostle Paul tells us that Jesus was the heir to whom all of Abraham's descendants pointed, the One in whom all God's promises are secured for us (Gal. 3:14–16). In 2 Corinthians 1:20 he says, "For all the promises of God find their Yes in [Christ]." Therefore, Paul says to believers, "Set your minds on things that are above, not on things that are on earth" (Col. 3:2).

---

3. John Powis Smith, cited in Martyn Lloyd-Jones, *The Life of Joy* (Grand Rapids: Baker, 1989), 103–4.

God's plan for history centered on the coming of Jesus Christ to bear the sin of the world and then to work a new principle into history through the faith of those who trust in him. That plan continues even now as the gospel is preached and lived out, as men and women come to faith, as parents pass faith on to their children. God's plan will continue until it culminates in the return of Christ in power, the judgment of all people, and the consummation of all things to the glory of God. This is what the plan of God is all about, as we are told in the Scriptures.

But the Bible also makes plain that God has a plan for individual people. Perhaps the statement of God's plan that is best known to believers comes from Jeremiah 29:11, where God said to the generation in exile: "For I know the plans I have for you, declares the LORD, plans for wholeness and not for evil, to give you a future and a hope."

Our passage in Hebrews 11 makes clear three things about God's plan, as Peter Lewis explains in his study of these verses. First, God's plan cannot be manipulated. The patriarchs knew a great deal of information about their future, yet that did not give them control over future events. Isaac illustrates this best. He wanted to give Esau the blessing, even though he knew God had foretold that it would go to Jacob. When he was old and blind, Isaac arranged to bless Esau, but the blessing was not Isaac's to give or to manipulate. Jacob's trickery in gaining the blessing may not commend him as an example of piety, but it does show God's ability to implement his own plan.

One reason we cannot manipulate God's will is that we cannot discern it except as he has spoken in his Word. As Isaiah says, "'For my thoughts are not your thoughts, neither are your ways my ways, declares the LORD'" (Isa. 55:8). Or as Paul said in his famous doxology: "How unsearchable are his judgments and how inscrutable his ways! 'For who has known the mind of the Lord, or who has been his counselor?'" (Rom. 11:33–34). Some people spend their time trying to figure out the details of God's plan, seeking to decipher things such as the exact timing of Christ's second coming. But given the information of the Old Testament, we could not have even figured out his first coming! The Messiah was to be born in Bethlehem, he was to be called a Nazarene, and he was to come out of Egypt. Who could make sense of that except the God who planned it?

If we know that God has a plan, but we cannot predict the future, what are we to do? We are to submit to God's Word. We are to trust and obey, step by step as God leads us through this world; like the pilgrims, we are on our long journey home.

The second point Peter Lewis makes from this passage is that God's plan cannot be taken for granted. Whenever we think we are sure of what God has in store for us, we are likely to be surprised. Joseph learned this lesson when he brought his two sons before Jacob to receive his blessing. Genesis 48 tells us how Joseph brought them before his father and carefully placed the older son, Manasseh, by Jacob's right hand, and Ephraim, the younger, by his left. The Bible describes what happened then: "But Israel reached out his right hand and put it on Ephraim's head, though he was the younger, and crossing his arms, he put his left hand on Manasseh's head, even though Manasseh was the firstborn" (v. 14 NIV). When Joseph saw his father's right hand on his younger son Ephraim, he protested, "Not this way, my father; since this one is the firstborn, put your right hand on his head" (v. 18). But Jacob refused, and his crossed arms provide a firm reminder that we cannot assume God's plan or take it for granted.

This means that we can expect to be surprised by God, and that we must keep our eyes focused on him always. He will start things in unexpected places, do things through unexpected people, all to show that he is the One who is orchestrating a plan that works according to his own secret will. How often it glorifies God to work in contrary ways, contradicting normal expectations. He takes the chief of sinners and persecutor of the church, Saul of Tarsus, and makes him Paul, the great apostle of grace. He takes a sin-obsessed monk like Martin Luther and through him returns the gospel to the church. Today he makes Christianity burn brightest in poor, downtrodden places in Asia or Africa. It glorifies God to work at cross-purposes to the wisdom of the world. He is "the God who gives life to the dead and calls into existence the things that do not exist" (Rom. 4:17).

Jacob's crossed arms remind us that God's plan is not subject to human standards and conventions. In the logic of the ancient world, the oldest son always received the chief blessing, but God operates differently. Indeed, none of the three figures in our passage were the oldest according to the flesh (that is, by birth). Isaac, Jacob, and Joseph were all younger sons, but they were also the ones who received God's blessing. They received their position according to grace, by faith, and this is how God operates in the world. Therefore, Philip Hughes rightly concludes, "The will of God cannot be forced into conformity with human patterns and preconceptions. His power manifests itself precisely within the sphere of human weakness. . . . The line of promise is not the line of the flesh but the line of faith."[4]

We all have plans. I have a plan for my life, and God has a plan for my life, and I need to realize that his plan is different from mine! My plan is one that goes forward in a straight line, each work building on another, small successes leading to large ones. My plan calls for achievement and blessing and worldly comfort. But though I have a plan, I can be sure that God's is different. He takes my plan, edits it with sorrows and failures and weaknesses, and gives it back to me one trial at a time. We cannot know what God has in store, except that we will receive trials and tribulations, all of which are overcome by faith. We cannot take God's plan for granted, but we may trust him implicitly. We cannot know what tomorrow brings, but we know the God who brings it. This is why Jesus warned us not to take our own plans too seriously:

> Therefore I tell you, do not be anxious about your life, what you will eat or what you will drink, nor about your body, what you will put on. Is not life more than food, and the body more than clothing? Look at the birds of the air: they neither sow nor reap nor gather into barns, and yet your heavenly Father feeds them. Are you not of more value than they? And which of you by being anxious can add a single hour to his span of life . . . O you of little faith? Therefore do not be anxious, saying, "What shall we eat?" or "What shall we drink?" or "What shall we wear?" For the Gentiles seek after all these things, and your heavenly Father knows that you need them all. But seek first the kingdom of God and his righteousness, and all these things will be added to you. (Matt. 6:25–33)

God's plan cannot be manipulated, and we must not take it for granted. But, third, this passage shows us that God's plan cannot fail. Isaac was a weak man, Jacob was a cheat, and Joseph was a victim. Yet through these three

---

4. Philip E. Hughes, *A Commentary on the Epistle to the Hebrews* (Grand Rapids: Eerdmans, 1977), 487.

generations God steadily wove his plan toward the end he had designed. Into Egypt went his people, right on his schedule. Isaac sought to give the blessing to Esau, but God's plan overruled; Joseph lined up his sons before his father, only to watch Jacob cross his arms. Years later Pharaoh would determine to hold Israel in slavery, yet God's people would carry out Joseph's body in the exodus. Nothing can change or thwart God's will and plan. "I am God, and there is no other," he says. "I am God, and there is none like me, declaring the end from the beginning and from ancient times things not yet done, saying, 'My counsel shall stand, and I will accomplish all my purpose'" (Isa. 46:9–10).

This means that we must not judge God's intentions by the appearance of our circumstances. God is working according to his plan, for the good of those who trust him. Peter Lewis writes, "One thousand years with him is like a day. Like Joseph we can be sure of God's future and therefore of our future for these are one in Jesus Christ. That future may seem less substantial than the present but it will be real and glorious when the pyramids of Egypt are dust and the empires of men forgotten."[5]

Of one thing we may be perfectly sure: Jesus Christ reigns now upon the throne of heaven, and history is leading to his exaltation as Lord of lords. "Worthy is the Lamb who was slain," sings the eternal choir, "to receive power and wealth and wisdom and might and honor and glory and blessing!" (Rev. 5:12). This is history's certain end, that "at the name of Jesus every knee should bow, in heaven and on earth and under the earth, and every tongue confess that Jesus Christ is Lord, to the glory of God the Father" (Phil. 2:10–11).

History has a revealed end in the exaltation of Christ. But history also has a central point, a fulcrum on which it turns, namely, that God's Son came and lived and died for us upon the cross. History is about him; it is "his story." Therefore, one thing is sure: God's plan leads us either to life through faith in Christ or death in condemnation for those who reject his name.

Finally, the certainty of God's plan tells us what we really need to know now, that we are to serve him who is the Lord of that great plan. We are to put God's Word into practice in our lives, bearing testimony to Jesus Christ,

---

5. Peter Lewis, *God's Hall of Fame* (Ross-shire, U.K.: Christian Focus, 1999), 94.

who shows us God's plan fulfilled. "I am making all things new," he says (Rev. 21:5). "It is done! I am the Alpha and the Omega, the beginning and the end. To the thirsty I will give from the spring of the water of life without payment. The one who conquers will have this heritage, and I will be his God and he will be my son" (Rev. 21:6–7).

46

FAITH CHOOSING GOD

Hebrews 11:23–26

By faith Moses, when he was born, was hidden for three months by his parents, because they saw that the child was beautiful, and they were not afraid of the king's edict. By faith Moses, when he was grown up, refused to be called the son of Pharaoh's daughter, choosing rather to be mistreated with the people of God than to enjoy the fleeting pleasures of sin. He considered the reproach of Christ greater wealth than the treasures of Egypt, for he was look-ing to the reward. (Heb. 11:23–26)

Undoubtedly the two most prominent figures of the Old Testa-ment are Abraham and Moses. It is no surprise, then, that when the writer of Hebrews turns to the Old Testament for models of faith, he dwells longest on these two great men. Hebrews 11 tells us five things that Abraham did by faith, and when it turns to the life of Moses, there are also five statements that begin "by faith." The account of Moses starts by telling us of his parents' faith, and ends with the faith of the generation that followed Moses. Like all of us, his faith was the product of others' influence on him, and his mark was made in the faith of those he influenced for the Lord.

The faith of Moses was particularly useful for the author's purpose, since the grand design of the Letter to the Hebrews is to persuade Jewish Christians not to abandon Christ for Moses. Moses, the author shows us, aligned himself with Christ, even in disgrace, and if people really wanted to follow Moses' example, they would have to do so as Christians and not as Jews.

MOSES' CHOICE

Faith will always make itself known through its choices, and Moses is commended here for a choice he made. "By faith Moses, when he was born, was hidden for three months by his parents, because they saw that the child was beautiful, and they were not afraid of the king's edict. By faith Moses, when he was grown up, refused to be called the son of Pharaoh's daughter, choosing rather to be mistreated with the people of God than to enjoy the fleeting pleasures of sin. He considered the reproach of Christ greater wealth than the treasures of Egypt, for he was looking to the reward" (Heb. 11:24–26). This seems to refer to an incident that took place when Moses was forty years old (see Acts 7:23). Exodus 2:11–12 tells us that he took the side of the Israelites against the Egyptians, thus forfeiting his status as son of Pharaoh's daughter: "One day, when Moses had grown up, he went out to his people and looked on their burdens, and he saw an Egyptian beating a Hebrew, one of his people. He looked this way and that, and seeing no one, he struck down the Egyptian and hid him in the sand."

Moses' story is well known. Pharaoh, fearing the growing numbers of the Israelites, had decreed that all Hebrew baby boys be killed. So after he was born, Moses' Hebrew parents concealed him in a basket, which they cast drift upon the Nile, trusting their baby to the Lord's care rather than letting him be killed by Pharaoh's soldiers. As a result of God's providential working, Moses was found by Pharaoh's daughter and raised in the royal household. Stephen summarizes the advantages this brought: "Moses was instructed in all the wisdom of the Egyptians, and he was mighty in his words and deeds" (Acts 7:22).

As he came to maturity, it seems that Moses realized he had a choice before him, one that would determine his destiny. The choice was straightforward: would he identify himself with the Hebrew slaves or their Egyptian masters? This is the kind of choice faith demands, and it involves both a yes and a no.

People today want to make everything yes; if you say no, you are narrow and negative. But Moses knew that a yes required a no. He said yes to his identity as an Israelite, as a son of Abraham and a follower of Yahweh, and very deliberately said no to his status as a prince of Egypt, a son of Pharaoh's daughter, and a servant to the gods of the Nile.

Consider all that Moses left by siding with the people of God. First, he left worldly honor and power behind. He "refused to be called the son of Pharaoh's daughter" (Heb. 11:24). According to some traditions, Pharaoh had no sons of his own, and so Moses stood in line to ascend the throne. This is possible but not certain. What *is* certain is that he was aligned with the royal house in an age when royalty stood next to divinity. Phenomenal power and exaltation were his if he would retain his position in Pharaoh's house. Second, he turned his back on the pleasures of sin, which are always available to such a high person, and which it seems were part and parcel of life in Pharaoh's court. Third, he turned his back on "the treasures of Egypt," which we know were vast beyond human reckoning.

That is an enormous amount to give up, so it must have been something very attractive that took Moses' eye off those things! Moses gave it all up for two things: first, for the privilege of mistreatment with the people of God, and second, to share in the disgrace of Christ. This is the choice Moses made. Charles Spurgeon says to him:

> O Moses, if you must needs join with Israel there is no present reward for you; you have nothing to gain but all to lose; you must do it out of pure principle, out of love to God, out of a full persuasion of the truth, for the tribes have no honors or wealth to bestow. You will receive affliction, and that is all. You will be called a fool, and people will think they have good reason for so doing.[1]

What an advertisement that is for Christianity! But it is a substantially true one! People will often try to evangelize others with promises of how wonderful it is to be a Christian. But Moses presents a truer picture. To be a Christian you must give up the world to embrace the cross. Once a teacher came to Jesus offering to follow wherever he went. Jesus replied, "Foxes have

---

1. Charles Haddon Spurgeon, "Moses' Decision," in *Metropolitan Tabernacle Pulpit*, 63 vols. (Pasadena Tex.: Pilgrim Publications, 1971), 18:427.

holes, and birds of the air have nests, but the Son of Man has nowhere to lay his head" (Matt. 8:20). He exhorted his disciples to count the cost of following him, saying, "Any one of you who does not renounce all that he has cannot be my disciple" (Luke 14:33). Moses' choice is the choice all must make who would follow Jesus: the pleasures and treasures of Egypt or affliction with the people of God and fellowship in the cross of Christ.

But our present loss does not go uncompensated: it gains spiritual peace now and untold riches later. Moses' choice cost him honor with men but brought him honor with God and, as our passage shows, a name that will be praised forever. As one scholar puts it, "Whatever Moses' social position if he had remained on as a member of Egyptian society all we would know of him now would be as a name on a mummy in the British Museum."[2] But instead we find his name in the hall of God's own beloved heroes.

MOSES' FAITH

What is it that causes a man to make a choice like this? Our passage tells us it was "by faith" that Moses chose reproach over power and Israel over Egypt. When people encounter a choice like Moses', they often ascribe it other motives, yet there are no other motives that credibly explain what he did.

For instance, we might think it was blood loyalty that forced Moses' choice. But blood is hardly thick enough to go from prince to slave. Nor does the Bible give this as Moses' motive. Well, then, it may have been a quirk in his character, an eccentricity that led him to choose so ridiculously. But everything points in the other direction: Moses was a man of distinction among the Egyptians, a man of respect among the rulers. Perhaps, then, it was a sudden enthusiasm; perhaps he heard some fiery preacher and became idealistic for a time. But having forty years afterward to consider what he did, Moses never repented or regretted his choice. What, then, can account for a man making a choice like that Moses made? The only answer is faith.

What was it that Moses believed? Mainly, he believed that the Israelites, though enslaved, were the people of God. He understood that the Egyptians, though wielding power and enjoying wealth, were in opposition to the true

---

2. G. A. F. Knight, cited in Peter Lewis, *God's Hall of Fame* (Ross-shire, U.K.: Christian Focus, 1999), 102.

God. Their pleasures were sinful ones and Israel's afflictions were holy ones. Surely this means that he knew Israel's God, Yahweh, to be the true God, and the many gods of the Nile to be empty idols. If this was true, he knew it was better to be one of God's people, even in a state of affliction.

Where, we might ask, did such faith come from? The first answer is provided in our text: it came from his parents. Verse 23 summarizes their trust in the Lord: "By faith Moses, when he was born, was hidden for three months by his parents, because they saw that the child was beautiful, and they were not afraid of the king's edict."

Pharaoh had ordered the murder of Hebrew baby boys, so Moses' parents, Amram and Jochebed, hid him for three months after his birth, not fearing Pharaoh's decree. Verse 23 says they did this because they saw he was "no ordinary child." The Greek text says they saw that he was "beautiful." In some way, they looked at Moses and saw that he was special, and thus determined to risk themselves to save his life. Amram and Jochebed were motivated by something more than normal paternal love; they had faith that the Lord had given them a special child.

According to the Jewish historian Josephus, Amram had received a dream in which he was told that this child would deliver Israel. If that is true, it is consistent with what the Old Testament shows of other notable births, such as that of Jacob, and later of Samson and Samuel, and ultimately of Jesus Christ. At the very least, Moses' parents saw in the striking beauty of their son a sign of divine grace that motivated them to take their stand. Hebrews 11:23 says it was by faith that they guarded him, and it was surely by faith that they later sent their newborn into the Nile, where he was discovered by Pharaoh's daughter.

One detail lends credence to the idea that Moses' parents knew he was born to be a deliverer and that they later told him. In Acts 7:25 Stephen speaks of Moses' murder of the Egyptian and says: "He supposed that his brothers would understand that God was giving them salvation by his hand, but they did not understand." Moses' choice to take a stand with Israel, therefore, was at least partly motivated by his knowledge of his calling as deliverer.

Moses got his faith the old-fashioned way: from his parents. He got it from what they taught him about the Lord and his covenant with Israel and his promises of a land and a multitude of seed. He got it, most especially, from their example of faith. The very thing that Moses is commended for in verse 27, that he did not fear the king's anger, is first ascribed to his parents. This is how we pass on the faith to our children: by our words, but more pointedly by our actions. Children are either hardened by the hypocrisy of their parents, or like Moses they are inspired by the consistency between word and deed. If we are unforgiving with our children and show an unwillingness to admit our sins, then we communicate a lack of grace to them. If we spend all our money on ourselves, begrudging the church and those in need, or if we speak harshly of people, seeming to rejoice in their failures and follies, then we communicate a religion other than that of Christianity. But when we are quick to repent and ready to forgive, when we trust the Lord for our own provision and give freely to others, and when we speak graciously of other sinners—to list just a few practical applications—we show our children our belief in a God who is merciful and kind and mighty to save.

Even in Pharaoh's household, Moses' faith was strengthened by the providence of God. One of the great problems of state in that day was the problem of the Hebrew slaves. That was why Pharaoh tried to kill Moses and his generation of babies, because in keeping with God's promise to Abraham they were increasing like the sands on the seashore. The Book of Exodus begins with the problem that confronted the Egyptians, as described by Pharaoh himself: "Behold, the people of Israel are too many and too mighty for us. Come, let us deal shrewdly with them, lest they multiply, and, if war breaks out, they join our enemies and fight against us and escape from the land" (Ex. 1:9–10).

How many times Moses must have heard of this problem in the schools and palaces of Pharaoh. He may have attended seminars on "the Israelite problem," with tips on how to oppress and afflict them, all qualified with the fact that nothing seemed to keep them down. Moses must have thought about the things his parents taught him, that the true God was with the people of Israel, that he had promised them great increase, and what is more, that he had promised them a home in a land of promise. This, too, is how parents pass on faith to their children: by teaching them to think biblically about the world and their times.

Because of his parents' faith, Moses grew up conscious of his own identity and believing the promises of the Lord to the afflicted people of Israel.

They gave Moses that which is most needful to any child: faith in the Lord. It was "by faith" that Moses chose to be identified with the people of God.

Faith's Calculation

We have seen a number of examples in Hebrews 11 of the relationship between faith and works. Faith always works, as we saw in the example of Noah. Noah's belief that the flood was coming caused his axe to chop down trees and his hammer to build the ark. Abraham believed God's promise, and so he offered Isaac, as God commanded. Moses, too, had faith, and his faith "reckoned," that is, it made calculations and they led to his actions.

Moses' action was the result of faith's calculation. Verse 25 says, "he chose," and verse 26 tells us why: "he considered." According to faith's calculation, Moses "considered the reproach of Christ greater wealth than the treasures of Egypt, for he was looking to the reward." Moses is yet another example of the principle of Hebrews 11:6, that faith believes God rewards those who earnestly seek after him. Moses wanted what was best, as we all do, and according to the calculation of faith he chose present affliction over pleasure, the disgrace of Christ over the treasures of Egypt. He put these side by side, and by faith he reckoned contrary to sight, considering the one as greater than the other.

Moses looked upon the honor of being the son of Pharaoh's daughter, and by faith he saw that this distinction meant apostasy from God. To be Pharaoh's daughter, even if it meant gaining the throne and crown of Egypt, meant losing his status as an Israelite, and therefore losing the covenant with God. So by faith Moses reckoned that he was choosing between Pharaoh, a king, and Yahweh, the one true God. On the basis of that calculation he made his choice.

Likewise, he looked on the carnal pleasures of Pharaoh's court. J. C. Ryle comments: "Faith told Moses that worldly pleasures were 'pleasures of sin.' They were mingled with sin, they led on to sin, they were ruinous to the soul, and displeasing to God. It would be small comfort to have pleasure while God was against him. Better suffer and obey God, than be at ease and sin."[3] Reckoning that way, he was willing to give up a life of pleasure. The same is

3. J. C. Ryle: *Holiness* (Darlington, U.K.: Evangelical Press, 1979), 138.

true of the vast treasures that would be his as an Egyptian prince. They were worldly treasures, temporary treasures, of no account compared to the spiritual and eternal riches that come through faith in God.

Many will look upon Moses' choice and cry, "What a fool! To have all that—honor, power, pleasure, wealth—and throw it away! These are the very things vast multitudes spend their lives seeking to gain only a portion of! And here Moses throws it all away! What folly! What a tragedy!" What would Moses say to all that? I think he would say two words from verse 26 in our text: "of Egypt." What treasures did he cast away? They were treasures that he knew, treasures of Egypt which he then compared to the riches of God. Then Moses would have added two more words from verse 25: "fleeting pleasures." The pleasures of sin he rejected would last only for a short time. Or, as Spurgeon put it, they were "for a season." He speaks for Moses when he hears a bell ringing in the air behind those words: "Did you hear the tolling of a bell? It was a knell. It spoke of a new-made grave. This is the knell of earthly joy—'For a season!' Honoured for doing wrong—'For a season!' Merry in evil company—'For a season!' Prosperous through a compromise—'For a season!' What after that season? Death and judgment."[4]

This is how Moses' faith made its calculation, and once we accept his principle we do not marvel at his choice. What did faith tell him but that there was a reward in heaven that far outweighed any treasure of Egypt? As Paul said, "For I consider that the sufferings of this present time are not worth comparing with the glory that is to be revealed to us" (Rom. 8:18). Faith showed Moses a crown that does not fade, a glory that shines with heaven's light. And faith showed Moses how to reckon the afflictions of God's people. J. C. Ryle puts it this way:

> Faith told Moses that affliction and suffering were not real evils. They were the school of God, in which He trains the children of grace for glory; the medicines which are needful to purify our corrupt wills; the furnace which must burn away our dross; the knife which must cut the ties that bind us to the world. . . .
>
> Marvel not that he refused greatness, riches and pleasure. He looked far forward. He saw with the eye of faith kingdoms crumbling into dust, riches making to themselves wings and fleeing away, pleasures leading on to death

4. Spurgeon, "Moses: His Faith and Decision," in *Metropolitan Tabernacle Pulpit*, 34:359.

and judgment, and Christ only and His little flock enduring for ever. . . . He saw with the eye of faith affliction lasting but for a moment, reproach rolled away, and ending in everlasting honour, and the despised people of God reigning as kings with Christ in glory.[5]

This is what faith showed Moses as he looked upon the kingdoms of this world, upon the pleasures and treasures of the Nile. I wonder what your faith sees as you look around you. Do you see things here that you must have? Do you see things now that you must enjoy? Do you see the affliction of God's people and turn away, the reproach of Christ of which you want no part? Then you see with different eyes, a different faith than Moses did, and you shall have a different reward.

Moses might have thought very differently, and few would have objected. He might have thought that to spurn the love of his adoptive mother was surely an evil thing. But instead he knew that God is greater than any mother or father or lover or friend; when there was a choice to be made, he had to choose for God. Or he might have listened to the thought that by remaining an Egyptian, by suppressing his convictions, by concealing his allegiance, he could do more good than he could by leaving. He might have been like those who stay where they have no business, like Lot sitting in Sodom's gate. This is the myth of influence that afflicts so many out-of-place believers today. "It is true that I am allied with unbelief, with injustice, with evil," they say, "but it is worth the good that I can do." Moses did not rationalize this way. He might have thought of the example of Joseph before him, who stayed in Pharaoh's court, though Joseph was able to do so without participating in sin or without apostasy. But Moses knew his situation was different, his times were different, and his conscience cried against the thought of association with evil.

Sometimes believers are called to serve in worldly courts. Obadiah rescued the prophets as chamberlain to wicked King Ahab, but he served there in great fear and at the daily risk of his life. Daniel served the king of Babylon—not in honor and wealth and pleasures of sin, but in the den of lions and with his heart daily turned toward Jerusalem. Some believers may be called to serve and aid the Pharaohs of this world. The choice facing Chris-

5. Ryle, *Holiness,* 139.

501

tians is not always as stark as the one before Moses, since Pharaoh represented an explicitly idolatrous enterprise. The organizations Christian serve (and may even lead) today will vary in the godliness of their ends and means. Like Moses, every believer will have to ask whether he or she is honoring God or betraying him, compromising with sin or restraining it, and serving his neighbor or exploiting his fellow man. Christ calls his followers to be salt in the world—and this requires most Christians to work in worldly institutions—but he then warns them against losing their own saltiness in the process (Matt. 5:13). In Moses' case—knowing his times and his own heart—his faith called him to take a sacrificial stand against the world and for the Lord.

Moses might have sought a compromise to avoid so costly a choice, such an unpleasant decision and costly separation. He might have been Moses the Israelite in the court of Pharaoh. But surely he knew that if the Lord is God, he must serve him and not the gods of Egypt. If the Hebrews were his people, then he must not wear Egyptian colors. If affliction as a slave was his calling, then he must not seek pleasure and honor. This was Moses' calling for Moses' own situation. But let us realize how greatly his way of thinking cuts across the grain of our own relativistic age, our age of tolerance, and our age of easy belief, of yes and no together. To Moses' everlasting credit, for him there was no half-hearted allegiance, no faint commitment, no looking back upon the city of sinful pleasure. He knew what James would later say, that God will not reward the double-minded man (James 1:8). By faith Moses chose "to be mistreated with the people of God than to enjoy the fleeting pleasures of sin. He considered the reproach of Christ greater wealth than the treasures of Egypt, for he was looking to the reward" (Heb. 11:25–26).

"WITH CHRIST"

Consider the remarkable statement that Moses shared "the reproach of Christ." In what sense can we say that Moses believed on Jesus, who came so many centuries later? This is an important point for the writer of Hebrews, since it was his design to motivate his Jewish-Christian readers to follow Moses' example of suffering for the name of Christ.

There are a couple of ways we might think of Moses looking to Christ, the first of which recognizes the parallel in this passage between the people of God and Christ himself. In Hebrews 11:26 mistreatment with God's people is seen as essentially the same as disgrace for Christ's sake. Perhaps the writer of Hebrews had in mind Psalm 89:50–51, which says, "Remember, O Lord, the reproach of Thy servants . . . with which Thine enemies have reproached, O LORD, with which they have reproached the footsteps of Thine anointed" (NASB). "Anointed" is what *Christ* means, and in the psalm it is applied not to Jesus specifically but to the people of God.

Moses did not choose affliction as such, but rather affliction "with the people of God." And what a difference those few words make: the difference between sorrow and joy, between loss and the greatest gain. Spurgeon writes, "'Affliction' nobody would choose; but 'affliction with the people of God,' ah! that is another business altogether. . . . Affliction with the people of God is affliction in glorious company. . . . 'With the people of God': that is the sweet which kills the bitter of affliction."[6]

"With the people of God" is where you always want to be, because that is where God is working with a purpose for good. That is where true wonders are seen, where saving grace is found, where flowers bloom in the desert, where a river flows that makes glad the city of God, either in blessing or affliction. To the mind of faith, "with the people of God" is always the place to be, where we belong, and where we will be so far as we are able to choose. If need be, we will be with the people of God as slaves in Egypt, so that we might also be with them as God's royal children in glory forever.

This is one way of looking at Moses' sharing in disgrace, but for the writer of Hebrews the "Christ" unquestionably means the Lord Jesus Christ. His point is that Moses' faith was faith in Jesus. This is something plainly stated in the Gospels. When Nathanael brought his brother Philip to meet Jesus, he did so with these words: "We have found him of whom Moses in the Law and also the prophets wrote, Jesus of Nazareth, the son of Joseph" (John 1:45). Later, Jesus said to the Jews, "If you believed Moses, you would believe me; for he wrote of me" (John 5:46). And on the mount of transfiguration, who was standing with Christ and Elijah, appearing in glory and speaking about the cross to come, but Moses (Luke 9:30)! Much, or even most, of what

6. Spurgeon, "Moses: His Faith and Decision," 357–58.

Moses came to know about Jesus came after his decision to leave the house of Pharaoh. But this much he surely knew: that God would send a Savior to bring a kingdom. By faith, he also knew that before the crown there lay a cross.

Moses' disgrace was one with that of Christ. It fit the pattern that Christ would later perfect in obedience and suffering. "He knew that the prizes of earth were contemptible compared with the ultimate reward of God"[7]—and that is the way of Christ, the way of fellowship in his sufferings. "Blessed are you," Jesus said, "when others revile you and persecute you and utter all kinds of evil against you falsely on my account. Rejoice and be glad, for your reward is great in heaven" (Matt. 5:11–12). This is the choice that Moses made and the reward that he sought. Thus he could say along with Paul in Philippians 3:8, "I count everything as loss because of the surpassing worth of knowing Christ Jesus my Lord. For his sake I have suffered the loss of all things and count them as rubbish, in order that I may gain Christ."

This is a choice that each of us must make, and faith will make it wisely. Jesus said, "Everyone who acknowledges me before men, I also will acknowledge before my Father who is in heaven" (Matt. 10:32). Acknowledging Christ is always costly; it means not just yes to him, but also yes to the affliction of his people, and yes to his disgrace before the world. And it brings a no as well, for Jesus also said: "Whoever does not take his cross and follow me is not worthy of me. Whoever finds his life will lose it, and whoever loses his life for my sake will find it" (Matt. 10:38–39). Both the yes and the no of faith in Christ will be richly rewarded, for in Christ there is greater wealth than all the treasures of this Egyptian world.

---

7. William Barclay, *The Letter to the Hebrews* (Louisville: Westminster/John Knox, 1976), 157.

47

FAITH PASSING THROUGH

Hebrews 11:27–29

By faith he left Egypt, not being afraid of the anger of the king, for
he endured as seeing him who is invisible. By faith he kept the
Passover and sprinkled the blood, so that the Destroyer of the
firstborn might not touch them. By faith the people crossed the
Red Sea as if on dry land, but the Egyptians, when they
attempted to do the same, were drowned. (Heb. 11:27–29)

ebrews appeals to a number of Old Testament examples, some positive and others negative. Chief among the negative examples is the generation that left Egypt in the exodus. The writer of Hebrews dwelt on them in chapters 3 and 4, repeatedly referring to their complaints and rebellions. His main text there was Psalm 95, which warned later generations against such unbelief: "Today, if you hear his voice, do not harden your hearts as in the rebellion, on the day of testing in the wilderness" (Ps. 95:7–8; Heb. 3:7–8).

The exodus is the great event of the Old Testament and the dominant New Testament paradigm for Christian salvation. Now, in Hebrews 11, the author's record of faith brings us to the time of Moses and the generation he led out of Egypt. Despite their many failures and rebellions, that generation did perform one great act of faith: the exodus itself and the passage through the Red Sea.

The focus of these verses, however, is on Moses himself, the leader of God's people in the exodus. His example shows that godly leadership is made courageous by faith, and that such leadership is able to reproduce its faith in the lives of others.

FROM FEAR TO FAITH

Hebrews 11:27 presents an exegetical problem having to do with Moses leaving Egypt. Verse 27 says, "By faith he left Egypt, not being afraid of the anger of the king, for he endured as seeing him who is invisible." The question is: to which of Moses' departures does this refer? Is it his first departure, after he had killed the Egyptian overseer (Ex. 2:15), or the much later departure in the actual exodus (Ex. 12:33–51)?

An initial reading suggests the earlier departure, since this keeps the verses in historical sequence. The chief problem is that this seems to contradict the Old Testament record. Exodus 2:14 explicitly says that Moses was afraid, and verse 15 shows him "fleeing" from Pharaoh. Hebrews, however, says he did not fear the king's anger when he fled, and for this reason many commentators insist that this must refer to the later occasion. Among these are John Calvin, John Owen, and B. F. Westcott. According to their view, this must refer to the time of the exodus, when Moses so courageously stood before Pharaoh and sent the plagues from God.

This assessment also has problems, however. First, if verse 27 refers to the exodus, it is out of order with verse 28, which mentions the keeping of the Passover. The writer of Hebrews has been following a straightforward historical progression, which now would be broken.

A second problem is far more serious. Why did the writer of Hebrews go out of his way to make the point about Moses not fearing Pharaoh? There is no reason to mention Moses' lack of fear in reference to the exodus, since by then Pharaoh and the Egyptians were pleading for the Israelites to leave. But, if this refers to the earlier departure, we see very well why the writer of Hebrews mentions it. Given the importance of Moses' faith to the overall argument of this letter, the writer would seek to explain the statement of Moses' fear in Exodus 2:14. Yes, the Exodus account says Moses was afraid, but, he clarifies, we should not think it was fear of Pharaoh; his leaving then was by faith, since he knew that God had called him to deliver the people. True, Moses' abortive attempt to free the people had failed; and, yes, Moses became afraid, but his faith in God overcame his fear and he left to await the Lord.

Following this reasoning, verse 27 likely refers to the earlier departure, when Moses was forty years old, and therefore serves as a fitting conclusion to what was said in verses 25 and 26. Five statements in this record of Moses begin with the words "by faith," and together they chronicle his life and ministry. By faith his parents hid him; by faith he chose God's people over Pharaoh's house; by faith he left Egypt for Midian; by faith he kept the Passover (which sums up the whole period of his return as deliverer); and by faith he led the people through the Red Sea waters.

This interpretation of verse 27 cannot be certain, but we can be sure of the writer's point in this verse. Remember that this letter was written to Jewish Christians undergoing the presence or at least the threat of persecution. If the setting was Rome, and persecution from Caesar could be avoided by renouncing Christ and returning to Judaism, then there was a striking parallel between Moses' experience and their own. The writer of Hebrews is therefore using this example to make the point that fear must be met with faith. This is a strong theme in the Moses account. We are told that his parents hid him because "they were not afraid of the king's edict" (v. 23). Now Moses left Egypt, not fearing the king's anger but "seeing him who is invisible." Likewise, these Christians must not shrink back in the hour of their trial. In the face of Caesar's persecution, a king not at all unlike Pharaoh, they must stand firm in their faith in God.

How was it that Moses stood firm, and that the Jewish Christians could expect to do the same? The answer is given at the end of verse 27: "he endured as seeing him who is invisible." This is always how God's people triumph over threatening circumstances. It was how David defeated Goliath. The giant mocked young David, but he replied, "You come to me with a sword and with a spear and with a javelin, but I come to you in the name of the LORD of hosts" (1 Sam. 17:45). This is how Daniel's three friends stood firm before the king of Babylon, even to the point of being cast into the blazing furnace. They saw their Lord, invisible to sight but evident to faith. When the king saw them untouched amidst the flames, he cried out, amazed that a fourth figure who looked like God was with them (Dan. 3:25). This was also how Moses faced his early failure, his impulse to flee rather than fight, and his long decades waiting God's timing as he lived in the desert. The New Testament statement of this principle is given by Paul in 2 Corinthians 5:7: "We walk by faith, not by sight."

A great Christian example comes from the Scottish Reformer John Knox. When asked how he could so boldly confront the Roman Catholic queen, Knox replied, "One does not fear the Queen of Scotland when he has been on his knees before the King of Kings." It is said that Napoleon would sometimes call his generals in one by one before a great battle to gaze on them without speaking and let them look upon his face. In a similar way, the man or woman of frequent communion with God in prayer and in his Word will see his face in the midst of the fight, thereby finding courage and a strong incentive to faith.

FAITH KEEPING GOD'S WORD

The statement that Moses "saw him who is invisible" may be pointing to the burning bush, the awesome and pivotal event when Moses first saw God. The emphasis, however, seems to be on a continuing spiritual perception. This is fully in keeping with the point of this chapter, that faith is "the conviction of things not seen" (v. 1). Moses was sure of God's promise, and therefore certain of the future. He left Egypt awaiting God's timing for that future to be made real.

Undoubtedly, the years of waiting were longer than Moses thought possible—forty years in all, as Acts 7:23 tells us. Initially the change of scenery might have been refreshing, but ten years and advancing age would have tried Moses' faith. As the ten years turned to twenty, and then thirty, and finally forty, his confidence must have drained away, his sense of calling all but vanished into a dim if not bitter memory. Yet God was working with a purpose in his life, until the time had come for Moses to go back. Peter Lewis comments:

> Moses had to learn to be a servant not a master, a prophet not a prince, the friend of God not of Pharaoh. And so God stripped him of his advantages

and began his apprenticeship in spiritual leadership.... Moses spent his first forty years becoming a somebody, then his second forty years becoming a nobody and then God could use him.... It was an apprenticeship in faith.[1]

Moses, no doubt impressed by the burning bush and the dramatic calling to return as Israel's deliverer, went back knowing that his leadership must be marked by faith, for it was faith that gave him endurance for those long and difficult years. Exodus 4 to 10 shows his bold confrontation with Egypt's king, in which he delivered one plague after another against unbelieving Pharaoh. Hebrews 11:28 points to the end of this drama, the tenth and final plague on the firstborn. God had said to Moses: "One plague more I will bring upon Pharaoh and upon Egypt. Afterward he will let you go from here. ... About midnight I will go out in the midst of Egypt, and every firstborn in the land of Egypt shall die, from the firstborn of Pharaoh who sits on his throne, even to the firstborn of the slave girl who is behind the hand mill, and all the firstborn of the cattle" (Ex. 11:1, 4–5).

Thus was celebrated the first Passover, which verse 28 refers to as an incident of great faith by Moses. God told Moses the Israelites were to sacrifice a lamb without defect and to spread its blood on the doorframe of their houses. The angel of death, seeing the blood, would pass over and the terrible plague would not visit them (Ex. 12:1–13). This was done under Moses' direction, and Israel was thus spared, while loud laments filled the homes of Egypt.

There are a number of ways we see Moses' faith at work here. First, the various plagues pitted the visible gods of Egypt against the invisible God who stood behind Moses. One after one, the Egyptian idols were disgraced in the plagues: Hapi, god of the Nile, Hekht the frog, Amen Ra the sun god. These and the other Egyptian gods were mocked by the various plagues God sent: the plague of blood in the river, the plague of frogs, the plague of darkness, and so on. Moses feared not a god fashioned out of visible materials, but the unseen and true God. Moses believed the Word of the Lord, and he and his people were saved. But Pharaoh hardened his heart, and by his unbelief he and his people were broken.

---

1. Peter Lewis, *God's Hall of Fame* (Ross-shire, U.K.: Christian Focus, 1999), 105.

It is unclear how well Moses perceived the significance of the first Passover. He was told that the blood of the lamb would cause the destroyer angel to pass over, and probably without fully understanding, he nonetheless acted out of faith. This seems to be the main point of this verse, that Moses by faith acted in careful observance of what God had said. Therefore, when we put verses 27 and 28 together, we see a clear contrast. Faith does not fear or listen to the world, to its powers and rulers, but faith does fear and listen to God, carefully obeying all his Word. Moses kept God's Word, just as he was told, and in this manner he and countless others were saved from the wrath of God. The same is true for everyone who hears God's Word and believes.

THE PASSOVER LAMB

Another way verse 28 speaks of great faith has to do with the blood of the lamb. We can imagine the thoughts of the Egyptians when the Israelites brought the lambs into their homes, then killed them and spread the blood around their doorposts. They were familiar with animal sacrifices, but as the Book of Hebrews has pointed out in 10:1–4, the Israelites must have realized that the blood of a helpless animal was no protection, no real help against what was coming. It was the eyes of faith that saw another, greater sacrifice, one that is necessary because of our sin and that protects us forever from the holy wrath of God.

Regardless of how well Moses' generation understood the full meaning of the Passover lamb, the connection would have been quite clear to the original Christian readers of this letter. To them the point would be made that they must be saved the same way Moses was. God's wrath will come upon the city of man, and it will certainly fall on their godless oppressors. But if they wanted to escape the death that such judgment brings, they like Moses must be found secure under the blood of Jesus Christ. Philip Hughes explains the connection:

> As the Passover lamb was required to be perfect and unblemished and its sacrifice was the moment of the people's moving from bondage to liberty, so Christ is the fulfillment of all that was symbolized by this event: he is "the Lamb of God" (Jn. 1:29, 36), "our paschal lamb" (1 Cor. 5:7), whose

precious redeeming blood is "like that of a lamb without blemish or spot" (1 Pet. 1:19), and who through his death has destroyed the power of the devil, our spiritual Pharaoh, and delivered us from lifelong bondage (Heb. 2:14).[2]

This being the case, faith's most important act is to lay hold of Christ as Lamb of God to remove our sin and preserve us against the coming of God's sure and holy wrath. Hughes quotes John Chrysostom, who long ago said:

> If the blood of a lamb then preserved the Jews unhurt in the midst of the Egyptians and in the presence of so great a destruction, much more will the blood of Christ save us, for whom it has been sprinkled not on our doorposts but on our souls. For even now the destroyer is still moving around in the depth of night; but let us be armed with Christ's sacrifice, since God has brought us out from Egypt, from darkness and from idolatry.[3]

It was this that Moses laid hold of by faith in the Passover lamb's blood. Therefore, if these Jewish Christians were to fall back on to Moses from Christ, from the new covenant back to the old, they would be abandoning that by which Moses himself was saved: his faith in Christ's work for salvation.

FAITH PASSING THROUGH

Verse 29 concludes the account of Moses and his generation by speaking of their departure from the land of Egypt: "By faith the people passed through the Red Sea as on dry land; but when the Egyptians tried to do so, they were drowned" (NIV).

This account is well known. After the plague of the firstborn, Pharaoh and all the Egyptians insisted on Israel's departure, even supplying them with great riches for the journey. Yet Pharaoh's heart was hardened once again, and he chased after them with his chariots. The Israelites were horri-

---

2. Philip E. Hughes, *A Commentary on the Epistle to the Hebrews* (Grand Rapids: Eerdmans, 1977), 150.

3. Ibid., 151.

fied, and cried out against Moses that God was allowing their destruction. Then Moses gave his great reply, one that resounds all through the Bible, being echoed by the faithful in generations to come: "Fear not, stand firm, and see the salvation of the LORD, which he will work for you today. For the Egyptians whom you see today, you shall never see again. The LORD will fight for you, and you have only to be silent" (Ex. 14:13–14).

Given the fact that the Egyptians were bearing down from the rear, and that ahead of them lay the impassable Red Sea, this was quite a statement of faith. But Moses had learned that God's promise to deliver was certain of success. It was by faith that he exhorted the people, and God rewarded Moses with this response:

> Lift up your staff, and stretch out your hand over the sea and divide it, that the people of Israel may go through the sea on dry ground. And I will harden the hearts of the Egyptians so that they shall go in after them, and I will get glory over Pharaoh and all his host, his chariots, and his horsemen. And the Egyptians shall know that I am the LORD, when I have gotten glory over Pharaoh, his chariots, and his horsemen." (vv. 16–18)

Here was the point of no return, and though the people needed prodding, they stepped forward into the divided sea. Like many other believers, they saw no way of escape until God revealed it to the eyes of their faith.

This is one of the great pictures of God's salvation, a salvation by grace alone that nonetheless requires us to step forward in saving faith. This is the only way anyone ever is saved: God makes a way of escape from the raging fury of his wrath. It points us to Jesus Christ, who said, "I am the way, and the truth, and the life" (John 14:6). Just as Moses' staff parted the waves, so Christ Jesus was lifted up "that whoever believes in him may have eternal life" (John 3:14–15).

John of Damascus, writing in the eighth century, used this example of God's saving grace as an incentive to Christian praise:

> Come, ye faithful, raise the strain
>   of triumphant gladness;
> God hath brought his Israel
>   into joy from sadness;
> loosed from Pharaoh's bitter yoke

Jacob's sons and daughters;
led them with unmoistened foot
through the Red Sea waters.[4]

Moses himself understood the Red Sea passage as a singular and epochal deliverance. Exodus 15 records his song to the Lord, a song that celebrates a sovereign grace and mighty salvation:

I will sing to the LORD, for he has triumphed gloriously;
the horse and his rider he has thrown into the sea.
The LORD is my strength and my song,
and he has become my salvation. . . .
The LORD will reign forever and ever. (vv. 1–2, 18)

That was the right conclusion, and the goal of the exodus, that God's people should praise him and rest their faith on his saving power that will protect them from every foe.

SALVATION BY FAITH

Moses was a pivotal figure in some of the most dramatic scenes in redemptive history. This makes him worthy of our study. First, we should consider Moses as a leader. The key aspect of Moses' leadership, as with all Christian leadership, was his faith. What, after all, do Christian leaders seek but to inspire and instill faith in others? Moses' success as a godly leader consisted not only in his own salvation but in passing his faith on to others.

Moses shows us the value of leadership that inspires faith. He was himself the recipient of that kind of inspiration. We saw this in Joseph, who ordered that his bones be taken up out of Egypt with the exodus, as an intentional reminder to his descendants of God's promise of deliverance. Moses remembered that promise, because when he left he took Joseph's bones; the patriarch's faith must have made a strong impression on him. Moses' parents also set a strong example of faith, and their impact was felt through the faith of their son, who led so many others out to their salvation. His exam-

4. John of Damascus, "Come, Ye Faithful, Raise the Strain," trans. John Mason Neale, 1853.

ple is an excellent reminder to every Christian leader along the lines of what Paul later wrote to Timothy: "Keep a close watch on yourself and on the teaching. Persist in this, for by so doing you will save both yourself and your hearers" (1 Tim. 4:16).

Second, we should reflect on the way faith served as the antidote to fear and danger. This is the main point of these verses in Hebrews 11. We have already noted that this passage corresponds powerfully to the original readers' situation as they were facing persecution. Moses, like his parents, set an example of fearless courage in the face of worldly power. But the greatest encouragement comes in verse 29, where we see God intervening for the sake of his people. John Owen rightly comments on the death of the Egyptians in the Red Sea: "When the oppressors of the church are nearest unto their own ruin they commonly rage most, and are most obstinate in their bloody persecutions. So it is at this day among the anti-Christian enemies of the church.... This destruction of the Egyptians, with the deliverance of Israel thereby, was a type and pledge of the victory and triumph which the church shall have over its anti-Christian adversaries."[5]

Third and finally, Moses' example makes very plain the difference between faith and unbelief. Unbelief fears the king, cringes before worldly powers, shrinks back from trouble and trial, caves in before pressure and opposition and danger. But the eyes of faith look upon this world with very different eyes. First of all, they see a God who is invisible. Others may not see God. Our employers may not see God, and may not consider the realities of God's justice in making decisions. Friends and neighbors and family members may not understand the choices Christians will make, simply because they are blind to the reality and glory of God. But faith sees God and delivers us from the fear of every other power. It should be our prayer for all those whom we know that God would open their eyes, even as we pray that we would see and know and act upon the presence of God in our lives. Seeing him drives out fear, for one mightier than Pharaoh is with us. As the writer of Hebrews will say in chapter 13: "For [God] has said, 'I will never leave you nor forsake you.' So we can confidently say, 'The Lord is my helper; I will not fear; what can man do to me?'" (vv. 5–6).

---

5. John Owen, *An Exposition of the Epistle to the Hebrews*, 7 vols. (Edinburgh: Banner of Truth, 1991), 7:174.

Faith allows us to look upon this world and see it the way God sees it. Ours is a world under judgment; as the destroyer of the firstborn once visited Egypt, so must God's holy wrath visit all the ungodly in the end. This is what the Red Sea waters symbolized: God's judgment pouring over his enemies, destroying them and casting them forever into a dark pit of death. The same waters that saved Israel destroyed the Egyptians, and this is what the New Testament says about the gospel, which it describes as a two-edged sword (Heb. 4:12; Rev. 1:16). To one it is a fragrance of life, but to another the fragrance of death (2 Cor. 2:16). This is what Peter said in his first epistle, where he referred to Christ as the cornerstone of God's spiritual temple. "Now to you who believe," he wrote, quoting the prophet Isaiah, "this stone is precious. But to those who do not believe . . . 'A stone that causes men to stumble and a rock that makes them fall'" (1 Peter 2:7–8 NIV). Here we see the difference between faith and unbelief in the gospel.

The Red Sea waters are an especially apt symbol of Christ's second coming, as were the waters of Noah's flood. Like the passing of God's people through the sea, Christ's coming will bring blessing on his people at the same time that it brings judgment on their enemies. As Paul wrote to another persecuted group of Christians, God will be vindicated in that day to come,

> when the Lord Jesus is revealed from heaven with his mighty angels in flaming fire, inflicting vengeance on those who do not know God and on those who do not obey the gospel of our Lord Jesus. They will suffer the punishment of eternal destruction, away from the presence of the Lord and from the glory of his might, when he comes on that day to be glorified in his saints, and to be marveled at among all who have believed, because our testimony to you was believed. (2 Thess. 1:7–10)

What a difference faith makes! Now it means the difference between fear and courageous perseverance, the very thing the early Christians needed and we so badly need today. But it will mean even more on that great day to come when the heavens part as the Red Sea once did, and Jesus comes back to bring salvation to those who trusted in him and judgment on the world that turned away. "Surely, I am coming soon," he says at the very end of the Bible. And all those who look to him in faith, afflicted in this world but not destroyed, cry out in reply, "Amen. Come, Lord Jesus" (Rev. 22:20).

48

FAITH CONQUERING

Hebrews 11:30–40

All these, though commended through their faith, did not receive
what was promised, since God had provided something better for
us, that apart from us they should not be made perfect.
(Heb. 11:39–40)

inally we come to the last Old Testament example of faith. The
verses that finish Hebrews 11 look back on the last verse of
Hebrews 10, where the writer says of these persecuted Christians, "But we are not of those who shrink back and are destroyed, but of
those who have faith and preserve their souls" (10:39). Salvation is by believing; failure to believe or shrinking back from faith because of hardship or
opposition leads to judgment and destruction. This is what motivated the
writer of Hebrews in all these studies of faith: not just interesting and encouraging tales, but a matter of eternal life or death. Now he briefly offers two
last examples—Joshua and Rahab—followed by a list of others whose faith
conquered and endured to the end.

THE WALLS FALL DOWN

Verse 30 points to a famous example of faith conquering through God's power, namely, the fall of Jericho under the godly leadership of Joshua. The writer of Hebrews moves forward forty years from his last example, pointedly skipping the rebellion of those who perished in the desert, whom he earlier employed as an example of unbelief. Forty years passed after the crossing of the Red Sea before finally God brought Israel to the Promised Land. Moses died at the age of 120, and Joshua son of Nun took over as Israel's leader. The Book of Joshua, which gives this account, begins with the transfer of authority. In a famous passage, God gave Joshua his charge to leadership and also to faith: "Be strong and courageous, for you shall cause this people to inherit the land that I swore to their fathers to give them. . . . Be strong and courageous. Do not be frightened, and do not be dismayed, for the LORD your God is with you wherever you go" (Josh. 1:6, 9).

Joshua's first challenge was to capture the fortress city of Jericho, which dominated the entrance into the land of Canaan, and it is for this that Hebrews 11:30 remembers his faith. Joshua's first action toward this objective was to send spies to reconnoiter the enemy position, and these spies would be the vehicles by which Rahab's name is joined to Joshua's.

Before the battle, Joshua encountered a mysterious figure who named himself as "the commander of the army of the LORD." Many identify him as the preincarnate Christ. First, he stated that the Lord had delivered Jericho into Joshua's hands. But then came instructions that must have seemed bizarre, to have the people simply march around the city for seven days, on the seventh day blowing trumpets, after which the walls would fall (Josh. 6:3–5). Joshua and the people under him did just as they were told and, just as God had said, when the trumpets sounded, the walls fell down and the Israelites put the city to the sword (Josh. 6:20–21).

Verse 30 memorializes this as a great moment in the record of faith: "By faith the walls of Jericho fell down after they had been encircled for seven days." This is faith trusting the promise of God and obeying carefully the commands he has given. Here we have perhaps the classic portrait of faith drawing forth the very power of God, and from it Christians have long drawn the conclusion John Chrysostom expressed in the ancient church: "Assuredly the sound of trumpets is unable to cast down stones, though one blow for ten thousand years, but faith can do all things."[1]

Coupled with Joshua's exploit is the faith of Rahab, a Canaanite prostitute: "By faith Rahab the prostitute did not perish with those who were disobedient, because she had given a friendly welcome to the spies" (Heb. 11:31). Before the battle, Joshua's spies had been detected by Jericho's leaders, and Rahab hid them at the risk of her life. One commentator says of her: "At the moment . . . there seemed not one chance in a million that the children of Israel could capture Jericho. These nomads from the desert had no artillery and no siege-engines. Yet Rahab believed—and staked her whole future on the belief that God would make the impossible possible."[2] Rahab explained why: "I know that the LORD has given you the land . . . we have heard how the LORD dried up the water of the Red Sea before you when you came out of Egypt . . . for the LORD your God, he is God in the heavens above and on the earth beneath" (Josh. 2:9–11). On the basis of that faith, Rahab asked the spies to guarantee her family's survival when the city was taken. She arranged to tie a scarlet cord in her window to mark her house. Although there is no evidence regarding what Rahab intended by the choice of color, Christian commentators have long understood the scarlet cord as a type of the atoning blood of Jesus. One of the church's earliest commentators, Clement of Rome, wrote that this sign foreshadowed "that through the blood of the Lord all who trust and hope in God shall have redemption" (1 Clem. 12:7).

Joshua and Rahab make quite a pair! In so many significant ways they were completely different. Joshua was a man, an Israelite, Moses' successor as Israel's leader, and the conqueror of Jericho. Rahab was a woman, a member of the cursed Amorite race, a prostitute, and a citizen of the condemned city. They had only one thing in common: they believed on the Lord and trusted his power to save. We look back centuries later and none of their differences seem to matter at all; what counts is their faith and the salvation they received by it.

---

1. Cited in Philip E. Hughes, *A Commentary on the Epistle to the Hebrews* (Grand Rapids: Eerdmans, 1977), 502.

2. William Barclay, *The Letter to the Hebrews* (Louisville: Westminster/John Knox, 1976), 161–62.

FAITH CONQUERING

At this point, it seems the writer of Hebrews looks where he is in his narrative, scans back over the vast biblical territory he has covered in this chapter, looks forward to all that he hopes to relate, and decides it is time for a change of strategy. It is comforting to know that I am not the only preacher whose ambitions are curbed by time constraints, and perhaps by the attention span of the audience! Verse 32 tells us, "And what more shall I say? I do not have time to tell about Gideon, Barak, Samson, Jephthah, David, Samuel, and the prophets" (NIV). Lacking time for these great tales of faith, the author merely mentions the names of their heroes and, in the remaining verses of this chapter, recounts some of the varied exploits of faith. His point is that the Old Testament is filled with accounts of faith, each of which is enough to inspire us to imitation. This final section may be divided into two categories: in verses 32–35a, we see faith conquering in success over obstacles, and in verses 35b–38 faith is shown conquering through perseverance in great suffering.

Let's begin by perusing this list of six great names. Gideon gave Israel victory over the Midianites with his force of just three hundred men. Obeying God's command, he armed them with torches in earthen jars; when the trumpets were blown they smashed the jars and God threw the enemy into a panic (see Judg. 7). Joined to his name is that of Barak, another leader from early in Judges. Spurred on by the prophetess Deborah, Barak led the united tribes in their victory against Sisera and the mighty Canaanite chariot army.

Next come Samson and Jephthah, also from the Book of Judges. Jephthah's foolish vow cost his daughter's life, but he too was a man of faith. Despite his beginning as an unwanted child and his later career as a bandit, through faith he led the tribes in battle against the Ammonites. Samson was hardly a paragon of virtue; he is particularly known for his fatal weakness for foreign women. Nonetheless, he belongs in this list of heroes of faith because of his one-man war against the Philistines, and especially for the way he ended his life, achieving by faith in his death what he had failed to do during his life because of unbelief.

Finally, we have two great heroes of the Old Testament, David the king and Samuel the prophet. Samuel's long career as judge and prophet was a crucial one, bridging the years of turmoil under the judges to the early monarchy he did so much to create. Even his birth tells a story of great faith, with his barren mother Hannah crying out to God for help and offering her child for the Lord's service. Without Samuel's faithful ministry, Israel would surely have fallen into disarray, the Philistines would have subjugated them, and David would have died an unknown shepherd.

The most recognizable name on this list is that of David, Israel's greatest king, "a man after [God's] own heart" (1 Sam. 13:14), who slew the giant Goliath by faith and whose career is one of the main Old Testament types for Jesus Christ. Although David was a very great sinner, he was also the quintessential Old Testament man of faith.

Having run through this list of names, the writer of Hebrews next turns to the mighty deeds that faith enabled these and others to do. The list is organized into three groups of three, starting in verse 33: "who through faith conquered kingdoms, enforced justice, obtained promises." The number of warriors on the list of names we just considered perhaps leads the writer to state first that by faith they "conquered kingdoms." Certainly this could be said of Joshua, David, and Solomon; indeed, victory in battle was probably the most common achievement produced by faith during this early period of Israel's history.

It is quite possible, however, to succeed in battle without faith in the Lord. Therefore, we read that these heroes "enforced justice" as well. The Greek literally says that they "established righteousness." This was certainly a hallmark of Israel's faithful judges and kings. They did not merely win battles, but they also served God by establishing his righteousness within their domains. This is always a mark of godly leadership, as was said of David: "David reigned over all Israel. And David administered justice and equity to all his people" (2 Sam. 8:15).

Because of faith, these believers "obtained promises." One of the stresses in this chapter is the point made in verse 39: "these, though commended through their faith, did not receive what was promised." This is also stated in verse 13, that Christian faith looks for promises that will not ultimately be fulfilled until heaven. But it is also the case that these heroes of faith did see many promises come true. Joshua saw the walls fall down; Rahab was saved from death; David was made king as promised; and so forth. Their experience encourages us that our faith in the great promises of the gospel will be fulfilled in God's timing just as their promises were.

The second trio of achievements runs from verse 33 to 34: they "stopped the mouths of lions, quenched the power of fire, escaped the edge of the sword." David and Samson both slew lions, but this seems to be about Daniel, who refused the king's edict to stop worshiping the Lord. When Daniel was thrown into the lions' den for punishment, God stopped the mouths of the lions and he emerged safe. His three friends Shadrach, Meshach, and Abednego similarly refused to obey a king's command to deny God. When they were thrown in the raging fire, God went with them. He protected them and they emerged safe. Surely the writer of Hebrews would encourage us to remember their great testimony of faith: "Our God whom we serve is able to deliver us from the burning fiery furnace, and he will deliver us out of your hand, O king. But if not, be it known to you, O king, that we will not serve your gods or worship the golden image that you have set up" (Dan. 3:17–18).

Verse 34 adds that others "were made strong out of weakness" through faith. Here Samson comes to mind, having forfeited his strength through folly but regaining it at the end through faith. This is a common biblical theme, but a notable example is Jehoshaphat, who "became mighty in war, put foreign armies to flight" (Heb. 11:34). When confronted by a vast enemy invader, Jehoshaphat stood before God in the assembly of the nation. Praising God for his might, he pointed out the threat of the invading armies and concluded, "O our God, will you not execute judgment on them? For we are powerless against this great horde that is coming against us. We do not know what to do, but our eyes are on you" (2 Chron. 20:12). The Scripture continues, "All Judah stood before the LORD, with their little ones, their wives, and their children" (2 Chron. 20:13). Jehoshaphat looked to God in his weakness and found strength. The Lord sent a prophet to reply to this great and godly king: "Do not be afraid and do not be dismayed at this great horde, for the battle is not yours but God's" (2 Chron. 20:14–15). If this is how God worked in times of old, it is also how we will find him working today if only we will look to him in the same kind of faith.

The writer of Hebrews completes his litany of achievement by saying, "Women received back their dead by resurrection" (Heb. 11:35). This statement speaks of two events, one from the ministry of Elijah and the other from Elisha. Elijah had sought shelter with the widow of Zarephath, a woman from pagan Sidon. She had trusted God by obeying the prophet's various commands, and through faith she received this miraculous display of God's blessing (1 Kings 17). In contrast to the widow of Zarephath, Elisha received help from a wealthy woman who had been unable to bear a child. God blessed her with a son, but when he subsequently died, she sought out the prophet to ask for God's intervention. Through her faith in Elisha's ministry, a ministry symbolic of Christ's, her son was restored to life (2 Kings 4).

The point of all this is that by faith God's people achieve what they never could have done otherwise. In openly miraculous ways, as well as in the more subtle and secret ways, the Lord puts his great power to work for those who trust in him. We might put this in the form of a question: How are we to overcome great obstacles? How do we who are so weak find the strength our circumstances require? What are we to do to overcome tragedies? The answer to all of these is the same. God's people are to have faith in him, finding deliverance and power and resurrection in the God we believe and trust.

Faith Enduring Suffering

If the account of faith were to stop right here, it might leave us with the dangerously false impression that faith keeps us from suffering in this world. This is the kind of thing we often hear today, that if we only have enough faith, we need never be sick or poor or troubled in any way. However, verses 35–38 refute such thinking, telling us about "others," that is, people who trusted God and yet were subjected to the greatest of trials. Theirs, however, was no less a triumphant faith, for it enabled them to honor God by faithfully enduring to the end: "Some were tortured, refusing to accept release, so that they might rise again to a better life. Others suffered mocking and flogging, and even chains and imprisonment. They were stoned, they were sawn in two, they were killed with the sword. They went about in skins of sheep and goats, destitute, afflicted, mistreated—of whom the world was not worthy—wandering about in deserts and mountains, and in dens and caves of the earth" (Heb. 11:35–38).

The first statement is a dramatic one, namely, that some of the faithful were tortured to death and refused to gain their deliverance by denying the faith. It is probable that the writer has the Maccabean martyrs in mind. These were the second century B.C. Jews who stood up to the Seleucid king Antiochus Epiphanes, who persecuted them by requiring them to eat swine flesh and sacrifice to Greek gods. A description in the apocryphal book of 2 Maccabees matches the particular Greek word for torture in our passage (*tympanizō*), one that means being stretched over a frame and beaten. The scene it depicts was well known in the author's time: the torture and murder of seven brothers in succession, each of whom refused to deny the Lord. The brutal tortures are graphically described and include scalping, mutilation, tearing out the tongue, and frying over the flames, most of which took place while they were stretched over the wheel of a catapult.

As our passage describes, these seven brothers accepted their deaths rather than renounce their faith, specifically because of their hope in a resurrection—a better one than experienced at the hands of Elijah and Elisha, which restored the dead only to this world, but a resurrection to eternal life in the world to come. One of the brothers spat out to his tormentors, "The King of the universe will raise us up to an everlasting renewal of life, because we have died for his laws" (2 Macc. 7:9). The last of the brothers to die confidently turned to the wicked king and assured him that his brothers, though dead, "after enduring their brief pain, now drink of ever-flowing life, by virtue of God's covenant" (see 2 Macc. 7:36).

This kind of sacrifice and fidelity is incomprehensible to the man who does not know God. But to the eyes of faith it is reckoned a fair bargain, however unpleasant, even a privilege and honor to suffer for God's sake. This is how another contemporary Jewish writing puts it: "The souls of the righteous are in the hand of God, and no torment will ever touch them. In the eyes of the foolish they seem to have died, and their departure was thought to be an affliction, and their going from us to be their destruction; but they are at peace. For though in the sight of men they were punished, their hope is full of immortality" (Wisdom of Solomon 3:1–4).

Hebrews 11:36 tells of those who were jeered and flogged, chained and put into prison. We might think of any number of prophets of whom this was true, as it was for our Lord Jesus. Verse 37 speaks of those who were stoned (as were many of the faithful and especially the prophets), or sawed in half (tradition holds that this was how the prophet Isaiah died at the hands of wicked king Manasseh), or put to death by the sword (as was the apostle James). "They went about in skins of sheep and goats, destitute, afflicted, mistreated ... wandering about in deserts and mountains, and in dens and caves of the earth" (Heb. 11:37–38). This may have the Maccabees in mind, for this is specifically said about them (1 Macc. 2:28; 2 Macc. 5:27, 10:6), although these things were also true of Elijah and Elisha.

Finally, we have this understatement: "of whom the world was not worthy" (Heb. 11:38). These men and women were thought unfit by the world because of their faith in God, when in reality this world—because of its unbelief—was not a fit place for them. "Therefore," Hebrews 11:16 tells us, "God is not ashamed to be called their God, for he has prepared for them a city." How well they remind us that, as the apostle John writes, "The world is passing away along with its desires, but whoever does the will of God abides forever" (1 John 2:17).

A PANORAMA OF FAITH

The visitors center at the Gettysburg battlefield presents a panorama depicting what took place there, a circular portrait within which an observer may stand to view the entire drama of the battle. Our writer has done the same thing for us in these verses. Here we stand within biblical history, among the heroes of faith, and we see what faith brings and what faith can do. What John said at the end of his first epistle would be a more than fitting inscription: "This is the victory that has overcome the world—our faith" (1 John 5:4).

We may draw four final conclusions about faith from this panorama. The first is that what matters is not the circumstances in which we find ourselves but our faith in God. It ought to be obvious that Christian faith does not guarantee us comfort in this world. Yes, God delivers some from trouble, but others he delivers in trouble. Faithful Elijah was spared Ahab's wrath, but numerous other faithful prophets died by his sword (1 Kings 19:10). Jeremiah escaped King Jehoiakim's hatred, but his fellow-prophet Uriah did not escape. If God sent an angel to break Peter's chains, he also allowed James, another of Christ's three closest disciples, to die at Herod's command. Understand, then, that God may place us on either of the two sides of this record: on the side of those who conquered in success or of those who conquered in defeat. What matters is not the circumstances—neither the blessing in this life, nor the trials. What matters is the faith by which we may conquer in all circumstances through the blood of Jesus Christ.

Second, faith suffices while we wait for God's promises to be fulfilled. Many blessings come to the Christian in this life, yet the great point of this entire chapter is the one found in verse 39: "And all these, though commended through their faith, did not receive what was promised." This is partly because the promises of God are beyond what can be received in this mortal existence. It is not in the flesh but in glory that we will be fit to receive what God has for us: "No eye has seen, nor ear heard, nor the heart of man imagined, what God has prepared for those who love him" (1 Cor. 2:9). Thus we are encouraged in our faith, knowing that just ahead lies an eternal weight of glory; beyond the cross there awaits a crown. What do we have while we wait, often in great difficulty? Faith suffices for the man or woman of God, for faith perceives and makes real the things that are yet unseen.

Third, and this is probably the main point the writer of Hebrews had for his original readers, times of trial especially demand faith. This letter was written to those tempted to fall back because of persecution. Earlier, the author reminded them of a time when their own heroes suffered some of the things recorded in this passage. It is only those who stand firm in faith, even in hardship, who are joined to this honor roll of salvation. Indeed, this is what trials do: they test and try our faith; they burn away the dross so that what is left is pure and glorious to God. Jonathan Edwards rightly comments: "The divine excellency of real Christianity is never exhibited with such advantage as when under the greatest trials; then it is that true faith appears much more precious than gold."[3]

In trials, we are encouraged by the knowledge of Christ's suffering for us and of the unbreakable bond created with him through our faith. This is why Paul could write, "Who shall separate us from the love of Christ? Shall tribulation, or distress, or persecution, or famine, or nakedness, or danger, or sword? As it is written, 'For your sake we are being killed all the day long; we are regarded as sheep to be slaughtered.' No, in all these things we are more than conquerors through him who loved us" (Rom. 8:35–37).

Fourth, and finally, let us remember that in the end, when all else is gone, what will matter is our faith. It is only through faith that we are saved. Look back over this list of names, and those associated with these descriptions, and think of the great variety there is among them. Some were Jews, others were not. Some were rich and others were poor. Some were men,

---

3. Jonathan Edwards, *The Religious Affections* (Edinburgh: Banner of Truth, 1961), 21–22.

some were women; some were loved, some were hated; some were successful, some were not. What is it, then, that puts their names on this blessed list of God's beloved? It is only one thing: faith. Someday we will look back and see how insignificant are so many things that we think so important now—our clothes, our cars, our houses, our reputations—just as we look back on the heroes of Hebrews 11 and realize that their faith is all that really mattered. With faith we gain Christ and his cross, the forgiveness of sin and life everlasting; without faith we are left to perish with the useless things of this world.

Are you rich? poor? popular? despised? Looked up to or looked down upon? What will it matter, compared to your faith? Labor, then, for eternal treasure through faith, which above all else is precious, because through faith your soul will be saved. The twentieth-century martyr Jim Elliot was right when he said: "He is no fool who gives what he cannot keep, to gain what he cannot lose."

This is the note on which our passage concludes: "All these [were] commended through their faith" (Heb. 11:39). Literally it says, "These were attested for their faith." In other words, their names are written here only because of their faith, and the same is true in the Book of Life in heaven, where their names are also found. It is only through faith in Christ that we are saved, and thus have our names recorded in the list of the redeemed. On the day of judgment this is all that will matter, and then indeed faith will be more precious than gold.

These men and women of faith died without receiving all that had been promised. Verse 40 concludes: "God had provided something better for us, that apart from us they should not be made perfect." The key word is "better." It is a key to the whole Book of Hebrews, which speaks of better things in Christ—a better plan, a better priest, a better covenant, a better sacrifice, better blood, a better home forever. These heroes of faith were waiting to see all these things that are better—things that can be seen only through faith in Jesus Christ. If these Old Testament saints could believe not seeing Christ—knowing only shadows and not the reality—not seeing with anything like our clarity the purchase price of our redemption by the cross—then how much more faith ought we to have than they, we who are called by his very name? Calvin writes, "A tiny spark of light led them to heaven, but now that the Sun of righteousness shines on us what excuse shall we offer if we still cling to the earth?"[4] Far from concluding from this great chapter that our circumstances make a smaller demand for faith, this argues that our greater privilege brings a greater responsibility. In light of the cross of Christ, this is how every believing heart must respond:

When I survey the wondrous cross
    on which the Prince of glory died,
my richest gain I count but loss,
    and pour contempt on all my pride.

Forbid it, Lord, that I should boast,
    save in the death of Christ my God:
all the vain things that charm me most,
    I sacrifice them to his blood. . . .

Were the whole realm of nature mine,
    that were a present far too small;
love so amazing, so divine,
    demands my soul, my life, my all.[5]

---

4. John Calvin, *New Testament Commentaries*, 12 vols. (Grand Rapids: Eerdmans, 1994), 12:185–86.
5. Isaac Watts, "When I Survey the Wondrous Cross," 1707, 1709.

49

FAITH FIXED ON JESUS

Hebrews 12:1–3

> *Therefore, since we are surrounded by so great a cloud of witnesses, let us also lay aside every weight, and sin which clings so closely, and let us run with endurance the race that is set before us, looking to Jesus, the founder and perfecter of our faith, who for the joy that was set before him endured the cross, despising the shame, and is seated at the right hand of the throne of God.*
> (Heb. 12:1–2)

*I*t has been rightly said that the story of our lives is only finished in the lives of other people, others we have loved and led, influenced and inspired. The same can be said of the great eleventh chapter of the Book of Hebrews, that it is only finished in the chapter that follows, in which the example of these heroes of the faith reaches out to us. The goal of chapter 11 was not mere history but exhortation. This is why chapter 12 begins with the key word "therefore," demanding that we deal with the implications of what we have learned, applying the lessons of faith to our own lives.

THE CONTEXT OF THE CHRISTIAN LIFE

There are four things we should notice from this passage, beginning with the context of the Christian life. It is often said that context is the key to interpretation, so the question is this: what is the context, what is the arena, in which you as a Christian should interpret your life? Do you think of yourself living in the midst of a secular society, with its testimony of materialism and sensuality and relativism? Or do you think of yourself as part of a particular corporation or organization with its own mandates to conformity? Do you think of yourself as part of the family in which you grew up, the neighborhood in which you live, a racial group, or a socio-economic class? However you answer, how you conceive of the context or arena of your life will dramatically shape your manner of living.

The writer of Hebrews suggests a far different context, namely, that Christians should think of themselves as "surrounded by a great cloud of witnesses" who bear testimony to faith in the Lord. If you are a believer, he says, this is the context in which you should see yourself. This is the body to which you belong, and whose approval you should court. This is the audience, as it were, before whom you live, a great arena filled with the beloved of God, the faithful of all ages, and now is the day when you are running your race to the sounds of their approval and encouragement.

This cloud of witnesses refers, of course, to the heroes of the faith presented in chapter 11: Noah, Abraham, Moses, and the others. Sometimes this is called the Westminster Abbey of biblical faith, comparing this chapter to the great church in England where so many of that nation's heroes are buried. But there is a great difference here, namely, that the writer of Hebrews does not see these as dead men to be remembered, but living witnesses to be heard. Though dead, they still live, and what was said of Abel can be said of them all: "Through his faith, though he died, he still speaks" (Heb. 11:4). John Owen writes, "All the saints of the Old Testament, as it were, stand looking on us in our striving, encouraging us unto our duty, and ready to testify unto our success with their applauses. They are placed about us unto this end; we are 'compassed' with them."[1]

---

1. John Owen, *An Exposition of the Epistle to the Hebrews*, 7 vols. (Edinburgh: Banner of Truth, 1991), 221.

This, then, is how you should conceive of your life. You belong to this noble company of God's people, living in this world but glorifying God through faith. This is the context of your life. You are surrounded by those with whom you will spend eternity, those who will be your brothers and sisters long after everyone else is consigned to judgment. You should hear their voices and conform to the pattern of their faith, not to the pattern of this world.

THE CALLING OF THE CHRISTIAN LIFE

This leads us to consider the calling of the Christian life. Verse 1 concludes by telling us that God has marked out a race for us. He has laid out a course for our lives. There are places we are to go, things we are to do, challenges we are to confront. We do not know where this course winds on its way to heaven, nor, frankly, is it important for us to know. Our calling is to "run with endurance the race that is set before us" (Heb. 12:1). Many Christians spend far too much effort trying to figure out what lies ahead, when our calling is to persevere in faith wherever God should lead us.

This metaphor of life as a race was common in ancient literature as well as in the Bible. Paul employs it in 1 Corinthians 9:24–25, where he tells Christians to "run in such a way as to get the prize . . . a crown that will last forever" (NIV). He describes his own life in similar terms, writing at the end of his life to his disciple Timothy: "I have fought the good fight, I have finished the race, I have kept the faith. Henceforth there is laid up for me the crown of righteousness" (2 Tim. 4:7–8).

The writer of Hebrews now applies the same terminology to us. First, he tells us that the stands are packed with the saints of old. He places them there not merely as spectators, but also as a cheering section. He tells us to pay attention to their testimony, to heed the encouragement they give us. There is Abel reminding us of the true sacrifice we are to trust. Out cries Noah that while the world is condemned there is an ark of salvation. Abraham cheers out for all who hope for promises yet unfulfilled, just the way he did for so many years in Canaan. Moses shouts out to those who, like him, must forfeit status and favor in the world, riches and rank, in order to follow the Lord. Their presence gives us the home-field advantage for our race, if only we will see them there by faith and hear their cries.

Earlier we saw that the context in which we envision ourselves has a great influence over our thinking, but how we conceive of our calling in life is even more vital. What is the purpose or goal of your life? Is it to attain a certain standard of wealth? Is it to rise to a position of influence and power? Is it to be popular or to enjoy maximum leisure and fun? These are the ways our unbelieving society defines success, but not how a Christian should think of his or her life.

How liberating it is for the Christian to realize that his or her true calling is the race of faith in the living God: to persevere in the various settings where God will place you, to hold fast your convictions and your obedience to God in different settings and seasons of life, to grow in grace and to glorify God through faith all the way to the end of your life. This is our victory: not worldly standards of success, but enduring in faith to the end.

This is not an easy calling, and just as if we were athletes training hard, the writer of Hebrews gives us training instructions: "Let us also lay aside every weight, and sin which clings so closely" (v. 1). He speaks here of two things, starting with weights or, as some versions put it, hindrances. In the ancient Greek games, a runner trained to make his body lean. Then, before the race began, he stripped off his long garments to run completely naked. The Greek word here for hindrances may be used in both of these ways: of excess body weight and of weighty garments. The writer of Hebrews tells us that anything that slows us down must be discarded if we are to run well.

This exhortation helps us with all sorts of decisions about our lives. People will say, "This is not technically a sin, so it must be all right for me." But here we read that anything that weighs you down, anything that hinders your spiritual progress, should be discarded. Perhaps it involves your lifestyle. For instance, many Christians today have bought into the entertainment culture, giving vast hours to mindless television, unwholesome literature, and objectionable movies. We should ask ourselves, "Is this a help or a hindrance to me spiritually?" Hindrances can be career ambitions, hobbies, associations and friendships, habits and preoccupations. Any of these may or may not be a problem, and it will vary from person to person. But each of us should look at the things in our lives and ask, "Is it a help? Is it a hindrance?" If it is the latter, then the wise believer will let the hindrance go, not wanting to be weighed down in the race.

When we turn to the matter of sin, the situation is far more serious. Hindrances weigh us down, but sin entangles our feet, possibly bringing us down to the ground. Notice how the writer puts it: "sin which clings so closely." The point is that sin entangles us. We take sin lightly at our great peril. Sin is deceitful, as we read in chapter 3, able to lead us off the path altogether. Therefore, we must be wise regarding sin, seeking grace from God to be free from actual sins that we know about, while shunning the temptations to sin that abound.

Think, for instance, how quickly and thoroughly a great man like King David fell into sin when he allowed his heart to lust after Bathsheba. How entangled he became, and what a horrible impact that sin had on his life and on his whole family, even the entire kingdom! He was running brilliantly, as almost no one had run before, but sin entangled him and took him down. Sexual sin and pride continue to entangle the feet of many today, including leaders in the church.

Therefore let us flee temptation and oppose all sin. Sin is the agent of death in our world; it is the master of untold slaves; sin is never profitable, and the pleasures it offers the unwise are all filled with deadly poison. Even true believers, whose debts are paid by the blood of the Lamb, can scarcely afford sin, for we have a race to run, a course marked out by God for these few short years of our lives, and unless we actively shun sin we will quickly find ourselves distracted and entangled.

This is our calling, the challenging race of a life of faith. Notice what kind of race we run. It is not a short sprint, and we will not finish it with a reckless burst of energy. It is a long-distance race, and our great virtue is not speed but perseverance. Many experience the flush of excitement at conversion, only to find that enthusiasm must be converted into endurance. What Jesus said to the church at Thyatira should be true for us as well: "I know your works, your love and faith and service and patient endurance" (Rev. 2:19).

THE ENCOURAGEMENT OF THE CHRISTIAN LIFE

This leads us to what I often call "the all-purpose Christian advice," from Hebrews 12:2, which gives the encouragement of the Christian life: I say this because there is no circumstance, no difficulty, no temptation for which this is not a reliable guide: "looking to Jesus." This is the "secret" of the Christian life, the encouragement we need for our faith: to place our eyes not on the world with its enticements and threats, not even on ourselves with our petty successes and many failures, but on him who is the source and fountain of all our spiritual vigor. John Owen writes:

> A constant view of the glory of Christ will revive our souls and cause our spiritual lives to flourish and thrive. . . . The more we behold the glory of Christ by faith now, the more spiritual and the more heavenly will be the state of our souls. The reason why the spiritual life in our souls decays and withers is because we fill our minds full of other things. . . . But when the mind is filled with thoughts of Christ and his glory, these things will be expelled. . . . This is how our spiritual life is revived.[2]

The writer of Hebrews has shown us the context of our life of faith, and the calling of our life of faith; now he sets before us the encouragement our faith requires: "looking to Jesus." There are three ways that this verse encourages us. First, it shows us Christ as the premier example for our faith. The Greek word translated as "founder" (*archēgos*) is better rendered "forerunner" or "pioneer." It describes one who goes ahead to blaze the trail and overcome barriers. Similarly, the word "perfecter" (*teleiōtēs*) connotes the idea that Jesus is the supreme and perfect example of faith, especially since the Greek text speaks of *the* faith rather than *our* faith.

It is noteworthy that this verse focuses on the ordeal of the cross, where Jesus' faith in God was put to the greatest test and given the most brilliant display. The religious authorities said of him on the cross, "He trusts in God" (Matt. 27:43). They were mocking him, yet how true it was. By faith Jesus pleased God as Enoch did. Like Abraham, Jesus looked forward to the city to come and, by faith, he was willing to make the supreme sacrifice. By faith Jesus, like Moses, set aside earthly glory that he might be numbered among the afflicted people of God and become their deliverer. By faith Jesus made the sacrifice Abel's faith presented. If the heroes of the Old Testament are lights testifying to faith in God, Jesus on the cross is a blazing sun bringing faith to its most dazzling expression.

2. John Owen, *The Glory of Christ* (Edinburgh: Banner of Truth, 1994), 167.

Jesus endured both suffering and shame on the cross. The Hebrew Christians were in danger of shrinking back from these very things, just as we find them so difficult to endure. It was by faith that Jesus "endured the cross, despising the shame," persevering to his appointed end and thus entering into his glory in heaven. He "is seated at the right hand of the throne of God," because he faithfully endured suffering and did not fear the world's contempt. This provides an example for us, that we would bear the cross in our own lives. First Peter 2:21 says, "To this you have been called, because Christ also suffered for you, leaving you an example, so that you might follow in his steps." How important, then, for us to fix our eyes upon him. James M. Boice wrote:

> The only thing that will ever get us moving along this path of self-denial and discipleship is fixing our eyes on Jesus and what he has done for us, coming to love him as a result, and thus wanting also to be with him both now and always. Jesus is our only possible model for self-denial. He is the very image of cross-bearing. And it is for love of him and a desire to be like him that we take up our cross and willingly follow him.[3]

Jesus is our example in perseverance, and also in spiritual joy: "for the joy that was set before him [he] endured the cross" (Heb. 12:2). That is an amazing statement and it says much about his faith. We may conceive of Jesus' joy before the cross in a number of ways. First, Jesus took joy in doing his Father's will. He said, "My food is to do the will of him who sent me and to accomplish his work" (John 4:34). William Newell writes, "There is no joy like the accomplishment of a noble task: and of the noblest task of all eternity, Christ was to say, 'I have finished it.'"[4]

Jesus also looked forward to his future reunion with the Father in heaven and to receiving his delight with the greatest of joy. He rejoiced at the knowledge of what his suffering and death would accomplish, namely, the redemption of a people for himself. In short, Jesus rejoiced because he saw the crown beyond the cross; he saw the purchase of his blood, even the church that would be his bride forever in the regenerated glory of the endless age to come. In the same vein, the apostle James writes to us, "Count it all joy, my

---

3. James M. Boice and Philip G. Ryken, *The Heart of the Cross* (Wheaton, Ill.: Crossway, 1999), 182.
4. William R. Newell, *Hebrews* (London: Oliphants, 1947), 403.

brothers, when you meet trials of various kinds, for you know that the testing of your faith produces steadfastness" (James 1:2–3). We should rejoice at trials, because by enduring we gain the crown that waits beyond the cross.

Jesus is not only the example for our faith, but he is also the object of our faith. He waits at the finish line for us; it is to him and for him that we run. We endure and persevere because we want to know him and join him and share the blessings of his salvation. This again explains why the cross is emphasized here, for the cross is not only the greatest example of Jesus' faith, but also the focus of our faith in him. We see his blood shed for our forgiveness; we see the wrath of God spent on him, and we find our safety there—our righteousness at his cross. To be a Christian, then, means to rely on his atoning blood, on his finished work for our salvation, and to hold this gospel as the great treasure of our heart. Henceforth we want to be faithful to him. We desire to please and serve him, and we would endure to the end so that we will spend eternity with him. This is what Paul says of his own ambition: "I press on to take hold of that for which Christ Jesus took hold of me. . . . One thing I do: Forgetting what is behind and straining toward what is ahead, I press on toward the goal to win the prize for which God has called me heavenward in Christ Jesus" (Phil. 3:12–14 NIV). We fix our eyes on Jesus because he is the example and object of our faith.

Third, we fix our eyes on Jesus because he is the source of our faith. It is in this sense that the translation "founder and perfecter of our faith" has real merit. Jesus is not merely an example, like some long-dead hero. Nor is he the object of our faith as a mere philosophical ideal. Rather, he is an active recipient of our faith, active in inspiring and empowering faith in us because he lives now. Faith in Christ produces union with a living Lord who reigns in the heavens, who is seated at the right hand of God's throne in power. Therefore, when we fix our eyes on him, he works in us by his power, sending God's Holy Spirit to sustain us in our trials. Thomas Watson says, "As the Spirit is at work in the heart, so is Christ at work in heaven. Christ is ever praying that the saint's grace may hold out. . . . That prayer which Christ made for Peter, was the copy of the prayer he now makes for believers. 'I have prayed for thee, that thy faith fail not' (Lk. 22:32). How can the children of such prayers perish?"[5]

---

5. Thomas Watson, *A Body of Divinity* (Edinburgh: Banner of Truth, 1958), 281.

This encouragement—"looking to Jesus"—is vitally important in such a difficult race as ours. Those who fix their gaze on the world and the things of the world will be conformed to its pattern. But in a still more powerful and reliable way, those whose gaze is fixed on Jesus will find themselves changed into his pattern—not merely because of the working of our own hearts, but because of his active and transforming work through the Holy Spirit. With our eyes fixed on him, we are, Paul says, "being transformed into [his] image from one degree of glory to another" (2 Cor. 3:18).

How essential it is that we grasp this principle! As Christians we live in the context of this great cloud of witnesses, with a race to run with endurance, a race that includes the suffering and shame of the cross. Therefore, we must remove every hindrance and entangling sin, for this is already more than the flesh can endure. Yet we are encouraged and empowered in our faith as we look to Jesus Christ, our great example of faith, the object of our faith, and the source of our faith, its author and finisher, as he reigns with power from on high in us and for us.

If you have never looked to Jesus in faith, if you have yet to enter this godly calling of those who follow him, this exhortation applies especially to you. Look to Jesus Christ, and you will find one who is altogether lovely, whose example of life and death transcends all others, and most important, who suffered death that you might be forgiven and have eternal life. Unless you look to Jesus in faith, you will never know the life that is of God, and though you may enjoy this world for a season, there will be no crown for you at the end, but only the judgment of God and the punishment your sins deserve.

A Cure for Weary Hearts

Lastly, we find in this passage a cure for weary hearts. This is what verse 3 says: "Consider him who endured from sinners such hostility against himself, so that you may not grow weary or fainthearted." Here the writer of Hebrews anticipates a problem and prescribes its cure.

This verse assumes something believers know all too well, namely, that from time to time Christians grow weary and become downcast. If you feel this way, you are not exceptional; this is something you should expect. Especially when faced with prolonged difficulty or trials, even the strongest

Christian can experience spiritual depression. The cure for this, he says, is to consider Jesus in his own struggle with the opposition of the world.

This may sound similar to the exhortation in verse 2 to fix our eyes on Jesus, but there is a difference in emphasis here. In verse 2 the Greek word *aphoraō* meant to look away from one thing to another; the emphasis was to keep looking away from distractions and to fix our eyes on Jesus. Here in verse 3 the writer uses a different word, *analogizomai*, which means "to consider intently." This is an accounting term related to the English word "logistics"; when we speak of "logging" something in, we mean that a record should be kept of what transpired. The point here is that we should meditate on or reflect on, take stock of Jesus' life and death as it relates to our own struggle, and especially remember how God ordained his suffering for his and our glory. We are to remember that beyond the cross there lies a crown; it was so for our Lord, and so it will be for us. As Paul writes, doing the very thing our text suggests, "I consider that the sufferings of this present time are not worth comparing with the glory that is to be revealed to us" (Rom. 8:18). That is the cure for our hearts when we grow weary in the long race of this life of faith.

How do we consider Jesus? By consulting what the Bible says about him. We read the Gospel accounts and learn what Jesus said and did and how God delivered him. We read the Epistles, which explain the significance of his life and death and resurrection. Indeed, in the Old Testament we see Christ in his work, as he is prophesied and represented by various types and symbols.

This is the very thing we find our Lord doing for his disciples in the Gospel accounts. Perhaps the worthiest way to conclude these studies of faith in Hebrews 11, especially as we are reminded here that they all direct us to Jesus, is with an account that appears in Luke 24. There we learn of two downcast disciples walking away from Jerusalem on the very day that Jesus was resurrected. They were weary and had lost heart, but unbeknownst to them, Jesus himself, risen from the grave, came alongside them on the road. Jesus asked what they were talking about; Luke tells us, "they stood still, looking sad" (v. 17). This is how Jesus finds us sometimes, discouraged and standing still instead of running the race. The two disciples told Jesus about a man from Nazareth they thought would be the Messiah. But, they added, he had been arrested and killed, and they did not understand the confusing reports they had heard about him being seen afterward.

Jesus responded by pointing them to Scripture: "Beginning with Moses and all the Prophets, he interpreted to them in all the Scriptures the things concerning himself" (Luke 24:27). What Jesus did for them, we are to do for ourselves, seeking and finding him and contemplating his life and ministry in the pages of Scripture.

When the party arrived at their destination, Jesus revealed himself to the disciples and then miraculously disappeared. Yet, in spite of this direct encounter with the risen Lord and his dramatic disappearance, the two disciples, now greatly encouraged, marveled not at this supernatural experience but at the things they had seen in the Scriptures! "They said to each other, 'Did not our hearts burn within us while he talked to us on the road, while he opened to us the Scriptures?'" (Luke 24:32).

This is what we will find when our hearts have grown cold on the long and sometimes difficult race that is our calling as Christ's disciples. We open the Scriptures and Jesus teaches us of himself, no less than he did for those two disciples, and as we consider him in his sufferings for us, his victory over sin and death, our hearts too are warmed and even burn within us. This is what makes us rejoice as we should, singing words of confident faith:

> My hope is in the Lord who gave himself for me,
>> and paid the price of all my sin at Calvary.
> For me he died, for me he lives,
>> and everlasting life and light he freely gives.[6]

If you want to live that way, with that kind of joy and power, then you must fix your eyes on Jesus, not on this world or anything in it, and consider how great a Savior he really is.

---

6. Norman J. Clayton, © 1945 Wordspring Music, LLC. All rights reserved. Used by permission.

PART 5

Concluding Exhortations

50

DISCIPLINED AS SONS

Hebrews 12:4–13

For the Lord disciplines the one he loves, and chastises every son
whom he receives." (Heb. 12:6)

he great preacher Alexander Maclaren compared Hebrews
12:4–13 to a lighthouse. It gives the kind of teaching that we
don't notice much when the sun is shining. Like the light from
a lighthouse, it doesn't stand out very well in the day. But when night comes,
and storms begin to blast against us, it suddenly blazes with a light that is
essential if we are to find our way. These verses are like that because they
speak of divine discipline: the biblical teaching that God chastises and trains
his children by means of the difficulties and hardships of life. This is a topic
we hardly care about when God does not seem to be doing it; but when his
hand of chastisement falls, Christians greatly need the encouragement and
instruction found here.

A PASTOR'S CONCERN

These verses arise out of a pastor's concern that his readers would fail to
think rightly about the troubles they were experiencing. His chief purpose in

this letter is to exhort Christians to be steadfast under trial, to hold fast to the faith. To that end, he reminds them that they have yet to suffer to the extent that Jesus did, or even as martyrs had done for the faith: "In your struggle against sin, you have not yet resisted to the point of shedding your blood" (v. 4). Notice that their struggle is against sin, not against the Roman persecutors or the Jewish community that was afflicting them. Verses 1–3 portray the Christian life as a race to be run with perseverance, and now verse 4 conceives of it as a boxing contest, another Greek sporting event, in which we contend through trials against our opponent, sin. If only we could be rid of our sin, God would have no purpose in allowing us to enter hardship; and when sin finally is gone from the world, then, but only then, will there finally be peace on earth.

After briefly making this point, the writer moves quickly to his main concern. Given that his readers were enduring hardship, his principal concern was that they not draw the wrong conclusion from their trials. How easy it is for us to think we are out of God's favor when circumstances turn against us; indeed, there is nothing more perilous in trials than to conclude that God has forgotten or betrayed us. Therefore, verse 5 begins by making a statement that probably is intended as a question: "Have you forgotten the exhortation that addresses you as sons?" This refers to Proverbs 3:11–12, which says, "My son, do not despise the LORD's discipline or be weary of his reproof, for the LORD reproves him whom he loves, as a father the son in whom he delights." Understanding this, the readers should not lose heart when God rebukes them through affliction.

The assumption bound up with the message of these verses is that when Christians experience trials it is not because God is unable to protect them. God can preserve us from every trial. He is sovereign over every aspect of our lives. Jesus put it this way: "Are not two sparrows sold for a penny? And not one of them will fall to the ground apart from your Father. But even the hairs of your head are all numbered" (Matt. 10:29–30). Therefore, when we enter into trials, God has allowed them and even ordained them. It is this realization that sometimes causes believers to question their relationship with God when times get tough.

FATHERLY DISCIPLINE AND CORRECTION

With that introduction, we now turn to the important teaching delivered in this passage, namely, that "the Lord disciplines the one he loves, and chastises every son whom he receives" (Heb. 12:6). Divine chastisement is a sign of sonship, a term that applies to both male and female Christians and speaks of our adoption into the family of God. "For what son is there whom his father does not discipline?" verse 7 asks. Verse 8 continues: "If you are left without discipline, in which all have participated, then you are illegitimate children and not sons." In the ancient world, discipline was the unquestioned prerogative and duty of a father. It was not a sign of favor when a child was not disciplined by his father, but of neglect or rejection. Fatherly love and discipline go together, and this awareness ought to transform the way Christians think about our trials. Andrew Murray puts it this way: "In every trial, small or great: first of all and at once recognize God's hand in it. Say at once: My Father has allowed this to come; I welcome it from Him; my first care is to glorify Him in it; He will make it a blessing. We may be sure of this; let us by faith rejoice in it."[1]

The writer tells us two things God does to raise us right, beginning with fatherly discipline. The Greek word for this is *paideia*, from the word *pais*, meaning "child," and speaks of the raising of a child. This is the primary way we should think about God's treatment of us in our trials. Just as a parent trains up a child, subjecting him or her to a process of education and arranging demanding experiences designed to spur development, so God also leads us through this life. As with a son or daughter in childhood, our whole lives are preparation for the age of maturity that waits for us in the life to come. This explains so many of our trials. God sends us challenges and hardships, not out of spite, but out of paternal love. Trials are designed to make us stronger, to apply force against the muscle of our faith to push us forward toward our spiritual potential.

Sometimes, however, God employs chastising hardships to punish sin in our lives. Along with discipline, God employs fatherly correction. This is not to be thought of as the damning wrath of God, but rather as the corrective punishment of a parent. Verse 6 tells us of these heavenly spankings: "[He] chastises every son whom he receives." The key word is *mastigoi*, which means scourging or whipping as an intense form of punishment. If we think God would never do that, we are obviously mistaken. While we are not judicially

---

1. Andrew Murray, *The Holiest of All: An Exposition of the Epistle to the Hebrews* (Grand Rapids: Revell, 1993), 507.

punished by God as Judge—Christ having borne all the penalty of our sin on the cross—God as Father gives painful, corrective punishment the way any loving parent does, because he wants us to grow up the right way. Many Christians have gratefully testified that the only way God got through to them in their sin and stubbornness was to allow a painful ordeal—the loss of a job, a severe illness, persecution for their faith. Eventually they recognized this as a sign of fatherly care, the kind that only beloved children receive from God.

The writer's point is that, as Calvin puts it, "the scourges of God bear witness of His love towards us."[2] J. C. Ryle comments:

> By affliction He teaches us many precious lessons, which, without it we should never learn. By affliction He shows us our emptiness and weakness, draws us to the throne of grace, purifies our affections, weans us from the world, makes us long for heaven. In the resurrection morning we shall all say, "It is good for me that I was afflicted." We shall thank God for every storm.[3]

Any Christian with much experience knows that we need this kind of training and discipline, for without fear and anxiety and loss we forget God and heaven all too easily. On our own we become comfortable with the world and even with sin. As C. S. Lewis famously put it, "God whispers to us in our pleasures, speaks in our conscience, but shouts in our pains: it is his megaphone to arouse a deaf world."[4] And J. I. Packer was certainly right when he said: "This is the ultimate reason, from our standpoint, why God fills our lives with troubles and perplexities of one sort or another—it is to ensure that we shall learn to hold Him fast. . . . God wants us to feel that our way through life is rough and perplexing, so that we may learn thankfully to lean on Him. Therefore He takes steps to drive us out of self-confidence to trust in Himself."[5]

What a difference it makes that God relates to us as his own beloved children. In the terms of the ancient world, God relates to us specifically the way a father did to his sons—those who would inherit from him, represent him

---

2. John Calvin, *New Testament Commentaries*, 12 vols. (Grand Rapids: Eerdmans, 1994), 12:190.

3. J. C. Ryle, *Expository Thoughts on Mark* (Edinburgh: Banner of Truth, 1994), 83.

4. C. S. Lewis, *The Problem of Pain* (New York: Macmillan, 1978), 81.

5. J. I. Packer, *Knowing God* (Downers Grove, Ill.: InterVarsity, 1979), 227.

in life, and bear his name in the world. This means that God's own heart is bound up with us, that we are the apple of his eye. Surely this ought to be the most welcome of news, even if coupled with the hardships by which God is raising us as his own.

King David was not a very good father. He set a terrible example with his sin against Bathsheba and her husband Uriah, an example his son Amnon would emulate against one of David's daughters (see 2 Sam. 13:1–19). It does not appear that David spent much time disciplining his children, perhaps because he had lost his credibility as a role model. The result was that his children grew up to be a veritable brood of vipers.

For all the poor example David was when it came to raising his children, it is clear that he loved them. Indeed, even the son who betrayed him never fell out of his love. One of his older sons was Absalom, who rebelled against David's rule so that David's army had to meet his army in battle. Absalom's revolt gravely threatened David's kingdom and put David's life in jeopardy. All that David had worked for all his life hung in the balance as the battle was fought against his son. As the day wore on, news came from the front that the battle was won and the usurper son had fallen. The Bible says that when David heard the news, he went upstairs into a room and wept: "O my son Absalom, my son, my son Absalom! Would I had died instead of you, O Absalom, my son, my son!" (2 Sam. 18:33). To the dismay of his generals, David felt no joy in the victory, but only remorse for the fallen rebel leader, his son.

If that is how David felt about a son he had not even given the time to raise properly, how must God therefore care for each of us, the beloved little children he is so carefully raising. Isn't this the greatest of all news, that God loves us as sons? How much this should motivate us to accept and profit from the discipline he so lovingly gives!

Enduring Discipline as Sons

There are a number of ways Christians can and do respond to God's discipline when it takes shape in difficult circumstances. One is the response of the stoic, who grimly seeks to accept what he cannot avoid. Such a person responds with defiant resignation, certainly without gratitude, seeking simply to get the struggle over with. This, it seems, is one of the concerns on the writer's mind, for he says in verse 5, "Do not regard lightly the discipline of the Lord." Such a person sees no purpose in suffering and therefore seeks to learn none of its lessons. He just wants to get through the storm to sunnier days.

Others respond to trials with self-pity and anger. We hear this sort of thing when people lash out, "What did I ever do to deserve this?!" This, too, is a concern to our writer, for he says, "Nor be weary when reproved by him." Some believers manifest abounding joy when God is blessing them with worldly goodness, but quickly resort to sullen resentment when God is blessing them with trials. Such Christians will never make much progress, because they fail to realize that trials are part and parcel of the Christian life, that they are a sign not of God's neglect but of his fatherly involvement. Affliction is a sign that we are children, that our conduct is important to God and has a bearing on his glory.

This leads to a third kind of response, the one commended in verse 7: "It is for discipline that you have to endure. God is treating you as sons." The point here is to see the purpose in our trials. There may be any number of reasons we are suffering, but one of them is always sure: God is training us for godliness. It is productive discipline we are going through, just as Peter writes in his first epistle: "As was necessary, you have been grieved by various trials, so that the tested genuineness of your faith—more precious than gold that perishes though it is tested by fire—may be found to result in praise and glory and honor at the revelation of Jesus Christ" (1 Peter 1:6–7). Along similar lines, James is perfectly serious when he writes, "Count it all joy, my brothers, when you meet trials of various kinds, for you know that the testing of your faith produces steadfastness. . . . Blessed is the man who remains steadfast under trial, for when he has stood the test he will receive the crown of life, which God has promised to those who love him" (James 1:2–3, 12).

A COMPARISON OF FATHERS

Our passage began with a pastor's concern that his suffering flock might draw mistaken conclusions from their trials. Next, he moves to a comparison, making an argument from the lesser to the greater, comparing the discipline of our earthly fathers to the discipline of our Father in heaven.

Hebrews 12:9 compares the father of our flesh to the father of our spirit, that is, our earthly father to our heavenly Father. Experience shows that parents grow in respect when they are involved in their children's lives, when they set clear boundaries and enforce them with discipline. Parents who try to win their children's affection by treating them as peers and friends, giving them what they want and neglecting discipline, not only fail in their duty but gain contempt instead of admiration. If discipline causes us to respect our earthly fathers, then the same should be true with regard to our heavenly Father.

We should "be subject to the Father of spirits and live" (Heb. 12:9). Parents teach their children to look both ways before crossing a street to avoid getting hit by cars, and in the same way God's discipline protects us from danger and leads us onward in life. The point is that like little children guided and guarded by a parent's disciplining hand, we should realize that our lives are on the line—our eternal lives—and thus revere God for the care he gives to our souls.

Furthermore, discipline makes all the difference in the quality and the usefulness of our lives. William Lane comments, "God is training his children for the enjoyment of life in its fullest sense,"[6] and we ought therefore to respond eagerly, perceiving the dangers of disobedience and the benefits of God's disciplining care.

The Hebrew readers who originally received this letter and knew the Old Testament law would have made another connection with this statement about life. They would surely have remembered the words of God in the giving of his law to Israel:

> See, I have set before you today life and good, death and evil. If you obey the commandments of the LORD your God that I command you today, by loving the LORD your God, by walking in his ways, and by keeping his commandments and his statutes and his rules, then you shall live and multiply, and the LORD your God will bless you in the land you are entering to take possession of it. . . . I have set before you life and death, blessing and curse. Therefore choose life, that you and your offspring may live, loving the LORD your God, obeying his voice and holding fast to him. (Deut. 30:15–20)

6. William L. Lane, *Hebrews 9–13* (Dallas: Word Books, 1991), 423.

Even more than our earthly fathers, God in heaven is worthy of our worship and reverence because of his governing influence over our lives. Undoubtedly, the word "life" also recalls the fifth commandment, "Honor your father and your mother, that your days may be long in the land that the LORD your God is giving you" (Ex. 20:12).

The second point of comparison is found in verse 10, namely, that our earthly discipline has value for this world, for a short life of however many years, but God's discipline is of eternal value for a life that never ends. Alexander Maclaren writes, "The earthly parent's discipline trains a boy or girl for circumstances, pursuits, occupations, professions, all of which terminate with the brief span of life. God's training is for an eternal day.... The writer's intention [is] to dwell upon the limited scope of the one and the wide and eternal purpose of the other."[7]

Third, the writer says that our fathers "disciplined us . . . as it seemed best to them." Every father makes mistakes, operates out of mixed motives, acts in sin toward his children in one way or another, and yet is still to be revered by his children. Even a bad father often exerts a positive influence on children by means of the discipline he gives.

When it comes to God, we have no such problem to overcome: "[God] disciplines us *for our good*, that we may share his holiness" (v. 10). What a difference it makes to realize that God, who is good, has only good for us in his manner of discipline. However difficult it is for us to perceive, he is making "all things work together for good" in our lives (Rom. 8:28). Since God is holy, all his intentions for us are also holy. They are pure, they are for our benefit, and they bring credit to him.

Because God is love, even when the worst afflictions pour upon our heads, behind them is a hand moved by love. God's love also means that he enters into our afflictions with us. A favorite passage of Christian comfort makes this very promise: "When you pass through the waters, I will be with you; and through the rivers, they shall not overwhelm you; when you walk through fire you shall not be burned, and the flame shall not consume you. For I am the LORD your God, the Holy One of Israel, your Savior" (Isa. 43:2–3). The Puritan Richard Sibbes therefore could say: "If God brings us

---

7. Alexander Maclaren, *Expositions of Holy Scripture*, 11 vols. (Grand Rapids: Eerdmans, 1959), 10:219.

into the trial he will be with us in the trial, and at length bring us out, more refined. We shall lose nothing but dross (Zech. 13:9). From our own strength we cannot bear the least trouble, but by the Spirit's assistance we can bear the greatest."[8]

God disciplines us for our good, and that good is our growth in holiness. Indeed, verse 10 tells us that he would have us share in his holiness in order that we would be like him, pure and holy. In verse 11 the writer makes this conclusion to his argument: "For the moment all discipline seems painful rather than pleasant, but later it yields the peaceful fruit of righteousness to those who have been trained by it." Of course discipline is painful at the time, which is why it gets our attention. But the Christian, whose eye is on the horizon of a life to come, perceives a reward at the end of the trial, a great gain from the present pain.

The famous football coach Tom Landry put it this way, "The job of a coach is to make men do what they don't want to do, in order to be what they've always wanted to be."[9] That is not a bad description of what God is doing for and in us because of his desire for our good. He is making us what we were meant to be, and what in our sanest moments we want to be, by means we would never choose on our own. This being the case, we will think of God's discipline according to what we think of holiness. If we long to be made holy—if we cry out to have hearts renewed, for sin to be removed, to be like God in our thoughts and desires—then we will not flinch when he enters us into afflictions, since they are the regimen of his training for all who would be holy. J. I. Packer describes this well:

> In this world, royal children have to undergo extra training and discipline, which other children escape, in order to fit them for their high destiny. It is the same with the children of the King of Kings. The clue to understanding all His dealings with them is to remember that throughout their lives He is training them for what awaits them, and chiseling them into the image of Christ. Sometimes the chiseling process is painful, and the discipline irksome; but then the Scripture reminds us—"Whom the Lord *loveth* he chasteneth, and scourgeth *every son whom he receiveth*. If ye endure chastening, *God dealeth with you as with sons.* . . . Now no chastening for the

8. Richard Sibbes, *The Bruised Reed* (Edinburgh: Banner of Truth, 1998), 55.
9. Cited in Ray Stedman, *Hebrews* (Downers Grove, Ill.: InterVarsity, 1992), 141.

present time seemeth to be joyous, but grievous; nevertheless afterward it yieldeth the peaceable fruit of righteousness . . ." (Heb. 12:6 ff.).[10]

A FERVENT EXHORTATION

Our passage concludes in verses 12 and 13 with a fervent exhortation that flows from the logic of the writer's argument: "Therefore lift your drooping hands and strengthen your weak knees, and make straight paths for your feet, so that what is lame may not be put out of joint but rather be healed." This means Christians should show determination in their struggle and fatigue, understanding the purpose of their trials and God's fatherly care. Verse 12 borrows its words from Isaiah 35:3—"Strengthen the weak hands, and make firm the feeble knees"—which then goes on to say, "Say to those who have an anxious heart, 'Be strong; fear not! Behold, your God will come. . . . He will come and save you.'" Like runners who see the finish line ahead, the readers of Hebrews are to take heart, lifting up their arms and legs to run the race to the end.

Verse 13 then echoes the words of Proverbs 4:26–27, telling us to make level paths, not swerving to the right or left. Here we are reminded of our Lord's own teaching, that the broad lane, followed by many, leads to destruction, but the narrow path, a path of turning away from sin, leads to life. Verse 13 ends with a reminder that our example has an influence on others, especially helping or hindering those who are lame or weak in the faith.

With these challenges set before us, surely we will not resent the reproofs God gives through Scripture or through other Christians, or his chastisement in circumstances that are hard. Instead, we should receive them with thanksgiving, eagerly repenting and seeking God's grace for power to change. He is working "for our good, that we may share his holiness."

But more important than this, and surely this is the main emphasis of our passage, what a difference it makes to know the love of God with assurance. Do not forget that you are sons, God's beloved children, through faith in Jesus Christ. John 1:12 says, "To all who did receive him, who believed in his name, he gave the right to become children of God." On the one hand, this means that if you have not yet turned to God through faith in Christ,

---

10. J. I. Packer, *Knowing God* (Downers Grove, Ill.: InterVarsity, 1979), 201–2.

you are not his child. You do not have the comfort of knowing that your trials are governed by God's loving care. Unless you turn to God through faith in Christ, the wrath of God abides upon you still, and you are alienated from this love we have been speaking about. Your trials are merely the bitter fruit of sins—yours and others—without any saving purpose, until you repent, believe, and come to God as a child through faith in Christ.

But if you are a Christian, you can fix your eyes on Jesus, glorified now in heaven, and see that God in his love sent a Savior to die for your sins. For Jesus, there was a cross before the crown. Though his cross took away your sins once for all, his pattern of trial before glory will be your pattern as well.

This is something William Cowper learned in his greatly troubled life. Cowper's mother died when he was a little boy, and he was deeply scarred by abuse he received in the years that followed at boarding school. The result was severe depression that afflicted him many times. In his early thirties, a series of events—the death of his father and his stepmother, the drowning of his closest friend, and his utter failure to secure a livelihood—caused a mental collapse. Many people exhorted Cowper, but one minister took the time to explain to him the gospel, the good news that God had sent his own Son to die for Cowper's sins. It was in a mental asylum that Cowper became convinced of this from the Scriptures. Years later he told of the day God's love set him free:

> I flung myself into a chair near the window and, seeing a Bible there, ventured once more to apply to it for comfort and instruction. The verse I saw was the 25th of the 3d of Romans, "Whom God hath set forth to be a propitiation through faith in his blood, to declare his righteousness for the remission of sins." . . . Immediately I received strength to believe it and the full beams of the Sun of Righteousness shone upon me. I saw the sufficiency of the atonement He had made, my pardon was sealed in His blood. . . . I could only look up to heaven in silent fear, overwhelmed with love and wonder.[11]

Cowper would still struggle in years to come, but it would never be quite the same now that he knew God's love for him, a love that was greater than his trials and gave meaning to them all. He found God's love proved in the

11. Cited in Elsie Houghton, *Christian Hymn Writers* (Glamorgan, U.K.: Evangelical Press of Wales, 1982), 149.

gift of his Son to take away our sins. Cowper's testimony is recorded in a hymn he wrote, entitled "Hark, My Soul! It Is the Lord." He imagined his loving God speaking to him of grace:

> I delivered thee when bound,
>   And, when bleeding, healed thy wound;
> Sought thee wandering, set thee right,
>   Turned thy darkness into light.[12]

Are you in hardship and toil, difficulty and sorrow? If you are not, you will be in due time. What a difference it makes to know that God loves us through faith in Christ! What a joy it is to learn that in our sorrows God is training us by his love, that his loving hand is preparing us for an eternity of glory in heaven. It makes all the difference between wandering aimlessly and running a race with conviction, between darkness of soul and the light of the gospel.

12. William Cowper, "Hark, My Soul! It Is the Lord," 1768.

51

A CALL TO HOLINESS

Hebrews 12:14–17

*Strive for peace with everyone, and for the holiness without which
no one will see the Lord.* (Heb. 12:14)

O f all the young men and women who tragically died in the assault
on Columbine High School in April 1999, none has touched the
lives of more people than Cassie Bernall. Cassie has been rightly
described as a martyr; that is, as one who died for her Christian faith. She
perished in her high school library when one of the two young murderers
put his automatic rifle to her head and asked, "Do you believe in God?"
Some think Cassie might have been praying, thereby drawing their attention and prompting the question. But the issue was not one of mere theological speculation. When they asked, "Do you believe in God?" they were
challenging her willingness to die for Christ. With the rifle muzzle pressed
against her forehead, the young woman pondered her response.

Cassie answered loudly and clearly, for another teenager, crouched
under a desk twenty-five feet away, heard her distinct reply. He later
recalled: "One of them asked her if she believed in God. She paused, like
she didn't know what she was going to answer, and then she said yes.
She must have been scared, but her voice didn't sound shaky. It was

strong."[1] She said yes, and with that the young killer pulled the trigger, and Cassie Bernall entered an eternal reward with the God she acknowledged in the face of death.

Cassie Bernall is famous for dying for Christ, but what is perhaps less well known is that in the months prior to her death she had been living for Christ. Two years earlier, in fact, Cassie had been much like the two angry youths who later shot her: caught up in the teen underworld of Gothic darkness with its trappings of disturbed music, wild rage, and flirtation with suicide. She had committed her soul to Satan in a dark ritual; she and a friend were plotting the murder of a teacher they despised and wrote letters seriously discussing the idea of killing her parents. When they found these letters, her parents dramatically intervened, among other ways by sending her to a nearby church's youth group. Cassie stuck out among the Christian kids, both by her dress and her demeanor, and attended unwillingly. But after finally making a Christian friend, Cassie was dramatically converted to Christ at a youth retreat. God brought the gospel of his love and forgiveness and power for life into her heart. Cassie returned home and exclaimed, "Mom, I've changed."

After two years of living for Christ, this young woman was willing to die for Christ. Her mother writes, "The real issue raised by Cassie's death is not what she said to her killers, but what it was that enabled her to face them as she did. . . . Cassie didn't just die on April 20, but died daily over the previous two years."[2] By faith she had been giving her life over to Christ, and that is how this young Christian was able to face death on his behalf.

A Holy Calling

This is the way the writer of Hebrews was thinking in this passage. If there was one concern on his mind, it was that his Christian readers stand firm when the day of testing came, perhaps as suddenly as it came to Cassie Bernall. The whole letter makes clear that he expected suffering and persecution in their immediate future. This was part of his message

1. Misty Bernall, *She Said Yes: The Unlikely Martyrdom of Cassie Bernall* (Farmington, Pa.: Plough, 1999), 13.
2. Ibid., 119.

when he exhorted them to look to Jesus "who for the joy that was set before him endured the cross, despising the shame" (12:2). In Hebrews 12:4 the author pointed out that they "have not yet resisted to the point of shedding your blood," which clearly implied that they might soon face that same kind of trial.

Hebrews 12 begins with the race that Christians are to run, shedding every hindrance and fleeing sin so as to endure to the end with our eyes fixed on Christ (vv. 1–3). Verses 4–13 then speak of God's discipline as he trains his children for a harvest of righteousness.

Verse 14 continues this discourse, giving the specific guidance Christians need. This straightforward instruction is what a young believer like Cassie Bernall especially requires in order to know how to live as a Christian. But it is also something more seasoned believers need to recall. It consists of an exhortation to pursue two specific aims: "Strive for peace with everyone, and for holiness." The first of these has to do with our relationship with other people, and the second with our relationship with God.

Christians are commanded to live peacefully with the people around them, to be peacemakers in the world. This is what our Lord Jesus emphasized when he taught, "Blessed are the peacemakers, for they shall be called sons of God" (Matt. 5:9). This is something Paul stressed in his Letter to the Romans: "If possible, so far as it depends on you, live peaceably with all" (Rom. 12:18).

This is what all of us must pursue in Christ's name: "Strive for peace with everyone." This is a sustained and determined pursuit; as one hunts prey, so Christians are to seek after peace. We should think of this peace in broad terms, as the effect of the gospel upon society as it is transmitted through our lives. Psalm 34:14 puts it this way: "Turn away from evil and do good; seek peace and pursue it."

The Chinese evangelist Watchman Nee tells a story that illustrates our calling to peace. A Christian who had a rice field on a hill had to hand-work a pump to bring water up from the irrigation stream that ran at the base of the hill. Beneath him was a neighbor who made a hole in the dividing wall so that when the Christian tried to pump water into his field it drained down into the neighbor's. The Christian became understandably frustrated at this repeated theft. Consulting his Christian friends he asked, "What shall I do? I have tried to be patient and not retaliate. Isn't it right for me to confront him?" The Christians prayed, and then one of them noted that as Christians they surely had a duty to seek more than justice for themselves, but to live in such a way as to be a blessing to others.

Armed with this advice, the Christian pursued a different strategy. The next day he went out and first pumped water into his neighbor's fields and then went on to do the additional labor for watering his own fields. Before long, this procedure brought the neighbor out to ask why the Christian would act in this way, and as a result of the relationship that ensued the neighbor became a Christian himself.[3]

That is the kind of attitude our passage exhorts, that which puts peace with our neighbors and being a blessing to others ahead of our own rights and prerogatives. The apostle Peter argued this way: "Christ also suffered for you, leaving you an example, so that you might follow in his steps. . . . When he was reviled, he did not revile in return; when he suffered, he did not threaten, but continued entrusting himself to him who judges justly" (1 Peter 2:21, 23).

The Christian life is not only focused on our relations with other people, but it also has a vertical dimension: our relationship with God. Therefore, the writer adds, "Strive . . . for the holiness without which no one will see the Lord" (v. 14). The Greek word translated "holiness" is elsewhere rendered "sanctification," that process by which Christians are freed from the power of sin and transformed into godliness. Sanctification is God's work in us, but one in which we are active by faith. Holiness means "set apart": set apart *from* the sinful world and *to* God for his pleasure and service.

This is not an option for the believer, but as Paul puts it, "Let everyone who names the name of the Lord depart from iniquity" (2 Tim. 2:19). Christian salvation is not caused by our holiness, but it necessitates our holiness, for this is God's very purpose in saving us, that we might "be conformed to the image of his Son" (Rom. 8:29). Holiness is necessary for us to be saved. It is not necessary as a *condition* of our acceptance with God, since we are justified by faith in Christ alone, apart from works. But it is necessary as a *consequence* of our acceptance with God, so much so that the apostle James mocks the idea of being saved by a faith that fails to produce good works. "Faith by itself," he writes, "if it does not have works, is dead" (James 2:17).

3. Cited from James Montgomery Boice, *Ephesians* (Grand Rapids: Zondervan, 1988), 111–12.

Holiness has been a major emphasis of the writer of Hebrews. Christ was perfected as our Savior so that he might perfect us to enter the fullness of the salvation God has provided. Hebrews 10:14 says, "By a single offering he has perfected for all time those who are being sanctified." Christ's sacrificial death has imputed to us his own perfect righteousness, and also entered us onto the path of increasing holiness; these two always go together. James M. Boice writes: "Real Christianity leads [a believer] to Jesus Christ. And that means that the Holy Spirit comes to live within the Christian, giving the person a new nature, creating love for God and a desire to obey him, and providing the ability to do what God requires. In other words, the gospel leads to an internal transformation."[4]

It is the advance of this progressive work that Christians are zealously to seek in this life. Therefore, although we are to be a blessing to the world, a source of peace to those around us so far as we are able, it is never by compromising with the world, or by becoming worldly. Indeed, Christians are the most good to the world when we are least like the world: when we are godly, when we have light to bring into the dark realm of sin. Our striving after peace and holiness go together.

Of course, this is a struggle for sinners like us, which is why the text exhorts us to "make every effort" (v. 14 NIV). Paul speaks in similar terms: "Not that I have already . . . been made perfect, but I press on to take hold of that for which Christ Jesus took hold of me. Brothers, I do not consider myself yet to have taken hold of it. But one thing I do: Forgetting what is behind and straining toward what is ahead, I press on toward the goal to win the prize for which God has called me heavenward in Christ Jesus" (Phil. 3:12–14). This is how a Christian pursues holiness, longing more to reflect God's character and to see the death of sin in our hearts by the power of his grace.

For a teenager like Cassie Bernall, that meant learning to think differently from other kids at school: not to think in terms of popularity or image or to put herself first. Instead, she was called to live out her love for God and his love for people, to think about how God would have her act in various situations, and to be willing to go out of her way for the sake of someone else. It is not much different for any of us; young and old, we are all called to "strive for peace with everyone, and for holiness."

---

4. James M. Boice, *Amazing Grace* (Wheaton, Ill.: Tyndale House, 1993), 114–15.

Three Dangers to Christians

The writer of Hebrews goes on to list three threats to Christians, both individually and corporately. The first is found in verse 15: "See to it that no one fails to obtain the grace of God." This is the writer's overarching concern, that someone might fall behind or drop out of the race.

The writer has expressed this concern about apostasy a number of times in Hebrews, that there would be people among his readers who under trial would deny Christ and fall away. In chapter 2 he wrote of believers "drifting away" from faith on the current of worldly unbelief. Chapter 3 warned of sin's deceitfulness, which hardens the heart so that people "fall away from the living God" (v. 12). In chapter 6 he wrote of people who had gone far enough into Christianity to have been enlightened by it, to have "tasted the heavenly gift," and even to have experienced the power of God's Spirit among the people of God. It is possible to fit even that description and yet have only a superficial commitment to Christ so that you fail to persevere. Chapter 10 then exhorted, "You have need of endurance, so that when you have done the will of God, you may receive what is promised" (v. 36). Now, in this fifth exhortation against apostasy, the writer of Hebrews returns to the same theme, describing it as missing or falling back from the grace of God.

This reminds us that while the Bible teaches that all true Christians are secure in God's saving work—we are "kept by God's power" (1 Peter 1:5)—the Bible also teaches that the reality of our faith is proved by our perseverance to the end. A true Christian will persevere, however he may stumble, just as Paul assures us in Philippians 1:6 that God will complete a work that is truly begun by him. Psalm 37 speaks of God's care for his true child: "The steps of a man are established by the LORD, when he delights in his way; though he fall, he shall not be cast headlong, for the LORD upholds his hand" (Ps. 37:23–24).

If you are weak, this should comfort you; as Jesus said of his true sheep, "I give them eternal life, and they will never perish, and no one will snatch them out of my hand" (John 10:28). But if your Christian life is superficial, perhaps you should be concerned, for this makes clear that there are many who make a profession of faith in Christ yet fall back from God's grace, especially when the going gets tough.

Verse 15 includes an antidote for this first danger, namely, the pastoral care of Christians for each other: "See to it," the author writes, "that no one fails to obtain the grace of God." He means that the Hebrew Christians are to actively beware of this danger, no doubt especially as they are facing tribulation. One of the early Greek commentators, Theophylact, puts it in terms of a band of travelers engaged in a journey and notes that they must periodically make sure that everyone is still there. "Has anyone fallen out?" he asks. "Has anyone been left behind while the others have pressed on?"[5]

The Greek word for "see to it" is *episkopeō*, from which comes *episkopos*, one of the main New Testament words for an elder or minister. The writer is not restricting this duty to officers in the church, but surely this is one of a minister's principal duties: to check up on the flock, to make sure all are coming along, and especially to take note of any who have disappeared. In our passage, this obligation, which especially applies to ministers and elders, is given generally to all Christians. We are to seek out those who seem to have fallen back or turned away, to inquire about their struggle, to exhort and encourage them in the truth of the gospel, and in that way we are used by God for the perseverance of those who are his own.

Verse 15 notes a second danger. See to it, he adds, "that no 'root of bitterness' springs up and causes trouble, and by it many become defiled." This is an allusion to Deuteronomy 29:18, where Moses said, "Beware lest there be among you a man or woman or clan or tribe whose heart is turning away today from the LORD our God to go and serve the gods of those nations. Beware lest there be among you a root bearing poisonous and bitter fruit." The danger is that a group might arise in the church to promote unbiblical teaching and practices.

Such a root is not merely bitter in that it tastes bad, but it is deadly poison that brings spiritual death. It causes trouble and defiles—that is, it excludes people from God's presence, so that the concern, again, is about apostasy, this time because of heresy in the church. This is why today we need oversight when it comes to teaching and practice, lest bitter roots grow in our midst and cause the fall of some in our ranks. Paul began his letter of instruction to Timothy with just this concern, to "charge certain persons not

---

5. Cited in William Barclay, *The Letter to the Hebrews* (Louisville: Westminster/John Knox, 1976), 182.

to teach any different doctrine," and to beware of those who "promote speculations rather than the stewardship from God that is by faith" (1 Tim. 1:3–4).

Verse 16 brings a third warning, against sensual and godless patterns that cause people to turn away from the eternal to the worldly: "See to it . . . that no one is sexually immoral or unholy." These two terms describe a profane attitude about life, namely, that which is sensual and earth-bound, that which pursues carnal cravings of all sorts, sexual and otherwise, rather than spiritual blessing. This attitude is all around us today; indeed, our nation's economy is practically built upon these twin pillars of worldliness: the sensual and the godless.

One prime example of this mindset, as well as a good warning against it, comes from the life of Esau, the elder son of the patriarch Isaac and the brother of Jacob. Esau was sensually oriented, which is why he took pagan wives and thus grieved his godly parents. But the grossest example of his sensuality came with his willingness to trade his birthright—the covenant of salvation with the Lord—for a bowl of stew. This is what Hebrews 12:16 highlights, that he "sold his birthright for a single meal," a dreadful act of folly recorded in Genesis 25:29–34. Genesis says that "Esau despised his birthright"—that is, his covenant relationship with God. Surely that is the height of disdain for the things of God, and yet it is a choice that is repeated by the hour in our own time. Our job as Christians, says the writer of Hebrews, is to make sure that this kind of secular attitude finds no place in the church, and that every believer is warned against it.

Hebrews 12:17 tells us why Esau's sensual frame of mind is so greatly to be avoided: "Afterward, when he desired to inherit the blessing, he was rejected, for he found no chance to repent, though he sought it with tears." This refers to Esau's predicament when, years later, the covenant blessing he had despised was actually given to Jacob instead of him. Genesis 27 records that Esau regretted having given away something so valuable. He wasn't sorry for his sin or depraved attitude, but only for its consequence. But he was unable to undo what he had done, and in the same way people with a sensual and godless attitude today are unable to undo their many foolish choices, however many tears they shed. How many people even blame God for not helping them, when they have first rejected him in favor of the world, a world that turns out not to live up to its glittering promises. See to it, we are commanded, that this attitude and its terrible toll of tears do not find a place in the Christian community.

These are real dangers facing us today, as always. First is the general concern that some will fall away; second is the threat of heresy within the church; and third is the danger of sensual godlessness, a threat we must take very seriously, especially with our young people and others who are prone to being easily influenced by worldly values.

"Without Holiness No One Will See the Lord"

There is one statement that dominates this passage. The writer says we are to strive for holiness "without which no one will see the Lord" (Heb. 12:14). This is a verse that has caused many Christians to lose sleep, because they infer from it that salvation results from our moral attainment. If you are thinking that, let me remind you that no one is saved because of his or her own perfect holiness. We are not saved by our works, which are uniformly tainted by sin and thus are unacceptable to God, but rather by the perfect work of Jesus Christ. This is the great message of the Book of Hebrews, that Christ has made perfect what must be presented to God. He achieved the righteousness God demands and offers it to God on behalf of all who come through faith in him. Hebrews 7:26–27 says of Christ, "It was indeed fitting that we should have such a high priest, holy, innocent, unstained, separated from sinners, and exalted above the heavens. . . . He [sacrificed] once for all when he offered up himself." What is more, Jesus was raised from the dead to show that God accepted his atonement for sin, and he now lives and reigns in heaven to ensure our perseverance. Hebrews 7:24–25 says, "But he holds his priesthood permanently, because he continues forever. Consequently, he is able to save to the uttermost those who draw near to God through him, since he always lives to make intercession for them."

Therefore, the point of Hebrews 12:14 is not that you must be saved by your own holiness, a teaching that can only drive you to despair. But the point of this statement is nonetheless quite direct and serious. It is about the necessity of sanctification for everyone who calls himself a Christian and seeks to be saved. What it says is true: "Without holiness—without sanctification—no one will see the Lord." Jesus made this point in positive terms in the Sermon on the Mount: "Blessed are the pure in heart, for they shall see God" (Matt. 5:8).

In heaven Christians will see God; that is, we will have blessed communion with him by virtue of our perfect participation in his holy character. The apostle John writes of this in his first epistle and even intimates that it is seeing Christ in death that will finally eradicate any vestige of sin from us. "Beloved," he writes, "we are God's children now, and what we will be has not yet appeared; but we know that when he appears we will be like him, because we shall see him as he is" (1 John 3:2). The Westminster Shorter Catechism puts this in especially lovely terms, asking, "What benefits do believers receive from Christ at death?" and answering, "The souls of believers are at their death made perfect in holiness, and do immediately pass into glory" (Q/A 37). Having begun our holiness in this life, we will enjoy its perfection in the life to come, and we will gaze upon God in the beauty of holiness.

This being true, there are three ways in which Hebrews 12:14 exhorts us to a present pursuit of that holiness which alone enables us to see the Lord. First, we are exhorted to holiness because holiness is our preparation for heaven. The only ones who will be perfected in holiness then are those who are being perfected in holiness now, however slowly and with however much difficulty. J. C. Ryle argues this persuasively:

> We must be holy, because without holiness on earth we shall never be prepared to enjoy heaven. Heaven is a holy place. . . . Suppose for a moment that you were allowed to enter heaven without holiness. What would you do? What possible enjoyment could you feel there? To which of all the saints would you join yourself, and by whose side would you sit down? Their pleasures are not your pleasures, their tastes not your tastes, their character not your character. How could you possibly be happy, if you had not been holy on earth?[6]

How better, then, to prepare for the eternal blessings of holiness forever in heaven than to seek holiness in our lives now.

Second, we must persevere in our faith if we want to be saved, and perseverance is not possible without holiness. This is why Hebrews 12:1 begins this section of teaching by telling us to "throw off everything that hinders and the sin that so easily entangles" (NIV). If we do not strive against sin, we will be overcome and will not finish the race. In chapter 2 we are told that sin is a current that drags us out to sea; chapter 3 says our hearts are hard-

6. J. C. Ryle, *Holiness* (Darlington, U.K.: Evangelical Press, 1979), 42.

ened by sin's deceitfulness. Unless we do what this passage commands, therefore, making every effort not only to live in peace but also to be holy, we will not see the Lord because we will not persevere in the faith. As in the case of Esau, a secular and sensual mindset is one that goes on to despise the Lord and his blessings. People shun holiness because they love the world, and this love will keep them from heaven.

Third, and finally, we must press on in holiness because our present actions have eternal implications. This, too, is the lesson of Esau; his careless actions led to ultimate alienation from eternal riches in God. On the one hand, there is no sin that cannot be repented of, no attitude that cannot be nailed to the cross through faith in Christ. Cassie Bernall once offered her soul to Satan in earnest, yet finished her life professing faith in God to a gun-wielding killer. The point is not that sin cannot be repented of and forgiven, because it can be. The point is that we must pursue holiness because what we think and say and do now matters eternally. Paul writes, "The one who sows to his own flesh will from the flesh reap corruption, but the one who sows to the Spirit will from the Spirit reap eternal life" (Gal. 6:8). It is often put this way: "Sow a thought and reap an action; sow an action and reap a habit; sow a habit and reap a lifestyle; sow a lifestyle and reap a character; sow a character and reap a destiny." That is the epitaph on many a ruined soul, and we must make every effort—all in the power of God's grace received through faith in Christ—to advance in holiness, without which we shall never see the Lord.

This is something Cassie Bernall obviously came to realize. There is an epitaph on her life, and it is the title of the book her mother wrote to tell her story: *She Said Yes*. In that book her youth pastor wrote, "The world looks at Cassie's 'yes' of April 20, but we need to look at the daily 'yes' she said day after day, month after month."[7] Cassie would surely have agreed, because shortly before her death she underlined a sentence in a book she was reading: "All of us should live life so as to be able to face eternity at any time."

That is a message for each of us, not only because like her we may face death at any moment, but because this is what lies ahead for all who are in Christ. The life in store for us is a holy life. Therefore, let us make every effort to be holy, for it is with holiness that someday we will see our precious Lord, and it is with holiness that others can see him now in us.

---

7. Bernall, *She Said Yes,* 119.

52

THE MOUNTAIN OF GRACE

Hebrews 12:18—24

*But you have come to Mount Zion and to the city of the living
God, the heavenly Jerusalem, and to innumerable angels in festal
gathering, and to the assembly of the firstborn who are enrolled
in heaven, and to God, the judge of all, and to the spirits of the
righteous made perfect, and to Jesus, the mediator of a new
covenant, and to the sprinkled blood that speaks a better word
than the blood of Abel. (Heb. 12:22–24)*

*T*he Book of Hebrews presents to the reader a brilliant tour of
biblical history and geography. The writer takes us to various
places in Bible history, recalling what happened and
always relating what we see to the person and work of Christ, and then
to the life of Christian faith. In different chapters we find ourselves in
the exodus wilderness, in Abraham's tents, before the veil in the tabernacle, in the courts of Melchizedek, at the gates of the Garden of Eden,
and in the ark with Noah above the flood. This tour de force gives a compelling variety and interest to the Book of Hebrews.

In this way the writer also makes his point that the Old Testament, like the New, is all about Jesus Christ. Wherever we go in the Bible, he shows, the message is to turn to Christ in faith. The promises and prophecies of the Old Testament all find their "Yes" and "Amen" in Jesus and in the New Testament church he is building. In all this great unfolding panorama, therefore, there is one consistent message, namely, that we must hold fast to Christ as Savior, whatever difficulty or trial might befall us.

THE MOUNTAIN OF GOD

Hebrews 12 concludes by taking us to another stop in our Biblelands tour, this time to Mount Sinai, where Moses brought Israel out in the exodus to meet with God. We remember that when God delivered his people from bondage in Egypt, he did not just turn them loose to do whatever they wanted; he brought them out to the mountain where he dwelt so they could worship him. "Let my people go," Moses cried to Pharaoh, "that they may hold a feast to me in the wilderness" (Ex. 5:1).

This is an excellent reminder that the purpose of our deliverance, the purpose of the church, is to worship and serve God—not to please the world, not to market goods and services to the secular culture, but to please God through our living worship. But it is not to Mount Sinai in the desert that Christians are told that they have come. Mount Sinai is brought into the picture, but only to present a contrast by which the mount of our salvation may be seen more clearly. It is a contrast between Sinai and Zion, between Moses and Christ, between the law and the gospel:

> For you have not come to what may be touched, a blazing fire and darkness and gloom and a tempest and the sound of a trumpet and a voice whose words made the hearers beg that no further messages be spoken to them. For they could not endure the order that was given, "If even a beast touches the mountain, it shall be stoned." Indeed, so terrifying was the sight that Moses said, "I tremble with fear." (Heb. 12:18–21)

The author of Hebrews is writing for effect, piling description upon description to make clear the situation of Judaism, the situation to which

565

Moses brought the twelve tribes and to which the writer warns the Hebrew Christians not to return. This is the old covenant situation, and it does not come across as a very attractive one.

The descriptions in Hebrews 12:18–21 come from the books of Exodus and Deuteronomy. First, the writer says, "For you have not come to what may be touched." This recalls Exodus 19:12, where God told Moses, "Set limits for the people all around, saying, 'Take care not to go up into the mountain or touch the edge of it. Whoever touches the mountain shall be put to death.'" When man came to God at the mountain of the law, there was a separation between man and God, a separation made necessary by our sin and his holiness.

Second, the mountain was "a blazing fire." This was not the painted fire of a decorative fireplace! This was a fire that could be felt, which menaced the people with its hot, destructive power. Its message was the same one delivered by the flaming sword of the angel at the gate to the Garden of Eden. It was a barrier to access, and a deadly one.

Third, there was "darkness," the mountain of the shadow of death. It was draped with "gloom and a tempest," we are told. This is what it meant to come to God under the administration of the law, under the old covenant. There were a trumpet blast and a voice of thunder that terrified the people. They could not bear the voice of God, so they sent Moses up to mediate for them.

To get the full effect, we have to rattle these items off one after another, the way the writer of Hebrews does: the mountain is roped off; it is blazing, dark, gloomy, and storm-ridden; from it blast a trumpet and a voice that makes the people beg it to stop, lest they die. Even their spiritual leader Moses, a true giant of the faith, a man set apart by God and for God, cried out, "I tremble with fear." This is the mountain to which Israel had been brought, having been delivered from the bondage of Egypt. B. F. Westcott comments: "That which the writer describes is the form of the revelation, fire and darkness and thunder, material signs of the nature of God. Thus every element is one which outwardly moves fear. . . . The mountain is lost in the fire and smoke. It was, so to speak, no longer a mountain. It becomes a manifestation of terrible majesty, a symbol of the Divine Presence."[1]

---

1. B. F. Westcott, *The Epistle to the Hebrews* (London: Macmillan, 1903), 412.

This is the writer's point: You in the church were likewise brought to the presence of God himself. You were brought to a mountain—but not to *that* mountain! There is a positive comparison here. The church, like Israel, has been delivered out of bondage, brought to the presence of God for the purpose of consecration to him. But there the comparison stops and the contrast begins. Philip Hughes writes:

> Such were the terrors of Sinai, the mount of God's law, where because of their sinfulness the people were unable to draw near to God's presence. How different are the circumstances of Zion, the mount of God's grace, where, thanks to the perfect law-keeping and the all-sufficient sacrifice of himself offered by the incarnate Son in our stead, we are invited to draw near with boldness into the heavenly holy of holies.[2]

"You have not come to *that* mountain," the writer says, "but instead to Mount Zion, to the heavenly Jerusalem, the city of the living God." We are reminded here of a comparison Paul made in Galatians 4. There the old covenant is Mount Sinai, and her children, Paul says, comparing her to Abraham's illegitimate mate Hagar, are slaves. This is Judaism, this is the old covenant. But we are "the Jerusalem above" that is free (see Gal. 4:21–26). This freedom, this access to God in Christ, is visually presented here in Hebrews 12:22–24, as the writer turns to the situation of the new covenant believer.

THE CITY OF GOD

Christians, through faith in Christ, have come into the presence of God himself, the place where God exercises sovereignty and from which he sends deliverance. This Zion is his acropolis, the seat of his throne. What we see in these verses is a mountain-city; indeed, it is "the city that has foundations, whose designer and builder is God" (Heb. 11:10), solid in its foundations as a great mountain arising from the earth. We are led to this new mountain, remembering the former one that was covered with darkness and fire and gloom. Now, all of that has been pierced, blown aside by

2. Philip E. Hughes, *A Commentary on the Epistle to the Hebrews* (Grand Rapids: Eerdmans, 1977), 543.

the wind of the gospel, torn open like the veil in the temple before the holy of holies, and what we see is a shining city, the city of the living God.

Sinai prohibited the entrance of sinful man. No man, woman, or child could even set foot on that mountain. But here on the mountain of grace is a city in the clouds, where God's people dwell. The sight of Sinai produced fear, but this is a scene of great encouragement. From Sinai boomed forbidding threats, but from this mountain sounds a voice of invitation. To approach the former mountain was to tremble with fear—even Moses felt it. To draw near to this mountain is to find hope renewed with every lightened step. This is the difference made by the coming of Jesus Christ, who has removed all that stood opposed to us with God, who has taken away the darkness and fire and gloom, who transforms the mountain of fear into the mountain of grace. What a magnificent portrayal of the difference it makes that Christ has come to take away our sin.

Upon the mountain is the City of God. One cannot help thinking of Saint Augustine's great book by that name, which said there are two cities with two loves. The City of Man is based on the love of self, which means enmity to God; the City of God is built on love of God in the place of self-love. In this world, God's city is weak and lowly, but there she is, presented to our faith, high upon the mount of God, wreathed in glory.

Abraham, we remember, lived in tents. He was a pilgrim in a land of promise. But all that time he was yet a part of this high city, and on it he set his gaze. He and his family dwelt in dry places, but all the while the promise of Psalm 46:4 was true through their faith: "There is a river whose streams make glad the city of God, the holy habitation of the Most High." By faith Abraham drank from that river, even the Spirit of God as he sends forth the gospel, refreshing our souls and planting our roots beside streams of living water.

In the last chapter of the Bible our Lord Jesus pronounces his last beatitude: "Blessed are those who wash their robes, so that they may have the right to the tree of life and that they may enter the city by the gates" (Rev. 22:14). With this pronouncement goes the last invitation of the Bible: "Whoever is thirsty, let him come; and whoever wishes, let him take the free gift of the water of life" (Rev. 22:17 NIV). These are the things within that city. Engraved upon her walls is this inscription, says Ezekiel: "The LORD is there" (48:35). Everything within it, says Zechariah, is inscribed "Holy to the LORD" (Zech. 14:20).

To this you have come, says our text, if you are a Christian. You have come to this mountain and this city. Look upon it, he says, with the eyes of faith. All that is there is yours, all the blessings of God and even God himself.

The Church of the Firstborn

The writer of Hebrews then proceeds to describe the inhabitants of the city: "You have come . . . to innumerable angels in festal gathering" (v. 22). In chapter 2 we noted that the old covenant was given through angels; they were the ones blaring the trumpets and stoking the fires on Mount Sinai. The angels were the ones clothed in darkness and gloom, working their ministry of despair before any who might draw near. But now, the author says, upon this mountain to which we have come in Christ, multitudes of angels are to be seen, all in festal array. They are now a welcoming party, inviting us to join their glad worship of the Lord.

Furthermore, what we find in the city—and what a welcome sight!—is something to which we ourselves belong: the "assembly of the firstborn who are enrolled in heaven" (v. 23). The term "firstborn" tells us the character and composition of this church. "Firstborn" has several connotations, all of them wonderful. The firstborn received a double portion of an inheritance, and here we have a whole city of such heirs. Heirs receive their portion by birth, not by achievement or deserts. So, too, these firstborn come into their rights by the new birth in Christ. This status is realized solely by faith: "To all who did receive him, who believed in his name, he gave the right to become children of God" (John 1:12).

Furthermore, the firstborn are those especially beloved of the Father. This is what God said of Israel in his demand to Pharaoh: "Israel is my firstborn son. . . . Let my son go that he might serve me" (Ex. 4:22–23). These citizens are those beloved of God, defended and delivered by his might for fellowship with him and to worship him forever.

We think back to Egypt and the exodus, and we remember, too, that the firstborn sons were redeemed by the blood of the lamb. Surely this is on the writer's mind as he compares Sinai to Zion. The angel of death came to the land of the Nile, and the only doors passed over were those marked by the redeeming blood of the lamb. And so, too, this church in God's city is filled with those redeemed by the saving blood of Christ. Just as Israel's

569

firstborn sons later had to be redeemed from God (see Ex. 13:13), so these too belong to him, are set apart for him, for his glory and service.

Finally, we remember that our Lord Jesus is the "head of the body, the church. He is the beginning, the firstborn from the dead" (Col. 1:18). He is, as Paul writes in Romans 8:29, "the firstborn among many brothers," to whom all the children of God are to be brought into conformity. In this city, Jesus is the cornerstone who sets the pattern for everyone else; he is the first-born and all the saints are "conformed to the image of [God's] Son."

The writer of Hebrews goes on to say that the firstborn "are enrolled in heaven" (v. 23). When Moses brought the children of Israel out to Sinai in the exodus, he was to enroll their names in the annals of the nation (Num. 3:40–43). This was an enrollment on earth; but the firstborn are recorded in heaven, a source of great rejoicing and praise. As the church father Athanasius exclaimed, "Who would not wish to enjoy the high companionship of these! Who would not desire to be enrolled with these, that he may hear with them, 'Come, ye blessed of my Father, inherit the kingdom prepared for you from the foundations of the world!'" (Matt. 25:34).[3]

Of course, if this is the City of God, then God himself must be there. And to him the writer draws our attention: "You have come . . . to God, the judge of all." This was also something the Israelites found on Mount Sinai: a judging God, a law-giving God, a God who gave the Ten Commandments upon the mount. For sinners, this is a sight that chills even the warmest welcome. Yet this is clearly not the meaning here.

Indeed, the point is quite the opposite of condemnation. For here we see God as judge, yet the fire and smoke and dark and gloom, the threatening blare of trumpets—all the trappings of condemnation—are gone! Indeed, what we see with this judging God is not hell but heaven, not those arrested and punished, but "the spirits of the righteous made perfect" (Heb. 12:23). The host around this God and Judge have been acquitted in his court; they are judged righteous and are made perfect. This is the host to which we belong, if we have come through faith in Christ. Philip Hughes writes, "This Judge is also the God of our Lord Jesus Christ, whose perfect sacrifice is . . . the first ground of our acceptance and justification. . . . To him the Chris-

3. Cited in Hughes, *Hebrews*, 549.

tian believer comes gladly and with confidence, knowing that what is for others a throne of judgment is for him a throne of grace" (Heb. 4:16; 10:22).[4]

For this host God stands as judge, not to condemn, but to vindicate. Indeed, the very fact that he is the Judge increases our comfort all the more, for he will be righteous in accepting us in Christ, who already paid the entire debt of our sin. This is what Paul was getting at in Romans 8:31–34:

> What then shall we say to these things? If God is for us, who can be against us? He who did not spare his own Son but gave him up for us all, how will he not also with him graciously give us all things? Who shall bring any charge against God's elect? It is God who justifies. Who is to condemn? Christ Jesus is the one who died—more than that, who was raised—who is at the right hand of God, who indeed is interceding for us.

THE MEDIATOR OF THE NEW COVENANT

Finally, the writer of Hebrews tells us that as Christians we "have come to . . . Jesus, the mediator of a new covenant." This is placed last for emphasis, as the climax of all we have already seen. Moses was the mediator who stepped toward the other mountain in fear and trembling. Jesus is the mediator of a new covenant in his blood, one who takes away our fear, strips away the clouds of fury and opens wide the gate to Paradise for all who come in faith.

We remember the point of the Letter to the Hebrews, and we see what this passage is teaching. What folly it would be to go from this mediator, Jesus, to the old mediator, Moses, from this mountain of grace to the mountain of fear and darkness that was Sinai!

This passage speaks joy to our hearts as well, most of which, I suppose, have never been tempted to revert to Judaism. The writer of Hebrews goes on to mention "the sprinkled blood that speaks a better word than the blood of Abel" (v. 24). Moses sprinkled the blood of sacrifices on the people when the old covenant community was being formed, and Jesus now is seen doing the same for the new covenant community.

Jesus' blood, we are told, speaks a better word than the blood of Abel. Again, we have an Old Testament reference, one that has the blood not just

---

4. Ibid.

sprinkled but actually speaking. In Genesis 4 we read of Cain, the first child of Adam and Eve, murdering his brother Abel, who received God's favor through faith. God tracked Cain down and exclaimed to him, "The voice of your brother's blood is crying to me from the ground" (Gen. 4:10). God therefore cursed Cain, and the blood of Abel spoke a word of vengeance. In the heart of Cain, the voice of Abel's blood resounded with despair all the long years of his cursed life. In great contrast, Westcott observes, "The blood of Christ pleads with God for forgiveness and speaks peace to man. The blood, that is, the abiding virtue of Christ's offered life, is in heaven; inseparable from the glorified King and Priest."[5]

What a contrast there is between Abel's blood and Christ's! Both were killed by their brothers: Abel by Cain, and Jesus by his fellow Jews, and no less by the sins of those firstborn brothers who will share eternity with him. Jesus was killed by us, his brothers. But what a different message Jesus' blood proclaims! Abel's blood brought storms upon the earth, while Jesus' blood cries, "Peace, be still!" Just as those words calmed the winds and waves when Jesus spoke them from the boat, so too does the voice of his blood drive away the mountain storms, the fire and tempest of Mount Sinai, to make Mount Zion a place of peace and calm and joy forevermore.

YOU HAVE COME

The passage that follows provides the writer's application to this marvelous description of the benefits and blessings for all who come to God through Jesus Christ. His main application is this: "See that you do not refuse him who is speaking" (v. 25). That is, ensure that you do not turn away from a salvation like this, since there is no other.

But we should also consider what this passage says about what it means to be a Christian. What are we to understand about the Christian life? The key to this is found in verse 22, which says, "You *have come*." The writer of Hebrews does not say, "You are coming" or "You will someday come." He says, "You have come." This is the dark glass taken away, so that we may have God's perspective on our own present existence as his people in the world. This is not merely a picture of your future reality—this is now your reality

5. Westcott, *Hebrews,* 419.

if you are a Christian. You have come to this mountain, where the threatening flames burn no more. You have come to this city, in which the worship of angels surrounds the people of God. You have come to this church, vindicated by God, proclaimed righteous and made perfect in Christ. Why? This is where our passage leads us—all of these things are true because of this one and essential thing, because "you have come . . . to Jesus, the mediator of a new covenant" (Heb. 12:22–24), to his better-speaking blood. You have come to Jesus and all of this is found in him. John Owen rightly says: "We have here a blessed, yea, a glorious description of the universal church, as the nature and communion of it are revealed under the gospel. . . . We have here the substance of all the privileges which we receive through the gospel."[6]

Think about this the next time you sit down in church. Perhaps you will find yourself next to a weak, sinful Christian, perhaps one who has just about worn out your patience, has plumb dried your reservoir of Christian love. Think about this next time at Bible study when new believers come in, ignorant of the Bible and only two steps down the road of sanctification. They are, if they really have believed on Jesus Christ, destined not just for improvement, but for glory. If you could see them now—those people whom you require so much effort to live amongst in the church, who let you down, who struggle with sin—if you could see them now as they will certainly be in the city to which they now belong, you would marvel at the glory God has prepared for those who love him. They are destined for glory, to be perfected, conformed to the image of their firstborn brother, Jesus Christ. They have become citizens of God's mountain city because they have come in faith to Christ.

Think about this, too, when you look at yourself, when you despair over besetting sins, when you find yourself so weighted down with filth and weakness and doubt and fear. Here God pulls aside the veil and shows you what he already sees in you: "the spirit of the righteous made perfect."

A Christian bumper-sticker reads, "I'm not perfect, I'm just forgiven." But in God's sight that statement is not true. Yes, there is much to be done, a whole network of sin to be thrown out and replaced by truth and grace. Yet so sure is this final perfecting in Christ that the writer of Hebrews could say,

---

6. John Owen, *An Exposition of the Epistle to the Hebrews*, 7 vols. (Edinburgh: Banner of Truth, 1991), 7:329.

"We have been sanctified through the offering of the body of Jesus Christ once for all. . . . By a single offering he has perfected for all time those who are being sanctified" (Heb. 10:10, 14). We are not just forgiven, but we are made perfect in Christ. This is how God sees us now in Christ, and this is our destiny according to the power of God's saving grace.

Never forget, if you have come to faith in Christ, that you have come "to Jesus, the mediator of a new covenant," to the blood that speaks a word of grace and not of condemnation. Jesus is a better Savior than you are a sinner. Therefore he rests enthroned in his city, his saving work secure in your life. He calls us to rest our hearts in him, and with thanksgiving to offer to God the worship of our lives.

53

WHAT CANNOT BE SHAKEN

Hebrews 12:25–29

Therefore let us be grateful for receiving a kingdom that cannot be shaken, and thus let us offer to God acceptable worship, with reverence and awe, for our God is a consuming fire. (Heb. 12:28–29)

In Hebrews 12:18–24, we observe a dramatic scene in our tour of Bible geography. The writer of Hebrews has shown us two mountains in succession. First was Mount Sinai, from which the law was given to the exodus generation. It was a mountain of foreboding, striking out with lightning and fire, darkness and gloom. Its message was the danger of drawing near to God in his holiness. Even Moses, we are reminded, trembled with fear at the sight.

Then we were shown the same scene after Christ came to take away the storms of judgment, after the darkness was pierced with the light of the gospel. Sinai became Zion, the mount on which rest the City of God and the church of his firstborn. Cries of fear have given way to songs of joy. The festal voices now invite us to draw near in faith unto eternal life.

On the basis of what we have seen, the writer of Hebrews intends for us to make some reflections about life and eternity. With this sight in our eyes,

575

and this sound in our ears, he exhorts us, "See that you do not refuse him who is speaking" (Heb. 12:25). Given the glorious prospect set before us in the gospel, it would be, he says, the gravest folly to gaze upon this, to hear this call, and yet to turn away.

"SEE TO IT"

Hebrews 12:25–29 completes the fifth and final exhortation against the danger of apostasy, a concern that has preoccupied our writer throughout this letter. "See to it," he says, "that you do not refuse him who speaks" (v. 25 NIV). "See to it" is a favorite expression of his, denoting watchfulness for a real and grave danger. In chapter 3 he charged his readers, "Take care [NIV: See to it], brothers, lest there be in any of you an evil, unbelieving heart, leading you to fall away from the living God" (v. 12). This is his great concern, that among the number of professing believers in this community, some might deny the faith under the threat of persecution.

The point he makes in verse 25 is one he has made before. He is arguing from the lesser to the greater, in this case from Mount Sinai to Mount Zion. If the Israelites did not escape the most severe punishment when they hardened their hearts toward God's revelation from Mount Sinai, how much greater is the punishment for those who do not heed the gospel, which comes to us from the heavenly Mount Zion! This is similar to what he argued in chapter 2: "For since the message declared by angels proved to be reliable and every transgression or disobedience received a just retribution, how shall we escape if we neglect such a great salvation?" (vv. 2–3).

There is no middle ground in the things of God. George H. Guthrie rightly says, "The Word must be received or rejected. . . . For those who reject the Word, there exists no escape from God's judgment. At the end a person either resides as a citizen of God's unshakable kingdom or perishes with the rest of the universe."[1]

Many people draw a mistaken conclusion about the New Testament and Christianity. They conclude that since Jesus speaks of grace and peace, God must no longer be as serious about obedience as he was in the Old Testament. People compare Moses and Jesus, and they think that Jesus is a nicer

---

1. George H. Guthrie, *Hebrews* (Grand Rapids: Zondervan, 1998), 425.

fellow who will be more tolerant of their sin and rebellious unbelief. But they are badly mistaken. According to the New Testament, the same Jesus who so tenderly ministers to his own flock will return in vengeance to judge the world that crucified him in unbelief. The apostle Paul puts this is the starkest terms, writing of Christ's return "from heaven with his mighty angels in flaming fire, inflicting vengeance on those who do not know God and on those who do not obey the gospel of our Lord Jesus. They will suffer the punishment of eternal destruction, away from the presence of the Lord and from the glory of his might" (2 Thess. 1:7–8).

Many people draw a similar conclusion when they compare the authority of Jesus with other authorities in this world. This was surely how Pontius Pilate, the Roman governor in Judah, felt when Jesus, though his prisoner and though displaying outward weakness, declared that he ruled a kingdom. "You? Are *you* a king?" Pilate wondered sarcastically. Jesus replied, "My kingdom is not of this world" (John 18:33–36). Jesus' kingdom is a spiritual one. Does that mean that while we must respect and fear earthly powers, we can afford to ignore Jesus' spiritual authority? If Jesus' rule is merely spiritual, does that mean it has nothing to do with people who don't choose to be religious? James M. Boice replies:

> Nothing is farther from the truth, for when we say that Christ's kingdom is not of this world, what we are really saying is that Christ's kingdom is of heaven and therefore has an even greater claim over us than do the earthly kingdoms we know so well. . . . Over these is Christ, and we flout his kingship not merely at the peril of our fortune and lives but at the peril of our eternal souls.[2]

The gospel presents the highest obligation to obedience, bringing a greater punishment for disobedience than even Moses' law. William Barclay says: "If a man merits condemnation for neglecting the imperfect message of the law, how much more does he merit it for neglecting the perfect message of the gospel? Because the gospel is the full revelation of God, there is laid on the man who hears it a double and a terrible responsibility; and his condemnation must be all the more if he neglects it."[3] That being the case, our writer's warning to "see to it" is very reasonable. Because they disobeyed

---

2. James Montgomery Boice, *The Gospel of John* (Grand Rapids: Zondervan, 1985), 1278.
3. William Barclay, *The Letter to the Hebrews* (Louisville: Westminster/John Knox, 1976), 188.

God's earthly revelation, an entire generation of Israelites was forced to wander and die in the wilderness. The penalty for refusing the gospel witness from heaven, as it is preached and read from the Bible, is considerably greater, even eternal condemnation.

WHAT CANNOT BE SHAKEN

Verse 25 argues from the lesser to the greater, from the law to the gospel. Our writer hopes to impress upon his readers the eternal significance of the choices that lie before them. This leads him to a second argument: "At that time his voice shook the earth, but now he has promised, 'Yet once more I will shake not only the earth but also the heavens'" (Heb. 12:26). Here is another comparison, starting with the violent scene at Mount Sinai. There God shook the earth. As Psalm 68 says, "The earth quaked, the heavens poured down rain, before God, the One of Sinai" (v. 8). That shaking of the earth at Sinai, the writer says, pointed forward to a greater shaking, one that will impact everything: "At that time his voice shook the earth, but now he has promised, 'Yet once more I will shake not only the earth but also the heavens'" (Heb. 12:26). The writer of Hebrews gives the explanation for this: "This phrase, 'Yet once more,' indicates the removal of things that are shaken—that is, things that have been made—in order that the things that cannot be shaken may remain" (Heb. 12:27). This is a quotation of Haggai 2:6–7, which says, "Yet once more, in a little while, I will shake the heavens and the earth and the sea and the dry land. And I will shake all nations, so that the treasures of all nations shall come in, and I will fill this house with glory, says the LORD of hosts."

We are reading a prophetic history lesson, a reminder that one day this present created realm will be shaken by God, leaving only those eternal things that are of him. This point is made by practically all the New Testament writers. John writes in his first epistle, "The world is passing away along with its desires." All the things that people live for, all that we strive toward that is of the world will ultimately come to nothing. In contrast, John exhorts, "But whoever does the will of God abides forever" (1 John 2:17). Peter likewise writes of the judgment that will come upon the world after Christ returns: "The heavens will pass away with a roar, and the heavenly bodies will be burned up and dissolved, and the earth and the works that are done on it will be exposed" (2 Peter 3:10). Paul puts it perhaps most succinctly: "For the present form of this world is passing away" (1 Cor. 7:31).

This is one point at which the Christian view is sharply at odds with that of the world. It is hard to underestimate the importance of this matter. All through our lives we are taught that the things of substance, those things that are lasting and stable, are the worldly things. Ideas, beliefs, spiritual commitments—these things come and go, we are told. What matters is cold hard cash, giant edifices of stone and steel, achievements in the world of nations and commerce and arts. Believe whatever you like about spiritual matters, we are told, since they are of secondary consideration. But do not let them interfere with the lasting things of the world.

Under this view, a practical person would abandon Christianity in the face of opposition, ridicule, and especially persecution. The Hebrew Christians stood in danger of having their property confiscated. They might lose their houses for the gospel; they might lose their jobs for Christ; they might be imprisoned and even die, when all this could be avoided by merely changing their religious position. What lunacy that is if the things of this world are the things that really matter!

But this world is not what ultimately matters. If it did, then our commitment to Christ might well be secondary. But God, who shook the earth when he descended on Mount Sinai, is going to shake the heavens and the earth—all things—when Christ comes again in glory and power. The day will come when everything that is of this world will pass away, and those who have their hopes and dreams, their security and their salvation rooted in this world, will find themselves brought to utter ruin with it.

A Tale of Two Kingdoms

Perhaps the greatest example of the folly of placing worldly priorities ahead of spiritual ones is provided by the Roman Empire. Rome's dominating power controlled the entire known world when this letter was written. This epistle was probably written to Jewish Christians living in Rome; the threat to them came from the Roman government with the help of the Jewish synagogue. What could have been more impressive in that day, more stable, or more lasting than the Roman Empire? If one had asked, "Which is going to last? The Roman Empire or Christianity?" people would have laughed! They would have cried, "Rome will last forever!" They would have pointed to its pomp and pageantry as mere symbols of its eternal power and glory.

But from our perspective things look quite different. In time, Rome would pit all its strength against the gospel and the followers of Jesus Christ. But in the end it was Rome that capitulated. Before long, the "eternal city" was overrun by barbarians, its statues crashed to the ground, and its buildings were looted and burned and crumbled. But the gospel of Jesus Christ, that voice that comes from heaven, has endured to this day and it shall endure forever. It endures because it is built on truth, not on worldly pretensions— because it *is* truth. It endures because it is the Word of God. The prophet Isaiah put it well: "All flesh is grass, and all its beauty is like the flower of the field. . . . The grass withers, the flower fades, but the word of our God will stand forever" (Isa. 40:6–8).

Today Rome's great power, which the Christian readers of this letter understandably feared, is but a memory. Meanwhile the kingdom of Christ is with us still, its strength unabated. The impact of the two kingdoms has been described quite cleverly by comparing Nero, the emperor who probably was involved in this persecution, and the apostle Paul, whom he had put to death. "Today people name their dogs after Nero," it is said, "but they name their sons after Paul."

The voice we most need to hear is that of Jesus himself. He said, "Heaven and earth will pass away, but my words will not pass away" (Matt. 24:35). Therefore, a Christian's priorities are opposite from those of the world. It is not that worldly things are of no importance to us. Christians may well be involved in the erection of great buildings and in worldly efforts of one sort or another. But far from putting spiritual things second, it is our allegiance to Christ that we place first. When worldly commitments and agendas, particularly as they involve sin, get in the way of our obedience to Christ, then we must be prepared to let the world go, remembering which kingdom will pass and which will last.

Furthermore, Christians are taught by the apostle Paul in 1 Corinthians 3:13–15 that all of our work "will become manifest, for the Day will disclose it . . . it will be revealed by fire, and the fire will test what sort of work each one has done. If the work that anyone has built on the foundation survives, he will receive a reward. If anyone's work is burned up, he will suffer loss, though he himself will be saved, but only as through fire." That being the case, why would any of us want to give ourselves to things that will perish? Christians may and in many cases should be involved in worldly endeavors, but wise believers will do so in a manner that is pleasing to God, that serves God's kingdom, and thus will offer up every labor for his inspection and approval.

Verse 28 says we are "receiving a kingdom that cannot be shaken." This is what we are taught to pray, "Your kingdom come"—that is, that God's rule should extend further and deeper into our lives and into this world. That is what history is about, and if we are wise, we will value our participation in Christ's spiritual kingdom far above any worldly calling.

Sadly, there are some whose false profession of faith will be revealed by their choice of the world over Christ. An example of this comes from the time of the Reformation in France. There, as elsewhere, the spread of the gospel brought tumult and even war. The evangelical Christians, known then and now as the Huguenots, had as one of their leaders a man named Henry of Navarre. Henry was a member of the French royal family, which was Roman Catholic, but he had heard the gospel, professed faith in Christ, and sided with the Reformed church. When, in 1593, the opportunity came for Henry to be crowned king of France, his profession was put to the test. To consolidate his political position, he would have to revert back to Roman Catholicism, at least officially. This is the kind of test the readers of this Letter to the Hebrews were facing. Would they compromise their faith? Would they make their allegiance to Christ secondary to worldly interests?

For Henry of Navarre it was the choice between a royal crown on earth and the crown awaiting God's people in heaven. Henry chose the world. Explaining his willingness to revert to Roman Catholicism, he callously remarked, "Paris is worth a mass." But Paris is not worth a mass. A promotion in the workplace is not worth betraying Jesus Christ, nor is a romance worth a compromise with the world, nor is any earthly treasure worth our eternal salvation. These are all things that will be shaken, that will fall to the ground in the end, while we by faith are receiving a kingdom that will not and cannot be shaken because it is of God.

WITH REVERENCE AND AWE

So far we have been exhorted to see to our faith because of the consequence of rejecting the gospel and because of the fleeting nature of every worldly kingdom and treasure. Verses 28 and 29 conclude our passage with a third argument and an accompanying exhortation: "Therefore let us be grateful for receiving a kingdom that cannot be shaken, and thus let us offer to God acceptable worship, with reverence and awe, for our God is a consuming fire."

While the gospel gives us a better revelation than that received at Mount Sinai, a salvation through God's grace in Jesus Christ, it is not a different God who speaks in this age. God is unchanging. He is now as he always has been, and that means that he is still holy and exalted, awesome in his glory. He is still "a consuming fire."

The gospel invites us to draw near to God, to live upon his mountain in the city he has prepared. Yet it is also true that God's holiness places an eternal distinction between the Creator and the creature. Verse 29 reminds us of Exodus 3, where Moses saw the fire burning within the bush. God called Moses to come near, but then said to him, "Do not come near; take your sandals off your feet, for the place on which you are standing is holy ground" (Ex. 3:5). The imagery of God as a raging fire speaks of his holiness and the reverent fear with which we must always treat him. God can never be taken lightly. Even when the threat of his wrath has been removed by the cross of Christ, he himself is not a tame God; he is always dangerous.

This truth is famously depicted by C. S. Lewis in his *Narnia* series of children's fantasies. Lewis uses the figure of Aslan, the giant and majestic lion, to depict the Lord. At one point, one of his heroines, the adventurous girl Jill, comes upon a stream of water. She has been lost and is dying of thirst. But as she comes forward, she spies the lion sitting calmly before the water. Terrified, she stops in her tracks. The lion invites her, "If you are thirsty, come and drink." Dying of thirst, and drawn by the rippling gurgle of the stream, the girl steps a bit forward. "Will you promise not to—do anything to me, if I do come?" she meekly asks. "I make no promise," said the lion. Drawn closer by the refreshing sounds of water, she wonders aloud, "*Do* you eat girls?" "I have swallowed up girls and boys, women and men, kings and emperors, cities and realms," he replies. Jill recoils at this, concluding, "I daren't come and drink." "Then you will die of thirst," said the lion. "O dear!" cries Jill, drawn yet a step closer by her need of refreshment, "I suppose I must go and look for another stream, then." But the lion responds, "There is no other stream."[4]

If you are going to have the thirst of your soul filled by the waters of eternal life, then you are going to have to deal with this kind of God. He will not move out of the way for you. He will not become a more palatable, a chummier kind of God. He will never be safe. But he is the Savior, the God of majesty and grace, the God who shakes the heavens and earth but gives to his own a kingdom that cannot be shaken.

Hebrews 12:29 recalls the fires of Mount Sinai, citing a statement made by Moses in Deuteronomy 4:24. Moses was warning the tribes about apostasy and idolatry, a betrayal of the true God for the false gods of this world. "Take care," he said, "lest you forget the covenant of the LORD your God, which he made with you, and make a carved image, the form of anything that the LORD your God has forbidden you. For the LORD your God is a consuming fire, a jealous God" (Deut. 4:23–24). Never think that allegiance to God is a light matter, for he is jealous of the affections of his people. He is a consuming fire, who purifies all with whom he comes into contact.

God being the kind of God he is, the two essential ingredients to true spirituality are those found in verse 28, namely, gratitude and awe. "Therefore let us be grateful for receiving a kingdom that cannot be shaken, and thus let us offer to God acceptable worship, with reverence and awe." As creatures before the Creator, we must tremble with fear, we must reckon on his holiness with a godly awe that produces reverence in all our dealings with him. But to awe we must add thanksgiving. We are sinners redeemed by the hand of mercy, enemies who are reconciled by love, rebels who are made children and heirs of God's eternal kingdom. Realizing this must surely draw forth gratitude from our hearts for the gifts we have not deserved. These two attitudes are given in the Bible as the yardsticks by which we may assess all our worship, all our works, all our lives as they are offered up to him. "Let us be grateful," not wishing for the world and stirring his jealous anger; "let us offer to God acceptable worship, with reverence and awe," not forgetting that this is the holy God of heaven, "a consuming fire."

4. C. S. Lewis, *The Silver Chair* (New York: HarperCollins, 1953), 21–23.

INVESTING IN ETERNITY

Everyone is faced with a great choice in this life, a choice that is tested and refined later on. Into the cacophony of this world, into our busy lives, into the ever-present hum of trivial human endeavors, God is speaking. God calls to this world; he calls to each of us. At Mount Sinai he spoke from the earth, but in the gospel today he speaks from heaven. Our choice is a simple one: will we heed that voice? Will we receive and obey the God who breaks into our worldly affairs? It is not easy to heed the call of God in a world like ours, to live for a world that is yet to come, that is invisible to our sight and evident only to our faith. But God does not intend for it to be easy, for it is the costly devotion of our hearts that he seeks. It is always that way: we must lose our lives in order to save them, we must give up the world to gain the kingdom of God.

One man who judged things rightly, who understood the relationship between this present world and the world to come, was Jeremiah, God's prophet in Jerusalem at the time of its destruction. The Babylonians had laid siege to the city, establishing the camps of their vast army in the surrounding towns, which they had trampled down. God then came to Jeremiah and told him to take his money and make an investment. Land had come up for sale in his hometown of Anathoth, one of those villages then being ground to dust by the enemy army. No doubt the real estate market was somewhat depressed there. But in accordance with God's Word, a man came to Jeremiah, saying, "Buy my field that is at Anathoth in the land of Benjamin, for the right of possession and redemption is yours; buy it for yourself" (Jer. 32:8). The cost was seventeen shekels of silver, and Jeremiah eagerly paid out the money, took the deed of purchase, and made provision for its safekeeping.

This is the kind of thing God is asking us to do. There are plots available in the kingdom of God, but they do not look very promising according to the market analysts of the world. In fact, like Jeremiah, we can buy low because people are hardly knocking down the doors to get in on the deal. But there is a catch. To invest in God's development, we must divest from the world. We cannot serve both God and mammon. We must choose between God's city, the new Jerusalem, and the city of this world, with its presently attractive offerings. Jeremiah paid seventeen shekels, which was not a great sum, and he expected a vast profit from that plot of heavenly soil; indeed, he expected an eternal weight of glory. God offers to us an inheritance in his kingdom for free—all we have to do is forsake all other kingdoms and all other gods.

Jeremiah was glad to buy his land. "I am buying low," he might have said, "but I will be selling high in that day to come." He foresaw a day when the kingdoms of this world will be shaken, and everything that is not stamped with God's royal seal will be removed forever. A place in God's kingdom is free, through faith in Jesus Christ, but it will cost us everything else in this world—and what a bargain that is! "The kingdom of heaven," Jesus said, "is like treasure hidden in a field, which a man found and covered up. Then in his joy he goes and sells all that he has and buys that field" (Matt. 13:44). Therefore, seeing a shaking of the heavens and earth, and receiving by faith a kingdom that cannot be shaken, we ought to live in reverent thanksgiving. This is what Peter advised:

> Since all these things are thus to be dissolved, what sort of people ought you to be in lives of holiness and godliness, waiting for and hastening the coming of the day of God, because of which the heavens will be set on fire and dissolved, and the heavenly bodies will melt as they burn! But according to his promise we are waiting for new heavens and a new earth in which righteousness dwells. (2 Peter 3:11–13)

May all our hope rest on Jesus Christ, whose coming is soon, who is worthy of all that we can give, and who is more than able to preserve all we place into his hands.

54

JESUS CHRIST THE SAME

Hebrews 13:1—8

[God] has said, "I will never leave you nor forsake you." So we
can confidently say, "The Lord is my helper; I will not fear; what
can man do to me?" Remember your leaders, those who spoke to
you the word of God. Consider the outcome of their way of life,
and imitate their faith. Jesus Christ is the same yesterday and
today and forever. (Heb. 13:5–8)

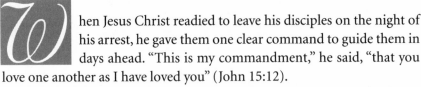hen Jesus Christ readied to leave his disciples on the night of
his arrest, he gave them one clear command to guide them in
days ahead. "This is my commandment," he said, "that you
love one another as I have loved you" (John 15:12).

We have come to a similar point in the Book of Hebrews. This letter
was sent to a body of Jewish believers who were tempted to revert from
Christianity back to Judaism in order to escape persecution. The great
refrain of Hebrews is both a warning against apostasy, against a falling
away from the faith, and an exhortation to hold fast to Christ for salvation. Five times this warning is given in one form or another, including

the one at the end of chapter 12 referring to the voice of God in the gospel: "See that you do not refuse him who is speaking" (v. 25).

Now, not unlike Jesus on the night of his departure from the twelve disciples, the writer of Hebrews prepares to leave his readers, and in this last chapter he gives his final words of exhortation. It is no surprise, therefore, that he begins in the same manner as Jesus did, exhorting them in verse 1: "Let brotherly love continue."

We might organize this final chapter into four sections. First, there is life within the church community, which is what we will consider in this study. Next is the belief of the church in the midst of an unbelieving world, in verses 9–14. Starting in verse 15 there is a call to lives offered sacrificially to the Lord. Finally, the chapter concludes with one of the great benedictions of the New Testament, in verses 20 and 21.

A LOVING COMMUNITY

Hebrews 13 begins, then, with a command Christians are required to take seriously: "Let brotherly love continue." Christians are to live continually by this principle. Christianity is the family of God; the church is to be a community characterized by family love.

One person who wrote much about Christian love was Francis Schaeffer. Much of his life was caught up in church disputes that were quite divisive. Schaeffer was known as a powerful defender of Christian doctrines, yet at the same time he strove to maintain love within the body of believers. One of his books begins with these words: "Through the centuries men have displayed many different symbols to show that they are Christians. They have worn marks in the lapels of their coats, hung chains about their necks, even had special haircuts. . . . But there is a much better sign. . . . It is a universal mark that is to last through all ages of the church until Jesus comes back."[1] That mark is love among Christians, and Schaeffer proves it with Jesus' teaching of John 13:35: "By this all people will know that you are my disciples, if you have love for one another." There are both a condi-

---

1. Francis A. Schaeffer, *The Mark of the Christian*, in *The Complete Works of Francis A. Schaeffer* (Wheaton, Ill.: Crossway, 1982), 4:183.

tion, an "if," he points out—namely, if we love one another—and a result, that people will see this as the mark identifying the disciples of Jesus.

In another book Schaeffer writes: "Evangelism is a calling, but not the first calling. Building congregations is a calling, but not the first calling. A Christian's first call is to . . . return to the first commandment to love God, to love the brotherhood, and then to love one's neighbor as himself."[2] We are to show love as an essential part of our witness, but more importantly because God is love and we are called to Godlikeness in the world. The apostle John puts this in challenging terms, writing in his first epistle: "Beloved, let us love one another, for love is from God, and whoever loves has been born of God and knows God. Anyone who does not love does not know God, because God is love" (1 John 4:7–8). Loving others is an outflowing of our relationship with God, and it is how we show gratitude for his love to us.

Love is always expressed in concrete actions, and our passage provides two important examples. First, "Do not neglect to show hospitality to strangers" (Heb. 13:2). Here we find that the scope of our family love is to be broad indeed, just as Jesus taught in the parable of the Good Samaritan. A Pharisee had asked, "Who is my neighbor?" Jesus showed him that his neighbor is anyone in need and that we must show mercy to others as we have received it from God. That same principle animates the call to hospitality in the Book of Hebrews.

The main idea here is bringing people into our homes. In the ancient world, where traveling was dangerous and there were few inns, this was an important ministry. Today, with our compartmentalized lives, hospitality is no less significant. Here is a diagnostic question: How many people could describe the inside of your home? If you are married, are there any singles who could give directions to your dinner table? If you are single, are there any widows or children who have seen the park where you go to unwind? Are there any people you have entertained simply because you were looking on them as brothers and sisters in the family of God and have sought to minister to their loneliness or need for encouragement and support? This exhortation applies not only to other Christians, but it also includes all sorts of people whom, even if they are strangers, we must embrace with the love of God through Christian hospitality.

2. Francis A. Schaeffer, *Genesis in Space and Time*, in *Complete Works*, 1:85.

The second example has to do with those in prison: "Remember those who are in prison, as though in prison with them, and those who are mistreated, since you also are in the body" (v. 3). If the first example is that of hospitality, here is the principle of sympathy for the trials experienced by others. It is probable that this refers to fellow Christians jailed and mistreated for their faith, but again we have no warrant for limiting this teaching only to believers. Ray Stedman writes, "Even those imprisoned justly merit Christian help, since Jesus ministered to the guilty and the condemned simply because they were human beings."[3] In this ministry Jesus is both our example and the ultimate recipient of our acts of love. "Truly, I say to you," he said, "as you did it to one of the least of these my brothers, you did it to me" (Matt. 25:40).

Two key verbs go together here. Verse 2 says, "Do not neglect to show hospitality to strangers." Verse 3 adds, "Remember those who are in prison." Do not neglect . . . remember. It seems that the problem is the way we view our lives and each other—the difficulty is that we forget to love other people, probably because we are too wrapped up in ourselves.

Verse 2 includes an interesting statement about the spiritual value of these acts of love: "thereby some have entertained angels unawares." The most prominent examples of this, of course, are Abraham and Lot. Seeing strangers, Abraham rushed from his tent and slaughtered a calf for them, only later learning that they brought good news as messengers of the Lord. Lot defended two angels who visited him from the lustful mob of Sodom, and ended up being delivered from that city's destruction by those he had served (see Gen. 18–19).

The point is that there may be more to the people we meet than meets the eye. It is possible that when you sit in church, the person next to you will really be an angel, but he or she is likely something even more wonderful. There beside you in the pews is probably a saint of God in light. Across the room are those destined to serve as priests and kings in the very presence of the living God, who are now being prepared for their glorious raiment. To meet an angel might be wonderful, but in the church are those whom angels are "sent out to serve" and "who are to inherit salvation" (Heb. 1:14). There is a work going on in their lives that angels wonder at and rejoice to see.

---

3. Ray Stedman, *Hebrews* (Downers Grove, Ill.: InterVarsity 1992), 150.

C. S. Lewis in his essay "The Weight of Glory" remarked on what an extraordinary thing it is to live among those in whom eternal destinies are being worked out:

> The dullest and most uninteresting person you can talk to may one day be a creature which, if you saw it now, you would be strongly tempted to worship, or else a horror and a corruption such as you now meet, if at all, only in a nightmare. . . . There are no *ordinary* people. You have never talked to a mere mortal. . . . It is immortals whom we joke with, work with, marry, snub, and exploit—immortal horrors or everlasting splendours.[4]

The most powerful force in the lives of such creatures, made in God's image, is love. Christopher Morley said, "If we all discovered that we had only five minutes left to say all that we wanted to say, every telephone booth would be occupied by people calling other people to stammer that we love them."[5] Our job is to meet them outside the phone booth in the real world, there to contrast the self-gratifying love of the world with the self-sacrificing love of Christ.

A HOLY COMMUNITY

The church is called to love, but also to purity and freedom from sinful corruption. Love is not the only virtue, but it stands together with the holiness that is of God, who said, "You shall be holy, for I am holy" (1 Peter 1:16). Francis Schaeffer again puts it well:

> The Christian really has a double task. He has to practice both God's holiness and God's love. . . . Not His love without His holiness—that is only compromise. Anything that an individual Christian or Christian group does that fails to show the simultaneous balance of the holiness of God and the love of God presents to a watching world not a demonstration of the God who exists, but a caricature of the God who exists.[6]

The church, as well as the individual Christian, is God's own dwelling, his temple. Therefore Paul writes, "Let everyone who names the name of the

---

4. C. S. Lewis, *The Weight of Glory and Other Addresses* (New York: Macmillan, 1975), 19.
5. Cited in Ravi Zacharias, *Can Man Live without God?* (Dallas: Word, 1994), 105.
6. Francis A. Schaeffer, *The Mark of the Christian*, 193–94.

Lord depart from iniquity" (2 Tim. 2:19). Again, our passage provides concrete examples, first the purity of marriage: "Let marriage be held in honor among all, and let the marriage bed be undefiled, for God will judge the sexually immoral and adulterous" (Heb. 13:4).

The first readers of this letter were in a position similar to ours, within a depraved society awash in sexual perversion and indulgence. Yet it has always been a mark of Christian purity that we should be dramatically different in just this area. Paul strongly denounces sexual immorality in many of his letters, often listing it first among the sins we must shun. On one occasion, he wrote of the sexually immoral, "I warn you, as I warned you before, that those who do such things will not inherit the kingdom of God" (Gal. 5:21). Our text likewise says, "God will judge the sexually immoral and adulterous." God is judging, even now, the wantonness of our society, as well as supposedly Christian churches that espouse or tolerate it. Unless Christians are willing and able to be different at precisely the point of our society's greatest depravity, we cannot expect our testimony to be taken seriously, and our own profession of faith is brought into question.

Who is to honor marriage? All of us, says Hebrews 13:4. The whole church. We have a special interest in upholding the institution of marriage and the actual marriages among us. Marriage is the first institution established by God and the basic building block of the church and society. There may be no better gauge today for the spiritual health of a congregation than the health of its marriages. Husbands and wives hold a precious trust before the Lord and the church. One of our great needs today is the example of strong and godly marriages to encourage those who have never seen true love and to provide them with a model. One of the greatest witnesses in our age will be Christian couples who faithfully meet the struggles of marriage with the grace and power of God. Along with that is the astonishing witness, as our world now judges it, of Christian singles who keep the marriage bed pure through self-control and godly restraint. Most importantly, God is honored when married couples honor the vows they made to him, and when all Christians honor marriage.

The second example of holiness has to do with contentment versus greed: "Keep your life free from love of money, and be content with what you have" (Heb. 13:5). In view here is an attitude toward possessions, the love of money contrasted with the grateful contentment that flows from faith. Paul described greed as "idolatry" (Col. 3:5), and it may also be said that contentment is one of the purest signs of true worship of God. In his priceless book *The Rare Jewel of Christian Contentment*, Jeremiah Burroughs wrote: "You worship God more by [contentment] than when you come to hear a sermon, or spend half an hour, or an hour, in prayer, or when you come to receive a sacrament. These . . . are only external acts of worship. . . . But [contentment] is the soul's worship, to subject itself thus to God . . . by being pleased with what God does."[7] Arthur Pink adds: "Contentment is the product of a heart resting in God. . . . It is the blessed assurance that God does all things well, and is, even now, making all things work together for my ultimate good."[8]

If this seems challenging, our passage contains an extraordinary promise that transforms our thinking. Verses 5 and 6 tell us: "For he has said, 'I will never leave you nor forsake you.' So we can confidently say, 'The Lord is my helper; I will not fear; what can man do to me?'" Here is the engine that drives Christians to both love and holiness, namely, God's faithful presence as our sustainer and helper.

This is faith's soliloquy: If God is my helper, then what can man do to me? The point here is that given God's promise to be with us—the God who gave us his only Son and therefore surely will give us everything else he has—then God is my helper, and he never will leave or forsake me. If that is true, then why should I be afraid? Here is the antidote to the fear of man which otherwise so dominates our lives, which leads us from God and into sin.

If God is our helper, then what can man do to us? People can lead us into temptation, of course; but if God is my helper, I shall not fall, and if I stumble, he will surely lift me up. People can bring us into trials—they may threaten our temporal peace and prosperity, but is not God able to provide for our needs? People may shun us, but do we not have the love of God and the family love of the church? People may lock us up and mistreat us, but will not God come to find us? Does not God, right here, command his people so that they will seek us out to give us aid and comfort and joy? What can man do to me if God is my helper?

7. Jeremiah Burroughs, *The Rare Jewel of Christian Contentment* (Edinburgh: Banner of Truth, 1964), 120.
8. Arthur W. Pink, *Comfort for Christians* (Grand Rapids: Baker, 1976), 85–86.

AN IMITATING COMMUNITY

The knowledge of God's presence and help is the greatest of our encouragements, but there is also the example of Christians who have lived before us. In them, in the outcome of their life and death, we see living testaments to the faithfulness of God and the blessedness of trusting in him. This is what Hebrews 13:7 commends to us: "Remember your leaders, those who spoke to you the word of God. Consider the outcome of their way of life, and imitate their faith."

This is the third thing we are to exhorted to do. First is the call to love, then to be holy, and now to remember that we are not the first to have tried this kind of life. We have excellent examples of how a Christian is to live and what kind of life that is. Think back, Hebrews says, to the people who taught you the Word of God. Perhaps it was a parent or a teacher in school, perhaps a Christian who became your friend. We are to search the example of leaders in the church, and especially among them the preachers of God's Word.

Note what we are to learn from them. Not their personalities, or their ministry techniques, but "the outcome of their way of life." The text seems to be pointing to both their lives and their deaths and asks, "What is the lesson to be learned from these?"

If we think we are living in the only time when the flesh is weak, when even pastors and well-known church leaders fall into sin, make grievous mistakes, disgrace themselves and scandalize the church, then we are greatly mistaken. But the writer's confidence is not in men of God; it is in the God of men. God, in the course of his people's lives, and especially in the lives of those set apart for his service, reveals the glad result of walking with him in faith for the course of a lifetime. I personally find great solace and motivation from the older ministers it is my privilege to know. I know from them that the best of men are men at best. But I also see in their spiritual character what God can do in a man over a lifetime of faith.

Note what it is we are to imitate in leaders and teachers of God's Word: not their worldly methods, not their sins—some of which we may come to know—not their fancies or foibles, but their faith. Imitate their faith. Study and reflect upon the times in their lives when they relied on the Lord and boldly stood with and for him. Observe that it was faith that gave their ministries power; it was faith that sustained them to the end. Through their example, resolve to trust the Lord, to firmly stand on his Word and to rely completely on his matchless grace, especially when others are giving way and times are hard. This is the greatest legacy any of us can impart from the pattern of our lives, and it is by providing such examples that Christian leaders most powerfully serve the Lord and his church. This is why, as Paul shows us in 1 Timothy 3, the qualification for an elder in the church is not money or stature in the world, but faith in Christ that issues forth in a godly example for others.

JESUS CHRIST THE SAME

Verse 8 completes our passage, and without it everything we have said might be lost on us. Times change, we say. What was good for others may not be good for us. What worked before might fail in our time. Against such concerns the writer points out this vital truth: "Jesus Christ is the same yesterday and today and forever." The point is not just that Jesus, being the second person of the eternal Godhead, remains today as he ever was before, true though that is. The point is what this says about our passage, namely, that we may confidently embrace the pattern of the Christian life taught by the Bible because Jesus is the same.

This means that if you are a Christian, these commands are not given as just some ideal or program, some bygone philosophy that served a prior generation. Rather, by this kind of life, you are now serving and following Jesus Christ himself, who was and is and is to come, who lives and reigns now in the heavens and by his Spirit on the earth. The Leader you truly follow, the Lord you serve and trust is none other than Jesus Christ himself, who in his Word speaks to you as he did before to others, and whose call will never be superseded or set aside.

Three vital implications flow from this verse. First, since Jesus Christ is the same, his ministry and call are the same as they ever were. The Christ you see in the Gospels—cleansing the leper, raising the dead, stilling the storms, feeding the hungry, speaking words of forgiveness to sinners—is our own Lord, the Son of God, mighty to save. Similarly, the demands he placed on his first disciples are fully valid today, for he is still the same: "If anyone would come after me, let him deny himself and take up his cross daily and follow me" (Luke 9:23). That call to the cross is still the same today. So, too, is Christ's offer of blessing: "Come to me, all who labor and are heavy laden, and I will give you rest" (Matt. 11:28).

Second, the Christian life is ever the same, unchanged in all generations. The stories and teachings in the Bible are not irrelevant to modern or postmodern man. In the face of the world's complaint that ours is an outmoded creed, this is our reply: "Jesus Christ is the same." This is why we should study church history and Christian biographies, because other lives of faith are examples for us. A. W. Tozer wrote, "One of the most popular current errors, and the one out of which springs most of the noisy, blustering religious activity in evangelical circles, is the notion that as times change the church must change with them."[9] In contrast, our wisdom is that of Jeremiah 6:16, which says, "Stand at the crossroads and look; ask for the ancient paths, ask where the good way is, and walk in it, and you will find rest for your souls" (NIV).

Because Jesus Christ is the same, now is our turn to live as Christ's people in a manner that would be recognizable to those who came before us. They will not accept the excuse that our times are different from theirs, nor should they. All times are different in some ways, but Jesus Christ is always the same. If we could interview the faithful forefathers of our churches, is there anything that would delight them more than to know that the gospel they preached is the gospel we preach, or that the life of faith they displayed is now the pattern for us as we walk with the Lord? If that is true of mere men and women who lived in generations past, what a blessing must it be for our Lord Jesus, who lives still, to see us display in our lives and in our churches the truth and love and purity to which he called his disciples from the earliest days!

Third, because Jesus Christ is the same today as ever, it is Jesus we represent and display before our own generation. It is not a tradition, not a philosophy of man we serve, but Jesus Christ the Savior of sinners, the Son of God who bears his love in our world, who calls men and women through us to a living hope as he did in ages past.

Ravi Zacharias tells of an evangelist named Jakov, who preached the gospel in communist-held Yugoslavia. In those days the formal church was a pawn of the cruel regime and a haven for wolves in sheep's clothing. Because of

---

9. Cited in D. Martyn Lloyd-Jones, *Old Testament Evangelistic Sermons* (Carlisle, Pa.: Banner of Truth, 1995), xvi.

this, Jakov had a hard time getting people to listen to his claims about the love of Christ. One day an old man named Cimmerman sharply upbraided him on account of the terrible record of those who called themselves Christians. "They wear those elaborate coats and caps and crosses," he exclaimed, "signifying a heavenly commission, but their evil designs and lives I cannot ignore." Jakov replied by posing a hypothetical situation. Suppose a man stole Cimmerman's coat, put it on, broke into a bank, and ran off into the distance. "What would you say to the authorities if they came to your house and accused you of breaking into the bank?" he asked. Cimmerman responded angrily, and Jakov went on to continue his work. Zacharias concludes the story:

> Jakov continued to return to the village periodically just to befriend Cimmerman, encourage him, and share the love of Christ with him. Finally one day Cimmerman asked, "How does one become a Christian?" and Jakov taught him the simple steps of repentance for sin and of trust in the work of Jesus Christ and gently pointed him to the Shepherd of his soul. Cimmerman bent his knee on the soil with his head bowed and surrendered his life to Christ. As he rose to his feet, wiping his tears, he embraced Jakov and said, "Thank you for being in my life." And then he pointed to the heavens and whispered, "You wear His coat very well."[10]

If we are to wear the genuine mark of Jesus Christ in this world, it will have to be in the manner of these verses from Hebrews 13. It will be through love and purity before the world, shining, as Paul said, "as lights in the world, holding fast to the word of life" (Phil. 2:15–16). In that manner, it will then be Jesus we truly and faithfully proclaim, displaying his mark of love and wearing his righteous robe.

---

10. Zacharias, *Can Man Live without God?* 102.

55

OUTSIDE THE CAMP

Hebrews 13:9—14

Jesus also suffered outside the gate in order to sanctify the people through his own blood. Therefore let us go to him outside the camp and bear the reproach he endured. (Heb. 13:12–13)

n our previous study, we saw that the writer's appeal to the unchanging character of Christ grounded his teaching on the Christian life. The Christians were to live in love and purity, as did those from whom they learned the faith, because "Jesus Christ is the same yesterday and today and forever" (Heb. 13:8). Because Jesus stays the same and lives forever, the way of discipleship to him is a constant one. The same can be said for Christian truth. If Jesus Christ is the same always, then the doctrines of our salvation always remain unchanged, grounded as they are in his person and work. Having given instructions on Christian living in verses 1–8, the writer now turns to the matter of Christian belief.

A WARNING AGAINST FALSE TEACHING

One of the marks of spiritual maturity is to stand firm in the presence of diverse and strange doctrines. Paul said that Christians who are mature in their knowledge of Christ are no longer like "children, tossed to and fro by the waves and carried about by every wind of doctrine, by human cunning, by craftiness in deceitful schemes" (Eph. 4:14). One of the problems with the Christians who received the Letter to the Hebrews was that they were not yet so mature. We know this because of what is said in 5:11–14, that though by now they ought to be teachers, they were still like children when it came to the truth. That being the case, we see why Hebrews 13:9 warns them: "Do not be led away by diverse and strange teachings." This warning is always needed, but especially when the church is weak in grace and shallow in understanding, as certainly is the case in our own time. Notice how the writer puts it: there is a danger that these lightweight Christians will get carried away by strange teachings, just as a strong wind blows away chaff, or as rolling waves toss around a ship that is not well anchored.

Like the Hebrews, one thing we can be sure of is that false teaching will come along. This was Paul's warning to the Ephesian elders during his last visit to them, recorded in Acts 20. "I know," he said, "that after my departure fierce wolves will come in among you, not sparing the flock." Paul identifies the nature of their attack: "men speaking twisted things, to draw away the disciples after them" (vv. 29–30). Knowing this, Christians—especially those entrusted with stewardship over the church—need to be always on their guard to defend the truth.

This was also Paul's emphasis to Timothy: "Follow the pattern of the sound words that you have heard from me, in the faith and love that are in Christ Jesus. By the Holy Spirit who dwells within us, guard the good deposit entrusted to you" (2 Tim. 1:13–14). Paul stressed that this will be the great threat to the church in years to come, that shallow people in the church "will not endure sound teaching," but instead "will accumulate for themselves teachers to suit their own passions" (2 Tim. 4:3), and thus will turn many away from the truth.

When you point this out today, you are likely to be labeled a divisive, uncharitable critic, who must have some psychological deficiency that explains such a paranoid attitude. Nonetheless, the Bible instructs us to take this warning very seriously.

One reason why this danger of false teaching is so constant is that Christians have an active, aggressive enemy—namely, the devil—who constantly schemes to weaken or overthrow our faith. The devil has two main strategies, both of which are seen in the Book of Hebrews. The first is persecution, Satan's assault on the church from without. The writer of Hebrews identifies this threat and worries that some will betray the faith to avoid suffering. However, in light of the history of the church, persecution really is not a very effective strategy. It has always been the case that "the blood of the martyrs is the seed of the church," so that persecution makes the church grow stronger.

But Satan has another strategy, and this is to work from within the church: the strategy of infiltration. He sends false teachers to don Christian garb and stir up falsehood and error within the church, and by this means he has succeeded in doing a great deal of harm over the years. Indeed, given that Christians in America have experienced so little persecution, we should not be surprised to realize that the devil has been quite busy working from within, employing, as Paul describes them, "false apostles, deceitful workmen, disguising themselves as apostles of Christ. And no wonder, for even Satan disguises himself as an angel of light" (2 Cor. 11:13–14). This is a very grave threat in our own time, and one we should be constantly on our guard to combat.

Verse 9 gives a telling description of false teaching. The New International Version describes it as "all kinds of strange teachings," which removes some of the original flavor. Two words are used here in the Greek, the first of which is *poikilais*, which is best translated as "diverse." The word is used of clothing woven with many colors; the Septuagint (the Greek translation of the Old Testament) uses this word for the multicolored coat Jacob gave to his favored son Joseph (Gen. 37:3). This is what false teaching is like: it is dazzling to behold; in the place of plain truth it presents something enticing from every viewpoint. In metal working, this word is used of alloys like brass; so, too, false teaching mixes the heavenly with the worldly, divine revelation with human reason; it blends and collaborates rather than preserves the pure substance. Things described by this word are complex and not clear, intricate and not plain.

Of course, this is much of the attraction when it comes to new and false teaching. It is alluring because it takes a clever angle on an old theme; it is enticing to the mind; it appeals to our intellectual pride. This is always a temptation for those engaged in academic work, which is why scholars often produce teaching of the sort that does great damage to the church. You will never be declared the latest genius, your dissertation will not likely make a splash in intellectual circles, if you are not willing to engage in teaching described by this word. There is, of course, a valued place for true and even original scholarship, yet we always want to ensure we are following the example Paul explained in 2 Corinthians 4:2, "setting forth the truth plainly" (NIV) so that men might be brought to consider God and not us.

The second description given in verse 9 is *xenais*, which means "alien" or "strange." This was the word Greeks used for those who were citizens of another nation, for foreigners, and even mercenary soldiers. The word was also used of things not previously known, things unheard of and unfamiliar. False teaching is alien and foreign; it is not native to God's Word. Here we are warned against novelty in theology, which like the diverse is always appealing to our fallen minds.

Both of these terms—diverse and alien—aptly describe much of what is entering the minds of Christians today in sermons, on the radio, and over the counters of Christian bookstores. Just as in our worldly society, so also in our worldly church, the "new" is thought to be better. We have new perspectives and new paradigms, new models for Christian living, new prayers that promise abundant blessing. Given such a savage assault from within the church—which is exactly what American evangelicalism is experiencing today—it is no wonder we are losing spiritual power for true godliness.

The question surely arises, "How do we tell the difference?" How do we judge doctrine? By the sincerity of the teacher? On the basis of his or her personality? Because it is popular and everybody is buying it? That is how many consumers shop for truth. But what our passage says about false teaching tells us how we should discern matters of truth. Beware teaching that is alloyed, that mixes God's Word with the word of man. Beware doctrines that are new, that boast to have discovered what the foolish church never grasped before.

The charge of novelty was leveled against the Protestant Reformers by the Roman Catholic Church in the sixteenth century. The Reformers took the charge seriously, acknowledging that if it were true, it would condemn their teaching. They were eager to show, and did so effectively, that theirs were not new but rather the old and original doctrines of Christianity. The truths of the Reformation were found in the writings of the early church fathers and derived from the apostles and prophets in the Bible.

Ultimately this is our only sure guide when it comes to matters of truth: Does it agree with the clear teaching of Scripture? If it presents a new interpretation of Bible passages, does it square with what we read elsewhere in God's Word? Does it suggest a way of approaching and relating to God other than what was set forth by our Lord and by the agents of biblical revelation? This was Paul's approach in his Letter to the Galatians. Shortly after he had established that church, they were drawn aside by teachers of new and persuasive doctrines. Paul replied, "Even if we or an angel from heaven should preach to you a gospel contrary to the one we preached to you, let him be accursed" (Gal. 1:8). That is quite a statement. No matter how impressive the speaker or the speech, even if he appears as an angel from heaven—and of course, Satan can give just such an appearance—any teacher is to be rejected if what he says is contrary to the prophetic and apostolic teaching of the Scripture.

FOOD FOR THE SOUL

Hebrews 13:9 gives a general warning against false teaching, but goes on to speak of a specific threat to that church: "It is good for the heart to be strengthened by grace, not by foods, which have not benefited those devoted to them." We do not know the precise error this warning concerns. Judaism emphasized the importance of eating or not eating certain types of food. The warning here does not seem to be about abstention but rather about eating sacramental meals that supposedly provide spiritual benefit. The writer probably had the Passover meal in mind, as well as the many other sacrificial feasts prominent in Jewish religious life.

The New Testament reveals that religious scruples over food did not die easily in the early church. Acts 10 shows us how hard it was for God to get the apostle Peter to abandon such views, commanding him three times through a vision to eat what he had previously considered unclean food. Paul seems to have fought these kinds of views practically everywhere he went. In 1 Corinthians 8:8 he wrote, "Food will not commend us to God. We are no worse off if we do not eat, and no better off if we do." To the Colossians he wrote, "Let no one pass judgment on you in questions of food and drink" (2:16). To the Romans he said: "The kingdom of God is not a matter of eating and drinking, but of righteousness and peace and joy in the Holy Spirit" (14:17).

The point is that spiritual strength does not come to us by what we eat, but by grace, which is received through faith. Indeed, we may extend the principle to say that no outward activities in themselves provide spiritual blessing, but only the exercise of faith in Christ. This directly opposes a contrary principle that has been prominent in the history of the church. The principle is expressed by the Latin phrase *ex opere operato*, which means, "By the doing, it is done." That statement originated to defend Roman Catholic sacramentalism, which taught that one benefits from outward participation in the sacraments, and especially the mass, regardless of the inward disposition of the heart. That principle is also found in revivalistic evangelicalism, with its reliance on altar calls, fasts, specially worded prayers and the like, which are ascribed an almost magical power simply by doing them. "Just do it!" is the motto of this approach to spiritual blessing, with very little emphasis on how or why it is done.

Many commentators imagine that the Hebrew Christians were criticized for avoiding Jewish feasts, that Christianity was derided because it did not offer an altar or outward sacrifices. The attack might have gone something like this: "Your religion doesn't even have an altar. You don't even offer sacrifices. You don't get meals to eat for spiritual blessing." To that kind of criticism, the writer responds: "We have an altar from which those who serve the tent have no right to eat" (Heb. 13:10). The use of the word "altar" refers to the whole system of religion that Christians have in the place of Judaism. This verse helps date the Book of Hebrews, since it speaks in the present tense of the temple service, indicating that it was written before the destruction of Jerusalem in A.D. 70.

In the case of many Old Testament sacrifices, the meat from the sacrifice was given afterward to the priests to eat (see Lev. 19:5–6; 22:29–30). But when it came to the sacrifice offered on the day of atonement, the day once a year when the high priest offered a sacrifice for the sins of all the people, that sacrifice was not permitted to be eaten. Instead, it was taken outside the camp and burned (Lev. 16:27). Verses 11 and 12 make the point that this was the sacrifice to which Christ's death corresponded—the one the old covenant priests could not consume but which those who have left Judaism to follow Christ receive as their food: "For the bodies of those animals whose blood is brought into the holy places by the high priest as a sacrifice for sin are burned outside the camp. So Jesus also suffered outside the gate in order to sanctify the people through his own blood" (Heb. 13:11–12). These verses form a powerful polemic from the Levitical regulations themselves against the idea of remaining in Judaism after the true sacrifice has come, and they make a strong reply the Christians could give to their Jewish critics.

Notice that the writer of Hebrews passes by the opportunity to commend the Christian sacrament of the Lord's Supper. Indeed, all through this letter our author seems to overlook excellent opportunities to connect his teaching to this sacramental meal. For instance, when speaking of Melchizedek in chapter 7, he failed to mention that this priest-king fed Abraham with wine and bread, the very elements of the communion ritual. Given this trend, and the concern about an emphasis on foods, it may be that one of the problems in this Hebrew church was an overemphasis on the sacraments. One writer says: "It is likely that, even this early, there were those who took a mechanical view of the sacraments, forgetting that no sacrament in the world avails anything by itself and that its only use is that in it the grace of God meets the faith of man. It is not the meat but the faith and the grace which matter."[1]

Our passage condemns any view that Christ enters into men and women simply by their eating food. This especially confronts the Roman Catholic teaching of transubstantiation, that the elements of the Lord's Supper are literally and physically the body and blood of Jesus Christ, and that we partake of Christ and his grace simply by eating and drinking the elements, even apart from faith. Indeed, this teaching can become so divorced from any spiritual consideration of Jesus and his saving work that many Roman Catholic churches practice the veneration of the elements themselves, so that long vigils are held adoring the pieces of bread and cups of wine. Far from commending an emphasis on a Christian sacramental altar, our passage roundly condemns and refutes the entire mechanical sacramental system of religion.

1. William Barclay, *The Letter to the Hebrews* (Louisville: Westminster/John Knox, 1976), 198.

The argument here is familiar to people who convert from Roman Catholicism to biblical Christianity today. They are told, "But you won't be able to partake of the sacraments. You will be denied confession and penance and especially the mass." To this believers may rightly reply in the manner of these early Christians to the Jews, "We have Christ in their place. We receive him by grace and through faith. In him we have an altar at which the unbelieving priests have no right to eat."

We might extend the principle to everyone who places the reality of religion in any outward form. Archbishop William Laud, the English champion of the high church, went to Scotland in 1633, and finding no cathedrals or other outward displays of religious grandeur, he reported that Scotland had "no religion at all that I could see—which grieved me much."[2] But the Scots had Christ by faith, and that is true religion indeed. The same is found today where there are no big screens, no dancing fountains, no altar to which people are begged to come—none of the rest of today's machinery of religious persuasion—but where there is simple faith in Jesus Christ. For eternal life comes by none of these external means, but only by the heart inclined to the cross through simple faith in God's Word.

We cannot be sure what the exact problem was among the Hebrews, yet we see in the answer a principle we may use as a general rule. Unless a system of religion relies utterly on the work of Christ in his substitutionary work of atonement, it is alien, it is foreign, to the true religion of Scripture, which is by grace alone, through faith alone, in Christ alone, and especially in his redeeming blood.

OUTSIDE THE CAMP

It is clear from what follows that the writer of Hebrews does not expect his readers to become popular by standing firm against false teaching. He therefore adds a statement that connects our disgrace to the disgrace of the cross, which was erected "outside the camp." He writes, "Jesus also suffered outside the gate in order to sanctify the people through his own blood. Therefore let us go to him outside the camp and bear the reproach he endured" (vv. 12–13).

2. Cited in F. F. Bruce, *The Epistle to the Hebrews*, rev. ed. (Grand Rapids: Eerdmans, 1990), 379.

Because Jesus taught the truth about God, about man, and about the only way of salvation, he was despised and rejected by men, and was literally cast outside the city gates. There he was put to death as one accursed. Jesus' whole ministry and message were outside the pale of worldly religion, and so he became an object of scorn and abuse. Outside the gate he suffered and died. In that separation, a principle is established for all who would come to God through him. Outside the camp is where we go to find the grace of God, for that is where the cross was raised, where God meets with us to forgive our sin and to accept us in the righteousness of the Son whom the world despised.

This means that if you want acceptance in the courts of respectable academia, if you want to be admired in the cocktail lounges of conventional and progressive worldly wisdom, and especially if you want to avoid the scandal of a religion that man rejects, then you may not have fellowship with this Jesus Christ. You may not approach his cross by staying within the safe confines of the worldly city, for the cross is found outside the camp. But if you go outside the gates of worldly acceptance, not because you have some grudge against the world but because you see Jesus there, you will gain the salvation he bought with his blood to make you holy unto God.

Since salvation is found in Jesus Christ and in him alone, the writer exhorts us, "Therefore let us go to him outside the camp and bear the reproach he endured" (v. 13). This is an often suppressed truth about Christianity, that the blessings of salvation cannot be had without the disgrace of Jesus' cross. Paul wrote, "Jews demand signs and Greeks seek wisdom, but we preach Christ crucified, a stumbling block to Jews and folly to Gentiles, but to those who are called, both Jews and Greeks, Christ the power of God and the wisdom of God" (1 Cor. 1:22–24). To Timothy he wrote, "All who desire to live a godly life in Christ Jesus will be persecuted" (2 Tim. 3:12). Jesus made it quite clear that following him means rejection by this world. He said to the disciples, "If the world hates you, know that it has hated me before it hated you. If you were of the world, the world would love you as its own; but because you are not of the world, but I chose you out of the world, therefore the world hates you" (John 15:18–19). If we want to be joined to Christ and his salvation, there is no way for us to avoid bearing the disgrace with which he was sent outside the camp.

It is possible there is an allusion here to Moses. The same word used for the disgrace we must bear is used of him in Hebrews 11:26: "He regarded disgrace for the sake of Christ as of greater value than the treasures of Egypt, because he was looking ahead to his reward" (NIV). Like Moses, by accepting such disgrace we will lose out in the terms of this world, only to receive from God a great deliverance. Furthermore, this idea of going outside the camp may also recall an event that took place during the exodus. Moses was on the mountain receiving God's law, while the people were worshiping a golden calf they had made. Exodus 33:7 tells us that when Moses returned, he pitched his tent outside the camp of the people, who had rejected God, and that is where God came in his cloud of glory to meet with his faithful followers. F. F. Bruce completes the analogy:

> Now, in the person of Jesus, God had again been rejected in the camp; his presence was therefore to be enjoyed outside the camp, where Jesus was, and everyone who sought him must go out and approach him through Jesus. In this context the "camp" stands for the established fellowship and ordinances of Judaism. To abandon them, with all their sacred associations inherited from remote antiquity, was a hard thing, but it was a necessary thing. . . . What was formerly sacred was now unhallowed, because Jesus had been expelled from it; what was formerly unhallowed was now sacred, because Jesus was there.[3]

So it is today, that wherever Jesus is denied as the only Savior for sinners, whether in false churches, in families, or in the world at large, all who stand with him must be willing to go outside the camp. But to those who do decide to follow him, Jesus says, "Truly, I say to you, there is no one who has left house or brothers or sisters or mother or father or children or lands, for my sake and for the gospel, who will not receive a hundredfold now in this time, houses and brothers and sisters and mothers and children and lands, with persecutions, and in the age to come eternal life" (Mark 10:29–30).

LOOKING FOR THE CITY TO COME

Verse 14 concludes this exhortation, not so much with an incentive as with a reminder, lest the resolve of the readers be weakening because of the difficulty of their calling. "For here we have no lasting city," the author reminds them, "but we seek the city that is to come." The point is clear: "Do

---

3. Bruce, *Hebrews*, 381–82.

not forget, as you are called to forsake the world, that it is a passing world and that your inheritance is found in the place to which you are going." We naturally think of the world as a safe place; we think of security in established worldly institutions. The fact is, however, that security is found with the One whose victory has already secured our salvation. Wherever Jesus is, there is hallowed ground, there is peace, there is security, there are hope and life eternal.

It is hard not to fit into the world in which we are living, and like the twelve disciples we often find ourselves challenged not to go the way of the world. How well we are represented by Simon Peter when Jesus asked him, after the crowds had gone away, "'Do you want to go away as well?' Simon Peter answered him, 'Lord, to whom shall we go? You have the words of eternal life, and we have believed, and have come to know, that you are the Holy One of God'" (John 6:67–69). And yet Christians need often to be reminded that "our citizenship is in heaven" (Phil. 3:20), that we, like the men and women of faith who went before us, are "looking forward to the city that has foundations, whose designer and builder is God" (Heb. 11:10).

We need to remember the heavenly situation that corresponds with our being outside the camp with Jesus. The writer of Hebrews has referred to this, our heavenly situation, as being within the veil (6:19; 10:20). We are brought near to God, with Christ in his heavenly dwelling, as God's children, his people, his flock. Therefore by faith we see that outside the camp is truly within the veil with Christ. This is what Paul meant when he said, "For you have died, and your life is hidden with Christ in God" (Col. 3:3). Yet the day will come when what is hidden will be revealed to the eyes of all. The day will come when the gates of this earthly city will be closed for judgment and destruction, and we will be glad to be outside those gates. Then what has seemed such a weak, ignoble place where now we are found in the shadow of a cursed cross, will be manifested in the glory of the new heavens and new earth as the cornerstone of a city that will never pass away, bathed in the light of the open tomb of Christ's resurrection morn. "Behold," he says, "I am coming soon!" Then speaking of the enduring city, that which is to come, he cries, "Blessed are those who wash their robes, so that they may have the right to the tree of life and that they may enter the city by the gates" (Rev. 22:12–14).

For now the gates are open. We may still go outside the camp by following Christ, and thus inside the veil to the city to come through faith in his blood. "Come," he says today, "and let the one who hears say, 'Come.' And let the one who is thirsty come; let the one who desires take the water of life without price" (Rev. 22:17).

56

A SACRIFICE OF PRAISE

Hebrews 13:15—19

*Through him then let us continually offer up a sacrifice of praise
to God, that is, the fruit of lips that acknowledge his name.*
(Heb. 13:15)

Often a single verse captures the message of a book of the Bible, especially one of the New Testament epistles. The Book of Romans gives its theme up front, in one of the Bible's great statements: "In [the gospel] the righteousness of God is revealed from faith for faith, as it is written, 'The righteous shall live by faith'" (Rom. 1:17). The message of Galatians is succinctly given in 2:16, "We know that a person is not justified by works of the law but through faith in Jesus Christ." First John 2:3 gives the message of that letter: "We know that we have come to know him, if we keep his commandments." If we were to pick a single verse to synthesize the Book of Hebrews, it might well be the first verse from our passage in this chapter: "Through him," that is, Jesus, "let us continually offer up a sacrifice of praise to God."

Sacrificial Living

Unlike Romans or Galatians, Hebrews is not focused on the doctrine of justification. It certainly agrees with that great teaching, and even advances beyond it. But as William Newell accurately states:

> The subject of Hebrews is not our justification, not our being delivered from condemnation: but our being brought into the glad company who are worshiping and praising God, Christ leading this worship. . . . In Hebrews as in no other book, is set forth a believing human being left here for a few years of pilgrim existence as to earth, but really occupied with Heaven, with the throne there . . . with the Great High Priest there, Jesus, the Son of God.[1]

This can be demonstrated by a brief summary of the book's contents. No sooner does chapter 1 establish the supremacy of Christ than chapter 2 gives Jesus his main designation in this book, the forerunner or pioneer of our salvation (2:10; 12:2). This is what Hebrews teaches about Christ, that he goes before us, blazing the trail we are to follow into the presence of God, removing every obstacle, satisfying every requirement, actually bringing all those he saves as worshipers before the Father in heaven. Hebrews 2:12–13 places the words of Psalm 22 on Jesus' lips: "'I will tell of your name to my brothers; in the midst of the congregation I will sing your praise.' . . . And again, 'Behold, I and the children God has given me.'"

In chapters 3 and 4 the main exhortation is that we should not do as the Israelites did before us, turning back from the Land of Promise, but rather we should press on in faith, following Christ to our heavenly destination. Chapter 6 tells us that God's covenant oath is anchored in heaven as our great hope, and it is secured by Jesus, who has gone before us (vv. 19–20). Chapter 9 uses the illustration of the tabernacle, with the inner sanctum sealed off by the veil from the outer room; the point is that now Jesus has opened up the way to the holy of holies, where God himself dwells. Unlike the Jewish priests, who brought only the blood of bulls and goats, which could not remove the curtain, Jesus opened the way once for all by bringing his own blood. His own perfect sacrifice not only removes the barrier, but also sanctifies us to draw near to God; it serves to "purify our conscience

---

1. William Newell, *Hebrews Verse by Verse* (London: Oliphants, 1947), 453, 455.

from dead works to serve the living God" (9:14). Hebrews 10:19–22 concludes from this: "Therefore, brothers, since we have confidence to enter the holy places by the blood of Jesus, by the new and living way that he opened for us through the curtain . . . and since we have a great priest over the house of God, let us draw near with a true heart in full assurance of faith." That being the case, the author now says, "Through [Jesus] then let us continually offer up a sacrifice of praise to God" (Heb. 13:15).

These words, together with the whole body of teaching in Hebrews, make clear how futile it is to offer service or sacrifice to God except "through Jesus." Apart from the trail he has blazed by his life and his death, apart from the access he has won for us with his blood, all the obstacles of our sin and God's holiness stand firm against us. God's wrath remains in deadly opposition to us, so that no one is received by God except "through him." This verse makes clear what "through Jesus" the Christian life is all about: drawing near to God and living sacrificially unto him, offering a sacrifice of praise.

This statement comes on the heels of yet another defense of Christianity against the accusations of Judaism. This has been a constant concern in this book, that the Hebrew Christians should not fall back into former ways, ways that no longer provided access to God because of their rejection of Jesus. The Jews, it seems, had been deriding Christianity because it lacked the outward rites in which they took so much confidence. Hebrews 13:9 indicates that the Jews scoffed because the Christians did not partake of their sacred feasts and observe their scrupulous laws concerning food. But the writer says in verse 10, speaking of faith in Christ, "We have an altar from which [they] have no right to eat." Apparently the Christians were ridiculed because they offered no sacrifices to God. Our writer responds by pointing out the all-sufficient sacrifice already offered by Jesus in our place: "Jesus also suffered outside the gate in order to sanctify the people through his own blood" (Heb. 13:12). Nevertheless, he now points out, Christians do have a sacrifice we offer to God, namely, the spiritual offering of our whole lives, a sacrifice not for forgiveness of sin but of gratitude and praise.

In terms of Old Testament Judaism, this sacrifice refers to the thank offering, which was offered not to make atonement for sin but in gratitude for salvation and for the many gifts God has given. In fact, the Greek words used in verse 15 for "sacrifice of praise" are the exact words used by the Septuagint (the Greek translation of the Old Testament used by the early church) in Leviticus 7:12–13, which prescribes the performance of such thank offerings. Jews wishing to express gratitude to God offered bread or cakes or grain to be used by the priests in God's service. This is the kind of sacrifice Christians offer to our Lord: we freely offer our goods and our selves for his service and praise. This was the highest expression of religion in Judaism, an occasional and special mark of piety, but now it is to characterize the whole of our lives as children of God. Paul, in Romans 12:1, speaks in this way of our whole response to the grace of God in the gospel: "I appeal to you therefore, brothers, by the mercies of God, to present your bodies as a living sacrifice, holy and acceptable to God, which is your spiritual worship."

What a contrast this is to the way many view Christianity. For many, the highest aspiration is simply to "get saved." If they can just make it into heaven, that will be good enough for them. But this is not all that Christianity is about. Justification, a doctrine we rightly emphasize, is not the end of our salvation, but rather the means to a life of pleasing service unto God. Justification is often called the hinge on which the door of the gospel turns, and that is certainly true, but it is a door that is meant to be opened, to give us entrance into the presence of God, that we may live with joy and awe as royal children in this world, and offer our lives as sacrifices of praise for his service and pleasure. Jesus said that the Father is seeking worshipers to worship him in spirit and in truth (John 4:23–24). It is for this that we are saved, to live sacrificially unto him, to offer a lifestyle of worship, for the blessing of others and for the glory of his name.

Does this mean that Christians are to engage only in religious work, that all of us are to quit our secular careers and enter vocational Christian ministry? The answer is No. Instead, this means that all work really is religious, involving the worship of one god or another. For followers of Christ, it means we can no longer live for ourselves, but as Paul says in Colossians 3:17, "Whatever you do, in word or deed, do everything in the name of the Lord Jesus, giving thanks to God the Father through him."

People complain that some Christians are "too heavenly-minded to be of any earthly good." But the opposite is more accurate, that many professing Christians are "too earthly-minded to be of any heavenly good." Our passage says, "Let us continually offer up a sacrifice of praise to God"—that means seven days a week and in every kind of human endeavor.

THE CALVES OF OUR LIPS

When Paul spoke in Romans of our lives being offered as living sacrifices, he went on to make the general statement that we are to live in a godly rather than a worldly manner. "Do not be conformed to this world," he wrote, "but be transformed by the renewal of your mind" (Rom. 12:2). The writer of Hebrews focuses this specifically on the manner of our speech: "Let us continually offer up a sacrifice of praise to God, that is, the fruit of lips that acknowledge his name" (Heb. 13:15).

The basic point is that we are to praise God and profess the Christian faith with our lips. This is not just about our gatherings for corporate worship, but encompasses our whole manner of speaking, all of which either confesses or denies his name. Through our speech, our whole attitude is revealed with devastating accuracy. Jesus said, "Out of the abundance of the heart the mouth speaks" (Matt. 12:34). What is in your heart will come out your mouth; the only way, therefore, to have a clean mouth is to have a clean heart. Clean and wholesome speech, therefore, indicates a whole life lived to the praise of God.

So powerful is our speech as a gauge of our true spiritual condition that Paul used it in Romans 3 as a summary of natural man's depravity: "'Their throat is an open grave; they use their tongues to deceive.' 'The venom of asps is under their lips.' 'Their mouth is full of curses and bitterness'" (Rom. 3:13–14). That alone sufficiently describes Western culture today; behind the veneer of our prosperity, the common manner of speech reveals a rot of the soul.

Some of the worst sins committed against God are committed by the tongue. Some of the greatest harm done to other people is done by the tongue. "Sticks and stones may break my bones," we say, "but words can never hurt me." That is simply untrue. James says, "The tongue is a fire, a world of unrighteousness. The tongue is set among our members, staining the whole body, setting on fire the entire course of life, and set on fire by hell. . . . It is a restless evil, full of deadly poison" (James 3:6, 8). All of us can think of things said to us, perhaps recently, perhaps years ago, that have scarred us deeply, that have created a whole world of evil in our lives. We likely have done the same to others. Words are powerful weapons, but also powerful instruments of blessing and worship.

Verse 15 uses the expression "the fruit of lips." This is a quote from Hosea 14:2, which speaks of God's people offering him "the calves of our lips" (KJV). The obvious reference is to sacrificial offerings, and our lips are seen as altars upon which our hearts give worship to the Lord.

Far more valuable to God than any outward religious display we offer, is that we should sacrificially devote our speech to him. This is something we should seek in prayer and cultivate as a Christian duty. Ask God to sanctify your lips, that they would be servants of his will and a source of pleasure to him. Of course, this will require the sanctification of your heart, which is the whole point. In large part we measure our heart sanctification by the sanctity of our speech, as gossip and coarse joking and cursing and complaining give way to encouraging, edifying, wise, and God-praising words.

One hard-driving, foul-mouthed military officer was converted to faith in Jesus Christ. Right away he realized that his mouth required a radical renewal, and he turned to the Lord for grace. A few years later a junior officer who had served under him years before was transferred into his unit. After some weeks the younger officer asked to meet with him and said this: "I used to hate you because you were so hard on us and you spoke so harshly. But I have been watching you and from the way you interact with people and the way you speak, it is obvious that some radical change has come over your life. I wanted to ask you what it is." Obviously, the Christian officer was greatly encouraged by this assessment of his changed life and was glad for the opportunity to speak about Jesus Christ and his power to save and transform. In the same manner, Christians are to testify to Christ, whether we happen to be talking about him or not.

The Goodness of Sharing

Verse 15 speaks of our lips as instruments of worship, but verse 16 turns to practical deeds of love and kindness, and especially to generosity with our material wealth: "Do not neglect to do good and to share what you have, for such sacrifices are pleasing to God." This includes an eagerness to act kindly toward others, and to work for the spiritual and temporal benefit of other people. It especially speaks, however, of a readiness to show generosity to those in need, to give freely of our wealth because we know that this pleases and glorifies God, and because we love others more than our money.

False religion is always exposed by its attitude toward possessions. "You cannot serve God and money," Jesus said (Matt. 6:24). James 1:27 adds, "Religion that is pure and undefiled before God and the Father is this: to visit orphans and widows in their affliction, and to keep oneself unstained from the world." This is not works-righteousness, but the true and spiritual worship that God demands all through the Bible. The prophet Micah also dealt with this contrast between external religion and true religion. Micah is asked, "With what shall I come before the LORD, and bow myself before God on high? Shall I come before him with burnt offerings, with calves a year old?" To this he replies, "He has told you, O man, what is good; and what does the LORD require of you but to do justice, and to love kindness, and to walk humbly with your God?" (Mic. 6:6–8).

We see from this how practical, how earthy, true spiritual worship is. George Guthrie writes, "Money is an area that tests the authenticity of our devotion to God. The heart that is too close to the back pocket is out of place and grows numb to the good gifts and provisions of God. [Our use of money] provides an arena in which great spiritual vitality can be grown and demonstrated."[2] Just as with our speech, it is only when the heart has been weaned from the world and drawn close to God that we can use our money as an instrument of sacrificial worship and service.

Ultimately, it is for God that we seek to live like this, since such true spiritual worship will often go unnoticed and unheralded in the world and even in the church. It is God we serve when we minister to others, and put their well-being ahead of our own financial gain. Corrie ten Boom tells a story about the example set by her father, a poor but godly shopkeeper. One morning their family had gathered for prayer, asking God to send them a customer to buy a watch, so they could pay bills that had come due. A customer did come, picking out a quite expensive watch, casually remarking as he paid that another merchant had sold him a defective watch. Casper, Corrie's father, asked to examine that watch, and pointed out that only a minor repair was needed. Assuring the man that he had been sold a fine-quality watch by the other merchant, Corrie's father refunded the money as the man returned the watch he had intended to buy.

2. George Guthrie, *Hebrews* (Grand Rapids: Zondervan, 1998), 448–49.

Little Corrie asked, "Papa, why did you do that? Aren't you worried about the bills you have due?" Her father replied, "There is blessed and unblessed money," adding that God would not be honored if he allowed another man's reputation to be wrongly harmed, especially since the other merchant was also a believer. He assured the little girl that God would provide, and just a few days later a man came and bought the most expensive watch they had, the sale of which not only paid their bills, but also paid for two years of Corrie's education.[3] What an excellent reminder this is that in the context of financial pressures and temptations our godly use of money will teach our children what it is to trust the Lord, while also revealing to God the fervency of our own trust and devotion.

FOLLOW THE LEADER

Our passage ends with an exhortation to submit to spiritual leaders established in the church. This seems to be distinct from the calling to offer spiritual sacrifices, and serves to conclude the exhortation that began in verse 7 with an earlier reference to leaders. Especially in a self-reliant culture like our own, submission to God-ordained authority is a true spiritual exercise and an element of our worship of the Lord.

In the Bible, all submission, whether of citizens to rulers, children to parents, or wives to husbands, is done unto the Lord. It is a sacrificial act of worship and trust. Verse 17 gives two commands, accompanied by compelling reasons for godly submission: "Obey your leaders and submit to them, for they are keeping watch over your souls, as those who will have to give an account. Let them do this with joy and not with groaning, for that would be of no advantage to you."

The first of these commands—"obey"—mainly speaks of receiving the teaching given by spiritual leaders. The Greek verb (*peithesthe*) is also used for "being persuaded." "Submit" speaks of yielding to proper authority established by God. These we offer to God as worship, receiving the truth and yielding to our leaders.

Six reasons are given for this obedience and submission. The first is found in the word "leaders," which may also be translated as "guides." True spiri-

---

3. Cited in ibid., 449.

tual leaders are those who go before the flock into the Word of God, into prayer, and into the Christian life. Just as the great message of Hebrews is that Jesus is our all-sufficient guide leading us to God, so also our Lord has appointed leaders in the church to guide us on his behalf. This is especially linked to the idea of being persuaded, because Christian leaders are guides into the Word of God. We should not say, "I believe it because Reverend or Doctor So-and-so said so," but rather, "I have been taught that this is the Word of God, it has been explained to me by my pastor, and my conscience now is bound to God to believe and obey."

Second, we submit to spiritual leaders because their authority comes from Christ. Ephesians 4:11–12 says, "He gave the apostles, the prophets, the evangelists, the pastors and teachers, to equip the saints for the work of ministry, for building up the body of Christ." This authority is spiritual and moral, not temporal or worldly. As Jesus said, "My kingdom is not of this world" (John 18:36). Since Christian leaders, particularly deacons and elders, are called to serve the church, we are to receive them as authorities established by Jesus himself.

Third and fourth, these leaders "are keeping watch over your souls, as those who will have to give an account." Many people have a security company to help them protect their possessions. When the company gives advice about the security of the house, the homeowner obediently responds. Others have a financial advisor who watches over their wealth. If the advisor sends information, the investor reads it and takes action on it. If advised to change investments, the investor does so. But the leaders mentioned in Hebrews watch over our very souls. They are gifted by God for rule and Christian teaching. They lie awake at night—that is what the verb "keeping watch" literally means—pondering our spiritual well-being, how they might help and support us in the faith. What better reason could there be for us gladly to follow their teaching and rule? Furthermore, as undershepherds they must give an account to the Chief Shepherd. They are not serving for their own benefit but for ours, and they are called to give an account. Our response, then, is to help them through obedience and faith.

Fifth, our obedience is what makes spiritual leadership a joy and not a burden. Without a doubt, the single greatest discouragement any pastor faces is a congregation that will not believe what he is teaching from the Word of God. This is what wears a minister down: not hard hours of labor, but frustration with a hard-hearted flock. The greatest gift a Christian can give to a spiritual leader is a readiness to believe and to obey God's Word.

Finally, this verse concludes that it is no advantage to us for our ministers to be burdened by division and strife and unbelief in the church. The text uses a market term and says, "That would be of no advantage to you." Surely there are few richer blessings in life than a unified, godly, spiritual church to which we belong, and each of us plays a vital role in building up such a body.

If we turn this verse around, it serves as a useful primer for those who would undertake spiritual leadership. We are to be guides in the Word of God and the Christian life, practicing what we preach and setting a godly example. We bear the burden of authority and therefore of responsibility. It will keep us up at night, thinking about the sermon to preach and the sheep who may be going astray, knowing the sorrows of many hearts and weeping for those who suffer. No wonder that the church has long considered as a prime illustration of Christian leadership the shepherds who were keeping watch over the flock on the night Jesus was born. Hugh Latimer, the great English Reformer, said, "Now these shepherds . . . they keep their sheep, they run not hither and thither, spending the time in vain and neglecting their office and calling. . . . I would that clergymen . . . would learn this lesson by these poor shepherds; which is this, to abide by their flocks and by their sheep, to tarry amongst them, to be careful over them . . . and feed their sheep with the food of God's Word."[4] To this we add the knowledge that we will give account for our care of our flocks. Ministers should think about that when tempted to sin or neglect; though we bear authority, it is in Christ's name and therefore must be Christ-like.

Even the strongest of men realizes his need of grace for a calling like this. Paul himself said, "Who is sufficient for these things?" (2 Cor. 2:16). No wonder, then, that the writer of Hebrews goes on to say, "Pray for us" (Heb. 13:18). If obedience is our duty to Christian leaders, surely prayer is the greatest ministry anyone can offer for a pastor or elder or deacon. The writer of Hebrews adds, "We are sure that we have a clear conscience, desiring to act honorably in all things" (Heb. 13:18). Surely this comment only thinly veils a desire for prayer in just these matters. "I see what is the duty of a pastor

---

4. Cited in Philip E. Hughes, *A Commentary on the Epistle to the Hebrews* (Grand Rapids: Eerdmans, 1977), 586–87.

and I think I am on target," the pastor is saying, "but please pray that I might be faithful, serving God with a clean conscience and living honorably as an example to the others."

If you do not pray for these things regularly for your pastors, then you fail to realize both their importance for the church and the frailty of their sinful nature, which like yours is flesh in all its weakness. We are living in a time marked by gross sins among spiritual leaders, the damage of which has been inestimable, and we should cry to God that such a thing should not occur in our church. We need to pray for the protection of our leaders, both from spiritual attack and the normal dangers of life in this world. After the death of a famous and outstanding Christian leader, a member of his congregation said to me, "It never occurred to me that a man like him needed my prayers." Let the lesson sink in, and pray for your leaders.

HEAVEN ON EARTH

At the funeral of the great Puritan Richard Sibbes, Izaak Walton remarked, "Of this blest man, let this just praise be given: heaven was in him, before he was in heaven."[5] This should certainly be true of Christian leaders whom God provides to teach and lead his flock. Whenever the church is strong, whenever she boldly stands for God, there always are such leaders, bold and true to his Word, setting the example and preaching persuasively in the power of the Holy Spirit.

The writer of Hebrews was able to direct his readers to the memory of such leaders among them, "who spoke to you the word of God" and whose example was worthy of imitation (Heb. 13:7). But the best of leaders will always be frustrated in ministry unless the people of God gladly hear what is taught from the Word, believe and put it into practice, committing their lives to God through prayer and worship and service. This is the whole of the Christian life, and it is a mighty, blessed thing. Indeed, when shepherds and sheep live in harmony before the Lord, what Walton said of Sibbes may be true of us all, that heaven will be in us even while we walk upon the face of this earth.

---

5. Izaak Walton, commenting on Richard Sibbes, cited in Richard Sibbes, *The Bruised Reed* (Edinburgh: Banner of Truth, 1998), viii.

57

BENEDICTION OF PEACE

Hebrews 13:20–25

Now may the God of peace who brought again from the dead our Lord Jesus, the great shepherd of the sheep, by the blood of the eternal covenant, equip you with everything good that you may do his will, working in us that which is pleasing in his sight, through Jesus Christ, to whom be glory forever and ever. Amen.
(Heb. 13:20–21)

hat we call the Book of Hebrews is actually a letter. It was written by an apostolic figure in the early church to address real concerns and to teach things actual people needed to hear. We have now reached the end of this letter, and we can learn a great deal from its closing. Usually, the way a letter ends, as well as how it begins, reveals the attitude of the writer toward his readers, his intentions and his personality, and the kind of relationship they have.

Along these lines, we first see that there is a warm pastoral relationship between this writer and his readers. He is in close fellowship with their leaders and is well enough known to send greetings to all the people of God there. He writes to them as "brothers" (v. 22), and in verse 19 asks for prayer so that he can be restored to them soon. We don't know what is keeping him from the church, but his fervent wish is to be reunited with the flock he has taken such an interest in.

Verse 22 describes this letter as a "word of exhortation." It is a sermon written and sent from a pastor to a congregation. The writer describes it as a short letter. It has been observed that it would take just under an hour to read this epistolary sermon—so apparently this is the Bible's idea of a "short" sermon!

These closing remarks also indicate a likely relationship between the writer and the apostle Paul. Many have identified the writer as Paul, but I have earlier stated my view that this is not likely. The Greek text of Hebrews is strikingly different in style and vocabulary from the known Pauline epistles. Furthermore, in 2:3 the writer speaks of having learned of the Lord secondhand, "by those who heard," which is not the way Paul received the gospel. On the contrary, in Galatians 1:16 Paul insists that he "did not immediately consult with anyone," but received the gospel firsthand from the Lord.

Nevertheless, the writer of Hebrews must have had a close relationship with Paul, as these concluding verses show. He writes in verse 23 of Timothy, who was Paul's aide. In verse 20, he writes of "the God of peace," an expression that often occurs in Paul's letters, generally very near the end (see Rom. 15:33; 16:20; 2 Cor. 13:11; 1 Thess. 5:23; Phil. 4:7). Furthermore, the final benediction in verse 25, like all of Paul's benedictions, speaks of the grace of God, and is identical to Paul's closing line in his letter to Titus. For all its originality, the Letter to the Hebrews shows these marks of familiarity with Paul's writings, along with an overall theological framework that also reveals Paul's influence.

Furthermore, these closing remarks shed some light on the location of those who received this letter. The main options are that these were Jews living in Palestine directly under the influence of the Jerusalem authorities, or that they were Christians converted from among the Jews of the Diaspora, either in Turkey or even in Rome itself. I have argued that the latter is most likely: this was a church composed of Jewish Christians living in or near Rome. The Roman Jews held a special protected status, owing to their support of Julius Caesar against Pompey some one hundred years before. But now the Hebrew Christians were not only losing that protection, but were also experiencing persecution at the hands of Jews.

The mention of Timothy especially strengthens the theory that these readers might have been in Rome: "You should know that our brother Timothy has been released, with whom I shall see you if he comes soon." If Hebrews was written in the mid-to-late 60s, as most scholars think, then it would not be a surprise for the readers to be intimate with Timothy. We know from Paul's prison letters (Ephesians, Philippians, Colossians, and Philemon) that Timothy had been with Paul during his first Roman imprisonment. From there, Timothy had been sent by Paul to lead the important church at Ephesus (in western Asia Minor), but was summoned back to Rome by Paul shortly before his execution, as shown in 2 Timothy 4:21. Paul warned his young protégé about enemies in Rome, like Alexander the metalworker, and perhaps such people had Timothy taken under arrest, from which Hebrews 13:23 tells us he has just been released. Verse 24 adds, "Those who come from Italy send you greetings." It is possible that this refers to people living in Italy, but the most natural way to take it is that some Italians who lived where the writer was sent their greetings, in which case it makes the most sense that the location of the recipients was in Italy.

A GREAT BENEDICTION

These are all interesting points, and to some extent helpful in understanding Hebrews, but the main message of our passage comes through the great benediction of verses 20 and 21. "Benediction" means "good word," and all the New Testament letters include a benediction at the end, some more elaborate than others. A benediction is a prayer to God on behalf of the readers, and that is especially appropriate here since in the preceding verses the writer has asked for their prayers for himself.

This benediction is rather long and involved, yet its purpose is simple and direct. The letter is a "word of exhortation," namely, that through Jesus Christ the congregation would stand firm in the faith and live in a manner pleasing to God. Verse 15 summarizes this whole thrust: "Through him then let us continually offer up a sacrifice of praise to God." The benediction likewise summarizes the whole letter, namely, that the readers might do God's will and please him with their lives.

There is something important here for us to notice. The writer has hopes for how the readers will respond, for how they will live in their difficult setting, but ultimately it is not to them that he appeals, but to God himself. While we have the responsibility and moral agency, we lack the power to carry out what God commands. Our writer has exhorted these Christians frequently, but ultimately he must appeal to God for the good things needed for doing his will.

This is the Bible's message to people today, just as it was to people in the time of the letter. What is going to enable men and women to lead lives that are different from the world, lives that are pleasing to God and do his holy will? For instance, what is going to enable you to cease living for yourself, to stop using other people but instead to love them as God commands, serving them with true goodwill and following through from good intentions to actual good works? What is going to enable you to factor God into the equation, to really lead a devout life in the truest sense? Are any of these things going to happen as the result of human effort? The Bible's answer is a resounding No! We are corrupted by sin. Paul says it very directly in Romans 3: "None is righteous, no, not one; no one understands; no one seeks for God. All have turned aside; together they have become worthless; no one does good, not even one" (vv. 10–12).

This can be proved even without the Bible. We have spent centuries trying to civilize man and the world. Especially in the last one or two hundred years, humanity has seriously proposed a heaven on earth, either through education or social reform or political action. We have had Enlightenment, democracy, communism, fascism, and now secular humanism. Yet look at the chaos of the world! Consider the confusion and torment, not just in little tyrannies in some far-off corner of the globe, but at the center of civilization, here in America and elsewhere, where the gods of humanism most boldly stride. Look at what is going on in our schools and shopping malls, look at television and see what is coming out, see what it is that people are drawn to watch. Look closer, into our families, apart from the grace of God, and see the futility of striving for real change by the power of man, for real blessing and peace and joy and fruit that is pleasing to God. Apart from God's direct intervention, these things remain beyond our grasp in any true and lasting sense.

Then look at yourself, in your own heart. The Bible proclaims that apart from the grace of God, apart from God's Holy Spirit entering into a man or woman who has come to faith in Christ, the heart is a self-serving, self-

623

deceiving, and ultimately self-destroying monster. Salvation and blessing are "not by might, nor by power," said the prophet, "but by my Spirit, says the LORD" (Zech. 4:6).

And yet, through Jesus Christ, the writer of Hebrews has real hopes for God's good and pleasing will taking root in the lives of his readers. Why? Because he appeals on their behalf to the "God of peace." Whereas man is gripped in his own chaos, God has within himself true peace to give. Furthermore, God is seeking peace with us and offers peace to this world, even while it remains at war with him.

The message of Christianity is not that we must do God's will and then we can be at peace with God. We can never do his will until we first receive his peace. Paul puts it most eloquently in Romans 5:6–8, "While we were still weak, at the right time Christ died for the ungodly. . . . God shows his love for us in that while we were still sinners, Christ died for us." You do not have to earn or negotiate peace with God, but only to receive it through his Son Jesus Christ. Out of his peace comes every good thing for doing his will, even the peaceable fruit of godliness and the joy that it brings.

GOD'S ETERNAL COVENANT WITH JESUS CHRIST

The Book of Hebrews is perhaps the most Christ-centered of all the Epistles, and accordingly we find Christ at the center of its closing benediction. Our writer is seeking transformed lives that will stand firm in the faith, and if the source of this transformation is God's own peace, the means through which it is received is the ministry of the Lord Jesus Christ. It is "through Christ" that every spiritual blessing comes.

Verse 20 sees Jesus as "the great shepherd of the sheep," so that it is only by following Christ, by being a part of the flock that he shepherds, that anyone attains the blessings of salvation. Jesus said, "If you abide in my word, you are truly my disciples, and you will know the truth, and the truth will set you free" (John 8:31–32). It is the call of Christ as it is made effectual by God's Holy Spirit that leads us out of our sin, in the same way that God led Jesus out of the grave in his resurrection.

Indeed, to walk with Jesus is to experience a spiritual resurrection that anticipates the rising of the dead unto life at the final day. This is what Paul says in Ephesians 1:18–20, where he prays that the Christians would know the riches they have in Christ, and "the immeasurable greatness of his power toward us who believe." That power, he says, is like the working of God's mighty strength which raised Jesus from the dead. Therefore, Paul can say of us, "If anyone is in Christ, he is a new creation. The old has passed away; behold, the new has come" (2 Cor. 5:17). Of his own experience he writes, "It is no longer I who live, but Christ who lives in me" (Gal. 2:20). A new and godly life is realized as we follow Christ as our great Shepherd and as he works in us with spiritual power from on high.

Verse 20 sees all this as the result of a covenant between the Father and the Son: it was "through the blood of the eternal covenant" that God "brought again from the dead our Lord Jesus." This is a remarkable and instructive statement. A covenant is a binding agreement; it provides the terms according to which two parties come together in a relationship. In the ancient world, a conquering lord would impose terms upon his new vassals who, by accepting the terms, entered into a covenant relationship. Likewise, business partners might enter into a covenant with certain specified obligations. The covenant relationship we are most familiar with is marriage, a relationship that comes into being through the solemn swearing of formal vows.

The parties in this covenant are quite evidently God the Father and his Son, the Lord Jesus Christ. It is called an eternal covenant, which means its effects reach forward everlastingly. Christ was raised from the dead once for all into an eternal life he is able to give to his own. Hebrews 7:25 tells us, "He is able to save to the uttermost those who draw near to God through him, since he always lives to make intercession for them." Because Jesus lives and reigns forever, he is able to offer a secure and eternal salvation. Through faith we are made "heirs of God and fellow heirs with Christ" (Rom. 8:17), and this inheritance is thus an eternal one. Paul writes to Titus that God has poured out his Spirit on us "so that being justified by his grace we might become heirs according to the hope of eternal life" (Titus 3:7). It is through Christ, therefore, that God makes covenant with us, saying in Ezekiel 37:26, "I will make a covenant of peace with them. It shall be an everlasting covenant." The new covenant in Jesus' blood, which the writer of Hebrews outlined in chapter 8, is eternal, and its benefits—namely, forgiveness of sin, sanctification by the Holy Spirit, and fellowship with God—last forever.

At the same time, this covenant is eternal in the other direction, reaching forever into the past. The Bible gives ample testimony of a covenant between

God the Father and God the Son established in their own eternal and precreation council. Peter speaks of Christ as the "lamb without blemish or defect ... chosen before the creation of the world" (1 Peter 1:19–20 NIV). Revelation 13:8 calls him "the Lamb that was slain from the creation of the world" (NIV).

Theologians call this the covenant of redemption. God the Father laid upon the Son a charge that he voluntarily accepted, with promises that would be bestowed upon its success. Thus Jesus prayed shortly before his arrest, "[Father,] I glorified you on earth, having accomplished the work that you gave me to do" (John 17:4). The biblical data show that Christ accepted the following conditions: (1) that he should take up human flesh, being born of a woman and under the law; (2) that he should fulfill the whole law of God on behalf of his elect people, achieving for them a full righteousness where Adam failed; and (3) that he should receive in their place the punishment his people had deserved by their sins, shedding his own blood for them on the cross. In return, God promised him the salvation of all the elect as his brothers adopted into him, as well as dominion over all things through his resurrection from the grave.[1]

Isaiah 53:11–12 referred to this eternal covenant eight centuries before Christ's birth:

> Out of the anguish of his soul he shall see and be satisfied; by his knowledge shall the righteous one, my servant, make many to be accounted righteous, and he shall bear their iniquities. Therefore I will divide him a portion with the many, and he shall divide the spoil with the strong, because he poured out his soul to death and was numbered with the transgressors; yet he bore the sin of many, and makes intercession for the transgressors.

This covenant agreement between God the Father and God the Son explains why, as Hebrews 12:2 says, it was "for the joy that was set before him" that Jesus "endured the cross, despising the shame, and is seated at the right hand of the throne of God." In the shadow of the cross, our Lord could see the victory that would enable him to gather us into his eternal love.

1. See A. A. Hodge, *The Confession of Faith* (Edinburgh: Banner of Truth, 1958), 127; and Herman Witsius, *The Economy of the Covenants between God and Man*, 2 vols. (Phillipsburg, N.J.: Presbyterian and Reformed, 1990), 1:171.

The Puritan John Flavel, preaching on this text, imagines the conversation that must have taken place before the worlds were born, and he uses it to exhort us to the highest devotion to the God who thus arranged our salvation. The Father says of us, "My Son, here is a company of poor miserable souls, that have utterly undone themselves, and now lie open to my justice! Justice demands satisfaction for them, or will satisfy itself in the eternal ruin of them: What shall be done for these souls?" Christ replies, "O my Father, such is my love to, and pity for them, that rather than they shall perish eternally, I will be responsible for them as their Surety; bring in all thy bills, that I may see what they owe thee; Lord, bring them all in, that there may be no after-reckonings with them; at my hand shalt thou require it. I will rather choose to suffer thy wrath than that they should suffer it: upon me, my Father, upon me be all their debt." "But my Son," says God, "if thou undertake for them, thou must reckon to pay the last mite, expect no abatements; if I spare them, I will not spare thee." And Christ replied, "Content, Father, let it be so; charge it all upon me, I am able to discharge it: and though it prove a kind of undoing to me, though it impoverish all my riches, empty all my treasures . . . yet I am content to undertake it."

Flavel concludes from this exchange, which agrees with the biblical picture, that we must blush to be ungrateful to one so pure who bore our stain, to one so rich who took our poverty, to one so innocent who paid the penalty for our guilt because of his love. How can we, he asks, ignore so great a salvation or complain under the yoke of obedience to him? Flavel writes, "O if you knew the grace of our Lord Jesus Christ in this his wonderful [compassion] for you, you could not do it."[2]

The Precious Blood of Christ

Verse 20 is very direct in focusing Christ's work upon the cross, according to that eternal covenant. It was through his blood that he fulfilled his part of the covenant, having first appeared as a spotless lamb, perfect and without any blemish of his own, and therefore able to offer himself for others. The Book of Hebrews is soaked in the blood of Christ; a great portion of its teaching has to do with the unique and saving efficacy of the blood of

2. John Flavel, *The Works of John Flavel*, 6 vols. (Edinburgh: Banner of Truth, 1968), 1:61.

the Son of God, that is, how far it surpasses and fulfills the meaning of the blood of bulls and goats, daily offered by Jews for so many centuries. This, the writer says, is how Christ saves us: Not by setting a moral example; not by simply enlightening our minds with his own philosophy; and not by seizing power to implement a better political agenda. Hebrews 13:12 puts it directly, "Jesus . . . suffered outside the gate in order to sanctify the people through his own blood."

The atonement is a repulsive subject to many; they flinch to think that God would require blood-shedding in order to achieve his goals. There is hardly a more arresting sight than that of human blood being spilled. People see blood and they faint. They stumble upon a crime scene, perhaps, or a traffic accident, and stop dead in their tracks to realize they are looking at a stain of human blood upon the ground. Blood is the very presence of death and suffering and lament. Yet it is with the shedding of his own Son's precious blood that God makes his most important and essential and final statements to this world, statements we must hear and receive if we are to come to God for salvation.

The first statement that the blood of Christ makes is God's holy judgment on our sin. It is only, really, when we see the blood of the Son of God spilled upon the earth that we comprehend anything of the sinfulness of sin. The Puritan Jeremiah Burroughs wrote: "From hence we see what is the evil of sin. How great it is that has made such a breach between God and my soul that only such a way and such a means must take away my sin. I must either have lain under the burden of my sin eternally, or Jesus Christ, who is God and man, must suffer so much for it."[3] J. C. Ryle adds, "Terribly black must that guilt be for which nothing but the blood of the Son of God could make satisfaction. Heavy must that weight of human sin be which made Jesus groan and sweat drops of blood in agony at Gethsemane and cry at Golgotha, 'My God, My God, why hast Thou forsaken Me?' (Matt. 27:46)."[4]

Second, the blood of Christ also shows the great magnitude of God's love for us. It is in dimensions appropriate to a cross that Paul speaks of God's love in Ephesians 3:18, praising its width and length and height and depth. J. I. Packer writes:

3. Jeremiah Burroughs, *Gospel Worship* (Morgan, Pa.: Soli Deo Gloria, 1990), 353.
4. J. C. Ryle, *Holiness* (Darlington, U.K.: Evangelical Press, 1979), 6.

The measure of love is how much it gives, and the measure of the love of God is the gift of His only Son to be made man, and to die for sins, and so to become the one mediator who can bring us to God. No wonder Paul speaks of God's love as "great," and passing knowledge! (Eph. 2:4, 3:19). . . . The New Testament writers constantly point to the Cross of Christ as the crowning proof of the reality and boundlessness of God's love.[5]

Third, the blood of Christ proclaims God's full involvement in our world, at every level. People like to complain today about the biblical view of a holy and good and sovereign God as impossible to believe in a world such as ours. "Where is God in all this sorrow and suffering!" they accuse. "If there is a God, why doesn't he do something!" We are pointing our fingers at God, while in his courts of justice the situation is quite reversed—it is we who are under just accusation. And yet it is not to us that God himself points as his wrath goes forth, but to his own beloved Son.

In a manner more arresting than any we could conceive, God has done the most astonishing thing. We want a divine wave of the wand to take our troubles all away. But God, whose holiness makes such a farce unthinkable, demanding a full accounting for our sin, has himself come into our world to personally deal with sin and death. This is important to the writer of Hebrews, that God the Son came and experienced all that we experience, all the difficulties and humiliations of life in a sinful world, all the temptations of the flesh, even death itself. God enters into the very depths of this fallen realm; he tastes the bitterest dregs of all that is wrong and twisted in the creation he made good. The writer of Hebrews put it this way: "He had to be made like his brothers in every respect, so that he might become a merciful and faithful high priest in the service of God, to make propitiation for the sins of the people. For because he himself has suffered when tempted, he is able to help those who are being tempted" (Heb. 2:17–18).

In light of the cross of Christ, the accusation that God is far off and aloof from the reality of this world is in fact the greatest of all blasphemies. For the cross displays God's involvement in this world in a way that is not only far greater than we could demand, but is far more gracious than we could imagine. God made a covenant far off in eternity, far before time and cre-

5. J. I. Packer, *Knowing God* (Downers Grove, Ill.: InterVarsity, 1979), 114.

ation, that his will would be done. But he also entered into our world in the person of his Son, spilling his own blood and taking death onto himself that he might seek and save those who were lost.

FROM HIM AND THROUGH HIM AND TO HIM

We have been calling this a great benediction, but at the conclusion of verse 21 it becomes a great doxology, a song of praise that makes a fitting climax to everything we have learned in Hebrews. Speaking of Jesus, the writer concludes, "To whom be glory forever and ever. Amen."

There is a striking similarity here with what is perhaps the apostle Paul's greatest doxology. Paul concluded Romans 11 by saying of God, "For from him and through him and to him are all things. To him be glory forever. Amen" (Rom. 11:36). How fitting it is, since the Book of Hebrews has as its great theme the deity and the surpassing greatness of Jesus Christ, who brings us to God, that this same formula should be applied to God the Son. Verse 20 speaks of his blood as the source of our salvation: it is *from* Jesus Christ that we gain all things with God. Verse 21 asks for Christians to be empowered to serve and please God *through* Jesus Christ, who is our great Shepherd and leader in salvation. Then the last words of the benediction tell us that all this is also *to* Jesus Christ, who as God incarnate is the recipient of all our worship and praise.

The opening verses of the Book of Hebrews made the point that God's final and ultimate revelation to man is through his Son, who in his resurrection has received supremacy over all things. Since the Son is the revelation of the Father, far from stealing praise from God when we worship Jesus Christ, we are in fact worshiping God in the manner he has prescribed. Burroughs rightly says, "Jesus Christ is the Altar upon whom all our spiritual sacrifices are to be offered."[6] John Owen adds, "The Father communicates all his love to us through Christ and we pour out our love to the Father only through Christ. . . . Christ is the priest into whose hand we put all the offerings that we wish to give to the Father."[7] God the Father's first and chief love is in his Son, both as the delight of his own soul and also as the Mediator

6. Burroughs, *Gospel Worship*, 147.
7. John Owen, *Communion with God* (Edinburgh: Banner of Truth, 1991), 20.

who brings us to God; and therefore it is God's chief delight that worship should be given to his Son our Lord. Jesus said, "I am the way, and the truth, and the life. No one comes to the Father except through me" (John 14:6). All our salvation and all of our worship are *from him* and *through him* and *to him*, all to the glory of God the Father.

If this is true, then the one thing absolutely essential is to hold fast to Jesus Christ. These early Christians were seeing their world change right before their eyes, just as we do. Their security, their peace, and their prosperity in the world were falling away in the face of sin and death. Meanwhile, they were commanded to live the kinds of lives they could hardly imagine: doing everything according to God's will, and pleasing him in all things. No wonder the writer of Hebrews concludes, "Grace be with you all" (v. 25), because they were going to need God's favor and help in every way. This is the one great and stable power to which the Christian can hold, firm and secure, an anchor within the veil—the grace of almighty God. And it is *from* Christ's blood that grace is made available to us. It is *through* his present ministry that we find grace for the trials of the day. It is *to* him who is enthroned at the right hand of the Majesty on high that we offer all the fruits of this grace.

"Therefore," says the writer of Hebrews, with words that are surely fitting to conclude our study of his great epistle, "let us lay aside every weight, and sin which clings so closely, and let us run with endurance the race that is set before us, looking to Jesus, the founder and perfecter of our faith, who for the joy that was set before him endured the cross, despising the shame, and is seated at the right hand of the throne of God" (12:1–2). To him be glory forever and ever, to the praise of his Father in heaven. Amen.

Index of Scripture

633

Index of Subjects and Names

Puritans, 428
purity, 255–56, 263

Qumran, 182

race, Christian life as, 530–32, 542, 555
Rahab, 516–18
rainbow, 246–47, 425
reading, 179
realized eschatology, 125–26, 128, 131
rebellion, 97, 105
reconciliation, 35, 149, 263, 298
Red Sea, 506, 512–15
redemption, 398
reformation, 133–34
Reformers, 164, 581, 600
refuge, 215
regeneration, 193
relativism, 9–10, 14
relics of saints, 266
remembering, 380, 383–84, 593
repentance, 109, 181, 191
representation, 156
reproach of Christ, 501, 502–4
rest, 118, 119–21, 124, 126, 443
resurrection, 475–78, 521–22, 523, 624–25
revelation, 11–14
reverence, 151, 152, 583
revival, revivalism, 105, 134, 195
reward, 202, 419–21, 422–23
rich young ruler, 166
righteousness, 34, 165–67, 171, 174, 178,
    224–25, 227, 229–30, 286, 425, 520
  of Christ, 169–73
  from faith, 431–33
  as infused, 167–69
"Rock of Ages" (hymn), 172–73
Roman Catholic Church, 164–65, 265–66,
    270, 581
  on infused righteousness, 167–69
  on justification, 201
  mass, 240
  on priesthood, 224

on Reformers, 600
  sacramentalism of, 602–4
Roman Empire, 542, 579
Rutherford, Samuel, 215
Ryle, J. C., 49, 146, 198, 399, 450, 499, 500,
    544, 562, 628

Sabbath, 119, 126–30
sacraments, 189, 191, 602–4
sacrifice, 71, 255, 260, 301–3, 324–25,
    404–5
  of Isaac, 473–80
sacrifice of praise, 609–12
sacrificial system, 337–38
Salem, 224–25
salt, Christians as, 502
salvation, 35, 49
  pictured in exodus, 512
  as rest, 118–19, 120–21, 125
  source of, 165–74
  sufficiency of, 244
Samson, 519, 521
Samuel, 337–38, 339, 519–20
sanctification, 50–51, 68–69, 142, 173, 182,
    183, 295, 348–49, 556–57, 573–74,
    614
Sarah, 447, 451, 453–56, 458, 462, 476
Satan, 91, 599, 601
Saul, King, 337–38
Saul of Tarsus, 42, 489
saving faith, 181, 194–95, 512
scarlet cord, 518
Schaeffer, Francis, 68, 357–58, 359, 363,
    420, 587–88, 590
Scougal, Henry, 87
seal, 248
Second Adam, 61, 67
secular humanism, 623
secularism, 9
seeing Jesus, 89–90
seeking God, 421–23
self-control, 199
self-pity, 546